Jews and the Civil War

Jews and the Civil War
A Reader

EDITED BY

Jonathan D. Sarna and Adam Mendelsohn

NEW YORK UNIVERSITY PRESS
NEW YORK AND LONDON

This book was published with the support of
the Braun Chair Research Fund, established through the generosity
of Mr. Lawrence E. Glick and Mrs. Nancy S. Glick.

NEW YORK UNIVERSITY PRESS
New York and London
www.nyupress.org

© 2010 by New York University
All rights reserved
First published in paperback in 2011.

Library of Congress Cataloging-in-Publication Data
Jews and the Civil War : a reader /
Edited by Jonathan D. Sarna and Adam Mendelsohn.
p. cm.
Includes bibliographical references and index.
ISBN: 978-0-8147-7113-6 (pb : alk. paper)
ISBN: 978-0-8147-4091-0 (cl : alk. paper)
1. United States—History—Civil War, 1861–1865—Social aspects.
2. United States—History—Civil War, 1861–1865—Jews. 3. United
States—History—Civil War, 1861–1865—Participation, Jewish. 4. United
States—Ethnic relations—History—18th century. 5. United States—Ethnic
relations—History—19th century. 6. Slavery—United States—History. 7.
African Americans—Relations with Jews—History—19th century.
8. Jews—United States—History—19th century. I. Sarna, Jonathan D.
II. Mendelsohn, Adam D., 1979-
E468.9.J49   2010
973.7'08924—dc22   2009050086

New York University Press books are printed on acid-free paper,
and their binding materials are chosen for strength and durability.
We strive to use environmentally responsible suppliers and materials
to the greatest extent possible in publishing our books.

Manufactured in the United States of America

c 10 9 8 7 6 5 4 3 2 1
p 10 9 8 7 6 5 4 3 2 1

To Andrea
With love
—ADM

To Lawrence E. Glick and Nancy S. Glick
With appreciation and thanks!
—JDS

Contents

	Preface	ix
	Introduction: Before Korn: A Century of Jewish Historical Writing about the American Civil War Adam Mendelsohn	1
	Overview: The War between Jewish Brothers in America Eli N. Evans	27
PART I	**Jews and Slavery**	**47**
1	Jews and New Christians in the Atlantic Slave Trade Seymour Drescher	51
2	Jews and Negro Slavery in the Old South, 1789–1865 Bertram W. Korn	87
PART II	**Jews and Abolition**	**123**
3	Revolution and Reform: The Antebellum Jewish Abolitionists Jayme A. Sokolow	125
4	The Abolitionists and the Jews: Some Further Thoughts Louis Ruchames	145
PART III	**Rabbis and the March to War**	**157**
5	Isaac Mayer Wise and the Civil War Sefton D. Temkin	161
6	Baltimore Rabbis during the Civil War Isaac M. Fein	181

PART IV Jewish Soldiers during the Civil War — 197

7   Divided Loyalties in 1861: — 201
    The Decision of Major Alfred Mordecai
    Stanley L. Falk

8   Jewish Confederates — 227
    Robert N. Rosen

9   From Peddler to Regimental Commander in Two Years: — 253
    The Civil War Career of Major Louis A. Gratz
    Jacob Rader Marcus

PART V The Home Front — 265

10 Eugenia Levy Phillips: The Civil War — 267
    Experiences of a Southern Jewish Woman
    David T. Morgan

11 Shifting Veils: Religion, Politics, and Womanhood in — 279
    the Civil War Writings of American Jewish Women
    Dianne Ashton

PART VI Jews as a Class — 307

12 "Shoddy" Antisemitism and the Civil War — 311
    Gary L. Bunker and John J. Appel

13 Jewish Chaplains during the Civil War — 335
    Bertram W. Korn

14 That Obnoxious Order — 353
    John Simon

15 Civil War Exodus: The Jews and Grant's General Order No. 11 — 363
    Stephen V. Ash

PART VII Aftermath — 385

16 The Post–Civil War Economy in the South — 387
    Thomas D. Clark

17 Candidate Grant and the Jews — 399
    Joakim Isaacs

For Further Reading — 411
Index — 419
About the Editors — 435

Preface

A grand exhibit entitled "The American Jew in the Civil War" opened at the Jewish Museum in New York on December 11, 1960, to mark the centennial of the Civil War. A metal silhouette of Abraham Lincoln, based on a statue by the Jewish sculptor Max Kalish, dominated the foyer. The galleries featured true-to-life replicas of the tomb of a Confederate Jewish soldier and the Jewish Civil War memorial at Salem Fields, Long Island; a photographic mural of a bloody Georgia battlefield; and a dramatic three-dimensional tent for the wounded tended by Jewish physicians. Fully 260 photographs, documents, and objects appeared in the multigallery exhibit. It was the largest display of Jewish Civil War memorabilia ever assembled.

The once-in-a-lifetime spectacle challenged "Civil War *aficionados* and enthusiasts of American Jewish history to get to work," the great historian of Jews and the Civil War Bertram W. Korn declared in his epilogue to the catalogue published for the occasion. His own *American Jewry and the Civil War*, first issued in 1951 and reissued for the centennial, had disrupted earlier hagiographic narratives of the Jewish experience of the conflict, shifting focus from Jewish "contributions" to the war effort and displays of patriotism to such uncomfortable subjects as Jews and slavery and Civil War–era antisemitism. But the historian's work, Korn knew, was never done: "We need to know much more than we know now," he wrote in the catalogue epilogue, "before we can feel that we are fully aware of the experiences of Jews during the Civil War and of the influence of those experiences on succeeding generations."

In the decades since the centennial exhibit, some of the work that Korn called for has been accomplished. This research, produced over five decades, is scattered across a range of journals. Several articles and essays, unfortunately, have languished in obscurity.

This volume rescues, organizes, and assembles choice examples of this literature. It explores themes familiar to readers of Korn (including two of his essays) and introduces readers to others that have received attention from historians since 1961. The opening historiographic chapter reviews scholarship prior to Korn, and the concluding essay—"For Further Reading"—surveys important books and articles that could not be included here but that have enriched our knowledge of Jews in the Civil War era. Throughout this volume, we also point to themes that cry out for additional research.

Eli Evans's eloquent survey, "The War between Jewish Brothers in America," begins the historical treatment of the subject. Each of the book's subsequent parts—"Jews and Slavery," "Jews and Abolition," "Rabbis and the March to War," "Jewish Soldiers during the Civil War," "The Home Front," "Jews as a Class," and "Aftermath"—deals with a central theme of the Jewish Civil War experience. By presenting multiple scholarly voices, rather than just one expert, we hope to deepen readers' understanding of these themes. Each section is also individually introduced by the editors.

Even as we focus on Jews, the essays in this volume invite comparison to broader developments within Civil War historiography. Scholars of social and cultural history, for example, have long since invaded territory once the province of military historians. They have explored the social experience of soldiering, troop culture and camaraderie, popular religion within the ranks, the origins of courage and cowardice, and ethnic divisions within the Union and Confederate armies. They have also broadened Civil War research beyond the battlefield to include, among many others, studies of patriotism, nationalism, and solidarity; social, regional, and racial cleavages; the gendered experience of the conflict; struggles on the home front; death and suffering; memory and commemoration. Likewise, scholars of ethnicity have revealed the particular challenges and opportunities that the war presented to immigrant communities including Irish and Germans. Historians of religion have examined the impact of the conflict on belief and practice in North and South and the role of faith and worship in motivating soldiers and civilians. These themes have important implications for the study of Jews and the Civil War. Today, no less than fifty years ago, there are many areas where "we need to know much more than we know now."

As the United States approaches the sesquicentennial of the Civil War, we expect that the essays collected in this volume will inform and instruct our readers. Much as the centennial exhibit did, we hope that this book inspires young and old alike to become "aware of the experiences of Jews during the Civil War and of the influence of those experiences on succeeding generations."

Introduction
Before Korn: A Century of Jewish Historical Writing about the American Civil War

Adam Mendelsohn

The history of scholarship on the American Jewish experience of the Civil War can be neatly divided into two eras. From the 1880s—when Jewish participation in the conflict first attracted sustained attention—until 1950, the field was dominated by enthusiastic amateur historians. A second era began in 1951, when Bertram Korn, an ordained rabbi who had served as a Marine Corps chaplain in the latter stages of World War II, published *American Jewry and the Civil War*, based on his doctoral thesis at Hebrew Union College in Cincinnati.[1] In spite of producing several other significant volumes, Korn is best remembered for this single work written at the beginning of his career. The book simultaneously debunked the thriving mythology about Jewish involvement in the war and raised new questions concerning the challenges that the conflict posed to Jews on both sides of the struggle. As the present volume demonstrates, Korn's research agenda continues to influence and define major work on Jews and the Civil War to this day.[2]

Despite a flowering of scholarship in fields first sown by Korn, an earlier hagiographic tradition, described in detail in this introduction, has proven remarkably resilient. Several specious themes have proven difficult to uproot from collective memory and popular history. This introduction examines the genesis of this earlier literature on Jews and the Civil War

---

This introduction was adapted from *American Jewish History* 92:4 (2007): 438–454, copyright © 2007 by the American Jewish Historical Society; reprinted with permission from The Johns Hopkins University Press.

and speculates on the reasons why a number of factually incorrect but alluring ideas have endured. It focuses on the period before American Jewish history became an academic field and explores how amateur historians crafted a consensual understanding of the meaning and importance of the Civil War for Jews. For the most part, this was popular history written with one eye closely focused on the present. These historical works—many of them textbooks and primers—were written for broad audiences, intended to introduce a primarily immigrant population to American Jewish history, to instill pride and create a common past, and to counter charges that Jews were unworthy of their American freedoms.

All these filiopietistic tendencies came under sustained assault in the decade following the Holocaust, as the professionally trained students of Salo W. Baron at Columbia University and Jacob Rader Marcus at Hebrew Union College began to challenge and rewrite the standard narratives of the American Jewish experience. Bertram Korn was trained by Marcus and adopted his mentor's empirical methodology. His first book was squarely aimed at a bastion of mythologizing and romanticism in American Jewish historical writing: the Civil War.

By the time Korn composed his landmark book, the Civil War had spent decades as one of the most contested areas in American historiography. Barely had the guns fallen silent at Appomattox, indeed, before politicians, polemicists, and historians mustered to refight the political battles of the war. Even though the Confederacy's armies lost on the battlefields, it won many of these initial intellectual skirmishes.[3] Much of this early debate was fiercely partisan and occurred outside the academy. Although the period following the conflict was marked by the slow and steady institutionalization and professionalization of the field of history, until the first decades of the twentieth century many of the most significant contemporary works of American history were produced by those who had had no formal training as historians.[4]

The same was certainly true in the field of American Jewish history. Amateur historians of American Jewry were, however, slow to develop a sustained interest in the Civil War. This changed in the 1880s and the 1890s with the publication of several articles and books that touched on the subject. These early efforts to interpret the Jewish experience of the war established the tone and approaches adopted almost uniformly until Korn broke the mold. This introduction traces the origin and evolution of these durable yet malleable tropes. What Jews wrote about the Civil War, we shall see, reveals much about their community's position and self-perception. What they omitted proves no less revealing, highlighting controversial and uncomfortable subjects thought best avoided.

These works also expose the relationship between American Jewish historical writing and the American historiographic mainstream. Most accounts of Jewish participation were written under the influence of an "impartial" consensus view of the conflict that captured the center of the historical establishment in the 1890s. This consensus, presented most forcefully by John Ford Rhodes, Woodrow Wilson, William Dunning, and John Bach McMaster, reflected significant changes within the American historical profession: a postwar generational shift, a radical reevaluation of race and Reconstruction, and a drive for objectivity.[5] Those who sought the "nationalization of historical perspective"—the creation of a cohort of professional historians guided by the principles of objectivity and impartiality—eschewed what were perceived as the earlier partisan and sectional accounts of the conflict and its aftermath. In their stead, Rhodes, Wilson, Dunning, and McMaster offered a reconciliationist interpretation of the war that squared with both the political climate and the quest for objectivity within the profession. The consensus view that they created was rooted in a racist repudiation of Reconstruction and a relatively favorable reassessment of slavery and the Southern cause.[6]

For much of the period between 1890s and the 1950s, Jewish representations of the war were closely tethered to these historiographical orthodoxies. Unlike the broader American historical field, however, Jewish historians steered clear of discussion of the period of Reconstruction, a major arena of debate and writing within the wider field. They were probably wary of addressing the stereotype of the Jewish carpetbagger and dealing with a period that offered more opportunities for controversy than contribution. It was also expedient (and easy) to steer clear of the subject of slavery, given the limited extent of Jewish slaveholding in the antebellum South and the sensitivity of this topic. Instead, accounts of the war provided opportunities to demonstrate the loyalty of American Jewry, to recount episodes of Jewish bravery, and to extol the contribution of Jews to the war effort. Beyond these goals, Jewish amateurs held limited ambitions as historians. Most did not seek to produce original research, interact with the wider historiography, court controversy, or challenge the mythology of the Jewish role in the conflict. In effect this meant that much Jewish historical writing was almost entirely disconnected from iconoclastic currents that rippled through American historiography between the 1890s and the 1950s. There is little evidence that the accounts written by Jewish amateurs were influenced by the movement toward Progressive history, the revisionism initiated by the *Journal of Negro History*, nor by the publication in 1935 of W. E. B. Du Bois's epochal *Black Reconstruction in America, 1860–1880*.[7]

The first book by a Jewish author to attempt a comprehensive examination of the Jewish involvement in the war was Isaac Markens's *The Hebrews in America*, published in 1888.[8] Markens assembled a collection of his newspaper articles into a chronicle celebrating Jewish success in America. His boosterism presented the rapidly expanding community as the obverse of its critics' unfavorable descriptions. Yet Markens's paean to progression and prosperity was laced with an implicit warning of the need for Jews to contribute conspicuously to broader American society.[9] This same concern was evident in his representation of the Civil War. His listings of Jewish soldiers, interspersed with tales of heroism and sacrifice, highlighted Jewish loyalty and offered an ideal of Jewish-Christian fellowship. Here Markens echoed both the parochialism of pre-professional American historians and those arguing for a reconciliationist revision of wartime memory. In place of the North-South conciliation pushed by some professional historians, Markens offered an imagined idyll of Jewish-Christian comity. Although sketchily presented, Markens's uncomplicated depiction contained some of the core elements of future representations, including the fact that he all but ignored antisemitism and slavery.

Whereas Markens treated the Civil War in a perfunctory manner, skirting controversial issues, Katie Magnus's *Outlines of Jewish History*, reissued in 1890 by the Jewish Publication Society with new chapters on American Jewry written by Henrietta Szold and Cyrus Adler, avoided the conflict entirely. Markens had originally been approached to write the new section, but his contribution was judged unsatisfactory.[10] However, his exultant and optimistic tone, but not his attention to a still divisive war, was reproduced in the new volume. Szold and Adler seem to have studiously avoided the subject, even as they did not demur from extolling Jewish loyalty and bravery in "furthering the patriotic cause" in the War of Independence and the War of 1812.[11] Their discussion of Michael Heilprin, a figure rarely described elsewhere without mention of his support for abolitionism, neglected this aspect of his biography. Perhaps the troubling dimensions of the war interfered with Szold and Adler's buoyant presentation of American Jewish history. They discussed antisemitism in America as an alien import—"legal rubbish, brought over from Europe" that was "swept away forever" in the early nineteenth century—an interpretation that was incompatible with evidence of its surge during the Civil War period. Moreover, their focus on the themes of "unification, elevation and advancement," and their presentation of Americans as a people "who have never failed to ignore speculative differences when the common good requires united action," would have been difficult to reconcile with a recent fratricidal conflict. The apparent avoidance of the Civil War may be both an indication that the conflict remained contentious and that the ascendant reconciliationist interpretation had yet to diffuse into popular writing. With an uncertain legacy a decade after the retreat from Reconstruction—a decade that saw the incremental reinstitution of a racial caste system and blossoming adherence to the Lost Cause—the war may have been too controversial for inclusion in a textbook history that was both the first publication of the newly reconstituted Jewish Publication Society and intended for a broad audience. This was perhaps hinted at in the conclusion, where Szold and Adler argued that it was "not practicable to enter upon a discussion which will involve comparative values of current movements."[12]

Simon Wolf, the B'nai B'rith's representative in Washington, provided a dramatically different approach in *The American Jew as Patriot, Soldier and Citizen*, published in 1895.[13] Whereas Szold and Adler shied away from the conflict, Wolf embraced it. The book was an omnibus of articles and lists, running to over 550 pages, heralding the heroism and fidelity of American Jewry. It was intended to serve explicit political ends. Wolf's effort was spurred by an angry exchange of letters in the *North American Review* in 1891.[14] The controversial correspondence was initiated after Goldwin Smith, a respected historian and public figure, cited Judah Benjamin's flight from the Confederacy as an illustration of how "the Jew changes their country more easily than others."[15] Isaac Bendavid wrote a lengthy rebuttal to this aspersion, describing Jewish Civil War service in detail.[16] The December issue contained a response to Bendavid entitled "Jewish Soldiers in the Union Army," written by a veteran who claimed not to

> remember meeting one Jew in uniform, or hearing of any Jewish soldier. . . . [Nor had I met] any who remembered serving with Jews. I learned of no place where they stood, shoulder to shoulder, except in General Sherman's department, and he promptly ordered them out for speculating in cotton and carrying information to the Confederates.[17]

The letter "attracted unusual attention," feeding into a current of nativism and antisemitism that targeted Jews as an unwelcome and inassimilable group. It was "widely quoted and commented on by the newspaper press," attaining, to Wolf's mind, "a degree of publicity out of all proportion to its merits or its authorship."[18] Wolf set out to provide evidence to counter these charges of Jewish clannishness and disloyalty. While centering his account on the Civil War, he offered evidence that in "free America" Jews had "stood from the very beginning 'shoulder to shoulder' with their fellow citizens of every creed, in every movement that has made for freedom and for liberty, for culture and charity."[19] Wolf provided his readers with a pantheon of Jewish bravery—battalions of stiff-backed Jewish heroes intended to replace the ghetto-bent refugee in the popular imagination. He solicited support for these claims from officers "entirely non-Jewish in their origin." Moreover, according to Wolf, these heroic Jews were distinctly Jewish, their "keen and responsive sense of duty" rooted in "Torah and Talmud." Implicitly Wolf was defending the community against an indirect attack on Jewish immigration from Eastern Europe, arguing that new immigrants would rapidly become loyal American citizens, as they were but a part of a "history of the Jewish people" that was "one long tragedy of personal sacrifice and heroism." Wolf felt confident in concluding that the "proportion of Jewish soldiers is, therefore, [not] only large, but is perhaps larger than that of any other faith in the United States."[20]

Wolf's polemic reflected and was aided by broader shifts in thinking about the war. The new representations of the conflict by Rhodes and his peers emphasized the themes of reconciliation, shared sacrifice, and common cause. Echoing the dominant political discourse, many American historians were starting to present the conflict less as a war between the states than as a struggle to build a new nation.[21] This nationalist reappraisal of the conflict was evident in Wolf's approach. He wrote of the war as a "struggle which has ended so beneficently as to have brought prosperity to both antagonists and dispelled the cause of discord."[22] His work also reflected a related innovation drawn from these new interpretations of the conflict. Contemporary popular historians, led by Rhodes, sought to integrate Southern and Northern experience into a shared, nonpartisan national history.[23] This trend served Wolf's political and polemical purposes well, allowing him safely to point to Jewish service in both the armies of the North and South as evidence of Jewish loyalty and adaptability. The service of Southern Jews in the army of the Confederacy was proof that "while retaining his racial and religious distinctiveness, [the

Jew] identifies with the people among whom he dwells, if he is not deliberately excluded from doing so."[24]

The themes of service and loyalty that Wolf emphasized were echoed in many subsequent accounts. In 1896, Max Kohler, a New York lawyer and amateur historian, penned the revealingly titled "Incidents Illustrative of American Jewish Patriotism," a catalogue of episodes "all tending to show that the Jew has ever been ready to battle for the cause of his adopted country."[25] Tellingly, the Hebrew Union Veterans Organization (later the Jewish War Veterans of the United States) was established in the same year by Jewish veterans of the Civil War. The *Jewish Encyclopedia*, published in the first years of the new century (and edited by Cyrus Adler, who had conspicuously ignored the war in his contribution to *Outlines of Jewish History*), repeated Wolf's claim that "the services rendered by the Jews to the states of their adoption or nativity have largely been in excess of their proportionate share."[26] Later representations drew equally heavily on Wolf's collection of often picaresque and romanticized stories, even while they sometimes sought to inflate his figures.[27] While the pool of available anecdotes remained shallow, the attention given to this aspect of the war fluctuated substantially, resurfacing as an area of major interest in periods of crisis.

The surge of broad popular interest in the Civil War at the turn of the century was reflected in the activities of the American Jewish Historical Society. Max Kohler, a mainstay of the organization and frequent contributor, wrote two trendsetting articles for its journal. The first examined the question of Jewish responses to slavery. Kohler recognized that this was a sensitive subject, particularly since the Civil War period was "barely past." Despite his misgivings, he found reassurance in the "great activity in the writing of the Civil War and its chief actors" that he saw around him, surely evidence that

> to-day we have reached a point from which we can view with intelligent appreciation and judgment the deeds of '61, so that the mere fact that such treatises involve praise or blame for some still in our midst, should weigh but little against these other considerations, in the mind of the historian whose sole purpose is to set forth the truth.[28]

Kohler's disclaimer mirrored the manifesto of the reconciliationist school of professionally trained historians who sought to reexamine the conflict objectively. Some of these historians, most notably Ulrich Bonnell

Phillips, also offered a radical reassessment of slavery. The issue of slavery presented a serious obstacle to reimagining the war as a largely blameless conflict. By removing much of the stigma from slaveholding—presenting slavery as a benevolent institution and, when necessary, distinguishing individual owners from the institution, downplaying personal responsibility, and blaming structural factors—these historians shaped an inclusive and neutral new history of slavery. Abolitionism was a victim of this new reconciliatory interpretation, accused of fomenting fanaticism and friction between North and South.[29] Kohler's article reflected both the problems and opportunities that this shift presented for Jewish historians. The new approach made it possible for Kohler to present a thorough examination of Southern Jewish slaveholding. During the war, antisemites lashed the Northern Jewish community with evidence of Judah P. Benjamin's and other Southern Jews' ownership of slaves.[30] Ironically, instead of engendering embarrassment, an honest appraisal now proffered political advantages. It provided further demonstration of Jewish adaptability and regional loyalty. Kohler argued that Jewish slaveholding demonstrated that Jews were "receptive and assimilative" to their environment, not the clannish and inassimilable outsiders of hostile depiction. They were "as actively identified with the institution as any other class of settlers."[31]

However, Kohler's primary focus, and sympathies, lay with opponents of slavery. While he lambasted the "revolutionary and impractical or anarchistic ravings of certain abolitionist leaders," his tone was inflected with obvious admiration for Jewish supporters of abolitionism. David Einhorn's "uncompromising, rigorous, earnest and convincing" stand against slavery, and his subsequent flight from Baltimore, was contrasted favorably with Morris Raphall's defense of slavery on biblical grounds.[32] Kohler proudly claimed that Judaism "contributed its share to the awakening and development of these moral forces and sentiments" and pointed to "numerous influences at work among the Jews of the United States in favor of the abolition movement." Yet he positioned the bulk of the community on unassailable high ground: "antagonism or aloofness on the part of many American Jews to or from anti-slavery agitation was due to love for the Union, and fear of its disruption, to which the Abolitionist propaganda at one time threatened to lead, rather than to any sympathy for slavery."[33] Kohler's pioneering work in this area encouraged little further exploration. Instead, for almost half a century, his work on slavery seemed to mark a historical cul-de-sac. Later works of popular Jewish history remained largely reticent on the causes of the war. This mirrored a trend within the mainstream literature on the conflict into the 1930s, which tended to focus more closely on Reconstruction. When slavery was discussed, it was primarily to demonstrate Jewish sympathy for abolition or the sectional loyalty of Southern Jews or to recount David Einhorn's flight from Baltimore.[34] The subject was only substantially revisited in the 1940s, when a new political imperative demanded a reassessment of the lessons of slavery.

Kohler's second groundbreaking article had a more sustained impact. Kohler set out single-handedly to resurrect the standing of Judah P. Benjamin as the "most distinguished statesman, orator and lawyer, that American Jewry has produced."[35] As with slavery, it had become acceptable, and even politically expedient, to reconsider a sensitive subject. Benjamin's wartime conduct had come under attack in a number of memoirs, including the widely read *The End of an Era*, published in 1899. The book described Benjamin as

> oleaginous, . . . his keg-like form and over-deferential manner suggestive of a shopkeeper. But his eye redeemed him and his speech was elegantly polished, even if his nose was hooked and his lips shone red amidst the curly black of his semitic beard. . . . [He had] more brains and less heart than any other civic leader in the South. He was an English Jew and a lawyer of the first rank. . . . If his client was in any case hanged . . . likely as not, he would be having a bottle of Madeira and a cigar at his club the moment the hanging was taking place. . . . When a case was lost, he did not bemoan it; he found another. . . . The Confederacy and its collapse were no more to Judah P. Benjamin than last year's birds nest.[36]

In spite, and probably because of, Benjamin's ambivalent position in both Confederate and American Jewish history, Kohler launched a defense of his reputation as a politician and as a Jew. Kohler paid little attention to Benjamin's term as secretary of war—service that earned him censure from the Confederate Congress and the enmity of Southerners and Northerners—instead focusing on his less controversial tenure in the Senate, term as secretary of state for the Confederacy, and postwar career in England. While Kohler was intent on restoring Benjamin's tarnished image, he also sought to reclaim him as a Jew. This was an equally difficult task. Benjamin had intermarried and evinced negligible interest in the Jewish community. Undeterred, Kohler assembled a litany of mostly apocryphal episodes to demonstrate that Benjamin was a closet Jew by convenience and not conviction. These examples entered Benjamin lore, an oft-repeated mythology that remained unchallenged until the late 1940s: a Hebrew psalter at Yale, Isaac Mayer Wise's account of a theological discussion, and a riposte, also attributed to Disraeli, to an antisemitic remark.[37]

Although Kohler conceded that Benjamin was "little more than a race Jew," he did find evidence of the "influence of Jewish antecedents and traits in moulding his career."[38] Implicitly, one of these traits was intelligence. Kohler reinterpreted what was originally intended as a critical comment—that Benjamin was the cold and manipulating "brains of the confederacy"—into a statement celebrating a valorized Jewish attribute. Kohler expanded on this theme in his entry on Benjamin in the *Jewish Encyclopedia*. He cited Benjamin's London *Times* obituary as affirmation from an authoritative non-Jewish source of this claim of positive innate Jewishness:

> His inheritance of that elastic resistance to evil fortune which preserved Mr. Benjamin's ancestors through a succession of exiles and plunderings, and reappeared in the Minister of the Confederate cause, together with the same refined apprehension of logical problems which informed the subtleties of the Talmud.[39]

Kohler thus transformed Benjamin into a communal hero:

> Benjamin's attitude did not represent that of a majority of his race, but fortunately, time has healed old wounds. We can do justice to-day to the views of the leaders of that differed from the prevailing policy, and instead of being ashamed to be identified with Benjamin, American Jewry can to-day point with pride to the remarkable career of the greatest statesman, orator and lawyer it has yet produced, notwithstanding his identification with the "Lost Cause."[40]

Subsequent accounts of the Jewish involvement in the Civil War gave Judah P. Benjamin pride of place, drawing heavily on, and often parroting, Kohler's depiction.[41] However, Benjamin was forced to share the limelight with his nemesis, Abraham Lincoln. In an article read to the American Jewish Historical Society on Lincoln's birthday in 1904, Myer Isaacs laid the foundations for a fourth dominant theme, adding to those introduced by Wolf and Kohler. While Isaacs wrote about the chaplaincy controversy—the efforts of the Northern Jewish community to alter a congressional statute that stipulated that army chaplains be of a "Christian denomination"—the conceptual framework that he applied, alongside the subject itself, became a staple of later Jewish representations of the war. Isaacs's impact came from the formula he provided for understanding this and other troubling dimensions of the conflict. For Isaacs, the episode served primarily as a reminder of the "momentous events in which the great Lincoln was the principal figure, as typical of the American who loved his country and was near to the 'common people.'"[42] Isaacs was producing a Jewish version of the cult of Lincoln, casting "Father Abraham" as the central character of Jewish Civil War experience.[43] He warned that

> profane hands, even now, touch the ark which holds sacred the memory of the beloved and martyred President. We of the Jewish Historical Society reverently place our tribute of gratitude by the side of the myriad chaplets in honor of the American who was too great to be sectarian, whose motto was "Malice toward none—charity for all," "doing the right as God gave him to see the right," whose idea of atonement was the Jewish inspiration, "let the oppressed go free."[44]

Although Jewish idolization of Lincoln was not in itself new, the novelty came from the way in which Isaacs refracted the chaplaincy controversy through the Lincoln lens. Isaacs introduced a tendency for episodes of wartime antisemitism—for example, Grant's General Order No. 11 that had expelled the "Jews, as a class" from the Department of Tennessee—to be portrayed less as crises of acceptance and integration than as vehicles for demonstrating Jewish links with Lincoln.[45] This focus on Lincoln meant that wartime antisemitism was decontextualized, treated as an episodic and isolated phenomenon. If anything, attention to a limited number of antisemitic incidents served primarily to embellish the Jewish Lincoln mythology.

Isaac Markens's article "Lincoln and the Jews," published in 1909 to mark the centenary year of Lincoln's birth, reinforced this nascent Lincoln-centered representation of the war.[46] Markens offered a catalogue of "touching" stories, revealing the mutual regard shared by Lincoln and his Jewish citizens, as well as the president's personal interest in the community.[47] He also trumpeted the role of Jews in a glorified national history. According to Markens, it was a Jew, Edward Rosewater, who "with his own hands transmitted to the world from the telegraph office of the War

Department in Washington Lincoln's Emancipation Proclamation."[48] Lincoln entrusted Isachar Zacharie, his chiropodist, with the "role of peacemaker" in a mission to Richmond. With subsequent retelling, Zacharie became the most (and only?) celebrated chiropodist in Jewish history.[49] Citing Isaac Mayer Wise, Markens even suggested that Lincoln himself may have been

> one of the chosen people: "Abraham Lincoln believed himself to be bone of our bone and flesh of our flesh. He supposed himself to be of Hebrew parentage, *he said so in my presence*, and indeed he possesses the common features of the Hebrew race both in countenance and features."[50]

The community, by associating itself with the iconic and revered figure of Abraham Lincoln, could burnish its own image and self-perception. This theme reached its apogee in the publication of *Abraham Lincoln: The Tribute of the Synagogue* in 1927. Emanuel Hertz, a bibliophile and the brother of England's chief rabbi, compiled a 682-page compendium of sermons, eulogies, and writings by rabbis and prominent communal leaders on Lincoln.[51] However unlikely the match, "Father Abraham," an adopted patriarch, and Judah P. Benjamin, a reclaimed wayward son, dominated Jewish Civil War historical writing.

These foundational tropes, introduced over the course of a decade, remained remarkably stable and durable into the 1950s, even as the broader historiography was roiled and gradually revised by the work of iconoclasts such as C. Vann Woodward and W. E. B. Du Bois. It was a formula that was repeated with little variation in children's literature, school text books, and works of general American Jewish history into the 1950s. Max Raisin's *A History of the Jews in Modern Times*, published in 1923 and marketed as a companion volume to Graetz's *History of the Jews*, provides an example of the assimilation of these themes. America's Jews had "rendered invaluable services in the Union as well as the Confederate armies" yet, "like their Christian fellow-citizens," were "a house divided against itself on the question of slavery." Some Southern Jews were "stanch believers in the slavery institution," but "probably owing to their natural tenderness which has ever been the marked characteristic of the race, they treated their slaves with greater consideration than did the non-Jews." By contrast, the Northern Jewish community produced some of the "greatest champions of the anti-slavery cause, . . . tireless in [sic] behalf of the emancipation movement." Lincoln counted "numerous personal friends among the Jews." So did the Confederate president: at the "right hand of President Jefferson Davis, sat a Jew to whom was attributed the distinction of being the 'brains of the Confederacy,'" a man "almost fanatical in his Southern patriotism, . . . who never for a moment lost the confidence of the President who, more than upon any other member of his official family, leaned upon him in all the weightiest of problems."[52] Northern and Southern antisemitism was barely mentioned.

Simon Glazer's *History of Israel* (1930), another attempt to capitalize on the success of "Graetz-Dubnow," provided a similar summary but paid less attention to the already unreliable facts.[53] Max Margolis and Alexander Marx's *A History of the Jewish People* (1927), Paul Masserman and Max Baker's *The Jews Come to America* (1932), Ismar Elbogen's *A Century of Jewish Life* (1944), Solomon Grayzel's *A History of the Jews* (1947), and Anita Lebeson's grandiloquent epic *Pilgrim People* (1950) also followed this general pattern in describing the war.[54] Philosemite Samuel Walker McCall, a former governor of Massachusetts, wrote *Patriotism of American Jewry* (posthumously published in 1924), which repeated these same entrenched themes in discussing Jewish war service. The book was intended as a response to those who, clamoring to close America's doors to Jewish immigrants, argued "that the Jew can be true to no country and is lacking in the capacity for patriotism."[55] Charles Eliot, former president of Harvard University, added his voice to McCall's opposition to the imposition of immigration quotas, although his endorsement came with reservations.[56]

These themes were most strongly expressed in literature intended for younger audiences. Lee Levinger's high school textbook *A History of the Jews in the United States*, issued in 1930, used the same material for instructional purposes.[57] Subsections in the chapter on the Civil War included "The Sympathies of the Jews" (three pages), "Abraham Lincoln and the Jews" (four pages), "Jews in the Armies" (three pages), and "Judah P. Benjamin" (five pages).[58] Special note was taken of Benjamin's work habits and chivalrous demeanor.[59] While praised as a proud Jew—"quick to resent an insult, whether against him or his people"—he and Benjamin Disraeli were gently rebuked for thinking "more of the achievements of their ancestors than they did of serving their people."[60] Oscar Leonard's *Americans All: Grandfather Tells Benny How Jews Helped in the Discovery and Building of America*, published in 1945, placed a wartime spin on Lincoln and Benjamin.[61] Franklin Roosevelt was portrayed as the latter-day Lincoln, "not only *our* champion of liberty—he's a symbol for the whole world, bringing light and new hope to the enslaved nations." Lincoln's lessons of tolerance and "true humanity lives for us today. We have a big fight on our hands—and it's good to remember Lincoln and what he stood for."[62] The chapter "They Were Friends of Lincoln" was followed by the story of the "Brains of the Confederacy." Benjamin was introduced as a Moses-like figure, the allusion crystallized in an illustration of a stylized Benjamin, drawn to look like Lincoln, seizing the whip hand of an overseer about to lash a kneeling slave.[63] The attention lavished on Benjamin suggests that he was particularly useful as an aspirational and inspirational role model, success story, and figure of pride at a time of increasing antisemitism and reduced opportunity. His was a malleable Jewish tale, even reconfigured into an immigration story—arriving old and penniless in Britain after his flight from the defeated Confederacy and regaining prominence, acceptance, and wealth.[64]

World War II and its uncertain aftermath also generated a barrage of historical writing by Jewish veterans. These volumes reproduced the traditional Jewish Civil War narrative. Sydney Gumpertz, winner of the Congressional Medal of Honor in World War I, offered a blood-soaked portrait of Jewish involvement in the Civil War—a "whole people of the same blood struggling to the death in the defense of ideals"—in his *Jewish Legion of Valor*. Above all, he stressed that Judaism was Americanism: "Deep rooted in the heart of the American Jew lies a spirit that is the American creed and he again drew his sword for an ideal that was his ideal, a creed that was his creed."[65] As with Wolf before him, Gumpertz treated the cause of the Confederacy and Union as equally worthy of Jewish sacrifice and service.[66] While the substance of these representations of the Civil War remained largely unchanged, the threat that these books were intended to address did change. For example, J. George Fredman and Louis Falk's *Jews in American Wars*, a volume that was reprinted four times during World War II, recounted Jewish involvement in the Civil War in order to combat the "moral havoc wrought by the weapon of [Nazi] propaganda."[67] A new edition, published in 1954, had an altered agenda, urging its readers to recognize the "treasonous ideology of Communism and to take steps to arouse the nation to combat it." A substantial amount of new material was added to the Civil War section, including, on the Confederate side, the claim that "a Jew fired the first gun against Fort Sumter, and another gave the last shelter to the fleeing President and Cabinet of the falling Confederacy."[68] As the centenary approached, more and more the Civil War had become a Jewish war.

The Brains of the Confederacy · JUDAH P. BENJAMIN · 1811 TO 1884 · BORN IN THE WEST INDIES

This stylized depiction of Judah P. Benjamin seizing the hand of an overseer about to whip a kneeling slave is emblematic of the rehabilitation of Judah P. Benjamin in American Jewish popular memory. During and after the war Benjamin became the focus of antisemitic venom. From the beginning of the twentieth century, Jewish historians sought to reclaim Benjamin as a Jewish hero. This illustration, which appeared in a children's book in 1945, recast Benjamin as a Moses-like figure. © Behrman House., Inc., reprinted with permission www.behrmanhouse.com.

While World War II appeared to reinforce the traditional Jewish approach to representing the Civil War, it also inspired a radically different assessment of the subject. For the first half of the century, Jewish Civil War historiography had been insulated from the revisionist currents that challenged the dominant nationalist interpretation of the war. It remained a field of enthusiasts and amateurs. Now for the first time a professionally trained historian reexamined Jewish involvement in the conflict. Philip Foner, a labor historian fired from the City College of New York in 1941 for membership in the Communist Party, published a short popular volume entitled *The Jews in American History* in 1945.[69] Nearly half the book was devoted to the Civil War, drawing on a substantial amount of new research. Foner's reinterpretation of the war bore the hallmarks of the revisionist approach to slaveholding and Reconstruction pioneered by W. E. B. Du Bois, and it echoed the progressive racial agenda of fellow Communist historians Herbert Aptheker and James Allen. While Foner repeated some staple elements of the Jewish mythology of the conflict, he centered his account on the iniquities of slavery. The Jewish role was measured according to its commitment and contribution to the antislavery cause. Foner's second innovation was to give substantial attention to the role of Jewish women in the abolitionist movement and on the home front.[70] By contrast, Southern Jewry and Judah P. Benjamin received brief and unfavorable treatment. Foner's representation of Abraham Lincoln did not vary from the traditional approach.[71] For all its innovation, the work was tendentious. Foner's message was of the necessity of Jewish steadfastness and sacrifice for a progressive cause. However, unlike the conservative priorities of the contemporaneous accounts produced by veterans, Foner's preferred cause was suggested in his approving references to Jewish activists who "did not flinch before the 'red baiters' of the 1850s."[72] Foner was substituting one polemical reading of the war for another. His history concluded with an implicit cri de coeur for Jews to support the struggle for black civil rights in the United States once World War II ended. Referring as much to the present as to the past, he wrote that the

> Civil War was over but the battle for the full freedom of the Negro people in America was just beginning. It was to be expected that the Jewish people would participate in this struggle. For as Rabbi Bernhard Felsenthal pointed out, any discrimination against the Negro people affected the status of Jews in America, since it was impossible to deny one minority its full rights without injuring the rights of all minorities. . . . Freedom for one minority would bring increased freedom for others.[73]

Although a forerunner of later academic treatments of the subject, Foner's work was significant foremost as a first break with the filiopietism and amateurism of the past, rather than as a predictor of the directions in which this new Jewish Civil War history would move.[74] Bertram Korn and, to a lesser extent, Morris Schappes and Jacob Rader Marcus were the pioneers of this new history. Their work paralleled a broader revisionist reappraisal of the Civil War that had begun in the 1930s, particularly the work of historians interested in the nativism and racism that the war spurred.[75] Korn's myth-deflating article on Judah P. Benjamin, followed by his groundbreaking book *American Jewry and the Civil War*, the first full-scale academic treatment of the subject, reshaped the historical representation of Jewish involvement in the conflict.[76] His account shed the romanticism of his predecessors, carefully analyzing Northern and Southern antisemitism, thoroughly investigating Jewish attitudes toward slavery and abolition, and perhaps most heretically of all, contending that "*Benjamin had no positive or active interest in Jews or Judaism.*"[77] Korn's work replaced Wolf's, Kohler's, and Isaacs's as the benchmark study of Jews and the Civil War. His depiction was popularized as the tercentenary of Jewish settlement in America, followed by the centenary of the war itself, generated a boom in interest in the Civil War. A substantial museum exhibition, relying heavily on his research, was mounted to memorialize the conflict. The centennial also spurred other Jewish historians to reexamine the war.[78]

In spite of the professionalization of the writing of American Jewish history, earlier themes were difficult to uproot from Jewish popular memory, particularly as some of these themes again became politically useful in the 1960s. The centenary of the Civil War coincided with a period when Jewish loyalties in the South were once more disputed. In Alabama, the State B'nai B'rith deployed Judah P. Benjamin—a Louisianan—to fight its cause. The organization devoted a session of its annual convention in 1962 to the "commemoration of the Jewish contribution to the War between the States." The event featured Jefferson Davis biographer Hudson Strode speaking on "Jefferson Davis and His Jewish Confederates."[79] The *Huntsville Times* reported that the convention would "kick off with a Banquet and Dance Saturday night, with the theme, 'Judah P. Benjamin Nite.'"[80] J. S. Gallinger, the State B'nai B'rith president, entitled his annual report "The Covenant Confederacy Annual Convention." More significant than the pageantry was the decision to sponsor the erection of a monument at the capitol in Alabama in honor of the "merits of Judah P. Benjamin, as a son of the Jewish people."[81] A century after the end of the war, a malleable past was still being marched out in defense of the present.

Although the revanchist memory embraced by the Alabama B'nai B'rith contrasted sharply with the mainstream of the historical profession in the 1960s—typified by the new work on slavery and the Civil War produced by C. Vann Woodward, Kenneth Stampp, and Eugene Genovese—this instance of Southern Jewish manipulation of memory to serve political purposes was in step with a century of past practice. The amateur historians—Wolf, Kohler, and Isaacs—who entrenched the themes that dominated Jewish representation of the Civil War for the first half of the twentieth century, as well as some of the first professional historians who challenged these motifs—Foner and Schappes—were responding to political imperatives. In each case, their representations were facilitated and legitimized by developments within the broader historiography of the Civil War. Jewish historical writing about the war evolved slowly alongside this general historiography, assimilating themes and approaches that could be used to bolster the image of the Jewish community or, in the case of Philip Foner, to impel it into action. For the most part, this was a self-serving use of history. The key elements of the dominant depiction of the war—loyal Jewish service to both North and South, the reciprocated Jewish love of Lincoln, and the braininess of Benjamin—echoed the reconciliatory spirit of the broader historiography in the early decades of the twentieth century.

Jewish historical writing hardly strayed from this nationalist interpretation offered in popular form by Rhodes and his professional colleagues from the 1890s, foremost because this account was convenient. This attachment to the conservative mainstream of American historiography facilitated a politically expedient Jewish reading of the war. It allowed a superficial discussion of Southern Jewish slaveholding that avoided troubling questions about morality and responsibility and enabled the resurrection of Judah P. Benjamin as a communal hero. Moreover, it allowed amateur historians, keen to extol Jewish patriotism and bravery, to present both Northern and Southern Jews as heroes. As the Alabaman example suggests, once adopted, these politically useful depictions have been difficult to displace, even when challenged by changes in mainstream historical thinking. Some Jewish historians continue to prefer the blameless war of Rhodes, Wilson, Dunning, and McMaster to the altogether more complicated and troubling version offered by Du Bois, Woodson, Woodward, and their historical heirs.

Although Korn's *American Jewry and the Civil War* failed to uproot completely misperceptions and myths from collective memory and popular history, his work planted the seeds for a new era of serious scholarship. The essays included in this volume represent the best of this literature. Almost all bear his imprint. Although these and other authors (whose work is detailed in "For Further Reading") have discovered new sources, offered fresh perspectives, and added considerable nuance—enriching our understanding of rabbinic attitudes, revealing the challenges facing women on the home front, and contextualizing Grant's Order No. 11—for the most part scholarship has not strayed far from the questions Korn originally raised. Historians have supplemented rather than revised his themes and conclusions. (His understanding of the Jewish relationship with abolitionism is one important exception.) As a result, several areas that received little attention in *American Jewry and the Civil War* remain underexplored. Korn, perhaps wary of military history, paid strikingly little attention to Jewish soldiering during the war. Likewise, we are still largely ignorant of the impact of the conflict on Jewish civilians caught in the destructive war zone, and equally so about the experience for Jews in Northern cities roiled by social and political tension. Aside from the canard of the Jewish carpetbagger, we know little about Jews and Reconstruction. Nonetheless, in the half century since the last major anniversary of the Civil War, professional historians have almost uniformly abandoned the parochial and politically expedient approaches that characterized writing about Jews and the Civil War in the decades before 1950. As we approach the sesquicentennial of the conflict, we await a fresh synthesis by a new generation of historians.

NOTES

1. Bertram W. Korn, *American Jewry and the Civil War* (Philadelphia, 1951).
2. This essay draws on and revises my article "'A Struggle Which Ended So Beneficently': A Century of Jewish Historical Writing about the American Civil War," *American Jewish History* 92:4 (December 2007): 438–454.
3. For the historiography of the war, see Thomas Pressley, *Americans Interpret Their Civil War* (Princeton, NJ, 1954); David Blight, *Race and Reunion: The Civil War in American Memory* (Cambridge, MA, 2001); David Blight, *Beyond the Battlefield: Race, Memory, and the American Civil War* (Boston, 2002); Paul Shackel, *Memory in Black and White: Race, Commemoration, and the Post-Bellum Landscape* (Walnut Creek, CA, 2003); Hugh Tulloch, *The Debate on the American Civil War Era* (Manchester, UK, 1999).
4. Peter Novick, *That Noble Dream: The "Objectivity" Question and the American Historical Profession* (Cambridge, UK, 1999), 49–50.

5. John Ford Rhodes, *History of the United States from the Compromise of 1850* (New York, 1892); Woodrow Wilson, *Division and Reunion, 1829–1889* (New York, 1893); William Dunning, *Essays on the Civil War and Reconstruction and Related Topics* (New York, 1897); John Bach McMaster, *History of the People of the United States: From the Revolution to the Civil War* (New York, 1883–1913).

6. See Novick, *That Noble Dream*, 72–80.

7. W. E. B. Du Bois, *Black Reconstruction in America, 1860–1880* (New York, 1935).

8. Isaac Markens, *The Hebrews in America: A Series of Historical and Biographical Sketches* (New York, 1888).

9. While Jews had "made themselves felt throughout the land to an extent far greater than any like number of people . . . [and] are recognized as among the most useful of our citizens," they had to remain "enterprising and foremost in all public movements looking to the welfare of the entire people, patriotic and law abiding, cosmopolitan in their charities, and permitting none of their people to become a burden on the State or city, [so that] their presence is welcomed and their power is extending year after year." Ibid., v. See also ibid., 126–138, 177–179.

10. See Jonathan Sarna, *JPS: The Americanization of Jewish Culture, 1888–1988* (Philadelphia, 1989), 29–33.

11. "All these good officers were treasured by the people at large, and the time was soon to come when it was well that the Jews had a fair reputation for patriotism set to their credit in the historical ledger of the American nation." Katie Magnus, *Outlines of Jewish History* (Philadelphia, 1890), 348–350.

12. The war was neglected in later editions of the book. Ibid., 352, 366–367.

13. Simon Wolf, *The American Jew as Patriot, Soldier and Citizen* (Philadelphia, 1895).

14. The exchange is discussed at length in Sylvan Morris Dubow, "Identifying the Jewish Servicemen in the Civil War: A Re-appraisal of Simon Wolf's *The American Jew as Patriot, Soldier and Citizen*," *American Jewish Historical Quarterly* 59 (1969): 357–369. See also Esther Panitz, *Simon Wolf: Private Conscience and Public Image* (Cranbury, NJ, 1987), 178–179.

15. Goldwin Smith, "New Light on the Jewish Question," *North American Review* 153:2 (1891): 129–143. On Goldwin Smith, see Gerald Tulchinsky, "Goldwin Smith: Victorian Canadian Antisemite," in Richard Menkis and Norman Ravvin, eds., *The Canadian Jewish Studies Reader* (Markham, ON, 2004).

16. Isaac Bendavid, "Goldwin Smith and the Jews," *North American Review* 153:3 (1891): 257–271.

17. J. M. Rogers, "Jewish Soldiers in the Union Army," *North American Review* 153:6 (1891): 761–762.

18. Wolf, *American Jew as Patriot, Soldier and Citizen*, 2–3, 544–564. Mark Twain repeated this claim in his article "Concerning the Jews" in *Harper's Magazine* in March 1898: "He [the Jew] is a frequent and faithful and capable officer

in the civil service, but he is charged with an unpatriotic disinclination to stand by the flag as a soldier." Later, based on Wolf, he published an addendum with a correction.

19. Ibid., 566. His purpose, according to his collaborator Louis Levy, was to "combat one of the most obstinate of all obstinate prejudices. . . . His impelling motive has been to enforce a recognition of the Jewish people as a militant force in the upbuilding of the State, and of Judaism as a primal force in the furtherance of civilization." Ibid., vii.

20. Ibid., 6. Wolf even suggested that a single mysterious Jew had single-handedly preserved the nation by halting British intervention. Ibid., 87–89.

21. See Pressley, *Americans Interpret Their Civil War*, 121–134, 150–162, 187–192; Blight, *Race and Reunion*, 343–360; Blight, *Beyond the Battlefield*, 124–146; Shackel, *Memory in Black and White*, 26–39; George M. Fredrickson, "Nineteenth Century American History," in Anthony Molho and Gordon S. Wood, eds., *Imagined Histories: American Historians Reinterpret the Past* (Princeton, NJ, 1998), 166–170.

22. Wolf, *American Jew as Patriot, Soldier and Citizen*, 10.

23. Rhodes, *History of the United States from the Compromise of 1850*; Wilson, *Division and Reunion, 1829–1889*; see also Pressley, *Americans Interpret Their Civil War*, 135–148.

24. Wolf, *American Jew as Patriot, Soldier and Citizen*, 104.

25. Max J. Kohler, "Incidents Illustrative of American Jewish Patriotism," *Publication of the American Jewish Historical Society* 4 (1896): 104.

26. *The Jewish Encyclopedia* (New York, 1906), 363.

27. Isaac Markens thought that Wolf had underestimated the number of Jewish soldiers by half. Max Raisin estimated that "fifteen to twenty thousand" served in the Union and Confederate armies. Max Raisin, *A History of Jews in Modern Times* (New York, 1923), 278; Isaac Markens, "Lincoln and the Jews," *Publication of the American Jewish Historical Society* 17 (1909): 157.

28. Max J. Kohler, "The Jews and the American Anti-Slavery Movement," *Publication of the American Jewish Historical Society* 5 (1897): 137.

29. See U. B. Phillips, *American Negro Slavery: A Survey of the Supply, Employment and Control of Negro Labor as Determined by the Plantation Régime* (New York, 1918); see also U. B. Phillips, *Life and Labor in the Old South* (Boston, 1929); *The Slave Economy of the Old South: Selected Essays in Economic and Social History* (Baton Rouge, LA, 1968); Novick, *That Noble Dream*, 72–80; Pressley, *Americans Interpret Their Civil War*, 143–146; Blight, *Beyond the Battlefield*, 130–140; Tulloch, *Debate on the American Civil War Era*, 6–7.

30. Kohler lamented this as a "most unjustified identification of Jews with the pro-slavery cause in the public mind." Max J. Kohler, "Judah P. Benjamin: Statesman and Jurist," *Publication of the American Jewish Historical Society* 12 (1904): 83.

31. Kohler, "Jews and the American Anti-Slavery Movement," 140–141.

32. David Einhorn was Kohler's maternal grandfather.

33. Max J. Kohler, "The Jews and the American Anti-Slavery Movement II," *Publication of the American Jewish Historical Society* 9 (1901): 45–53.

34. For example, Lee Levinger maintained in *A History of the Jews in the United States* that Jewish (and Christian) immigrants were "ardent for every kind of liberty, including that of the negro." Elma Levinger's children's book *The Golden Door* offered a melodramatic retelling of Einhorn's escape from Baltimore, presented through the (blind) eyes of an adoring slave (a "tall Negress who might have been a queen in her native Africa") who dies to save Einhorn's life. Lee Levinger, *A History of the Jews of the United States* (Cincinnati, 1930), 192–193; Elma Levinger, *The Golden Door: Stories of the Jews Who Had a Part in the Making of America* (New York, 1947), 188–198.

35. Quoted in Kohler, "Judah P. Benjamin," 63.

36. Quoted in Eli Evans, *Judah P. Benjamin: The Jewish Confederate* (New York, 1989), 148.

37. See Isaac Wise, *Reminiscences* (Cincinnati, 1901), 184–185. For a later repetition, and embellishment, of these same myths, see Herbert Ezekiel and Gaston Lichtenstein, *The History of the Jews of Richmond from 1769 to 1917* (Richmond, VA, 1917), 169. For the debunking of these claims, see Bertram Korn, "Judah P. Benjamin as a Jew," *Publication of the American Jewish Historical Society* 38:3 (1949): 153–171.

38. Kohler, "Judah P. Benjamin," 83.

39. Max J. Kohler, "Benjamin, Judah Philip," in Isidore Singer, ed., *The Jewish Encyclopedia* (New York, 1906), 28–31. Ironically, an admiring Richmond contemporary thought that Benjamin was "Hebrew in blood, English in Tenacity and grasp of purpose." Quoted in Evans, *Judah P. Benjamin*, 138.

40. Kohler, "Judah P. Benjamin," 85.

41. For example, Max Raisin wrote that at the "right hand of President Jefferson Davis, sat a Jew to whom was attributed the distinction of being the 'brains of the Confederacy,'" a man "almost fanatical in his Southern patriotism . . . who never for a moment lost the confidence of the President who, more than upon any other member of his official family, leaned upon him in all the weightiest of problems." Raisin, *A History of the Jews in Modern Times*, 279–281.

42. Myer Isaacs, "A Jewish Army Chaplain," *Publication of the American Jewish Historical Society* 12 (1904): 136–137.

43. For the cult of Lincoln (and Lee), see Pressley, *Americans Interpret Their Civil War*, 188.

44. Isaacs, "Jewish Army Chaplain," 137.

45. For Lincoln's interactions with Jews, see Bertram Korn, *American Jewry and the Civil War* (New York, 1970), 189–216. Simon Wolf, a political supporter of President Grant, had, in a series of newspaper articles, previously sought to absolve

Grant of all blame for Order No. 11, "which was issued over the signature of General Grant, but of which he, at the time, had absolutely no knowledge." Writing in 1909, Joseph Lebowich questioned the accuracy of Wolf's interpretation but concluded that "Grant's dealings with Jews, both before and after the issuing of Order No. 11, showed not only his freedom from the slightest taint of antisemitism but proved that he was a friend of the Jew. . . . [He] was singularly free from race prejudice." Joseph Lebowich, "General Ulysses S. Grant and the Jews," *Publication of the American Jewish Historical Society* 17 (1909): 71–79. The official papers of Ulysses S. Grant easily refute these claims and prove that quite the opposite was true. John Y. Simon, ed., *The Papers of Ulysses S. Grant*, vol. 7, (Carbondale, IL, 1979), 50–56; John Y. Simon, ed., *The Papers of U.S. Grant*, vol. 19 (Carbondale, IL, 1995), 18–22.

46. Isaac Markens, "Lincoln and the Jews," *Publication of the American Jewish Historical Society* 17 (1909): 109–165.

47. For example, the award of "numerous appointments and promotions in the military service" attested "Lincoln's appreciation of the services rendered by the Jews." Ibid., 157.

48. Ibid., 161.

49. See, for example, Charles Segal, "Isachar Zacharie: Lincoln's Chiropodist," *Publication of the American Jewish Historical Society* 43:1 (1953).

50. Markens, "Lincoln and the Jews," 111. In 1860, Wise had opposed Lincoln in *Die Deborah*, describing him as a "country squire who would look queer in the White House with his country manner." Jonathan Sarna and Nancy Klein, *The Jews of Cincinnati* (Cincinnati, 1989), 53.

51. Emanuel Hertz, ed., *Abraham Lincoln: The Tribute of the Synagogue* (New York, 1927).

52. Raisin, *A History of Jews in Modern Times*, 276–281.

53.
> When the American nation was confronted by the Civil War the Jews were the first in the Union and Second to none in the Confederacy. Over three thousand Jewish soldiers, from every denomination, were among the boys in blue, and who does no know what Jadah [sic] P. Benjamin did for the confederacy? The Jews of the Civil War have primarily observed Jeremiah's instructions to the exiles of Nebuchadnezzar: "And seek the peace of the city whither I have caused you to be carried away captive and pray unto the Lord for it." Those of the south prayed for the gray, and those of the north entreated God for the blue. *But this was the first time in the history of Israel in exile that his sons fought against one another for a country worthy of sacrificing their lives, for a country worthy to die for and good to live in.* Many Jewish generals on both sides have distinguished themselves in numerous engagements and the bravery of the Jewish soldiers received the acclaim of their American fellow-citizens unstintingly.

Simon Glazer, *History of Israel* (New York, 1930), 338–339 (italics added).

54. Paul Masserman and Max Baker, *The Jews Come to America* (New York, 1932), 202–211; Max Margolis and Alexander Marx, *A History of the Jewish People* (Philadelphia, 1927), 677; Solomon Grayzel, *A History of the Jews* (Philadelphia, 1947), 627–627; Ismar Elbogen, *A Century of Jewish Life* (Philadelphia, 1944), 118–121; Anita Lebeson, *Pilgrim People* (New York, 1950), 255–295.

55. Samuel McCall, *Patriotism of the American Jew* (New York, 1924), 7.

56. Ibid., 11–13.

57. Lee Levinger, *A History of the Jews in the United States* (Cincinnati, 1930), 192–209. The book probably had more influence on public knowledge of American Jewish history than any other textbook before or since. See Jonathan Krasner, "Representations of Self and Other in American Jewish History and Social Studies Schoolbooks: An Exploration of the Changing Shape of American Jewish Identity" (Ph.D. diss., Brandeis University, 2002), 391–407.

58. The review section at the end of the chapter included such leading questions as "Did the Jews serve in the Civil War in proportion to their number in the general population?"; "Tell one story of contact between Lincoln and some Jew"; and "What was Abraham Lincoln's attitude toward religion? Toward various peoples of different race or religion from his own?" Levinger, *A History of the Jews in the United States*, 208.

59. "He used to be at his desk at eight in the morning and leave it, day after day, at one or two in the morning; through it all he preserved his calm, his courtesy, and his cheerful smile." Ibid., 205.

60. Ibid., 209.

61. Oscar Leonard, *Americans All: Grandfather Tells Benny How Jews Helped in the Discovery and Building of America* (New York, 1945), 114–130.

62. Ibid., 115, 122. Elma Levinger offered a similar lesson, spoken by a schoolteacher in her story: "He [Lincoln] is not one of our people, yet I believe he is more like our Hebrew prophets than any man, Jew or Christian, living today." Elma Levinger, *The Golden Door: Stories of the Jews Who Had a Part in the Making of America* (New York, 1947), 188.

63. The chapter started with an entirely fictional account of Benjamin intervening to halt the whipping of a slave:

> Suddenly he stopped talking and jumped the carriage. He ran toward the sound of a cruel, angry voice and the swift lashing of a whip. The fury in Benjamin's voice was controlled as he spoke in low, steady tones. "Who gave you the right to beat a helpless slave?" Before him stood his overseer, a whip now hanging limply at his side, and a frightened, trembling Negro. The man stammered hesitantly. "But he sassed me . . ." "You know my wishes in these matters. Complaints are to be brought before me. I will not tolerate whippings on my plantation. Is that clear?" The overseer muttered:

"I worked on plantations before, for gentlemen . . ." Benjamin's face was severe as he cut in. "I know. You never worked for a Jew before."
Leonard, *Americans All*, 124.

64. See Tina Levitan, *The Firsts of American Jewish History, 1492–1951* (New York, 1952), 74.

65. He set out in "glowing language [to] paint brilliant pictures of feats of prowess, of unselfish devotion, of supreme sacrifice. A picture with colors of unfading hue that will live for all time, a perpetual monument to the valor of Jewry." Sydney Gumpertz, *The Jewish Legion of Valor* (New York, 1946), ix, 81–83.

66.
> A supreme principle was involved, the sentiments of the combatants were enlisted on the side of the ideals. . . . It is not our intention to present a case of right or wrong, to censure or commend the North or South, but it is a source of additional pride that Jews in their thousands again proved their manhood by flocking to the Stars and Stripes of the United States and the Stars and Bars of the Confederacy.

Ibid., 81–83.

67. The world "must realize that he [Hitler] was moved not so much by hatred as by the fear that Jewish ideals, which are an integral part of our Judeo-Christian civilization, were the greatest obstacle to the success of his barbaric 'new order.'" J. George Fredman and Louis Falk, *Jews in American Wars* (Hoboken, NJ, 1946), 5.

68. For the new material, see pages 48–66 in the 1954 edition.

69. Philip Foner, *The Jews in American History, 1654–1865* (New York, 1945). For Foner, see Ellen Fitzpatrick, *History's Memory: Writing America's Past, 1880–1980* (Cambridge, MA, 2002), 226–227; Novick, *That Noble Dream*, 225, 327.

70. Foner, *Jews in American History*, 54–57, 70–72.

71. Ibid., 72–75.

72. Ibid., 57.

73. Ibid., 76.

74. Tina Levitan's *The Firsts of American Jewish History*, published in 1952 and intended for a young audience, followed Foner's lead in reinterpreting the Civil War to teach progressive lessons. Levitan, *The Firsts of American Jewish History*, 74.

75. See Tulloch, *The Debate on the American Civil War Era*, 18. For a critique of Marcus's treatment of Jewish slaveholding, see Jonathan Schorsch, "American Jewish Historians, Colonial Jews and Blacks, and the Limits of *Wissenschaft*: A Critical Review," *Jewish Social Studies* 6:2 (2000): 108–111.

76. Korn, *American Jewry and the Civil War*; Korn, "Judah P. Benjamin as a Jew."

77. Korn, *American Jewry and the Civil War*, 168 (italics in the original).

78. For the Civil War Centennial Jewish Historical Commission, see *American Jewish Historical Quarterly* 53:4 (1964): 324–325; and *American Jewish Historical Quarterly* 50:4 (1961): 427. For the Civil War exhibition, see Isidore Meyer, ed., *The American Jew in the Civil War: Catalog of the Exhibit of the Civil War Centennial Commission* (New York, 1962). See also *Journal of the Southern Jewish Historical Society* 1:1 (1963).

79. See also *B'nai B'rith Voice,* January 1962, 4, 10; Proceedings of Annual Convention, 1953–1954, B'nai B'rith collection, MS 180, American Jewish Archives.

80. *Huntsville Times*, March 8, 1962.

81. Resolutions Presented at the 1963 Annual Convention of the Alabama State Association of B'nai B'rith, 20–21 April 1963, box 13, MS 180, American Jewish Archives.

Overview
The War between Jewish Brothers in America

Eli N. Evans

For Jews in America, the Civil War was a watershed that involved Jewish soldiers from all over the nation. Jews served in both armies and helped in the war effort in many other ways. Serving their countries under fire and fighting side by side with their Gentile comrades in arms accelerated the process of acculturation, not only through their self-perceptions, but also because of the reactions of the community around them. Jewish immigrants who had only recently arrived in America and thought of themselves as Germans came to see themselves not only as Americans, but as Americans who belonged. And the veterans were largely treated that way when they returned home.

By 1860, with a Jewish population of 150,000 (more than 100,000 new immigrants having arrived since 1850, mostly from Germany), there were at least 160 identifiable Jewish communities with synagogues in America, which meant that Jewish families with sons from cities and towns all across the country were involved in the Civil War. There were thirty congregations in New York City, but congregations also existed in cities and towns such as Albany, Utica, Rochester, Syracuse, and Buffalo, New York, as well as Savannah and West Point, Georgia, and Springfield, Illinois.

Slavery evolved into the lightning rod and the sword that made a civil war on this divided continent inevitable. The divisive political, economic, social, and moral upheavals brought about by the struggle over slavery

---

Reprinted, with minor abridgement, with permission of Eli N. Evans from *From Haven to Home: 350 Years of Jewish Life in America*, ed. Michael Grunberger (New York: George Braziller, in association with the Library of Congress, 2005), 47–67, copyright © 2005 by the Library of Congress.

gripped the nation for decades. There was no one Jewish position on slavery, but German Jews, who in 1848 had begun the great journey to America in search of religious liberty, gravitated to the newly formed Republican Party in the North. There were many Jews who stood up for what they believed in on all sides of the issues, but on the whole Jews in both sections of the country, especially the struggling new immigrants, preferred political neutrality to outspoken participation in the bitter arguments over abolition. In the end, as Naomi Cohen pointed out in *Encounter with Emancipation*, "geographical location determined which army they fought in; for whom the women rolled bandages, and for which side the rabbis invoked divine aid." Finally, as the war clouds gathered, Jewish neutrality was tested from an unexpected quarter—an improbable clash of rabbis impassioned by Old Testament interpretation.

The War Years

Anti-Semitism, or what one historian refers to as "Judaeophobia," during and in the aftermath of the Civil War was as great as anytime in American history. That Jews didn't fight, but just made money off the war, is a canard that gained great currency in the press during and in the years after the war. The charges took on the coloration of the fierce regional divisions that were at the core of the conflict. When the presence of Jews in the South during the Civil War was even acknowledged, the image in the Northern press was often of the cunning merchant-cheat and the speculator. The Southern press depicted Jews as "scavengers" who were unpatriotic and therefore "un-Southern," outsiders safely behind the lines, feeding off the troubles of the South in its most desolate time. In the North as well, the Jews were accused of undermining the war effort and Jewish financiers of making money off the war. The truth for both sides is a more dramatic story of participation and sacrifice.

Shocked by the charges that Jews avoided the dangers of the war and that no Jews even fought in the war, in 1895 Simon Wolf, a lawyer who had supported Abraham Lincoln and was the major lobbyist for Jewish causes in Washington, assembled a list of as many Jewish soldiers as he could find and published it in his book, *The American Jew as Patriot, Soldier and Citizen* (which contains 300 pages of lists and biographical data taken from his interviews with families, citing their recollections, Jewish names, testimony, and other inexact sources). Wolf estimated that approximately twelve hundred Jews served in the Confederacy, including twenty-four army officers and eleven navy officers. But his contacts were not as good in the South as they were in the North. Confederate Secretary of War James A. Seddon placed the number in the South as high as 10,000. However, most scholars have concluded that the figure is closer to between 2,000 and 3,000, but no accurate number has ever been established.

In the North, 6,000 Jews served, according to Wolf's account, but only sixteen were officers. (Eight hundred more names were listed but not classified.) There were six Jews awarded the Congressional Medal of Honor for bravery in battle. In the South, Jews even organized two Jewish companies—at West Point, Georgia, in the first month of the war, and at Macon, Georgia, in 1862, for the stated purpose of the defense of Savannah. Jewish companies were also organized in the North—in Chicago and Syracuse. However, most Jews, Northern and Southern, were reluctant to separate themselves as Jews and chose to enlist in the regular army units.

The South

All over the South, Jews rallied to the Confederacy as ardent Southerners. Now that fate had cast the gauntlet, they would fight for the glory of the Southern flag, as steeped in the honor and insult as the other white men they fought with.

In Charleston, 180 Jews joined the Confederate Army; M. C. Mordecai's steamer *Isabel* was outfitted into a blockade runner; Benjamin Mordecai organized the "Free Market of Charleston," which was supporting more than six hundred families at a cost of $8,000 a month by late 1862; and David Lopez, a talented builder and architect, constructed one of the torpedo boats, *David*, which in 1863, in Charleston harbor, seriously damaged the federal warship *New Ironsides* in the first successful torpedo attack in naval history.

In Montgomery, Alabama, Mayer Lehman was cut off from his brother Emanuel in New York City, but because the Lehman family was so trusted by the Governor of Alabama, Emanuel was sent to England to raise funds for the Confederacy. (Little wonder then that Mayer named his eighth child after his friend Hillary Herbert, Confederate colonel and congressman from Alabama. Herbert Lehman would become Governor and U.S. Senator from the State of New York.)

In Chattanooga, Tennessee, the war split the Ochs family. Julius Ochs (the father of Adolph Ochs, who would ultimately buy and build the *New York Times*) joined the Union Army, but his wife Bertha remained loyal to the Confederacy and was once arrested for trying to smuggle quinine in a baby carriage to wounded Confederate soldiers. Bertha was a charter member of the Chattanooga Chapter of the United Daughters of the Confederacy, and when she died she requested that a Confederate flag be placed on her coffin. Julius was buried next to her in a coffin draped with the Stars and Stripes.

Down in the ranks, the stories of bravery would be passed from generation to generation as Southern Jewish families swelled proudly at the portraits of Confederate infantrymen over their mantels.

Max Frauenthal, from Port Gibson and Summit, Mississippi, served as a member of the 16th Mississippi Infantry and distinguished himself at Bloody Acute Angle during the Battle of Spottsylvania Court House in Virginia. A veteran from his company remembered Frauenthal as "a little Jew, who, though insignificant, had the heart of a lion in a battle. For several hours, he stood at the immediate point of contact amid the most terrific hail of lead, and coolly and deliberately loaded and fired without cringing. . . . I now understand how it was that a handful of Jews could drive before them a hundred kings—they were all Fronthals." It would not be the last time that a Jewish name was mispronounced; for years in Mississippi, Confederate veterans referred to any brave man as "a regular Fronthal."

Private Isaac Gleitzman of Arkansas fought under the daring command of Nathan Bedford Forrest. While the Confederacy awarded him its Cross of Honor for "conspicuous gallantry in the field," he was proudest that he had never eaten any *trefa,* or nonkosher food, during his entire four years of military service. His family retains to this day the two mess kits he carried with him during the war, one for meat and one for dairy.

Robert Rosen reports in *The Jewish Confederates* that there were "Jewish Johnny Rebs," who were the enlisted men in the trenches who did the fighting as well as the unglamorous work of the army. They were "cooks, sharp shooters, orderlies, teamsters, foragers . . . who dug trenches, cut trees, guarded prisoners, and served on picket duty." And they were the infantry, casualties at every major battle of the war. The book records the story of family after family with losses of sons and fathers and quotes from the unintended poetry of diaries. There is the story of Simon Baruch, the father of Bernard Baruch, a Prussian immigrant from Camden,

South Carolina, who served as a surgeon (with the equivalent rank of major), treating the wounded of the 3rd South Carolina Battalion, known as Kershaw's Brigade, and others wounded at Gettysburg for weeks after the battle. Baruch later wrote that Union doctors shared their supplies. And there is the very poignant story of Lieutenant Joshua Lazarus Moses, a Citadel graduate and one of five brothers to serve in the Confederacy. He was killed in action at Fort Blakely, outside of Mobile, Alabama, on April 9, 1865, the same day that Lee surrendered at Appomattox.

The Levy Sisters of Charleston

Eugenia and Phoebe Levy were Jewish Southern belles who became legends in the South from their unusual adventures during the Civil War. We know a great deal about them because of Eugenia's wartime diary in the Library of Congress collection and Phoebe's book written after the war, *A Southern Woman's Diary* (1875). Eugenia's 1902 obituaries noted the two Confederate Jewish sisters as "toasts of the day" and that "two more brilliant women . . . could not be found."

T. C. Deleon, writing in his *Belles, Beaux and Brains of the Sixties* (New York, 1909), a paean to Southern women during the war, wrote that "Eugenia . . . was one of the most picturesque personages in Confederate history, . . . most potent and popular," and that Phoebe "was a belle and early a widow, she made herself loved in the army camps by that good work of her Chimborazo Hospital."

They were raised in a prominent family of considerable wealth in Charleston, with all the privileges of young women of their class, and especially the self-confidence and high-spirited élan for which Southern women have been celebrated in Southern literature.

Both married well, as one would expect, but Eugenia, after being pursued by many, at the age of sixteen married Philip Phillips, a twenty-nine-year-old brilliant young Jewish lawyer in Charleston who moved her to Mobile, where he represented the major commercial interests and eventually was elected to Congress from Alabama.

When the war broke out, they remained in Washington for a time because Phillips was opposed to slavery and secession, while Eugenia was an outspoken Confederate patriot. Korn called her "a fire-eating secessionist in skirts." She even enlisted in a form of female espionage, using her charms on gullible Union officers and politicians to get information that she managed to deliver clandestinely to the young Confederate government. She and others were arrested by Union authorities, and Mary Chesnut referred to her and fellow spy Rose Greenhow as "saints and martyrs and patriots."

Moving with their nine children to New Orleans, which they thought would be a relatively safe haven far from the battlegrounds of Virginia, she became embroiled in the episode which sealed her story in the annals of Confederate history. When New Orleans fell to the Union Navy in early 1862, Major General Benjamin Butler of Massachusetts took over the occupation and eventually became known as "Beast" Butler for the harshness of his administration. Accusing Eugenia of teaching her children to spit from the balcony of their home on Union officers and "laughing at and mocking" the passing remains of a Union officer during a solemn funeral procession, Butler decided to make an example of her. He reported that when he confronted her as to why she had done those things, she replied, "I was in good spirits that day." T. C. De Leon reported, "it was Mrs. Phillips' contempt of the general and her cool sarcasm that caused her imprisonment." Butler ordered her to be isolated till further orders on Ship Island, sixty-five miles from New Orleans, an isolated prison site infested with mosquitoes and the threat of disease, certainly no place for a "lady" among so many male soldiers acting as guards. She would later complain that "their conversation, evidently to insult me, was of the basest and foulest character." When notified of her sentence, she replied, "It has one advantage over the city, sir; you will not be there." And when informed it was a yellow fever station, she stated, "It is fortunate that neither the fever nor General Butler is contagious."

News of her imprisonment spread all over the South—for Butler had challenged the code of Southern chivalry. After all, he had warned in his notorious "The Woman Order" that if the Confederate women of New Orleans insulted the occupying forces in any way, they would "be treated as a woman of the town plying her avocation." Diaries of the time indicate that such language and attitude inflamed women across the South, and Eugenia became a symbol of injustice for standing up to the Union occupation. Moreover, her fervently patriotic letters from the island were widely circulated, and she became an overnight heroine for her unflinching loyalty to the cause and her acid tongue. When she was released three and a half months later (some said by intervention of friends in Washington) she and her husband were greeted with standing ovations and cheers everywhere they went. Crowds made pilgrimages to their home, and a relative wrote to her, "future historians will vie with each other for the honor of writing your biography." Robert N. Rosen summarized her life as follows: "raised nine children, incarcerated twice for her pro-Southern sympathies, and lived to the age of eighty-three."

Her younger sister, Phoebe Yates Pember, widowed shortly after her marriage, was drawn to serve the cause after the war began and worked herself up from simple nursing tasks to become the first female administrator of the sprawling Chimborazo Hospital. It was a remarkable achievement for a Southern woman, especially one from the aristocracy, for this was the largest hospital in the world at that time, at its height with 150 wards and over the course of the war serving 76,000 patients. In truth, all of Richmond became a vast hospital, with thousands of bloodied and bandaged men hobbling back to the city, some blinded and missing limbs, helped by comrades or in carts, wagons, and litters. Inside the wards, it was a scene of unspeakable carnage and suffering, as the wounded and dying were brought to the hospital from surrounding battlegrounds to be treated, or into the amputation room to be hacked or sawed and then cauterized with a hot poker, or just left to die if they were too far gone.

It was inconceivable for most Southerners to imagine a woman of such fine upbringing as Phoebe Pember in such circumstances, and she later wrote that many thought "such a life would be injurious to the delicacy and refinement of a lady." But she had a strong character that enabled her to be around death and misery all day and still summon the strength to read to the suffering wounded from the Bible, give a sip of water or soup, hold a hand, or bind a wound, or write a farewell letter home for the illiterate soldiers. In her book, she wrote that she was not prepared or trained to be a Florence Nightingale. Instead she was able to call on a forceful nature fueled by an unlikely combination of moral outrage and warm humanity in the face of the agony all around her, possessed of an extraordinary determination and resilience, not unlike her sister. One of the most famous scenes portraying the role of women in the war described her standing guard over the whiskey barrel, with a pistol on her hip, protecting it from thievery so that it would be available for the wounded and those facing the surgeons. "Hers was a will of steel," De Leon wrote.

The North

There were also legendary Jewish immigrants who fought for the Union, whose stories are better documented, both in the better-staffed Northern newspapers and by Simon Wolf's interviews. Wolf tracked down the stories of six Jewish soldiers of the Union Army who received the first Congressional Medal of Honor, created by President Lincoln "to reward non-commissioned officers and privates as shall most distinguish themselves by their gallantry in action." Sergeant Leopold Karpeles was born in Prague and in 1850, when he was twelve years old, came to the United States to live with his brother in Texas. He joined the Union Army at Springfield, Massachusetts, and received the Congressional Medal for "rallying the men of the 57th Massachusetts Volunteers around his flag" in a major battle, "turning retreat into victory."

Private Abraham Cohen, of the 68th New York Regiment, rose in the ranks to be a sergeant major and won the Congressional Medal "for conspicuous gallantry displayed at the Battle of the Wilderness, in rallying and forming, under heavy fire, disorganized troops"; also "for bravery and coolness in carrying orders to advanced lines under murderous fire." After rising to the rank of captain of his regiment, sickness and wounds caused surgeons to declare him "unfit for service" and he was given an honorable discharge. But after an extended recovery, he reenlisted as a private in the 6th New Hampshire Volunteers and served with such distinction at the Battle of Petersburg, once again risking life and limb by "carrying orders from and to advanced outposts under a barrage of fire," that he received new promotions in a second career.

Wolf counted fourteen families in both armies who gave the ultimate sacrifice of no less than fifty-one lives: families who lost three, four, and five brothers; a father and three sons; a father and four sons, all of whom were "volunteers in a deadly strife."

Many others with roots in one region fought for the other side. On September 2, 1891, former Captain Joseph B. Greenhut, a Jewish Union officer recalling the unforgettable panorama of death and courage seared into his memory of his service as a twenty-year-old in the Illinois 82nd Infantry, walked the fields of Gettysburg to Cemetery Hill to deliver the dedication at the unveiling of the monument to the soldiers of the Illinois 82nd who fought there. Appointed by the governor of Illinois as one of three veterans to erect the monument, it must have been difficult for Greenhut to imagine that the boy born in Austria in 1843, who immigrated with his

Maximilian Heller, a Jewish surgeon in the Union army, sits for a formal portrait. The military uniform served as a mark of pride for a recent immigrant, displaying his patriotism toward his adopted homeland. Courtesy of Jonathan D. Sarna and Ruth Langer.

parents to Chicago at the age of nine, worked for several years in Mobile, Alabama, but returned North after secession to join the Union Army as an eighteen-year-old recruit, twenty-eight years later would be standing in the middle of the battlefield where he saw unbelievable carnage and tragedy that he never thought he would survive.

The two highest-ranking Jews in the Union Army were Brigadier Generals Edward Solomon and Frederick Knefler. Solomon left Germany at the age of eighteen, settled in Chicago in 1854, and at the outbreak of the war joined the 14th Illinois as a second lieutenant. By the summer of 1862, as a major, he was instrumental in organizing the all-Jewish company for the new 82nd Illinois with a full complement of ninety-six men, supported by funds raised by the local community. Praising the patriotism of "our Israelite citizens," the *Chicago Tribune* trumpeted that "the rapidity with which the company was enlisted has not its equal in the history of recruiting. . . . Can any town, city or state in the nation show an equally good two days work?" Solomon became a lieutenant colonel and led his company through the battles at Chancellorsville and the three-day battle at Gettysburg (possibly firing at Proskauer in the 12th Alabama). Looking back thirty years later, Major General Carl Schurz told Simon Wolf: "He was the only soldier at Gettysburg who did not dodge when Lee's guns thundered; he stood up, smoked his cigar and faced the cannon balls." At the end of the war, in June of 1865, Secretary of War Edwin Stanton, with the ratification of the U.S. Senate, awarded him the rank of brigadier general.

At the age of twenty-six, Frederick Knefler of Hungary immigrated to the United States and arrived in 1859 on the eve of the outbreak of the Civil War. He enlisted as a private in the Army in response to Lincoln's first call for volunteers in the 79th Regiment of the Indiana Volunteers. He took part in many battles over the course of the war with the Army of the Cumberland and served for a time under General Grant. For heroic conduct in the bloody Battle of Chickamaugua, he attained the rank of major general and subsequently joined General William Tecumseh Sherman in the "total war" March to the Sea that broke the back and the spirit of the South.

With regard to Jews in the government, the South would reward with its highest honors the generation of Sephardic Jews, by 1860 almost totally assimilated, made up of men who had married outside their faith and drifted away from Judaism until they blended smoothly into the slave-holding plantation life of the aristocracy—men like Judah

P. Benjamin, who served as U.S. Senator from Louisiana before becoming Attorney General, Secretary of War, and Secretary of State to the Confederacy; Henry Hyams, the Lieutenant Governor of Louisiana; and Dr. Edwin Moise, the Speaker of the Louisiana legislature. Even though they were indistinguishable from other Southerners in style and language, they could retain a cultural curiosity about their Jewishness, both an awareness and a respect, that would astound a visitor who had assumed they had long since abandoned any consciousness of their roots.

Just before the war, Salomon de Rothschild of the Parisian branch of the noted banking family traveled to New Orleans, where he met with Benjamin, Hyams, and Moise. "What is astonishing here," he wrote home, "or rather what is not astonishing, is the high position occupied by our coreligionists, or rather by those who were born into the faith and who, having married Christian women, and without converting, have forgotten the practices of their fathers, . . . and what is odd, all these men have a Jewish heart and take an interest in me, because I represent the greatest Jewish house in the world."

Judah P. Benjamin

There is much that is intriguing about how deeply Jews and Southerners are alike—stepchildren of an anguished history—and yet different. Whereas the Jewish search for a homeland contrasted with the Southerners' commitment to place, Southern defenders of the Confederacy often used Old Testament analogies in referring to themselves as "the chosen people," destined to survive and triumph against overwhelming odds. Judah P. Benjamin was called "the dark prince of the Confederacy" by Stephen Vincent Benet in *John Brown's Body*. He was an extraordinary figure in the Civil War who achieved greater political power than perhaps any other Jewish American in history. Benjamin was the first acknowledged Jew in the U.S. Senate, and after Secession he became Jefferson Davis's right-hand man, serving initially as Attorney General, a job that expanded because the president needed a prodigious administrator to help organize the government. Subsequently, Davis appointed him Secretary of War, to which he was named because Davis wanted to have a dependable and trusted friend who would not question the president's decisions and yet would accept the blame for military defeats. Even after the harsh denunciations of Benjamin for failures on the battlefield, Davis once again appointed him to a third cabinet post, Secretary of State, which put him in charge of all efforts to bring England and other nations into the war and fatefully, as it would turn out, involve him in the spy efforts in Canada and elsewhere. Yet this brilliant, cultured man, who came to be called "the brains of the Confederacy," has been largely overlooked by history because he chose obscurity by burning his papers in the closing days of the war. Still, he left letters to others, thousands of official documents, and many impressions.

Judah P. Benjamin was fascinating because of the extraordinary role he played in Southern history and the ways in which Jews and non-Jews reacted to him. He was the prototype of the contradictions in the Jewish Southerner and the stranger in the Confederate story, the Jew at the eye of the storm that was the Civil War. Objectively, with so few Jews in the South at the time, it is astonishing that one should appear at the very center of Southern history. Benjamin himself avoided his Jewishness throughout his public career, though his enemies in the Southern press and in the halls of the Confederate Congress never let the South forget it. The virulence of the times, which saw an outpouring of anti-Semitism such as had existed in no previous period in American history, required a symbolic figure as a catalyst for an ancient hostility and perhaps contributed to his intentional elusiveness.

Judah Benjamin would abandon formal Judaism, but neither the South nor the North would allow Judaism to abandon him. Cruelly, anti-Semitism stalked him throughout his career, as if to mock his success with ancient hatreds. When the South began to sink in despair, Benjamin, as Secretary of War, emerged as a convenient target of attack for the military failures, the lack of supplies, and the gathering disillusionment with the cause. Thomas R. R. Cobb, a brigadier general and member of the Provisional Congress of the Confederacy, said, "a grander rascal than this Jew Benjamin does not exist in the Confederacy, and I am not particular in concealing my opinion of him." In the Confederate House of Representatives, Congressman Henry S. Foote of Tennessee affirmed that he "would never consent to the establishment of a supreme court of the Confederate States as long as Judah P. Benjamin shall continue to pollute the ears of majesty Davis with his insidious counsels." A writer to the *Richmond Enquirer* believed it "blasphemous" for a Jew to hold such high office and suggested that the prayers of the Confederacy would have more effect if Benjamin were dismissed from the cabinet.

Blamed by the South for its miseries, Benjamin also was bitterly denounced in the North and rarely mentioned in the Northern press without some reference to his being a Jew. Other senators bitterly attacked both him and another Jew, Florida Senator David (Levy) Yulee, known as the "Florida fire-eater" because of the passion of his proslavery views. Andrew Johnson, as a senator, later to succeed Lincoln as the seventeenth president, told Charles Francis Adams of Boston, "There's that Yulee; miserable little cuss! I remember him in the House—the contemptible little Jew—standing there and begging us to let Florida in as a state. Well, we let her in, and took care of her and fought her Indians, and now that despicable little beggar stands up in the Senate and talks about her rights." The future president also had choice words for Judah Benjamin: "There's another Jew—that miserable Benjamin."

Isachar Zacharie

In a private meeting in 1863 in Richmond, Judah P. Benjamin met with Isachar Zacharie, who was the closest Jewish friend to President Abraham Lincoln. Lincoln had personally issued Zacharie a pass to cross Confederate lines to make an unofficial visit to explore peace talks after Gettysburg and the fall of Vicksburg and had sent one of his closest confidants on the mission. The two Jews closest to their respective presidents met for the discussion, and subsequently with other members of the Confederate Cabinet as well.

It was an improbable choice of emissary on Lincoln's part. Zacharie was an English immigrant and a chiropodist, or foot doctor, who had periodically visited the president to remove bunions and treat other presidential foot ailments. But Zacharie was also a man of great intelligence and enormous charm, who used language with flair and knew America well, since he had family in Savannah and had traveled widely in his profession. As the president was being treated, Zacharie sensed Lincoln's loneliness and need for companionship and began to converse with Lincoln about all manner of subjects including affairs of state and the condition of the Jewish community. Zacharie also must have had much Washington gossip to report because his medical specialty had enabled him to treat the most influential feet in the capital—other members of the cabinet such as Secretary of State Seward and Secretary of War Stanton, and Union generals McClellan, Banks, and Burnside, as well as members of Congress such as Henry

Clay and William Cullen Bryant. Zacharie clearly intrigued the president. In 1864, the *New York World* reported that Zacharie "enjoyed Mr. Lincoln's confidence, perhaps more than any other private individual . . . [and was] perhaps the most favored family visitor to the White House."

He did not pass through Washington unnoticed. The *New York Herald* described him as "a man distinguished by a splendid Roman nose, fashionable whiskers, an eloquent tongue, . . . great skill in his profession, an ingratiating address, . . . and a plentiful supply of social moral courage." On the other hand, the *World* disparaged Zacharie as a "toe-nail trimmer" and reported, "the President has often left his business-apartment to spend an evening in the parlor with his favored bunionist."

A year before Zacharie's trip to Richmond, after the fall of New Orleans to the Union, realizing that a foot doctor could move with ease between social classes as well as among the influential in the Confederacy, Lincoln had sent Zacharie to New Orleans on a sensitive mission to interview local people, including Jewish friends, to assess public opinion in the aftermath of General Nathaniel P. Banks's assumption of command as a successor to the hated General Benjamin "Beast" Butler. Zacharie treated the feet of General Banks and numerous other leading citizens of New Orleans to seek information and frequently wrote letters back to Lincoln describing what he discovered. (He also sent the President baskets of bananas, oranges, and pineapples, addressing him as "My Dear Friend.") The letters, which are preserved in the Library of Congress, tell an extraordinary tale of spying and observation, even observing Confederate troop movements to uncover future military plans. With $5,000 in Confederate currency issued by the military quartermaster, Zacharie employed and outfitted as peddlers Jewish businessmen who had lost their livelihoods, who could, thus disguised, move around the countryside as familiar figures on the rural landscape.

Zacharie also was able to befriend and help Jewish visitors from the North who had been unable to return home from New Orleans after the Union capture of the city, as well as numerous concerned Southern Jewish families who had relatives there now living under Union rule. Among them had been the sister of Judah P. Benjamin, for whom Banks had arranged safe passage out of the city. One of Zacharie's missions to Richmond was to obtain the South's approval to allow General Banks to discuss possible peace negotiations, and Zacharie wrote back to General Banks, "Benjamin . . . spoke of you *in the kindest manner* and said . . . he was under obligation to you for your kindness *toward his sister*."

Zacharie claimed that he was the originator of the so-called peace plan that he brought to Richmond, but the politically ambitious General Banks also claimed authorship and wanted to represent the Union in any subsequent peace talks. (Banks was one of Lincoln's notorious "political generals" with no military training who was given military command because he had served before the war as Governor of Massachusetts, a two-term congressman from the state, and Speaker of the U.S. House of Representatives.) The plan became known and ultimately was ridiculed by the Northern press as the product of an overactive imagination. The idea, discussed over two days in Richmond, and later reported in the *New York Herald*, was that Jefferson Davis, with Union support and supplies, would assemble 150,000 soldiers of the Confederate Army to attack Napoleon III's French troops in Mexico, conquer that country, and oust Emperor Maximilian. Davis would then proclaim himself president of the Mexican republic, after which the seceding states would be readmitted to the Union, thereby ending the Civil War.

It was a grand scheme that had a certain breathless naiveté to it. Though Zacharie wrote that he discussed the matter for two hours with President Lincoln behind closed doors, ultimately it was also opposed by Stanton and other hard-liners in the Cabinet.

In 1864, after campaigning for Lincoln's reelection among Jews across the North, and hinting in almost every letter to Lincoln of his merit and hope of future recognition, Zacharie was honored by Jewish leaders at a testimonial evening in New York. He responded to the praise in remarks stating that "in this republican and enlightened country, where we know not how soon it may fall to the lot of any man to be elevated to a high position in the government, why may it not fall to the lot of an Israelite as well as any other?" Bertram W. Korn asked in *American Jewry and the Civil War*: "Did he conceive of himself as another Jewish premier, like Judah P. Benjamin, wielding the power of statecraft for an affectionate President? It is not altogether unlikely."

In an interesting footnote to the story, Henry Wentworth Monk, described by Korn as a "strange . . . Canadian born Judeophile" and "early Zionist . . . visionary," once went to Washington to discuss still another peace plan with Lincoln and mentioned "his pet project" of the Jewish return to their ancient biblical homeland in Palestine. It was reported that Lincoln agreed that it "was worthy of consideration" and that "I myself have regard for the Jews. My chiropodist is a Jew and he has so many times 'put me on my feet' that I would have no objection to giving his countrymen 'a leg up.'"

Korn sums up Zacharie's role in history as a man Lincoln listened to, trusted enough to send on missions, read reports from, and accepted on merit as a Jewish foreigner who had no "mass following or well-placed backers" and was "unknown and unimportant." Korn concludes that "whatever his role—sycophant, court jester, politician, spy or sincere friend—his relationship with Lincoln was one of the strange corners of the personal and public life of the Civil War President."

As the war dragged on and the structure of the South began to unravel, the romantic dreams of easy victory turned to blood, death, starvation, and destruction; and the nation, at its most desperate moment, erupted with the most virulent explosion of anti-Semitism that America had yet experienced. The press and officials in the North and the South, including Union officers, attacked the Jews. In the North, the Jews were the secessionists, the "rebel spies," the "speculators," the "counterfeiters driving Anglo-Saxon firms out of business," the "cause of the inflation," the dark and shadowy presence behind all the troubles. An Associated Press writer in New Orleans wrote an article stating that "the Jews of New Orleans and all the South ought to be exterminated. They run the blockade and are always to be found at the bottom of every new villainy."

Of course, the anti-Semitic charges against Jews ignored the nature of the crisis in the Southern economy after the outbreak of hostilities. As an agricultural economy, the South imported most of what was needed from the North and from Europe. Once the Northern blockade became the "anaconda" that was designed to strangle the South, all imports were cut off. With instantaneous shortages of every kind of goods imaginable and rapid inflation, blockade runners and smugglers were able to earn fantastic fortunes for their cargoes; and everyone who bought and sold commodities benefited from the scarcity—farmers, merchants, tradesmen, shop owners, farm supply storekeepers—whether they were Jews or Gentiles, native born or foreigners, patriots or traitors. The South needed scapegoats, and who better than the Jews, who had served such a role for centuries and whose dishonesty and vilification were part of the church preaching on Sundays and holidays.

General Order No. 11: "the most sweeping anti-Jewish regulation in all American history"

The South lay in ruins, decimated by fire and plunder, its ports isolated for years by blockade, its factories turned to charred rubble by a deliberate scorched-earth policy, its money worthless, and its economy in turmoil. Without foodstuffs or farmers to raise food in the midst of battle, the scarcity sent prices soaring beyond imagination to make a broken people more miserable. In Memphis, on the Mississippi River, at the line of battle, thousands of bales of cotton sat in the warehouses, half hostage and half gold, the target for speculators and adventurers and Yankee soldiers, who saw unprotected cotton as a way to steal whatever the South had left of any worth. But cotton could be turned into a huge profit by selling it in the North to the reopening textile factories so long deprived of Southern cotton. President Lincoln told a friend, "The army itself is diverted from fighting the rebels to speculating in cotton." Charles A. Dana wrote to the Secretary of War, "Every colonel, captain, or quartermaster is in secret partnership with some operator in cotton; every soldier dreams of adding a bale of cotton to his monthly pay."

Generals Ulysses S. Grant and William Sherman considered all the speculators as leeches on the system, bringing in gold for cotton that would be convertible into arms. Sherman had earlier complained of "swarms of Jews and speculators" who were flocking into Memphis. For Sherman, the terms were synonymous.

On December 17, 1862, Grant issued what Bertram Korn called in his volume, *American Jewry and the Civil War*, "the most sweeping anti-Jewish regulation in all American history," General Order No. 11, providing that "the Jews, as a class violating every regulation of trade established by the Treasury Department and also department orders, are hereby expelled from the department [of Tennessee] within twenty-four hours from the receipt of this order."

Southern Jews who had lived in Tennessee for decades, even former Union soldiers, were forced to pack up their families hurriedly and leave. When one man and his wife questioned a soldier, they were told, "It's because you are Jews and neither a benefit to the Union nor the Confederacy." But the political struggle to rescind the order would not be argued on behalf of the Jews in the South; instead it would be based on the more blatant injustices to Jewish loyalists to the Union cause.

Cesar Kaskel of Paducah, Kentucky, had seen thirty men, some with Union military service, and their families deported, without trial or hearing, and he hastened to Washington to see President Lincoln. He stopped in Cincinnati to ask the assistance of Rabbi Isaac Wise, and together they began to stimulate petitions, letters of protest from Jewish leaders to Washington, and resolutions demanding revocation of the order. Congressman Gurley of Ohio, a friend of Rabbi Wise, arranged an appointment with the president, and Kaskel brought affidavits from leading Republican Party members and military authorities. Korn's book reported the following quiet conversation with the president—almost charming in view of the intensity of his visitor.

> LINCOLN: And so the Children of Israel were driven from the happy land of Canaan?
> KASKEL: Yes, and that is why we have come unto Father Abraham's bosom, asking protection.
> LINCOLN: And this protection they shall have at once.

Lincoln walked over to a big table and wrote a note to the General-in-Chief of the Army, Henry W. Halleck, directing him to telegraph instructions canceling the order. He wished Kaskel well and told him that he was free to return home. When a delegation of rabbis and other Jewish leaders called on the president to thank him, Lincoln told them that he could not understand what compelled the general to issue it. "To condemn a class is, to say the least, to wrong the good with the bad. I do not like to hear a class or nationality condemned on account of a few sinners." In Allan Nevins's words, "All honor to Lincoln!"

The *New York Times* referred to the order as "one of the deepest sensations of the war" and criticized Grant, saying, "men cannot be condemned and punished as a class without gross violence to our free institutions." Most newspapers gave the popular general every shadow of a doubt; some, like the *Washington Chronicle*, called the Jews "the scavengers ... of commerce," while others criticized the general as "thoughtless," while praising his military record. The order followed Grant into politics and became one of the major issues in his election as president in 1868. He never apologized or explained, though he wrote a congressman during the campaign, "I have no prejudice against sect or race, but want each individual to be judged by his own merit. Order No. 11 does not sustain this statement, I admit, but I do not sustain the order. It would never have been issued if it had not been telegraphed the moment it was penned and without reflection."

The *Cincinnati Enquirer* suggested that Grant and Sherman had been influenced by powerful cotton buyers and their officer cohorts in the army to make way for larger profits. The price of cotton was lowered from forty cents a pound to twenty-five cents a pound the day after the order was issued; thus the speculators who remained profited from the order. Isaac Wise charged in his journal a few months after the order, "The Jews bought cotton from planters at forty cents a pound; the military authorities with their business partners, agents, clerks, porters, etc., intended to buy that staple at twenty-five cents a pound . . . they could sell it in Eastern cities just as high as the next man—and the Jews must leave, because they interfere with a branch of military business."

Lincoln's cancellation of the order diminished greatly the rising fear of Jews in the South that the Union victory would thrust them again into the kind of anti-Semitism they had fled from in Europe. The Northern Jewish community had stood beside the Jews in the South, demonstrating a sense of community that transcended sectional bitterness. Northern Jews had publicly petitioned their government to revoke an order by its most popular general in the midst of a war, and the head of the nation had agreed. For Northern and Southern Jews who had escaped from countries where such unfairness would have been shrugged off, the decision by Lincoln made them know that they had found a home in the new land, and that its paper promises as the protector of minorities were real and concrete. The war itself had given Jews on both sides the opportunity to stand and fight with their neighbors, and when it was over, for most of them, they were much more "American" than when it began. The Civil War had been a totally American battle without foreign troops or clash of foreign ideology—only brothers could fight. Bitter as that experience was for the nation, it enabled Jews in the North and the South to taste the fire of American dissension and be welcomed by other Americans into the bosom of the nation.

The Aftermath of the War

After years of struggle and turmoil, the devastated and wrecked Southern economy began to show signs of life. A recovering South suggested opportunity to the new Jews streaming from Russia and Poland to the "Promised Land"—2.8 million from 1881 to 1924—crowding into the pushcart pandemonium of the Lower East Side of New York City, packing the tenement houses, and scrambling for wages in the sweatshops of the streets.

Only fifteen years after the end of the Great War almost four million black slaves were newly freed, Atlanta was just beginning to rebuild from the devastation of Sherman's march, and the South was still smoldering in the lawlessness and racial violence of Reconstruction. Only the most foolhardy or the most desperate immigrants would take the chance. But why not try? First, stock a peddler's pack at the Baltimore Bargain House—little risk in that—then look for a place to settle and send for the family. Surely then his relatives would come.

Another generation of Jews was poised to play out the drama again.

Part I

Jews and Slavery

The twelve-volume *Jewish Encyclopedia* (New York, 1901–1906), the first comprehensive work embracing all aspects of Jewish history, religion, and life, contained no article about slaveholding among American Jews but a significant article on the "Antislavery Movement in America." While the article acknowledged Jewish slaveholding ("it is not hard to account for the fact that so receptive and assimilative a people as the Jews should have adopted it from the people among whom they were living"), it focused on those Jews who opposed the "peculiar institution." It credited the rise of antislavery sentiments among Jews "for the enormous number of Jewish soldiers who enlisted in the Union army during the Civil War."

Much twentieth-century scholarship concerning Jews and Blacks echoed the *Jewish Encyclopedia*. Writers acknowledged that Jews in the Caribbean, in colonial America, and in the antebellum South had owned slaves, but they focused on Jews who opposed slavery. During the heyday of the "Black-Jewish Alliance" in the 1950s and '60s, this historiography provided activist Jews with the comfortable assurance that they were carrying forward a long and noble tradition.

A tract published in 1991 by the Nation of Islam disturbed this comfort. Entitled *The Secret Relationship between Blacks and Jews*, it proclaimed that Jews funded, masterminded, and dominated the Atlantic slave trade. Jews, the publication concluded, bore "monumental culpability" for all that slavery wrought.

The controversy over the Nation of Islam's claims stimulated a bumper crop of fresh scholarship concerning Jews and the slave trade. Although the tract's overwrought claims were quickly demolished, scholars who looked anew at the evidence painted a more nuanced portrait of Jewish involvement in the slave trade, raised surprising questions, and set forth a whole new way of thinking about Blacks and Jews in the New World.

Seymour Drescher, who spent a lifetime studying the Atlantic slave trade, summarizes much of this new scholarship in his 2001 article reprinted here. "It is unlikely that more than a fraction of 1 percent of the twelve million enslaved and relayed Africans were purchased or sold by Jewish merchants," he concludes (this volume, 67). In a 1993 article in *Immigrants and Minorities*, he observed that "the Atlantic slave system was more important to certain segments of early modern Jewry than early modern Jews were to the Atlantic slave system." Indeed, drawing on Eli Faber's exhaustively researched *Jews, Slaves and the Slave Trade* (1998), Drescher wonders why, given Jews' significance in other realms of trade, they actually played so *small* a role in the slave trade. For example, the great Newport Jewish merchant Aaron Lopez, historian Virginia Platt showed in a 1975 article in the *William and Mary Quarterly*, dispatched well over two hundred trade voyages between 1760 and 1776, but only fourteen of them went to Africa for the purpose of gathering slaves. Why Lopez and other Jewish merchants traded far fewer slaves than comparable non-Jewish traders remains unclear.

Drescher concludes, as historian David Brion Davis did, that the New World proved highly beneficial to Jews but catastrophic to Blacks. Jews, with their mercantile skills and wide kinship networks, proved highly valuable to New World colonies. As a result, Jews found their "threshold of liberation" in the New World, winning an array of rights in the Americas that they could not have enjoyed back in Europe. By contrast, since New World economies depended on slave labor, Blacks were brought to the New World in chains. They became the principle out-group and objects of prejudice and hatred, while Jews greatly improved their lot, particularly in places where skin color determined status and Jews won acceptance as whites.

Such was the case in the Old South, the subject of Bertram W. Korn's classic article reprinted in chapter 2. First published in 1961 for the Civil War centennial, the article anticipated many themes of subsequent research and remains the single best study of Jews and Black slavery in the antebellum United States. Korn exhaustively surveyed "Jews as planters, and as owners of slaves; the treatment of slaves by Jews; the emancipation of slaves by Jews; Jews as harsh taskmasters; business dealings of Jews with slaves and free Negroes; Jews as slave dealers; cases of miscegenation involving Jews and Negroes; and opinions of Jews about the slave system" (this volume, 87–88). New documents have subsequently appeared, and thanks to Jonathan Schorsch's *Jews and Blacks in the Early Modern World* (2004) we also now know much more about the period prior to the American Revolution. Korn's basic conclusion, however, remains unchallenged. When it came to slavery, Jews "were in no appreciable degree different from . . . their non-Jewish neighbors" (this volume, 115).

1

Jews and New Christians in the Atlantic Slave Trade

Seymour Drescher

In studying the westward expansion of Europe after 1500, "the development of an Atlantic economy is impossible to imagine without slavery and the slave trade."[1] During three and a half centuries, up to twelve million Africans were loaded and transported in dreadful conditions to the tropical and subtropical zones of the Americas. This massive coerced transoceanic transportation system was only one element of a still broader process. Probably twice as many Africans were seized within Africa for purposes of domestic enslavement or transportation to purchasers in the Eastern Hemisphere during the same period. The coerced movement of Africans long exceeded the combined voluntary and involuntary migrations of Europeans. By the beginning of the nineteenth century, between two and three Africans had been landed in the Americas for every European who crossed the Atlantic.[2]

This major human migration involved the direct and indirect participation of many individuals and institutions in Europe, Africa, Asia, and the Americas. It required an enormous number of interlocking activities, within and between continents. Although tens of thousands of direct participants involved Muslims, Christians, Jews, and others who could be classified by religion, and scores of groups that could be classified by ethnic affiliation, the history of the slave trade is usually considered in terms of geography and state sponsors. Geographically, the trade is analyzed in

---

Reprinted, without accompanying maps, with permission of Seymour Drescher from *The Jews and the Expansion of Europe to the West, 1450–1800*, ed. Paolo Bernardini and Norman Fiering (New York: Berghahn Books, 2001), 439–470, copyright © 2001 by The John Carter Brown Library.

terms of a triangular trade in which Europeans provided capital, organization, and the means and manpower of transoceanic transportation; Africans provided the captives and the means of intra-continental movement; and Europeans in the Americas provided the means for redistributing transported captives to productive occupations in various regions.[3]

Politically, the slave trade is usually framed in terms of a succession of national entities drawn into and dominating the trade as suppliers, carriers, and purchasers. Although every European polity bordering the Atlantic attempted to enter into the Atlantic slave trade between 1450 and 1800, a small number of states dominated the European-sponsored enterprises. Chronologically, the trade as a whole is generally broken down into three phases. Each succeeding phase of the slave trade was numerically larger than its predecessor. In the century and a half of the first phase (1500–1640), 788,000 Africans were embarked on the "Middle Passage," or about 5,600 per year. During the course of the second phase (1640–1700), 817,000 left Africa, or about 13,600 per year. In the final phase, between 1700 and British abolition in 1807, 6,686,000 were exported, or about 62,000 per year. Thus, four out of every five Africans transported to the New World between 1500 and 1807 were boarded in the final phase.[4]

For most scholars of the slave trade, economic, demographic, and political categories are the most significant variables in determining the coerced movement of Africans. They look to economics or political economy to explain the flow of people from Europe to the coast of Africa and of captive Africans from the coast of Africa to the Americas. Price, mortality, health, age, sex, provenance, destination, and occupation are the key variables. Economic and demographic conditions, inflected by political attempts to bend those conditions in favor of one nation or another, define the priorities of analysis.[5]

This essay, however, deals with the impact of a particular religious minority upon economic and demographic developments in the Atlantic world over three centuries. Analyzing the role of religious or ethnoreligious groups in the African slave trade within the familiar framework of nations and regions presents unusual methodological difficulties. Historians are acutely aware that the trade involved tens of thousands of perpetrators. Among them were pagans, Muslims, Catholics, Protestants, and Jews. Those who were involved may be further divided into scores of groups by ethnic designation, including every major entity ever defined as a "race." Scholars incorporate these entities contingently as they analyze the core processes of the trade itself. Even in regard to the study of slave

TABLE 1.1
Coerced African Migrants Leaving for the Americas by National Carrier
(in thousands)

1500–1700 (Phases I and II)

Carrier	Before 1580	1580–1640	1640–1700
Spanish	10	100	10
Portuguese	63	590	226
British	1	4	371
Dutch	0	20	160
French	0	0	50
Total	74	714	817

1700–1800 (Phase III)

Carrier	Totals
British	3,120
Portuguese	1,903
French	1,052
Dutch	352
American	208
Danish	51
Total	6,686

Sources: David Eltis, *The Rise of the African Slave Trade in the Americas* (Cambridge, U.K., 2000), 9, table I-I; and David Richardson, "Slave Exports from West and West-Central Africa, 1700–1810: New Estimates of Volume and Distribution," *Journal of African History* 30 (1989): 10, table 4.

trading collectivities, it is rare that historians regard the religious affiliation of the European participants as of more than limited significance, compared with economic relationships. The trade flowed easily from one religious and commercial entity to another. Culturally defined identities may have had some impact upon the fundamental choice of viewing Africans as enslavable, but over the whole period of its rise the transatlantic slave trade appears to have been an activity extraordinarily responsive to cost-benefit calculations.[6]

Analyzing the specific relation of Jews to the Atlantic slave trade is warranted by a peculiar historiographical tradition. "Scarcely were the doors of the New World opened to Europeans," declared the economist and historian Werner Sombart, "than crowds of Jews came swarming in. . . . European Jewry was like an ant-heap into which a stick [expulsion from Spain] had been thrust. Little wonder, therefore, that a great part of this heap betook itself to the New World. . . . The first traders in America were Jews," as well as "the first plantation owners" in African Saõ Tomé and the first transplanters of sugar and slaves across the Atlantic. Jews were the "dominant social class [*die herrschende Kaste*]" of Brazil. Along with Portuguese criminals, they constituted almost the entire population of that colony, which reached its peak of prosperity only with "the influx of rich Jews from Holland." In support of his interpretation, Sombart drew heavily upon accounts by Jewish historians and encyclopedists. As Jewish migration to the Americas swelled at the end of the nineteenth century, writers sought to establish the earliest possible Jewish presence of their ancestors in the New World and to magnify their role in the grand narrative of European westward expansion. The search for Jewish preeminence in Atlantic development continues to find supporters among authors with dramatically contrasting motives.[7]

Sombart's hyperbolic account was correct in one respect. Three centuries of cumulative expulsions of Jews from Atlantic maritime states reached their climax as Europe's great westward expansion began in the fifteenth and sixteenth centuries. The simultaneous departure of both the Columbian expedition and Jews from Spain in 1492 was merely emblematic of a broader movement in European Jewish history. By 1500, Jews had been expelled from the kingdoms of England, France, Spain, and Portugal. Two generations later they had also been excluded from most of the Habsburg Netherlands, from the Baltic seacoast, and from large parts of Italy. This meant that by the time Africans began to be exported to the Americas in significant numbers (ca. 1570), Europe's rulers had forced the overwhelming mass of European Jewry eastward to Poland, Lithuania, and the Ottoman Empire. Neither the rulers nor the merchants (including the Jewish merchants) of those new regions of settlement were involved or interested in the Atlantic slave trade.[8]

Jews could not live openly or securely anywhere along the European Atlantic seaboard during the first century after the Columbian expedition, the century in which the Euro-African coastal supply systems and the Iberian-American slave systems were created. Jews were consequently prohibited from openly participating in co-founding the institutions of the slave trade at any terminus of the triangular trade, or in the transoceanic "Middle Passage." One characteristic of this "religious cleansing" of Europe's Atlantic littoral also carried over into the second phase of the slave trade (1604–1700). African forced migration was dominated by political entities that tried to limit the slave trade to their own sponsored contractors in Europe, Africa, and the Americas. Success in long-distance and long-term voyages, as Europeans discovered, was initially enhanced by access to politically privileged monopolies in Europe, trade enclaves on the African coast, and colonial settlements in the Americas. Until the end of the seventeenth century, governmental agencies or quasi-public trading companies aspired to monopoly positions.

The greater the advantage offered by official patronage in any European polity, the less likely there was to be a Jewish presence. In a confessionally intolerant Europe and its overseas extensions, it was virtually impossible for Jews to hold the principal managerial positions in official slave trading entities. During three centuries, Spanish slave trade licenses and *asientos* (monopoly contracts for the delivery of slaves to the Spanish colonies) were never awarded to Jews. Apparently, this was as true in the Portuguese, Dutch, English, and French trades as it was for the Spanish *asiento*. Jews could, at most, exercise occasional influence at the margins of these official agencies as negotiators and consular intermediaries. Even subcontracting to Jewish merchants for the delivery of slaves contributed to the refusal of the Spanish government to renew the *asiento* to the Portuguese Royal Guinea Company at the beginning of the eighteenth century.[9]

Phase One

The Portuguese Atlantic slave trade to the Americas was an offshoot of their fifteenth-century slave trade from the African mainland to offshore islands and metropolitan Portugal. Historians of this pre-Columbian migration stream always emphasize the high degree of state control over this trade. It was conducted under the auspices of a crusading monarchy that was engaged in almost continuous religious warfare with North African Muslim kingdoms. Those who participated in the African coastal voyages of exploration by supplying capital, ships, or manpower included English, French, Polish, and Italians, as well as Iberians. None of the historical accounts of the Portuguese slave trade during the pre-Colombian period discusses a Jewish slaving dimension. The only accounts of a prominent Jewish presence in this initial process of oceanic exploration and trade are related to the scientific and cartographic experts mobilized by Prince Henry the Navigator to track his African exploratory expeditions.[10]

If Jews could play no role in the initial political and legal foundations of the European transatlantic slave trade, the elimination of Jewry from the Iberian Peninsula created a major economic niche for some genetic descendants of the Jews. In 1497, the forced mass conversion of one hundred thousand Iberian Jews residing in Portugal created a novel situation.

As Christians, ex-Jews were free to take full advantage of the Portuguese seaborne empire, the first fully global network of its kind in human history. The Portuguese trading network expanded explosively along the coasts of Africa, into South Asia, and to the east coast of South America. For nearly a century after the 1490s, the Portuguese held a virtual monopoly in the trades to Europe from these areas.

In one respect, Portugal's post-conversion legislation tended to enhance and prolong the commercial orientation of these legally designated "New Christians" in a society dominated by a traditional system of values and institutions. At the same time, however, Portugal's stigmatization of New Christians as members of a legally separate and inherited status also rendered its members subject to endless genealogical scrutiny, humiliation, confiscation, and violence from generation to generation.

The volatile nature of the New Christian position was symbolized by the first mass deportation of European children to the tropics. Following the flight of Jews to Portugal after the Spanish expulsion of 1492, the Portuguese monarch had two thousand children abducted from their Jewish families. They were baptized and deported to Saõ Tomé, an island off the coast of Africa at the latitude of the equator. In a few years, only six hundred children remained alive. The continent that was soon to be called "the white man's grave" was first a "white child's grave." This first cohort of New Christians in Africa was mated at maturity with Africans. Their descendants, along with New and Old Christian Portuguese immigrants who arrived both involuntarily and voluntarily, became Saõ Tomé's principal inhabitants and traders.[11]

New Christians were, of course, legally denied the opportunity to openly profess or transmit Jewish culture and ritual. The Inquisition's premise of "impure blood" and the alleged collective propensity to heresy and "Judaization" transformed descent and kinship linkages into socially explosive material. However, these descendants of Jews were far from being frozen within a rigid endogenous caste system. The idea that New Christians overwhelmingly maintained religious, cultural, or even genealogical continuity with fifteenth-century Iberian Jewry into the eighteenth century was a racial myth. Most of those who remained within the Iberian orbit in fact attempted to assimilate as rapidly as possible. Intergenerational studies of Portuguese and overseas New Christians have concluded that each generation became culturally and religiously more able to live among, practice with, and marry Old Christians. For more than two centuries, however, this trajectory toward assimilation was intercepted by waves of official and popular coercion. Of an estimated one hundred thousand Jews at the time of conversion in 1497 (one-tenth of Portugal's population), no more than sixty thousand New Christians remained in 1542, and perhaps half that number in 1604 (or 2 percent of the population) at the height of their influence in the Portuguese slave trade.[12]

This marginalizing and volatile environment has serious implications for anyone wishing to analyze the economic behavior of New Christians both in general and as slave traders in particular. Their reaction to stigmatization punctuated by purges was a complex pattern of social organization and behavior. Denied full legitimacy in the community of the faithful, New Christians tended to develop trading networks that, as a means of survival, were based above all on family connections, and also tended to narrow their loyalties only to kinsmen or, at the most, to other New Christians who were similarly marginalized. Their ties to a geographically and culturally distant Jewry were often as fragile as those to the more proximate Old Christians among whom they lived in uncomfortable conformity. Unpredictable purges created periodic crises of identity. Those with sufficient resources and anxiety sometimes exited from the Iberian orbit altogether. Small waves of individuals periodically fled to areas where they could escape the Inquisition's procedures.

Not all of those who left Iberia rejoined Jewish communities. Many fled under threat of Inquisitorial persecution to the domains of more tolerant Catholic princes, an indication of a propensity toward Christianization. Economic opportunities frequently took precedence over genealogical vulnerability, even among those who lived beyond the power of the Iberian Inquisitions. A considerable number of those arrested as crypto-Jews in Mexico between 1620 and 1650, for example, had lived unmolested in Catholic Italy and France before risking immigration to the Spanish empire. Moreover, the documented phenomenon of New Christians returning to Iberia from Africa, Asia, or the Americas after having made their fortunes indicates that most wealthy merchants and mercantile families were not necessarily inclined to resettle where they could openly practice Judaism or even practice syncretic brands of family religiosity.[13]

The exercise of caution in lumping together Jews and New Christians in Europe or America is further warranted by developments in Africa. During the late sixteenth century, at the height of their participation in the Atlantic slave trade, a number of New Christians were living as defectors, beyond the Portuguese zone of control in Africa. These New Christian *lançados*, notes John Thornton, established a whole chain of settlements "with posts in Kongo (and often positions in the church and administration of Kongo) and its eastern neighbors as well as in states in the Ndembu region and Ndongo." Thornton, however, makes no mention of the reestablishment of Jewish communities among these New Christian defectors living there or anywhere else beyond the power of the Inquisition and the exclusivist definition of Christianity prevalent in Portugal. On the American side of the Iberian empires, New Christian merchants in the seventeenth-century New World "could social-climb almost as well as Old Christian merchants; it simply took them another generation or two to reach their goal." That goal was "the foundation of an entailed estate and a patent of nobility as a *fidalgo da casa real*." We have no evidence that the Dutch, English, or French Caribbean islands constituted important places of refuge for New World New Christians who might possibly have wished to flee Inquisitorial threats in the nearby Spanish American mainland colonies.[14]

Neither in their social orientation nor in their approach to economic activity, can one differentiate significantly between New and Old Christians in the slave trade. The latter certainly did not shun that economic activity because of its association with crypto-Jews in the popular mentality. Especially in discussing economic activity in the early modern Iberian empire, there is no heuristic value in generically identifying New Christians more closely with Jewish merchants among whom they did not live, than with Old Christian merchants among whom they did live. To conflate two distinct social entities (Jews and New Christians) when attempting to assess the potential roles of religious formations simply begs the question of affiliation.[15]

In comparative terms, however, the early modern Iberian empires allowed New Christians to play a role in the Atlantic slave trade that was never to be matched by Jews in any part of the Atlantic world. When the first global trade network in the world formed at the beginning of the sixteenth century, the New Christians were positioned to become its first trade diaspora. If their quasi-pariah religious status kept them at least once removed from institutional power, that same status tended to make them most effective in a world in which opportunities for long-term credit were dependent upon kinship and trust.

The African slave trade depended upon a complex series of exchanges—from Europe to Africa to America to Europe—in which trustworthy interlocking agents and trained apprentices offered enormous advantages to competing traders. As Joseph Miller notes, slave traders always operated at the margins of the rapidly expanding Atlantic system: "To the extent that merchants from the metropole involved themselves at all in this early trade in slaves, they tended to come from New Christian circles then coming under heavy pressure from the Inquisition at home and seeking respite from persecution in flight to the remote corners of the empire or to Protestant Northern Europe."[16]

The slave trade, therefore, opened up transoceanic niches of entrée and refuge that gave New Christians an initial advantage in human capital over other merchants. Slaving was so valuable an activity in the eyes of rulers that its New Christian practitioners might hope to be specifically exempted from periodic group expulsions. In one purge, New Christians were allowed to remain in Angola only if they were merchants. As commodities, slaves themselves opened niches into the American empires at times when other types of goods were restricted or excluded. Slaving was long a privileged means of gaining a foothold in Spanish as well as Portuguese America, even though there was a tendency for slavers, once established, to switch to other economic activities.[17]

Given this balance of negative institutional, social, and legal coercion and their positive technical and familial advantages, New Christian merchants managed to gain control of a sizable, perhaps major, share of all segments of the Portuguese Atlantic slave trade during the Iberian-dominated phase of the Atlantic system. I have come across no description of the Portuguese slave trade that estimates the relative shares of the various participants in the slave trade by this racial-religious designation, but New Christian families certainly oversaw the movement of a vast number of slaves from Africa to Brazil during its first-century period. James Boyajian identifies one New Christian whose network was responsible for transporting more than 10,200 "pieces" to the New World.[18] Another individual, António Fernandes de Elvas, operated the Angola and Cape Verde contracts between 1615 and 1623. This was also the peak period for general attacks on the crypto-Jewish monopoly of Portuguese trade.

Phase Two

During the "second Atlantic system," about 1640 to 1700, the Iberian near-monopoly was definitively broken. The focus of the slave trade expanded northward from Portuguese Brazil to the Caribbean region. Most northern Atlantic and Baltic Sea states attempted to enter the transatlantic slave system: the Netherlands, England, France, Denmark, Sweden, Brandenburg, and Courland. In the second half of the seventeenth century, the sheer number of state-sponsored companies engaged in the transportation of African slave-laborers reached its peak. For the first time, Jews participated substantially in this more open and competitive environment and played their most tangible role in the slave trade.[19]

By the end of the sixteenth century, a small stream of New Christians had already moved northward from Iberia, settling (either as Christians or as Jews) along a string of Atlantic and North Sea ports from southern France to northwestern Germany (and, eventually, England).[20] Before full-scale Dutch entry, Jewish Sephardim residing in Amsterdam used their comparative advantage in Iberian contacts to begin the first African slaving voyages conducted by professing Jews. Before the founding of the Dutch West India Company, Amsterdam Jewish merchants chartered several vessels specifically for the slave trade from West Africa to Brazil and the Spanish Caribbean. The interest of Jewish merchants in the slave trade constituted a small part of their larger interest in the African and Brazilian trades to Europe.[21] Jews operating out of (or migrating from) the Netherlands still did not make a major contribution to the slave trade in most of the geographic segments of the system: fitting slave ships in Europe; managing slave factories, i.e., trading outposts, in Africa; or transporting slaves to the Americas.

During most of the seventeenth century, the Dutch transatlantic trade was conducted primarily by means of a chartered slaving monopoly given to the Dutch West India Company. That Company held on to the slaving monopoly long after it lost its exclusive rights over all other commodities. As Jewish merchants were unable to operate freely outside the Company and were excluded on grounds of religion from serving on its directorate, they could enter the Dutch slave trade in only two ways: as passive investors in the Company itself, or as illegal private traders (interlopers). In the first case, Jewish investment in the West India Company was remarkably small. It amounted to only a 1.3 percent share of the founding capital. At the peak of Dutch influence in the Atlantic slave trade between the early 1640s and the early 1670s, Jews appear to have constituted between 4 and 7 percent of the membership in the West India Company.[22] Jews were a much smaller segment in the Dutch overseas trade than were New Christians in the Portuguese global trade. Dutch society was comparatively much better endowed with capital, commercial skills, and entrepreneurial expertise. There remains, however, the possibilities of illegal, or interloper, trade. It is the one branch of the Dutch slave trade for which I have seen no quantitative estimate of Jewish mercantile participation. However, according to Johannes Postma's comprehensive quantitative estimate of the Dutch slave trade, interlopers accounted for no more than 5 percent of the total transatlantic trade.[23]

In terms of company-sanctioned slaving, Jews were hardly involved in the "Middle Passage." Throughout the period of the West India Company's slave trade monopoly, from 1630 to 1730, only a handful of Jewish merchants are recorded as having been given permission to sail on their own account directly to the African coast. In Africa itself, the rise of the Dutch empire seems to have contributed equally little to the establishment of a strong Jewish presence. The Dutch seizure in the 1630s and 1640s of many important Portuguese trading centers and possessions in Africa resulted neither in a great influx of European Jews nor in a sudden relapsing of resident New Christians (whose ranks, according to contemporary polemicists, were filled with crypto-Jews) into professing Jews.

The main Jewish link with Dutch and other slaving came at the New World terminus. The Dutch were fully launched as a slaving power after their conquests in Brazil and Africa during the 1630s and early 1640s. However, they lacked a metropolitan population eager or desperate enough to relocate to the American frontiers. It was at the first western margin of the Dutch transatlantic trade that Jews played their largest role. Around 1640, the Dutch briefly became Europe's principal slave traders. They welcomed Jews as colonizers and as onshore middlemen in newly conquered Brazil. During the eight years between 1637 and 1644, Jewish merchants accounted for between 8 and 63 percent of first onshore purchasers of the twenty-five thousand slaves landed by the West India Company in Dutch-held Brazil. Perhaps a third of these captives must have reached planters through Jewish traders. The progressive loss of Dutch Brazil to the Portuguese between 1645 and 1654 brought the Jewish presence to an end. The recapture of Brazil also revealed the degree to which religious affinities between Dutch Jews and Portuguese New Christians were limited by overriding economic interests. It was the New Christians who financed the Portuguese expedition to recapture Brazil. The ritual public burning of one of Brazil's captured Jews in Lisbon marked a definitive point of cultural and commercial alienation between the Jewish community in Holland (which also suffered heavy economic losses from the reconquest of Brazil) and the New Christian merchants in Portugal.[24]

Jewish merchants took up a similar activity at another margin of the Dutch empire, in the Caribbean colonies. Even in the relatively tolerant

TABLE 1.2
Estimated Traffic and Destination of Slaves Delivered by the Dutch to Curaçao, 1658–1732

Period	Number of Slaves
1658–1674	24,555
1675–1699	25,399
1700–1730	23,716
1731–1795	15,587

Source: Johannes Menne Postma, *The Dutch in the Atlantic Slave Trade, 1600–1815* (Cambridge, U.K., 1990), 35, 45, 48, 223.

Dutch empire, Jews were initially more welcome in tropical areas of polyglot European and slave colonization than in temperate zone areas originally designed to be outposts of Dutch culture, including the Reformed religion. Refugees from Brazil and Europe were resettled primarily in Dutch-controlled islands and in Suriname on the coast of South America. By the end of the seventeenth century, the island of Curaçao contained the largest Jewish settlement in the Americas. From Curaçao, Jews engaged extensively in a transit trade with the British and French islands, and, more significantly, with the Spanish mainland. Over the course of the century between Curaçao's establishment as a Dutch colony in 1630 and the virtual end of its transit slave trade in the 1760s, Jewish merchants settled or handled a considerable (but not yet precisely defined) portion of the eighty-five thousand slaves who landed in Curaçao, about one-sixth of the total Dutch slave trade.

As in other sectors of the slave trade, the West India Company's local agents were invariably Christians, and the island's commercial life was dominated by the Protestant majority. Just when Curaçao's participation in the transit slave trade was reaching its zenith at the end of the seventeenth century, wealthier Jews in the Netherlands were forging strong business ties with the island. Sephardic Jewish investors were involved in shipments of slaves from West Africa and in Dutch participation in the Spanish *asiento*. One Jewish family acted as Amsterdam factors for the Portuguese Guinea Company and as its delegates to the Dutch West India Company. Jewish mercantile influence in the politics of the Atlantic slave trade probably reached its peak in the opening years of the eighteenth century. During the War of Spanish Succession (1702–13), the whole trade of Spanish America seemed open to the Dutch. Both the political and the economic prospects of Dutch Sephardic capitalists rapidly faded, however, when the English emerged with the *asiento* at the Peace of Utrecht in 1713.[25]

Less discussion is necessary regarding the Jews in the other colonies of the seventeenth-century Caribbean region. Jewish mercantile activity in the British colonies was a more modest replication of the pattern in the Dutch Antilles. As in the Dutch case, metropolitan Jews played a minor role as passive investors in the seventeenth-century chartered slaving monopolies. Jewish merchants did not invest in the first such company, the Royal Adventurers Trading into Africa, which lasted from 1660 to 1672. Nor did they initially invest in its successor, the Royal African Company (RAC), until the 1690s. Eli Faber's assiduously researched study of Jewish participation in British imperial slavery shows that the peak of Jewish mercantile investment in the Royal African Company lasted from the mid-1690s to the second decade of the eighteenth century. Owning about 10 percent of the RAC's shares during the period when the company accounted for about 20 percent of the English slave trade, Jewish merchants accounted for about 2 percent of metropolitan slaving capital. With the removal of charter restrictions on the Anglo-African trade in 1712, the Jewish metropolitan role declined still further.

During the third quarter of the seventeenth century, Jewish merchants also established a presence in some of the English West Indies, especially Barbados and Jamaica. In neither island did they acquire a large proportion of the island's slaves as planters. However, like non-Jews who resided in the urban areas, they bought a small percentage of less desired slaves, often known as "refuse slaves" for resale and redistribution in the Caribbean transit trade. Eli Faber calculates that Jews purchased 7.1 percent of the slaves landed by the Royal African Company in Jamaica between 1674 and 1700. A corroborating study by Trevor Burnard calculates the Jewish share at 6.5 percent for the slightly longer period of 1674–1708. As in the Dutch Caribbean, Jews were most prominent in the intra-Caribbean branch of the slave trade. Jewish merchants in the English islands never attained the significance of the Curaçao merchants in the Dutch Caribbean. Nowhere in the English Atlantic colonies did Jews own much more than 1 percent of the slaves.[26]

Jewish participation in the French slave trade was more evanescent. In the French Caribbean colonies, a Jewish presence established in the 1660s and 1670s was virtually eliminated by expulsions in the mid-1680s. As slave traders in the French colonies, Jews never approached the significance of their counterparts in the Dutch Antilles. Jews also played marginal roles in the efforts of smaller Northern European maritime states to become players in the Atlantic economy. At a moment when access to this second

Atlantic system seemed open, the rulers of Denmark, Sweden, Courland, and Brandenburg all attempted to enter it. Jews of Hamburg and Amsterdam were sought out for advice or expertise. Again, one must note the relatively modest role of even the most prominent of Europe's mercantile Jews in the formation of Atlantic trading enterprises. When the Brandenburg African Company was formed, late in the seventeenth century, its subscribers were principally the elector of Brandenburg, the elector of Cologne, and Benjamin Raule (Zeelander and director-general of the Brandenburg navy). Smaller sums were offered by several of the elector's privy councilors. Raule's own share was underwritten by Dutch investors, presumably including Jews. As in the Dutch case, Jewish participation was auxiliary and nonmanagerial. Jews played an even more marginal role in another slave trade project. In 1669, the Count of Hanau wished to found a slave-labor colony within the Dutch West India Company's colonial sphere in South America. His agent made contact with the Company's executive in Amsterdam through a Jewish intermediary. Neither the German prince nor the West India merchants thereafter required the Jew's services.[27]

During the same period, however, other Jews occasionally had more important roles as agents and intermediaries. "The Nunes da Costa, in Amsterdam and Hamburg, were leading participants in setting up of the Portuguese Brazil Company. They also aided the colonial schemes of Duke James of Courland. The Belmontes were closely connected with Dutch bids for the Spanish slaving *asientos*." This flurry of activity coincided with the peak of Jewish entrepreneurial activity in the last third of the seventeenth century.[28] At the height of this second phase of the Atlantic slave trade, the Jewish mercantile influence on its development in Europe, in Africa, and on the Atlantic remained modest. The real importance of the sojourn of Jews in Brazil was that it gave some of them an initial technological advantage in their movement into the Caribbean. Elsewhere, Jewish capital and organization never approached the level of significance attained by that of New Christians in the Americas during the previous century and a half of Jewish exclusion.

Phase Three

The long eighteenth century (1700–1807) witnessed the absolute peak of the Atlantic slave trade in terms of annual slave departures and arrivals. With some local exceptions, the Jewish presence in the slave trade declined rapidly. Intensive research into each of the national trades has failed to turn up more than a handful of Jewish individuals or mercantile families in any of the great slaving systems of the eighteenth century. Research on the French trade has turned up detailed records of a few Jewish families in a trade dominated by merchants of other religious groups. In Bordeaux, the center of Jewish activity in the French colonial trade, Jewish traders accounted for only 4.3 percent of the slaves exported to the New World by the merchants of that city. One Jewish family, the Gradis, ranked among the seven major slavers in eighteenth-century Bordeaux. The prominence of the Gradis family was yet one more demonstration that special political influence was a significant comparative advantage for dealers in slaves. The Gradis family had greater access to institutional centers of power, both on the African coast and in France, than other Jewish mercantile families in the port.[29]

Concerning Britain, Faber shows that the Jewish share of Britain's African trade declined from its minor role in the Royal African Company. Jewish shareholders accounted for less than 1.6 percent of the original capital of the South Sea Company in 1714. As independent investors and ship-owners, the metropolitan Jewish capitalists never accounted for more than 1 percent of Britain's African trade during the last fifty years before slave trade abolition. Eighteenth-century Jews were equally marginal as receivers of consignments of slaves in the colonies. Only an occasional Jewish factor can be identified in any of the islands. Jewish merchants continued to occupy their traditional niche as purchasers of slaves for resale. According to British Naval Office records, 5.9 percent of the twenty-four thousand slaves reexported from Jamaica between 1742 and 1769 were carried on Jewish-owned vessels. Only in two British colonies did Jewish participation rise above the 6 to 7 percent share level of seventeenth-century traders. During the third quarter of the eighteenth century, the combined African slaving voyages of the Rivera and Lopez families of Newport, Rhode Island, accounted for 9 percent of that colony's slaving activity. During the century before Anglo-American abolition in 1807, Jews accounted for about 2 percent of Newport's transatlantic slave trade.

In Jamaica, the Jewish role was more volatile. The revival of the slave trade after the war of the American Revolution was accompanied by a rise of Jewish mercantile participation in the reexport trade. During the mid-1760s, as in the metropolis, fewer than 1 percent of the ships in Jamaica's ports belonged to Jews. Twenty years later, their ownership share had increased to 4.3 percent. In the late 1780s, an unprecedented 26.7 percent of reexported slaves were carried in their vessels. Thereafter, their share fell to the seventeenth-century level of 6 percent before British slave trade abolition. The post–American Revolution recovery also stimulated a dramatic increase in the role of Jamaican Jewish merchants as slave factors. From the mid-1790s until 1802, the Jewish-Christian partnership of Alexandre Lindo and Richard Lake was responsible for between 22 and 37 percent of Africans advertised for sale in Kingston, Jamaica.[30]

The eighteenth-century Iberian slave trade is equally notable for the declining significance of its New Christians. They seem to have rapidly disappeared from the discourse of the South Atlantic slave trade. At the beginning of the seventeenth century, Portuguese polemicists inveighed against the New Christian monopoly of the Portuguese trade. By the 1680s, however, the most serious petition against African slavery and the slave trade ever to be laid before the Roman *curia* failed to evoke the old charge of New Christian preponderance. The anti-slavery petitioner had no qualms about invoking Iberian racial prejudice toward the descendants of Jews in support of his case against African enslavement. It was scandalous that impure crypto-Jewish masters held black Christians of pure blood in bondage. The petitioner, however, remarkably failed to assail the predominance or to mention the function of contemporary New Christians in the African slave trade.[31]

Flights of New Christians from the Iberian orbit dwindled in proportion to the decline of Inquisitorial persecutions. The last century and a half of the Portuguese-Brazilian slave trade is a period in which New Christians simply faded into obscurity.

When the Iberian Inquisitorial period came to an end and freedom of religion was introduced in Latin America after the wars of independence, former New Christians did not reemerge as Jews, Protestants, or marranists. Roman Catholicism remained the overwhelming locus of communal religious identity, whatever the genealogical composition of the inhabitants. Except in some isolated villages in Portugal and the Americas, crypto-Jewry had to be rediscovered or reinvented in the late twentieth century.

Conclusion

During the first three centuries of Atlantic slaving, Europeans landed eight million African captives in the Americas. By 1800, three million African-American slaves toiled in houses, shops, farms, and plantations from the Hudson River Valley to the Rio de la Plata. If it is impossible to imagine the expansion of the early Atlantic economy without the slave trade, can the same be said about the role of Jewish merchants in that trade? Had the return of the Jews to Europe's Atlantic ports been postponed until the 1790s instead of the 1590s, the volume of enslavement or distribution of Africans in the Atlantic system would hardly have been altered. The "Jewish presence" in the slave trade was too ephemeral, too localized, and too limited to have made an appreciable difference.

The economic, social, legal, and racial pattern of the Atlantic slave trade was in place before Jews made their way back to the Atlantic ports of northwestern Europe, to the coasts and islands of Africa, or to European colonies in the Americas. They were marginal collective actors in most places and during most periods of the Atlantic system: its political and legal foundations; its capital formation; its maritime organization; and its distribution of coerced migrants from Europe and Africa. Only in the Americas—momentarily in Brazil, more durably in the Caribbean—can the role of Jewish traders be described as significant. If we consider the whole complex of major class actors in the transatlantic slave trade, the share of Jews in this vast network is extremely modest.

Considering the number of African captives who passed into and through the hands of captors and dealers from capture in Africa until sale in America, it is unlikely that more than a fraction of 1 percent of the twelve million enslaved and relayed Africans were purchased or sold by Jewish merchants even once. If one expands the classes of participants to include all those in Europe, Africa, Asia, and the Americas who produced goods for the trade or who processed goods produced by the slaves, and all those who ultimately produced goods with slave labor and consumed slave-produced commodities, the conclusion remains the same. At no point along the continuum of the slave trade were Jews numerous enough, rich enough, and powerful enough to affect significantly the structure and flow of the slave trade or to diminish the suffering of its African victims.[32]

The same conclusion does not hold true for the New Christian merchants during one phase of the trade. The foundations of the Atlantic slave trade were indeed firmly in place before New Christians began to appear in the documents of the sixteenth-century Portuguese Afro-European slave trade. They again rapidly diminished in significance by the eighteenth century; however, their role in the development of the slave trade to the Americas must be given its full weight. When Portuguese merchants became the first fully global trading diaspora in the history of the world, New Christian merchants were prominent in the growth of the Atlantic economy.³³ Distrusted by Old Christian political and religious elites, New Christians found a precarious niche in the Atlantic system. Less as a religious group than as a loose network of trading families, they were pioneers in the formation of the European-Asian-African-American complex that supported the New World's first African-based slave economies.

I lack the basis for a quantitative breakdown of New Christians in the Atlantic system. However, they seem to have had a more significant function in the operations of the slave trade than would be indicated by their numerical proportion of the Portuguese or Ibero-American populations. During the period when Portugal dominated the slave trade to the Americas (1570–1630), New Christians dominated important segments of Portuguese long-distance trade. The majority of these New Christians successfully effected their own disappearance into African, Iberian, or Ibero-American identities. A minority worked their way northward or eastward into various forms of Christianity, Judaism, or a syncretistic amalgam of both religious systems. In assessing the economic links between African slaves, New Christians, and Jews in the Americas, one must bear in mind that although Jews and New Christians shared some common ancestors, the differences between them became progressively deeper.³⁴ Economically speaking, in any given area of the Iberian orbit, New and Old Christian slave traders constituted denser networks of interaction than those that remained between Jews and New Christians across great geographical distances.

Viewing the Atlantic system over the whole period from 1500 to the age of the American revolutions, it is clear that merchant families of Jewish ancestry possessed their greatest comparative economic advantage at the beginning of the transatlantic slave trade. In 1500, they found themselves trapped and forcibly converted in a poor country where mercantile skills and capital were at a premium. They also found themselves at the center of a trading network that circled the globe in a single generation. The network deepened and broadened when the Portuguese and Spanish empires were ruled by a single monarch between 1580 and 1640. New Christian families were represented in all zones of the early Atlantic trade—in Europe, Africa, and Latin America.

During the second phase of the Atlantic slave trade, when observant Jews first entered the system, they found that their relative advantages and significance were both sharply reduced in comparison to those of New Christians within the Iberian orbit. They played minor roles in the

European, African, and transoceanic branches of the Northern European trade. Their mercantile communities were far smaller in proportion to Christian networks in Northern Europe than were those of New Christians to Old Christians in Iberia. Their working capital was correspondingly less significant. Finally, any technical advantages that Jewish traders enjoyed over their Dutch, English, or French Christian competitors was far more restricted than had been those of the New Christians in sixteenth-century Iberia.[35]

Only in the Dutch orbit did Jews play a durable, if modest, role. In part, their brief prominence depended as much upon their availability as refugee "risk-takers" in tropical frontier colonies as upon their experience as merchant entrepreneurs in Europe. They were, as the English essayist Joseph Addison correctly noted, "pegs and nails" rather than architects and master builders in the second Atlantic system after 1640. During the third phase of the trade, the significance of Jewish capitalists declined further. When the Afro-American slave trade reached its absolute peak toward the end of the eighteenth century, both Jews and New Christians had nearly disappeared from the records of the transatlantic slave trade.

There is one final indicator of the Jews' eighteenth-century marginality. At two important flashpoints, one in the history of British Jewry, the other in the history of the British slave trade, the empirical insignificance of the relationship between Jews and the Atlantic slave trade was matched by its insignificance in contemporary discourse. In 1753, a bitter debate erupted over a bill to naturalize foreign-born Jews residing in England. A friendly pamphleteer cited as many Jewish contributions to the welfare of the British nation as he could, pointedly including Britain's overseas trades with East India, Jamaica, and Spanish America. There was no mention of Africa or the transatlantic slave trade.[36]

Thirty-five years later, the first European abolitionist crusade began in Great Britain. By the end of the American Revolutionary and Napoleonic wars, its target had expanded to include the entire Atlantic slave trade, symbolized by a declaration against the trade at the Congress of Vienna in 1815. Yet, steeped as they were in the Christian tradition, European abolitionists never sought to add a specifically "Jewish" dimension to their rhetorical attack on the slave traders. Nor did they shift religious responsibility for the traffic from the overwhelming majority of Christian traders toward the few Jewish traders in their midst. Still more significantly, British and French abolitionists never responded to the temptation offered by the mentality of the Iberian Inquisitions. They did not attempt to rewrite the history of the Atlantic slave trade within an antisemitic framework, or to construct a Jewish or crypto-Jewish creation myth. Sombart's later variant of this myth did not draw nourishment from the main current of European antislavery sentiment.

I have not touched upon another large historiographic question—the relation of the eighteenth-century slave trade to the British Industrial Revolution. Suffice it to say that if the Jewish role in the slave trade was meager, the slave trade's role in generating capital for the British Industrial Revolution (or for the prior Dutch "Golden Age") was equally modest. The Jewish merchants' share of the slave trade's share in accounting for European economic expansion and industrialization was a small fraction of a small fraction. Here again, Iberian New Christian merchants presumably played a much larger role in a trade that probably made them much more important to Portuguese commerce than Jews had been to any early modern European economy. To conclude from this, however, that the slave trade "helped" Portugal to achieve sustained economic progress would be absurd. After three hundred years of sponsoring colonial slavery, neither the Portuguese nor their observers could detect much in the way of economic development in Portugal.[37]

Thus far I have considered what Jewish and New Christian merchants did to expand the flow of Africans within the Atlantic system. But what did the slave trade do for the expansion of European Jewry to the Americas? I noted the important function of the slave trade as an escape hatch for New Christians in Africa and in Latin America, and for Jews in the Caribbean region. One common historiographic inference is that the settlement and liberty of Jews in the New World (albeit on a far smaller scale and less completely than that of other European migrants) was aided by the forced migration of enslaved Africans. The most significant point, from this perspective, is not that a few Jewish slave dealers changed the course of Atlantic history, but that Jews in general found their "threshold of liberation" in regions newly dependent upon black slavery. In this scenario, Sephardic Jews and New Christians who engaged in the European slave trade were pioneers of Jewish resettlement in the early modern world, blazing a path for the liberation of their co-religionists.[38]

A still more intriguing historical question has begun to emerge in scholarly discourse on the role of Jews in the African slave trade. If the empirical record makes it relatively easy for historians of the trade to verify empirically that Jews did not dominate this segment of the Atlantic economy, historians of Jewry have begun to ask why Jews were not more involved than they were in the trade. If there was no special religious inhibition against buying and selling human beings among early modern Jews, why didn't Jewish merchants maximize their presumed advantages: a transoceanic ethno-religious network, and a facility with the important trading languages of the early Atlantic world? From the perspective of a historian of the slave trade, the response might be that these putative advantages were not the significant ingredients for success in the transatlantic slave business. In ethno-religious terms, there was no Jewish communal network on the coasts of Africa. Nor did Jewish multilingualism extend to any special competence in the languages of Africa, although it probably helped in the Caribbean transit trade, where they did find a niche. Success in the African trade depended far more on up-to-date intelligence about the changing tastes of Africans, translatable into rapid business decisions about the optimum assortment of goods for slaving voyages.

Even in most of the Americas, there is ample evidence that the Jewish mercantile network probably counted for little in Atlantic slaving. The evidence of Jewish involvement in the eighteenth-century slave trade presents us with a trail of inter-religious networks as keys to success. In case after case, Jewish merchants who participated in multiple slaving voyages or similar long-term activities linked themselves to Christian agents or partners. In Newport, Barbados, Jamaica, New York, Philadelphia, and Charleston, the pattern was replicated throughout the century before British abolition. A close study of Jews in the slave trade seems to confirm the main focus of slave trade historiography during the past half-century. Economic and demographic variables, inflected by political conditions, remain the decisive elements. It was not as Jews but as merchants that Jewish traders ventured into one of the significant enterprises of the early modern world.[39]

In light of the above analysis, we need to reconsider older assessments of New Christian and Jewish participation in European expansion to the Americas. Tens of thousands of Portuguese New Christians emigrated from Portugal after 1500. If we suppose that they departed from the metropolis at least proportionately to their estimated share of the Portuguese population (10 percent), then seventy thousand of the seven hundred thousand who left Portugal between 1500 and 1700 were New Christians. The movement of Spanish *conversos* would only add to this total. From a cultural perspective, however, three centuries of New Christian migration to the Ibero-Americas and to Ibero-Africa resulted only in the disappearance of New Christians, almost always in favor of fusion with other

Catholics. There is no evidence of a rapid reappearance of distinctive marrano (still less of a "New Jewish") religiosity when Ibero-American citizens were finally allowed freedom of worship after their successful wars of independence. At best, New Christian crypto-Jews remained as a smattering of isolated families in the Americas, with a secretive "culture of difference," rather than a web of Jewish or marrano cultural formations. The migratory wave of seventy thousand New Christians to the New World left less of a cultural or communal trace in the Atlantic world of 1800 than a Jewish migration one-tenth as large.[40]

Professing Jews, by contrast, did gain a foothold in the Americas by 1800. Their largest and most successful communities were located in non-Iberian colonies dominated by slave agriculture. Even with the assumption that the Sephardic archipelago was indebted to the Atlantic slave trade for its expansion, it would be truly hyperbolic to say that European Jewry had gained much demographic or cultural advantage from their economic involvement. Nowhere in the Atlantic world did Jews collectively identify themselves in terms of some of their co-religionists' presence in the slave trade. Nor did their economic activities depend more heavily upon that trade than those of other European or African ethnic groups. Even in Curaçao, "it was textiles and hardware which were the backbone" of the trade of Jewish merchants with Spanish America. Demographically, of the nearly two million Europeans migrating across the Atlantic from 1500 to 1800, far less than 1 percent could conceivably have been Jews. In 1800, the fraction of world Jewry and wealth on the western shores of the Atlantic was smaller still. No Jewish settlement in the Americas had yet gained repute among European Jewry as a vital center of religious or cultural eminence. The appeal of the transatlantic world to the European Jewish imagination before 1800 seems to have been limited.[41]

Even before the onset of revolutions for independence in the Americas, the largest Caribbean Jewish communities were in decline. Curaçao and Suriname were already stagnant colonies in a minor empire. In the latter case, the late eighteenth-century movement of Jews into the tropical Atlantic eerily echoed the coerced migration with which it had begun from Portugal three centuries before. After 1750, Jewish arrivals in Suriname only barely exceeded departures because of a semicoerced migration from Amsterdam.[42]

As the volume of the transatlantic slave trade moved toward its peak on the eve of the Saint-Domingue revolution of 1791, the Jewish presence in that trade had long since shrunk even from its modest dimensions of

TABLE 1.3
Jewish Population Centers in the Western Hemisphere, 1500–1800

Area	Census Date	Population (est.)
Recife, Brazil	1645	1,450
Barbados	1699	250
Martinique	1685	96
Curaçao	1745	1,500
Jamaica	1770	900
Nevis	1678	25
Saint-Domingue	1765	120
New Amsterdam	1654	100
Rhode Island	1774	120
Savannah, Georgia	1733	41
Charleston, South Carolina	1800	600
Suriname	1787	1,292

Source: Malcolm H. Stern, "Portuguese Sephardim in the Americas," *American Jewish Archives* 44 (1992): 141–78; R. van Lier, *Samenleving in een grensgebied. Een Sociaal-historische studie von Suriname* (Deventer, the Netherlands, 1972), 24; cited in Jan Lucassen, "The Netherlands, the Dutch, and Long-Distance Migration in the Late Sixteenth to Early Nineteenth Centuries," in *Europeans on the Move: Studies on European Migration, 1500–1800*, ed. Nicholas Canny, 153–91 (Oxford, U.K., 1994).

the previous century. Above all, no Jewish community in the Americas had emerged as a magnet for the Jewish populations living in the heartland of Jewry—Eastern and Mediterranean Europe. When a second and far greater wave of Jewish migration flowed to the New World a century after 1800, it owed nothing to the slave trade or to plantation slavery. It began after the demise of the Atlantic slave trade, and it largely avoided the great arc of the Caribbean basin that had once been the center of Sephardic settlement. When the mass Jewish and mass African migrations finally converged in the late nineteenth-century Americas, they were the voluntary migrations of two peoples, among many, yearning to breathe free.

NOTES

1. P. K. O'Brien and S. L. Engerman, "Exports and the Growth of the British Economy from the Glorious Revolution to the Peace of Amiens," in *Slavery and the Rise of the Atlantic System,* ed. Barbara L. Solow (Cambridge, U.K., 1991), 177–209, esp. 207.

2. For estimates, see Philip Curtin, *The Atlantic Slave Trade: A Census* (Madison, Wis., 1969); Paul E. Lovejoy, "Volume of the Atlantic Slave Trade: A Synthesis," *Journal of African History* 23 (1982): 473–501; David Eltis, "Free and Coerced Transatlantic Migrations: Some Comparisons," *American Historical Review* 88 (1983): 251–80;

David Richardson, "Slave Exports from West and West-Central Africa, 1700–1810: New Estimates of Volume and Distribution," *Journal of African History* 30 (1989): 1–22; David Richardson, review essay, "Across the Desert and the Sea: Trans-Saharan and Atlantic Slavery, 1500–1900," *Historical Journal* 38(1) (1995): 195–204; and David Eltis, Stephen D. Behrendt, David Richardson, and Herbert S. Klein, *The Trans-Atlantic Slave Trade*, a database on CD-ROM (Cambridge, U.K., 1999).

3. See Henry A. Gemery and Jan S. Hogendorn, eds., *The Uncommon Market: Essays in the Economic History of the Atlantic Slave Trade* (New York, 1979); Barbara L. Solow, ed., *British Capitalism and Caribbean Slavery* (Cambridge, U.K., 1991); J. I. Inikori and S. L. Engerman, eds., *The Atlantic Slave Trade: Effects on Economics, Societies, and Peoples in Africa, the Americas, and Europe* (Durham, N.C., 1992); and John Thornton, *Africa and the Africans in the Making of the Atlantic World, 1400–1680* (Cambridge, U.K., 1992), 152–82, 206–53. On the Asian dimension of the Atlantic trade, see Sandra Lee Evenson, "A History of Indian Madras Manufacture and Trade Shifting Patterns of Exchange" (Ph.D. diss., University of Minnesota, 1994). Evenson maintains that Indian madras was a "currency that financed two major global trade networks," including the slave trade.

4. For estimates, I have relied upon David Eltis, *The Rise of African Slavery in the Americas* (Cambridge, U.K., 2000), 9, table 1; Eltis, "Free and Coerced Transatlantic Migrations," 251–80; and Richardson, "Slave Exports from West and West-Central Africa," 10, table 4.

5. See essays in Gemery and Hogendorn, *Uncommon Market*; Herbert Klein, *The Middle Passage: Comparative Studies in the Atlantic Slave Trade* (Princeton, N.J., 1978); Julian Gwyn, "The Economics of the Transatlantic Slave Trade: A Review," *Social History* 25 (1992): 151–62. For examples of systematic analysis, see Robert W. Fogel et al., *Without Consent or Contract: The Rise and Fall of American Slavery*, 4 vols. (New York, 1989–92); David Eltis, *Economic Growth and the Ending of the Transatlantic Slave Trade* (New York, 1987). For the cultural context of the selection of Africans as the primary labor force in the plantation Americas between the sixteenth and the early nineteenth centuries, see Eltis, *Rise of African Slavery*, chaps. 1 and 3.

6. William A. Darity, "A General Equilibrium Model of the Eighteenth-Century Atlantic Slave Trade: A Least-Likely Test for the Caribbean School," *Research in Economic History* 7 (1982): 287–326; Hilary McD. Beckles, "The Economic Origins of Black Slavery in the British West Indies, 1640–1680: A Tentative Analysis of the Barbados Model," *Journal of Caribbean History* 16 (1982): 35–56; Raymond L. Cohn and Richard A. Jensen, "The Determinants of Slave Mortality Rates on the Middle Passage," *Explorations in Economic History* 10(2) (1982): 173–76; David W. Galenson, "The Atlantic Slave Trade and the Barbados Market, 1673–1723," *Journal of Economic History* 42(3) (1982): 491–511; Gemery and Hogendorn, *Uncommon Market*; Klein, *Middle Passage*; Gwyn, "Economics of the Transatlantic Slave Trade"; and Inikori and Engerman, *Atlantic Slave Trade*.

7. Werner Sombart, *The Jews and Modern Capitalism,* trans. M. Epstein, with an American edition by Bert F. Hoselitz (Glencoe, Ill., 1951), 32–33, 363nn. 61–70. For more recent scholarly assertions of Jewish dominance in the early Atlantic slave system, see note 12 below. For polemical accounts of Jewish dominance, see *The Secret Relationship between Blacks and Jews* (Chicago, 1991) and the commentary of Harold Brackman, *Ministry of Lies: The Truth behind the Nation of Islam's "The Secret Relationship between Blacks and Jews"* (New York, 1994), esp. 15–17. In scholarly perspective, David Brion Davis notes "the negative but legitimating review" of *The Secret Relationship* by Winthrop D. Jordan in *Atlantic Monthly* (September 1995): 109–14; see David Brion Davis, "Constructing Race: A Reflection," in *William and Mary Quarterly,* 3rd series, 54(1) (January 1997): 7–18, esp. 11 and note; and the letters of commentary and reply in the January 1996 issue of the *Atlantic Monthly,* 14–15. For a survey of ascriptions of Jewish domination of the slave trade, see Saul S. Friedman, *Jews and the American Slave Trade* (New Brunswick, N.J., 1998), esp. 1–15, 235–52. Early Jewish historiography on the Americas affirmed the active participation of Jews in transatlantic slavery: "The Jews settled in the American colonies were as actively identified with the institution as any other class of settlers." Max Kohler, "The Jews and the American Anti-Slavery Movement," *Publications of the American Jewish Historical Society* 5 (1897): 137–55. Jewish slave traders in Brazil were also the focus of historical scholarship. See Herbert I. Bloom, "A Study of Brazilian Jewish History, 1623–1654," *Publications of the American Jewish Historical Society* 33 (1934): 43–125. Jews, while subjected to civil and political disabilities, were always considered to be non-enslavable "Europeans," rather than enslavable Africans. See Eltis, *Rise of African Slavery,* 60. Ironically, the tradition of "Jewish difference" was sometimes exaggerated by Jewish historians to explain the lack of early Jewish opposition to transatlantic slavery. Max Kohler, no less "Orientalist" than his non-Jewish contemporaries, attributed Jewish acceptance of slavery during the colonial period to "oriental customs," which did not tend "to make the Jew an enemy of slavery." See Kohler, "Jews and the American Anti-Slavery Movement," 145. Jews were rather less distinct from their European, American, and African contemporaries than Kohler imagined. See, inter alia, Eltis, *Rise of African Slavery,* chaps. 1 and 3.

8. Jonathan I. Israel, *European Jewry in the Age of Mercantilism, 1550–1750,* 2nd ed. (Oxford, U.K., 1989), 5–34. In Polish Lithuania, Jews settled away from the Baltic seaboard provinces (ibid., 27).

9. On the establishment of a transoceanic slaving network well before the end of the fifteenth century, see John Vogt, "The Lisbon Slave House and African Trade 1486–1520," *Proceedings of the American Philosophical Society* 117(1) (1973): 1–17. For a brief period, from 1698 to 1701, the bulk of Dutch investments in the Spanish slave trade *asiento* also came from Portuguese Jews in the United Provinces. See Wim Klooster, "Contraband Trade by Curaçao's Jews with Countries of Idolatry, 1660–1800," *Studia Rosenthalia* 31 (1977): 58–73.

10. Charles Verlinden, who magnified the role of Jews in the early medieval slave trade, no longer treated them as significant actors in the late medieval period and the transition to the Atlantic system. See Charles Verlinden, *L'Esclavage dans l'Europe Médiévale*, 2 vols. (Brugge and Ghent, 1955–77); and idem, *The Beginnings of Modern Colonization: Eleven Essays with an Introduction*, trans. Y. Freccero (Ithaca, N.Y., 1970). On the Genoese as the principal financiers of the Spanish slave trade of the sixteenth century, see Ruth Pike, *Enterprise and Adventure: The Genoese in Seville and the Opening of the New World* (Ithaca, N.Y., 1966). The only reference to Jewish involvement in the African trade prior to 1500 that I have come across is a Portuguese license for trading to Guinea in precious minerals and animals from 1469 to 1474. Complaints against a Jewish presence in the Portuguese empire before the expansion to the Americas were directed toward their participation in the sugar trade. See Bailey W. Diffie and George D. Winius, *Foundations of the Portuguese Empire, 1415–1580* (Minneapolis, 1977), 307.

11. Timothy Joel Coates, "Exiles and Orphans: Forced and State-Sponsored Colonizers in the Portuguese Empire, 1550–1720" (Ph.D. diss., University of Minnesota, 1993). On the rapid intermixing of Africans and Europeans, see *Omanuscrito Valentim Fernandes*, ed. Joaquim Bensaúde and António Baião (Lisbon, 1940), 122. Robert Garfield concludes that by 1530 most of the surviving original children were probably Christian in fact. At the peak of Saõ Tomé's role in the New World slave trade, it had "a thoroughly Portuguese mulatto population." A. H. de Oliveira Marques, *History of Portugal*, 2 vols. (New York, 1972), vol. 1, 374–75.

12. On the New Christian population of Portugal, see Oliveira Marques, *History of Portugal*, vol. 1, 287. On the complexity of New Christian identity over three centuries, see Anita Novinsky, "Sephardim in Brazil: The New Christians," in *The Sephardi Heritage*, ed. R. D. Barnett and W. M. Schwab, 2 vols. (Grindon, U.K., 1989), vol. 2, 431–44; Martin A. Cohen, "The Sephardic Phenomenon: A Reappraisal," *American Jewish Archives* 44 (1992): 1–80; and B. Netanyahu, *The Origins of the Inquisition* in *Fifteenth-Century Spain* (New York, 1995), xix, 1041–42. One historiographic tradition, represented by José Goncalves Salvador, *Os Magnatas do Tráfico Negreiro XVI e XVII* (Sao Paulo, 1981), 6, is very similar to Gilberto Freyre's earlier portrayals of Jewish merchants as essentially running the Portuguese economy. The state was merely "an obligatory client of the Portuguese Sephardim." Salvador, in an extensive series of racial-cultural categories, places Jews, Semites, ethnic Hebrews, Sephardim, New Christians, and the Jewish race in opposition to Aryans and Old Christians. In this perspective, Salvador claims that by 1600 most of Brazil's churches were run by New Christian Hebrews (Salvador, *Os Magnatas*, 86), and sees the "Jewish" presence as pervasive in Iberian and Ibero-American commercial institutions. Indeed, Spain's "tolerance" for Jews in the seventeenth century is offered as a major reason for

Portugal's reassertion of independence in 1640. Compare Salvador's perspective with those of C. R. Boxer, *The Portuguese Seaborne Empire, 1415–1825* (New York, 1969), 269–72; and Anita Novinsky, "Padre Antonio Vieira, the Inquisition, and the Jews," *Jewish History* 6(1–2) (1992): 151–62. Novinsky found that Brazilian New Christians integrated more fully into the local society than those who went east or north from Iberia. See Anita Novinsky, "A Posição dos Cristãos Novos na Sociedade Bainana," in *Cristãos Novos na Bahia* (Sao Paulo, 1972), 57–103, esp. 57–58. Novinsky and Günter Böhm both deem it significant that when a Jewish community formed in Bahia during the period of Dutch occupation, New Christians did not hasten en masse to join the Dutch Jewish community. See Günter Böhm, Los *sefardies en los domenios holandeses de America del Sur y del Caribe, 1630–1750* (Seville, 1977), 21. On the refusal of many *conversos* to be circumcised so that they could return to Iberia, see Yosef Kaplan, "Wayward New Christians and Stubborn Jews: The Shaping of a Jewish Identity," *Jewish History* 8 (1994): 27–41. On the return of many wealthy New Christians from Brazil to Iberia in the 1600s, see Vitorino Magalhães Godhino, "Portuguese Emigration from the Fifteenth to the Twentieth Century: Constants and Changes," in *European Expansion and Migration: Essays on the Intercontinental Migration from Africa, Asia and Europe,* ed. P. C. Emmer and M. Mörner (Oxford, U.K., 1992), 17. On hasty ascriptions of "Judaization" elsewhere in Europe, see Rose-Blanche Escoupérie, "Sur quelque 'Marchands Portugais' établis à Toulouse ala fin du XVII siècle," *Annales du Midi* 106(205) (1994): 57–71. David M. Gitlitz, *Secrecy and Deceit: The Religion of the Crypto-Jews* (Philadelphia, 1996), 76, also concludes that those who assimilated substantially outnumbered those who identified as Jews. It must be emphasized that Jewish historiography in the United States sometimes fused "Marranos, New Christians, or Secret Jews," "whose astonishing tenacity, nay admirable obstinacy," for centuries was verified by the record of Inquisitional confessions, processions, and executions. See M. Kayserling, "The Colonization of America by the Jews," *Publications of the American Jewish Historical Society* 2 (1894): 73–76. Kayserling was a major authority for Sombart. The casual conflation of Jews and New Christians occasionally continues in otherwise well-researched histories of slavery.

13. See Jonathan I. Israel, *Empires and Entrepots: The Dutch, the Spanish Monarchy and the Jews, 1585–1713* (London, 1990), 328. In economic, as in religious, assessments, the conflation of New Christian and Jewish traders relies on elusive combinations of expansive metaphors and fragmentary "for example" evidence. Among the most notorious and entrepreneurial Portuguese Sephardic families, the Nunes da Costa, one prominent slave trading member (Diogo Peres da Costa) ended his days in Safed having eluded the Inquisition. Another slave trader (Francisco de Victoria), however, remained a sincere Christian, the only New Christian to become a bishop in sixteenth-century America. See Jonathan I. Israel, "Duarte Nunes da Costa (Jacob Curiel) of Hamburg, Sephardi Nobleman

and Communal Leader, 1585–1664," *Studia Rosenthalia* 21 (1987): 14–34. Daniel M. Swetschinski, "Kinship and Commerce: The Foundations of Portuguese Jewish Life in Seventeenth-Century Holland," *Studia Rosenthalia* 15 (1981): 52–74: "We can no longer take the proverbial interdependence of the Sephardic diaspora for granted. If and when such interdependence existed, it had little to do with shared 'Sephardichood' *per se*, but derived more precisely from an intricate network of personal kin relations" (67). In the economic sphere, "Commercial interests of separate families were paramount" (ibid., 74n.). Chains of commercial-familial links, like chains of Inquisitorial-familial associations, present quite similar conceptual temptations to envision the presence of Portuguese traders as the tip of a "Jewish" or "crypto-Jewish" iceberg: "The problem thus becomes one of trying to imagine from a view of the proverbial tip of the iceberg the contours and size of its invisible larger part." Daniel M. Swetschinski, "Conflict and Opportunity in 'Europe's Other Sea': The Adventure of Caribbean Jewish Settlement," *American Jewish History* 72 (1982): 212–40, esp. 215. The iceberg does not travel too well in those tropical waters where we have more precise records of the role of Jews in the slave trade.

14. See Thornton, *Africa and the Africans,* 61–62; idem, "The Development of an African Catholic Church in the Kingdom of Kongo, 1491–1750," *Journal of African History* 25 (1984): 146–67; David Grant Smith, "Old Christian Merchants and the Foundation of the Brazil Company, 1649," *Hispanic American Historical Review* 54(2) (1974): 233–59. Some New Christians in Spanish America confessed to being introduced to the "law of Moses" in Angola, or going to Angola out of fear of the Inquisition because they belonged to the "Jewish Nation." See Boleslao Lewin, *Singular Proceso de Salomón Machorro* [Juan de Léon]: *Israelita liornés condenado por la Inquisición* [Mexico 1650] (Buenos Aires, 1977), xii–xviii; and Manuel Tejado Fernandez, *Aspectos de la vida social en Cartegna de Indias durante el seiscientos* (Seville, 1954), 186. These works were kindly brought to my attention by Jonathan Schorsch.

15. See David Grant Smith, "The Mercantile Class of Portugal and Brazil in the Seventeenth Century: A Socio-economic Study of the Merchants of Lisbon and Bahia, 1620–1690" (Ph.D. diss., University of Texas, 1975), 103: "the distinction between New and Old Christian is quite irrelevant to their functions as merchants and merchant bankers . . . engaged in precisely the same kinds of operations, as often as not in partnership with each other." David Grant Smith and Rae Flory, "Bahian Merchants and Planters in the Seventeenth and Early Eighteenth Centuries," *Hispanic American Historical Review* 58(4) (1978): 571–94; James C. Boyajian, *Portuguese Bankers at the Court of Spain, 1626–1650* (New Brunswick, N.J., 1983), esp. chaps. 1–3; idem, "New Christians Reconsidered: Evidence from Lisbon's Portuguese Bankers, 1497–1647," *Studia Rosenthalia* 8 (1978): 129–56; and Oliveira Marques, *History of Portugal,* vol. 1, 287–88. On the insignificance of the migratory flow of New Christians from Latin America to the Northern

European-controlled Caribbean, see Swetschinski, "Conflict and Opportunity," 212-40. On Africa, see Robert Garfield, "Public Christians, Secret Jews: Religion and Political Conflict on São Tomé Island in the Sixteenth and Seventeenth Centuries," *Sixteenth-Century Journal* 21(4) (1990): 645-54. Garfield concludes that Jews had vanished from the community a century before the outburst of conflict between Old and New Christians. Even in northwestern Europe, "the cultivation of Iberian cultural habits and aristocratic pretensions became a strong distinguishing feature of their Jewish communities." *Conversos* within the peninsula were often regarded "as practicing Catholicism out of prudence, conviction, or inertia." See Miriam Bodian, "'Men of the Nation': The Shaping of *Converso* Identity in Early Modern Europe," *Past and Present* 143 (1994): 48-76, esp. 66 and 74; and idem, *Hebrews of the Portuguese Nation: Conversos and Community in Early Modern Amsterdam* (Bloomington, Ind., 1977), 30-52. Dutch suspicion of Catholics may have encouraged Amsterdam's original Sephardic settlers to hasten conversion to Judaism, even when its practices were still largely unfamiliar to them. Kaspar von Greyerz finds that sixteenth-century New Christians who settled in the Upper Rhine show evidence of an Iberian subculture, but evidence of a "deviant" religious subculture is lacking. "Judaizing" by *conversos* in that region was, as in many other cases, a projection of the Inquisitorial imagination. See Kaspar von Greyerz, "Portuguese Conversos on the Upper Rhine and the Converso Community of Sixteenth-Century Europe," *Social History* 14(1) (1988): 59-82. In Brazil, the concept of hidden "Jewish characteristics" could paradoxically subvert all distinctions between "Christian" and "Jewish" practices. The Inquisition's assumptions rendered all religiosity suspect, conformist as well as deviant. In Bahia, the more ostentatiously one wore rosaries and effigies, the greater might be the suspicion of crypto-Judaism. See Pierre Vergier, *Trade Relations between the Bight of Benin and Bahia from the Seventeenth to Nineteenth Century*, trans. Evelyn Crawford (Ibadan, Nigeria, 1976), 69n. On the often unsuccessful attempt to enforce the "congruence of legally defined ethnic and racial categories with social realities," see Stuart B. Schwartz, "Spaniards, *Pardos,* and the Missing Mestizos: Identities and Racial Categories in the Early Hispanic Caribbean," *New West Indian Guide* 71(1-2) (1997): 5-19.

16. Joseph C. Miller, "A Marginal Institution on the Margin of the Atlantic System: The Portuguese Southern Atlantic Slave Trade in the Eighteenth Century," in Solow, *Slavery and the Rise of the Atlantic System*, 120-50, esp. 122-23, 126. See also James C. Boyajian, *Portuguese Trade in Asia under the Habsburgs, 1580-1640* (Baltimore, 1993).

17. Felipe de Alencastro, "The Apprenticeship of Colonization," in Solow, *Slavery and the Rise of the Atlantic System*, 151-76, esp. 162-63. On the utility of slave trading as an entrée to Mexican residency, see Israel, *Empires and Entrepots*, 322-23; and Boyajian, *Portuguese Bankers,* 13, 33. "Only the Portuguese, who controlled the principal slave stations of West Africa could satisfy the escalating

demands of both Brazil and the Spanish colonies for black slaves," and draw Asian commodities into the economic expansion of the Americas (Boyajian, *Portuguese Trade*, 15). On the Atlantic network to Spanish America, see Enriqueta Vila Vilar, "Aspectos Maritimos del commercio de esclavos con Hispanoamerica en el siglo XVII," *Revista de Historia Naval* 5(19) (1987): 113–31. Within Europe, Jews also entered trades not blocked by guilds, including newly imported commodities (Israel, *European Jewry*, 62).

18. Boyajian, *Portuguese Bankers*, 32, 233n.; Oliveira Marques, *History of Portugal*, vol. 1,363, 373; Boxer, *Portuguese Seaborne Empire*, 331, 333.

19. See P. C. Emmer, "The Dutch and the Making of the Second Atlantic System," in Solow, *Slavery and the Rise of the Atlantic System*, 75–96.

20. See Israel, *European Jewry*, chap. 2.

21. Israel, *Empires and Entrepots*, 438–40. Herbert Bloom, whose richly documented study seeks to maximize the Jewish role in Dutch economic activity, does not list slave trading as an occupation of Jews of Amsterdam during the "Golden Age." Herbert Bloom, *The Economic Activities of the Jews of Amsterdam in the Seventeenth and Eighteenth Centuries* (Williamsport, Pa., 1937), chap. 1. In all ambiguous cases, Bloom favors a Jewish identity (see, for example, p. 133n. 52). It is worth noting that of the dozen early seventeenth-century Dutch Sephardim described by Jonathan Israel as traders "on any scale" with the Iberian Peninsula, only Diogo Nunes Belmonte (Ya'akov Israel Belmonte) is identified as a slave trader. See also Jonathan Israel, "Spain and the Dutch Sephardim, 1609–1660," *Studia Rosenthalia* 12 (1978): 1–61, esp. 5–6. Although the Portuguese imperium was central to the commercial activities of New Amsterdam's Portuguese Jews, slaving seems to have been peripheral to those activities. (See also Swetschinski, "Kinship and Commerce," 52–74.) Jews entered the slave trade primarily as intermediaries in the distribution process once slaves were landed in the Americas.

22. See Jonathan I. Israel, *The Dutch Republic and the Hispanic World, 1606–1661* (Oxford, U.K., 1982), 127; José António Gonsalves de Mello, *Gente da nação* (Recife, Brazil, 1987), 208; and Stephen Alexander Fortune, *Merchants and Jews: The Struggle for British West Indian Commerce, 1650–1750* (Gainesville, Fla., 1984), 178n. 34.

23. See Johannes Menne Postma, *The Dutch in the Atlantic Slave Trade, 1600–1815* (Cambridge, U.K., 1990). Some who have argued for a larger Jewish role in Dutch African slaving than is indicated by Jewish investment in the Dutch West India Company invoke private trading as an alternative activity. Postma, however, estimates the entire Dutch interloper trade in slaves at only 14,000 out of 286,000 Africans delivered to America by Dutch ships between 1600 and 1738, or about 5 percent of the total (ibid., 110). Even if one were to discover that Jews were heavily represented in the private Atlantic trade, the vast majority of the Dutch interlopers on the African coast were interested in the Euro-African commodity trade and not the slave trade (ibid., 80). Odette Vlessing asserts that

Portuguese Jews had an enormous influence on the development of the Dutch "Golden Age." See Odette Vlessing, "New Light on the Earliest History of the Amsterdam Portuguese Jews," in *Dutch Jewish History*, ed. Joseph Michman (Assen, the Netherlands, 1993), 43–76, esp. 64. Vlessing makes no reference to the magnitude of the Portuguese-Jewish share in the Dutch slave trade. Herbert Bloom indicates that some Jews, in partnership with a Spanish national, financed private slavers to the Spanish colonies (Bloom, *Economic Activities of the Jews of Amsterdam*, 147 and note). In Bloom's example, however, the slaver's itinerary included Curaçao, where the ship's slaves would have been recorded in the island's imports and in Postma's estimate of interloper traders. See also note 12 above.

24. See Arnold Wiznitzer, *Jews in Colonial Brazil* (New York, 1960); Gonsalves de Mello, *Gente da nação*, 233; and Jonathan Israel, "Dutch Sephardi Jewry, Millenarian Politics, and the Struggle for Brazil, 1640–1654," in *Skeptics, Millenarians and Jews*, ed. David S. Katz and Jonathan I. Israel (Leiden, 1990), 76—97. See also Günter Böhrn, *Los Sefardies en los dominios holandeses del Sur y del Caribe, 1630–1750* (Seville, 1977), 75. The Dutch occupied part of northeastern Brazil from 1630 to 1654. Jews clearly played a dominant role as wholesale purchasers of slaves from the Dutch West India Company during five of those years. Egon Wolff and Frieda Wolff, in *Dicionário Biográfico: Judaizantes e Judeus no Brazil 1500–1808* (Rio de Janeiro, 1986), show that virtually all Jewish purchases of slaves were clustered between 1641 and 1645. On the dearth of the Jewish merchant involvement in the transatlantic slave trade to the Caribbean, see also Zvi Loker, *Jews in the Caribbean: Evidence on the History of Jews in the Caribbean Zone in Colonial Times* (Jerusalem, 1991), 48–49.

25. The landing in the Americas usually marked the end of the worst horrors of the slaves' coerced migration, but the captives had to endure long and repeated physical inspection by prospective buyers. The healthiest and strongest slaves went first. The remaining ("refuse") slaves were sometimes taken on to other ports for resale. Those whose family and kinship contacts had survived the "Middle Passage" might be subject to a final separation at this point. See Seymour Drescher, "The Atlantic Slave Trade and the Holocaust: A Comparative Analysis," in *From Slavery to Freedom: Comparative Studies in the Rise and Fall of Atlantic Slavery* (New York, 1999), 312–38. On Jewish merchants in Curaçao's slave trade, see especially Klooster, "Contraband Trade," 61–63. The heyday of Curaçao's transit trade occurred later in the eighteenth century, when it was decreasingly dependent on slaves. See P. C. Emmer, "'Jesus Christ Was Good, but Trade Was Better': An Overview of the Transit Trade of the Dutch Antilles, 1634–1795," in *The Lesser Antilles in the Age of European Expansion*, ed. Robert L. Paquette and Stanley L. Engerman (Gainesville, Fla., 1996), 206–22; and Postma, *The Dutch in the Atlantic Slave Trade*, 26—55, 197–200, 268–72. Compare these modest assessments of Curaçao's role with Yosef Hayim Yerushalmi's in "Between Amsterdam and New Amsterdam: The Place of Curaçao and the Caribbean in

Early Modern Jewish History," *American Jewish History* 7(2) (1982): 172–92. Yerushalmi maximizes the value of Curaçao to European expansion from the perspective of a historian of Jewry. On the reception of Jewish refugees in New Amsterdam, see James H. Williams, "An Atlantic Perspective on the Jewish Struggle for Rights and Opportunities in Brazil, New Netherland, and New York," in *The Jews and the Expansion of Europe to the West, 1450–1800*, ed. Paolo Bernardini and Norman Fiering, 439–70 (New York, 2001). On Jewish involvement in European diplomacy and the politics of the slave trade, see Jonathan I. Israel, *Conflicts of Empires: Spain, the Low Countries and the Struggle for World Supremacy 1585–1713* (London, 1997), 392–401. For the latest calculations on the role of Sephardic capital in the Dutch West India Company, see Klooster, "Contraband Trade," 63. By the 1650s, the share of Jews investing in the West India Company had risen to around 4 percent, sufficient perhaps for the company to protect Brazilian refugees in New Amsterdam from Governor Peter Stuyvesant's expulsion orders. By 1674, Jews owned about 5 percent of the Dutch West India Company's stock.

26. On Jewish merchants in the early English slave trade, see, above all, Eli Faber, *Jews, Slaves, and the Slave Trade: Setting the Record Straight* (New York, 1998), esp. 11–56; and Trevor Burnard, "Who Bought Slaves in Early America? Purchasers of Slaves from the Royal African Company in Jamaica, 1674–1708," *Slavery and Abolition* 17(2) (August 1996): 68–92. See also Fortune, *Merchants and Jews*, 48.

27. See Israel, *European Jewry*, 139; Adam Jones, *Brandenburg Sources for West African History, 1680–1700* (Stuttgart, 1985); and Pamela Smith, *The Business of Alchemy: Science and Culture in the Holy Roman Empire* (Princeton, N.J., 1994), 151. On Portuguese Jewish participation in various African voyages from Baltic ports in the seventeenth century, see Georg Nørregard, *Danish Settlements in West Africa, 1658–1850* (Boston, 1966), 11, 12, 53, 54, 57.

28. Israel, *European Jewry*, 139. Jeronimo Nunes da Costa (1620–1697) seems to have been unusually active among Jews of Northern Europe in his ability to direct mercantile capital toward the Guinea trade of Baltic states at the end of the seventeenth century. He was frequently involved in slaving expeditions from Brandenburg, Glückstadt, and Copenhagen. See Jonathan I. Israel, "An Amsterdam Jewish Merchant of the Golden Age: Jeronimo Nunes da Costa (1620–1697), Agent of Portugal in the Dutch Republic," *Studia Rosenthalia* 18 (1984): 21–40, esp. 35–37.

29. On the French slave trade, see Robert Louis Stein, *The French Slave Trade in the Eighteenth Century: An Old Regime Business* (Madison, Wis., 1979). In Bordeaux, "only two Jewish families, Gradis and Mendez, fitted out more than one slave ship each during the entire eighteenth-century" (ibid., 159). See also Silvia Marzagalli, "Atlantic Trade and Sephardim Merchants in Eighteenth-Century France: The Case of Bordeaux," in Bernardini and Fiering, *Jews and the Expansion of Europe to the West*, 268–86; Eric Saugera, *Bordeaux, Port Négrier*

XVIIe–XIXe siècles (Biarritz, 1995), 229–34; Richard Menkis, "The Gradis Family of Eighteenth-Century Bordeaux: A Social and Economic Study" (Ph.D. diss., Brandeis University, 1988). Silvia Marzagalli kindly brought these last two studies to my attention. Across the Atlantic, Jews of Saint-Domingue constituted about 1 percent of the colony's white population in the late eighteenth century. See Pierre Pluchon, *Nègres et Juifs au XVIII siècle: Le racisme au siècle des Lumières* (Paris, 1984), 19–93. As with the Gradis family in France, one should note the similarly atypical involvement of Amsterdam's Jeronimo Nunes da Costa in the slave trade of the previous century. His access to the Saõ Tomé and Guinea trades probably depended upon his status as the agent of the Portuguese crown in the Dutch Republic and on his personal link to Portugal's Brazil Company. Thus privileged, Jeronimo seems to have been far more involved in the sugar trade than in the slave trade of Saõ Tomé and the African coast. Jonathan Israel regards this African extension of Jeronimo's economic activity as exceptional (see Israel, "An Amsterdam Jewish Merchant," 30–37).

30. See Faber, *Jews, Slaves, and the Slave Trade*, 73–82, 113–23.

31. See Richard Gray, "The Papacy and the Atlantic Slave Trade: Lourenço da Silva, the Capuchins and the Decisions of the Holy Office," *Past and Present* 115 (May 1987): 52–68. Joseph Miller, a historian of the eighteenth-century Luso-Brazilian slave trade, observes that New Christians were no longer a subject of discussion in this period (mail communication of 14 June 1996). In Miller's monumental *Way of Death: Merchant Capitalism and the Angolan Slave Trade, 1730–1830* (Madison, Wis., 1988), "New Christians" is not an indexed term. Martin Klein, a historian of Africa, has never seen a reference to Jewish slave traders on the African coast in the final period of the Atlantic slave trade (e-mail communication, 22 December 1995). On the general reduction of New Christian influence in the metropolitan Portuguese economy during the second half of the seventeenth century, see Carl A. Hanson, *Economy and Society in Baroque Portugal, 1668–1703* (Minneapolis, 1981), 218.

32. Of the fifty to sixty million working Europeans during the peak of the slave trade in the 1780s, up to two million might have been implicated in the trade in one way or another, or in the importation of slave-grown products. In the Americas, a still larger proportion of the descendants of Europeans must have been similarly involved in the same range of economic activities. Given the far larger numbers of those who were enslaved in Africa compared to those who were deported, a large proportion of the active West African population (perhaps twenty-eight million in 1820) must also have been direct participants in the slave trade and its collateral activities along the coast of Africa. For these estimates, see Olivier Pétré-Grenouilleau, *La Traite des Noirs* (Paris, 1997), 42–50; and Eltis, *Economic Growth,* 67 and notes.

33. Boyajian, *Portuguese Trade,* 17. For those who view New Christians interchangeably with Jews, it may indeed be impossible to imagine the Atlantic

system without Jewish slave traders: "So we see therefore that if it were not for the high percentage of ships in the hands of men of the Hebrew nation, commerce in the South Atlantic would be almost impossible and therefore likewise the sugar industry and African slavery" (Salvador, *Os Magnatas*, 96). For Salvador, Jews were the proverbial nail for want of which American sugar, African slavery, and the entire black Atlantic diaspora would never have existed.

34. Germán Peralta Rivera, *Los Mecanismos del comercio negrero* (Lima, 1990), 280. For recent attempts to rediscover a vanished Jewish presence in Africa, see Yossi Halevi, "Looking for Jews off Africa's Coast," *Central African Zionist Digest* (April 1995). The recent revival of interest in Jews hidden during the Holocaust seems to find an echo in a rekindled interest in marrano ancestry. Recently, a society for crypto-Judaic studies was formed by people seeking to reclaim a Jewish heritage. See Mary Rourke, "In Search of Hidden Jews," *Los Angeles Times*, 8 February 1997.

35. Greater degrees of human diversity in Africa than on other continents meant that market breakdowns, costly violence, and trade customs varied greatly from region to region. Divergent trading rules had to be learned in Africa, which put a premium on local factors. The Euro-African trade "had to get by without the cross-cultural diasporic merchant communities that [Philip] Curtin describes for other parts of the globe" (Eltis, *Rise of African Slavery*, 154, 164–92).

36. See Faber, *Jews, Slaves, and the Slave Trade*, 35–36 and 271n.

37. See Eltis, *Rise of African Slavery*, 265–66; and Kenneth Maxwell, *Pombal: Paradox of the Enlightenment* (Cambridge, U.K., 1995), 17. Jonathan Israel notes that apart from the trade in diamonds and coral and the Spanish Caribbean trade via Cadiz, Jewish activity in general counted for relatively little in England's eighteenth-century rise to commercial dominance (Israel, *European Jewry*, 242). That characterization equally applies to Jewish activity in the British slave trade. Stephen Alexander Fortune claims "a striking discovery" in finding "a close business relationship" between the South Sea Company and Jamaican Jews. He also notes that Jews were stockholders of the company in England and had contacts in the Caribbean (Fortune, *Merchants and Jews*, 137–38). Fortune does not offer any estimate of the amount or proportion of capital so invested by English Jews, or their relative importance as agents or factors in the transoceanic chain of commerce. John G. Sperling, in *The South Sea Company: An Historical Essay* (Boston, 1962), is silent on any Jewish role, as is Colin Palmer, in *Human Cargoes: The British Slave Trade to Spanish America, 1700–1739* (Urbana, Ill., 1981). As for the Netherlands, by the late eighteenth century, its "Portuguese" Jewry was recognized as having abandoned trading in favor of stock-brokering. See Charles Wilson, *Anglo-Dutch Commerce and Finance* (Cambridge, U.K., 1966), 14–15.

38. See, above all, David Brion Davis, *Slavery and Human Progress* (New York, 1984), 101; Seymour Drescher, "The Role of Jews in Transatlantic Slave Trade," *Immigrants and Minorities* 12(2) (July 1993): 113–25; David Brion Davis,

"The Slave Trade and the Jews," *New York Review of Books,* 22 December 1994, 14–17; and Yosef Hiam Yerushalmi, "Between Amsterdam and New Amsterdam," 177.

39. Gleaned from Faber's accounts of slave traders in *Jews, Slaves, and the Slave Trade.* I have discovered no evidence of a link between metropolitan religious movements and any documented unease about Jewish transatlantic slaving. See Seymour Drescher, "The Long Goodbye: Dutch Capitalism and Antislavery in Comparative Perspective," in *Fifty Years Later: Antislavery, Capitalism and Modernity in the Dutch Orbit,* ed. Gert Oostindie (Leiden, 1995; Pittsburgh, 1996), 25–66, esp. 35n. 22. For a detailed study of Jewish and black interaction during the initial period of European overseas expansion, see Jonathan Schorsch, "Jews and Blacks in the Early Colonial World, 1450–1800" (Ph.D. diss., University of California, Berkeley, 2000).

40. For an estimate of overall Portuguese emigration after 1500, see Stanley L. Engerman and João César das Neves, *The Bricks of an Empire, 1415–1999: 585 Years of Portuguese Empire* (Lisbon, 1996), WP22-96, 12. The estimate is based upon data in V. M. Godinho, "L'Emigration Portugaise (XV–XX siècles)—une constante structurale et les réponses aux changements du monde," *Revista de História Económica e Social* 1 (1978). They estimate the total outflow from Portugal for the years 1500 to 1760 at about 1.3 million. Magnus Morner and Harold Sims, in *Adventurers and Proletarians: The Story of Migrants in Latin America* (Pittsburgh, 1985), 10 (also citing Godhino), estimate the total net emigration from Portugal to Brazil between 1500 and 1760 (the limits of Inquisitorial concern with New Christians) at 790,000. A much smaller flow of *conversos* may have emigrated from Spain to the New World. I follow Boyajian in assuming that New Christian emigration from Portugal was at least proportionate to their share of the Portuguese population in 1500 (10 percent). Anita Novinsky finds that at one point New Christians represented 10 to 20 percent of the population of Bahia (see Novinsky, "A Posição dos Cristãos Novos," 57–103, esp. 65).

41. For an estimate of early modern European migration to the Americas, see Eltis, "Free and Coerced Transatlantic Migrations," 255. Based upon Robert Swierenga's estimates, the Jewish population of the New World in about 1800 could not have exceeded 10,000, and no more than that number migrated from Europe to the Americas between 1500 and 1800. Swierenga estimates that the Jewish population of the Caribbean was five times its counterpart in the United States in 1790. See Robert P. Swierenga, *The Forerunners: Dutch Jewry in the North American Diaspora* (Detroit, 1994), 36. In a study of Dutch emigration, Jan Lucassen estimates that as many as fifteen thousand Netherlanders may have emigrated "to the colonies in South Africa, the Caribbean, and West Africa" before 1800. Only one-quarter of that total would have landed before 1750 (the high tide of Jewish migration). See Jan Lucassen, "The Netherlands, the Dutch, and Long-Distance Migration, in the Late Sixteenth to Early Nineteenth Centuries," in *Europeans on*

the Move: Studies on European Migration, 1500–1800, ed. Nicholas Canny (Oxford, U.K., 1994), 153–91, esp. 175–78. Regarding New Christians, the destruction of the genealogical records by the Portuguese government in 1773 completed the official fusion of Old and New Christians and "the disappearance of the Jews and their descendants from Portugal and Brazil." In 1797, the Portuguese government explicitly invited Suriname's Portuguese Jews back: "where you would enjoy the greatest security and peace. For presently . . . none of the reasons which occasioned your expatriation exists any longer" (quoted in Swetschinski, "Conflict and Opportunity," 212). Swetschinski does not mention any Jewish migration in response to the belated invitation. Nor does he indicate any "internal immigration" by descendants of the New Christians within Portugal or Brazil into the Jewish fold. See also Oliveira Marques, *History of Portugal,* vol. 1, 380. There is no evidence to indicate that any large group of Latin Americans rejoined the Jewish community when a continuous Jewish migration to Ibero-America resumed early in the nineteenth century. See Judith Laikin Elkin, *Jews of the Latin American Republics* (Chapel Hill, N.C., 1980), 14–20. The deeper Jewish and African relationship began, of course, where the transoceanic slave trade finally deposited its victims. Whatever the transatlantic world's attractions for seventeenth-century Sephardim, it seems to have appealed much less to the literary imagination of Ashkenazi Jewry. Natalie Zemon Davis notes in her biographical sketch of Glikl bas Judah Leib, a merchant of Metz, that Glikl's autobiography was written "at a time when . . . Jews were among the new owners of sugar plantations and of African and Indian slaves in Suriname" and when Menasseh ben Israel, of Amsterdam, played with the idea "that the Amerindians were the descendants of the Lost Tribes of Israel." See Natalie Zemon Davis, *Women on the Margins: Three Seventeenth-Century Lives* (Cambridge, Mass., 1995), 41. Yet when Glikl chose to weave an exotic tale about the seafaring quest of a wise Talmudist, she had her hero board a boat bound for the East Indies.

42. See Wim Klooster, "The Jews in Suriname and Curaçao," in Bernardini and Fiering, *Jews and the Expansion of Europe to the West,* 350–68. On Suriname, see Robert Cohen, *Jews in Another Environment: Surinam in the Second Half of the Eighteenth Century* (Leiden, 1991), 18–20, 175–80.

2

Jews and Negro Slavery in the Old South, 1789–1865

Bertram W. Korn

Introduction

Slavery was the dominant social and economic fact of life in the Southern states. It was also the focus of the increasing strife between the North and South which culminated in the secession of the Southern states, the formation of the Confederate States of America, and the effort of the North and West to reform the Union which, in its military phase, is known as the Civil War. While it is true that there were many other factors which contributed to the outbreak of the Civil War, it is equally true that there would have been no armed conflict if slavery had not been the integral aspect of the economic and social life of the South. Slavery was the single indigestible element in the life of the American people which fostered disunion, strife, and carnage, just as the concomitant race problem has continued to an important degree to be a divisive force in American life to this very day.

This chapter is an effort to assess the experiences of Jews with slavery, to evaluate their participation in and acceptance of the system, and to establish the relationship of Jewish status in the Southern states to the existence of the institution of slavery, during the period from the adoption of the Constitution to the end of the Civil War. The following themes are treated in detail: Jews as planters, and as owners of slaves; the treatment of

---

Reprinted, in abridged and somewhat revised form, with permission from *Publications of the American Jewish Historical Society* 50 (1961): 151–201, copyright © 1961 by the American Jewish Historical Society.

slaves by Jews; the emancipation of slaves by Jews; Jews as harsh taskmasters; business dealings of Jews with slaves and free Negroes; Jews as slave dealers; cases of miscegenation involving Jews and Negroes; and opinions of Jews about the slave system.[1]

I. Jews as Planters and as Owners of Slaves

Only a small number of Jews in the Old South were planters. Sociological and economic factors explain why so few Jews achieved this characteristic Southern status of ownership and occupation. History had ordained that European Jews could not own land; the selection of occupations in which Jews could train their sons was severely delimited. Most Jews, out of natural inclination and the pressure of circumstances, felt safer in urban areas, where they could share each other's fellowship and find support in each other's presence. If Jews desired to be loyal to their ancestral faith, they could fulfill this need only where other Jews resided, not in the rural areas. An additional pressure was the poverty which accompanied most immigrant Jews when they came to America. The average Southern Jew was, therefore, a peddler or store-keeper, with comparatively slim resources, who tended to live in a town or city, and would not even think of aspiring to the ownership of a plantation.

Some Jews found their way to the highest rung of the economic and social ladder through prosperous careers as merchants or professional men. Among this small number of men, probably the best-known was Judah P. Benjamin, the brilliant New Orleans attorney, who purchased an extensive plantation twenty miles south of the city in 1844, in partnership with Theodore Packwood, who served as the resident manager. Not content with the rather smallish mansion house, Benjamin rebuilt Bellechasse into a magnificent house which finally fell victim to a housing development in 1960. Benjamin's home, in which he installed his sisters after his wife and daughter moved to Paris, was an elegant example of ante-bellum grace, with "great, double-leveled porches, almost fifteen feet across, a parade of massive, rectangular pillars and everything else in proportion; curving stairways of mahogany, massive carved decorations, silver-plated doorknobs, extensive rose gardens between the house and the levee, and an enormous bell into which Benjamin was said to have dropped five hundred silver dollars during the melting, to 'sweeten the tone.'" Though Benjamin continued to practice his legal profession, he devoted great interest to his plantation, unlike the typical absentee landlord, and wrote articles and delivered speeches on the problems of sugar-planting. Bellechasse was staffed with one hundred and forty slaves, of whom about eighty were field-hands. Benjamin sold the plantation after his election to the Senate.[2]

Another well-known Jewish planter was Major Raphael J. Moses, who owned land at Esquiline Hill, near Columbus, Georgia. Moses, who became Chief Commissary Officer of Longstreet's Corps during the war, wrote in his memoirs that "when the war broke out, I had forty-seven slaves, and when it ended I had forty-seven freedmen—all left me except one, old London, who staid with me until he died."[3]

Other Jewish planters were: Nathan Nathans, who was a President of Beth Elohim Congregation of Charleston, South Carolina, with a plantation on the Cooper River; Isaiah Moses, who worked thirty-five slaves on his farm at St. James, Goose Creek, South Carolina; Mordecai Cohen, who had twenty-seven slaves on his plantation at St. Andrews, South Carolina, and his two sons, Marx and David, both of whom owned nearby farms; Isaac Lyons, of Columbia, South Carolina; Barnet A. Cohen of King's Creek, South Carolina; and Chapman Levy, who turned from the law to planting when he moved to the Mississippi Territory. Various members of the Mordecai family had plantations in North Carolina and Virginia. Among other large plantation holdings, Moses Levy owned a magnificent home, "Parthenope," on a plantation at the juncture of the Matamzas River and Moses Creek, in Florida, which he sold to Achille Murat, the French refugee. One of the few lady planters was Abigail Minis, who had a small plantation near Savannah on which she employed seventeen slaves. The only Louisiana planter other than Benjamin whom we have been able to discover was J. Levy of Ascension Parish, with forty-one slaves working his fields.[4]

There were probably a number of other Jewish owners of plantations, but altogether they constituted only a tiny proportion of the Southerners whose habits, opinions, and status were to become decisive for the entire section, and eventually, for the entire country. In contradistinction, it is astonishing to discover even one Jew who tried his hand as a plantation overseer even if only for a brief time. He was the much-traveled, restless, and adventurous Solomon Polock, a member of the well-known Philadelphia family, who worked on a plantation near Mobile in the late 1830s.[5]

But the typical Jew had no thought of working on a plantation, much less of owning one. He was likely to be a petty trader, trying to eke out a marginal living in an occupation which ranked quite low on the social scale of the Old South. He considered himself fortunate if he could pay his bills on time, and rated it a high accomplishment to own his shop with a few rooms on the floor above where his family could live. If he were as yet unmarried, he and a brother or uncle or nephew would live in a room behind the store, and the men would try to save up enough money to make their future more secure. Such men as these had no reason to invest their small capital in a slave, nor had they any need for a slave's services. Take, for example, young Samuel Adler and his brother, who had a store in Talladega, Alabama. These two men, both unmarried, slept in the room behind their store, while two or three young clerks lived upstairs. They sent their laundry out, and ate their meals at a local hotel, except on Sunday, when their food was sent over to the store. What would the Adlers have done with a slave even if they could have afforded one?[6] Or consider the fourteen Jewish men who lived in a Mobile, Alabama, boarding house. They were all between the ages of nineteen and thirty-nine, and earned their living as shopkeepers or clerks, with one tailor added for good measure. These men might be served at table by a slave, but this was the extent of their need. Furthermore, a slave would only be in the way in their little stores.[7]

On the other hand, Jews who were more firmly established in a business or professional career, as well as in their family relationships, had every reason to become slave-owners, although, of course, some socially prominent families took pride in employing white servants in their homes. Precise statistics concerning the ownership of slaves by Jews are hard to locate. Census records must be used with caution, because certain Jews known from other sources to be resident in a specific area at a given time were not listed at all; peddlers and traveling merchants, for example, were apt to be on the road when the census was taken; some of the manuscript census returns are quite illegible; and, in addition to frequent misspelling, the identification of Jewish names will always constitute a problem.

It would seem to be realistic to conclude that any Jew who could afford to own slaves and had need for their services would do so. Jewish owners of slaves were not exceptional figures. Slavery was an axiomatic foundation of the social pattern of the Old South. Jews wanted to acclimate themselves in every way to their environment; in both a social and psychological sense, they needed to be accepted as equals by their fellow-citizens. It was, therefore, only a matter of financial circumstance and familial status whether they were to become slave-owners.

II. The Treatment of Slaves by Jews

How did these Jewish slave-owners treat their Negroes? What did they feel towards them as human beings? Were they inclined to be lenient masters, motivated by tender sympathy, or were they, like other Southerners, sometimes kindly, sometimes harsh—but always masters?

It is obviously hard to secure answers to these questions. But some indication of the feelings of Jews towards their slaves may be derived from a detailed study of wills.

Apologists for the slave system have often contended that the cruel master was an exception, and that most slave-owners were considerate, kindly, and thoughtful. Much depends on the definition of a word like *consideration*. However kindly a man might be as a master, what of the future of his slaves after his death? Of the thirty-three wills assembled at the American Jewish Archives that pertain to identifiable Southern Jews who died during the period of our interest and refer to the ownership and disposition of slaves, slaves were merely bequeathed to relatives or friends without specific instructions in nineteen wills; in five, the executors were instructed to sell them. In the majority of these wills, then, slaves were treated like other property, to be retained if convenient and expedient, to be sold if that seemed the judicious course. The word *kindness* surely cannot encompass any relationship where a faithful servant could be torn away from familiar moorings and sold to a stranger who might or might not be a "good" master. It was probably typical that the executor of the estate of Emanuel Stern, who died in New Orleans in 1828, sold off his twelve-year-old slave, Mathilda, at auction, for $400. This was a profitable transaction, for in the inventory, Mathilda was valued at $250.[8]

On the other hand, although the kindly feelings of some slave owners cannot possibly be regarded as justification for the slave system, it is important to realize that some masters went far beyond a commercial attitude in their relationships with slaves. The proof of this is to be found in numerous cases of loyalty even after the emancipation which was produced by the Civil War. One example of this reciprocated regard is to be found in old London's decision to stay with his former master, Major Moses. Another is revealed in a letter which Emma Mordecai received in 1867 from a former slave, Sarah P. Norris. The letter itself, beautifully composed and written, is evidence of Emma's opinion of the law which forbade whites to teach reading and writing to slaves. Sarah sends Emma news of the family and acquaintances in Richmond. But more, she assures her erstwhile mistress that she and her husband are looking after the family graves in the Richmond cemetery, and that all is well. "I never could forget my people," she writes. "I loved them then, I love them now."⁹ It would be pure prejudice to gainsay the humane motivations of slave-owners like Miss Mordecai.

Nine of the wills in the American Jewish Archives contain specific provisions relating to Negroes which reflect feelings of warm generosity. In his last testament, proved on February 18, 1796, Philip Hart of Charleston bequeathed freedom to his slave Flora. Jacob Cohen of Charleston emancipated his slave Tom, in his will proved on June 6, 1800. Samuel Jones of Charleston, in his will proved on January 20, 1809, instructed his executors to emancipate his slave Jenny and her son Emanuel, if he had not already done so in his lifetime, and bequeathed to Jenny his "Bed, Sheets, Bedstead, Blankets, Tables, Pots, Plates, Chairs, Looking Glass," allowing two other slaves such part of these possessions as they might desire. Jones also bequeathed the income from certain properties to Jenny and her son, and to six slaves who were not to be emancipated. A further provision stipulated that "it is my further desire not to drive Jenny and her children out of my House in King Street, until they have time to Procure a Place for their abode." Jones gave no indication of his reason for failing to emancipate his other slaves.

Col. Chapman Levy's mother, Sarah Levy of Kershaw District, South Carolina, who died in 1839, revealed a special affection for two old slaves in her will. "It is my directions, desire and earnest request," she wrote, "that old Kennedy shall be kept with his wife and each treated with kindness and all reasonable indulgence and if my son Chapman Levy shall desire to purchase him to add to his happiness it is my directions that he shall have him at the price of three hundred dollars." Rachel D'Azevedo of Charleston, whose will was proved on February 23, 1843, did her best to assure the contentment of her slaves, Maria, Rose, Dinah, and Flora, despite the adamant provisions of state law. She bequeathed these slaves and their issue to her daughter, Mrs. Sarah A. Motta, with the express, and particular conditions, that immediately after the death of the said Mrs. Sarah A. Motta, "the Servants aforesaid with their issue or increase Shall work for their own use and time or services, being the same to all intents and purposes as if they were entirely free." She also asked that her executor, Abraham Moïse, act as "a kind protector to my Servants Should they require his Valuable Services."

Dr. Jacob De La Motta of Charleston, whose will was proved on February 22, 1845, directed that his sister Rachel treat his slaves, Ann Maria Simmons, and her son Augustus, "with lenity," that she allow them to work at their own option, that they pay her only "moderate" wages, "and on no account to be sold on account of their being family servants born and bred in the same."

Benjamin Levy, the New Orleans printer and publisher, directed in his will, probated just after his death on January 10, 1860, that his slave Richard White, a barber, be given the opportunity to purchase his freedom for $500. If this were not possible during his son, Alexander Levy's lifetime, White was to be set free after the son's death. Levy furthermore stipulated that the slave was "never to be sold, Mortgaged, or hired out for a longer term than one Year at a time, and never to be hired out of the State of Louisiana." Another provision in Levy's will expressed his hope that a token of esteem be given by his family to each of the eight slaves who had been his property, and now belonged to other members of the family, as a "Small Memorial of their old Master."

Two of the wills refer to free Negroes. Benjamin Davis of Charleston, in his last testament, which was proved on September 26, 1831, bequeathed one hundred and fifty dollars "for her faithful Services" to "a free colod woman named Elsey." Far more unusual was a provision in the will of David Perayra Brandon of Charleston, proved on April 24, 1838:

> I recommend my faithful Servant and friend Juellit or Julien free Negro, to my dear Rachel [his stepdaughter] and W. C. Lambert [her husband] my friend and request them to take him under their protection to treat him as well as they would do me and to give him Such portion of my Cloths as they will think useful to him and never forsake him being the best friend I ever had.

How many white men in the Old South would have wanted to describe a Negro as their "best friend" in the most permanent document of their lives, and how many would have dared do so?

These wills are ample evidence that some Jewish Southerners were deeply sensitive to the human character of their Negroes, and thought of them as fellow men rather than as cattle or merchandise.

III. Emancipation of Slaves by Jews

No matter what kindnesses were bestowed upon slaves by their masters, only one gift was permanently meaningful, the gift of freedom. Fortunately, Samuel Jones, Jacob Cohen, Philip Hart, and Benjamin Levy were not the only folk who wanted to emancipate their slaves. Isaiah Isaacs of

Charlottesville, Virginia, whose firm had once been compelled to take a Negro slave as security for a debt, outlined an elaborate program for the freeing of his slaves in his will, which was proved in April, 1806:

> Being of opinion that all men are by nature equally free and being possessed of some of those beings who are unfortunate[ly] doomed to slavery, as to them I must enjoin upon my executors a strict observance of the following clause in my will. My slaves hereafter named are to be and they are hereby manumitted and made free so that after the different periods hereafter mentioned they shall enjoy all the privileges and immunities of freed people. My slave Rachel is to go free and quit all manner of claim of servitude from and after the first day of January, which shall be in the year [1816], James from and after the first day of January [1820], Polly on the first day of January [1822], Henry on the first day of January [1830], and William on the first day of January [1834], and should either of my female slaves Rachel or Polly have a child or children before the time they become free such issue is to serve to the age of thirty-one, and then to be discharged from servitude; the said slaves are not to be sold, but to remain the property of my children and to be divided in the same manner as directed as to the division of my real estate; each one of my slaves are to receive the value of twenty dollars in clothing on the day of their manumission.[10]

No comparable Jewish will exists, with so complete a plan of emancipation, but in 1796, Samuel Myers of Petersburg, Virginia, purchased a mulatto woman, Alice, from the trustees of the estate of a neighbor, with the obvious intention of emancipating her, which purpose he fulfilled a little over a year later.[11] A similar case of purchasing a slave for rapid emancipation was that of Joseph Tobias of Charleston, who, on July 23, 1798, bought a slave named Jenny for $500 from Dr. James Cletherall, and promptly freed her "for former services rendered me." Perhaps she had nursed him during an illness while she was still the physician's property.[12] In the same year, Solomon Raphael of Richmond, and his partner, freed their slave Sylvia and her child; and six years later Raphael emancipated another slave, Priscilla.[13] In 1812, Solomon Jacobs, also of Richmond, freed his slave Esther.[14]

A Northern owner of Southern slaves, Jacob I. Cohen, formerly of Richmond, and now of Philadelphia, provided for the emancipation of his slaves in his will, which was probated in Philadelphia on October 31, 1823. Cohen directed that his slaves

Dick, Spencer, Meshack, Fanny and Eliza together with their children be manumitted from slavery immediately after my decease; and I do give and bequeathe to the said Dick, Spencer, Meshack, Fanny and Eliza twenty-five dollars each. But if any of my said Negroes will not accept their freedom I do then will and direct that they have the choice of their own master.

Cohen also directed that the children of Mary Andrew, a slave who was to be freed at a later time, be regarded as "free from their birth."[15]

It will be noticed, of course, that these examples of emancipation were all quite early. This is no coincidence, since most of the Southern states gradually tightened their restrictions until it was virtually impossible to free a slave except through stratagem or deceit. Those who believe that the Civil War could have been avoided through a general realization of the coming collapse of the slave economy ought to be compelled to read the enactments of the various states which were contrived to make the slave system a one-way street with no escape. It is quite possibly true that the expansion of slavery was economically unfeasible, but there is no indication that Southern leaders and framers of law were prepared to make emancipation easy. To the contrary, they bent every effort to keep the slaves in chains, and gradually encroached on the lives and activities of free Negroes, as well.

IV. Jews as Harsh Taskmasters

Acts of kindness towards Negroes were the only relief in the reality of a system which placed white masters in a position of absolute and total control over their slaves. Jews participated in every aspect and process of the exploitation of the defenseless blacks. The most extreme case on record was the murder of a slave by Joseph Cohen of Lynchburg, Virginia, in 1819, a crime for which he was indicted, tried, and convicted—although of course the penalty for the murder of a Negro by a white was much less severe than the penalty for a trivial misdemeanor committed by a Negro.[16]

Crimes of violence against slaves by Jews were probably quite rare, since most of these occurred in rural areas where there were few Jews. But Jews in the towns and cities appear to have been quite content to abide by the excessively cruel punishments meted out to blacks who were caught by the law. These are a few examples of the testimony of Jews against Negroes taken from the Richmond court records. In 1798, Polly, a mulatto slave, was tried for taking a loaf of white sugar worth two dollars from Benjamin Solomon's home, and was sentenced to five lashes on her bare back and ordered to be branded on her left hand.[17] Two years later, Joseph Darmstadt had "a bag and lot of beeswax," valued at fifty shillings, stolen from his store by Daniel Clayton, a free Negro, and heard Clayton sentenced to thirty-nine lashes on the bare back.[18] Another free Negro was accused of stealing two silver watches valued at $32 from Myer Angel in 1832, and the culprit was sentenced to five years' imprisonment, six months of which was to be a spent in solitary confinement.[19] Benjamin Wolfe's store was broken into in 1797, and $500 in merchandise was stolen. Three slaves were tried for the crime, but only one was convicted. He was sentenced to be hung.[20]

Not only did Jews bring slaves to court as private citizens, but they also participated as public officials in legal action against slaves. In 1792, for instance, Mordecai Sheftall of Georgia was responsible for issuing warrants for the arrest of runaway slaves in his district.[21] A large number of Charleston Jews held public positions which required their constant involvement in the apprehension and punishment of Negroes: Lewis Gomez was Turnkey of the Jail in 1802; Moses Solomon (1802), Nathan Hart (1821), and Solomon Moses (1822) were Constables; Samuel Hyams was Keeper of the Jail in 1822; Elisha Elizer (1802), Mark Marks (1822), and Solomon Moses, Jr. (1822) were City Deputy Sherrifs.[22] Moses Levy, also of Charleston, achieved a state-wide reputation as the most successful detective on the city's police force.[23] Moses N. Cardozo, who had a plantation near Richmond, was also the Jailer of Powhatan Courthouse. One of his responsibilities was the incarceration and disposition of runaway slaves.[24] J. S. Cohen was City Marshal of Mobile in 1841. In connection with ordinary bankruptcies, Cohen was required to supervise the sale of Negro slaves for the account of the creditors. In the *Mobile Daily Advertiser and Chronicle* of November 4, 1841, he offered ten Negroes for sale for immediate cash, including "a first rate mantua maker, and several good cooks, washers and ironers."

From testifying against Negroes in court, to apprehending a runaway slave, to inflicting punishment upon a convicted Negro, these Jews were thoroughly a part of their society.

V. Business Dealings of Jews with Slaves and Free Negroes

Jewish merchants were probably more likely than others to have dealings with slaves and free Negroes, because large numbers of immigrant

German Jews in the Southern states were marginal traders. Frederick Law Olmsted commented on the large numbers of Negroes who paraded the streets of Richmond on Sunday, wearing "the cast-off clothes of the white people, . . . purchased of the Jews, whose shops show that there must be considerable importation of such articles, probably from the North." Olmsted was not, of course, an unbiased observer; he manifested a constant antipathy to Jews in all of his books. But there was probably some truth to his assertion that Jews in many Southern towns engaged in "an unlawful trade with the simple Negroes, which is found very profitable."[25]

Not all business dealings with Negroes were illegal. Slaves were frequently authorized to make purchases with their own small savings; sometimes they were sent on errands for their masters. Free Negroes, and even slaves who were permitted to hire themselves out for work, could transact business in stores where they were well-known. The difference between Jewish and non-Jewish merchants was probably this: that the Jewish traders displayed somewhat less reluctance to do business with Negroes. Such, at any rate, was the impression of those who wrote of the post-bellum transactions of Jewish merchants with former slaves.[26] There is no question that this observation applied to Lewis B. Levy of Richmond, a manufacturer and vendor of "Servants' Clothing," who publicly solicited the patronage of slave traders, and masters who were selling or hiring out their slaves.[27]

A number of law cases record difficulties which some Jews encountered in their business dealings with slaves. In 1836, Daniel Becker was convicted of illegal liquor sales to Negroes in South Carolina.[28] In 1843, Samuel F. Isaacs was convicted of selling a horse to a slave without permission, in the same state. But this case was based on a technicality which reveals the rigidity of laws relating to slaves: the overseer had given verbal consent to the slave and to Isaacs, but the law required written permission.[29] In 1859, Charlotte Levy of New Orleans leased a house to a slave, and was hauled into court over the illegal transaction.[30]

All merchants had perennial troubles with the law over the question of Sunday sales, both to whites and to Negroes, but slaves were particularly involved because Sunday was generally their only shopping day. In 1806, when the Richmond officials conducted a special campaign against merchants who did business on Sunday, two of the thirty-one merchants who were prosecuted were Jews, Marcus Levi and Reuben Cantor.[31] Among many other subsequent cases, Walter Thalheimer was fined $20, in 1847, for selling goods to slaves on Sunday without the consent of their owners.[32] But these business dealings with Negroes pale into insignificance compared to the major business involvement with slaves, namely, slave-trading itself.

VI. Jews as Slave-Traders

Everyone who owned slaves participated in the barter of human beings. There were three classes of people so involved. The first group were those who purchased and sold slaves only in connection with their own personal needs. There was hardly a slave-owner who had never bought or sold a slave; only as an heir to a sizeable workforce could he fail to do so. But there were few who did not see fit at some time or other to dispose of a few superfluous slaves, or to increase their holdings through additional purchases. And even if one treated his slaves with the utmost of kindness, short of outright emancipation, which was forbidden in most Southern states in the last two decades before the Civil War, no one could predict the fate of his slaves after his death. A particularly tragic case was that of "A Negro named Sam, about Eighty Years of age, diseased, and a Negro Woman named Sylvie about Seventy five years of Age," who were sold for ninety dollars in 1852 by Benjamin D. Lazarus, as Executor of the estate of Dr. Jacob De La Motta.[33] This was the same Dr. De La Motta who gave directions in his will for kindly treatment to other slaves. Perhaps the estate required cash, and undoubtedly the slaves were too old for any useful purpose, but what future could they have at the hands of a purchaser who would be compelled somehow to regain his investment?

After Solomon Jacobs, Acting Mayor of Richmond in 1818–1819, died in 1827, his family composed a tombstone epitaph which described him in most sentimental fashion:

> Fond as a Husband.
> Indulgent as a Father.
> Kind as a Master . . .

If these were more than words, what would Jacobs have thought of his widow, Hetty, who in 1829 succeeded in having a special law passed by the Virginia House and Senate, allowing the sale of a number of female slaves and children because the "conduct of said slaves towards their mistress . . . was so very malevolent and very objectionable"?[34]

Thin though it may have been, there was still a line of demarcation between persons who bought or sold slaves as individuals, and those who dealt in slaves as part of their occupational pursuit. The second group of those who participated in the sale of Negroes were those merchants who dealt in many commodities, including slaves. Philip Sartorius of Louisiana and Mississippi, for instance, recalled the time in 1850 that his partner Sam Rothschild "gambled all our money off and sold [our trading] boat and stock to another flat boat man for a Negro girl, took her to New Orleans and traded her off for tobacco."[35] To Sam Rothschild, there was little difference between buying and selling a slave girl and any other kind of merchandise.

Sometimes Jewish store-keepers would take a flier at an investment in slaves for purely speculative purposes. An example of this activity was the purchase of three Negro slaves "named Joe William and Friendly" for $4,500, in July, 1863, by Jacob Adler and Herman Cone of Jonesboro, Tennessee. Adler and Cone lost their investment, however; the Union victories deprived them of both capital and property.[36] An outstanding example of this kind of speculator was Jacob Barrett, an early merchant in Columbia, South Carolina, and later a resident of Charleston. Barrett was a characteristic store-keeper of the time, who carried a stock which included dry-goods, groceries, provisions, liquor, hardware, crockery, shoes, hats, saddles, horses, real estate, and when the opportunity presented itself, slaves as well. One of his clerks recalled the time when a gang of twenty Negroes was sent to him from Charleston; he promptly disposed of the slaves "at very large profits, keeping for his own use Armistead Booker, a goodlooking, active carriage driver and barber, who attended to his horses and in the store, and Aunt Nanny, a first rate cook." Barrett later married the daughter of his cousin, Jacob Ottolengui of Charleston, another speculator in Negroes, and claimed before the Civil War to have around a thousand slaves working his rice plantations near the Savannah River.[37]

Among this group of merchants were numerous Jewish auctioneers, commission merchants, and brokers. This was an avenue of commerce in which many Jews found their niche, because no stock of merchandise or investment of capital was required, at least at the beginning. As a merchant achieved a record in the community for sagacious advice, clever salesmanship, and financial reliability, he prospered, and then could build his own warehouses and auction rooms, and buy and sell for his own account as well as for his clients. Auctioneers were licensed by law in most communities;

they were, in a sense, public officials. Even if they disliked the traffic in human flesh, therefore, they could not avoid it; they were expected by the public to deal in slaves as readily as in any other sort of merchandise. To all intents and purposes, they were slave-traders, but not exclusively.

Members of Jewish communities who were dealers in slaves were not scorned by their fellow Jews. Both Jacob Levin and Israel I. Jones occupied particularly prominent positions in the Jewish life of their towns.

Levin was the acting rabbi and recognized leader of the Jews of Columbia. For many years he gave the main address at the annual public meetings and examinations of the Columbia Hebrew Sunday School, of which his wife was directress. His speeches, which were deemed important enough to be reported and even quoted at length in Rabbi Isaac Leeser's Philadelphia monthly journal, *The Occident and American Jewish Advocate*, were high-minded appeals to Jewish adults as well as children to devote themselves to the traditional ideals of Judaism. Levin was also an early Secretary and Treasurer of the Hebrew Benevolent Society of Columbia. His non-Jewish neighbors held him in equally high esteem: he was elected Illustrious Grand Master of the Masonic Council.[38]

Israel Jones was an even more distinguished leader. One of the first of Mobile's Jewish residents to cleave loyally to his faith, he was the President of the first congregation in Alabama, Congregation Shaarai Shomayim, from its founding in 1844 until 1873. During the few brief years of activity of the pioneering Board of Delegates of American Israelites, the first national Jewish organization for the purpose of national and international representation, Israel Jones was honored with the office of Vice-President. Jones took great pride in the fact that his daughter Emily married the talented Rabbi James K. Gutheim of New Orleans. Occupying a similar position of high repute in the general community, he was at various times a member of the City Council of Mobile, President of the Mobile Musical Association, and founder of Mobile's street car line.[39]

Slave-dealing obviously did not disqualify Jews from receiving the friendship and esteem of their co-religionists any more than it disqualified Christians; engaging in business transactions in Negro flesh was not regarded as incompatible with being a good Jew.[40]

Abraham Mendes Seixas was not a Jewish leader, but his brother was the famous rabbi of Colonial and early Federal New York and Philadelphia, Gershom Mendes Seixas. Abraham, like other auctioneers of slaves, was neither ashamed of nor apologetic about his offerings of Negroes. He even burst into doggerel about his slave merchandise:

ABRAHAM SEIXAS,
All so gracious,
Once again does offer
His service pure
For to secure
Money in the coffer.
He has for sale
Some Negroes, male,
Will suit full well grooms,
He has likewise
Some of their wives
Can make clean, dirty rooms.
For planting, too,
He has a few
To sell, all for the cash,
Of various price,
To work the rice
Or bring them to the lash.
The young ones true,
If that will do,
May some be had of him
To learn your trade
They may be made,
Or bring them to your trim.
The boatmen great,
Will you elate
They are so brisk and free;
What e'er you say.
They will obey,
If you buy them of me.[41]

The third group of those who dealt in Negroes were, of course, the full-time slave-traders, whose sole income was derived from purchasing, transporting, and selling slaves. None of the major slave-traders was Jewish, nor did Jews constitute a large proportion of traders in any particular community. Frederic Bancroft, who has made an exhaustive study of the business, attempted to classify all traders and auctioneers in the major Southern markets. In Richmond, according to his list, only three of seventy were Jews; in Charleston, four out of forty-four; in Memphis, only one of more than a dozen.[42] Other standard works limited to the investigation of the slave-trade in Kentucky and Mississippi list many dozens of slave-traders, among whom not a single Jewish name appears.[43] Probably all of the Jewish slave-traders in all of the Southern cities and towns combined did not buy and sell as many slaves as did the firm of Franklin and Armfield, the largest Negro traders in the South.

Slave-dealing was an extremely profitable business. Through natural increase, the upper South produced more slaves than its over-worked soil required, while the lower South needed constant recruits for an ever-increasing labor force on its newly developed plantations. When the price of cotton was high, slave-traders could double their investment by leading long coffles of slaves from one section of the South to the other, despite the expenses of fattening up their wares and giving them medical attention.

The largest Jewish slave-trading firm in the South seems to have been the Davis family of Petersburg and Richmond, including Ansley, Benjamin, George, and Solomon.[44] They were the only Jews mentioned by Harriet Beecher Stowe in her little-known commentary, *A Key to Uncle Tom's Cabin*. Mrs. Stowe quotes a letter by Dr. Gamaliel Bailey, referring to them:

> The Davises, in Petersburg, are the great slave-traders. They are Jews, came to that place many years ago as poor peddlers. . . . These men are always in the market, giving the highest price for slaves. During the summer and fall they buy them up at low prices, trim, shave, wash them, fatten them so that they may look sleek, and sell them to great profit.[45]

The Davis family traveled far and wide with their slave merchandise. The Davises were obviously well-prepared to do business in various Southern states, with legal forms already printed for their use. The family was also known in Georgia. Benjamin Davis advertised in the Columbus *Enquirer* of April 12, 1838, that he had for sale "Sixty Likely Virginia Negroes—House Servants, Field Hands, Blow boys, Cooks, Washers, Ironers, and three first-rate Seamstresses." Davis was remaining in Columbus, and assured the local folk that he would continue to receive shipments of additional bargains "by every arrival" for almost two more months.[46]

In these ways did Jews participate in the commercial components of the slave system.

NEGROES, NEGROES.

The undersigned has just arrived in Lumpkin from Virginia, with a likely lot of negroes, about 40 in number, embracing every shade and variety. He has seamstresses, chamber maids, field hands, and doubts not that he is able to fill the bill of any who may want to buy. He has sold over two hundred negroes in this section, mostly in this county, and flatters himself that he has so far given satisfaction to his purchasers. Being a regular trader to this market he has nothing to gain by misrepresentation, and will, therefore, warrant every negro sold to come up to the bill, squarely and completely. Give him a call at his Mart.

J. F. MOSES.

Lumpkin, Ga., Nov. 14th, 1859.

Here J. F. Moses, one of several Jewish slave dealers who operated in the South during the antebellum period, assured potential customers that "every negro sold" would "come up to the bill, squarely and completely." Such claims of honesty and propriety were not atypical in advertisements for slaves; traders were eager to burnish the reputation of a profession notorious for unscrupulous business practices. Courtesy of The Jacob Rader Marcus Center of the American Jewish Archives.

VII. Cases of Miscegenation Involving Jews

Inter-racial cohabitation was quite common in the South, but there is little available documentary evidence which can be utilized to establish statistical indices, either for the general white population, or for any minor division thereof.

A search in the available records for Jewish names borne by Negroes encounters the inevitable difficulty of distinguishing Jewish from non-Jewish names. Many, like Aaron, Abrahams, Benjamin, David, Davis, Emanuel, Hart, Isaacs, Lyons, Marks, Moses, Myers, Noah, Samuels, Salomons, and Stein, can be Jewish or Gentile, as the case may be. Nor have we any notion of whether Northern Negroes with names like Hannah Adler, Perry Cohen, Isaac Farber, Richard Levy, Peter Levy, Benjamin Levy, Isaac Nathans, Abraham Stern, and thirteen Negro Tobiases, went North before or after receiving their names. But it is likely that some of these Negroes did receive their names either from Jewish owners or Jewish fathers. This is probably also true of Sheldon Cohen of St. Peters Parish, South Carolina; Constance Herschell of New Orleans; Levy Jacobs of Fayetteville, North Carolina; George and Samuel Kauffman of King and Queen County, Virginia; Affey Levy of Charleston; Justine Moise of New Orleans; Harry Mordecai of Frankfort, Kentucky; Betty Rosenberg of Charleston Neck; and Catherine Sasportes of Charleston.[47]

There is no available data to help us to ascertain whether these Negroes took their names from Jewish masters, or fathers, or neighbors, or benefactors, or, in certain cases, from the Bible. But there are situations where a relationship of friendship if not of parentage seems quite likely, as for instance, George Darmstadt, a free Negro of Richmond, who, with his wife Patty, was given permission in September, 1816, to live in the city in recognition of his "faithful services, honesty, and good demeanor."[48]

We do not even have the help of religious affiliation in our investigation of this question, since Jewish congregations would not accept Negro members. The Richmond congregation required that its members be free; and the Charleston Beth Elohim constitution of 1820 accepted proselytes only if "he, she, or they are not people of colour."[49] There is only one reference to a Jewish Negro in all of Southern Jewish records, "a free man of color" who was converted to Judaism by his master, and was accustomed to attending services at the Charleston synagogue in 1857, during the tenure of Rabbi Maurice Mayer.[50] The fact that Jewish masters, with this exception, did not educate their slaves in the Jewish faith, and that synagogues did not welcome Negro worshippers, would seem to negate the contention that present-day Negroes who regard themselves as Jews are descended from slave-converts of Jewish masters.

There are actually only five instances in which documentary evidence indicates cohabitation of Jews with Negro women, and it is important to note that in each case they were free Negroes. In the first, the only one to be brought to court, David Isaacs and Nancy West, a free mulatto woman, were indicted in 1826 by the grand jury of Albermarle County, Virginia, "for outraging the decency of society . . . by cohabiting together . . . as man and wife, without being lawfully married." A higher court reduced the serious charge of the indictment to the lesser charge of fornication.[51]

In our second case, the evidence is less positive. Samuel Simons, whose will was proved in Charleston on February 13, 1824, left his entire estate to relatives and Jewish institutions in London, with the exception of an extensive bequest to his "House Keeper Maria Chapman a free woman of Colour." Simons left Maria "the Sum of fourteen hundred Dollars, two Negroes named Pompey and Peggy with the issue and increase of the females and also two Bedsteads bedding and six chairs." Negro concubines were frequently called "housekeepers," and Simons's bequest to Maria was extraordinarily large. The supposition would be that her employer had a much more personal relationship with Maria than would be mentioned in polite society.[52] This may also be true of other men whose generous bequests have already been noted, especially when the names of children are also mentioned.

The third instance is far more definite. The will of Moses Nunes of Savannah, who died on September 6, 1797, acknowledges "Mulatta Rose" as his concubine, and recognizes her children, Robert, James, Alexander, and Frances (married to George Galphin), as his own progeny. He bequeathed certain tracts of land, his home, furniture, and clothing, and thirteen Negro slaves, to Rose and his four children, in addition to "a full and perfect freedom from all Slavery and servitude in reward and as an acknowledgement of the faithful conduct and behaviour of the said Mulatta Rose towards me and my Children."[53] Moses Nunes's will became an important document in 1853 when it was exhumed in connection with a lawsuit which was carried through the courts during the next eleven years. The case concerned the legality of Moses's grandson, Joseph's, sale of five slave children, his own, by his Negro concubine, Patience. What was at stake was the question of Joseph's race, since his father, James Nunes, had passed for white, and had been married to a white woman. Many witnesses testified to their belief that both James and Joseph were of pure white ancestry. Unfortunately, however, the grandfather's will was strong evidence of mixed blood. But Sherman's march through Georgia made the entire question an academic one before the final appeal was adjudicated.[54]

A less complicated example, in certain ways, was that of the Negro branch of the Cardozo family, which produced two leading figures in Reconstruction governments. It is a moot question whether their father was Jacob N. Cardozo, the famous Southern journalist and economist, or his lesser-known brother Isaac, who for twenty-four years was a weigher in the Charleston Custom House. Historical writers seem to have favored Jacob's name, while present-day members of the family believe that Isaac was their ancestor.[55]

Our final example of miscegenation concerns the family of Barnet A. Cohen, who was born in 1770 in Bristol, England, had plantations in King's Creek, South Carolina, and died there on March 23, 1839. The fortunate preservation of a batch of family papers enables us to comprehend, in a uniquely personal way, the difficult social and psychological problems which faced a free mulatto.[56]

By 1810, when the first of these papers was drawn up, Barnet A. Cohen had fathered two children, Barnet Owens Cohen and Benjamin Phillip Owens Cohen, by a "free woman of Colour," Catherine Owens. A number of neighbors, including four Jews, signed a document attesting to the family relationship and the free status of the woman and her children. According to the second document, in March, 1822, Barnet A. Cohen, the father, as legal guardian for his son Benjamin, and on his behalf, purchased "a Negro wench named Sarah and her child Lina," the mother probably being bought as a concubine for Benjamin. The lot of a free Negro was far from simple; his choice of mates was extremely limited. Most frequently he had to buy his own women, and unless he could emancipate them, which was next to impossible, he was compelled also to own title to his own children.

In 1832, with the approval of his father-guardian, Benjamin Cohen purchased a nine-month-old Negro, "Alonzo," for $100. It would seem obvious that Alonzo must have been his own child by a slave woman whose owner refused to part with her; why else should he, or for that matter, anyone, buy a Negro infant?

In 1837, two years before his father's death, Benjamin purchased some land in Barnwell District, adjoining farms which belonged to his father and his mulatto brother, Barnet. By now, his white half brother, Moses A.

Cohen, was signing as his guardian. It is significant that the Negro and white members of this family lived in such close proximity and, apparently, harmony, as well. The father's white wife, Bella, died in 1836; and when the father died in 1839, there was no sign of strain in the family's feelings, at least on Barnet's tombstone, which commemorated "the virtues of a beloved parent . . . as a memorial of [his children's] love and veneration." What a shame that we have no way of telling whether Benjamin and Barnet had a hand in composing this epitaph!

From 1840 to 1850, Benjamin was worrying about the future of his slave family. He wanted to set them free, and thus assure their status after his own death, but he could not find the way. In 1840, he consulted an attorney, who informed him that "no Slave can be Set free in this State except by Act of the Legislature on a Petition. But it is *almost impossible* to have such a Petition granted—The Legislature almost always refuses them." If it was *"almost impossible"* in 1840, it became altogether so, on December 17, 1841, when the South Carolina legislature passed "An Act to Prevent the Emancipation of Slaves," a copy of which Benjamin secured and kept among his papers. According to this law, any effort through "bequest, deed of trust, or conveyance," to send slaves out of the state for the purpose of emancipation, was declared null and void. The act also prohibited any stratagem whereby "slaves shall be held in nominal servitude." In 1844, Benjamin Cohen consulted another lawyer, and, after paying a fee of ten dollars, received the categorical advice that "a free coloured man can purchase a Slave, but he cannot give her her freedom—the Slave and her children will always remain Slaves."

In 1850, Benjamin Cohen, free man of color but without the freedom to do very much, by then about fifty years of age or perhaps older, was altogether anxious to do something for his family. So he drew up a draft of a will—one of the most pathetic wills I have ever been privileged to read. After the usual formalities, including a request for "Christian burial," he bequeathes all his property to his "esteemed patron and benefactor, Samuel Cohen," who must have been another white half-brother. Then, in an effort to forestall the effects of the law of 1841, he offers this declaration of loyalty and disclaimer of intention:

SECONDLY. I give and devise unto the aforesaid Samuel Cohen, the following Slaves, viz—Jane, John, Susan, Benjamin, Alonzo, Moses, Dani[e]l, Emma, Sarah, and Frances, and as most of them are my offspring, and Jane my wife, it may be thought that this devise is intended to avoid and defeat, the laws of this commonwealth, which affords me protection, and to which I defferentially bow, in gratitude. I therefore declare and Solemnly asseverate that I intend no such unlawful act. I know that by the law, they are slaves, and must remain so. Wherefore through the means of this my will I choose their Master, preferring him, for my heir at Law to anyone else. Neither is there any understanding secret, or otherwise, that the above named Slaves are to be held in nominal servitude only.

Benjamin makes only one bequest—he provides for a gift of $100 to his niece Emily, the daughter of his deceased mulatto brother Barnet (or "Barney" as he calls him in this document). All other property is left to Samuel Cohen, "in consideration of my friendship and his many kindnesses to me." It was apparently no longer proper for a will to mention the familial relationship of Negroes and whites.

This is the final document which concerns Benjamin Philip Owens Cohen. A probated will cannot be discovered in the records of the Barnwell Court House. Only this rough draft has been preserved, together with his other papers, among the records of his half-brother Samuel, who lived into the 1870s and had a store in a town with one of the most remarkable names in the United States, Cohen's Bluff, South Carolina. But the fact that these papers relating to Benjamin were preserved by Samuel, without the inventories and other documents an executor would have needed to prepare, would seem to be convincing proof that the will was never executed in its present form. Perhaps Benjamin Philip Owens Cohen outlived the institution of slavery and was able to spend his last days with a family freed from involuntary servitude by the bloodshed which began in 1861.

VIII. Opinions of Jews about Slavery

This study has thus far traced a pattern of almost complete conformity to the slave society of the Old South on the part of its Jewish citizens. They participated in the buying, owning, and selling of slaves, and the exploitation of their labor, along with their neighbors. The behavior of Jews towards slaves seems to have been indistinguishable from that of their non-Jewish friends. This description also characterizes the opinions of Jews about slavery.

No Jewish political figure of the Old South ever expressed any reservations about the justice of slavery or the rightness of the Southern position.

Men like David Levy Yulee of Florida and David S. Kaufman of Texas were typical exponents of Southern views on states' rights and the spread of slavery.[57] Judah P. Benjamin of Louisiana was regarded as one of the most eloquent defenders of the Southern way of life. Though far from a fanatic, he stood squarely with his Senatorial colleagues every inch of the way that led from Washington to Montgomery and then to Richmond.

Benjamin did question the wisdom of entrusting Negro slaves with complicated agricultural machinery, and advised sugar planters to employ trained white mechanics, but he never admitted that this deterrent to progressive agriculture was an inevitable consequence of the slave economy. Despite his conservative views, however, he was the only notable Confederate leader who advocated the arming of slaves during the Civil War, and who urged that they be emancipated as reward for this effort. He seems to have been far ahead of most Southerners in his willingness to use any weapon for the deliverance of the Confederacy. "The true issue," he said, is, "is it better for the Negro to fight for us or against us?" He urged the adoption of his policy as an answer to the ever-present manpower shortage, but he also believed that "the action of our people on this point will be of more value to us abroad than any diplomacy or treaty-making." But most Southerners would rather lose the war than weaken the slave system in any way.[58]

Benjamin's proposal was certainly not a repudiation of slavery. Neither was the program which Judge Solomon Heydenfeldt of Alabama advocated in 1849 as an antidote to the problems created by the concentration of Alabama capital in slave property. Heydenfeldt first published his *Communication on the Subject of Slave Immigration, Addressed to Hon. Reuben Chapman, Governor of Alabama*, in the Huntsville *Democrat* on January 31, 1849, and subsequently in pamphlet form. The jurist questioned the economic wisdom of unlimited slave immigration and protested that the state would become impoverished through the uncontrolled "dumping" of slaves in Alabama. But his arguments were denounced by fellow Alabamians. One critic said, in the Wetumpka *Daily Stateguard* of February 12, 1849, that if Heydenfeldt's proposal were to be adopted, an artificial scarcity of slaves would be created, the prices of slaves would soar, and the rich would become richer, while the poor who hoped sometime to become slave-owners would be deprived of any expectation of economic advancement. Heydenfeldt was far from being the abolitionist some have imagined him to be.[59]

Long after the Civil War had been fought and lost by the South, Philip Phillips of Alabama, who for a time served in the House of Representatives and was perhaps the outstanding Jewish attorney of the ante-bellum South, said that he regarded emancipation as a new opportunity for the South. "So far as the loss of property in slaves was involved," he said, "I regard it as the greatest blessing. . . . A new generation with self-reliant spirit will create a new South, and crown it by their energy and industry, with all that enriches and enobles a land." But he never criticized slavery as an enemy of self-reliance and creativity while it was the accepted economic and social foundation of his state and section.[60]

Nor was there anyone among the many Jewish journalists, writers, and publicists of the Old South who questioned the moral, political, or economic justice of slavery. Jacob De Cordova, the Texas real-estate promoter, newspaper editor, and geographer, emphatically denied charges that he had given voice to "free-soil doctrines" during his 1858 lecture tour in the North, and "wish[ed] it distinctly understood that our feelings and education have always been proslavery."[61] Isaac Harby, the Charleston dramatist and political essayist, was writing in Charleston in opposition to "the abolitionist society and its secret branches," as early as 1824.[62] Jacob N. Cardozo, the editor and political economist, asserted that slavery was defensible both economically and morally. In the former respect, he maintained that "Slavery brought not only great wealth to the South, but to the slaves a greater share of its enjoyment that in many regions where the relation between employer and employee was based on wages." In regard to the ethical question, he placed the responsibility squarely on the Deity: "The reason the Almighty made the colored black is to prove their inferiority." After the Civil War, in his well-known *Reminiscences of Charleston*, Cardozo expressed his sympathy with the planters who were now suffering great privation:

> The owner of two hundred to five hundred slaves, with a princely income, has not only to submit to the most degraded employments, but he frequently cannot obtain them. In some instances, he has to drive a cart, or attend a retail grocery, while he may have to obey the orders of an ignorant and course menial. There is something unnatural in this reverse of position—something revolting to my sense of propriety in this social degradation.[63]

Edwin De Leon, the journalist and Confederate diplomat, devoted many pages of his reminiscences to an extended apologia for slavery.[64] His brother, Thomas Cooper De Leon, one of the most prolific Southern litterateurs of the second half of the nineteenth century, wrote many novels and other works in the Southern romantic style of which he was a major practitioner. In one of his most famous works, *Belles, Beaux and Brains of the Confederacy*, De Leon described all talk of cruelty in the slave system as propaganda and mythology; he underlined the fact that Harriet Beecher Stowe was compelled to ascribe a Yankee origin to her famous character, Simon Legree.[65] Samuel Mordecai, the bachelor journalist of Richmond, derived part of his income from his articles in Edmund Ruffin's *The Farmer's Register*, a journal devoted primarily to the interests of Southern employers of slave labor forces. Mordecai loved everything about old Virginia, and wrote tenderly of the old colored aristocracy, in his *Richmond in By-Gone Days*. He too regarded slavery as a natural and desirable condition of society.[66]

Even in the days of the secession crisis, and the subsequent prolongated war and eventual defeat, many Southern Jews believed slavery to be indispensable to their happiness and security. George W. Mordecai, born a Jew but now an Episcopalian banker, railroad executive, and plantation owner in North Carolina, wrote to a Northern Republican in December 1860: "I would much sooner trust myself alone on my plantation surrounded by my slaves, than in one of your large manufacturing towns when your labourers are discharged from employment and crying aloud for bread for themselves and their little ones."[67] In 1864, Private Eugene Henry Levy of the Confederate Army objected to the radical suggestion that Negroes be utilized in the war effort and be freed for this assistance. "The slaves," he said, "are in their proper sphere as they are at present situated within the boundaries of the Confederacy."[68]

After the war was over, some Southern Jews still believed that slavery had been a necessary foundation of human society. Eleanor H. Cohen, the daughter of Dr. Philip Melvin Cohen of Charleston, said in the innocent selfishness of young maidenhood: "I, who believe in the institution of slavery, regret deeply its being abolished. I am accustomed to have them wait on me, and I dislike white servants very much."[69] Perhaps no more concise and self-deceptive rationalization of slavery was ever written than the observations which were recorded by Solomon Cohen, the distinguished civic leader and merchant of Savannah, who had lost a son in the war, in a letter which he wrote to his sister-in-law, Emma Mordecai, shortly after the end of the war:

> I believe that the institution of slavery was refining and civilizing to the whites—giving them an elevation of sentiment and ease and dignity of manners only attainable in societies under the restraining influence of a privileged class—and at the same time the only human institution that could elevate the Negro from barbarism and develop the small amount of intellect with which he is endowed.[70]

Such sentiments might well be expected of members of families long resident in the South and thoroughly acclimated to its habits and assumptions. The De Leons, Mordecais, and Cardozos had lived with their neighbors long enough to share their ideas and attitudes. But what of the newly immigrant German Jews who came to the South in increasing numbers beginning in the 1840s? There is no evidence that they found it very difficult to adjust to the slave society of which they became a part. Julius Weis, of New Orleans, who came to the United States in 1845, recorded his shock at his first sight of a Negro "being whipped upon his bare back by an overseer. The sight of a human being punished in this manner was very repugnant to me, though living in the midst of a country where slavery existed. I afterwards got somewhat accustomed to it, but I always felt a pity for the poor slaves." But Weis's compassion seemed to be limited to this matter of punishment, for he owned several slaves during the period from 1853 to 1857, and bought a Negro barber in 1862. He notes that "I never found it necessary to punish them in such a manner," but his feeling of pity never led him to adopt a critical attitude toward the entire system of slavery.[71]

Louis Stix of Cincinnati wrote of a German Jewish immigrant to the South who became violent in his pro-slavery opinions. They met at a Jewish boarding-house in New York City; at dinner one night this unidentified Southern Jew said that "Southerners could not live without slavery." "I replied to this," wrote Stix, "by a very uncalled-for remark not at all flattering to our race who were living in the South. . . . The Southerner . . . drew his pistol to compel me to take back my words. . . . I hope [he] has since learned to do without slaves, or has returned to the place from which he came, where he was almost a slave himself."[72] But such a direct application of logic from Jewish experience in Europe to the situation of the Negroes in the South could only stem from the mind of a Northern Jew; it was never, to my knowledge, expressed in such blunt terms by a Southern Jew. To the contrary, the average Southern Jew would probably have agreed with Aaron Hirsch, who came to the United States in 1847 and worked through Mississippi and Arkansas, and who said that "the institution of Slavery as it existed in the South was not so great a wrong as people believe. The Negroes were brought here in a savage state; they captured and ate each other in their African home. Here they were instructed to work, were civilized and got religion, and were perfectly happy."[73]

Some Southern Jews, however, did not deceive themselves into thinking that the Negro slaves were "perfectly happy." These sensitive spirits were appalled at human exploitation of the life and labor of other human beings. Most of them reacted in a purely personal way, by avoiding the owning of slaves or by helping slaves. Major Alfred Mordecai of the United States Army, reared in the South and brother to planters and defenders of slavery, purchased only one slave in his life, simply to emancipate her. He believed that slavery was "the greatest misfortune and curse that could have befallen us." Yet he would do nothing to oppose slavery, and when the lines were drawn, he resigned his commission rather than fight for the North, without being willing to take up arms for the South.[74] Judah Touro, the New Orleans merchant, is reported to have emancipated many slaves whom he purchased solely for that purpose, and is even said to have established some of them in business at his own expense.[75] Another such spirit was Lazarus Straus, immigrant store-keeper of Talbotton, Georgia, who used to argue with local Protestant ministers about the Biblical grounds for the defense of slavery. According to his son, Oscar, hired slaves who worked for the Straus family would beg to be purchased by them. "As the result of such pleadings," Oscar said, "my father purchased household slaves one by one from their masters, although neither he nor my mother believed in slavery."[76] Probably many Jews as well as non-Jews were caught in the dilemma of purchasing slaves just because they did not believe in slavery; since emancipation was virtually impossible, all they could do was to become the most generous masters possible under the circumstances. But there is, of course, no way of telling what proportion of people who could not conscientiously condone slavery were included in the statistics of slave-owners.

The literature has preserved only one instance of Jewish participation in the dangerous game of taking a Negro slave to the North for clandestine emancipation. This was the risk taken by the Friedman brothers of Cincinnati, Ohio, and Tuscumbia, Alabama, who purchased Peter Still and conspired to take him North after he had earned enough money to refund his purchase price. This exciting story is told in Kate E. R. Packard's *The Kidnapped and the Ransomed*.[77] Joseph Friedman and his brother Isaac had been regarded by the townsmen with suspicion and dislike when they first came to Tuscumbia, but their behavior gradually overcame the local prejudices. Six or seven years later, Peter Still, beloved by his owners and by the community in general, prevailed on the Friedmans to hire him. After he felt certain that he could trust them, he confided to their ears his hope of obtaining freedom, so they purchased him from his owner. There was much criticism of the transaction in the town. People knew that the Friedmans had no use for a slave in their business, and that they maintained no home. The townsfolk therefore suspected that Joseph Friedman would ultimately sell Peter away from the community to some stranger who would mistreat him. Kate Packard quotes a child as saying, "Ma says he's a Jew, and she says *Jews will sell their own children for money.*" The author highlights the contrast between the behavior of "the slandered Jew," who is Peter's friend, and "the gaudy hypocrisy of his traducers," who "had bought and sold, and beaten and oppressed the poor until their cry had gone up to heaven." The plot succeeds: Peter saves up enough money to repay Joseph Friedman; the brothers close up their store and return to Cincinnati, taking Peter with them so that he can be freed. But the brothers never return to Alabama, for eventually their duplicity is revealed. Peter's well-wishers are indignant that the slave has been emancipated: that was carrying friendship too far! Joseph and Isaac Friedman are worthy of remembrance as anti-slavery activists: though other Southern Jews may well have risked fortune and reputation to evade state laws which restricted the emancipation of slaves, theirs are the only names recorded as having taken part in this risky venture.

We should not be surprised to discover that there was not a single abolitionist among the Jews of the South, but at least one did stem from this background. He was Marx E. Lazarus, eccentric scion of two distinguished Southern Jewish families, who was attracted to various radical social movements, including Fourierism, the North American Phalanx, Socialism, phrenology, spiritualism, and homeopathy. In 1860, Lazarus contributed a number of articles and translations to Moncure D. Conway's radical journal, *The Dial*, which was published in Cincinnati. One of these was entitled "True Principles of Emancipation," and was signed, "A Native of North Carolina and a Citizen of the World." In this article, Lazarus reminded his readers that Negro slavery was only one aspect of "the manifold cruelties that labor elsewhere suffers at the hands of capital, classes or castes, from their social superiors." He warned idealists against the "conversion of chattel slavery into that of labor for wages, changing the form, but not the facts, of slavery and oppression." "This prolonged crucifixion of a martyr race," he said, "demands a resurrection more humane than the liberty of selling oneself by the day, the cut-throat competitions of labor for wages, the outrages sanctioned by prejudice against color, careworn indigence or paralyzed pauperism." Despite these advanced views, Lazarus, in contrast to Major Mordecai, would not abandon the land of his birthplace; with the outbreak of war he returned home to enlist in the Confederate army as a private.[78]

But men like Marx Lazarus were outright anomalies. The Southern intellectual scene in the main, was a drab, monochromatic landscape of unquestioning adherence to the dominant Southern doctrine about slavery during the two decades before the Civil War. Jews not only accepted this doctrine; some of them helped to formulate and circulate it, although their role was by no means a significant one.

IX. An Evaluation

This investigation has traced Jewish participation in various aspects of the "peculiar institution" of the Old South. Jewish opinions about and relationships to the system of slavery were in no appreciable degree different from those of their non-Jewish neighbors. If more Jews owned slaves in terms of their numerical proportion of the population, it was because larger percentages of Jews lived in the towns and cities; if more Jews were auctioneers of slaves, it was because they were also auctioneers of every kind of merchandise; if fewer Jews were large-scale planters, it was for understandable social and economic reasons.

The significant thing is that being Jewish did not play any discernible role in the determination of the relationship of Jews to slavery. Except for the teachings of a very few rabbis like David Einhorn of Baltimore, Judaism in America had not yet adopted a "social justice" view of the responsibility of Jews towards society. Ante-bellum Southern Jews were more likely to quote the Talmudic maxim that "the law of the land is the law [for Jews]," and to regard the institution of slavery as part of the law which they were bound to uphold and follow, than they were to evaluate the failings of slavery in the light of the prophetic ethic.

Their acceptance of slavery as a natural aspect of the life of their section should not be regarded as a deliberately contrived "protective coloration," in order that they might remain inconspicuous. There is no iota of evidence, no line in a letter, no stray remark, which would lead us to believe that these Jews gave conscious support to the slave system out of fear of arousing anti-Jewish prejudice. Any such motivation for their behavior and attitudes, if it existed at all, was well hidden in the unconscious psyche.

It is true, however, that their small numbers militated against the creation of a distinctively Jewish approach to any political or social question other than anti-Semitism. Jews were only a fragment of the Southern population, thinly distributed throughout the area. Even in the largest cities, New Orleans, Charleston, Richmond, they were a tiny group. They would be entirely likely, therefore, to derive their opinions from discussions with non-Jewish neighbors, rather than with Jewish friends. This was especially true of the more prominent Jews, planters, attorneys, physicians, newspaper editors, merchants, whose associations with non-Jews were quite intimate.

Whatever prejudice there was in the South, before the Civil War aggravated every possible source of tension, was directed largely against the alien Jew, the immigrant peddler and petty store-keeper, the insecure newcomer, whose very survival was in the hands of his customers. He would, therefore, be inclined to adopt their opinions and attitudes, not because he was afraid to disagree with them, but because he wanted to succeed in his new home.

Slavery played an unacknowledged role in this question of Jewish status in the Old South, too. Although Southern society fostered a caste system which also applied to various classes of whites, and which distinguished the store-keeper from the wealthier merchant, the merchant in turn from the professional man, and the attorney and physician from the planter, the all-pervasive division was between the races. The Jews were white, and this very fact goes a long way towards accounting for the measurably higher social and political status achieved by Jews in the South than in the North. Foreign observers like Salomon de Rothschild and I. J. Benjamin were acutely aware of the sharp contrast between the South, where so many Jews were elected to high office, and the North, where Jews constituted a larger percentage of the population, yet had achieved fewer honors.[79] The Negroes acted as an escape-valve in Southern society. The Jews gained in status and security from the very presence of this large mass of defenseless victims who were compelled to absorb all of the prejudices which might otherwise have been expressed more frequently in anti-Jewish sentiment. As I. J. Benjamin said, "The white inhabitants felt themselves united with, and closer to, other whites—as opposed to the

Negroes. Since the Israelites there did not do the humbler kinds of work which the Negro did, he was quickly received among the upper classes, and early rose to high political rank." Although this was too broad a generalization, and not all Jews were treated so generously, the road to social and economic advancement and acceptance for many Jews was smoothed by the ever-present race distinction which imputed superiority to all whites. And even the path of the poor, foreign Jew was made easier by the institution of slavery. Oscar Straus remembered that when his father was peddling through the rural areas of Georgia, he "was treated by the owners of the plantations with a spirit of equality that is hard to appreciate today. Then, too, the existence of slavery drew a distinct line of demarcation between the white and black races. This gave to the white [peddler] a status of equality that probably otherwise he would not have enjoyed to such a degree."[80]

Slavery, therefore, played a more significant role in the development of Jewish life in the Old South, than Jews themselves played in the establishment and maintenance of the institution. The history of slavery would not have differed one whit from historic reality if no single Jew had been resident in the South. Other whites would have owned slaves; other traders and auctioneers would have bought and sold slaves; other political and intellectual leaders would have propagandized in behalf of slavery; a few slaves might have fared better or worse at the hands of other masters, but their feelings were immaterial details in the total story of the institution itself. But whether so many Jews would have achieved so high a level of social, political, economic, and intellectual status and recognition, without the presence of the lowly and degraded slave, is indeed dubious. How ironic that the distinctions bestowed upon men like Judah P. Benjamin, Major Raphael J. Moses, and the Honorable Solomon Cohen were in some measure dependent upon the sufferings of the very Negro slaves they bought and sold with such equanimity.

NOTES

1. The following abbreviations are used for works frequently cited: AJA = American Jewish Archives files; *AJAM* = *American Jewish Archives* (journal); E = Barnett A. Elzas, *The Jews of South Carolina* (Philadelphia, 1905); EL = Herbert T. Ezekiel and Gaston Lichtenstein, *The History of the Jews of Richmond* (Richmond, Va., 1917); HTC = Helen Tunnicliff Catterall, *Judicial Cases Concerning American*

Slavery and the Negro, 4 vols. (Washington, D.C., 1926–1936); *JNH* = *Journal of Negro History*; MC = Jacob Rader Marcus, *American Jewry: Documents, Eighteenth Century* (Cincinnati, 1959): ME = Jacob Rader Marcus, *Early American Jewry*, vol. II (Philadelphia, 1953); MM = Jacob Rader Marcus, *Memoirs of American Jews, 1775–1865*, 3 vols. (Philadelphia, 1955–1956): OCC = *The Occident and American Jewish Advocate*; PAJHS = *Publications of the American Jewish Historical Society*; R = Joseph R. Rosenbloom, *A Biographical Dictionary of Early American Jews* (Lexington, Ky., 1960); RE = Charles Reznikoff with Uriah Z. Engelman, *The Jews of Charleston* (Philadelphia, 1950).

2. Robert Douthat Meade, *Judah P. Benjamin* (New York, 1948), pp. 67, 63 and 90; J. Carlyle Sitterson, *Sugar Country: The Cane Sugar Industry in the South, 1753–1950* (Lexington, Ky., 1953), pp. 131, 154; *The Life of Judah Philip Benjamin*, A Publication of the Louisiana State Museum (New Orleans, 1937); Harnett T. Kane, *Deep Delta Country* (New York, 1944), pp. 68–69; Baton Rouge *Advocate*, March 27, 1960, magazine section, p. 1.

3. MM, vol. I, p. 184.

4. Addendum on "Absentee Ownership of Slaves in the United States in 1830," in Carter G. Woodson, *Free Negro Owners of Slaves in the United States in 1830* (Washington, D.C., 1924), p. 61; 1840 Mss. Census Returns for New Orleans and Vicinity, National Archives; RE, p. 92; E, pp. 51 and 143; R, pp. 25 and 89; ME, p. 385; A. J. Hanna, *A Prince in Their Midst: The Adventurous Life of Achille Murat on the American Frontier* (Norman, Okla., 1946), p. 86; Leon Hühner, "David L. Yulee, Florida's First Senator," *PAJHS*, no. 25 (1917), pp. 4–7. Hühner, however, reports that Moses Levy favored the abolition of slavery, despite his extensive ownership of slaves.

5. Letter, Barnett Polack to Sarah Polack, Sept. 6, 1836, in private collection of Edwin Wolf, 2nd.

6. We know about the Adler brothers' laundry and meals from 26 Ala. 145, quoted in HTC, vol. III, p. 201.

7. 1850 Mss. Census Returns for Mobile County, National Archives.

8. Data from Inventory of Estate of Emanuel Stern, Record Room, Civil District Court, New Orleans.

9. Letter, dated Nov. 23, 1867, Mordecai Collection, Duke University Library.

10. EL, pp. 15, 327–329.

11. Photostat of deed of emancipation, AJA. But Myers did not free all his slaves.

12. Deeds from vol. 3-L, p. 174, Miscellaneous Records, South Carolina Archives Department, Columbia, in Thomas J. Tobias's collection of photostats of family papers.

13. EL, pp. 78 and 80.

14. EL, p. 85.

15. EL, pp. 330–332.

16. Va. 158–159, cited in HTC, vol. I, p. 131. The records of the Lynchburg courts are so incomplete that it has not been possible to discover any details of Cohen's crime.

17. EL, p. 78.
18. EL, p. 79.
19. EL, p. 91.
20. EL, pp. 77–78.
21. MG, p. 63.
22. E, p. 142.
23. Jack Kenny Williams, *Vogues in Villainy, Crime and Retribution in Ante-Bellum South Carolina* (Columbia, S.C., 1939), p. 73.
24. Richmond *Enquirer*, May 21, 1805.
25. Frederick Law Olmsted, *The Cotton Kingdom*, ed. Arthur M. Schlesinger (New York, 1953), pp. 37 and 196.
26. E. Merton Coulter, *The South during Reconstruction, 1865–1877* (Baton Rouge, La., 1947), pp. 202–203.
27. Richmond *City Directory* for 1852, p. 27 of the advertising section.
28. Riley 155, cited in HTC, vol. II, p. 361.
29. 1 Spears 223, cited in HTC, vol. II, p. 385.
30. 15 La. An. 38, cited in HTC, vol. III, p. 676.
31. EL, p. 82.
32. EL, p. 98.
33. Bill of sale, dated May 11, 1852, in the author's collection.
34. EL, pp. 43 and 298.
35. MM, vol. II, p. 28.
36. Photostats of slave bills loaned to me by Ben Cone of Greensboro, North Carolina, Herman's grandson.
37. Edwin J. Scott, *Random Recollections of a Long Life* (Columbia, S.C., 1884), pp. 82–85.
38. *OCC*, vol. II (1844), pp. 83–87, 147–150; vol. IV (1846), pp. 387–389; vol. V (1847), p. 164; vol. VI (1848), p. 153; vol. VIII (1850), pp. 145–158; vol. IX (1851), pp. 268–269; vol. XII (1854), p. 326; Helen Kohn Hennig, *The Tree of Life . . .* (Columbia, S.C., 1945), pp. 3–4.
39. Bertram W. Korn, "An Historical Excursus," in *1844–1944, Congregation Shaarai Shomayim, Mobile, Alabama* (Mobile, Ala., 1944); Mobile City Directories for 1839, pp. iii, 24a; 1842, p. 64; 1850, p. 48; 1856, p. 57; Korn mss. files on Jones; letter, Myer S. Isaacs to Jones, Aug. 14, 1860, Board of Delegates Mss. Files, Library of the American Jewish Historical Society.
40. Nor, of course, did slave owning seem to be offensive in a rabbi. Bertram W. Korn, *American Jewry and the Civil War* (Philadelphia, 1951), p. 29, gives data on the Rev. George Jacobs's hiring of a slave woman. A. J. Marks, acting Rabbi of New Orleans in the 1830s, listed eleven slaves in his household in the 1840 census for New Orleans.

41. Quoted from the Charleston *South Carolina State Gazette*, Sept. 6, 1784, in E, pp. 129–130.

42. Frederic Bancroft, *Slave-Trading in the Old South* (Baltimore, 1931), pp. 97–98, 175–177, 251–252.

43. J. Winston Coleman, *Slavery Times in Kentucky* (Chapel Hill, N.C., 1940); and Charles Sackett Sydnor, *Slavery in Mississippi* (New York, 1933).

44. Data about these men is given in Louis Ginsburg, *History of the Jews of Petersburg* (Petersburg, Va., 1954), pp. 25, 31, 35–36; and EL, p. 143.

45. Harriett Beecher Stowe, *A Key to Uncle Tom's Cabin* (Boston, 1853), p. 151.

46. Cited in Ralph Betts Flanders, *Plantation Slavery in Georgia* (Chapel Hill, N.C., 1933), p. 185.

47. Carter G. Woodson, *Free Negro Heads of Families in the United States in 1880* (Washington, D.C., 1926). Eight of these Negroes, incidentally, owned a total of thirty-nine slaves: Woodson, *Free Negro Owners of Slaves*, pp. 4ff.

48. EL, p. 86.

49. ME, vol. II, p. 224; E, p. 153; Constitution of the Hebrew Congregation Kaal Kodesh Beth-Elohim, or House of God, Charleston, 1820 (reprinted Charleston, S.C., 1904), p. 16.

50. RE, p. 78.

51. HTC, vol. I, p. 145, citing 5 Randolph 634.

52. Will in AJA.

53. Will in AJA.

54. 14 Ga. 185–207; 20 Ga. 480–512; 33 Ga. 11–29, as cited in HTC, vol. III, pp. 33, 50–51, 87–88.

55. For Jacob N. Cardozo, see Alexander Brody, "Jacob Newton Cardozo, American Economist," *Historia Judaica*, vol. XV (1955), pp. 135–166; for Isaac, see E, pp. 161, 163–164, and 204; and Barnett A. Elzas, *The Old Jewish Cemeteries of Charleston, S.C.* (Charleston, S.C., 1903), p. 12.

56. These papers, in the author's collection, are dated April 4, 1810; March 30, 1822; Jan. 23, 1833; Nov. 13, 1837; May 2, 1840; April 8, 1844; no date, 1850. Data about Barnet A. Cohen from E, pp. 133 and 144; Cecil Roth, *The Rise of Provincial Jewry* (London, 1950), p. 41; R, p. 24; Elzas, *Old Jewish Cemeteries of Charleston*, pp. 5–6.

57. Speech of Hon. David S. Kaufman, of Texas, on "The Slavery Question," delivered in the House of Representatives, February 10, 1847 (Washington, D.C., 1847); Speech of Hon. D. S. Kaufman, of Texas, on "The Slavery Question and Its Adjustment," delivered in the House of Representatives, June 10, 1850 (Washington, D.C., 1850); Hühner, "David L. Yulee," pp. 14 and 20–22. Although Kaufman has generally been regarded as stemming from Jewish parents, there is no contemporary evidence for the assumption; all such testimony is of comparatively late date, as for instance, Henry Cohen et al., *One Hundred Years of Jewry in Texas* (Dallas, 1936), p. 8.

58. Sitterson, *Sugar Country*, pp. 131, 154; Meade, *Judah P. Benjamin*, pp. 92, 100ff.; Bell Irvin Wiley, *Southern Negroes, 1861–1865* (New Haven, Conn., 1938), pp. 152, 154, and 157; Speech of Hon. J. P. Benjamin, of Louisiana, delivered in the Senate of the United States, May 22, 1860 (Washington, D.C., 1860).

59. Morris U. Schappes, *Documentary History of the Jews in the United States, 1654–1875*, rev. ed. (New York, 1952), pp. 293–301 and 643–644; James Benson Sellars, *Slavery in Alabama* (Tuscaloosa, Ala., 1950), pp. 188–190.

60. MM, vol. III, p. 149.

61. Lecture on Texas delivered by Mr. J. De Cordova, at Philadelphia, New York, Mount Holly, Brooklyn, and Newark; also a paper read by him before the New York Geographical Society, April 15, 1858 (Philadelphia, 1858), pp. 2 and 24–25.

62. "Essays by Junius," vol. I, pp. 95 and 135, in Henry L. Pinckney and Abraham Moise, *A Section from the Miscellaneous Writings of the Late Isaac Harby, Esq.* (Charleston, S.C., 1829).

63. Jacob N. Cardozo, *Reminiscences of Charleston* (Charleston, S.C., 1866), p. 10; Brody, "Jacob Newton Cardozo," pp. 150–151.

64. Edwin De Leon, *Thirty Years of My Life on Three Continents* (London, 1890), vol. I, pp. 13–36.

65. Thomas Cooper De Leon, *Belles, Beaux and Brains of the Confederacy* (New York, 1909), pp. 15–16; see also his *Four Years in Rebel Capitals* (Mobile, Ala., 1890), p. 370.

66. "Writers of Anonymous Articles in *The Farmer's Register* by Edmund Ruffin," *Journal of Southern History*, vol. XXIII (1957), pp. 90–102; Samuel Mordecai, *Richmond in By-Gone Days* (Richmond, Va., 1946), pp. 354–355; letter, Samuel Mordecai to G. W. Mordecai, Dec. 17, 1860, Mordecai Mss., Duke University Library.

67. Quoted in Clement Eaton, *Freedom of Thought in the Old South* (Durham, N.C., 1940), p. 232.

68. MM, vol. III, pp. 308–309.

69. MM, vol. III, p. 368.

70. Letter, dated Jan. 8, 1866, Mordecai Mss., Duke University Library.

71. MM, vol. I, pp. 51 and 56.

72. MM, vol. I. p. 338.

73. MM, vol. II, p. 138.

74. Stanley L. Falk, "Divided Loyalties in 1861: The Decision of Major Alfred Mordecai," *PAJHS*, vol. XLVIII, no. 3 (Mar. 1959), pp. 149–150.

75. Leon Hühner, *The Life of Judah Touro* (Philadelphia, 1946), p. 69.

76. MM, vol. II, pp. 295–296.

77. First published in 1856 and reprinted in part in *AJAM*, vol. IX (1957), pp. 3–31, with notes and introduction by Maxwell Whiteman.

78. Caroline Cohen, *Records of the Myers, Hays and Mordecai Families from 1707 to 1918* (Washington, D.C., 1913), p. 56; Moncure Daniel Conway, *Autobiography, Memories and Experiences* (Boston, 1904), vol. I, pp. 313–314; Eaton, *Freedom of Thought,* p. 322; Frank Luther Mott, *A History of American Magazines, 1850–1865* (Cambridge, Mass., 1938), p. 535; letter, Marx E. Lazarus to George W. Mordecai, New York, March 24, 1846, Mordecai Mss., Southern Historical Collection, University of North Carolina Library; *The Dial,* vol. I (1860), pp. 219–228.

79. MM, vol. III, p. 104; I. J. Benjamin, *Three Years in America* (Philadelphia, 1956), p. 76.

80. MM, vol. II, p. 291.

Part II

|||||||||||||||||||||||||||||||||||||||||||||

Jews and Abolition

Although the American Jewish population was relatively small in the decades before the Civil War, Jews and Judaism held an outsized position in the cosmology of several leading abolitionists. Many abolitionists drew motivation and inspiration from their evangelical Protestant convictions. They moved in circles that sought the conversion of Jews to Christianity through active missionizing. And a handful of their voluble political antagonists, particularly Mordecai Noah and Judah P. Benjamin, were conspicuously Jewish. Anti-Jewish animus, as a result, surfaced occasionally, for example, when the leading abolitionists William Lloyd Garrison and Edmund Quincy mouthed unflattering stereotypes.

For the most part Jews reciprocated this suspicion and disfavor. Isaac Mayer Wise and most other American rabbis, even some who opposed slavery, considered abolitionists to be reckless agitators and warmongering Christian zealots. This distaste did not dissipate in the decades following the Civil War. If anything, a politically expedient public consensus hardened into the conviction that abolitionists were responsible for fomenting fanaticism and friction between North and South. Wise's *Reminiscences*, published in English in 1901, reinforced this interpretation of the relationship between Jews and abolitionists, accusing the latter of ethical inconsistency in harboring nativist and anti-Jewish sentiments.

Bertram Korn dedicated little attention to this subject in his *American Jewry and the Civil War* and did not challenge this dominant understanding of the interaction of Jews and abolitionists. Nonetheless, his book triggered a reappraisal of the entire issue. Barely months after its publication in 1951, a young rabbi and scholar named Louis Ruchames published a bristling defense of abolitionism. He felt Korn had unfairly echoed the prejudices of Isaac Mayer Wise in maligning abolitionists. Ruchames scythed through Wise's claims of abolitionist Judeophobia, gathering evidence instead of their Judeophilia. Ruchames, who later published a collection of abolitionist writings and edited the letters of William Lloyd Garrison, stood in the vanguard of a wave of new scholarship that gathered momentum in the 1960s, offering a far more sophisticated and favorable reassessment of abolitionism. Looking back at the end of his career, though, Ruchames concluded that the vigor of his apologia had blinded him to almost all contrary evidence. The essay included in chapter 4, first published in 1976, presents a more nuanced assessment of the diversity (and fluidity) of abolitionist views about Jews. Several leading abolitionists, including Garrison, turn out to have been "not without prejudices."

Ruchames did not address a second underlying assumption of earlier works on Jews and abolitionism—that no Jews had joined its ranks. Jews were understood to be leery of abolitionists for both their evangelicalism and their anti-Judaism, a damning double brand. Given this seeming incompatibility, it is unsurprising that the leading historian of American Jewry, Jacob Rader Marcus, doubted whether any Jews joined the front ranks of the movement. Although several prominent Jews including Rabbi David Einhorn and Michael Heilprin voiced support for emancipation in public, they were thought to have shied from formal association with abolitionism. The subject was not addressed systematically until 1984, when Jayme Sokolow published the essay included in chapter 3. Although Sokolow did not dispute the paucity of Jewish abolitionists before the 1850s, he assembled compelling evidence of a cohort of ideologically minded Jewish émigrés drawn to the slavery question in the decade before the Civil War. Since the publication of this essay, piecemeal evidence of Jewish support for abolitionism has grown. Perhaps the most important addition has been Chris Monaco's 2005 biography of Moses Levy of Florida (1782–1854)—the father of U.S. Senator David Yulee—a volume that reveals Levy's energy as activist and pamphleteer in service of abolitionism from at least the 1820s.

3

Revolution and Reform
The Antebellum Jewish Abolitionists

Jayme A. Sokolow

Many antebellum abolitionists condemned discrimination throughout the world and tried to enlist the aid of traditionally oppressed ethnic groups in the antislavery crusade. They were spectacularly unsuccessful, however, in soliciting Irish support.[1] The antebellum Jews' apparent unwillingness to participate in the emancipation struggle also puzzled and hurt the abolitionists. In the 1853 report of the American and Foreign Anti-Slavery Society, they wondered why the

> Jews of the United States have never taken any steps whatever with regard to the Slavery question. As citizens, they deem it their policy "to have everyone choose which ever side he may deem best to promote his own interests and the welfare of his country." . . . It cannot be said that the Jews have formed any denominational opinion on the subject of American slavery. . . . The objects of so much mean prejudice and unrighteous oppression as the Jews have been for ages, surely they, it would seem, more than any other denomination, ought to be the enemies of CASTE, and the friends of UNIVERSAL FREEDOM.[2]

The abolitionists' evaluation was essentially correct. Before the 1850s, there were only a few scattered examples of Jewish antislavery activities. While some Jews emancipated their slaves, most Southern Jews accepted

---

Reprinted, without accompanying table, with permission of Jayme A. Sokolow from the *Journal of Ethnic Studies* 9 (Spring 1981): 27–43. Jayme A. Sokolow is founder and president of the Development Source, Inc.

and defended slavery until the Civil War ended. They supported the peculiar institution because Southern Jews lived in a proslavery environment, profited economically and psychologically from slavery, and lacked Reform Jewish temples which might have challenged slavery. Most antebellum northern and midwestern Jews also maintained a discreet silence on the subject.

Their European experiences and religious traditions, their lowly economic and educational backgrounds, and the fear of antisemitic backlash made them politically conservative and detached from controversial causes outside the scope of Judaism.[3]

Previous scholars have examined the abolitionists' attitude toward antebellum Jews, but they have ignored any significant abolitionist activities by pre–Civil War Jews.[4] Bertram W. Korn, a prominent historian of nineteenth-century American Judaism, has contended that most abolitionist leaders were uninterested in defending the civil rights of Jews and sometimes uttered antisemitic statements because their obsessive concern for Blacks blinded them to the plight of the Jews.[5] Although the abolitionists could have been more vocal during the Mortara case and Grant's infamous 1862 Order No. 11 barring Jews from trading in Tennessee, Louis Ruchames's contentions appear valid: the antislavery crusade's attempts to help Blacks involved a considerable effort to understand and defend Judaism.[6]

In the 1850s, however, Jewish abolitionists emerged who publicly criticized slavery and participated in antebellum America's most controversial reform. By examining the social backgrounds, careers, and ideology of the Jewish abolitionists, we can better understand the origins and complexity of antebellum abolitionism and the momentous changes taking place in American Judaism, for with one exception all the Jewish abolitionists were Reform Jewish émigrés. While most native abolitionists were motivated by evangelical Protestantism and American democratic ideals, the Jewish abolitionists' decision to participate in antislavery activities was primarily a function of their European political and religious experiences.

Until the 1840s, Jewish immigration to America usually involved individuals and isolated families. After this period there was a mass migration of German and Eastern European Jews (Austria, Hungary, Poland, Bohemia) which raised America's Jewish population from 50,000 in 1850 to 150,000 by the Civil War. During this decade the number of congregations increased from 37 to 77; seating capacity almost doubled from 19,588 to 34,412, and there was a threefold increase in the value of religious property. In 1850 there were eleven states with congregations; by 1860, nineteen states, led by New York and Pennsylvania, registered congregations according to the second American Census of Social Statistics. Crop failures, the disruption of internal trade, the failures of the 1848 revolutions, and continuous outbreaks of antisemitic violence propelled Jews to America.[7] From these immigrant ranks came all the Jewish abolitionists.

The revolutions of 1848 encouraged two groups of Jews to enter America. The largest group migrated because they were determined to find the personal opportunity, economic freedom, and civic equality denied them in Europe. For these immigrants, the revolutions accelerated a process which had begun in the early nineteenth century. Earlier Jewish immigrants were Sephardim who often had mercantile connections in Europe and the Caribbean. The German and Eastern European Ashkenazic Jews, in contrast, arrived without significant business interests, were generally quite poor, and usually started their American careers as peddlers.[8]

The second, smaller group fled to America because they had participated in the 1848 revolutions or were opposed to the restoration of the conservative regimes. These revolutions, which occurred in areas inhabited by one-third of world Jewry, had a strong effect on the process of Jewish emancipation. Jews played prominent roles in the European revolutions. In Vienna they were among the leaders of the National Guard and the Students Legion. The Jewish delegates in the Austrian Diet campaigned for the annulment of the special taxes on Jews and argued for complete civic equality. And at the Frankfurt Parliament and the Prussian Assembly the Jewish representatives pleaded for equal rights. Throughout these struggles, the general principle of equality, rather than the peculiar situation of the Jews, was consistently invoked by protagonists of emancipation.[9] This was the attitude that the émigrés who became abolitionists would take in America.

Many of the Jewish political radicals never became involved in abolitionist activities. Sigismund Kaufman actively participated in the September 1848 Frankfurt uprising and then fled to England and later Brooklyn, where he practiced law after 1852. Although he became a dedicated member of the Republican Party, there is no evidence that abolitionism ever claimed his attention.[10] Isaac Hartman, who was imprisoned in Wurzburg after the revolutionaries were defeated, taught European languages in New York schools and shunned politics until he died of tuberculosis in 1855.[11] Some of the Jewish political refugees settled in the South and became proslavery advocates. Louis Schlessinger, a veteran of the Kossuth campaigns, joined the William Walker filibuster in Nicaragua and became the baron of a coffee plantation there. And Adolphus Adler defended slavery and was commissioned a Confederate colonel at the outbreak of the Civil War.[12]

Because there is little biographical information on the forty active Jewish 48'ers that migrated to America, it is unclear exactly why certain Jewish émigrés became abolitionists while others remained indifferent or defended slavery. I would suggest that the answer lies in their political-religious ideologies and social backgrounds, for all the refugee abolitionists came from emancipated, cosmopolitan homes where parents vigorously defended liberalism (in the mid-nineteenth-century sense, liberalism included a belief in individualism, civic equality, and representative government).

Probably the most dramatic and adventurous abolitionist was August Bondi. As a child in Vienna, he was tutored in an urbane, scholarly environment in Hebrew, German, French, Hungarian, and Latin. When the March 1848 Vienna revolution occurred, August had been in the Academic Gymnasium for five years and was accepted into the Students Legion at the age of fourteen. After the revolution his family prudently left Austria and moved to St. Louis, where August quickly became involved in antislavery rallies and activities. He tried a variety of trades but found them all boring, and so August migrated to frontier Kansas to start a farm: "I was most anxious for a strenuous life. I was tired of the humdrum life of a clerk. Any struggle, any hard work would be welcome to me. I thirsted for it, for adventure."[13] Soon afterwards he fought with John Brown in Kansas and participated in the battles of Black Jack and Osawatomie with two other Jewish immigrants, Theodore Weiner and Jacob Benjamin. When the Civil War began, Bondi enlisted in the Union Army and served with distinction until wounded in 1864.[14]

Michael Heilprin similarly moved from European revolutionary activities to American abolitionism. His father was a merchant scholar and an avid student of Jewish literature and the German romantics. Michael developed into a literary genius whose linguistic ability attracted the attention of distinguished Hebraists. When the 1848 Hungarian Revolution began, Heilprin's friendship with Louis Kossuth and other revolutionaries led to a literary post in the new government. After barely escaping capture by the Austrians, he migrated to Paris, then London, and eventually settled in Philadelphia, where he immediately became involved in the abolitionist movement. When an antislavery Democratic Party rally in Philadelphia's Carpenter's Hall was disrupted by proslavery forces in 1858, Heilprin arose from the front row, serenely mounted the stage, and in clear, vigorous German lambasted the proslavery Democrats![15] Fortunately he was quickly ushered out of the hall before any harm befell him. Heilprin later worked with William Lloyd Garrison, William H. Seward, and Charles Sumner, and criticized slaveholders in *The Nation* and the New York *Tribune*.

Isidor Busch, like Bondi and Heilprin, emigrated to America as a result of his revolutionary activities. As a young man in Vienna, he was active in the field of Jewish letters. From 1842 to 1847 he edited the first popular German-Jewish periodical in Austria, the *Kalender und Jahrbuch fur Israeliten*, which tried to publicize the scientific and literary accomplishments of leading Jewish scholars. During the Vienna revolution he published another journal that fiercely advocated revolution and the need for political and religious freedom. After the revolution failed, the young Busch family migrated to St. Louis, where Isidor distinguished himself in business, banking, agronomy, and politics.[16] An avowed abolitionist, Busch's greatest contribution to the antislavery cause came at the Missouri state conventions held between 1861 and 1863 to decide whether the state should remain in the Union or join the Confederacy. He led the abolitionist forces at the convention and consistently argued that the "position of our national affairs, the preservation of the Union, . . . the interest of the slave-owner, as well as humanity to the slaves, imperatively demand *speedy* emancipation."[17] His oratory and leadership were instrumental in keeping the state within the Union, and he helped develop the plan which freed Missouri slaves without compensating their masters.

Bondi, Heilprin, Busch, and the other émigré abolitionists had similar European backgrounds. They were raised in comfortable, stimulating homes, and their fathers were often involved in manufacturing, commerce, or publishing. In Europe these radicals were certainly not economically or socially oppressed. Recently emancipated, they were gaining status in mid-nineteenth-century Europe and America, tended to be occupationally versatile, and pursued careers which required broadly applicable skills. Their home environments and urban experiences propelled them into political activities that challenged the conservative order.

Abraham Jacobi neatly summarized these political beliefs when he characterized his friend and fellow abolitionist Ernst Krackowitzer. Jacobi had been active in the 1848 German revolution and was imprisoned for his role in the Bonn uprising. After escaping to America in 1853, Jacobi became an abolitionist and a pioneering pediatrics physician.[18] According to him, the former Viennese student council revolutionary Krackowitzer

> did not *drift* into politics; he was a born politician. . . . No oppression or injustice found grace before his eyes. Thus he was a free soiler, thus he was an abolitionist; no matter whether the chains to be broken were those of color, or religion, or sex. . . . He supported Fremont, supported Lincoln, supported energetically the war for the Union.[19]

Recent historians have developed a similar social portrait of the native American abolitionists that substantially modifies David Donald's theory about the abolitionists as a displaced social elite trying to reassert traditional values. According to Leonard L. Richards, Gerald Sorin, and James Brewer Stewart, the abolitionists were a broad and diverse group of farmers, urban manufacturers, tradesmen, and artisans who were gaining status during the Jacksonian era.[20] Although the Jewish abolitionists' backgrounds support Richards, Sorin, and Stewart, Donald's findings remain very suggestive as to the role of parental guidance. As numerous biographers have shown, the families of abolitionists placed a stern emphasis on moral righteousness and social responsibility. Wendell Phillips, the Tappen brothers, and William Lloyd Garrison internalized the religious dictates of dominating mothers. James G. Birney, Elijah P. Lovejoy, and Elizabeth Cady Stanton modeled their early lives to please their demanding fathers.

The Jewish abolitionists were also heavily influenced by strong father figures. Isidor Busch's father taught him scholarship, printing, and the need for political and religious freedom.[21] Samuel Morais was a devoted Italian republican ("even the boards of my bed are Republican") who transmitted a flaming liberalism to his son Sabato.[22] And Bondi claimed that he "became imbued with a hatred of spiritual and governmental tyranny. . . . We boys were fairly fanaticized with sympathy for the downtrodden of the globe." He did not marry a Southerner because Bondi "felt that my father's son was not to be a slave-driver."[23] The fathers of Jewish abolitionists inculcated a lasting liberal religious and social conscience in their sons. A strong sense of individuality and an earnestness about moral issues characterized the abolitionists in their youths. In their reminiscences, Jewish abolitionists often paid homage to strong fathers whose moral fervor dominated their households.

Aside from their familial and political experiences, religion was the other crucial factor which impelled émigré Jews to become abolitionists.

Except for the Orthodox rabbi Sabato Morais of Philadelphia, who had a similar background to the other Jewish abolitionists aside for his religion,[24] there were no Orthodox Jews in the antislavery movement. Only German Reform rabbis and Reform Jews became avowed abolitionists. It makes no sense to isolate Jewish radicals as William O. McCragg, Jr. has done, and ignore their religious experiences by merely portraying them as urban modernizers in revolt against a traditional agrarian society.[25] The conspicuous role played by Jews in nineteenth- and twentieth-century social movements can be partially explained by analyzing their social backgrounds, but historians who neglect religion by portraying Jewish rebels as liberal secularists miss the impact of religion on social reform. The abolitionists were Reform Jews because the issues surrounding abolitionism seemed related to the problems Reform Judaism faced in the mid-nineteenth century.

Until the late eighteenth century, European Jews in Central and Eastern Europe lived in self-governing Jewish communities and were regarded as part of one dispersed Jewish nation. But during the next hundred years Jewish communities were transformed in ways that changed their legal status, occupational distribution, cultural habits, and their religious perspective and behavior as Talmudic or Rabbinic laws were dissolved and Jews were allowed to become citizens. This dramatic revolution, variously called the period of Enlightenment, Haskalah, early reform, or emancipation, occurred when European states, with various degrees of success, gradually eliminated the special and separate status of Jews and their communities. Concurrently, high-social-status German Jews began a religious movement called Reform that tried to modify traditional Jewish religious practices and values in the direction of a more decorous, rationalistic faith freed from ancient Talmudic learning and rites. Its supporters accentuated those elements of Biblical and even Talmudic Judaism that had universalistic elements and neglected or omitted conflicting notions that were no less a part of that tradition. Finally, Reform Jews discarded Judaism as a set of revealed laws and instead perceived their religion as a body of dogma and moral teachings. For the Reformers, Judaism was now a confession of faith, and the Reform Jewish community was united by its adherence to an abstract body of teachings.[26]

In America, Reform Judaism rapidly captured the majority of American congregations for two reasons. First, in Europe Reformers had to contend with Orthodox Jews who still controlled many Jewish communities; in America the Reformers were leaders of independent congregations entirely free to translate their principles into action. And second, insofar as Reform implied the negation of ritual observances, the movement was aided by the tendency of the immigrants to drop cultural impediments to material success and to Americanization. By the Civil War, most American Jews believed that their religion was a form of ethical monotheism capable of indefinite development and expansion, were mildly antinomian and antiritualistic, and believed that Reform Judaism was in the vanguard of mankind's progress toward a universal religion of humanity.[27] David Einhorn, an abolitionist and one of the founders of German and American Judaism, summed up the new creed when he said that Reform Judaism believed "in one humanity, all of whose members, being of the same heavenly and earthly origin, possess a like nobility of birth and a claim to equal rights, equal laws, and in an equal share of happiness."[28] For many American Jews, the Haskalah, Jewish emancipation, and new conditions in America made Reform appear more appropriate than Orthodoxy.

Importantly, a similar religious development took place among the Garrisonian abolitionists, who also jettisoned revealed law and instead emphasized the progressive ethical nature of Christianity. Both the Garrisonians and the Reformers began as Biblical literalists. But changing social conditions and new ideologies encouraged both groups to modify their theologies. In the case of the Garrisonians, establishment Protestantism's unwillingness to embrace antislavery and the proslavery use of the Bible turned the New England abolitionists away from Calvinist orthodoxy toward a belief in the social gospel. They gradually downplayed Biblical literalism and began stressing natural law and conscience. For the Garrisonians, theological Christianity had to be judged pragmatically by its effects. Original sin and predestination were deemphasized as a vague ethical Christianity which was a rationale for social concern evolved. God became a name which was applied to the Garrisonians' perceptions of correct conduct: "*Humanity before all things*—before all books and before all institutions; and God in the soul is the only authority."[29]

As Richards, Sorin, and Stewart have explained, the abolitionists' northern opponents held leadership positions in traditional Protestant denominations such as the Episcopal Church and the old-school Presbyterian Church. The Protestant and Jewish abolitionists came from less distinguished religious stock; their religious beliefs stood in sharp contrast to their foes' sacramental elitism. For the Protestant abolitionists, evangelicalism often provided a break with tradition and a sense of immediatism and moral fervor. The Jewish abolitionists used reform to reject the dogmas of Orthodoxy; this dissenting attitude led to a crusading moral assertiveness and a searching reexamination of accepted Jewish, European, and American institutions. Reform Judaism's belief in the "approach of the realization of Israel's great Messianic hope for the establishment of the kingdom of truth, justice, and peace among all men" also encouraged Jews to "solve on the basis of justice and righteousness the problems presented by the contrasts and evils of the present organization of society."[30] This zealousness and dedication to a world mission, and not just the social position of mid-nineteenth-century Jewry, explains why fighting Reform Jews in Europe became abolitionists in America.

They used their liberal European beliefs and Reform Judaism to defend antebellum Blacks. One of the most formidable obstacles to abolitionism was the widespread popular and scientific belief in the innate inferiority of Blacks. Those abolitionists who believed that Blacks were not inherently inferior attacked the concept of racial inequality on two fronts: they attempted to demonstrate, from the Bible, science, history, and observed facts, the essential equality of the races, and they also tried to show that the unfavorable environmental conditions of slavery and segregation, rather than natural inferiority, had caused the disabilities of American Blacks.

The Jewish abolitionists were quite sensitive to these arguments. One reason was the proslavery use of the Bible, which relied on Mosaic law and ancient slavery to defend the peculiar institution. Since Reform Jews only accepted those Mosaic laws which would "elevate and sanctify"[31] their lives, they rejected any suggestions that the Bible could be used to defend modern slavery. The second reason was related to the position of nineteenth-century European Jews. During the emancipation struggle, the "Jewish question"[32] was whether Jews were innately inferior to Gentiles or whether the ghetto environment explained the Jews' "backward" social customs and traditions. Because Reform Jews believed that emancipation would elevate the position of European Jewry and expose the Gentiles to a superior religion purged of its excrescences and anachronisms, the Jewish abolitionists felt threatened by proslavery arguments. They ominously resembled antisemitic doctrines and could be used against American Jews. Therefore for religious and social reasons, Jewish abolitionists tried to weaken antebellum racial myths.

They did not deny that ancient slavery was sanctioned by the Bible. But the Jewish abolitionists did argue, using a Reform perspective, that Biblical bondage had to be interpreted in a historical context and could not be used to justify modern slavery. This approach was exemplified best in the famous debate over Rabbi Morris Jacob Raphall's 1861 proslavery sermon.

President Buchanan had proclaimed January 4, 1861, a National Fast Day in an effort to mobilize national sentiment against secession. On this day, Raphall, a famous and distinguished New York City Orthodox rabbi, delivered a sermon accepted by many as the Jewish position on the slavery question. Accusing the abolitionists of being "impulsive declaimers, gifted with great zeal, but little knowledge; more eloquent than learned; better able to excite our passions than to satisfy our reason,"[33] he proceeded to investigate three related questions. How far back could the influence of slavery be traced? Was slavery condemned as a sin in the Bible? And what were the condition of slaves in Biblical times? His answer to all three questions gave no succor to the abolitionists. Raphall believed that slavery existed before the flood and was nowhere contradicted by the Mosaic code or the New Testament. Thus he accused abolitionist preachers like Henry Ward Beecher of perverting the meaning of the Bible. Abraham, Isaac, Jacob, and Job all were slaveholders, and so the Bible was opposed to abolitionism. Although Raphall made a minor distinction between ancient and southern slavery—Hebrews could only be enslaved for theft or poverty—he triumphantly concluded that "slavery has existed since the earliest time," and thus "slaveholding is no sin" because "slave property is expressly placed under the protection of the Ten Commandments."[34]

Raphall's sermon contributed nothing novel to the slavery debate; since the colonial period proslavery apologists had used the Bible to sanction bondage, while the abolitionists continued to argue that slavery was a moral sin condemned in the scriptures. But Raphall was a prominent Orthodox rabbi, and so the sermon was used in the South to prove the Biblical sanction of slavery and the American Jews' sympathy with the secession movement.[35] Pro-Southern New York Democrats and the American Society for Promotion of National Unity had Raphall repeat his speech on January 17 and printed it in newspapers, pamphlets, and book form.[36] But even Raphall's mild distinction between ancient and modern slavery was too corrosive for the defenders of slavery. On the second occasion some people in the audience "required him to withdraw his remarks on the character of Southern slavery."[37]

Although Einhorn first attacked Raphall in his monthly magazine *Sinai*, the rebuttal probably reached a small audience because it was written in German.[38] Michael Heilprin's slashing criticism of Raphall attracted the most publicity because it was printed in the influential *New York Daily*

Tribune, where Horace Greeley described Heilprin as a "learned Jew" who had few living equals in "historical, philogical, and biblical knowledge."[39] The noted Jewish scholar used his linguistic and rhetorical skills to attack Raphall's interpretation of the Bible. First he argued that the proslavery rabbi had mistranslated the word "slave," which should have been rendered "servant" or "bondsman." Heilprin believed Raphall's Biblical quotations were inaccurate, for there was a "rigorously limited allowance" for the purchase of a freeman's life services.

Heilprin's second major point concerned the interpretation of Scriptures. In standard Reform fashion he argued there was much "contradictory, unjust, and even barbarous" material in the Bible that rabbis wisely rejected or ignored. It was nonsense to believe everything in the Bible retained a divine sanction. Heilprin challenged Raphall to "make your Bible, by some process of reasoning, to be pure, just, and humane," or else reject it as full of human frailty. It was shocking to Heilprin that any Jew would support slavery, for the "reproach of Egypt" was a stigma that had haunted Jews throughout history.[40]

Heilprin's argument was repeated by other abolitionists and even by rabbis indifferent to the antislavery cause. A telling poem entitled "Rabbi Raphall" asked, "He that unto thy fathers freedom gave— / Hath he not taught thee pity for the slave?"[41] Einhorn agreed with Heilprin and argued that since ancient slavery could not be eradicated immediately, regulations were introduced to limit its most serious abuses and even totally abolish it.[42] Protestant abolitionists supported Heilprin and Einhorn by translating and publishing the doctoral dissertation of Moses Mielziner, a German rabbi who had recently migrated to New York. Applying the contemporary methods of German Biblical criticism to the scriptural laws regarding slavery, Mielziner concluded that Hebrew slavery was definitely circumscribed and ceased with the destruction of the First Temple.[43] And even Isaac Mayer Wise, the pragmatic leader of American Reform who believed that Jewish abolitionists were schismatics threatening to disunify American Judaism, argued that the Scriptures did not sanction slavery.[44] Like most Orthodox and Reform rabbis of the period, though, Wise avoided controversial causes which might lead to increased antisemitism or weaken the congregational structure. Perhaps the most prudent and typical Jewish response to the Raphall-Heilprin debate was that of *The Jewish Messenger*, which refused to print Heilprin's remarks because they had "no desire to take part in a controversy of this nature."[45]

This debate transcended the slavery controversy; it was a major conflict between Orthodoxy and Reform Judaism. Raphall defended the traditional, literal interpretation of the Bible, while Heilprin wanted Biblical slavery passages analyzed historically in a critical, liberal spirit. Jewish abolitionism and Garrisonian theology, however, had already triumphed before the debate. The Republican Party, which condemned slavery in the territories but promised not to attack it in the southern states, endorsed the abolitionist Biblical interpretation in its 1860 campaign when it stated that the Mosaic code tried to soften slavery "among the rude tribes, among a people so ignorant, being just delivered from Egyptian bondage. . . . It is therefore, the opposite of the American system [which] is without a peer for its cruelty."[46] Although this statement might appear condescending or even antisemitic, it was substantially similar to the position of contemporary Reform rabbis who believed the Bible "reflected the primitive ideas of its own age" and thus had to be reinterpreted according to the "spirit of broad humanity of our age."[47]

The Jewish abolitionists not only denied the proslavery interpretation of the Bible, but they also rejected racialist thinking with its emphasis on contrasting stereotypes. The heightened consciousness about "white" racial characteristics, abetted by romanticism and national expansion, helped make it easier for many people on both sides of the sectional debate over slavery to accept a stereotype of Blacks that made them anti-Caucasians. During the 1830s, racialist arguments led to change in the character of the debate over Black personality and prospects. Until the 1840s, discussions about slavery occurred between environmentalist defenders of a single human species and proponents of inherent racial differences. In the two decades before the Civil War, the dialogue tended increasingly to start from the common assumption that the races differed fundamentally. Although many abolitionists argued that Blacks were different from Whites, they projected a flattering image of the slave; like Harriet Beecher Stowe's Uncle Tom, the slave seemed to be a childlike, innocent creature free of the lust for power and wealth.[48]

Other abolitionists believed that the adverse environmental effects of slavery and discrimination, rather than innate deficiencies, were responsible for the seeming inferiority of American Blacks. The Jewish abolitionists supported the environmentalist argument and rejected racialist thinking because they realized that even a flattering racialism could be transmuted into an overt doctrine of Black inferiority, distinguished from harsher forms of racism only by a certain flavor of humanitarian paternalism.

They perceived a strong similarity between European tyranny, discrimination against Jews, and slavery. Emphasizing that the question was not one of race, but of human rights, the Jewish abolitionists made frequent pleas for racial and political equality based on Jewish history and tried to counteract the growing popularity of racialist thinking among abolitionists and their opponents.

Bondi, for example, enlisted in the Union army because he believed that "as a Jehudi, I had a duty to perform, to defend the institutions which gave equal rights to all beliefs."[49] Busch described abolitionism as "part of that everlasting war between Ormuzd and Ariman, between light and darkness, between right and wrong."[50] And Ernestine L. Rose, the only female Jewish abolitionist, became a popular platform speaker partly because she dramatically linked women, Blacks, and Jews in the struggle against discrimination and oppression. At an 1852 women's rights convention, she delivered her standard argument:

> I am an example of the universality of our claims; for not American women only, but a daughter of poor crushed Poland, and the downtrodden and persecuted people called the Jews . . . I go for emancipation of all kinds—white and black, man and woman. Humanity's children are, in my estimation, all one and the same family.[51]

Perhaps the two most effective critics of racialist thinking were Rabbis David Einhorn and Bernhard Felsenthal. Einhorn, who was forced to flee both Hungary and Baltimore because of his liberal political beliefs, was one of the most prominent antebellum Jewish abolitionists. He believed there was a fundamental relationship between the rights of Jews and the rights of Blacks because there could be no freedom for minorities in an atmosphere of enslavement. Therefore he criticized the Know-Nothings and the proslavery forces because both groups were trying to exclude and degrade ethnic groups. Einhorn wanted democratic rights extended to Blacks not only because it was right but also to safeguard the status of other traditionally outcast groups like the Jews. Innate inferiority arguments were dangerous because they could be employed against any oppressed minorities as a reason for further oppression.[52]

Felsenthal, a midwestern abolitionist who had delivered many antislavery sermons and speeches before the Civil War,[53] explicitly made the same parallels between Jewish oppression and slavery. He had called slavery the "most shameful institution on earth."[54] Now he was angry about an 1862

Polish-born Ernestine Rose (1810–1892) was a leading advocate of two radical causes in the mid-nineteenth century: women's rights and the abolition of slavery. Rose toured the country as a public speaker, stirring controversy from the platform; her slogan was "agitate, agitate." In several instances, her anti-slavery speeches earned her vehement threats from hostile audiences in both the North and the South. Courtesy of The Jacob Rader Marcus Center of the American Jewish Archives.

bill declaring Blacks incompetent to act as witnesses in the District of Columbia. Felsenthal traced similar restrictions in the case of the Jews from Justinian to Russia and in the modern Germanic states. Again a minority group was being degraded, and their degradation then was used as an excuse to deny them equal rights: "What can justify such barbarism? Russia does not lie only between Kalisz and Kamchatka, but also on the shores on the Potomac and Lake Michigan."[55] The Jewish abolitionists made telling parallels between Poland, Russia, the Germanic states, and America; between women and Blacks, and Jews and Blacks. The Jewish antislavery crusade was extraordinarily sensitive to charges of innate inferiority and civic inequality. They believed that slavery was not only wrong but dangerous. Its defenders could use their arguments against other groups, and thus all minorities had a stake in showing that the Blacks' shortcomings had environmental, not racial causes.

Jewish abolitionism was a conditioned response to the existence of American slavery. But many strains of Western and Jewish thought converged in the mid-nineteenth century to produce the particular emotional and intellectual intensity of the Jewish antislavery movement. The Haskalah, emancipation, and the liberal ideas of the 1848 revolutions were all synthesized in an American environment. Reform Judaism absorbed elements from all these movements and added to them a moral, crusading fervor. Its adherents were particularly attracted to two prophetic ideas: the belief that Judaism had a special mission in the world, and the concept of social justice. As a result, European Jews who were emancipated, supported the Haskalah movement, and participated in European revolutionary activities continued their proselytizing in America on behalf of a race that resembled them in its social and political disabilities.

The Jewish abolitionists were involved in a wide variety of antislavery activities throughout the free states, Kansas, and Maryland. Bondi, Benjamin, and Weiner fought with John Brown in Kansas. Michael Greenbaum assisted fugitive slaves in Chicago.[56] Moritz Pinner and Wilhelm Rapp courageously edited abolitionist newspapers in Kansas City and Baltimore.[57] And abolitionist rabbis and their supporters publicly criticized slavery in St. Louis, New York City, Baltimore, Chicago, Philadelphia, Detroit, and Madison, Indiana. Although the Jewish abolitionists had a unique perspective on American slavery, they could not form separate organizations because of their small numbers. Instead, they worked with local and national abolitionists and reform organizations to destroy the peculiar institution.

These freedom fighters were an unusual group of individuals who came from urban cosmopolitan families and were active in European and American civic life; they also socialized with Gentiles and experimented in leading lives in the contemporary world while remaining Jews. An upwardly mobile immigrant group, the Jewish abolitionists used European liberalism and Reform Judaism to challenge established American institutions and ideas related to slavery because they were autocratic, discriminatory, and had antisemitic implications.

NOTES

1. Gilbert Osofsky, "Abolitionists, Irish Immigrants, and the Dilemmas of Romantic Nationalism," *American Historical Review*, 80 (1975), 889–912.

2. *The Thirteenth Annual Report of the American & Foreign Anti-Slavery Society, Presented at New York, May 11, 1853* (New York, 1953), pp. 114–115.

3. Robert G. Weisbord and Arthur Stein, *Bittersweet Encounter: The Afro-American and the American Jew* (Westport, Conn., 1970), pp. 19–26; Bertram W. Korn, "Jews and Negro Slavery in the Old South, 1789–1865," *Publications of the American Jewish Historical Society*, L (1961), 151–201; Hugh H. Smythe and Martin S. Price, "The American Jew and Negro Slavery," *Midwest Journal*, VII (1956), 315–319.

4. The only exceptions to this statement are Morris U. Schappes, ed., *A Documentary History of the Jews in the United States, 1654–1875* (New York, 3rd edition, 1971), which contains good primary material on the slavery controversy and the Jews, and the pioneering article by Max J. Kohler, "The Jews and the Anti Slavery Movement," *Publications of the American Jewish Historical Society*, V (1897), 137–155.

5. Bertram W. Korn, "Isaac Mayer Wise on the Civil War," *Hebrew Union College Annual*, XX (1947), 635–658; Bertram W. Korn, *American Jewry and the Civil War* (Philadelphia, 1951).

6. Louis Ruchames, "The Abolitionists and the Jews," *Publications of the American Jewish Historical Society*, XLII (1952), 131–156. Korn admitted in his preface to the 1961 paperback edition of *American Jewry* that Ruchames's article was a useful corrective to Wise's prejudices against the abolitionists, but Korn continued to insist that the abolitionists' humanitarian concerns were very limited. See Korn, *American Jewry and the Civil War* (Cleveland, 1961), xviii–xix.

7. Marcus Lee Hansen, *The Atlantic Migration, 1607–1860* (Cambridge, Mass., 1940), p. 280; Nathan Glazer, *American Judaism* (Chicago, 1957), p. 23; Guido Kisch, "The Jewish 'On to America Movement,'" *Publications of the American Jewish Historical Society*, XXVIII (1949), 185–234; Mack Walker, *Germany and*

the Emigration, 1816–1885 (Cambridge, Mass., 1964), pp. 42–133; Uriah Zwi Engelman, "Jewish Statistics in the U.S. Census of Religious Bodies (1850–1936)," *Jewish Social Studies*, IX (1947), 129–131; Max J. Kohler, "The German Jewish Migration to America," *Publications of the American Jewish Historical Society*, IX (1901), 87–105.

8. Nathan Glazer, "Social Characteristics of American Jews, 1654–1954," *American Jewish Year Book*, LVI (1955), 3–20; Rudolph Glanz, "The Immigration of German Jews up to 1880," *Yivo Annual of Jewish Social Science*, II–III (1947–1948), 81–99.

9. Salo W. Baron, "The Impact of the Revolution of 1848 on Jewish Emancipation," *Jewish Social Studies*, XI (1949), 195–248; Adolph Kober, "Jews in the Revolution of 1848 in Germany," *Jewish Social Studies*, X (1948), 135–164.

10. *The Sun*, September 17, 1870.

11. *The Asmonean*, August 24, 1855.

12. Bertram W. Korn, "Jewish 'Forty-Eighters' in America," *American Jewish Archives*, II (1949), 12–14.

13. August Bondi, *Autobiography of August Bondi* (Galesburg, Ill., 1910), p. 33.

14. Bondi, *Autobiography*, pp. 5–132; August Bondi, "With John Brown in Kansas," *Transactions of the Kansas State Historical Society*, VIII (1903–4), 275–289; Leon Hühner, "Some Jewish Associates of John Brown," *Publications of the American Jewish Historical Society*, XXIII (1915), 55–78.

15. Gustav Pollack, *Michael Heilprin and His Sons* (New York, 1912), pp. 3–12; *Jewish Exponent*, October 17, 1899.

16. Leon Ruzicka, "Isidor Busch," *Judisches Archiv*, I (1928), 16–21; James Wax, "Isidor Busch, American Patriot and Abolitionist," *Historia Judaica*, V (1943), 183–203.

17. *Proceedings of the Missouri State Convention Held in Jefferson City, June, 1863* (St. Louis, 1863), p. 135.

18. *Medical Life*, XXXV (1928), 214–258.

19. *American Medicine*, IX (1905), 243.

20. Leonard L. Richards, *"Gentlemen of Property and Standing": Anti-Abolition Mobs in Jacksonian America* (New York, 1970); Gerald Sorin, *The New York Abolitionists: A Case Study of Political Radicalism* (Westport, Conn., 1971); James Brewer Stewart, *Holy Warriors: The Abolitionists and American Slavery* (New York, 1976); David Donald, "Toward a Reconsideration of Abolitionists," in *Lincoln Reconsidered* (New York, 1956), pp. 19–36.

21. *The Jewish Tribune*, December 21, 1883; *The Menorah*, June, 1889, October, 1890, September, 1898.

22. Henry S. Morais, "Sabato Morais," *Proceedings of the Sixth Biennial Convention of the Jewish Theological Seminary Association* (New York, 1892), pp. 63–84. The quotation is from page 67.

23. Bondi, *Autobiography*, pp. 27, 24.

24. Although Morais was the only Orthodox rabbi to embrace abolitionism, his European history was similar to the other Jewish abolitionists. Samuel Morais was a liberal, scholarly individual who belonged to the Masonic order in Italy. Sabato became an ardent republican; Mazzini used Morais's passport when he was forced to travel throughout Europe in disguise. After his arrival in 1851, Morais became a bold, fearless advocate of abolitionism in Philadelphia. By the early 1870s, Morais, as chazan of Sephardic Mikveh Israel, had modified the religious services along Reform lines to achieve an "American Judaism more comfortable to our changed circumstances." Thus Morais's social background, political ideology, and religious beliefs were much closer to the Jewish abolitionists than to Orthodoxy. See Morais, "Sabato Morais," pp. 63–84; *The Jewish Messenger*, XXXVIII (November 12, 1875).

25. William O. McCragg, Jr., "Jews in Revolutions: The Hungarian Experience," *Journal of Social History*, 6 (1972), 78–105.

26. Jacob Katz, *Out of the Ghetto: The Social Background of Jewish Emancipation, 1770–1870* (Cambridge, Mass., 1973); "The Term 'Jewish Emancipation': Its Origin and Historical Impact," in *Studies in Jewish Intellectual History*, ed. Alexander Altman (Cambridge, Mass., 1964), pp. 1–25; *The Origins of the Modern Jew: Jewish Identity and European Culture in Germany, 1749–1824* (Detroit, 1967); Isaac Eisenstein-Barzilay, "The Ideology of the Berlin Haskalah," *Proceedings of the American Academy for Jewish Research*, XXV (1956), 1–37.

27. David Philipson, *The Reform Movement in Judaism* (New York, 1931); Martin B. Ryback, "The East-West Conflict in American Reform, 1854–1879," *American Jewish Archives*, II (1950), 3–14; Stephen Stein, "Reform Judaism: The Origins and Evolution of a 'Church Movement,'" *Journal for the Scientific Study of Religion*, V (1965), 117–129; Leon A. Jick, *The Americanization of the Synagogue, 1820–1870* (Hanover, N.H., 1976), pp. 79–97, 133–194.

28. David Einhorn, *Antirittspredight Gehalten in Tempel des Har Sinai Vereins* (Baltimore, 1855), p. 10.

29. *The Liberator*, March 30, 1855.

30. "Declaration of Principles Adopted by a Group of Reform Rabbis at Pittsburgh, 1885," *Yearbook of the Central Conference of American Rabbis*, XLV (1935), p. 200. Although the platform was drawn up after the Civil War, it is a rather moderate statement and thus would have been acceptable to the antebellum Jewish abolitionists.

31. "Declaration of Principles," *Yearbook of the Central Conference of American Rabbis*, p. 199.

32. For an excellent discussion of the "Jewish question" during the early struggle for emancipation, see Katz, *Out of the Ghetto*, pp. 8–103.

33. *The New York Herald*, January 5, 1861.

34. *The New York Herald*, January 5, 1861.

35. *Memphis Daily Appeal*, January 23, 1861; *Richmond Daily Dispatch*, January 7, 29, 1861.

36. *The New York Herald,* January 17, 19, 1861; *The Evening Post,* January 17, 1861.
37. *The New York Herald,* January 19, 1861.
38. *Sinai,* VI (February, March, April, 1861).
39. *New York Daily Tribune,* January 9, 1861.
40. *New York Daily Tribune,* January 15, 1861.
41. *The Independent,* February 21, 1861.
42. *Sinai,* VI (March, April, 1861); David Einhorn, *War with Amalek* (Philadelphia, 1864), pp. 4, 5.
43. E. M. F. Mielziner, *Moses Mielziner, 1823-1903* (New York, 1931), pp. 21-23, 64-103.
44. *The Israelite,* II (January 23, 1856), VI (January 18, 1861). Wise considered Whites superior to Blacks, but he never defended slavery. After the Civil War, he admitted that emancipation was desirable and progressive. See Jacob Rader Marcus, *The Americanization of Isaac Mayer Wise* (Cincinnati, 1931), pp. 10-18.
45. *The Jewish Messenger,* January 18, 1861.
46. William Henry Fry, *Republican "Campaign" Textbook* (New York, 1860), pp. 10-11.
47. "Declaration of Principles," *Yearbook of the Central Conference of American Rabbis,* pp. 199-200.
48. George M. Fredrickson, *The Black Image in the White Mind: The Debate on Afro-American Character and Destiny, 1817-1914* (New York, 1971), pp. 97-129; William R. Stanton, *The Leopard's Spots: Scientific Attitudes toward Race in America, 1815-1859* (Chicago, 1960); William R. Taylor, *Cavalier and Yankee: The Old South and American National Character* (New York, 1961), pp. 123-155, 279-294.
49. Bondi, *Autobiography,* p. 72.
50. *Journal of Missouri State Convention,* p. 326.
51. *The Proceedings of the Women's Rights Convention Held in Syracuse, September 8th, 9th and 10th, 1852* (Syracuse, N.Y., 1952), p. 63. For a similar argument, see her speech on the anniversary of West Indian emancipation in *The Liberator,* August 19, 1853.
52. *Sinai,* I (October, 1856), VII (June, July, August, 1861); Einhorn, *War with Amalek,* pp. 4, 5; David Einhorn to Samuel Adler, January 21, 1864, American Jewish Archives, Cincinnati, Ohio; Kaufman Kohler, ed., *David Einhorn Memorial Volume* (New York, 1911), pp. 403-455.
53. Emma Felsenthal, *Bernard Felsenthal, Teacher in Israel* (New York, 1924), p. 23; Bernard Falsenthal to Max J. Kohler, October 25, 1901, American Jewish Archives, Cincinnati, Ohio.
54. Bernard Felsenthal, "Die Juden und die Sclaveri," *Illinois Staatszeitung,* June 6, 1862.
55. Bernard Felsenthal, "Legislatoriche Barbarei, Nagerrecht und 'Juden-Recht,'" *Illinois Staatszeitung,* July 9, 1862.

56. Simon Wolf, *The American Jew as Patriot, Soldier and Citizen* (Philadelphia, 1895), pp. 425–426.

57. *St. Louis Republican,* February 13, 1860; George William Brown, *Baltimore and the 19th of April, 1861: A Study of the War* (Baltimore, 1887), p. 53; Dieter Cunz, *The Maryland Germans: A History* (Princeton, N.J., 1948), pp. 304–306.

4

The Abolitionists and the Jews
Some Further Thoughts

Louis Ruchames

About twenty-five years ago, in a paper presented at the annual meeting of the American Jewish Historical Society,[1] this writer delivered a rather vigorous critique of the views of Isaac Mayer Wise and Bertram Korn—especially of the latter's volume, *American Jewry and the Civil War*[2]—concerning the abolitionists and other antislavery leaders. The paper was essentially polemical in nature. It consisted, for the most part, of a defense of the antislavery movement against the accusations that had been made against it by Wise and Korn, who, in the words of this writer, pictured abolitionists "as power-hungry politicians, heedless of the welfare of minority groups other than Negroes, and guilty of prejudice and discriminatory acts toward foreigners and Jews."[3] It did not pretend to be a complete evaluation of all that had been written by antislavery men and women about foreigners and Jews. It sought rather to provide evidence warranting a different and more sympathetic interpretation of a misunderstood and much maligned group of American reformers. In essence, it argued,

> their efforts were concentrated upon helping the free Negro and the slave, for these were the most oppressed elements of the population of their day; but their devotion to equal rights extended also to the Jew, the foreigner and members of other minority groups. Although one sometimes finds in their letters and other writings expressions of racial stereotypes and preju-

Reprinted with permission of Ktav Publishing House from *A Bicentennial Festschrift for Jacob Rader Marcus*, ed. Bertram Korn (New York: Ktav, 1976), 505–516, copyright © 1976 by Ktav Publishing House, Inc.

dices, concerning both Negroes and Jews, these are infrequent and atypical, and do not affect their devotion to equal rights for Negroes and Jews.[4]

In the perspective of twenty-five years, a rereading of the essay evokes several thoughts. First, because of its limited theme and polemical nature, the essay presents a negative impression of Korn's volume, one that does not accord with this writer's view of the volume as a whole. For *American Jewry and the Civil War* is an important contribution to our understanding of the history of American Jewry during the Civil War, of the many political and social issues which it faced, and its relations to the broader American community. Whatever Korn's views of abolitionist attitudes toward the Jews, these constitute but a very small portion of the entire work, which is a distinguished contribution to the history of the period.

Second, although the essay mentioned abolitionist "racial stereotypes and prejudices," it emphasized that these were "infrequent and atypical" and did not weaken the abolitionist devotion to equal rights for Jews and Negroes. It may not be amiss, however, to discuss the nature of these stereotypes and prejudices, some of which are to be found in the writings of the most prominent abolitionist, William Lloyd Garrison. There are several references to Jews and Judaism in his letters and editorials, almost always of a religious and derogatory nature. Thus, on September 23, 1836, in a letter to Samuel May, a prominent abolitionist and Unitarian clergyman, who was then a minister in South Scituate, Massachusetts, Garrison writes as follows:

> O, the rottenness of Christendom! Judaism and Romanism are the leading features of Protestantism. I am forced to believe, that, as it respects the greater portion of professing Christians in this land, Christ has died in vain. In their traditions, their forms and ceremonies, their vain janglings, their self-righteousness, their will-worship, their sectarian zeal and devotion, their infallibility and exclusiveness, they are Pharisees and Sadducees, they are Papists and Jews.[5]

A year later, in another letter, he exclaims, "What an oath-taking, war-making, man-enslaving religion is that which is preached, professed, and practised in this country! . . . Its main pillars are Judaism and Popery."[6] Finally, in a reply to a newspaper editor in Boston, who had attacked him for Christian infidelity and for non-attendance at Sunday church services, Garrison writes: "It is one of your legal impostures to represent a building made of bricks and mortar as 'the house of God.' There is no such holy locality, or holy building on earth, and if you were not groping in Jewish darkness, you would perceive this truth."[7]

In these excerpts, Garrison expresses his abandonment of the Protestant Christian orthodoxy in which he was raised, and criticizes the emphasis upon ritual, ceremony, and attendance at formal church services as expressions of religion. But in his denunciation of Protestantism and orthodox Protestants of his day, he reveals his religious bias, absorbed in his youth, as a fundamentalist Protestant, taught to regard both Judaism and Catholicism as benighted religions representative of the most harmful religious attitudes and practices. The Judaism which Garrison has in mind is defined by certain New Testament writers, and although his mastery of the Old Testament, especially the prophetic portions, equaled his mastery of the New Testament, these are seen through the eyes of the New Testament writers. Thus, although time and again he attacks the priests and rabbis as representatives of Judaism, he nowhere appears to associate the Hebrew prophets, whom he quotes time and again, with Jews or Judaism. Garrison's view of Judaism, at least during the 1830s and 1840s, does not reveal any acquaintance with Jewish scholarship or Jewish sources concerning Jews and Judaism. Moreover, at no time does he draw a distinction between ancient Judaism and the Jews and Judaism of his own day; of these latter he seems to have no knowledge.

Any evaluation of Garrison's attitude toward Jews should include some reference to his relationships to two prominent Jews of the antebellum period: Ernestine Rose, the woman's rights advocate and abolitionist, and Mordecai Manuel Noah, Democratic leader, playwright, editor, opponent of the antislavery movement, and sometimes regarded as an apologist for slavery.

Garrison, apparently, first met Ernestine Rose in the early 1840s—she seems to have been the first Jew whom he knew personally—and although she was by no means always in agreement with his views on antislavery or woman's rights, he had a deep admiration for her abilities and idealism, referred to her in the most laudatory terms,[8] and often reprinted her speeches in the *Liberator*. Their friendship continued even after 1869, when Ernestine Rose and her husband left the United States to resettle in England. As late as 1877, about two years before Garrison's death, she sent a note of condolence to him on the death of his wife, Helen.[9]

Accounts of her speeches in the *Liberator* sometimes carried references to her Jewishness, and to the fact that her father was a rabbi. Although

Peter Still, redeemed from slavery by the Friedman brothers. Courtesy of The Jacob Rader Marcus Center of the American Jewish Archives.

she herself was an atheist and did not participate in any way in Jewish communal life or express publicly her views about the religion or culture of Judaism, she did sometimes write and speak about the oppression and discrimination which Jews have had to endure throughout history and in her own day and of the need for freedom and equality for her people.

But it is important to note that, although Garrison knew that Rose was Jewish and the daughter of a rabbi,[10] he rarely referred to her Jewishness and never intimated that her reformist activities and beliefs cast any credit upon the Jewish people or Judaism itself. In fact, when reprinting some of her speeches the *Liberator* identified her as "one born and educated in Poland,"[11] and as "a native of Poland,"[12] but made no mention of her Jewishness.

On the other hand, when referring to Noah and Noah's anti-abolitionist writings, Garrison did so in the most derogatory and antagonistic terms and rarely failed to mention Noah's Jewishness or the odium which, in his opinion, Noah's views and activities cast upon Judaism and the Jewish people. Thus, on May 20, 1842, Garrison reprinted in the *Liberator* a charge by Noah, who was then a judge in New York City, to the grand jury of the Court of Sessions of New York. The charge expressed sentiments hostile to the abolitionists. In commenting on it, Garrison refers to Noah as "a Jewish unbeliever, the enemy of Christ and Liberty." Several years later, in the *Liberator*,[13] Garrison reprinted a portion of an article by Noah from the *New York Sunday Messenger*, Noah's newspaper, and in his comments referred to Noah as "the miscreant Jew." In September of the same year, in the *Liberator*,[14] he refers to Noah as "that lineal descendant of the monsters who nailed Jesus to the cross between two thieves," and ends his comment with: "Shylock will have his 'pound of flesh' at whatever cost."

In his later years, i.e., during the 1860s and 1870s, Garrison's attitudes toward Jews and Judaism seem to have mellowed somewhat, and one notes signs of perhaps a greater recognition of the contribution of ancient Judaism to the spirit of antebellum reform. There is an interesting letter, written by Garrison when in England, dated Huntley Lodge, Edinburgh, July 15, 1867, to the Reverend S. Alfred Steinthal (1826–1910), a Unitarian minister of Bridgewater, England, active in the temperance movement and a longtime friend of Garrison. The letter expresses Garrison's regret over a misunderstanding that had occurred in Manchester, England, as a result of certain remarks that he had made in an address at a banquet in that city. The relevant extract is self-explanatory.

> Thanks for your letter of the 10th inst. The reading of it caused equal amusement, surprise, and regret—the regret having reference to the annoyance caused good Dr. Gottheil by the ludicrous perversion of the term I used, "Fourth of Ju-liars," (not Jew-liars) in my remarks at the Manchester [England] banquet, by such of his people as were not present. I am thus admonished that it is a hazardous thing to indulge in punning! As soon as I received your letter, I sent an explanatory note to Dr. G., showing that, so far from having cast any imputation upon Jewish veracity, I was "an

Israelite indeed, in whom there was no guile," in the matter referred to, and that they were those who professed to be Christians to whom my criticism was applied. I have given him liberty to publish my note in any way he may think best.[15]

The "Dr. Gottheil" referred to by Garrison was Gustav Gottheil (1827–1903), rabbi of the Manchester Congregation of British Jews from 1860 to 1873, and thereafter rabbi of Temple Emanu-El in New York for twenty-three years until his retirement as rabbi emeritus at the age of seventy-two. Garrison may have been especially solicitous of his feelings because of Gottheil's antislavery views, expressed in a volume entitled *Moses versus Slavery* and published in Manchester in 1861.

On his way to England in 1867, Garrison had an encounter aboard ship with three Jewish former slaveholders. He describes the incident in a letter to his wife dated May 15, 1867.[16] "Sitting opposite me at the table," he writes "are three German Jews, Louisiana planters, who have lost all their slaves by the rebellion, and who profess to regret their loss chiefly because their slaves, now that they are free, will be unable to take care of themselves! Of these Israelites it cannot be said that they are without guile; nevertheless, they are unobtrusive in manner and very respectful (as indeed all on board are) to Mr. Thompson and myself."

Most interesting of all, perhaps, is a letter by Garrison to the Reverend Samuel Hunt, a Protestant clergyman of Massachusetts, who assisted Henry Wilson, Republican senator from Massachusetts and vice-president of the United States during Grant's second term in office. Hunt had acted as private secretary to Wilson in 1873–75, assisted Wilson in writing the three-volume *History of the Rise and Fall of the Slave Power in America* (Boston, 1872–77; reprinted by Negro Universities Press, New York, 1969), and completed the work after Wilson's death in 1875. Hunt sent Garrison the page-proofs for chapter XLIX of volume III, entitled "Influence of Christian Churches and Associations." In his letter, dated Roxbury, December 26, 1876, Garrison offers the following criticism:

> On page 822 you say, "Antislavery was the child of Christian faith," but why any more so than of the Jewish faith? What can surpass the denunciations against oppressing the poor and needy that can be found in the Old Testament, "Deliver him that is spoiled out of the hand of the oppressor"—"undo the heavy burdens, break every yoke, and let the oppressed go free"—"your hands are full of blood; seek judgment, deliver the oppressed"—"he that

stealeth a man, and selleth him, or if he be found in his hand, he shall surely be put to death"—&c., &c. Quotations of this nature, and reiterated "in season and out of season," exerted a powerful influence in discussing the duty and necessity of abolishing slavery.[17]

The one abolitionist who equaled and probably even exceeded Garrison in his tendency to identify the negative characteristics of individual Jews with the entire Jewish people, and even with the principles of the Jewish faith, was Edmund Quincy, of Boston, who often edited the *Liberator* in Garrison's absence and was a prominent abolitionist leader. Quincy was a Boston blue-blood, his father having been a member of Congress, mayor of Boston, and president of Harvard University. A graduate of Harvard University in 1827, he joined the Massachusetts Anti-Slavery Society in 1837 and the American Anti-Slavery Society the following year. During the ensuing years, he was corresponding secretary of the Massachusetts society from 1844 to 1853 and vice-president of the national society in 1853 and 1856–59. He was also an editor of the Massachusetts *Abolitionist* in 1839, the *National Anti-Slavery Standard* in 1844 and subsequent years, and contributed numerous essays to these and other newspapers and journals.

As an example of Quincy's opinions of Jews and Judaism, one may cite an essay in the *Liberator*, August 10, 1848, signed "Q" for Quincy, entitled "A Jew and a Christian." Quincy cites certain of Mordecai M. Noah's opinions of the abolitionists, of blacks, and of slavery, and refers to Noah as "that Judge in Israel, Mordecai Manasseh Noah, the leader of the chosen seed into the land flowing with milk and honey on Grand Island, and the charger of grand juries to indict abolitionists for being mobbed." Quincy then gives his opinion of Noah: "It would be difficult even for American Christians to match this Jew for meanness and servility. We think none the worse of a man for being a Jew, but we must say, that if this Judge be a fair specimen of the race, it is no wonder they have been an insulted and despised people."

Quincy's opinions of Jews were expressed, too, in a novel that he wrote in 1854, *Wensley, a Story with a Moral* (reprinted in 1885 in *Wensley and Other Stories*). The only Jews in the novel are villains and obnoxious characters. They are Aaron Abrahams; his wife, portrayed as a loudmouthed shrew; and one son, whose name is also apparently Aaron. Quincy, it seems, did not know that in a traditional Jewish family, a son did not have the same first name as his father. The son, who is described as "a sort of

Jew lawyer," is the real villain. But the father is mentioned as having been a commissary to the American Army in 1777. He is described as follows by another character in the novel: "I guess I had reason to know him. I know he almost starved us; and would quite, had not a lot of our men threatened to burn his house down about his ears for him. They tried to do it, too. Ben Simpkins was hanged for it, poor fellow!" (p. 252). Referring to the Abrahams home during the Revolution, the same character remarks: "It was an awful wrecking-place, and old Abraham's house was full of cabin furniture and things. Folks said he had got rich by wrecking. He was rich, any way. But I don't believe such riches is any good to people" (p. 252).

Two other abolitionists deserve mention for their attitudes toward Jews: Samuel J. May and Nathaniel Peabody Rogers. The former, a native of Boston, was one of the pioneers of the antislavery movement, an early friend of Garrison, and a Unitarian minister highly respected and loved by all who knew him, friends and opponents alike. As a minister, he served churches in Brooklyn, Connecticut (1822–36), South Scituate, Massachusetts (1836–42), and Syracuse, New York (1845–67), where he spent the last years of his life. In a volume entitled *Memoir of Samuel J. May* (Boston, 1873), prepared by George B. Emerson, Samuel May, and Thomas J. Mumford, much of which consists of May's autobiography, there appears a sketch by May of his earliest relationships with Jews. The selection is worth quoting in its entirety.[18]

> If the children of my day were taught, among other things, to dread, if not despise, Jews, a very different lesson was impressed upon my young heart. There was but one family of the despised children of the house of Israel resident in Boston,—the family of Moses Michael Hays: a man much respected, not only on account of his large wealth, but for his many personal virtues and the high culture and great excellence of his wife, his son Judah, and his daughters,—especially Catherine and Slowey. His house, far down in Hanover Street, then one of the fashionable streets of the town, was the abode of hospitality; and his family moved in what were then the first circles of society. He and his truly good wife were hospitable, not to the rich alone, but also to the poor. Many indigent families were fed pretty regularly from his table. They would come especially after his frequent dinner-parties, and were sure to be made welcome, not to the crumbs only, but to ampler portions of the food that might be left.

Always, on Saturday, he expected a number of friends to dine with him. A full-length table was always spread, and loaded with the luxuries of the season; and he loved to see it surrounded by a few regular visitors and others especially invited. My father was a favorite guest. He was regarded by Mr. Hays and his whole family as a particular friend, their chosen counsellor in times of perplexity, and their comforter in the days of their affliction. My father seldom failed to dine at Mr. Hays's on Saturday, and often took me with him; for he was sure I should meet refined company there.

Both Uncle and Aunt Hays (for so I called them) were fond of children, particularly of me; and I was permitted to stay with them several days, and even weeks, together. And I can never forget, not merely their kind, but their conscientious care of me. I was the child of Christian parents, and they took especial pains that I should lose nothing of religious training so long as I was permitted to abide with them. Every night, I was required, on going to bed, to repeat my Christian hymns and prayers to them, or else to an excellent Christian servant woman who lived with them many years. I witnessed their religious exercises,—their fastings and their prayers,—and was made to feel that they worshipped the Unseen Almighty and All-merciful one. Of course I grew up without any prejudice against Jews,—or any other religionists, because they did not believe as my father and mother believed.

Nathaniel Peabody Rogers (1794–1846) was a well-known abolitionist in his day, a New Hampshire man, a lawyer, and, finally, editor of the *Herald of Freedom*, which he established in Concord, New Hampshire, in 1838. On April 25, 1845, in the *Herald of Freedom*, in an essay entitled "The Jews and Holy Land," he expressed his views of Mordecai Noah's efforts at Jewish restoration in Palestine. These views are especially interesting for what they reveal of the opposition of a radical Christian toward Zionism, an opposition repeated in almost the very same terms by many radicals, Jews and Christians, through the succeeding decades of the nineteenth and twentieth centuries. Rogers is opposed to nationalism as contrary to a universal humanity, he dislikes religious distinctions, he fails to understand the religious and nationalistic attachment of Jews to Palestine, and he regards any American Jewish effort to rebuild a Jewish Palestine as a weakening of the struggle for justice and equal rights in the United States. Because it appears to be the only extant evaluation of American Zionism by an abolitionist, the major portion of the essay is reproduced here.

Now, I desire most truly, that an end may be put to the religious persecution of the Jews. Christendom has persecuted them as barbarously as ever Jews did Christians. And it ought to stop. But then the rescue of the Jews, is of no more consequence than the rescue of any other people—of Turks, Greeks, Polanders, or American slaves. The intolerance and persecution inflicted on them, ought to cease, not because they are Jews,—nor because they are Old Testament people, but because they are men, women and children. It is not because they were a "chosen people," and had Abraham, Isaac and Jacob among them, and Moses and David. Nor because it was prophesied they would return. But, because they are sufferers under persecution, and it is base and bigoted and barbarous to inflict it upon them. Because persecution is grievous to be borne, and wrong to inflict.

As to the Jews flocking to Palestine, I would say of it, as I do of the slaves running to Canada,—and colored people "returning" to Africa. So long as Jews can't have quarter, any where out of Palestine, I should advise them to run there, and the slave to Canada, that is, if they could have quarter when they get there. But were I Major Noah, I would put in for a better destiny for my countrymen. I would go for their rights where they are. I will join him in an agitation for their liberation here, on the spot, as many of them as are in the country. It is their country, as much as it is anybody's. They need not run to "Holy Land." They have a right to this country. Not as Jews, against Americans, but as men. As all other people have a right here. And I would not go to Jerusalem, or Jordan. New England or New York is as good as Palestine, and a great deal better. And Connecticut River, or the Merrimack, or the Old Hudson, are either of them as good rivers as any Jordan that ever run into a dead or a live sea. And as "Holy," for that matter. The Jews had better stay where they are, every where, for all going to Jerusalem. If they can better their condition, by migrating, I would migrate. I would go East—West—South—any point of compass,—*to better my real condition*. But they better leave off being Jews and turn *mankind*. They will make as good folks as any body. And if these Americans won't tolerate them, or allow them human rights here, I tell Major Noah, the Herald of Freedom shall be at *their service*, for an agitation that shall shake Christendom—till its bigotry is shaken out of it! Not that the Herald can *alone* shake Christendom, unless Major Noah will help *us write for it*.

But, then, if Jews can't have a home, where they happen to be, the Major, and everybody else, ought to go in for a shaking of the Earth about it. And the Major would be better employed in carrying on such an agitation for Jewish Rights, than in summoning Israelites from the four quarters of the globe, to Palestine, Goat Island, or any other island in the Niagara River. . . .

And the idea of keeping up this Jewish distinction, is inhuman and unwise. It is time it was merged, and annihilated. In Humanity, as in "Christ Jesus," as Paul says, "there is neither Jew nor Greek." And there ought to be none. It is high time all these hostile distinctions were annihilated; these obstacles to the harmony and fellowship of mankind, done away. Down with all of them.

Much more may be said on the subject of abolitionist-Jewish relationships and attitudes, and much more research is needed. Although the abolitionists and other antislavery men and women were in the forefront of the effort to achieve a more just society, and opposed discrimination in all its forms, they were not without prejudices and some of the religious and racial stereotypes which prevailed in the society of their day. In part, these prejudices existed in the absence of any direct contact with Jews and a sparsity of Jewish inhabitants, especially in Boston. They were often the result of either literary influences, as was probably true of Edmund Quincy, or fundamentalist Protestant indoctrination, as with Garrison. Yet, while deserving condemnation, they must be seen within the context of the consistent devotion of the abolitionists to equal rights for all men in the United States and their opposition to discrimination in this country against any racial, religious, or national group.

NOTES

1. Subsequently printed as "The Abolitionists and the Jews," in *Publications of the American Jewish Historical Society,* XLII (December 1952), 131–55.
2. Philadelphia: Jewish Publication Society, 1951.
3. Ruchames, "The Abolitionists and the Jews," p. 131.
4. Ibid., p. 132.
5. Louis Ruchames, ed., *The Letters of William Lloyd Garrison,* vol. II, *A House Dividing against Itself, 1836–1840* (Cambridge, Mass., 1971), p. 178.
6. Letter dated August 14, 1837, to Oliver Johnson, ibid., p. 281.
7. Letter dated October 20, 1839, to the editor of the *Spectator,* ibid., p. 314.
8. In the *Liberator,* March 23, 1855, Garrison characterized her as "one of the most remarkable women, and one of the ablest and most eloquent public speakers in this country."

9. Yuri Suhl, *Ernestine Rose and the Battle for Human Rights* (New York, 1959), p. 271.

10. See the report in the *Liberator,* October 8, 1852, of the National Woman's Rights Convention at Syracuse, New York, which describes Ernestine Rose's speech, and notes that she was introduced as "a Polish lady" and as having had an early education "in the Jewish faith." It quotes her as saying that "even that downtrodden people, the Jews, were sensible of the wrongs inflicted upon woman."

On May 16, 1856, the *Liberator* reprinted from the *Excelsior* a short biographical sketch by "L. E. B.," which mentioned that "her father was a very pious and learned rabbi" and referred to her "strict observance of all the religious rites and ceremonies of the Jewish faith" in her youth.

11. June 1, 1855.
12. June 8, 1855.
13. May 18, 1849.
14. September 21, 1849.
15. The original is in the Boston Public Library.
16. The original is in the Boston Public Library.
17. The original of the letter is to be found in the Sophia Smith Collection, Smith College, Northampton, Mass. It may be noted that Hunt kept his original formulation. See vol. III, p. 718.
18. Pp. 15–16.

Part III

Rabbis and the March to War

The American Jewish community took no official position on slavery or secession. Since there was no chief rabbi of the United States, and Judaism in the country was not organized hierarchically, the great political questions of the Civil War era elicited a broad range of Jewish views, as many as there were rabbis and congregations. No individual rabbi spoke for the community at large.

Nevertheless, the voice of one prominent rabbi, Morris Raphall of New York, rang out louder than the rest. Speaking on the National Fast Day (January 4, 1861) called by President James Buchanan to promote national unity, Rabbi Raphall in a widely publicized address concluded that even if Southern slaveholders had acted wrongly, slaveholding as such was "no sin," for slave property was "expressly placed under the protection of the Ten Commandments." He promoted a literal reading of selected biblical texts that sanctioned slavery. Opponents of slavery, significant rabbis among them, vehemently disagreed. They read the Bible contextually, focusing on the spirit rather than on the letter of divine law. They considered slavery nothing short of blasphemous.

Reviewing more than sixty pronouncements delivered by rabbis on Civil War–related issues between 1861 and 1865, Bertram Korn concluded that "the rabbis participated in the various political currents which eddied through American life" but were far indeed from unanimity. Some sided with the South, some with the North; some promoted compromise for the sake of peace, others staked their claim on principle, even if that meant war.

Historian Isaac Fein, in an article first published for the Civil War centennial in 1961, demonstrates how divided rabbis were even in a single city—Baltimore, Maryland. That city was deeply riven during the war years, and its Jewish community echoed those divisions both at the leadership and at the lay levels. Some of the fractures among the city's four synagogues, Fein explains, were based on economics and politics. The "German elite," whose wealth depended on trade with the South, defended slavery, while the liberal "48ers," refugees from the Central European revolutions of 1848, recalled the political positions that they had championed in their youth and favored abolition.

Fein also points to a close identity, in Baltimore, between the religious positions of the city's rabbis and their political positions. The Orthodox Rabbi Bernard Illowy, a man leery of change, advocated the status quo in religion as well as in politics; he favored keeping religious rituals and slavery just as they were. By contrast, Rabbi David Einhorn, a Reform rabbi committed to upholding principles even at great cost, advocated far-reaching religious changes in Judaism and full-scale abolition of slavery; he was a radical in religion and politics alike. The two other active rabbis in Baltimore, Henry Hochheimer and Benjamin Szold, strove in both cases for the middle ground. Just as they sought to reconcile tradition and change in religion, so they sought to reconcile union and peace in politics. They advocated neither for slavery nor for war.

One of America's foremost rabbis, the Reform Jewish leader Isaac Mayer Wise of Cincinnati, sided with the Peace Democrats, the so-called Copperheads. His biographer, historian Sefton D. Temkin, explains why in the first article in this part. As in Baltimore, the local setting was important; Cincinnati borders the South and depended on Southern trade. Wise was also a "middle of the road man"—more like Szold than Einhorn—and he feared that abolitionists were "fanatics," opposed to immigrants and Jews alike. Most important of all, Wise felt that the status quo, the "live and let live" policy of Democrats like Stephen A. Douglas, had been good for Jews. He favored peace and sectional self-determination to uphold the union, even if that meant acquiescing to slavery.

Significantly, though, Wise was somewhat inconsistent in his views. For a brief time, in 1855, he identified as a Republican. After the war broke out, he proclaimed himself neutral and vowed to keep silent, explaining that "we have dear friends and near relations . . . in either section of the country." Then, in September 1863, he agreed to be nominated for the Ohio State Senate at the Democratic County Convention along with other Peace Democrats. At the stern behest of his congregation, he declined to run.

The ambivalence displayed by Wise and the range of views expressed by him and his fellow rabbis mirror the complexities of the Civil War era, the conflicting loyalties, sentiments, and ideals of Jews in all sections of the country. Orthodox and Reform religious leaders could be found on both sides of this struggle, and many, especially in border communities, searched for a middle ground where all sides might be reconciled. Rabbis were torn: some stood firm for cherished principles; others sought to compromise for the sake of union and peace.

5

Isaac Mayer Wise and the Civil War

Sefton D. Temkin

A Turbulence in Cincinnati

When, on April 12, 1861, the Confederate forces, by attacking Fort Sumter, kindled into flame the quivering feeling that had developed between North and South, Isaac Mayer Wise was forty-two years of age. He had arrived in New York from Bohemia fourteen years before, had settled in Albany shortly afterwards, and had removed to Cincinnati in April, 1854, there to serve as rabbi of Congregation B'nai Yeshurun and as headmaster of the Talmud Yelodim Institute attached to it. Within a month after arriving at Cincinnati, Wise had begun preparations for the publication of a Jewish weekly; the first issue of *The Israelite* appeared on July 15th. At that time a large proportion of the Jewish population of the United States was German-speaking, and twelve months after *The Israelite* made its bow Wise started a second Jewish weekly, *Deborah*, in German. The position which he had begun to carve for himself in the Jewish communities—admittedly new and unstable—of the West is indicated by the fact that in 1855 Wise had joined in the call for a conference of Jewish congregations. This conference had met in Cleveland, and Wise had been chosen as its president. This early effort at union proved abortive, except for the revision of the prayer book which, left in Wise's hands, was accomplished through the publication of *Minhag America* ("American rite") in 1857.

Wise was an energetic traveler, and in the course of his journeys he became acquainted with some of the country's leading politicians and publicists. His grandson and biographer declared that he probably had no

---

Reprinted, in somewhat abridged form, with permission from *American Jewish Archives* 15 (1963): 120–142, copyright © 1962 by the American Jewish Archives.

warmer friend than Salmon P. Chase, United States Senator from Ohio and later Secretary of War and Chief Justice of the United States.[1] He had taken part in a delegation to President James Buchanan on the Swiss Treaty question. Wise had shown that his horizons were not limited to the boundaries of his "parish," and he had made himself a figure of more than local significance.

Nevertheless, like the rest of mankind, Wise doubtless felt first of all the influences that were closest at hand. Fortunately, his immediate milieu was in itself conducive to his taking an extra-parochial view of his responsibilities and opportunities. Ohio was then the fourth state in the Union in point of population. At mid-century the state was predominantly rural, but Cincinnati, then far and away its largest city, was the leading industrial center of the West. Its importance as a manufacturing center was associated with its position as the great entrepôt of the Ohio Valley, and this reinforced with commerce the links with which nature had tied it to the South.

The 1860 census gave the population of Cincinnati as 161,044. The 1840 figure had been only 46,338, and thus the population had multiplied more than three times in twenty years. An increase of this order suggests heavy migration into the city; in fact, most of the immigrants were German.

Another feature of the population at this time was its youth. The 1850 census showed that persons under ten years of age constituted over 30 percent of the population, and those under forty almost 84 percent.

A sudden increase in population suggests overcrowding, and a heavy influx of immigrants suggests a population without roots. These factors, together with the youthfulness of the people, lead one to infer that life in Cincinnati was, to put it cautiously, as vigorous as the climate allowed; turbulent and excitable would probably be expressions equally apt.[2]

Cincinnati was also noteworthy for the comparative size of its Jewish population. It is estimated that in 1860 there were altogether some 150,000 Jews in the United States, of whom 40,000 lived in New York.[3] In numbers, the 10,000 Jews of Cincinnati lagged behind, but they still constituted one of the foremost Jewish communities in the country.[4] Moreover, its geographical position at the gateway to the still important South—before the South had been destroyed in war and before the East-West railroads passing through Chicago had removed the economic fulcrum—was important. The dates of the founding of the Cincinnati synagogues confirm that the Jewish community, like the general population, was of recent growth.[5]

Rabbi Isaac Mayer Wise (1819–1900) as he looked around the Civil War era. Courtesy of The Jacob Rader Marcus Center of the American Jewish Archives.

A Plague on Both Your Houses

Wise arrived in Cincinnati at a time of political flux, as the bitter controversies which preceded the Civil War mounted in force. Six years before, the Whigs had split on the slavery issue. Chase had led a Free Soil movement, and out of this grouping the state's Republican Party was born in July, 1855. Chase suggested that Wise attach himself to the newly-born Republican Party. Wise himself declared that he had "sat at the round table at which that party was born and baptized," but that "some wounded apostles of the atheistical stripe" drove him out.[6] Wise's subsequent actions, in any event, suggest no sympathy with its aims. Perhaps the strong anti-immigrant "Know Nothing" element which pervaded the Ohio party (Chase was an exception) repelled him. In the 1855 state election feeling in Cincinnati was hostile to the Republicans. Chase's attitude towards slavery won no support from the business community, concerned for its trade connections with the South, while his associations with "Know Nothings" earned the suspicions of the German element, even though it tended to be Abolitionist.[7] There is no direct evidence of the effect of these influences on Wise, but his position as an immigrant and as a rabbi in a community closely engaged in commerce makes it legitimate at least to speculate whether they may have been present.

The issues must have forced themselves on Wise's attention. Cincinnati stood on the border between free and slave states; its environs were the first stage on the "Underground Railroad" by which slaves were taken to Canada for liberation; it was near the scene of attempts, sometimes the cause of riots, to arrest and return slaves under the Fugitive Slave law.

Something of a panic followed the Presidential election of November, 1860. Wise took a "plague on both your houses—why all this fuss?" attitude. He insisted on regarding the situation as an "artificial panic which . . . is no more than the product of the present state of politics and the cunning contrivance of bankers, stock jobbers, brokers etc." And he forecast peace: "The republicans have turned lambkins, tender and innocent, immaculate and bashful. . . . They are as tame and obliging now as the peasant the first time in the city. . . . The same thing . . . is the case in the extreme south with fire eaters, seceders and political circus riders."[8]

The belief that the fires would cool was widespread, and Wise was by no means alone when he remarked that "the two extreme factions will be cooled down before the year ends."[9] However, there is some interest in the decided view of human nature on which Wise based his conclusion: "people care very little for abstract ideas, extreme views or false conceptions of honor when their material interests are neglected or even ruined."[10] And this worldly cynicism he backed with the affirmation that, threats of secession notwithstanding, he was still prepared to take payment for *The Israelite* in bills payable in any state of the Union.[11]

The crisis did not abate as Wise and others prophesied. South Carolina's secession occasioned a lengthy editorial in *The Israelite* of December 28, 1860: "The fanatics in both sections of the country succeeded in destroying the most admirable fabric of government. Under the pretext of progress and liberty, state rights and personal freedom they have made the beginning of destroying the proud structure of liberty to which all good men looked with hope and satisfaction."[12] Here, as before, the "a plague on both your houses" note is sounded, but as the article proceeds the balance shifts somewhat against the Abolitionists:

> Demagogues who sought offices at any price, red Republicans and habitual revolutionists, who feed on excitement and civil wars, German atheism and American puritanism who know no limits to their fanaticism, visionary philanthropists and wicked preachers who have that religion which is most suitable to their congregations, speculators in property, stock jobbers and usurers whose God is Mammon, thoughtless multitudes and hired criers in the South and North succeeded in breaking down the fortress of liberty, the great bulwark of our best hopes.

Wise continues in the pessimistic note: "either the republican party must be killed off forever by constitutional guarantees to the South, to make an end forever to this vexing slavery question, or the Union must be dissolved." For the desired course, the necessary majority of three quarters of the states cannot be obtained, "because we have too many demagogues and fantasts, therefore we maintain this Union is as good as dissolved."[13]

The dissolution of the Union is a theme to which Wise reverts when, in the following week's issue of *The Israelite*, he indulges in prophecy for the New Year:

> The year 1861 must witness either the end of the Republican party or the dissolution of the Union. The Republicans know this very well and talk quite freely of the final and perpetual separation of the North and South. All their manoeuvres are intended to that point. They want neither war nor coercion nor compromises. Separation is their final object. They maintain their object of Abolitionism can best be achieved by the separation of the South from the North.[14]

No Political Preaching

In December, 1860, President Buchanan had called upon all denominations to observe January 4, 1861, "as a day of fasting and prayer, that God might have mercy upon us and save this Union." In *The Israelite* of December 28th, Wise published a sarcastic reference to Buchanan's action, describing Buchanan as one of the principal agents of the calamity and as being possessed of "hatred and feelings of vengeance."[15] On the same page there was an announcement of a special service for the following Friday morning—the day appointed by the President—in the Lodge Street Synagogue, at which the "Rev. Doctors Wise and Lilienthal" would preach. However, some incident must have arisen which prevented Wise from using the pulpit of his own synagogue, for in an article headed "No Political Preaching," which he published in *The Israelite* of February 1st, Wise declared that it had been his fixed principle not to say a word in the pulpit on the politics of the day "and for that very reason refused to preach the fourth of January last, in order not to violate our principle."[16] No hint is given as to the issue which arose, but is it too much to assume that it may have been serious if it prevented the rabbi from addressing his own congregation? Perhaps, knowing the opinions to which he had given vent in *The Israelite*, the congregation expected some positive statement from the pulpit against secession and in favor of the Union; in view of the inflamed state of feeling, the absence of such a statement might have occasioned some disturbance. Nothing definite can be asserted.

In the course of a lengthy article, Wise, in giving his reasons for refusing to "preach politics," makes some scathing comments on the nature of politics:

> Politics in this country means money, material interests, and no more. The leaders of all parties are office-seekers or office-holders. They hold or seek offices, not in order to benefit the community, but to benefit themselves....
>
> Land speculators, who bought large tracts of land in Kansas, exercised every sort of influence to make her a free state, in order to increase the price of land. Other speculators ... exercised all their influence in order to make a slave state of Kansas, in order to direct the current of migration to such states or territories where they possessed land, so as to dispose of it at improved rates. Slaveholders favor the extension of slavery because it increases their wealth, and land speculators oppose it, because they find their present account by it. Politics and money are synonyms, however

holy, exalted or lofty these things may appear to the myriads of honest men who are dragged along by party leaders....

Politics is a business, and in many instances a mean business, which requires more cheat and falsehood than a vulgar scoundrel would practice. Philosophize over it as you please, ... it remains a vulgar business ... with which we are fairly disgusted on account of its dishonesty and violence.

In the context in which they were written—the issues before the American people just before the Civil War broke out, and the particular incident of the day of national prayer—these words convey an attitude towards those issues. The questions of freedom or servitude for the Negro, of Free Soil or the extension of slavery to the territories, of the right of secession or the indissolubility of the Union, seem to have been placed by Wise on the same level as controversies over the spoils of office or the granting of land to a railroad. A mountain peak looks more imposing when the traveler beholds it from a distance than when he is trudging up its lower slopes. Wise's vision during the weeks before the attack on Fort Sumter does not seem to have been directed to the loftier questions.

The Middle of the Road

The fact that Wise treated opposition to the extension of slavery as a pretext indicates that he did not regard slavery as an issue;[17] and his repeated verbal assaults on "fanatics" suggests that he looked upon the Abolitionists as disturbers of the peace. Some controversy has arisen as to whether Wise actually favored slavery. The issue was faced squarely by other Jewish teachers. David Einhorn and Sabato Morais expressed themselves against slavery; Morris J. Raphall, supported by Isaac Leeser, took the view that it was an institution sanctioned by Judaism. Writing many years afterwards, Max J. Kohler, whose relationship to one of Wise's antagonists should not be ignored, said that Wise, in *The Israelite*, expressed approbation of Raphall's stand.[18] This is not true. Alluding to press comments on Raphall's proslavery sermon, Wise wrote that "among all nonsense imposed on the Bible the greatest is to suppose the Negroes are the descendants of Ham, and the curse of Noah is applicable to them."[19] But, though he contested the view that Negro slavery was supported by scriptural texts, he did not attack slavery.[20] Indeed, the above quotations suggest that, in Wise's opinion, it was proper to perpetuate slavery in order to prevent secession.

A clue to Wise's positive attitude may be found in his fervent memorial tribute to Stephen A. Douglas, who died shortly after the conflict began.[21] Douglas, to be sure, had supported war as a means of preventing secession, and that was further than Wise was prepared to go;[22] but it was Douglas who had proposed that the question of slavery be left to the people of the territories to decide as they organized themselves into states.[23] All this corresponded to the kind of sentiment that was fairly strong in Ohio. Its mainspring may have been prudential considerations natural enough in a border state, but there are grounds for believing that Wise's feeling as a Jew played a part. Wise "was essentially a middle of the road man, not only in religion, but also in politics. The only exception was where politics touched Jewish emancipation and liberty. Then he was an implacable extremist and demanded immediate change."[24] Rightly or wrongly, Wise appears to have suspected some of the Abolitionists of a disposition to tamper with the guarantees of liberty and equality which he regarded as the crowning glory of the American state and Federal constitutions. Massachusetts was a center of Abolitionism; Massachusetts was also antialien—specifically anti-Irish, but what immigrant was to know where the canker would spread? Therefore, Abolitionists were hypocrites. Such a picture may be oversimplified to the point of caricature, but the lines are clear in Wise's view of the Abolitionists. He regarded them as ethically inconsistent for having adopted, in Massachusetts, in 1859, a law requiring of aliens seven years' residence and naturalization as qualifications for holding public office.[25]

Society in Ohio at that time may have reinforced an intense equalitarianism, which became charged with resentment at the least suggestion of any superiority of the Old American as compared with the New. The fact, however, that Abolitionism was espoused by the Christian clergy in the North did not endear the cause to Wise, because he suspected the political parsons of trying to inject Christianity into the Constitution.[26] Wise had known a system under which an authoritarian government interfered with every department of life and gave to the Jew a status inferior to that of the Christian. He was intoxicated with the liberty and equality afforded by the open frontier, the open society, and the political system of the United States. There, of all places, he seems to have felt, men should live and let live. He saw, in the Abolitionists, not men who wished to grant liberty to the slaves, but men who interfered with the liberty of the states. He lumped them together with those who would restrict the liquor traffic, enforce the observance of Sunday, and somehow make Christianity a legally established religion.[27]

So ardent a lover of the American system obviously deplored secession—"this is the most terrible blow the cause of humanity is likely to suffer in the year 1861," he wrote while the crisis was yet building up. Coercion, however, was not his line:

> Keep the Union together by the force of arms, some say; Lincoln will do it, Buchanan is a traitor, we do not want the affections of the people as long as we have the power. That is as practicable and just as the other planks of the Republican programme are.—By what means will you coerce eight or ten states to obey your mandates? How can you command so vast an area of land, how can you conquer it? . . . Force will not hold together this Union; it was cemented by liberty and can stand only by the affections of the people. Every state may appeal to that right by which this Union was cemented, the right of man, and withdraw from this Union when her rights are infringed upon. No free state has a right to force another free state to adopt repugnant measures. Force and liberty are antagonistic. Either must fall to the ground.[28]

So, though he deplored secession, Wise held that the right to secede was there. The foregoing was written in December, 1860. By March, 1861, an anti-Semitic aside in an attack on Judah P. Benjamin by Senator Henry Wilson of Massachusetts provoked Wise to look upon the act of secession in a more favorable light:

> With every passing day we get more and more convinced that the secessionists are right, they would not bow down to a set of fanatics who are blind in their zeal to do wrong, who care much less for the white man than for the Negro, and prove themselves faithful to one thing only, i.e., to fanaticism.[29]

Silence, Our Policy

On April 14, 1861, Fort Sumter surrendered to the Confederate forces. The fire of that bombardment fused into a single mass the diverse elements that had existed on each side. Lincoln's call for volunteers met with an overwhelming response. *The Jewish Messenger*, of New York, reported from Cincinnati that "the Jewish young men of this city have entered into the war excitement with considerable enthusiasm; over fifty of our first

Jewish young men have enlisted into actual service, and many more are about following."³⁰

A little before, Wise had expressed himself in a manner indicating something falling far short of enthusiasm. Under the heading "Silence, Our Policy," he had written:

> We are the servant of peace, not of war. Hitherto we thought fit to say something on public affairs, and it was our ardent hope to assist those who wished to prevent civil war, but we wasted our words. What can we say now? Shall we lament and weep like Jeremiah over a state of things too sad and too threatening to be looked upon with indifference? We would only be laughed at . . . or probably abused for discouraging the sentiment. Or should we choose sides with one of the parties? We cannot, not only because we abhor the idea of war, but also we have dear friends and near relations, beloved brethren and kinsmen in either section of the country, that our heart bleeds on thinking of their distress. . . .
>
> Therefore silence must henceforth be our policy, silence on all the questions of the day, until a spirit of conciliation shall move the hearts of millions to a better understanding of the blessings of peace, freedom and union.³¹

There is no need to question the genuineness of Wise's abhorrence of the war; but Abraham Lincoln, who felt the anguish of the situation no less keenly, steeled himself to the consequences of his belief that the Union was indissoluble, and sober citizens without number must have acted in the same spirit. Wise's comment is that of a man who was opposed to the war, but whose position did not allow him to speak his mind.

The outbreak of war must have embarrassed Wise personally, because many of the subscribers to *The Israelite* lived in the South and became cut off, and many of those in the North canceled their subscriptions. There is something quaint, however, in his lament, published in June, that the Postmaster General had stopped mails to the seceding states, and in his suggestion that this action was unconstitutional.³² Evidently the implications of total war still had to be grasped.

The absence of any support for the Union cause from Wise did not pass unnoticed in Cincinnati. In *The Israelite* of May 31, 1861, he refers to a sermon by the Rev. Moncure D. Conway "accusing *The Israelite* and another religious organ of this city, of unfair motives on account of the silence preserved on the present state of the country"—to which Wise replied that he never preached on politics: "Spread eagle and star and stripeism may sound agreeably at political gatherings; in the pulpit, however, it appears to me a violation of the contract between minister and congregation, and a misapplication of the Sabbath and the pulpit; there are plenty of opportunities for almost anybody to make patriotic speeches outside the pulpit."[33]

The weeks rolled on with only the faintest suggestion of a war penetrating the columns of *The Israelite*. The topic was avoided in the reflections which Wise wrote for the New Year 5622,[34] and twelve months later the same policy was observed.[35]

Although Wise placed the main issues of the war outside his purview, his thunder pealed forth when the rights or the honor of Jews were touched. His pen was as forthright as it could be when anti-Semitic accusations were made, when Congress denied Jews the right to have army chaplains, and when General Ulysses S. Grant ordered Jews to be expelled from his Department.[36] More surprising, however, was his sudden incursion into politics at a time of acute controversy and when the Union cause was greatly harassed by war-weariness and internal dissension.

Delenda Est Carthago

Writing of the American people some years after the Civil War, James Bryce observed that "they have what chemists call low specific heat; they grow warm suddenly and cold as suddenly; they are liable to swift and vehement outbursts of feeling which rush like wildfire across the country, gaining glow like the wheel of a railway car, by the accelerated motion."[37] When the guns roared at Fort Sumter a war fever spread through the North, a fever in which all parts of Ohio shared; when the war proved to be something less agreeable than a picnic, when the Union cause suffered in battle and recruits for the army had to be drafted, defeatism became open. In Ohio's state elections in 1861, the Union Party, a coalition of Republicans and War Democrats, carried the day, but the Regular Democratic organization, which, while not clearly opposed to the war, favored peace through a Constitutional convention, remained intact. This sentiment was fed by weariness with the fighting, dismay at maladministration, and resentment at the unaccustomed powers exercised by the Federal government. The outstanding leader of the Peace Democrats was Clement L. Vallandigham, who sat in the Congress as representative for the Dayton District of Ohio. His attacks on the Lincoln Administration were merciless, and it appeared as if he desired the defeat of the Union forces in order to achieve peace. In the 1862 Congressional election, the Democrats won fourteen districts out of nineteen.

Sympathy with Vallandigham's movement expressed itself early in 1863 in the less constitutional forms of desertion from the army and armed resistance to conscription. Vallandigham, who continued to demand conciliation and to attack what he described as the unconstitutional measures of the Lincoln Administration, was arrested by military order in May and sentenced to confinement by a military court. By Lincoln's intervention, he was sent behind the Confederate lines. From the South he made his way through the blockade to Canada and, establishing himself at Niagara Falls, continued his propaganda from there. The arrest of Vallandigham strengthened the hold of the Peace Democrats on the party organization, and almost unanimously he was nominated as candidate for the governorship.[38]

The election was bitterly fought, and it was under these conditions that Wise, who previously had been adamant in his refusal to talk politics, suddenly descended into the arena. Cincinnati's *Daily Enquirer*, of September 6, 1863, reported the Democratic County Convention held at Carthage on the previous day. It was a Saturday, and Wise had not been present, but he received 280 votes, out of a possible 312, in the ballot for nomination of a state senator. The newspaper, which was the leading supporter of the Vallandigham cause, commented: "Dr. Wise is a gentleman of learning and accomplishments—is well known as an estimable Hebrew rabbi of this city. He would make an excellent Senator."

The news must have agitated some part of Wise's congregation, because two days after this report—that is, on September 8th—there was a special meeting of the Board of Trustees "to take in consideration the nomination of Dr. I. M. Wise as State Senator." "After some discussion," the minutes of the meeting tell us, "a Committee of 3 . . . were on motion appointed to draft suitable resolutions, expressing the sentiments of the Board in relation to this matter, who reported the following communication to Dr. Wise, which was unanimously adopted and the Secy. ordered to forward the same, after which the meeting adjourned."

The letter appended to the minutes bears the date September 3, 1863— the day prior to the meeting—and under that date it was subsequently published.[39] It is couched in respectful terms:

Rev. Sir—By unanimous desire of the Board of Trustees of K. K. [Holy Congregation] Bene Jeshurun, I am instructed to communicate to you that the subject of your nomination as State Senator by a Convention held at Carthage, on the 5th inst., has been fully deliberated upon.

The Board feels greatly honoured by this demonstration of confidence bestowed upon you; they are also well aware of your sincere attachment to our common country; nevertheless, as it is an established law with us that our minister should be present in the synagogue whenever divine service is held, and also, your services otherwise being indispensably necessary in our congregation, as well as in the scholastic department, you are hereby politely, but most emphatically requested to decline the said nomination at once.

With due regard, I have the honor to be, Rev. Sir, your obedient servant,

Fred[erick]. Eichberg,

Sec'y of the K. K. Bene Jeshurun.

The polite tone of this letter does not conceal the "emphatically" and "at once" in its operative words.

Under the same date, the Board of Directors of the Talmud Yelodim Institute wrote to Wise, forwarding a resolution passed that day. This wears no velvet glove:

> The Rev. Dr. Wise is engaged as school superintendent, with a fixed salary attached, and the duties of the superintendent are such as to require his attendance almost daily at the school.
>
> Resolved, that we remonstrate to the acceptance, by the Rev. Dr. Wise, of the above named nomination.
>
> Resolved, that we desire the Rev. Dr. Wise to decline the nomination, and for particular reason, that the duties and obligations due to our Institute are paramount to any other engagements.

Peace Democrats and Shoddy Contractors

The trustees of the congregation held their quarterly meeting less than two weeks later, on September 19th, and a general meeting took place on September 20th. The minutes of neither meeting make reference to this incident. In the meantime, however, Wise had replied to the communications addressed to him, and the matter had spilled over into the daily press. In the course of his reply Wise stated:

> I beg leave to state that the duties I owe to the congregation and the school are prior to those of any other office to which I might be elected hereafter; therefore, as long as I am not dispensed of the first, I cannot enter upon any other. As you maintain you can not dispense with my humble services for the time I might be obliged to spend at the Capital of the State, and the law of the congregation especially ordains it so, I certainly feel obliged to decline a nomination so honourably tendered, notwithstanding my private opinion, that I might render some services to my country, not altogether unessential, especially as those who nominated me know well my sincere attachment to this country and government. God will save the Union and the Constitution; liberty and justice for all, without my active co-operation, being, after all, without any political aspirations—only an humble individual.

The tone is distinctly more chastened than that of the fighting editor of *The Israelite*. And perhaps the denial of political ambitions at the end only calls attention to that which it professes to disavow.

Some hint of these proceedings appears to have been dropped in the ear of the press. On September 8th, Cincinnati's strongly Unionist *Daily Commercial* remarked: "It is uncertain, we understand, whether Dr. Wise will accept the nomination." This hint may have encouraged further disclosures, for on September 10th, the *Daily Times*, an evening paper, published the correspondence, and on the following morning the pro-Vallandigham *Daily Enquirer* came out with this announcement:

> The Rev. Dr. Wise has been forced, by outside pressure, to decline the Democratic nomination for State Senator. Had his name been on the other ticket, the Shoddy Contractors, who have been so busy in pulling the wires to produce this result, would have been contented to let it remain. The names of these Shoddy Contractors do not appear on the record, but they are known nevertheless.[40]

That evening—September 11th—the *Daily Times* printed the *Daily Enquirer*'s comments and added its own in a somewhat naive vein:

> Relative to the above we have to say that when the letters announcing the declination of Dr. Wise were handed us yesterday, we asked if party feeling had anything to do with the matter. The committee assured us in the negative, but that they did not desire to release Dr. Wise even temporarily from his labors as a minister, but further, that it was against the tenets of their

denomination to recognize the right of their minister to take an active part in political life.

On the morning of September 11th, the Unionist *Daily Commercial* also had printed the correspondence without comment, but, having read the *Enquirer*'s acidly partisan observations, it returned to the subject on the following morning. Having quoted from the *Enquirer*, it proceeded: "The friends of Dr. Wise, who urged him to decline the nomination, will not be slow to appreciate this. The repetition of the phrase 'Shoddy Contractors' is intended to cast an imputation on all Israelites who do not sustain Vallandigham."

It is reasonable to assume that it must have been humiliating to Wise, not merely to be forced to retrace his steps, but to have the fact bandied about in the daily press. In *The Israelite* of September 18th, he printed the correspondence and stated that "these papers were not intended for publication, but having been done so in the *Times*, Sept. 10, we think proper to republish them." By way of comment, he reminded his readers that on November 5, 1854, the Bene Israel Congregation, of Cincinnati, had elected him its rabbi, preacher, and school superintendent, but that B'nai Yeshurun would not allow him to accept the office. Did he think that, therefore, he was entitled to make his own terms?

Apart from the explanation printed in *The Times* of September 11th, no evidence has come to light which amplifies the written exchanges between Wise and his officers. Obviously they were not going to admit to the press that they were actuated by party feeling. Jews who were prominent in the clothing trade might be said to have acquired a pecuniary interest in the stability of the Republican Administration by virtue of the war contracts which they were enjoying.[41] On the other hand, Cincinnati as a whole was not a pro-Vallandigham center; and the congregation's case against having its rabbi involved in a bitterly contested election,[42] and as a supporter of a man who had been exiled as a traitor, was, to say the least, plausible.

An Unsettled Era

What might look like inconsistency between Wise's attraction to the Republican Party in 1856 and his adherence to the Peace Democrats in 1863 is not important. Seven years lay between the two episodes; it was an unsettled era, and each party in its day may have seemed to represent the cause of freedom.

Moreover, if the character of Wise's writings is at all revealing, no single episode should be taken by itself as indicating the direction in which he was moving. He was impetuous, usually down to earth, often passionate; his style was crude; his opinion did not receive expression in considered, logical form. He was like an angry fly, buzzing, on a short-range view, first in this direction, and then in that; no single tack necessarily indicates the desired goal, but only out of a series can the direction be plotted.

Before this can be attempted, the investigation must be carried further. The source of Wise's opinions—and the influences which came to bear upon him—may emerge from a further reading of the publications, English and German, circulating in Cincinnati during the period under review. Thus far, one senses that his attitudes were molded by the feelings of an immigrant from Metternich's Austria, settled in a state which allowed no slavery and was, therefore, not involved in direct responsibility for the institution, but which was sufficiently connected with the South to make it difficult to take a high moral attitude. The United States, as seen from that position, gave peace and freedom, and the status quo was reasonably perfect. To interfere was unnecessary.

NOTES

1. Max B. May, *Isaac Mayer Wise* (New York: G. P. Putnam's Sons, 1916), p. 207.

2. Eugene H. Roseboom and Francis P. Weisenburger, *A History of Ohio* (Columbus, Ohio: Ohio State Archaeological and Historical Society, 1953), pp. 115–16, 119, 122–23, 216; Carl Wittke, ed., *The History of the State of Ohio* (Columbus, Ohio: Ohio State Archaeological and Historical Society, 1941–1944), IV, 57.

3. Bertram W. Korn, *American Jewry and the Civil War* (Philadelphia: The Jewish Publication Society, 1951), p. 1; Hyman B. Grinstein, *The Rise of the Jewish Community of New York, 1654–1860* (Philadelphia: The Jewish Publication Society, 1945), p. 469.

4. The Jewish population of Cincinnati is given as between 6,000 and 7,000 in *The Israelite*, November 14, 1856, and as 10,500–11,000 in the issue of March 29, 1861, both cited by James G. Heller, *As Yesterday When It Is Past* (Cincinnati: Isaac M. Wise Temple, 1942), p. 88. Charles Cist, *Sketches and Statistics of Cincinnati in 1859* (Cincinnati, 1859), pp. 197–98, calculates the Jewish population as 7,913.

5. Cist gives the oldest congregation ("Children of Israel") as having been founded in 1820, and the second ("Children of Jeshurun") as having been founded in 1845, and the other congregations as dating from 1847, 1850, 1854, and 1856.

6. Isaac M. Wise, *Reminiscences* (Cincinnati: Leo Wise and Company, 1901), p. 327.
7. Roseboom and Weisenburger, *A History of Ohio*, p. 173.
8. *The Israelite*, November 30, 1860, p. 172.
9. Ibid.
10. Ibid.
11. Ibid. The tone of Wise's approach is worth considering for its effect on a man like David Einhorn, in view of the latter's opposition to Wise and his works.
12. Ibid., December 28, 1860, p. 205. In this same article, Wise takes the stand against coercion mentioned later in this essay.
13. Ibid. Two weeks before, Wise had voiced his faith in the Union:
It is with the utmost regret that we record the fact of thousands of our fellow citizens speaking of the dissolution of the Union; they not only speak of but are actually zealous to accomplish it. . . . It is a lamentable evidence of the shortsightedness of man under the influence of passion, that there should be honest men in this country who, while European nations struggle after Union, should think of benefitting themselves by disunion. . . . Providence reserved this sea-girt continent for the last and highest triumphs of humanity. This great and blessed land was not reserved for schismatics and separatists; it is for God and freedom, for the highest interests of humanity which to protect we must have the power of union—union and peace, union of sentiment and fraternal feelings must be our watchword. We do not know by what policy, compromise or amendments this can be effected easiest and quickest, but we know and feel that the storm must abate and the union must be maintained. (*The Israelite*, December 14, 1860, p. 188)
14. *The Israelite*, January 4, 1861, p. 212.
15. Ibid., December 28, 1860, p. 206. Immediately below the editorial article is a letter signed "Amico," criticizing Buchanan's action, e.g., "Rocks are ahead, captain and officers take to boats and tell the crew to pray and save themselves."
16. Ibid., February 1, 1861, p. 244. The minutes of the Board of Trustees of K. K. B'nai Yeshurun make no reference to any incident in connection with this service.
17. Max B. May, in *Isaac Mayer Wise*, p. 243, states that Wise "did not zealously advocate the abolition of slavery." If May meant to imply that Wise advocated abolition, though not zealously, he does not support his contention with evidence.
18. *Publications of the American Jewish Historical Society* (*PAJHS*), V (1897), 150.
19. *The Israelite*, January 18, 1861, p. 230.
20. Max B. May, in *Isaac Mayer Wise*, p. 245, attacks Kohler's statement that Wise approved of Raphall's position, but does not make clear what Wise's position was. Korn, in "Isaac Mayer Wise on the Civil War," *Hebrew Union College Annual*, XX (1947), 638, states that Wise was "prepared to see slavery established

as a permanent American institution, to save the Union," but was not "proslavery." On p. 640, he observes: "Long after the final draft of the Emancipation Proclamation was issued, Wise finally gave an expression of his views on slavery in the Bible. He showed no unwillingness to state his beliefs once slavery had ceased to be a political issue. They are, of course, the ideas of a man opposed to slavery." Still, it would not prove that Wise was antislavery before the Emancipation Proclamation, even were he shown to be equivocally so afterwards. On p. 641, Korn adds: "Wise was still unwilling to come to grips with the evils of southern slavery which so infuriated the north, or with the economic conditions which perpetuated those evils."

21. *The Israelite*, June 7, 1861, p. 386.
22. See Wise's rejection of coercion later in this essay.
23. *Encyclopaedia of the Social Sciences* (New York: Macmillan Co., 1930–1935), V, 227.
24. Jacob R. Marcus, *The Americanization of Isaac Mayer Wise* (Cincinnati, 1931), p. 10. This has been laid under contribution generally for its assessment of Wise's political ideas.
25. *The Israelite*, January 25, 1861. The inconsistency would seem to be Wise's, since a parallel can hardly be drawn between a civic disability which disappears either automatically or by readily taken administrative action and an inborn state of personal servitude. But Wise's view does reflect an intense dislike of enacting distinctions between different sections of the population.
26. *The Israelite*, October 18, 1861, p. 124, despite its self-denying ordinance of April 19, 1861, contains an article in violent tone, headed "The Wrong Influence of the Church":

> who in the world could act worse, more extravagant and reckless in this crisis than the Protestant priests did? From the very start of the unfortunate difficulties, the consequences of which we now suffer so severely, the Protestant priests threw the firebrand of abolitionism into the very heart of this country.... Remember the violent abolition speeches and denunciations of all opponents from the [Henry Ward] Beecher and [Theodore] Parker factions and another host of eccentric minds.... Remember the petition to Congress by the Presbyterian synod of Pittsburgh, Pa., at the beginning of this war, praying to acknowledge God and Jesus, and abolish slavery.

27. *The Israelite*, January 24, 1862, p. 236:

> Years ago we knew nothing of prayer meetings, Sunday laws, Christian country, Christian legislations, and all that sort of new fangled theories, nay most of our eminent statesmen were not even baptized.... Now we have plenty (and yet more every day) of prayer meetings, Sunday laws, temperance laws, Christian states and legislations, Christian chaplains in the Army, Navy, hospitals, legislative halls and elsewhere, with a masterly inactivity, a lack of energy and vigor, a want of strength and honesty of purpose, plenty

of blunders, weakness, fraud and selfishness almost everywhere.... How sick is our moral nature, if we stand in need of such artificial means and priestly guardians, and submit to them! The better nature of moral freemen must revolt against the impertinence of men to be our guardians in religious matters, in matters between man and his God.

28. *The Israelite*, December 28, 1860, pp. 205–206.

29. Ibid., March 22, 1861, p. 386. In *The Israelite* of February 27, 1863, Wise again associates Abolitionism with attempts to Christianize the Constitution.

30. *The Jewish Messenger* (New York), May 3, 1861, p. 133.

31. *The Israelite*, April 19, 1861, p. 334. Evidently Wise's attitude in this respect came under criticism in Cincinnati. *The Israelite* of May 31, 1861, p. 380, contains a letter signed by Wise which was stated to have been sent to several dailies and refused publication. It opens by stating that a Rev. Mr. Conway, in one of his sermons published in the press, had accused *The Israelite* and another Cincinnati religious organ "of unfair motives on account of the silence observed on the present state of the country." Wise defends his attitude along the lines already indicated.

32. *The Israelite*, June 14, 1861, p. 396.

33. Ibid., May 31, 1861, p. 380.

34. Ibid., September 6, 1861, p. 76.

35. On this occasion the Civil War was alluded to, though without any opinion being expressed (*The Israelite*, September 26, 1862). A week earlier there had been a reference to the interruption in production caused by the proclamation of martial law in Cincinnati. Occasionally notes were sounded which might be considered ambivalent, e.g., "Should this war result in an entire restoration of this union to its former majesty and integrity" (*The Israelite*, February 21, 1862, p. 269); the reprinting "as somewhat of a curiosity" of a form of prayer for the Confederacy introduced by the Rev. Dr. Bernard Illowy into some of the synagogues of the South (ibid., February 14, 1862, p. 263); and an editorial headed "To Preachers," commending the vacant pulpit at Charleston, S.C. (ibid., March 7, 1862, p. 285).

36. This whole episode is dealt with in detail in Korn, *American Jewry and the Civil War*. See also Ellis Rivkin, "A Decisive Pattern in American Jewish History," in *Essays in American Jewish History* (Cincinnati: American Jewish Archives, 1958), pp. 37–38.

37. James Bryce, *The American Commonwealth* (London and New York: Macmillan and Company, 1888), II, 253.

38. Roseboom and Weisenburger, *A History of Ohio*, 282.

39. See *The Daily Times* (Cincinnati), September 10, 1863, p. 3.

40. *Daily Enquirer* (Cincinnati), September 11, 1863, p. 2.

41. The prominence of Jews in the clothing trade is mentioned in Roseboom and Weisenburger, *A History of Ohio*, pp. 122–23. *The Occident* (Philadelphia),

May, 1863, p. 94, had noted "many of the Israelites of Cincinnati have grown immensely rich, as we hear, from contracts and other business springing up in their favour from the dreadful war of desolation which now sweeps over the Southern section of the land." A sign of this prosperity was the building of the large Plum Street Temple which Wise's congregation embarked upon at this period.

42. Wise withdrew before election day, but the atmosphere of the contest had presumably developed before. Of this the following description is of interest:

> The campaign of 1861 was rancorous to the point of ferocity, and has never been equalled in this state for political ferocity either before or since. . . .
> The bitterness of that contest became so intense in many parts of the state that business relations between Democrats and Republicans were entirely severed. They would have nothing to do with each other. The political feud was carried into their families, and old friends and neighbours became strangers. Fist fights were of daily occurrence, and a pin or emblem of any kind worn by a Democrat was like a red rag to a bull before the eyes of a Republican. (Thomas C. Powell, *The Democratic Party of the State of Ohio* [Columbus, Ohio: Ohio Publishing Co., 1913], I, 148)

6

Baltimore Rabbis during the Civil War

Isaac M. Fein

The number of Jews in the United States tripled during the decade preceding the Civil War. From about fifty thousand in 1850, it grew to about one hundred and fifty thousand by 1860.[1] Since Baltimore was an important center, and a port of landing at that, the rate of growth of its Jewish population was, naturally, larger than that of the country at large. In 1840, there were in Baltimore less than two hundred Jewish families.[2] By 1855, only fifteen years later, the number grew about sevenfold, to between twelve to fifteen hundred families.[3] In 1859, the estimated number of individuals was between five to seven thousand,[4] and six years later, in 1865, this figure again doubled, and the estimated number was between ten to twelve thousand.[5]

In Baltimore, as in other American cities with large German populations, the Jews formed a colony within the larger German colony. Jewish youngsters attended German schools; adults belonged to all kinds of German Vereins, sport societies, etc. In this case the formula "*Wie es sich christelt so judelt es sich* [as go the Christians so go the Jews]" ought to be changed to: "*Wie es sich deutschelt so judelt es sich* [as go the Germans so go the Jews]." The majority of the Germans belonged to the Democratic party.[6] Their newspaper was *Der Deutsche Correspondent*, which, while not defending slavery as a "divine institution," was quite outspoken on the issue and defended it on a rational basis. The paper called upon its readers, immigrants in a new land, "never to forget that the Constitution of the United States in support of which every adopted citizen of the

---

Reprinted, in substantially abridged form, with permission of Rashi Fein from *American Jewish Historical Quarterly* 51 (1961): 67–86, copyright © 1961 by the American Jewish Historical Society.

Republic has sworn an oath of loyalty, sanctions and protects the institution of slavery."[7] From this the immigrant was to draw the only possible conclusion: Beware, live up to your oath, defense of slavery means good citizenship. To the Jews, and at that period practically all of them were German Jews, *Der Deutsche Correspondent* was the "Jewish paper." In it the Baltimore Jews found advertisements and reports of Jewish events in the city. Most of the Jews, like the non-Jewish Germans, were for the status quo on the issue of slavery.

At the two extremes were the German elite and the 48'ers. The elite was economically and socially related to the South. This group was outspoken for slavery without any reservations, and later it became secessionist. Slavery was defended by them on the basis of the Constitution and also because it was a "divine institution." There was a corresponding group among the Jews. The German 48'ers, however, were liberals who saw that "the same principles which were involved in Europe of 1848 are involved in America in 1861."[8] This quotation is from the strongly Republican Baltimore German daily, *Der Wecker*, the paper whose political stand was expressed by the statement: "Within the Union happy, outside the Union unhappy."[9] There were correspondingly Jewish 48'ers who felt the same way, and Rabbi David Einhorn's monthly *Sinai* expressed their sentiments, which were similar to those of the *Wecker*.

These various points of view found their expression in the sermons, writings, addresses, and discourses of the rabbis of those days. Whether the rabbis were independent in their opinions or were merely reflecting the point of view of their members,—an interesting problem in itself,—is not the issue here. There is no doubt, however, that their opinions were reflected in the community, and the records, which contemporary rabbis left behind, help us to understand the moods of the people and to learn about the life of the Jews at that time.

During the period we are discussing there were in Baltimore four synagogues.[10] The first charter giving the Jews in Maryland the right to establish a synagogue was granted in 1830. Five rabbis officiated during this period in those four synagogues. The first to come to the city, in 1840, Abraham Rice, was the first ordained rabbi to come to the United States.[11] Concerning him, Isaac Leeser declared: "We know of none in the country on whose shoulders the dignity of Rabbi could be more fittingly placed."[12] Rabbi Rice had, by the time now under discussion, very little influence. In private correspondence he expressed apprehension and prayed that God should "guard us in these times from all troubles and misfortunes, and that the whole thing should pass peacefully for the Jews."[13] The other four rabbis exercised considerable influence. Unfortunately, their sermons have not been recorded in the minute books of their respective congregations. Except for a telling remark about "unfortunate times which has befallen us,"[14] about "arrears in dues" and, what seems to be a natural concomitant, the reduction in the salaries of the rabbis,—such as a reduction in Rabbi Szold's salary from $125.00 to $75.00 per month, and a similar reduction in the salary of Rabbi Illowy,[15]—there is nothing to give any indication that there was a severe crisis, let alone a war going on. We have to depend on reports of the rabbis' sermons in the Jewish national press and the local English press. Full texts are rare in either case. We have, of course, more sermons of Rabbi David Einhorn, since he had his monthly magazine, *Sinai*, at his disposal.

In the oldest and most orthodox synagogue in the city, the Baltimore Hebrew Congregation, Rabbi Bernard Illowy defended the status quo. He took this position with regard to minutest rituals: nothing was to be changed; and he took a similar position in regard to the major social issue of the day,—slavery. In a sermon delivered on the National Fast Day, January 4, 1861, proclaimed by President James Buchanan, Illowy pleaded for "peace and harmony." He was not preaching secession but declared his open sympathy for the secessionists:

> The ends for which men unite in society and submit to government, are to enjoy security for their property and freedom for their persons ... who can blame our brethern of the South for their being inclined to secede from a society under whose government those ends cannot be attained and whose union is kept together ... by ... heavy iron ties of violence and arbitrary force? Who can blame our brethern of the South for seceding from a society whose government cannot or will not protect the property, rights and privileges of a great portion of the Union against the encroachments of a majority misguided by some influential, ambitious aspirants and selfish politicians who, under the color of religion and the disguise of philanthropy, have thrown the country into a general state of confusion, and millions into want and poverty?

This is followed by the usual strong appeal for states' rights, and Illowy went even so far as to compare the rights of the states with those of foreign countries as follows: "We have no right to exercise violence against the institutions of other states or other countries." As was usual with clergymen who favored slavery, Illowy too "proved" that the Bible approved of slavery, for "Why did not Moses . . . prohibit the buying or selling of slaves?" or "Where was ever a greater philanthropist than Abraham, and why did he not set free his slaves?" He insisted that "the country must free itself from the influence of some individuals who exert all their efforts to mislead it under the disguise of Religion and Philanthropy."[16] From the texts he quoted, it is obvious that he had in mind the Abolitionists. And all this on the Fast Day proclaimed as a day of prayer for the unity of the people. Illowy had in his congregation people who shared his views on this subject.

From the extreme right, we turn to the center. This position was taken by two rabbis, Henry Hochheimer and the more important one, Benjamin Szold. A careful reading of Szold's inaugural sermon of September, 1859, leaves no doubt that this rabbi was a man who would do everything in his power to bring peace among the various religious factions, and he, therefore, could not take a clear stand on major issues. He pleads time and again for "reconciliation" among the different groups. The young rabbi (Szold was thirty years old when he came to Baltimore) promises to lay down his "principles of belief . . . and show the causes of the dissensions that have arisen in the midst of Israel: the spirit of the time on one side and the tradition on the other."

He goes on to expound that on the one side there are those who claim that "time has no power over the divine commandments, they were holy to our forefathers and they must be holy to us. . . . We are not allowed to change them." As against these he points to those who believe that "free reasoning is the main thing . . . , that the religious life is dependent upon the influence of the time." He summarizes the opposing points of view as follows: "Many want to press all religious demands in obsolete garb. . . . The others again yield everything to the authority of the times." What, in the light of these diametrically opposing points of view, were Szold's "principles of belief"? "It is evident that in neither direction the exclusive truth is contained. The truth, in general, must lie in a right medium. . . . The truth, the full truth, is contained in both directions." And again, and again, he speaks of a "reconcilable sense," "conciliatory spirit,"[17] but fails to present a clear picture of his own religious philosophy, unless love of peace was, indeed, the mainstay of his thinking.

Szold's unwillingness to take a clear-cut position on most fundamental issues led at times to extremes. To cite but one, albeit an outstanding one: that Rabbi Szold was devoted to the idea of the restoration of the Jewish homeland in Palestine needs no proof. He found it, nevertheless, possible, no doubt, for "conciliatory" reasons, to introduce changes in his prayer book *Abodath Israel*, which do not square at all with his "Zionist" views. He omitted, for example, the prayers dealing with the Messiah; he introduced a special prayer for the Fast Day of the Ninth of Ab, not a prayer for restoration of the destroyed homeland, but:

> We do not unduly lament over the Temple that is destroyed. . . . We mourn not despairingly over the downfall of Jerusalem, for all places whither Thou hast sent us, shall be consecrated unto Thee through the worship of Thy name. . . . Thou hast given us another home in place of that which we lost in the land of our fathers.

He introduced many similar changes in his prayerbook.[18]

It was only natural for Szold and his middle of the road group to take an attitude of, so called, "neutrality" also on the issues of the Civil War. Szold spoke for that group when on December 22, 1860, he preached on "Peace and Union."[19] Again Szold expressed his hopes for "reconciliation." He quoted the Bible and the Talmud to substantiate his thesis that "peace is the angel of consolation," that "all . . . heartily long for . . . peace and reconciliation," that the warring sections should discuss their problems for "the language . . . proves itself the harbinger of peace and reconciliation, it is in the power of this heavenly gift [language] to reconcile. . . . The spirit of faith . . . is the holy language that proclaims peace and reconciliation to mankind." He reduced all of the troubles of the country to: "The land of the free and the home of the brave is the tumultuous arena of unbridled passions, mad partisans and hungry office seekers, [and he appealed to] the charming power of argument," but he failed to give any indication of his position in the "argument" except, of course, that he is for the Union. His position, while not spelled out, is quite clear: peace above all, peace at any price. A very popular position in those days.[20]

The middle of the road group was the careful group. The name of Rabbi Szold's congregation, Oheb Shalom, befits their philosophy and their activities.

The Jewish 48'ers, who saw in the Civil War issues the same issues that they had fought for in Europe, found their champion and spokesman in the Reform Rabbi, David Einhorn. In his inaugural sermon, delivered on September 29, 1855, he clearly stated his religious and social philosophy. He stated that "the old world is fast crumbling and a new world seeks to rise from its ruins. . . . The religious idea cannot persist in one and the same form." Turning from Jewish problems to general, he discussed

> a humanity, the members of which have one and the same right, possess the same claim to happiness and a state of blessedness which will be realized already here on earth. All men possess one and the same natural and spiritual origin, the same native nobility, and are, therefore, entitled to the same rights, the same laws. . . . To achieve this goal we need only indomitable courage in our battle against the forces of darkness.[21]

In his monthly *Sinai*, which he established only about six months after his arrival in Baltimore,[22] Einhorn fought against all defenders of slavery, especially those among the clergy, Jewish as well as non-Jewish. In reporting a meeting of Presbyterians in Cleveland who were told that in the South both clergy as well as lay leaders have slaves "on principle," since "slavery is a divine ordinance, sanctified by the Bible," Einhorn comments that the southern church defends slavery because the church "unfortunately is not a free agent, is not independent of the state, it follows the politics of the ruling party. . . . The church leaders read the Bible according to its letter, not according to its spirit."[23]

Einhorn was very careful to make a distinction between church and religion. The "church and the state have nothing in common," not so religion, which is "to permeate every phase of life." Since church and state are separate and have "nothing in common," Einhorn even criticized President Lincoln when the latter, in an order to the army, used the expression "Christian people."[24]

In *Sinai*, he published four articles[25] against Rabbi Morris Jacob Raphall, who preached in defense of slavery.[26] In these articles he castigated Raphall, called him all kinds of names, and Einhorn was, indeed, a master of name calling and bitter sarcasm. At the same time, however, Einhorn carefully examined and discussed the passages quoted by Raphall. His conclusion was that the "learned Rabbi" missed the whole point of the Mosaic attitude to slavery. Indeed, he regards Raphall's talk as both "shameful and senseless."[27] In bitterness, and perhaps more in pain, Einhorn wrote:

> A Jew, a sapling of that stem, which praises the Lord daily for the deliverance out of Egyptian yoke of slavery, undertook to defend slavery . . . "Alas for ears that hear such things."[28] We are obliged to reject such words because they are "a profanation of God's name."[29]

Bavarian-born Rabbi David Einhorn (1808–1879), a leading proponent of so-called Radical Reform Judaism, spoke out sharply against slavery from his pulpit in Baltimore, which he assumed in 1855. Threatened by the city's pro-slavery secessionists upon the outbreak of war, Einhorn was forced to flee for his life. Courtesy of The Jacob Rader Marcus Center of the American Jewish Archives.

Einhorn's articles were, naturally, discussed approvingly in the abolitionist daily, *Der Wecker*.[30]

Time and again Einhorn returned to the problem of slavery—"the cancer of the union."[31]

> Does the Negro have less ability to think, to feel, to will? Does he have less of a desire to happiness? Was he born not to be entitled to all these? Does the Negro have an iron neck that does not feel a burdensome yoke? Does he have a stiffer heart that does not bleed when . . . his beloved child is torn away from him?[32]

To those who feared that Negro emancipation might prove dangerous for the progress of humanity, Einhorn's answer was: "The end never justifies the means. Slavery is immoral and must be abolished."[33] While he was certain that slavery was to be fought against by everybody, he demanded and expected that Jews would be more sensitive to this issue than anyone else. He was shocked by the fact that "there are even immigrant Jews, who are so blinded as to be enthusiastic for secession and slavery."[34]

Einhorn sounds like a man of our era when he bewailed the state of religion in his days:

> There are enough churches, synagogues and temples, but there is very little religion, little morality . . . here [among the Jews]. Everything is empty, everything is glimmer. . . . Here, too, rules the golden eagle rather than the cherubim. . . . Here, too, all feelings of the heart and dreams are concentrated only on acquiring [things]. . . . There is only one thought: to make as much as possible.[35]

Einhorn took his religion and, what to him was synonymous with it, ethical conduct, very seriously. He demanded much of himself and expected others too, and especially rabbis, to live a moral life. Since to him it was immoral to defend slavery or to besmirch the name of the Jew, he denounced those rabbis whom he found wanting in this respect. To a report published in *Sinai* that Rabbi Simon Tuska of Memphis had compared the Jews, who had come there to do business with the military, with "greedy birds of prey," Einhorn added a long note reproaching Tuska: "A Jew in a responsible position, and especially a Rabbi, dares not be against the Union and make statements detrimental to the good name of the Jewish people." He expressed the hope that people would remember those Jews who stood by the republic in the hour of its "gravest danger" and those who by their deeds proved to be "detractors of their own stem."[36] A long and bitter correspondence ensued. Einhorn refused to accept ambiguous denials and was relentless in his denunciations.[37]

The word of a rabbi carried weight with both the pro-slavery as well as the anti-slavery elements. Rabbi Raphall's defense of slavery was widely distributed in the South.[38] One of Einhorn's patriotic sermons was published, and the profits from its sale went to the Sanitary Commission.[39]

Unlike Leeser, who anticipated the Haskalah slogan "Be a man in the world and a Jew at home"[40] by saying: "In the synagogue we want Jews, in public matters only Americans,"[41] Einhorn made no such division. He insisted that Jews, indeed, because they are Jews, are to be active in civic affairs. Civic affairs are to be their concern. In speaking of the War, he warned the Jews: "You, Israelites, stand more to lose . . . much, infinitely more than gold and silver. Do you comprehend your duties as members of the American people?"[42] Indeed, it is the duty of Jews as Jews to fight bigotry, for "Jews for thousands of years consciously or unconsciously were fighting for freedom of conscience."[43] The struggle of the Jews is not, however, a struggle for the improvement of their own lot. "Israel, the people of peoples, is called upon to fight against the whole world for the whole world."[44] Einhorn is convinced that the Jews and the United States have similar destinies. The Jews are to fight "for the whole world" and so does the United States: "America of the future will not rest on slave chains or belittling its adopted citizens. It will also give up its disinterestedness in the fate of other peoples of the world."[45]

Baltimore Jews, the right and the center, began to be concerned lest the Rabbi's pronouncements endanger their position. Baltimore was a city on a powder keg, and people whom Einhorn sarcastically characterized as "educated in politics and theology" called a protest meeting against Einhorn in a desire to disassociate the Jewish community from him.[46] Let us bear in mind that all this took place only about thirty years after Jews had been granted equality in Maryland in 1826. Jews feared that their loyalty was still being questioned. It was only a few years after Einhorn's predecessor in the Har Sinai Verein, the reader, Max Soutro, suggested to the Board, and the latter approved the suggestion, to do away with the commemoration of the Ninth of Ab because "Our Christian brothers with whom we form one social body may think that since we mourn and wail for the destruction of Jerusalem, that we yearn to return there and that our patriotism for our present abode is not a genuine, a real, an ardent one." And then, he added, "should our congregation become bigger and our principles more generally known, so that we would not have to be afraid any longer of misconceptions, we could then celebrate the 9th of Ab in a suitable fashion."[47]

Einhorn was accused of lacking a sense of responsibility for the well-being of the entire community. To this, Einhorn replied that he is aware that "for the crime of one of us, the entire community is held responsible," and it is, indeed, his concern for the community that obliges him to call upon the Jews to "behave decently, to fight against prejudices."[48] It was his sense of mutual responsibility that made him later, in his *War with Amalek*, call upon American Jews to "fight against Jewish smugglers to make war also upon the Amalek in our own midst. . . . They bring shame and disgrace upon us and our religious faith."[49]

Prior to these events, he had fought the mob rule of the Know Nothings when they were riding high in the state. Baltimore was in virtual control of the "Red Necks," "Rip Rads," "Black Snakes," and similar clubs of the Know Nothing party. It was the period when "roughnecks felt free to disturb balls, picnics, and other gatherings and break them up."[50] It was the period when in the election campaign of 1856 there were "scores of citizens insulted and severely beaten. Hundreds were wounded, shot and killed."[51] "A foreigner," according to the memoirs of a contemporary Jew, "could only cast his vote by running through a gauntlet of pistols, knives, and clubs."[52] Einhorn was convinced that "once we start to evaluate people by the country of birth, next will come an evaluation by religion and in this case surely, the Jews, the so-called crucifiers of the crucified, will be in great danger."[53] He called again and again to fight against the Know Nothings, for "the defeat of the Know Nothing will be the victory of the fundamental Mosaic law of equality of the stranger with the native before the law."[54]

The situation did not improve much with the defeat of the Know Nothings and the rise of the Republican Party. Baltimore, known as "mobtown," was even more in a turmoil than the rest of the country. There was fear of the new party, of the "Black Republicans." Again, in face of opposition and danger, Einhorn makes clear his position: "We are aware of the concern of those who fear that this party may lead to the dissolution of the Union. We don't share these views, if only because if the Union is based on immoral foundations, it is not fit to survive, nor is it worth surviving."[55] This was said at a time when, according to Hyman Spitz, a contemporary who lived in Baltimore during the Civil War: "The Union people had to keep still and had to pretend to be Rebels. In order to be treated right in school our [the word "our" no doubt, signifies either "Jewish" or "Foreign"] children were obliged to carry Rebel emblems."[56]

The political situation in the country generally, and in Maryland especially, continued from bad to worse. In the 1860 Presidential elections Lincoln, in Maryland, received only 2,294 votes out of a total of 92,502. The secessionist movement was very strong. The General Assembly of 1860 adopted a resolution that "should the hour ever arrive when the Union must be dissolved, Maryland will cast her lot with her sister states of the South and abide their fortune to the fullest extent."[57] Even as late as September 11, 1861, months after the start of the war, the Secretary of War, Simon Cameron, deemed it necessary to arrest all Maryland legislators to prevent the passage of an ordinance of secession.

Maryland remained with the North, not as a contemporary writer would have it, because "its population became mixed, the ancient stock having absorbed much bad blood,"[58] but because the Federal Army kept close watch over the state because of its tremendous geographic importance. Washington, D.C., was situated between secessionist Virginia and Maryland, and in addition, three railroads, by which loyal troops could reach the capital, converged in Baltimore. The situation in the city deteriorated rapidly. A great many citizens were arrested,—among them even the Mayor and the Marshal. On April 19th, Federal troops, on their way to Washington, were attacked. Among the six (!) arrested for "assaulting" was Joseph Friedenwald, a member of a leading Jewish family in the city.[59] A Jewish eye-witness relates that

> one soldier was . . . beaten to death by the mob and left on the sidewalk to perish. After the commotion ceased, mother went over to the store and ordered the clerks to bring the body in. This was done. The mob threatened to sack the establishment, and there was no relief until the police came. . . . Everyone expected . . . that the State of Maryland would secede.[60]

On the following day the shops of both abolitionist publications, *Der Wecker* and *Sinai*, were demolished. Einhorn's life was in danger. According to his version, he was "requested" by his congregation to leave town.[61] The congregation, however, asked him to make a correction in his report of the events. They claimed that "there had been no meeting of the congregation," that his "warm friends knew quite well that [his] sense of duty would not permit [him] to leave [his] congregation at such a time," and that only their "concern about [his] safety" made some of them make a remark that "the congregation in all probability would not mind" if he left town.[62] Be it as it may, Einhorn, with his family, fled to Philadelphia. Before long he began to publish his *Sinai* in that city and in the first issue gave a full account of the events which led to his flight from Baltimore.[63] The magazine continued in Philadelphia only for another year and a half. In the last issue Einhorn stated that "Sinai dies in the battle against slavery."[64]

Many members of Har Sinai were in sympathy with their Rabbi's views, even if much more cautious than he was. Three weeks after his escape, on May 12th, he was asked by the congregation to return with the understanding that "for the sake of your own safety as well as out of consideration for the members of your congregation," they were asking him "not to comment from the pulpit on the excitable issues of the time." They assured him that this request is dictated only by the prevailing "sad circumstances." As was to be expected, he rejected the invitation and rejected it again when a delegation from the Har Sinai Congregation waited on him on May 29th.[65] Fear was the characteristic of Baltimore. Even as late as 1864, Wise reported on a visit to the city: "In politics, of course, one must penetrate into the secrecy of private circles to learn the opinions held by various persons."[66]

That Einhorn was bitter, is quite understandable. In his correspondence with one of his staunch supporters, Reuben Oppenheimer,[67] he points an accusing finger against his opponents at his own temple:

> There is nothing so loathsome, indeed, than this riffraff of bacon reformers. The light of the Rabbis becomes a destroying torch in the hands of such people. Luther was right when he said in his own manner of speaking: "certain people are like a drunken horseman. If you help him mount the horse from one side, he will fall down from the other side."[68]

He is mindful that along "with much hatred [he] found much love in Baltimore." He is happy that many Baltimore friends, Jews and non-Jews, visit him in Philadelphia.[69] On the whole, however, he was bitter about his experiences in Baltimore:

> It would be bad if I found here [in Philadelphia] Jews who are as bad as those in Baltimore. . . . Baltimore made me, practically, unsociable. . . . A week from next Sabbath I am giving my first sermon in Keneseth Israel . . . [where he, in the meantime, had been elected Rabbi]. I hope that the

interval of three months will have been sufficient to cleanse myself from the dirt which the Baltimore orthodox and reformers have thrown on me.

In all his bitterness he comforts his friends and urges them to believe that "the next battles will leave a real blood bath, but slavery will be drowned in that bath." The most intimate personal matters are related by him to the war. Announcing the birth of his son, Einhorn says: "The boy started out by being anxious to take a look at America at the very moment they fought at Bull Run." The letter was written at the High Holiday season, and Einhorn declared: "Now comes the Holy Season and I hope that the Southern rebels will be sent to perdition, Amen!"[70]

Einhorn's extreme animosity toward the secessionists is, perhaps, best seen in his eulogy of President Lincoln. He regarded the martyred President as "the Messiah of his people," "the high priest of freedom." He did, however, find "one fault" with Lincoln, "He was too mild to the Rebels."[71]

NOTES

The following abbreviations are used in the notes:

AZJ   *Algemeine Zeitung des Judenthums*
BHC   Baltimore Hebrew Congregation (Baltimore)
Cyc   *Biographical Encyclopedia of Representative Men of Maryland* (Baltimore, 1879)
HSC   Har Sinai Congregation (Baltimore)
Isr   *Israelite* (Cincinnati)
JHSM   Jewish Historical Society of Maryland
JTSAL Library of the Jewish Theological Seminary of America (New York City)
Occ   *Occident* (Philadelphia)
OSC   Oheb Shalom Congregation (Baltimore)

1. Bertram Wallace Korn, *American Jewry and the Civil War* (Philadelphia, 1951), pp. 1 and 247, n. 1.
2. William S. Rayner, *Address at the Fiftieth Anniversary of the Har Sinai Congregation* (Baltimore, 1892).
3. *Isr*, July 27, 1855.
4. I. J. Benjamin, *Three Years in America*, 2 vols. (Philadelphia, 1956), vol. 1, p. 305.
5. *AZJ*, July, 1865, p. 617.
6. For a detailed discussion on the Germans in Baltimore during the Civil War see Dieter Cunz, *The Maryland Germans* (Princeton, N.J., 1948), pp. 284–315.

7. *Deutsche Correspondent*, May 13, 1891. The paper's stand on the Civil War problems, reviewed in the issue published on occasion of the Fiftieth Anniversary of the paper.

8. *Der Wecker*, June 18, 1861.

9. Ibid., Jan. 18, 1861.

10. The Baltimore Hebrew Congregation, for many years known as Lloyd Street Synagogue and Stadt Schul, established in 1830; Fells Point Hebrew Friendship Congregation, established in 1838; Har Sinai Verein, established in 1842; and Oheb Shalom Congregation, established in 1853.

11. Hyman B. Grinstein, *The Rise of the Jewish Community of New York, 1654-1860* (Philadelphia, 1945), p. 543, n. 14.

12. *Occ*, vol. XX, no. 4 (June, 1862), p. 142.

13. Letter by Abraham Rice, 1862. Collection of sermons and letters by Rabbi Abraham Rice in the Library of the Jewish Theological Seminary of America, New York.

14. BHC, Minute Book, April 6, 1862, p. 263.

15. OSC, Minute Book, March, 1861; BHC, Minute Book, July 29, 1861, p. 222.

16. *Occ*, vol. XVIII, no. 44 (Jan. 24, 1861), pp. 267-268.

17. Rabbi Benjamin Szold, "Inaugural Sermon," translated from the German by Sophie and Henrietta Szold (the Rabbi's wife and daughter, respectively), 1909. Manuscript in OSC, copy in JHSM.

18. Moshe Davis, *Yahadut Amerika Be-Hitpathutah* (New York, 1951), pp. 307-312.

19. *Isr*, vol. VII (Jan. 11, 1861), p. 220.

20. Rabbi Henry Hochheimer's sermons were in a vein similar to those of Rabbi Szold. *Occ*, vol. VII, no. 9 (Dec., 1859), pp. 444-453; vol. VII (Jan. 25, 1861), p. 236; *Sermons*, separately published, Nov. 4, 1865.

21. Dr. David Einhorn, *Inaugural Sermon*, 1855 (translated from the German by Dr. Abraham B. Arnold), also in Kaufmann Kohler, ed., *David Einhorn Memorial Volume* (New York, 1911), pp. 31-44.

22. The first issue of *Sinai: Ein Organ fur Erkentniss und Veredlung des Judenthums,* whose motto was את אחי אנכי מבקש ["I seek my brethren"], appeared in February, 1856.

23. *Sinai*, vol. II, no. 6 (July 1, 1857), p. 599.

24. Ibid., vol. VIII, no. 11 (Dec., 1862), p. 313.

25. Ibid., vol. VI, no. 1 (Feb., 1861), pp. 2-20; vol. VI, no. 2 (March, 1861), pp. 45-50, 60-61; vol. VI, no. 3 (April, 1861), pp. 99-100.

26. The discourse on the *Bible View on Slavery* was delivered at the B'nai Jeshurun Synagogue in New York on the occasion of the National Fast Day, Jan. 4, 1861.

27. *Sinai*, vol. VI, no. 2 (March, 1861), p. 45.

28. The Hebrew original reads: אוי לאזנים שכך שומעות.

29. The Hebrew original reads: חלול השם. Ibid., vol. VI, no. 1 (Feb. 1, 1861), pp. 9, 22.
30. *Der Wecker*, Feb. 6 and 7, 1861.
31. *Sinai*, vol. I, no. 9 (Oct., 1856), p. 259.
32. Ibid., vol. VII, no. 7 (Aug., 1862), p. 187.
33. Ibid., vol. II, no. 11 (Dec., 1857). p. 357.
34. Ibid., vol. VI. no. 3 (April, 1861), p. 95.
35. Ibid., vol. VII, no. 1 (Feb., 1861), p. 30.
36. Ibid., vol. VII, no. 7 (Aug., 1862), p. 199.
37. Ibid., vol. VII, no. 7 (Aug., 1862) , pp. 199–200; vol. VII, no. 8 (Sept., 1862), p. 227; vol. VII, no. 9 (Oct., 1862), p. 257; vol. VII, no. 10 (Nov., 1862), p. 284.
38. Korn, *American Jewry and the Civil War*, p. 250, notes 20–25.
39. Max J. Kohler, "The Jews and the American Anti-Slavery Movement," *Publication of the American Jewish Historical Society*, vol. V (1897), p. 151.
40. This slogan באוהלך היה אדם בצאתך ויהודי was introduced by the Hebrew poet Judah Leib Gordon in his poem "הקיצה עמי" ["Awake, my people"], in 1863. J. L. Gordon, *Writings* [Hebrew] (Tel Aviv, 1950), p. 17.
41. *Occ*, vol. VII, no. 11 (Feb., 1855), p. 558.
42. *Sinai*, vol. V, no. 1 (Feb., 1861), p. 23.
43. Ibid., vol. I, no. 11 (Dec., 1856), p. 355.
44. Ibid., vol. I, no. 12 (Jan., 1861), p. 367.
45. Ibid., vol. VII, no. 7 (Aug., 1862), p. 185.
46. Ibid., vol. VI, no. 1 (Feb., 1861), p. 32.
47. HSC, Minute Book, Aug. 3, 1845.
48. David Einhorn, "Sermon," April 30, 1863, in Kaufmann Kohler, ed., *David Einhorn Memorial Volume*, p. 120.
49. Quoted in Korn, *American Jewry and the Civil War*, p. 152.
50. Harry Friedenwald, *Letters and Addresses by Aaron Friedenwald* (Baltimore, 1906), pp. 29–30.
51. Matthew Page Andrews, *Tercentenary History of Maryland*, 4 vols. (Chicago-Baltimore, 1905), vol. 1, p. 781.
52. Simeon Hecht, *Memoirs*, p. 30. (Original manuscript is owned by the descendants of Simeon Hecht and covers the period 1824–1872. Photostats of the manuscript are located at the JHSM.)
53. *Sinai*, vol. I, no. 11 (Dec., 1856), p. 354.
54. Ibid., vol. I, no. 11 (Dec., 1856), p. 355.
55. Ibid., vol. I, no. 9 (Oct., 1856), p. 259.
56. Haiman Philip Spitz, "An Autobiography," in Jacob Rader Marcus, *Memoirs of American Jews, 1775–1865*, 3 vols. (Philadelphia, 1955), vol. 1, p. 300.
57. Andrews, *Tercentenary History of Maryland*, vol. 1, p. 818.
58. W. Jefferson Buchanan, *Maryland's Crisis: A Political Outline* (Richmond, Va., 1863), p. 15.

59. "Pratt Street Riots," *The Sun* (April 16, 1961), Magazine Section, p. 10.

60. Hecht, *Memoirs*, p. 38.

61. *Sinai*, vol. VI (June, 1861), p. 139.

62. S. G. Putzel, Secretary of HSC, letter to Rabbi Einhorn, Baltimore, June 11, 1861.

63. *Sinai*, vol. VI, no. 6 (June, 1861), pp. 135–142.

64. Ibid., vol. VII, no. 10 (Dec., 1862), p. 319.

65. Ibid., vol. VI, no. 6 (June, 1861), p. 160.

66. *Isr*, vol. X, no. 29 (Jan. 15, 1864).

67. Oppenheimer was one of Rabbi Einhorn's closest friends. Like his Rabbi, he, too, was for open discussion of political as well as religious questions. He published a protest against a resolution of The Richmond Young Men Literary Association that "political and religious questions of any kind are out of order." *Sinai*, vol. I, no. 3 (April, 1856), p. 69. The Einhorn-Oppenheimer correspondence is located at the American Jewish Historical Society.

68. Einhorn, letter to Oppenheimer, Philadelphia, Aug. 17, 1861.

69. Among the visitors was the liberal educator Friedrich Knapp, the principal of the Deutsche und Englische Schule. This school was attended by wealthy Jewish boys. Hebrew was taught in different classes. *Sinai*, vol. V, no. 10 (Nov., 1860), p. 322b.

A very interesting description of the Jewish students in this school, about the relationship between "the chosen and the *goyim*," about the Jewish boys "with Hittite noses, curly hair" is given by H. L. Mencken, who attended the school in the '80s. Mencken, who learned Hebrew there, relates how difficult it was to teach "these reluctant Yido-Americans the principles of their sacred tongue." H. L. Mencken, *Happy Days* (New York, 1955), pp. 23–25.

70. Letter of Einhorn to Oppenheimer, Aug. 17, 1861. The phrase he uses is "schlagen כפרות."

71. David Einhorn, "Eulogy on the Death of Lincoln," in Kaufmann Kohler, ed., *David Einhorn Memorial Volume*, p. 137.

Part IV

Jewish Soldiers during the Civil War

From the first, Jewish writing about the Civil War extolled (and enumerated) the participation of Jews in the conflict as soldiers and sailors, officers and enlistees. Paradoxically for a subject repeatedly foraged by historians, we know surprisingly little about the experience of Jews in the armies of the North. Partly this reflects the difficulty of assembling the sources necessary for writing a richly textured account of Jewish life in uniform. But primarily it suggests the vestigial legacy of several generations of historians who collected and collated material to serve political, apologetic, and presentist—rather than historical—agendas. The former approach is exemplified by Simon Wolf's *The American Jew as Patriot, Soldier and Citizen*, a massive compendium of articles and lists of servicemen published in 1895 in response to an antisemite's allegation that he could not "remember meeting one Jew in uniform of hearing of any Jewish soldier." Wolf's work has since served as a template (and sourcebook) for many others who have written about Jewish Civil War service.

Perhaps in reaction to these largely amateur efforts, scholars have largely avoided the subject of Jewish soldiering. Bertram Korn, in his magisterial work on the Civil War, offers only fleeting glimpses of Jewish life in the ranks. Korn deliberately eschewed the form of military history favored by many of his forebears who studied Jewish involvement in the war, preferring to write a social history of the American Jewish community's experience of the conflict. Aside from the publication of several memoirs and diaries of veterans, as well as a handful of scholarly accounts that have often echoed Wolf, the field of battle has been left surprisingly barren.

Historians of Jewish military service in the Civil War have fallen behind a broader historiography that has long since moved from recounting the exploits of military heroics to investigating the social and psychological experience of soldiering. Social historians of the Civil War have explored subjects that include the effects of trauma, the social lives of soldiers, popular religion within the ranks, troop culture and camaraderie, and the origins of courage and cowardice, as well as the ethnic and national divisions within the armies. It is within this latter category that studies of the Jewish experience of soldiering have most to contribute.

We still know surprisingly little of Jewish service for the Union. Thanks to Robert Rosen, we know more about those who fought for the Confederacy. By Wolf's unreliable estimates, close to eight thousand Jews served in uniform. All-Jewish companies were formed in Syracuse, Chicago, and Cincinnati, as well as two in Georgia. Other units, by virtue of geography and the connections between enlistees, were heavily composed of Jews. Yet we have no group portrait of those who chose to enlist (and those who opted to avoid conscription) in the Union armies. We have only a handful of anecdotal examples of the conflicts and compromises that service forced on those observing Jewish law—kashrut, worship, and burial—in the field. We know little of antisemitism and proselytizing in the ranks. Most strikingly, we have no broad sense of the impact of the war on the Jews who fought: the effects of billeting and serving alongside Christians, as well as the long-term impact of service on Jewish veterans' identities, religious observance and faith, integration and Americanization.

Although the essays by Stanley Falk and Jacob Rader Marcus included here do not engage with these issues systematically, they break substantively with a historiographic tradition that, above all, celebrated service. Marcus's study of the career of Louis Gratz, who arrived from Germany months before the outbreak of war, points to some of the advantages—and even attractions—of enlistment for recent immigrants. After struggling unsuccessfully as a peddler, Gratz found rapid advancement in an army desperately short of skilled officers and full of opportunities for capable young men fortunate to survive a perilous profession. Marcus describes how the army acted as an avenue for his integration: Gratz's period of service improved his command of English, provided rough socialization in American ways, deepened his sense of belonging, and broadened his postwar prospects. At the end of the war, Gratz settled in Knoxville, a town in which he had been stationed during the conflict, opened a legal practice (some soldiers had helped with his training in the latter months of the war), and married the daughter of a gentile fellow officer. Altogether the Civil War transformed the trajectory of Louis Gratz's life.

Robert Rosen offers a thorough accounting of the motivations of Gratz's counterparts in the South for enlisting and serving in the Confederate cause. In his essay included here, and in his book *The Jewish Confederates* (2000), he provides a lavish picture of Jewish service in the South. His assiduity in assembling sources demonstrates the riches that await future historians of Jews in the Union armies.

If Marcus's essay provides a somewhat alluring example of service, Stanley Falk describes how the war ended the career of a professional soldier with incompatible loyalties to both North and South. Falk recounts the inexorable dilemma of Southern-born Alfred Mordecai, a long-serving career soldier who was forced to choose sides at the outbreak of the war. The essay provides an usually detailed psychological portrait of the inner conflicts and moral quandaries that the internecine war created.

7

Divided Loyalties in 1861
The Decision of Major Alfred Mordecai

Stanley L. Falk

When Confederate batteries opened fire on beleaguered Fort Sumter on the morning of April 12, 1861, Major Alfred Mordecai, a senior officer in the Ordnance Department, United States Army, was testing artillery carriages at Fort Monroe, Virginia. He immediately hurried back to his post as commanding officer of Watervliet Arsenal, a major ordnance installation located just outside of Troy, New York.[1] Like thousands of other Americans, he found himself faced with the problem of divided loyalties.

Major Mordecai was a distinguished army scientist who had made great contributions in weapons development and ballistics during a military career that spanned more than four decades. Born in North Carolina in 1804, he had entered the United States Military Academy in 1819. After graduating at the top of his class, he had held a number of important positions and commands, had been sent by the War Department on several consequential missions, and, above all, had been an active and outstanding participant in the development of American military technology. In April, 1861, he was at the height of his long and distinguished career when the booming guns in Charleston harbor pushed him one step closer toward the inevitable and agonizing decision that would end his service in the United States Army. A sensitive, perceptive, gentle man, he was horror-stricken by the knowledge of what lay before him and his country.

Along with many of his fellow Army officers, Mordecai was forced by the advent of the Civil War to make a most difficult choice. Southern

---

Reprinted with permission from *Publications of the American Jewish Historical Society* 48 (1959): 147–169, copyright © 1959 by the American Jewish Historical Society.

born and oriented, he was sympathetic to the Southern position. The other members of his father's large family were scattered throughout Virginia, North Carolina, and Alabama, and Mordecai was closely bound to them by strong ties of loyalty and affection. On the Northern side, Mordecai had served the United States faithfully for more than forty years, and he loved and firmly believed in the Union. His wife, Sara, moreover, and their children were all Northern by birth and belief. And finally, he was, above all, a conscientious, sincere, and highly honorable man. Torn by divided allegiances, he postponed his choice as long as he could. But in the spring of 1861, when further delay was no longer possible, he made the only decision that logic and conscience allowed.[2]

Mordecai's views on the major questions dividing the nation can best be described as moderate or, in his own words, "conservative opinions." Above all, he desired the preservation of the Union and saw "no hope for the country if divided."[3] Such a division, he believed, would split the nation "into incoherent fragments, to become the inveterate foes of each other, and the scorn and contempt of the rest of the world." He had "no patience to think of the spectacle" that America would present under these circumstances, and "no disposition to join in the miserable strife" that would result.[4]

He viewed with growing annoyance, disgust, and apprehension the activities of extremists on both sides. In 1850, when he was still confident that a peaceful and satisfactory solution could be found to the problems dividing North and South, he suggested, as his own "favorite plan" for ending tensions, the hanging of "a dozen or twenty politicians—without being very particular in the choice of them either."[5] But as the heat of the intersectional dispute intensified, his jocular tone changed to one of growing dread. He condemned abolitionism, that "wide spread sentiment at the North, . . . grown to a fearful extent within a few years"[6] and at the same time denounced the "madness and folly" of Southern radicals.[7] The extremists were leading the country to civil war, a prospect "dreadful to contemplate,"[8] which must be averted by all means possible. "How much easier and better it would be to sit down in peace," he exclaimed, "than to purchase it with the horrors of revolution and civil war!"[9]

Mordecai saw the quarrel between North and South as basically "a struggle about the institution of slavery," and here, while he completely opposed the North "for attempting to interfere," he had "no sympathy" for the Southern "feeling, or doctrine rather, as lately inculcated."[10] From boyhood, he had looked upon slavery in the United States "as the

Alfred Mordecai in uniform. Courtesy of The Jacob Rader Marcus Center of the American Jewish Archives.

greatest misfortune and curse that could have befallen us," and he had often thought of how "prosperous" might have been the states of the upper South had they been "relieved from this incubus." That slavery had been maintained, however, he firmly believed to have been the result of Northern abolitionist activities. Furthermore, slavery had been "expressly protected" by the Constitution, and those who had retained it were "entitled to the enforcement of their constitutional rights with regard to it, both in the letter and the spirit."[11] Mordecai's Southern relatives had been slaveholders at least as far back as he could remember; indeed, his brother George, a wealthy Raleigh businessman, owned about one hundred slaves.[12] Yet, while Mordecai believed that Negroes were better off as slaves in America than "as savages in Africa, or than they would be as freemen," he "never wished to be one of the agents in thus bettering their condition." He had owned but one slave in his life, and he had purchased her only to free her.[13] In sum then, while deploring slavery, he had "no objection to its existence, under the circumstances in which we have it here," and, while condemning Southern extremism, he was "utterly averse to any participation in the schemes for destroying, or weakening, the hold of the masters on their slaves, unless they themselves shall be willing to abandon it."

He hoped, until the very end, that some solution might be found, that both sides might "yet see the utter madness" of the course they were pursuing to their "ruin." The South had a "duty" to "try all constitutional remedies, before resorting to the extreme of revolution." But Southerners also had "the right to judge of the injury" that they had sustained or with which they were threatened, and "of the remedy and redress" that they should seek. And should the majority of them believe their "existence and happiness" to be "inconsistent with the maintenance of the Union," then, declared Mordecai, "let them go in peace."[14]

It is not clear just when Mordecai first realized that Civil War was inevitable, and that it would force a fateful decision upon him. Until 1850, at least, he had no doubt that some "final adjustment" could be worked out,[15] and it was not until late 1859 that political questions began to intrude in his personal correspondence. Prior to that time, while becoming increasingly aware of the growing tensions, he tended to avoid discussion of the problems they raised. John Brown's raid on the Harpers Ferry Armory in October, 1859, however, brought home to him the extent of the growing schism. It raised dramatically the prospect of civil war, and filled him with "many anxious thoughts." Living as he was at Watervliet Arsenal, in the heart of the North, he found few kindred souls with whom to discuss the great questions of the day. Only to his family did he express his growing anxiety. In hopes of encouraging moderate views in the North, he sent to the editor of the *Albany Argus* part of a letter from his brother Samuel that had taken a critical but restrained view of the Brown incident. He saw in such moderate opinions, still evident in some areas of the North, the only hopes for avoiding an intersectional conflict.[16]

During 1860, he watched with growing apprehension and dread the increasing antagonisms on both sides. Nor was he encouraged by the nominations for that year's presidential election. Lincoln and his party, he believed, promised no good for the South. Stephen A. Douglas was, or would soon be, "driven into opposition," and might any day be seen "in the Republican ranks." Nothing could be expected of John Bell, the Unionist candidate. And even if John C. Breckinridge, "the only hope of peace and safety for the South," was elected, this would but postpone "the evil day" when the growing population of the North would make Republican success a certainty.[17] Mordecai himself was "willing to put up" with any party save the Republican, in hopes that the four years before the next presidential contest might bring some means of saving "our goodly fabric from ruin."[18] Apparently he felt that some temporary solution, at least, might be reached to prevent any political or economic upheaval, for during the summer and fall he made several investments in North Carolina state bonds.[19] And even when Lincoln was elected, he took heart from the fact that the Republicans were a minority in the new Congress and, as such, could do nothing "seriously injurious" to the South.[20] As late as mid-December, 1860, then, only three days before South Carolina seceded, Mordecai was still seeking to buy additional North Carolina bonds.[21]

By now, however, he had begun to think seriously about the course he should pursue in the event of the disruption of the Union. Eschewing any public declaration of his intentions, he condemned his fellow officers who had already taken actions or made statements that might tend to encourage those "trying to precipitate dissension." He, himself, intended to continue to discharge his duty and to "uphold conservative opinions" until the future was clear, believing that in this manner he would be doing his best "to discourage the mad proceedings of fanatics, North or South." Should "the worst" occur, it would then be time enough for him to act, "and you may be sure," he wrote his brother George, "that I shall not be found in opposition to my own people."[22]

In his attempt to follow a moderate course, Mordecai encountered no adverse pressure from friends and relatives. Some, like his old friend and colleague Major Benjamin Huger of South Carolina, later to accept a Confederate commission, urged moderation, patience, and hope.[23] Others, like Sara, his wife, and their children, remained silent, understanding the difficulty of the decision before him, and, by their restraint, assisting him in his attempt to maintain a neutral course.[24] While still others, like his sister Caroline, could only sympathize with his plight, but offer nothing in the way of a solution.[25] The fact that his mother, brothers, and sisters, and their families were living in the South was, in itself, an argument for Mordecai to make a quick decision in favor of the South. But it was for the most part a silent argument, for, until the spring of 1861, his relatives, despite their strong feelings, limited themselves to expressions of the Southern viewpoint, and at no time attempted to persuade Mordecai to cast his lot with them.

The first definite endeavor to bring Mordecai South was made by North Carolina's Governor John W. Ellis, on January 15, 1861. Knowing Major Mordecai to be a native of his state, he requested Representative Warren Winslow, also of North Carolina, to offer him "a good position and a good salary" if he would resign from the Army and take on "the work of putting N. C. on a war footing." Winslow forwarded this offer to Mordecai through a mutual friend, Captain Theodore T. S. Laidley, despite Laidley's advice that Mordecai would probably decline.[26]

Mordecai's reaction was as Laidley had predicted. Through Laidley, he informed Congressman Winslow that he was declining Ellis's offer, while at the same time he wrote George Mordecai, in Raleigh, asking him to inform the governor of his decision. The "controlling reason" for this, he told his brother, was that he refused to "do anything to sanction or encourage revolutionary measures," so long as there was "the least hope of an adjustment of our national trouble." On this course he was determined. "I shall continue to discharge my duty," he declared, "in the fervent hope that the calamity which has befallen us may yet be remedied without bloodshed, and that the alternative of choosing sides in a civil war may never be presented to me."[27]

In addition to the North Carolina offer, there was also some talk in Virginia of asking Mordecai to head an Ordnance Corps in a new state military organization. Here, however, there was doubt as to whether or not he would accept service in that state in preference to North Carolina, and no offer, even as informal and indefinite as that of Governor Ellis, was made. Mordecai learned of this through a nephew, who tended to take a disparaging view of the entire matter. Not only were the chances of an offer doubtful, he explained, but the salary was "no great shakes either."[28] Needless to say, Mordecai made no attempt to acquire further information. As he wrote his sister in early February about these Southern offers: "As long as there seems to be any *possibility*, (not to say *hope*!) of continuing to serve the *United* states, I shall make no other arrangement and give no encouragement to think that I shall make any other."[29]

In March, came another offer from the South, this one a definite and important one. On the 4th of that month, Colonel William J. Hardee of the new Confederate army, a former United States cavalry officer and a good friend of Mordecai's, wrote to extend an offer from President Jefferson Davis. Davis, who had known and respected Mordecai for many years, did not want "to seduce any officer from his allegiance," but he believed that Mordecai was "a true Southerner" in his feelings," and might prefer service in the Army of the Confederate States." There was to be a Corps of Engineers and a Corps of Artillery—the latter would be charged with Ordnance duties—and the President, Hardee informed Mordecai, "would be pleased to place you at the head of either as you may elect." If he desired to accept, Mordecai was to telegraph Hardee the words "I will," or "I will accept."[30]

Mordecai lost no time in replying to Hardee, and his answer was brief and to the point. While "truly grateful" to Davis "for this new proof of his good opinion," Mordecai was "compelled to decline entertaining" the President's offer. Nor would he explain his reasons. "I will only say," he added, "that my decision on the subject was made on the occasion of a previous proposition of a similar kind"—presumably the offer from North Carolina.[31] To his brother George, he explained that he was still "determined to remain at liberty to adopt, in my own time, such a course as my deliberate judgment on the progress of events may dictate."[32] His refusal of a Southern commission left Davis no choice but to offer the post of Chief of Ordnance to Captain Josiah Gorgas, the only other ordnance officer then available, who received the appointment by default.[33]

Not all of the pressures for Mordecai to join the Confederacy came from the South. As a Southerner commanding the most important arsenal in the country, he was subject to growing suspicion by those unfamiliar with his high standards of honor. This suspicion might well have driven a weaker or more self-interested officer South. But it did not affect Mordecai's determination to bide his time and then take only the course he knew to be right.

Until he made the final decision concerning his future, Mordecai, like most of the other officers facing a similar choice, continued to work and carry out his duties to the best of his ability. Beginning in mid-January, 1861, after Mississippi and Alabama had followed South Carolina from the Union, Watervliet Arsenal began to receive an ever-growing flood of orders for supplies. There were orders for artillery, carriages, and ammunition, for harnesses and small-arms cartridges, for muskets and for gunpowder. Everything that could be manufactured, taken from storage, purchased, or obtained from other nearby arsenals was being shipped in response to these orders. A large part, if not all, of the ordnance supplies for the projected expeditions to Fort Pickens and other Gulf forts were shipped from Watervliet. "We are fabricating and issuing, by day and night," noted one of Mordecai's officers.[34] More men were hired, the shops were lit by gas for night work, and Mordecai had little time for anything other than filling supply orders.

Despite his preoccupation with these duties, Mordecai was forced to interrupt his routine to answer charges by those suspicious of his Southern birth. In December, 1860, at the direction of the Ordnance Office, he had sold to Gazaway B. Lamar, a Southern purchasing agent, 10,000 old obsolete muskets that the Ordnance Department had long since declared to be useless for military service. There was nothing unusual about the sale—similar transactions had been carried out before with both Northern and Southern purchasers, when anyone could be found to buy the old weapons—and Secretary of War John B. Floyd has been cleared of charges that he was selling arms to the South with malice aforethought.[35] In December, 1860, however, many Northerners took a dim view of making any arms, however unserviceable, available for Southern use. Late that month, the New York *Evening Post* printed a rumor about Lamar's muskets, and asked caustically, "Where is General Wool?"[36]

Major General John E. Wool, a veteran officer with a distinguished career dating back to the War of 1812, commanded the Department of the East, which included New York State. In this capacity, he had no authority whatsoever over Watervliet Arsenal, which was responsible only to the Ordnance Department. Yet he was hardly a man to take a slur lying down, and he was used to having his way. Accordingly, after sending off a sharp note to the editor of the *Evening Post* explaining his lack of authority, he wrote another to Mordecai, demanding to know what was going on at the arsenal. Mordecai was then away from Watervliet on temporary duty, or else he would have certainly refused to answer Wool's peremptory demand. But the young lieutenant he had left in charge of the post failed to realize, or thought it more discreet to overlook, Wool's lack of authority, and sent the general a brief report of the arms transaction. This apparently satisfied Wool, but Mordecai would hear from him again.[37]

Before he did, however, in mid-January, 1861, he felt constrained to write a letter of explanation to Colonel Henry K. Craig, the Chief of Ordnance, about another matter of a similar nature. Already rumors had begun to spread about the dangers involved in leaving a Southerner in command of Watervliet Arsenal, about supplies being shipped to the Confederacy, and about the possibility "that Major Mordecai was unsound."[38] In 1859, the arsenal foreman had designed and built a new machine for the production of bullets. As was his custom in such cases, and as was perfectly permissible, Mordecai had allowed the foreman, on his own time and at his own expense, to have copies made of the plans of the machine and to sell them to a local machinist. But with a cautious eye to the heightened tensions of the day, Mordecai now wrote Craig an explanation of the entire matter, and offered to recall the plans. As he pointed out, however, there was no requirement for secrecy at the arsenals, and the machine could be seen by any visitor and, since it was not patented, reproduced by any intelligent mechanic.

Craig must have agreed, for there is no indication that any further action was taken on the matter. Nor does it seem to have started any rumors or gossip at the time. Later in the year, however, after Mordecai had left Watervliet, there were a few newspaper charges that he had "had a hand in a transfer of the patterns for the bullet machine . . . inconsistent with the interests of the Government."[39] But he was able to refute these charges effectively by sending each paper a brief explanation and a copy of his original letter to Craig. That letter undoubtedly saved him a good deal of trouble and embarrassment.

It did not, however, prevent an encounter with General Wool. The Ordnance Department had always procured from private manufacturers a large part of the supplies it distributed. In January, 1861, in order to ensure speedy fulfillment of the heavy supply orders suddenly pouring into Watervliet, Mordecai had contracted with two private workshops in Troy for the manufacture of brass fuze plugs for shells. News of this reached the suspicious General Wool in the form of rumors that a former employee of the arsenal, with the assistance of Mordecai's foreman, was manufacturing machines for making fuzes for the South. This time Wool was not satisfied to write Mordecai a letter, but instead sent his aide to the arsenal to check on the matter.

Mordecai had not forgotten the first instance of Wool's interference, and he was determined to set no precedent recognizing that Wool had any authority over him. Should he admit to any such authority, he would only invite continued interference by Wool in arsenal matters. The peremptory old general might seriously interfere with the smooth workings at Watervliet, at a time when the post was swamped with large and important supply orders. Accordingly, he told Wool's aide, to use that officer's words, that "he did not know anything of it [the matter of the fuzes], and really wished the General would address the authorities at Washington if he desired to know anything of the Arsenal"—and then cut short the interview.[40]

Temporarily thwarted, and probably fuming, Wool, without Mordecai's foreknowledge, sent for the arsenal foreman, who promptly denied that he knew anything of the matter.[41] After mulling on this for several weeks, Wool again took the bit between his teeth and decided to report the entire incident to Winfield Scott, the Army's aging Commanding General. Not only did he complain about Mordecai's "great want of courtesy to a superior officer," but he also dredged up the matter of the 10,000 old muskets sold to G. B. Lamar. There was only one way, wrote Wool, to stop such activities, and that was to make the arsenal subject to his "inspection"—or, in other words, his control.[42]

When Wool's report on Watervliet was referred to Colonel Craig, he immediately came to the arsenal commander's defense. "I feel confident," he wrote of Mordecai, "that he would not permit anything to be done, by anyone employed at the Arsenal, prejudicial to the interests of the United States." As further proof that Mordecai "appreciated the responsibilities resting upon him," Craig enclosed a copy of Mordecai's earlier letter concerning the bullet machine. Turning then to Wool's request that Watervliet be made subject to his inspection, the Chief of Ordnance chose to ignore the general's obvious effort to gain control of the arsenal. Instead, he merely pointed out that Ordnance regulations called for inspections to be made by an ordnance officer, and that the Ordnance Department had sufficient officers, properly trained, to carry out this task.[43]

Having taken care of Wool's complaint to Scott, Colonel Craig turned to Mordecai for his version of the matter,[44] which the Watervliet commander provided by return mail. In a lengthy letter to the Chief of Ordnance, Mordecai explained his handling of Wool's aide, pointed out that no ordnance establishment in the country had ever made any attempt whatsoever at conducting operations in secret, and stated that as long as the manufacture of cannon, small arms, ammunition, and other supplies was contracted to private manufacturers it was impossible to keep this material secret.

Mordecai was particularly disturbed by Wool's "imputation of censure" of his conduct as commander of Watervliet Arsenal. Since the general's letter to Scott had asked for control only of Watervliet, rather than of all the arsenals in the Department of the East, it was obvious, felt Mordecai, that he was being singled out for special attention. "I invite," he declared, "the most rigid scrutiny into my administration of the arsenal; and I trust that, in common justice, no effect will be given to the imputation referred to, until such a scrutiny shall have been made, by a Court of Inquiry or other competent authority."[45]

Craig forwarded Mordecai's letter to General Scott, with his own favorable concurring endorsement.[46] This ended the matter, and Mordecai had no more trouble from the fiery General Wool.

Despite the suspicions and difficulties Mordecai encountered because of his Southern birth, and despite the knowledge that the Confederacy offered him rank and position, the acceptance of which would be no dishonor, he continued to discharge his duties "faithfully and zealously, without any reservation or arrière-pensée."[47] The increasing volume of orders for supplies occupied him constantly at the arsenal, and there was no slackening in his efforts to carry them out. "I shall continue to execute them as fast as possible," he told Colonel Craig.[48]

But even as he labored on, the news from the South became more and more depressing. As, one after another, efforts to find a solution to the great problem splitting the country were unsuccessful, Mordecai became increasingly pessimistic.[49] By the middle of March, 1861, he realized that he could not put off a decision much longer. He still hoped to avoid one, but, if and when it became necessary, he now knew what he planned to do.

So far, he had given neither his relatives in the South nor his immediate family around him any more than a hint of what action he intended. On the morning of March 18th, he sat down with Sara and the children and read them a long letter that he had started the day before to his brother Samuel in Richmond. "In these calamitous times," he began, "it is well that relatives and friends should understand each other's positions, and as my views may not be fully known by our family, I will devote this leisure Sunday to communicating to you so much of them at least as may influence my own action in relation to public affairs."

The letter outlined his thoughts and feelings on the issues of the day: his belief in the South's constitutional right to maintain slavery, and his recognition of the North's abhorrence of that institution; his condemnation of extremists on both sides; his opinion that secession was unnecessary but legitimate; and his conclusion that splitting the nation would be a spectacular tragedy. He had "no disposition," he explained, "to join in the miserable strife which will result from the entire rupture of our Union. If I am doomed to witness that calamity . . . , you know that I would not take sides against the south; but . . . I should be almost equally reluctant to enter the ranks against those with whom I have been so long associated on terms of close intimacy and friendship." He hoped to avoid a decision, but, should civil war occur, his "first wish" would be to retire to private life, and find some "civil pursuit" by means of which he could support his family during the "miserable remnant" of his days. He wished that his "southern friends" would understand his position, and he knew that they would "appreciate" his motives "for adhering to the last, to the hope, even the most feeble, of a re-adjustment" that might "repair this incredible calamity." Should his "family relations with the north" exert any influence on his final decision, he knew that he would "not be liable to misconstruction" by those in the South.[50]

Having made up his mind, Mordecai could now only wait and hope and continue his work. Rumors that he would resign and join the Confederacy grew stronger in the area around Watervliet, and when he left for Fort Monroe, at Craig's direction, in early April, some of the local newspapers carried charges that he was deserting to the South. The fact that Sara and their daughter Laura accompanied him—in order to pay a long-promised visit to Mordecai's eighty-six-year-old mother in Richmond—seemed to lend credence to the accusations. Hardly had he reached Fort Monroe, however, when the attack on Fort Sumter recalled him to Watervliet. Stopping in Richmond on April 13th to pick up Sara and Laura, he heard the news of Sumter's surrender that day. His brother George urged him to resign from the Army immediately, and it was now clear to Mordecai that he could no longer postpone his decision.[51]

There remained one final chance of avoiding this decision. He telegraphed his old friend Major Benjamin Huger, himself in the process of resigning, to meet him in Baltimore, where the two conferred briefly and agreed on a possible solution. Then he hurried on to New York, where, on April 15th, as Lincoln issued his first call for volunteers, he took a few moments to send a hasty personal note to Colonel Craig. This letter contained his last hope of remaining in the United States Army.

Briefly outlining to the Chief of Ordnance his unwillingness to continue supervising the production of munitions to be used against his relatives and friends, Mordecai requested that he be relieved of command of Watervliet Arsenal and transferred to an area like California, where he believed he might be free from involvement in any possible military operations.[52] This, he felt, was the only way he could remain in the Army. He sought it, out of consideration for his family, in "the hope, however small, of better times."[53]

Back at Watervliet, Mordecai immediately threw himself into the heavy work at the arsenal while awaiting a reply from Craig.[54] Events beyond his control, however, now took a hand to remove his one last chance of staying in the Army. On April 19th, Craig wrote Mordecai that he "thought well" of his request for a transfer, and that he would write him "further on the subject."[55] But before he could so, or take any other action on the transfer, he fell ill. His absence from duty at this critical moment in the nation's history irked the new Secretary of War, Simon Cameron, who promptly assigned the post of Chief of Ordnance to the next senior ordnance officer, Lieutenant Colonel James W. Ripley. The change, ostensibly temporary, was, in fact, permanent, and Ripley was to take a different view of Mordecai's request than had Craig.[56]

Mordecai, meanwhile, continued to work frantically at the job of filling the large and urgent supply orders that were pouring into the arsenal. Despite his loyal and energetic efforts, he found himself more and more the object of local suspicion and mistrust, feelings increased, no doubt, by the secession of Virginia on April 17th.[57] On the 20th, still without an answer to his letter to Craig, he received a note from the Chief of Ordnance, dated the 18th, that only increased his frustration. Local founders around Watervliet, Craig said, had complained to the Secretary of War that Mordecai's orders for shot and shells from private workshops were going only to those who had been "busy in furnishing supplies to the seceding states." Without commenting on these complaints, Craig suggested that Mordecai so distribute his orders "as to give no cause for rumors" that they were being "given to the enemies of the Union."[58]

Craig's note only served to underline a letter that Mordecai had received a day or so earlier from Raleigh. In this letter, his brother George had urged him to resign his commission at once "and accept service in the Southern army." Furiously attacking Lincoln's "absurd and violent measures," George called for "every friend of the South and especially every Southern man to take a firm decided stand" against them. Then he outlined the practical reasons why Mordecai should join the Confederacy. Mordecai's ties, said George, were almost entirely with the South, and his feelings and opinions were Southern. If he resigned and remained in the North, he would be regarded with "jealousy and suspicion," and constantly insulted and abused, and might even be forced into a state militia to fight against the South. The Confederacy, on the other hand, offered "honor and distinction" in military service, or, if he desired, a much better opportunity for civilian employment, as well as the warm welcome of family and friends.[59]

There was considerable truth in George's reasoning, but to this letter, and a similar one written two days later, Mordecai could only reply with a plea for patience. "You have no adequate idea," he wrote, "of the state of things in this quarter."[60] At the Mordecai home in Richmond, meanwhile, the air was crisp with tension and "painful excitement." "Everybody anxiously inquires what is Major Mordecai going to do," reported Emma Mordecai, "and we answer we do not know."[61]

By April 23rd, having still received no reply to his request for a transfer, and unaware that on that very day Craig was being replaced as Chief of Ordnance,[62] Mordecai sent the colonel an angry and urgent letter. He was angry because Craig had seen fit to pay attention to what Mordecai rightfully felt were unjust criticisms of his purchases of ordnance supplies from private workshops. The mildness of Craig's note of the 18th on this subject had not disguised its implied rebuke. "It must be obvious to you," snapped Mordecai, "that if the commanding officer of the arsenal is to be subject to the surveillance of irresponsible persons, who are interested in misrepresenting his actions, and still more, if he have not the confidence of the head of the Ordnance Department, it is impossible for him to discharge his duties properly." His request of the 15th for a transfer, Mordecai continued, had been in anticipation of just such difficulties. On the assumption that Craig had not received that request, he was renewing it now. Since he himself could not leave the arsenal, he was giving his letter to Lieutenant Horace Porter, one of his officers, for delivery, and he begged Craig for a "prompt answer by the same officer."[63]

Craig's reply to Mordecai's original request for transfer, delayed when riots in Baltimore disrupted mail service in and out of Washington, reached Watervliet on April 24th, the day after Porter had left for the capital.[64] The brief but encouraging note must have lifted Mordecai's sagging spirits, for he still was unaware that Craig had been relieved, and he waited impatiently for Porter's return with the hoped-for transfer from Watervliet.

Lieutenant Porter, meanwhile, aware of the interruption to rail service through Baltimore, had boarded a troop transport in New York, to come by sea, and did not reach Washington until April 29th. Hastening to the Ordnance Office, he found Lieutenant Colonel Ripley in charge.[65] Ripley and his assistant, Captain William Maynadier, were both as busy as two men could be in trying to supervise and co-ordinate the vast flood of orders rushing in and out of the Ordnance Office, but they stopped for a minute to read Mordecai's letter, and to consider how to answer it. Unlike Craig, Ripley was unwilling to grant Mordecai's request for transfer. He regarded Mordecai as one of his ablest officers, and he needed him at Watervliet. There would be little left of military discipline and organization if assignments were to be based on personal wishes rather than on the needs of the service. Regretfully, but correctly, the Chief of Ordnance concluded that he must refuse the request, whatever the consequences.

Both Ripley and Maynadier knew and respected Mordecai, and they hoped to send him a reply that would, while denying him a transfer, dissuade him from resigning. To Maynadier, whose friendship with Mordecai was especially close, fell the task of composing a reply for Ripley's signature.

> Your application to be relieved from duty at Watervliet Arsenal [read the letter] is not founded on any grounds that would induce me to recommend a compliance with it, at any time, and especially now when your valuable services are so necessary. I am not aware of any failure on your part to give satisfaction to the government in your official capacity, and whatever idle rumors or vague charges may have arisen from the excitement of the times, or the pique or malice of disappointed or bad men, they have not, and shall not affect in the estimation of this Department, or elsewhere so far as I have the power to prevent it, the high character for capability, for industry and for intelligence in the discharge of your professional duties, and for integrity and fidelity in all things which you have established by useful and faithful service to the government of the United States during so many years. You may rest assured that the character and reputation of no officer shall suffer from any imputations that may be brought against him for the honest and faithful discharge of his duties to the United States Government, so far as my efforts to protect him can possibly be exerted.

Then, turning back to the business of preparing for war, the letter closed with an order for artillery equipment urgently needed in Washington.[66]

Lieutenant Porter returned to Watervliet with Colonel Ripley's letter on May 2nd.[67] Mordecai knew by now of Craig's relief,[68] so he may have already guessed at the contents of the letter Porter carried. At any rate, Ripley's tone of finality convinced Mordecai that there was "no hope of a different decision,"[69] and he wasted no time in replying.

First, he addressed a brief note to the Adjutant General of the Army: "I hereby tender the resignation of my commission as Major of Ordnance in the Army of the United States, and request that it may be accepted by the President."[70] Enclosing this in a letter to Ripley, he thanked the Chief of Ordnance for the "complimentary terms" of his letter of the 29th, and stated that "peculiar circumstances," unnecessary to explain further, made it impossible for him to remain at Watervliet. Since he no longer had any hope of being relieved, he was resigning from the Army. He was submitting his resignation through Ripley, so that the latter could pick a new arsenal commander before forwarding it to the Adjutant General. "After thirty-eight years of faithful service," wrote Mordecai, "I trust that I need not assure you that the public interests here will, in the mean time, be perfectly safe in my hands." He closed with the wish that his replacement would arrive soon, and that "a suitable inspection" might be made of the Arsenal before he departed. The letter was signed simply, "A. Mordecai," without the indication of rank and branch with which he had been closing official letters for nearly four decades.[71]

In a separate, personal letter to Ripley, Mordecai expressed his regrets at the step he had been forced to take. He recommended a successor for the Watervliet command, and assured Ripley that he would keep his resignation a secret until the new commander arrived, or until it was announced in Washington, so as not to interfere with operations at the arsenal. He had "no intention of joining the Southern army," but would take his family to Sara's home in Philadelphia, "and make arrangements for my future life."[72]

Having taken this final step, Mordecai threw himself back into the work at the arsenal, at which he continued until he was relieved.[73] Ripley received Mordecai's letters and resignation on May 5th, and, the next day, forwarded the resignation to the Adjutant General. By the 10th, it had been accepted by Secretary of War Cameron and President Lincoln, effective as of the 5th. A note from the Ordnance Office informed Mordecai that the officer he had recommended to replace him at Watervliet would be there as soon as he himself could be relieved. But on May 14th, even before Mordecai's successor arrived, a copy of the War Department order announcing Mordecai's resignation reached the arsenal. On that day, accordingly, he relinquished the Watervliet command to the next-ranking officer on the post and began preparations to leave.[74]

Mordecai's resignation produced varied reactions. Many of his friends, both Northern and Southern, were sympathetic and understanding, although some on both sides regretted his decision to remain neutral.[75] His fellow Army officers who knew him well were probably the most understanding of all. From Captain Maynadier, who, ironically, was promoted to major to fill the position vacated by his old friend, came a brief but warm note, regretting Mordecai's resignation, but expressing respect for his judgment. "I offer you no compliment," he said. "I would scorn to flatter such a man as I know you to be—but I cannot express the sorrow I feel at losing such a comrade and such an officer."[76] And a young lieutenant named Stephen Vincent Benet, then teaching at West Point and later to be Chief of Ordnance, summed up the feeling of many officers at the resignation of Mordecai and others like him:

> And so one by one [he wrote Mordecai] the shining lights of the Ordnance are being extinguished, and those of us who are left cannot but grieve at the sad necessity that forces our best officers from the Army. In your retirement you will at least have the consoling reflection that your honors have not equalled your deserts, and that your resignation received the approval of your own conscience.[77]

Not everyone was as kind as this, however. Some of the Troy and Albany newspapers picked up and published the news of Mordecai's resignation even before it was officially announced. Initial editorial comment was adverse, and in the Troy area the "lower class of the population," in Mordecai's words, "were in the greatest excitement," calling for his arrest and even threatening personal violence to prevent him from joining the Confederacy. Mordecai's friends among the "higher class of people" remained steadfast, however, and extended their sympathy and assistance.

As soon as the press published news of his resignation, Mordecai wrote letters of full explanation to the local editors, and released to them copies of some of the official correspondence concerning his resignation. He made it clear that he intended to sit out the war as a civilian. Publication of these letters, and of sympathetic editorials and other letters by his friends, helped to calm public sentiments. Mordecai himself, busy at the arsenal anyway, made a point of avoiding public appearances, and the excitement soon died down. Nevertheless, on about the 24th of May, when he and his family were packed and ready to go, they deemed it safer to leave the arsenal quietly and at night. And on at least two occasions, later in the year, Mordecai felt constrained to answer newspaper charges that he had turned over material to the South while at Watervliet.[78]

In the South, meanwhile, the other members of the Mordecai family had no word of their brother, and could only hope for his safety. They hesitated to communicate with him directly through the mails, lest correspondence from Richmond or Raleigh cause him to fall under suspicion, and sent their letters via circuitous channels.[79] A note from George urged Mordecai to come to North Carolina and accept a military command. The state he wrote, was "in a perfect sink of anarchy and confusion," and badly in need of a good military leader. Scarcely a day passed that he was not asked whether his brother "would come on and accept the appointment of commander in chief."[80] His sister Ellen also urged Mordecai to come where he was "not only desired, but needed in directing the military affairs" of North Carolina. The family made promises of assistance, and offered to provide a home for Mordecai and his family. Similar offers came from Southern friends.[81]

North Carolina officials trying frantically to organize the state's military forces took heart from Mordecai's resignation, and spoke confidently of "his probable advancement" to the position of major general in command of state troops.[82] In Richmond, President Davis was informed of the resignation even before it was officially announced or the implementing orders issued by the War Department. Still anxious to secure Mordecai's services, he asked Samuel Mordecai what his brother intended to do. Now that the major had at last left the Union Army, perhaps he could be persuaded to accept a Southern commission. But Samuel could only refer to Mordecai's statements published in the newspapers that he intended to retire to private life, an intention that Davis hoped would change.[83]

By early June, Mordecai and most of his immediate family were living in Philadelphia. For the first time since he had submitted his resignation, he was able to sit down and write his Southern relatives a lengthy letter, detailing the events of the preceding month, thanking them for their offers of assistance, and again declining to come South. Once more he described his feelings about the great question that had divided the nation, and begged his brothers and sisters to understand his point of view. He depreciated the possible value of his military services to the Confederacy, and pointed out that the loss of his assistance to either side was "by no means" as great as his friends, or his "unfriends," seemed to think. To his regret, his son Alfred, soon to graduate from the United States Military

Academy, was determined to accept his commission. Mordecai emphasized that this was not because of any urging on his part, but was due, rather, to the boy's West Point training and associations. Mordecai, himself, could only repeat that his Southern friends should be content with the "sacrifice" he had made. "Do not cease to love me," he begged.[84]

Mordecai's pleading notwithstanding, it was another two months before his family in the South could completely forgive him for the step he had taken. They did not blame the decision entirely on him, but rather were certain that Sara had persuaded or influenced him in his course. This he was quick to deny. She had acquiesced uncomplainingly in his decision, but had had no part in the making of it. Another sore point with those in the South was young Alfred's determination to fight in the Union Army, and Mordecai's unwillingness to attempt to dissuade him. George Mordecai pointed out that their brother Augustus had two sons in the Confederate Army, as did their brother Solomon, and, said George, "if it will afford Alfred any pleasure or gratification to take the chance of killing or being killed by them, I have nothing to say."[85]

Despite these feelings, the tie of family love and loyalty was too strong to be broken. Early in August, Mordecai received letters from his family that showed the understanding and love his brothers and sisters still bore for him. He read their words of forgiveness through "almost blinding tears" of relief.[86]

Mordecai's military career was now ended. Having taken the decisive step of resigning from the Army, and refusing to join the South, he was faced with the problem of supporting himself and his family. "You cannot know," he wrote his brother Samuel, "what I have sacrificed . . . : the labor of a whole life seems to be rendered useless . . . ; from the enjoyment of easy comfort, and even luxury, my family . . . may soon have to look poverty in the face."[87] Most of his savings were invested in the South, and the family would be dependent on his income. At the age of fifty-seven, for the first time in his life, he was seeking a job.

But what sort of a job? A soldier and a scientist, the only trade he knew was the preparation and testing of the tools of war. Yet he was determined that he would have nothing to do with the prosecution of the Civil War, and this to him meant avoidance of any occupation remotely related to military service. During the war, therefore, he refused many good positions. He declined to serve as a consulting engineer on the repair of Fort Delaware, near Philadelphia. He turned down offers to teach in or administer military schools. He would not accept the position of Inspector General of Kentucky and the job of organizing a force for defense of that state.

Any and all offers of this sort he gratefully but firmly refused.[88] Mordecai was not the only Army officer to resign his commission and refuse to fight for either side—indeed, there were at least thirty others[89]—but it is doubtful if many were as scrupulous in their neutrality as he.

Determined to avoid "all connection with Mil[itar]y Affairs,"[90] Mordecai and his family lived quietly in Philadelphia during the war years. He turned to teaching to support himself, but the bulk of the family income came from a school run by his three daughters.[91] With the end of hostilities, when passions had calmed and rancor eased, he began the search for a new and permanent career. "This great reverse of fortune, in the evening of life," he wrote, "I have endeavored to bear with philosophical patience; solaced by the companionship of my affectionate wife and by the love and good conduct of our dear children; not without also the comfort afforded by the sympathy and regard of many kind and esteemed friends."[92]

NOTES

1. Alfred Mordecai, "Personal Memoranda," p. 86, Alfred Mordecai Papers, Library of Congress, Washington, D.C. This collection is hereinafter cited as AMP. References in this essay to dates and events connected with the start of the Civil War are based on J. G. Randall, *The Civil War and Reconstruction* (Boston: D. C. Heath, 1937), chaps. iv–ix, passim.

2. For Mordecai's life and military career, see Stanley L. Falk, "Soldier-Technologist: Major Alfred Mordecai and the Beginnings of Science in the United States Army," Ph.D. dissertation, Georgetown University, 1959.

3. Mordecai to George Mordecai (a brother), Dec. 17, 1860, George W. Mordecai Papers, Southern Historical Collection, No. 522, University of North Carolina, Chapel Hill, N.C. These papers are hereinafter cited as GWMP. Mordecai's attitudes and feelings that led to his final decision can be reconstructed, in general, from correspondence in AMP and GWMP, especially for the period from Nov., 1859, through June, 1861. Also helpful is the correspondence in Jacob Mordecai Papers, Duke University, Durham, N.C. (hereinafter cited as JMP).

4. Mordecai to Samuel Mordecai (a brother), March 17, 1861, AMP.

5. Mordecai to George Mordecai, Aug. 19, 1860, GWMP.

6. Mordecai to Ellen Mordecai (a sister), Nov. 29, 1869, AMP.

7. Mordecai to Samuel Mordecai, June 2, 1861, AMP. See also Mordecai to [Samuel] Mordecai, Dec. 7, 1859, JMP, and to George Mordecai, Dec. 17, 1860, Jan. 9, 1861, GWMP.

8. Mordecai to Ellen Mordecai, Nov. 29, 1859, AMP.

9. Mordecai to George Mordecai, Jan. 6, 1861, GWMP.

10. Except as indicated, quotations in this paragraph are taken from Mordecai to Samuel Mordecai, June 2, 1861, AMP.

11. Mordecai to Samuel Mordecai, March 17, 1861, AMP.

12. Lizzie Wilson Montgomery, *Sketches of Old Warrenton, North Carolina* (Raleigh: Edwards and Broughton, 1924), pp. 186, 141; Mordecai, "Personal Memoranda," p. 4; "George W. Mordecai Account Book, 1858–1870," GWMP.

13. Mordecai, "Personal Memoranda," reverse of p. 24.

14. Mordecai to Samuel Mordecai, March 17, 1861, AMP.

15. Mordecai to George Mordecai, Aug. 19, 1850, GWMP.

16. Mordecai to Ellen Mordecai, Nov. 29, 1859, AMP, and to [Samuel] Mordecai, Dec. 7, 1859, JMP.

17. Mordecai to George Mordecai, Aug. 7, 1860, GWMP.

18. Mordecai to George Mordecai, Aug. 29, 1860, GWMP.

19. Rosa Mordecai (a daughter) to George Mordecai, Aug. 28, 1860, and Mordecai to George Mordecai, Aug. 29, Sept. 25, 1860, GWMP.

20. Mordecai to Samuel Mordecai, March 17, 1861, AMP. See also Mordecai to [Samuel Mordecai, Nov., 1860], JMP.

21. Mordecai to George Mordecai, Dec. 17, 1860, GWMP.

22. Ibid.

23. Ibid.; Huger to Mordecai, Jan. 11, 26, 1861, AMP.

24. Mordecai to "My dear sister," June 16, 1861, and Sara Mordecai to Ellen Mordecai, Aug. 9, [1861], AMP.

25. Caroline Mordecai to A. Mordecai, March 11, 1861, AMP.

26. Ellis to Winslow, Jan. 15, 1861, encl. to Laidley to Mordecai, Jan. 17, 1861, AMP; Winslow to Ellis (telegram), Jan. 17, 1860 [1861], *War of the Rebellion: A Compilation of the Official Records of the Union and Confederate Armies* (Washington, D.C.: Government Printing Office, 1880–1901), Ser. I, Vol. LI, Pt. 2, p. 7 (hereinafter cited as *Official Records*); Mordecai to George Mordecai, Jan. 20, 26, 1861, GWMP.

27. Mordecai to George Mordecai, Jan. 20, 26, 1861, GWMP. See also George Mordecai to Mordecai, Jan. 23, 1861, AMP.

28. Edmund [Myers] to Mordecai, Jan. 27, 1861, AMP.

29. Mordecai to "My dear sister," Feb. 10, 1861, AMP. Emphasis in original.

30. Hardee to Mordecai, March 4, 1861, AMP.

31. Mordecai to Hardee, March 10, 1861, AMP.

32. Mordecai to George Mordecai, March 10, 1861, GWMP.

33. Frank E. Vandiver, *Ploughshares into Swords: Josiah Gorgas and Confederate Ordnance* (Austin: University of Texas Press, 1952), pp. 52–54, 57, and passim.

34. Lt. George C. Strong to Col. H. K. Craig, April 9, 1861, Records of the Office of the Chief of Ordnance (Record Group 156): Watervliet Arsenal, Letters Sent, National Archives, Washington, D.C. (hereinafter cited as OCO / Watervliet, Ltrs Sent, and as NA). For arsenal work during this period, see other

correspondence in this file and also in OCO: Letters to Ordnance Officers (hereinafter cited as OCO /Ltrs to Ord Ofcrs) and OCO: Watervliet Arsenal, Register of Letters Received, NA.

35. Maynadier to Mordecai (telegram and letter), Nov. 24, 1860, OCO /Ltrs to Ord Ofcrs; Lamar to Mordecai, Dec. 1, 3, 1860, copies in AMP; Mordecai to Lamar, Dec. 2, 1860, OCO /Watervliet, Ltrs Sent; Lamar to Floyd, Nov. 21, 1860, and Floyd to Lamar, Nov. 24, 27, 1860, *Official Records,* Ser. III, Vol. I, pp. 6–7, 9–10; A. Howard Meneely, *The War Department, 1861: A Study in Mobilization and Administration* (New York: Columbia University Press, 1928), pp. 40–47. Copies of many official letters to and from Mordecai that concerned him personally during this period are filed in AMP. Often Mordecai's personal copies bear his own notations, with additional information. Where these have been used, they have been checked against the originals, if possible, or against other copies.

36. Maj. Gen. J. E. Wool to Floyd, Dec. 29, 1860, *Official Records,* Ser. III, Vol. I, p. 21.

37. Wool to Floyd, Dec. 29, 1860, *Official Records,* Ser. III, Vol. I, p. 21; Wool to Mordecai, Dec. 27, 1860, AMP; Lt. Geo. T. Balch to Wool, Dec. 27, 1860, OCO /Watervliet, Ltrs Sent.

38. *Troy Daily News,* May 8, 1861, clipping in AMP. This paragraph is based on this and other similar newspaper clippings from 1861, some unidentified, in AMP, and on Mordecai to Craig, Jan. 17, 1861, OCO /Watervliet, Ltrs Sent.

39. *Troy Daily News,* May 8, 1861, clipping in AMP. Some of the other newspapers that printed similar charges were the Albany *Evening Journal,* the New York *Evening Post,* and the Philadelphia *Inquirer.*

40. Lt. Richard Arnold to Wool, Feb. 1, 1861; Mordecai to Craig, March 2, 1861; copies in AMP.

41. Mordecai to Craig, March 2, 1861, copy in AMP.

42. Wool to Scott, Feb. 25, 1861, copy in AMP.

43. Craig to Lt. Col. L. Thomas, Feb. 27, 1861, copy in AMP.

44. Craig to Mordecai, Feb. 27, 1861, copy in AMP.

45. Mordecai to Craig, March 2, 1861, copy in AMP.

46. Craig to Lt. Col. L. Thomas, March 5, 1861, *A Collection of Annual Reports and Other Important Papers, Relating to the Ordnance Department,* prepared under the direction of Brig. Gen. Stephen V. Benet (4 vols.; Washington, D.C.: Government Printing Office, 1878–1890), III, 567.

47. Mordecai to Samuel Mordecai, March 17, 1861, AMP.

48. Mordecai to Craig, April 17, 1861, OCO /Watervliet, Ltrs Sent.

49. Mordecai to George Mordecai, March 10, 1861, GWMP.

50. Mordecai to Samuel Mordecai, March 17, 1861, and to "My dear sister," June 16, 1861, AMP.

51. Mordecai to Samuel Mordecai, March 17, June 2, 1861; clipping from *Troy Daily News,* May 8, 1861; Mordecai, "Resignation of Major Mordecai: A Card

of Explanation," May 8, 1861, *Troy Daily Whig*, May 9, 1861; Emma Mordecai (a sister) to Sara Mordecai, March 10, 1861; George Mordecai to Mordecai, April 16, 1861; all in AMP.

52. Mordecai made no copy of this letter for himself, and, since it was unofficial, Craig apparently retained or destroyed it, and did not place it in the Ordnance files. There is ample evidence, however, of the contents of the letter. Mordecai to Samuel Mordecai June 2, 1861, AMP; Craig to Mordecai, April 19, 1861, extract copy in AMP; Mordecai to Craig, April 23, 1861, and to Col. J. W. Ripley, May 2, 1861, OCO /Watervliet, Ltrs Sent; Mordecai, "Resignation of Major Mordecai: A Card of Explanation," May 8, 1861, *Troy Daily Whig*, May 9, 1861, AMP; Ripley to Mordecai, April 29, 1861, OCO /Ltrs to Ord Ofcrs; [Rosa Mordecai], biographical sketch of her father, Sept. 29, 1933, partial ms. in AMP.

53. Mordecai to Samuel Mordecai, June 2, 1861, AMP.

54. Ibid.; Mordecai to Craig, April 16, 17, 18, 23, 1861, OCO /Watervliet, Ltrs Sent.

55. Craig to Mordecai, April 19, 1861, extract copy in AMP.

56. Mordecai to Samuel Mordecai, June 2, 1861, AMP; Robert V. Bruce, *Lincoln and the Tools of War* (New York: Bobbs-Merrill, 1956), pp. 27–30.

57. Mordecai, "Resignation of Major Mordecai: A Card of Explanation," May 8, 1861, *Troy Daily Whig*, May 9, 1861, and Mordecai to Samuel Mordecai, June 2, 1861, AMP.

58. Craig to Mordecai, April 18, 1861, copy in AMP.

59. George Mordecai to Mordecai, April 16, 1861, AMP.

60. Mordecai to George Mordecai, April 22, 1861, GWMP.

61. Emma Mordecai to [Sara Mordecai], April 21, 1861, AMP.

62. Adjutant General's Office (hereinafter cited as AGO), Special Order No. 115, April 23, 1861, NA.

63. Mordecai to Craig, and to Lt. Horace Porter, April 23, 1861, AMP.

64. Mordecai's notation on extract copy of Craig to Mordecai, April 19, 1861, AMP.

65. [Rosa Mordecai], biographical sketch of her father, Sept. 29, 1933, partial ms. in AMP; Ripley to Mordecai, April 29, 1861, OCO /Ltrs to Ord Ofcrs.

66. Ripley to Mordecai, April 29, 1861, OCO /Ltrs to Ord Ofcrs; Maynadier to Mordecai, May 6, 1861, and P. E. Berlin [clerk?], Ord. Office, to Mordecai, May 5, 1861, AMP.

67. Notation on copy of Ripley to Mordecai, April 29, 1861, reproduced in unidentified, undated newspaper clipping in AMP.

68. A copy of the order replacing Craig with Ripley was apparently sent to Ordnance installations on April 23rd, its date of issue, or shortly thereafter. OCO /Ltrs to Ord Ofcrs.

69. Mordecai to Samuel Mordecai, June 2, 1861, AMP.

70. Mordecai to AG, May 2, 1861, copy in AMP.

71. Mordecai to Ripley, May 2, 1861, OCO /Watervliet, Ltrs Sent.

72. Mordecai to Ripley, May 2, 1861, in undated clipping from [New York?] *Herald,* AMP.

73. Correspondence to and from Mordecai, May 2–14, 1861, in OCO /Watervliet, Ltrs Sent, OCO /Ltrs to Ord Ofcrs, and OCO: Register of Letters Received, NA.

74. P. E. Berlin to Mordecai, May 5, 1861, and to [Sara Mordecai], May 7, 1861, AMP; Records of the AGO (Record Group 94): Register of Letters Received, No. M-289, 1861, NA; Records of the Office of the Secretary of War (Record Group 107): Register of Letters Received, No. A-347, 1861, NA; AGO, Special Order No. 130, May 10, 1861, NA; Mordecai to Ripley, May 14, 1861, OCO /Watervliet, Ltrs Sent.

75. Mordecai to "My dear sister," June 16, 1861, AMP. See also miscellaneous general correspondence for this period filed here.

76. Maynadier to Mordecai, May 6, 1861, AMP; AGO, General Order No. 24, May 22, 1861, NA.

77. Benet to Mordecai, May 13, 1861, AMP.

78. Mordecai to Samuel Mordecai, June 2, 1861; [Rosa Mordecai], ms. biographical sketch of her father, Sept. 29, 1933; and miscellaneous newspaper clippings, 1861; all in AMP.

79. Samuel Mordecai to George Mordecai, May 3, 1861, GWMP; George Mordecai to Samuel Mordecai, May 5, 1861, JMP; George Mordecai to Mordecai, May 6, 1861, AMP.

80. George Mordecai to Mordecai, May 5, 1861, AMP.

81. Ellen Mordecai to Mordecai, May 28, 1861; Mordecai to Samuel Mordecai, June 2, 1861; Miriam Cohen to Sara Mordecai [May, 1861]; G. Cohen to Mordecai [May, 1861]; A. Minis to Mordecai, May 19, 1861; all in AMP.

82. Maj. W. H. C. Whiting to Brig. Gen. S. Cooper, May 11, 1861, *Official Records,* Ser. I, Vol. LI, Pt. 2, pp. 83–86.

83. D. G. Duncan to Confederate Secretary of War L. P. Walker, May 9, 1861, ibid., p. 74: Samuel Mordecai to George Mordecai, June 9, 1861, GWMP.

84. Mordecai to Samuel Mordecai, June 2, 1861, AMP.

85. George Mordecai to Mordecai, June 26, 1861; Mordecai to Samuel Mordecai, June 2, 1861, to "My dear sister," June 16, 1861, and to "My dear brother and sister," Aug. 9, 1861; all in AMP.

86. Mordecai to "My dear brother and sister," Aug. 9, 1861, AMP.

87. Mordecai to Samuel Mordecai, June 2, 1861, AMP.

88. B. F. Green to Mordecai, Oct. 21, 1861; Benjamin Gratz to Mordecai, Oct. 28, 1862; Mordecai to Gratz, Nov. 4, 1862; Brig. Gen. J. G. Totten to Mordecai [May, 1868]; Mordecai to Totten, May 23, 1863; Mordecai to J. B. Tibbits, April 1, 1864; J. F. Lee to Mordecai, Feb. 9, 22, 1865; Mordecai to Lee (extract copy), Feb. 17, 1865; all in AMP.

89. Ellsworth Eliot, Jr., *West Point in the Confederacy* (New York: G. A. Baker, 1941), p. 11.

90. Mordecai to J. B. Tibbits, April 1, 1864, AMP.

91. [Rosa Mordecai], ms. biographical sketch of her father, and Mordecai to [Ellen Mordecai], Oct. 13, 1861, AMP; Samuel Mordecai to George Mordecai, Jan. 28, 1863, GWMP.

92. Mordecai, "Personal Memoranda," p. 37.

8

Jewish Confederates

Robert N. Rosen

In March 1865, Samuel Yates Levy, a captain in the Confederate army and a prisoner of war at Johnson's Island, wrote to his father J. C. Levy of Savannah, Georgia, "I long to breathe the free air of Dixie." Like the Levy family, southern Jews were an integral part of the Confederate States of America and had been breathing the free air of Dixie for more than two hundred years.

When the Civil War began, there were sizable Jewish communities in all of the major southern cities. Louisiana boasted more than five congregations. New Orleans had the seventh-largest Jewish population in the United States (Boston was sixth and Chicago eighth). In Charleston, South Carolina, home to three congregations (one Reform, one traditional, and one composed of Orthodox Polish immigrants) "Israelites occupy the most distinguished places," according to one Jewish traveler. The Jews of Savannah organized K. K. Mikve Israel in 1735, the third congregation in America, following those in New York and Newport, Rhode Island. There were Jewish communities in Richmond and Petersburg, Virginia; Atlanta, Macon, and Columbus, Georgia; Memphis and Nashville, Tennessee; and Galveston and Houston, Texas, and Jews lived in dozens of small towns throughout the South.[1]

Louisiana was emblematic of the acculturation and assimilation of Jews in the antebellum South. Judah P. Benjamin served as one of the state's U.S. senators. Lieutenant Governor Henry M. Hyams was Benjamin's cousin, having moved to Louisiana with Benjamin from Charleston in

---

Reprinted with permission of Robert Rosen from *Jewish Roots in Southern Soil: A New History*, ed. Marcie Cohen Ferris and Mark I. Greenberg (Lebanon, NH: University Press of New England, 2006), 109–133, copyright © 2006 by Brandeis University Press.

1828. Edwin Warren Moise, also from South Carolina, served as Speaker of the Louisiana House of Representatives and was about to become a Confederate judge. According to the youthful Salomon de Rothschild of the great French banking family, "all these men have a Jewish heart and take an interest in me."[2]

In 1860, Louisiana was home to at least 8,000 Jews, and likely many more. The total number of Jews in the eleven states of the Confederacy was between 20,000 and 25,000, which means that Louisiana was home to 25 to 40 percent of southern Jewry. New Orleans in 1860 was the South's largest city by far. Its population of 168,675 dwarfed Charleston's (40,522), Richmond's (37,910), Mobile's (29,258), and Savannah's (22,292). Like the growing cities of the North and West, New Orleans beckoned to immigrants, and they came.[3]

Southern Jews accepted regional customs and institutions, and most significantly, its greatest pathology, slavery. Oscar Straus put it best when he wrote in his memoirs: "As a boy brought up in the South I never questioned the rights or wrongs of slavery. Its existence I regarded as matter of course, as most other customs or institutions." Jews adopted the "southern way of life," including its code of honor, dueling, slavery, and notions about race and states' rights. In 1862, Bernhard Felsenthal, a northern abolitionist rabbi wrote that "Israelites residing in New Orleans are man by man . . . ardently in favor of secession" and that Jewish German immigrants favored slavery precisely because many non-Jewish German immigrants opposed it. "No Jewish political figure of the Old South ever expressed reservations about the justice of slavery or the rightness of the Southern position," Rabbi Bertram Korn concluded.[4]

Nor is there any evidence that Jews supported slavery as a result of intimidation or fear of reprisals. The Talmud taught Jews that "the law of the land is the law." According to many rabbis, North and South, the Hebrew Bible allowed for slavery. "How dare you . . . denounce slaveholding as a sin?" Rabbi Morris J. Raphall of New York thundered at the abolitionists. "When you remember that Abraham, Isaac, Jacob, Job—the men with whom the Almighty conversed, with whose names he emphatically connects his own most holy name—all these men were slaveholders." Solomon Cohen wrote to his aunt, Rebecca Gratz of Philadelphia, that "God gave laws to his chosen people for the government of their slaves, and did not order them to abolish slavery."[5]

As most Jews in the South in 1861 were struggling or poor immigrants from the German states or eastern Europe, they owned few slaves. Jewish southerners were peddlers, store clerks, innkeepers, cigar makers, teachers, bartenders, petty merchants, tradesmen, and tailors. But they lived in a slaveholding society, and they accepted the institution as part of everyday life. Jews in southern cities and towns who did own small numbers of slaves utilized them as domestic servants or as workers in their trades, or they hired them out. "Acceptance of slavery was," Leonard Dinnerstein writes, "an aspect of southern life common to nearly all its white inhabitants." Indeed, it was common to its free black inhabitants, who owned more slaves than southern Jews. The free blacks of Charleston owned three times the number of slaves owned by Charleston Jewry.[6]

In 1840, three-fourths of all heads of families in Charleston owned at least one slave, and the incidence of slaveholding among Jews likely paralleled that of their neighbors. In Richmond, a few Jewish auctioneers sold slaves, and there was one Jewish slave dealer, Abraham Smith. Richmond's rabbis supported slavery. George Jacobs of Richmond hired a slave to work in his home, although he owned no slaves. Reverend Max Michelbacher prayed during the Civil War that God would protect his congregation from slave revolt and that the Union's "wicked" efforts to "beguile [the slaves] from the path of duty that they may waylay their masters, to assassinate and slay the men, women, and children . . . be frustrated."[7]

Because Jews accepted southern customs and mores, southerners accepted Jews. Most southerners were tolerant of different religions. The Fundamental Constitution of Carolina written by John Locke in 1699 granted freedom of religion to "Ye Heathens, Jues [sic] and other Disenters." Jefferson's celebrated act of religious freedom asserted that "no man shall be compelled to frequent or support any religious worship, place, or ministry whatever." Southern aristocrats, influenced by the Anglican, Episcopalian, Presbyterian, Methodist, and liberal Protestant tradition, had few concerns about Jews in their midst. They found their Jewish neighbors to be law-abiding, educated, and cosmopolitan, characteristics they appreciated. Jewish peddlers, teachers, musicians, lawyers, doctors, druggists, merchants, and men of learning enhanced their quality of life. Because the South attracted few "foreigners," small numbers of white immigrants were more readily accepted. Finally, southerners believed fervently in the God of the Old Testament and respected their Jewish neighbors' knowledge of and historic connection to the Bible. Oscar Straus recalled how his father, who was well versed in biblical literature, translated passages from the Hebrew Bible for local ministers over dinner in their home.[8]

In 1859, the traveling journalist I. J. Benjamin explained Jews' acceptance in the South by noting that white inhabitants "felt themselves united with, and closer to, other whites. . . . Since the Israelite there did not do the humbler kinds of work which the Negro did, he was quickly received among the upper classes and easily rose to high political rank. For this reason, until now, it was only the South which sent Jews to the Senate. Benjamin came from Louisiana; [David Levy] Yulee from Florida." Yulee was born Jewish, married a Gentile, and disassociated himself from his Jewish roots.[9]

This is not to say that there was no antisemitism in the Old South, because there was. It was a fact of life in the nineteenth century. Emma Holmes of Charleston wrote in her diary that she disliked "Sumter [S.C.] very much from the prevalence of sand and Jews, my great abhorrences." By 1862, she blamed all of her ills on the Jews. Jews came into conflict with the majority Christian society on issues such as conducting retail businesses on Sunday. And, of course, southerners often found Jewish customs strange. Maria Bryan Connell of Hancock County, Georgia, had a Jewish houseguest. "I did not at all comprehend the trouble occasioned by their notions of unclean and forbidden food until I had a daughter of Abraham under the roof. She will not eat one mouthful of the finest fresh pork or the most delicate ham," she wrote. It was not, Connell concluded, "an unimportant consideration with her. Pray let this be entre nous, for I feel as if I am in some respect violating the duties of hospitality in speaking of it."[10]

The northern states were not as hospitable to Jews as was the South prior to the Civil War. The first known Jew in Boston was "warned out" in the 1640s. Unlike colonial Charleston, where Jews flourished, Jews were not allowed to live in early colonial Boston. John Quincy Adams referred to David Yulee as the "squeaking Jew delegate from Florida" and to Representative Albert G. Marchand of Pennsylvania as a "squat little Jew-faced rotundity." When the South seceded, the *Boston Evening Transcript*, a Brahmin publication, went so far as to blame secession on southern Jews. Calling Benjamin "the disunion leader in the U.S. Senate," and Yulee ("whose name has been changed from the more appropriate one of Levy or Levi") an ultra-fire-eater, the newspaper claimed that "this peculiar race . . . having no country of their own," desired "that other nations shall be in the same unhappy condition." By 1864, the *New York Times* castigated the Democratic Party because its chairman, August Belmont, was "the agent of foreign jew bankers."[11]

Not all southern Jews supported secession. Edwin De Leon was pro-secession, whereas his brother Camden De Leon, an officer in the army, was clearly uncomfortable with disloyalty to his government. Many were concerned about Lincoln's election and the elevation of an avowed opponent of slavery to the presidency. Simon Baruch, a Prussian immigrant and medical student, carried a lantern in a parade to celebrate secession bearing the words, "There is a point beyond which endurance ceases to be a virtue." After Lincoln's election, Solomon Cohen of Savannah wrote: "our enemies have triumphed." Cohen worried about control of the federal government by "those who hate us and our institutions."[12]

The irony of Jewish slaveowners was not lost on northern critics of slavery. The antislavery senator Benjamin Wade of Ohio referred to Judah Benjamin as an "Israelite with Egyptian principles."[13] The *Jewish Messenger* of New York City called upon American Jewry to "rally as one man for the Union and the Constitution." In April 1861, the Jews of Shreveport, Louisiana, responded with a denunciation of the newspaper and its editor. "[W]e, the Hebrew congregation of Shreveport scorn and repel your advice.... We solemnly pledge ourselves to stand by, protect, and honor the flag, with its stars and stripes, the Union and Constitution of the Southern Confederacy, with our lives, liberty, and all that is dear to us." Max Baer, president of the congregation, asked that newspapers friendly to the southern cause publish their resolution.[14]

Jewish southerners perceived New Englanders as abolitionists who were frequently antisemitic. Theodore Parker, a leading abolitionist minister, believed Jews' intellects were "sadly pinched in those narrow foreheads," that Jews were "lecherous," and "did sometimes kill a Christian baby at the Passover." William Lloyd Garrison, editor of the *Liberator*, once described Judge Mordecai Manuel Noah of New York as "the miscreant Jew," a "Shylock," "the enemy of Christ and liberty," and a descendant "of the monsters who nailed Jesus to the cross." Similar sentiments came from Edmund Quincy, Lydia Maria Child, William Ellery Channing, and Senator Henry Wilson of Massachusetts, all leading abolitionists. Child thought Judaism rife with superstition, claiming that Jews "have humbugged the world." John Quincy Adams opposed slavery and derided Jews.[15]

It is little wonder that there was no great love lost between southern Jews, who were accustomed to being treated as equals, and New Englanders. Isaac Harby, the Charleston journalist and pioneer of the Reform movement in the United States, denounced "the abolitionist society and its secret branches." It came as no surprise to South Carolina Jewry to see the following statement from the *Boston Journal* reprinted in their local newspaper in March 1861: "The Jew, [Benjamin] Mordecai, at Charleston, who gave ten thousand dollars to the South Carolina Government, had just settled with his Northern creditors by paying fifty cents on the dollar. The ten thousand was thus a Northern donation to secession." The *Charleston Daily Courier* called the story "a willful, unmitigated and deliberate falsehood."[16]

The question of why southern Jews fought for the Confederacy is not difficult to answer. "We of the South," Solomon Cohen wrote Rebecca Gratz, "feel that prudence and self-defense demand that we should protect ourselves." Jewish Confederates fought for liberty and freedom, including the right to own slaves. They fought to preserve the southern racial caste system. They fought invaders of their hearth and home. Private Simon Mayer of Natchez wrote to his family: "I sympathize with the poor victims of abolition despotism."[17]

Jewish Johnny Rebs were also motivated by a sense of duty and honor, powerful emotions in Victorian America. "Victorians," James McPherson writes, "understood duty to be a binding moral obligation involving reciprocity: one had a duty to defend the flag under whose protection one had lived." Corporal Isaac Valentine, a fallen Jewish Confederate, was mortally wounded in the same battle as his comrade Gustavus Poznanski Jr. On his deathbed Valentine believed he had done his duty and died for his country.[18]

Letters, memoirs, and obituaries all reflect Jewish soldiers' chief reasons for fighting: to do their duty, to protect their homeland, to protect southern rights and liberty and, once the war began, to support their comrades in arms. Philip Rosenheim of Richmond had just returned home from marching to the Chickahominy and had "fallen into sweet slumber" when his sister Rebecca awoke him. The bells had tolled, informing his militia company to gather. "I was very weak and had a severe headache," he wrote to his family, "but still I dressed myself, buckled on my accouterments, thinking I would not shrink from my duty and would follow the company wherever it goes, as our Flag says, when duty calls tis ours to obey." "We were thoroughly imbued with the idea," Moses Ezekiel of Richmond wrote in his memoirs, "that we were not fighting for the perpetuation of slavery, but for the principle of State's rights and free trade, and in the defense of our homes, which were being ruthlessly invaded."[19] Many a Jewish youth left the German fatherland to avoid military service only to enlist voluntarily in the Confederate army soon after arriving in Dixie.

Isaac Hirsch of Fredericksburg, Virginia, a soldier in the 30th Virginia, visited the battlefield at Second Manassas, where Stonewall Jackson defeated General Pope's army. "It is bad," he wrote in his diary, "that the dead Yankees could not be buried as I don't like to see any human being lay on the top of the earth and rot, but it is a fit emblem for the invader of our soil for his bones to bleach on the soil he invades, especially of a people that wish to be left alone and settle down to their own peaceful pursuits."[20]

Mothers and sisters encouraged Jewish men, like other southern men, to fight. At the start of the war, Catherine Ezekiel, Moses's mother, said that "she would not own a son who would not fight for his home and country." In May 1862, Mary Chestnut wrote of her friend "Mem" Cohen's dedication to the cause in her diary: "Our soldiers, thank God, are men after our own heart, cries Miriam of the house of Aaron." Phoebe Pember recalled that the "women of the South had been openly and violently rebellious from the moment they thought their states' rights touched. . . . They were the first to rebel—the last to succumb."[21]

The social pressure to enlist was also a strong factor in many young Confederates' decision to join the army. According to Gary Gallagher, 75 to 85 percent of the Confederacy's available draft-age white population served in the military. Any young white southern male had a difficult time in 1862 and 1863 explaining why he was not in uniform. Simon Baruch, a Prussian from Schwersenz (and Bernard Baruch's father), immigrated to Camden, South Carolina, as did his younger brother Herman. When Simon enlisted, he admonished Herman to stay out of the war. But Herman joined the cavalry because, as he told Simon, "I could no longer stand it. I could no longer look into the faces of the ladies."[22]

There was also the adventure of war and the bounty paid in advance. Young men unhappy in their work saw a chance to escape. Lewis Leon was such a clerk. An unmarried immigrant, Leon spoke German as well as English and at age nineteen enlisted for six months in the Charlotte Grays, Company C, 1st North Carolina. (Most southerners believed the war would be over in six months.) He was issued a fine uniform. "We were all boys between the ages of eighteen and twenty-one. . . . Our trip was full of joy and pleasure, for at every station where our train stopped the ladies showered us with flowers and Godspeed."[23]

Jewish Confederates, like other immigrants and African Americans, had a special burden during the war. They had to prove that Jews could fight. One of the tenets of nineteenth-century antisemitism was that the Jews were disloyal, unpatriotic, and cowardly. The "Wandering Jew" was the symbolic image of antisemitism. This stereotype labeled Jews as ghetto dwellers from Europe, who refused to assimilate with their neighbors and had fled their homelands to avoid military service. Southern Jewish soldiers set out to disprove these calumnies.[24]

Other Jews fought to make a place in southern society for those who would come after them. Philip Whitlock wrote in his memoir that "especially when I was of the Jewish Faith I thought that if I am negligent in my duty as a citizen of this country, it would unfavorably reflect on the whole Jewish race and religion." Charles Wessolowsky said after the war that "sometimes he felt like a Jewish missionary among the Gentiles to show the way for other Jews to follow." Early twentieth-century Jewish historians were anxious to defend the courage and bravery of the generation that preceded them. "There existed no occasion to threaten the young or, for that matter, the middle-aged, with the 'white feather,'" Ezekiel and Lichtenstein write in *The History of the Jews of Richmond*. "None held back or hesitated."[25]

Finally, Jewish tradition also played a part. From the Book of Esther and Jeremiah ("Seek the welfare of the city to which I have exiled you," Jer. 29:7) to rabbinical law, Judaism taught respect and obedience to the established government. Jews had always aligned themselves with monarchs and conservative regimes for self-protection from the masses. The traditional Jewish prayer for the government, dating to the sixteenth century, called upon God to bless the king and inspire him with benevolence "toward us and all Israel our brethren." As the new Confederacy was now their lawful government, Jewish tradition demanded loyalty to it.[26]

Thus, Jewish Johnny Rebs went off to war for patriotism and love of country, yearning for a fatherland they could believe in, defense of their new homeland, and demonstrating to the North that their rights could not be assailed. Equally compelling were the social pressures to enlist, the frenzy of secession and war, the desire to escape home and see the world, the lure of adventure and money, and to prove that Jews were fighters. "The Jews of the Confederacy had good reason to be loyal to their section," Rabbi Korn concludes. "Nowhere else in America—certainly not in the ante-bellum North—had Jews been accorded such an opportunity to be complete equals as in the old South."[27]

From the top of the social ladder to the bottom, southern Jews supported the Confederate cause. Former Senator Judah Benjamin, one of the South's most brilliant lawyers (President Millard Fillmore nominated him to the Supreme Court, but Benjamin declined the honor), became attorney general of the new Confederate States of America. "A Hebrew of Hebrews, for the map of the Holy City was traced all over his small, refined face," Thomas Cooper DeLeon later recalled, "the attorney-general was of the highest type of his race."[28]

There was little legal work for the new attorney general, and Benjamin rapidly became a close confidant of and political adviser to President Jefferson Davis. A wit, a gourmand, and a raconteur, Benjamin was a popular member of Richmond society. When the secretary of war resigned, Davis asked Benjamin to take his place. Unfortunately Benjamin had no military background. He did bring his well-known capacity for hard work and organization to the War Department, but his tenure was marked by notable failures in the field, for which he received (and accepted) the blame. After the disastrous fall of Roanoke Island, Virginia, in early 1862, Davis promoted Benjamin to secretary of state in "the very teeth of criticism."

Benjamin's Jewish heritage (he did not practice the Jewish religion) was a lightning rod for critics of the Davis administration. Congressman Henry S. Foote of Tennessee, a rabid antisemite, referred to Benjamin as "Judas Iscariot Benjamin" and the "Jewish puppeteer" behind the "Davis tyranny." John M. Daniel of the *Richmond Examiner* reacted to Benjamin's appointment as secretary of state by remarking that "the representation of the Synagogue is not diminished; it remains full." These, however, were minority opinions.[29]

Benjamin continued to serve as Davis's secretary of state. He was to the civilian government what Robert E. Lee was to the military: a loyal, stalwart, indefatigable, and uncomplaining patriot. He was the best-known Confederate official next to the president and vice-president and third in order of succession. Varina Howell Davis called Benjamin her husband's "right arm." Historians have described him as "the President's most intimate friend and counselor." Eli Evans portrayed Benjamin as Davis's alter ego.[30]

As the war dragged on, the Confederacy's options dwindled. On February 12, 1864, the Confederate Congress voted in secret session to create "bodies for the capture and destruction of the enemies' property." The Bureau of Special and Secret Service came into existence, and funding for these operations went to the State Department. Benjamin, as secretary of state, was the likely head of the bureau and chief of Confederate covert activities. Shortly thereafter, important agents of the Confederacy arrived in Montreal. "A few months later," according to Roy Z. Chamlee Jr., "John Wilkes Booth opened a bank account in the same Montreal bank used by the Rebels."[31]

This engraving from around 1864 positioned Judah P. Benjamin prominently among the Confederate chieftains. Courtesy of The Jacob Rader Marcus Center of the American Jewish Archives.

Benjamin took on the most dangerous assignment Davis had given him, that of spymaster. This would be his last assignment for the Confederacy. He established spy rings and sent political propagandists to the North and to Canada. He enlisted the seductive Belle Boyd, the "Cleopatra of Secession," in the cause. He sent agents to Ireland to stem the tide of Irish volunteers entering the Union army. He planned the burning of federal medical stores in Louisville, Kentucky, and bridges in strategic locations across the occupied South. He also oversaw the suppression of treason against the Confederacy. Special commissioners who investigated and arrested those disloyal to the government reported to Benjamin. Colonel Henry J. Leovy, a close friend of Benjamin's from New Orleans, served as a military commissioner in southwest Virginia, where he searched for traitors.[32]

Benjamin, like many other Confederate leaders, believed Northerners would not support Lincoln indefinitely. Serious efforts were made to exploit the difference between eastern and western states, to increase public disaffection in the North for the war, and to raid prisoner-of-war camps. Provocateurs attempted to capture federal property in the far north. Confederate agents tried to disrupt the monetary system by urging people to convert paper money to gold. There was even an attempt—probably unknown to Benjamin but involving his agents—to set New York City on fire. Benjamin oversaw the most ambitious mission, a one-million-dollar covert operation in Canada headed by Jacob Thompson. When the war ended, Benjamin fled Richmond with Davis and the Confederate cabinet.[33]

The common Jewish soldier in the field matched Benjamin's commitment to the Confederate cause. There were about 2,000 Jewish Confederate servicemen. Simon Wolf, a prominent Jewish lawyer, published a book in 1895 containing a list of Jews who served in the Union and Confederate armies. His list reflects the preponderance of service in the infantry. Of the 1,340 men listed, 967 served in the infantry, 116 in the cavalry, 129 in the artillery, and 11 in the navy or marines. Rabbi Barnett Elzas's list of Jewish South Carolinians shows 117 in the infantry of a total of 167 men. In their study of Richmond's Jews, Ezekiel and Lichtenstein noted 70 of 100 soldiers in the infantry. Eric Brock's list of Confederate Jewish soldiers in Shreveport, Louisiana, comes to similar conclusions.[34]

There were Jewish Johnny Rebs in every aspect of the war. They were privates in infantry units all over the South and in every major campaign. They were cooks, sharpshooters, orderlies, teamsters, and foragers. They dug trenches, cut trees, guarded prisoners, and served on picket duty. Most of the historical information about Jewish Confederate soldiers is contained in the letters, diaries, reminiscences, and biographies of well-known, powerful, and older men, such as Judah Benjamin and Raphael Moses, a prominent commissary officer. There is little documentation for the average soldier.[35]

The average Confederate soldier was in his twenties, and this was undoubtedly true about Jewish Johnny Rebs. We know little about these young men except their names and units, but there is enough information about men in the ranks to make some generalizations. The majority enlisted in hometown companies with men whom they knew, often fellow Jews. They preferred serving in units with their friends and relatives. There were seven Rosenbalms in Company H of the 37th Virginia. Philip Rosenheim of the Richmond militia was proud of his service and his friends: "Charley Marx and David Mittledorfer, Julius Straus, Moses Hutzler, Sam and Herman Hirsh, Simon Sycles, Gus Thalheimer, Abr. Goldback, and a good many other Yuhudim all belonged to the same company, which I did."[36]

But unlike Irish and German immigrants, who formed ethnic companies, Jews did not form distinctively Jewish companies because they fervently desired to be seen as citizens of their state and nation, not as a separate nationality. They did not want to stand out as they had been forced to do in Europe. There were no Catholic or Lutheran units in the Confederate army, and, therefore, no Jewish units either. As a practical matter, there were few wealthy Jewish men with the military background and political influence needed to organize a company of troops. The majority of Jewish Confederates were recent young immigrants. They were followers, comrades-in-arms, not leaders.[37]

The majority of Jewish Confederates served as privates or corporals in the infantry, but there were Jews in all branches of the service and in all departments. One hundred and five Jews served in the Alabama infantry and twenty-one in the cavalry. There were almost as many Jews in the Arkansas cavalry as in the infantry. Leopold Levy and his brother Sampson served in Company G, 1st Virginia Cavalry, commanded by Colonel J. E. B. Stuart. Texas had seventy-three Jewish infantry men and twenty-one Jewish cavalrymen.

Jews also served in artillery units such as the Washington Artillery of New Orleans. Texas and Alabama each had five Jewish artillerymen; Arkansas had eight. Edwin Kursheedt and Eugene Henry Levy served in the artillery. Marx Cohen and Gustavus A. Cohen served in James F. Hart's Company (Washington Artillery, South Carolina), initially a part of Hampton's Legion, as did five other Cohens from South Carolina. Perry Moses of Sumter served in a number of units, including Culpepper's Battery. In 1863, Moses was in charge of a twelve-pound Napoleon cannon and later that year wrote to his mother, Octavia Harby Moses: "I fought a battery of four guns for over an hour, giving them gun for gun."[38]

Some Jewish Johnny Rebs served in militia or home guards, which were organized for local self-defense. At the beginning of the war, many men who did not want to leave home or serve in the regular army joined the militia. As the war progressed and conscription was instituted, the home guards consisted of those too young, too old, or too infirm to serve, as well as those exempt by virtue of their occupations or political office. When Richmond, Virginia, was attacked in the summer of 1863, young Philip Rosenheim served in the local militia. In a letter to his sister and brother-in-law, Amelia and Isaac Meinnart, Philip stated, "I, as well as all the Boys rallied to the call and we stood firmly at our Flag ready to meet the foe."[39]

Jewish soldiers came from varied backgrounds. Some were recent immigrants, and some were from old families. Strong evidence of the southern Jewish immigrant's contribution to Confederate military service can be seen in Shreveport, Louisiana, in 1860. Eric J. Brock estimated that three hundred Jews lived in Shreveport at that time and that seventy-eight served in the Confederate armed forces. Almost all were recent immigrants who arrived in Louisiana in the 1850s. Most, like Marx Baer, were born in one of the German states or Alsace and Lorraine. Some were from Poland: Jack Citron, Company I, 3rd Louisiana, from Koval; and Jacob Gall, Company D, 19th Louisiana, from Meschisko. Some were from France: Marx Israel of Company 5, 3rd Regiment, European Brigade, was from Onepie near Metz.[40]

Leading Jews of Richmond, Virginia, had been members of the Richmond Light Infantry Blues for generations. The unit participated in quelling the Gabriel Prosser slave revolt in 1800 and was called into service in 1807 when the British man-of-war *Leopard* attacked the *Chesapeake* off Norfolk. When the Richmond Blues left the city for the war on April 24, 1861, fifteen of its ninety-nine members were Jewish, including Ezekiel J. ("Zeke") Levy, its fourth sergeant.

The Blues served as Company A, 46th Virginia, in West Virginia and saw combat at Roanoke Island in February 1862. "Soon a ball [bullet] came from the Yankees," the company's record states, and "one of our boys, Mr. L. Wasserman, replied." Henry Adler was mortally wounded. Isaacs, Lyon, Levi Wasserman, and Joseph Levy were captured and exchanged for Union prisoners that August. After suffering a great deal from his wounds, Adler died at the naval hospital in Portsmouth and was buried by the Blues, who turned out en masse to honor their first private killed in the war. The Blues served in Virginia and North Carolina, and also fought in the defense of Charleston, Richmond, Petersburg, and finally in Appomattox. With the Blues' captain killed and first lieutenant wounded, Lieutenant Ezekiel J. Levy became commanding officer in June 1864.[41]

There were dozens of Jewish officers in the Confederate service, including the quartermaster general of the Confederate army, Colonel Abraham Charles Myers, the great-grandson of the first rabbi of K. K. Beth Elohim in Charleston. After graduating from West Point, Myers became a career army officer and served in the Second Seminole and Mexican Wars. Fort Myers, Florida, was named in his honor by his father-in-law, General David Emanuel Twiggs. In 1861, Myers set up his offices on the southwest corner of 9th and Main Streets, near Capitol Square in Richmond. The Quartermaster Department included quartermasters in each state, paymasters and quartermasters in the field, manufacturing plants, special units such as the Tax-in-Kind Office, depot and post quartermasters, and purchasing agents posted abroad. Colonel Myers reported to the secretary of war.[42]

As the war continued, public concern, followed by anger and then outrage at the Commissary and Quartermaster Departments, plagued the Confederacy. It was understandable, if unjustified, that officers in charge of food, clothing, and supplies were blamed for the army's ills. The head commissary officer was the scapegoat of the Confederate Congress. His nomination to full colonel and confirmation as commissary general provoked heated debate. Myers's nomination to full colonel and confirmation as quartermaster general was immediately approved. T. C. De Leon believed that Myers's "bureau was managed with an efficiency and vigor that could scarcely have been looked for in so new an organization." Early in the war, Myers enjoyed a good reputation as a competent and honest department head.

It soon became clear that the war would not be short and that supplying an army of four hundred thousand men would be a formidable task. Prices rose as the blockade tightened and northern supply sources dwindled. States' rights played a part in the Confederacy's problems. The state government of North Carolina supplied uniforms for its troops with the understanding that the quartermaster would not purchase clothing from North Carolina factories, and thereby deplete their inventories. The southern economy could not keep pace with the army's huge appetite for supplies.

The Union victories of 1862 were a disaster for the Confederacy and especially for the quartermaster general. The loss of New Orleans, key border states, coastal areas, and the Mississippi Valley limited the areas from which supplies, manufactured goods, and raw materials could be obtained. Blockade-running was severely curtailed, interfering with the importation of European goods. By August 1862, Lee complained that his army lacked "much of the materials of war, . . . [was] feeble in transportation, the animals being much reduced, and the men . . . poorly provided with clothes, and in thousands of instances . . . destitute of shoes."[43]

As the war dragged on, the Quartermaster Department came under severe criticism. The *Savannah Daily News* noted "that peculation and plunder, and misuse of authority for private purpose, have often been put before public duty and public service." The *Richmond Enquirer* complained that "quartermasters sometimes get rich. . . . Unfaithful, incompetent, or dishonest quartermasters or commissaries could plunge the country into ruin." Historian Richard Goff concludes that despite the criticism, under Myers's leadership, the Quartermaster Department was "as well organized and as efficient as circumstances would allow."[44]

Myers's friends in Congress sought to promote him to brigadier general, and in March 1863, the Congress passed a law providing that the rank and pay of the quartermaster general "shall be those of Brigadier General in the provisional army." Seventy-six members of Congress sent the president a letter recommending that Colonel Myers be promoted to general. Ironically, Jefferson Davis used the law to dismiss Myers from office. On August 7, 1863, he replaced Abraham Myers with his old friend Alexander R. Lawton.

Davis argued that the dismissal of Myers was in the interest of efficiency, and there was some basis for the charge. But Myers and Davis had feuded many years before, in the army, and according to Richmond gossip, the true reason for the controversy lay between the men's wives. Marian Myers, who considered herself the social superior of Mrs. Davis, had called the president's wife "an old squaw," referring to Davis's dark complexion. Assistant Secretary of War A. T. Bledsoe passed along the insult in early 1862. "The Congress of 1863," Mary Chestnut wrote, "gave up its time to fighting the battle of Colonel Myers—Mrs. Myers."[45]

There is no evidence that antisemitism played any role in Myers's firing, despite sentiments expressed by John Beauchamp Jones, a clerk in the War Department. In his memoir, *A Rebel War Clerk's Diary* (1866), Jones called Myers the "Jew Quarter-Master General" and claimed the officer said, "let them suffer," when told of soldiers' pleas for blankets. But Sallie Putman, who had no love for the Jews, thought Myers was mistreated. Most important, Jefferson Davis not only had no prejudice against Jews but, to the contrary, maintained warm relationships with many southern Jews.[46]

Adolph Proskauer of Mobile was among the few Jewish immigrants who became a high-ranking Confederate officer. Proskauer was educated at the gymnasium in Breslau before coming to the United States. In May 1861, he enlisted for twelve months in Captain Augustus Stikes's company, the Independent Rifles, and was appointed first corporal. In Richmond, the Independent Rifles became Company C, 12th Alabama Infantry. The 12th Alabama was a cosmopolitan regiment that included German, French, Irish, and Spanish soldiers, as well as young men from the mountains of north Alabama. Captain Robert Emory Park, an officer in the regiment, recalled their talent for foraging, stating that "the vast majority of them suffered very little from hunger" despite limited rations.

By December, Proskauer was promoted to sergeant. In April 1862, he was commissioned as a first lieutenant. He served in that rank for only twenty-six days before being promoted to captain in May, replacing Stikes, who became a major of the regiment. Proskauer was remembered as a handsome captain, the "best dressed man in the regiment." He participated in some of the fiercest battles of the war, such as the Siege of Yorktown in the late spring of 1862. He also helped lead the 12th Alabama at the Battle of Seven Pines, where it made a "gallant charge . . . into the very jaws of death."

Proskauer and his regiment marched north in Lee's Maryland campaign as part of Rodes's brigade. He was in combat at the Battle of South Mountain and Sharpsburg (Antietam), where he was wounded. On September 17, 1862, the single bloodiest day in the Civil War, Lee's Army of Northern Virginia faced George B. McClellan's Army of the Potomac: 4,710 men were killed; 18,440 men were wounded. Proskauer was shot in the abdomen during intense fighting along the Sunken Road, later called the "Bloody Lane." He recuperated and later returned to his company at Orange Court House, Virginia.

Proskauer was also at the Battle of Chancellorsville in May 1863, when the 12th fought as a part of Stonewall Jackson's famous flanking attack on

Major General Hooker's Union army. On the morning of May 3, Proskauer led the regiment, as Colonel Pickens assumed leadership of a portion of the brigade after the commander was wounded. Wounded in the battle, Proskauer was promoted to major by Colonel Pickens while he was in the hospital, and his promotion was later confirmed by the Confederate Congress in early 1864.

Major Proskauer returned to his command at the Battle of Gettysburg on July 1, 1863. A part of Rodes's division, the 12th suffered heavy casualties at Oak Ridge, northeast of Gettysburg. Years later, Captain Park wrote to Mrs. Proskauer: "I can see him now, in mental view, as he nobly carried himself at Gettysburg, standing coolly and calmly, with cigar in his mouth, at the head of the Twelfth Alabama, amid a perfect rain of bullets, shot and shell. He was the personification of intrepid gallantry, of imperturbable courage."

On July 4, 1863, Lee retreated from Pennsylvania. Major Proskauer and the 12th Alabama, "suffering, wet and anxious," on a dark, dreary, rainy night retreated south. During the remainder of the summer of 1863 they camped near Orange Court House. Fighting continued in Virginia, and in October, Proskauer led half the regiment on a mission to destroy railroad tracks near Warrenton Junction. In late December, he led the regiment to Paine's Mill to saw planks for the Orange Road. The regiment saw action again on May 8 at Spotsylvania Court House, where Proskauer was wounded once more, ending his involvement in the war.[47]

Like the officers and enlisted men in the field, southern rabbis supported the Confederate war effort. Rabbi Max Michelbacher of Beth Ahabah Synagogue in Richmond and the Confederate capital's Jewish community assisted Jewish soldiers. Michelbacher saw to the soldiers' needs, requested furloughs on their behalf for Jewish holidays, and even published a "prayer of the C[onfederate] S[tates] Soldiers." Beginning with the Shema, it called upon the God of Israel to "be with me in the hot season of the contending strife; protect and bless me with health and courage to bear cheerfully the hardships of war. . . . Be unto the Army of this Confederacy, as thou wert of old, unto us, thy chosen people!"[48]

Rabbi James K. Gutheim of New Orleans was also a vocal supporter of the Confederacy. The spiritual leader of Dispersed of Judah congregation, Gutheim refused to swear allegiance to the Union when the federal army occupied the Crescent City. Along with many of his congregants, Gutheim left the city for Montgomery, Alabama, where he prayed from the pulpit, "Regard, O Father, in Thine abundant favor and benevolence, our beloved country, the Confederate States of America. May our young Republic increase in strength. . . . Behold, O God, and judge between us and our enemies, who have forced upon us this unholy and unnatural war."[49]

The revolution wrought by the Civil War—the freeing of the slaves; the collapse of the ancien régime; the death, destruction, and impoverishment of southern cities—was devastating to southern Jewry. Those most committed to the cause lost the most. Judah Benjamin left the country for Europe. Union officials tried to implicate him in Lincoln's assassination. Abraham C. Myers's career was ended. Many families lost fathers, brothers, and sons. Businesses suffered, and many were destroyed. Those Jews who had owned slaves, lost them. Reconstruction was as bitter for the Jewish community as it was for the rest of the white South. In a letter to a family member in April 1868, Henry Hyams, the former lieutenant governor of Louisiana, wrote, "As Israelites, we are passing through another captivity which relives and reenacts all the troubles so pathetically poured forth by the inspired Jeremiah." Emma Mordecai of Richmond could not abide the occupying army. "Richmond is a strange place," she confided to her diary. "Everything looks unnatural and desecrated."[50]

Like other southerners, Jewish southerners licked their wounds, rebuilt their lives, and memorialized their honored dead. The Jewish women of Richmond formed the Hebrew Ladies Memorial Association for the Confederate Dead. A circular was sent out "To the Israelites of the South" seeking funds to create a cemetery and to erect a monument to the Jewish Confederate dead. Time was of the essence. "While the world yet rings with the narrative of a brave people's struggle for independence," the circular stated, the soldiers' graves were neglected. Southern Jews could not abide this situation. They were urged to remember "the myriads of heroes who spilled their noble blood" in defense of the "glorious cause." The circular appealed to southern Jews' fear of antisemitism: "In time to come," it concluded, "when the malicious tongue of slander, ever so ready to assail Israel, shall be raised against us, then, with a feeling of mournful pride, will we point to this monument and say: '*There* is our reply.'"[51]

NOTES

1. Yates Levy to J. C. Levy, March 16, 1865, Phillips-Myers Papers #596, UNC; Robert N. Rosen, *The Jewish Confederates* (Columbia: University of South Carolina Press, 2000) (hereafter "Rosen"), 9–31; Eli Faber, A *Time for Planting: The*

First Migration, 1654–1820 (Baltimore: Johns Hopkins University Press, 1992). Important works on local southern Jewish history include Mark I. Greenberg, "Becoming Southern: The Jews of Savannah, Georgia, 1830–1870," *American Jewish History* 86 (March 1998): 55–75; Myron Berman, *Richmond's Jewry, 1769–1976: Shabbat in Shockoe* (Charlottesville: University Press of Virginia, 1979); Steven Hertzberg, *Strangers within the Gate City: The Jews of Atlanta, 1845–1915* (Philadelphia: Jewish Publication Society of America, 1978); Ruthe Winegarten and Cathy Schechter, *Deep in the Heart: The Lives and Legends of Texas Jews* (Austin: Eakin Press and Texas Jewish Historical Society, 1990); James W. Hagy, *This Happy Land: The Jews of Colonial and Antebellum Charleston* (Tuscaloosa: University of Alabama Press, 1993); Belinda Gergel and Richard Gergel, *In Pursuit of the Tree of Life: A History of the Early Jews of Columbia, South Carolina, and the Tree of Life Congregation* (Columbia, S.C.: Tree of Life Congregation, 1996); Bertram Wallace Korn, *The Jews of Mobile, Alabama, 1763–1841* (Cincinnati: Hebrew Union College Press, 1970), and *The Early Jews of New Orleans* (Waltham, Mass.: American Jewish Historical Society, 1969); Selma S. Lewis, *A Biblical People in the Bible Belt: The Jewish Community of Memphis, Tennessee, 1840s–1960s* (Macon, Ga.: Mercer University Press, 1998); Janice O. Rothschild, *As But a Day: The First Hundred Years, 1867–1967* (Atlanta: Hebrew Benevolent Congregation, The Temple, 1967); Melvin I. Urofsky, *Commonwealth and Community: The Jewish Experience in Virginia* (Richmond: Virginia Historical Society and Jewish Community Federation of Richmond, 1997); Rabbi Newton J. Friedman, "A History of Temple Beth Israel of Macon, Georgia" (Ph.D. diss., Burton College and Seminary, 1955).

2. Rosen, 23–25; Jacob Rader Marcus, ed., *Memoirs of American Jews, 1775–1865* (Philadelphia: Jewish Publication Society of America, 1955–56), 3:104.

3. Rosen, 25; Richard C. Wade, *Slavery in the Cities: The South, 1820–1860* (Oxford: Oxford University Press, 1964), appendix; Elliott Ashkenazi, *The Business of Jews in Louisiana, 1840–1875* (Tuscaloosa: University of Alabama Press, 1988), 9–11.

4. Greenberg, "Becoming Southern," 57–58; Rosen, 37; Bertram W. Korn, *Jews and Negro Slavery in the Old South, 1789–1865* (Elkins Park, Pa.: Reform Congregation Kenesseth Israel, 1961), 123.

5. Rosen, 37. Numerous rabbis and Jewish leaders in the North answered Rabbi Raphall's defense of slavery. The majority of northern Jews opposed slavery, and there were a number of northern Jewish abolitionists. Michael Heilprin, a Polish Jewish-American writer, was outraged by Raphall's "sacrilegious words." "Have we not had enough of the 'reproach of Egypt'? Must the stigma of Egyptian principles be fastened on the people of Israel by Israelitish lips themselves?" Bertram W. Korn, *American Jewry and the Civil War*, 2nd ed. (Philadelphia: Jewish Publication Society of America, 1957), 18–23.

6. Rosen, 382–83; Korn, *American Jewry and the Civil War*, 15–31, and *Jews*

and Negro Slavery, also published a chapter entitled "Jews and Negro Slavery in the Old South, 1789–1865," in *Jews in the South*, ed. Leonard Dinnerstein and Mary Dale Palsson (Baton Rouge: Louisiana State University Press, 1973), 89–134; Hagy, *This Happy Land*, 93; Abraham Barkai, *Branching Out: German-Jewish Immigration to the United States, 1820–1914* (New York: Holmes and Meier, 1994), 109–11.

7. Rosen, 16; Wade, *Slavery in the Cities*, 20; Michelbacher quoted in Korn, *Jews and Negro Slavery*, 111–13; Korn, *American Jewry and the Civil War*, 29.

8. Rosen, 15, 31–33; Howard M. Sachar, *A History of the Jews in America* (New York: Alfred A. Knopf, 1992), 26–27; Oscar S. Straus, *Under Four Administrations: From Cleveland to Taft* (Boston: Houghton Mifflin, 1922), 10.

9. Rosen, 31; I. J. Benjamin, *Three Years in America, 1859–1862*, Vol. I, ed. Oscar Handlin, translated from German by Charles Reznikoff (Philadelphia: Jewish Publication Society of America, 1956), 76.

10. Rosen, 34; John F. Marszalek, ed., *The Diary of Miss Emma Holmes, 1861–1866* (Baton Rouge: Louisiana State University Press, 1979), 162, 209, 306; Carol Bleser, ed., *Tokens of Affection: The Letters of a Planter's Daughter in the Old South* (Athens: University of Georgia Press, 1996), 343.

11. Quotes from Rosen, 35. See also Jacob Rader Marcus, *Early American Jewry* (Philadelphia: Jewish Publication Society of America, 1951), vol. 1, chap. 5 ("it is . . . a matter of record that the New Englanders, with rare exception, had no use for Jews. The original Puritans were interested in Hebrew and in ancient Hebrews . . . but not in their descendants as long as they remained Jews").

12. Rosen, 35; Cohen quoted in Gergel and Gergel, *In Pursuit of the Tree of Life*, 33–35; *Confederate Veteran* 23, no. 8 (August 1915): 343. This is in a letter from Simon Baruch to the *Confederate Veteran*. Samuel Proctor and Louis Schmier, eds., with Malcolm Stern, *Jews of the South: Selected Essays from the Southern Jewish Historical Society* (Macon, Ga.: Mercer University Press, 1984), 37; Schmier, "Georgia History in Pictures. This 'New Canaan': The Jewish Experience in Georgia," *Georgia Historical Quarterly* 73, no. 4, pt. 2 (Winter 1989); Greenberg, "Becoming Southern"; Lewis, *A Biblical People*, 34.

13. Quoted in Eli N. Evans, *Judah P. Benjamin: The Jewish Confederate* (New York: Free Press, 1988), 96–97.

14. Rosen, 38; Baer quoted in Morris U. Schappes, *Documentary History of the Jews in the United States 1654–1875*, rev. ed. (New York: Citadel Press, 1952), 436–41.

15. Rosen, 38; Korn, *American Jewry and the Civil War*, 250n. 48; Frederic Cople Jaher, *A Scapegoat in the New Wilderness: The Origins of Anti-Semitism in America* (Cambridge, Mass.: Harvard University Press, 1994), 138, 200–203, 215. John Weiss, *Life and Correspondence of Theodore Parker* (New York: D. Appleton, 1964): Theodore Parker, "Journal," March 1843, 1:214, and Parker to Dr. Francis, May 26, 1844, 1:236, "Letter to the Members of the 28th Congregational Society

of Boston" (1859), 2:497, and "Some Thoughts on the Charities of Boston" (1858), 1:397, and to Rev. David Wasson, December 12, 1857, 1:395–96. See also Egal Feldman, *Dual Destinies: The Jewish Encounter with Protestant America* (Urbana: University of Illinois Press, 1990), 56–59; and *Liberator* 15 (May 20, 1842): 1; and 19 (May 18 and September 21, 1849): 77, 751.

Edmond Quincy, "A Jew and a Christian," *Liberator* 18 (August 11, 1848): 126. Quincy, a Boston Brahmin and a cousin of John Quincy Adams, wrote a novel, *Wensley: A Story without a Moral* (1854), in which the villain is a forger and cheat named Aaron Abrahams. The book is laced with every cliche of old-fashioned Boston antisemitism: the Jew as a liar, cheat, and coward. See also Jonathan D. Sarna, "The 'Mythical Jew' and the 'Jew Next Door' in Nineteenth-Century America," in *Anti-Semitism in American History*, ed. David A. Gerber (Urbana: University of Illinois Press, 1986), 57–78; David A. Gerber, "Cutting Out Shylock: Elite Anti-Semitism and the Quest for Moral Order in the Mid-Nineteenth Century American Market Place," *Journal of American History* 69, no. 3 (December 1982): 615–37.

Lydia Maria Child, *Letters from New-York* (New York: Charles Francis; Boston: James Munroe, 1843), 12–13, 26–29, 31, 33–34, 217–18, 225 ("Judaism was rife with superstition, vengeance, blindness"; its ceremonies "strange . . . spectral and flitting"). See also Patricia G. Holland and Milton Meltzer, eds., *Guide to the Collected Correspondence of Lydia Maria Child, 1817–1880* (New York: Kraus Microform, 1980), s.v. "Jews," especially letters to Louisa Gilman Loring (September 4, 1846) and Ellis Gray Loring (March 5, 1854).

As to Henry Wilson's views, see *The Congressional Globe*, 36th Cong., 2d sess., February 21, 1861, 1091; and 37th Cong., 2d sess., February 13, 1862, 789; Korn, *American Jewry and the Civil War*, 168; Robert Douthat Meade, *Judah P. Benjamin: Confederate Statesman* (London: Oxford University Press, 1943), 139; Jacob Rader Marcus, *United States Jewry, 1776–1985* (Detroit: Wayne State University Press, 1989–93), 3:36.

16. Rosen, 121; Sachar, *A History of the Jews in America*, 73; and *History of the Jews of Louisiana: Their Religious, Civic, Charitable and Patriotic Life* (New Orleans: Jewish Historical Publishing Company of Louisiana, 1903), 33; Scherck to J. L. Meyer, Columbus, Ga., September 9, 1864, American Jewish Archives, Cincinnati (hereafter "AJA"); *Charleston Daily Courier*, March 11, 1861.

17. Rosen, 13–14, 49–54; Mayer quoted in Schmier, "Georgia History in Pictures," 820; Isaac Hermann, *Memoirs of a Veteran Who Served as a Private in the 60S in the War between the States: Personal Incidents, Experiences, and Observations* (Atlanta: Byrd Printing, 1911), 192–93. Letter, April 17, 1864, Simon Mayer Papers, box I, Tulane University.

18. James M. McPherson, *For Cause and Comrades: Why Men Fought in the Civil War* (New York: Oxford University Press, 1988); Mel Young, *Where They Lie Someone Should Say Kaddish* (Lanham, Md.: University Press of America), 39.

19. Rosen, 49. Letter dated July 8, 1863, addressed to "Dear Brother Isaac and Sister Amelia" (Mr. and Mrs. Isaac Meinnart) in Richmond from Philip Rosenheim, AJA. Leo E. Turitz and Evelyn Turitz, *Jews in Early Mississippi*, 2nd ed. (Jackson: University Press of Mississippi, 1995), xvii. Typewritten autobiography of Sir Moses Ezekiel, 75–76, Beth Ahaba Archive (Richmond, Virginia). See also Joseph Gutman and Stanley F. Chyet, eds., *Moses Jacob Ezekiel: Memoirs from the Baths of Diocletian* (Detroit: Wayne State University Press, 1975); *VMI Alumni Review* (Spring 1973): 1; Stanley F. Chyet, "Moses Jacob Ezekiel: A Childhood in Richmond," *Publications of the American Jewish Historical Society* 62 (1973): 286–94.

20. Quoted in Berman, *Richmond's Jewry*, 194–95.

21. Rosen, 50; typewritten autobiography of Moses Ezekiel, 75–76; C. Vann Woodward and Elisabeth Muhlenfeld, eds., *The Private Mary Chestnut: The Unpublished Civil War Diaries* (New York: Oxford University Press, 1984), 350; Phoebe Yates Pember, *A Southern Woman's Story: Life in Confederate Richmond*, ed. Bell Irvin Wiley (Jackson, Tenn.: McCowat-Mercer Press, 1959; reprint, Wilmington, N.C.: Broadfoot Publishing, 1991), 24.

22. Rosen, 52; Gary W. Gallagher, *The Confederate War* (Cambridge, Mass.: Harvard University Press, 1997), 28; Bernard M. Baruch, *My Own Story* (New York: Henry Holt, 1957), 5.

23. Lewis Leon, *The Diary of a Tar Heel Confederate Soldier* (Charlotte, N.C.: Stone Publishing, 1913), 1; Schappes, *Documentary History*, 481; Marcus, *Memoirs of American Jews*, 3:197; and Schappes, *Documentary* History, 481, 707–8.

24. Jaher, *Scapegoat in the New Wilderness*, 3–4, 117–18, 135–36.

25. Philip Whitlock, MS, autobiography, Virginia Historical Society, Richmond, 92. Wessolowsky quoted in Herbert Ezekiel and Gaston Lichtenstein, *The History of the Jews of Richmond from 1769 to 1917* (Richmond, Va.: Herbert Ezekiel, 1917), 183, 16, 175.

26. Jonathan D. Sarna, "American Jewish Political Conservatism in Historical Perspective," *American Jewish History* 87 (June and September 1999): 113–22.

27. Bertram W. Korn, introduction to "The Jews of the Confederacy," *American Jewish Archives* 13, no. 1, "Civil War Centennial Southern Issue" (April 1961): 4.

28. Rosen, chap. 2; Thomas Cooper DeLeon, *Belles, Beaux, and Brains of the '60's* (New York: G. W. Dillingham, 1909), 91–93.

29. Richard S. Tedlow, "Judah Benjamin," in *"Turn to the South": Essays on Southern Jewry*, ed. Nathan M. Kaganoff and Melvin I. Urofsky (Charlottesville: University Press of Virginia, 1979), 46; Evans, *Judah P. Benjamin*, 147–49; S. I. Neiman, *Judah Benjamin: Mystery Man of the Confederacy* (Indianapolis: Bobbs-Merrill, 1963), 145–46; Meade, *Judah P. Benjamin*, 235; George C. Rable, *The Confederate Republic* (Chapel Hill: University of North Carolina Press, 1994), 130.

30. A. J. Hanna, *Flight into Oblivion* (Richmond, Va.: Johnson Publishing, 1938), 194; Louis Gruss, "Judah Philip Benjamin," *Louisiana Historical Quarterly* 19, no. 4 (October 1936): 1046; Pierce Butler, *Judah P. Benjamin* (Philadelphia: W. G. Jacobs, 1907), 332; Robert Selph Henry, *The Story of the Confederacy* (Indianapolis: Bobbs-Merrill, 1931), 85, 87; Charles P. Roland, *The Confederacy* (Chicago: University of Chicago Press, 1960), 83, 111; Davis quoted in Evans, *Judah P. Benjamin*, xi–xxi.

31. Roy Z. Chamlee Jr., *Lincoln's Assassins: A Complete Account of Their Capture, Trial, and Punishment* (Jefferson, N.C.: McFarland, 1990), 401.

32. Meade, *Judah P. Benjamin*, 297–305; Evans, *Judah P. Benjamin*, 193; Rosen, 137. Col. Henry J. Leovy's activities are briefly described in William M. Robinson Jr., *Justice in Grey: A History of the Judicial System of the Confederate States of America* (Cambridge, Mass.: Harvard University Press, 1941), 409–11. His activities as a special commissioner are described in the Official Records IV, 4:802–15 and Kenneth W. Noe, "Red String Scare: Civil War Southwest Virginia and the Heroes of America," *North Carolina Historical Review* 69, no. 3 (July 1992): 301–22. Noe has Leovy's name as "Leory" because the Official Records made the same mistake. On the flight of the cabinet, see Hanna, *Flight into Oblivion*. See Leovy's obituary, *Daily Picayune*, October 4, 1902, 10, col. 2; letters from Jefferson Davis to Leovy dated May 26, 1877, and November 10, 1883, Historic New Orleans Collection (Henry J. Leovy Papers, 1859–1900).

33. Meade, *Judah P. Benjamin*, 301–4; William A. Tidwell, *Come Retribution: The Confederate Secret Service and the Assassination of Lincoln* (Jackson: University Press of Mississippi, 1998), chap. 8; William A. Tidwell, *April '65: Confederate Covert Action in the American Civil War* (Kent, Ohio: Kent State University Press, 1995), 127–29.

34. Simon Wolf, *The American Jew as Patriot, Soldier, and Citizen* (Philadelphia: Levytype, 1895); Barnett A. Elzas, *The Jews of South Carolina from the Earliest Times to the Present Day* (Philadelphia: Lippincott, 1905); Ezekiel and Lichtenstein, *The History of the Jews of Richmond*; list of Shreveport Jewish Confederate soldiers compiled by Eric Brock, Rosen Papers, Jewish Heritage Collection, College of Charleston Library; Ezekiel and Lichtenstein, *History of the Jews of Richmond*, 176–88. The authors, writing in 1916, believed their list of Jewish Confederate soldiers to be "the best that has ever been printed, and it is safe to assume that no more complete or accurate one will ever be published" (176). Bell I. Wiley, *The Life of Johnny Reb: The Common Soldier of the Confederacy* (Garden City, N.Y.: Doubleday, 1971), 331.

35. Rosen, 162–63.

36. Rosen, 419.

37. Rosen, 163–65.

38. Wolf, *The American Jew,* passim, as to Cohens, see 374; Ashley Halsey Jr., "The Last Duel in the Confederacy," *Civil War Times Illustrated* 1, no. 7 (November 1862): 7; Elzas, *Jews of South Carolina,* 226; Joseph H. Crute Sr., *Units of the Confederate Army,* 2d ed. (reprint, Gaithersburg, Md.: Olde Soldier Books, 1987), 271–72; Moses quoted in Dorothy Phelps Bultman, "The Story of a Good Life" (November 1863, Sumter, S.C.), 1, Jewish Heritage Collection, College of Charleston.

39. Ernest B. Furguson, *Ashes of Glory: Richmond at War* (New York: Alfred A. Knopf, 1996), 212. Letter dated July 8, 1863, from Philip Rosenheim to the Meinnarts, Korn file, AJA.

40. Rosen, 174–75; Eric Brock, "The Jewish Cemeteries of Shreveport, Louisiana" (Shreveport, La.: privately printed, 1995), Jewish Heritage Collection.

41. John A. Cutchins, *A Famous Command: The Richmond Light Infantry Blues* (Richmond, Va.: Garrett and Massies, 1934), passim; quote from company record in Berman, *Richmond's Jewry,* 93–97; Ezekiel and Lichtenstein, *History of the Jews of Richmond,* 129, 149–52; Darrell L. Collins, *46th Virginia Infantry* (Lynchburg, Va.: H. E. Howard, 1992), 151.

42. Rosen, 118–25. The best source on Abraham C. Myers is Richard D. Goff, *Confederate Supply* (Durham, N.C.: Duke University Press, 1969). Walter Burke Jr. has written a useful pamphlet entitled "Quartermaster: A Brief Account of the Life of Colonel Abraham Charles Myers, Quartermaster General C.S.A.," published in 1976. William C. Davis, *Breckinridge: Statesman, Soldier, Symbol* (Baton Rouge: Louisiana State University Press, 1974); William C. Davis, *Jefferson Davis: The Man and His Hour* (New York: HarperCollins, 1991); and William C. Davis, *A Government of Our Own: The Making of the Confederacy* (New York: Free Press, 1994). Thomas Cooper DeLeon, the irrepressible author of *Belles, Beaux, and Brains of the '60s* and *Four Years in Rebel Capitals: An Inside View of Life in the Southern Confederacy, from Birth to Death* (Mobile: Gossip Printing, 1890), knew Myers personally and was well acquainted with his family, as was true of Mary Chestnut, who was also from South Carolina and knew the Jewish community through her close friendship with Miriam DeLeon Cohen. Her diary is a good source on Myers: Mary Boykin Miller Chestnut, *Mary Chestnut's Civil War,* ed. C. Vann Woodward (New Haven, Conn.: Yale University Press, 1981). See also Karl H. Grismer, *The Story of Fort Myers: The History of the Land of the Caloosahatchee and Southwest Florida* (Fort Myers: Southwest Florida Historical Society, 1949); Samuel Bernard Thompson, *Confederate Purchasing Operations Abroad* (Chapel Hill: University of North Carolina Press, 1935); Clement Eaton, *A History of the Southern Confederacy* (New York: Macmillan, 1954); Ellsworth Eliot Jr., *West Point in the Confederacy* (New York: G. A. Baker, 1941); Robert C. Black III, *The Railroads of the Confederacy* (Chapel Hill: University of North Carolina Press, 1952); John Beauchamp Jones, *A Rebel War Clerk's Diary at the Confederate States Capital,* 2 vols., ed. Howard Swiggett (New York: Old Hickory Bookshop, 1935).

43. Quoted in Rosen, 121.

44. Rosen, 132, 142; Goff, *Confederate Supply*, 59–60.

45. Eaton, *History of the Southern Confederacy*, 138; Davis, *Jefferson Davis*, 537–38; Goff, *Confederate Supply*, 142; Chestnut, *Mary Chestnut's Civil War*, 437n. 5.

46. Chestnut, *Mary Chestnut's Civil War*, 532; Sallie B. Putnam [A Richmond Lady], *Richmond during the War: Four Years of Personal Observation* (New York, 1867; reprint, Alexandria, Va.: Collector's Library of the Civil War, Time-Life Books, 1983), 275. Jones was a native of Baltimore. *A Rebel War Clerk's Diary*, condensed ed., ed. Earl Schenck Miers (New York: Sagamore Press, 1958), 1:186, 2:8; Berman, *Richmond's Jewry*, 187.

47. Rosen, 107–10; Joseph Proskauer, *A Segment of My Times* (New York: Farrar, Straus, 1950). Adolph Proskauer's daughter Jenny Proskauer wrote an unreliable recollection in 1948, which is at the AJA. The chief source of this material is Robert Emory Park, *Sketch of the Twelfth Alabama Infantry of Battle's Brigade, Rodes Division, Early's Corps, of the Army of Northern Virginia* (Richmond, Va.: W. E. Jones, 1906), originally printed in *Southern Historical Society Papers* 33 (January–December 1905): 193–296. The details of Proskauer's military career are derived from his compiled service record at the National Archives as well as the Official Record, where his name is misspelled "Proskaner." See ser. 1, vol. 25, pt. 1, 960 (Reports of Col. Samuel B. Pickens, 12th Alabama, May 5, 1863); ser. 1, vol. 36, pt. 1, 1083 (May 9, 1864); 1:27, 563; 1:25, 950–53 (Reports of Col. Edward A. O'Neal, May 12, 1863); 1:29, 891–92 (Reports of Maj. A Proskaner, January 22, 1864). Also see Young, *Where They Lie*, 76, 78–79; Robert K. Krick, *Lee's Colonels: A Biographical Register of the Field Officers of the Army of Northern Virginia* (Dayton, Ohio: Morningside House, 1992), 266; Korn, *American Jewry*, 176; obituary of Adolph Proskauer, AJA (the AJA has an extensive file on Proskauer); Park, *Sketch of the Twelfth Alabama Infantry*, 5.

48. Quoted in Rosen, 209–13.

49. Quoted in Rosen, 249, 256–57.

50. Rosen, 333–37; letter from Hyams dated April 19, 1868, to "My Dear Caroline," AJA; Mordecai quoted in Marcus, *Memoirs of American Jews*, 3:341.

51. Undated clipping, George Jacobs scrapbook, AJA; Rosen, 338–40 (the circular is reproduced on p. 339). See also Korn, *American Jewry*, 110–12.

9

From Peddler to Regimental Commander in Two Years
The Civil War Career of Major Louis A. Gratz

Jacob Rader Marcus

Early in 1861 a German Jewish immigrant, not yet twenty-two years of age, landed in New York City. The name by which he was to be known in this, the land of his adoption, was Louis A. Gratz. Judging by the surname, which was Grätz in German, the original home of his family was either in the Austro-Silesian town of Grätz or in the German-Polish town of the same name in the province of Posen. Although there is no conclusive evidence by any means, the likelihood is that the Louis A. Gratz family stemmed from this latter town, the same city that in all probability once sheltered an ancestor of Heinrich Grätz, the classical Jewish historian, and an ancestor of the Gratz brothers, notable Philadelphia merchants of the eighteenth century.

We do not know where Louis A. Gratz was born, but we do know that some years before his emigration he went to live with an uncle by the name of Kurtzig in the Posen town of Inowrazlaw. He made his home with this family for several years, and when later he joined the long stream of wanderers to these shores, he wrote back to his beloved relatives, describing his life and adventures in the new world. These German letters—some of which have been preserved—are the source of our knowledge of his career during the years 1861 to 1869.

Reprinted, in abridged form, with permission of Jacob Rader Marcus's literary executor from *Publications of the American Jewish Historical Society* 38 (September 1948–June 1949): 22–45, copyright © 1949 by the American Jewish Historical Society.

Uncle Aron Kurtzig and Aunt Emma Kühlbrand Kurtzig were engaged in the manufacture of oil from rapeseed, and it was in the pursuit of this task that Kurtzig introduced the first steam engine and modern industry into his district. This was no mean task, for the nearest railroad was at Bromberg, twenty-six miles away, and all the heavy boilers and machines had to be dragged over the miry roads. The sticky mud of this part of the country was far famed, and tradition had it that when Napoleon I was once bogged down in the neighborhood, he is reported to have said ironically: "And they call this a fatherland!"

Inowrazlaw, situated in the midst of a rich grain district, was a typical isolated German-Polish town. There was very little water in town—just a few wells—and the luxuries of life were conspicuously absent. When the children in the Kurtzig house once received an orange from one of the neighboring gentry, they did not eat it, but put it under glass where they could look at it as much as they wanted and inhale its wonderful perfume. The town, in the decade of the 1850s, sheltered some 5,000 people, almost half of whom were Jews. Most of the latter were orthodox and observant; the Kurtzigs we know were, and it was in this rigidly religious environment that young Gratz spent considerable time. We may safely assume that he was given the usual Jewish education and hence enjoyed some familiarity with the Hebrew language and ritual.

What induced this young man to leave his Polonized German town to go to America? Although he lived under rather comfortable circumstances at home—he was by no means faced by want—he was induced by a friend to go to America in the hope of becoming rich. This was the lure that led him to say yes to the solicitation of his companion; the realities he found on his arrival were a grim disappointment.

The eight-week voyage on a sailing vessel almost took all the starch out of him; bad food and bad quarters left him shaken in body and soul when he arrived. He visited a cousin but was shabbily received and probably never called again; he knew no English, had no trade, and soon became so discouraged that he was almost disconsolate. His one friend, the man who had accompanied him here, soon left him in the lurch to take a job with a relative. His total fortune was ten dollars, not a great deal for a stranger in a strange land, a frightened, lonely young man of twenty-one. His board in a good Jewish family, where the dietary laws were no doubt observed, cost him two and one-half dollars a week, and at that rate he knew his little nest egg would not last very long. The eager immigrant tried desperately to get a job, but nobody had anything for him; everyone with whom he spoke discouraged him, and finally he turned to the last—if not the first—resort of every unskilled but intelligent German Jewish immigrant: he became a peddler.

He invested part of his meager store of money in a basket of shoe laces, thimbles, and stockings, and started climbing up and down stairs, and knocking at doors in the great metropolis of New York. By dint of hard labor he earned enough to pay his daily board. That meant he earned about thirty-five cents a day. By this time—his first week in the country—he knew the names and prices of the goods he carried. One of the merchants who sold him his supplies helpfully suggested that he would do better peddling in the countryside and even offered him five dollars' worth of goods on credit. The young man accepted the kind offer, trudged out to the farms in the outlying districts, and did a little better until he ran into rain. There could be no peddling while the mud in the roads was knee-deep; he had to go back, and he walked the twenty-five miles to the city carrying his pack on his back. The net result of this first expedition on the road to fortune was a bad fever and an infected leg.

Now his troubles really began. Instead of resting—how could he afford to do this?—he started peddling again until he was confined to bed with a constant fever. In the meantime his money was dwindling away because of his expenditures for food and medicine. There was but one thing to do: go to a public hospital reserved primarily for the poor, a hospital where conditions were indescribably bad and where the surgeons operated experimentally on his legs twice a week. There is no indication that he went to Jews' Hospital—later Mount Sinai—and it is difficult to understand why he did not take advantage of its resources, unless, of course, he did attempt to do so, but was refused admittance for one reason or another. For six weeks he lay in the hospital, and when he was finally discharged, he returned to his former quarters, uncured and depressed. Fortunately he soon found a physician who did cure him, and again, for lack of something better, he took up his peddler's pack. The scene of his new labors was Carbondale in the coal country, and here he went to work in partnership with a New York clerk, originally a compatriot from Inowrazlaw, who had a capital of fifty dollars. During his nights and spare time, Gratz devoted himself to the study of English, for he realized the importance of a fluency in the vernacular, and like other ambitious men he was resolved to get ahead.

All these experiences were crowded into a few busy months, a half year at the most. In the meantime war broke out, and Abraham Lincoln had issued his call for volunteers. Young Gratz—Lewis he called himself, no doubt for the homonymous Löb or Levi—joined up in Pittston, Luzerne County, where many of his fellow Germans were to be found. What had he to lose in a ninety-day enlistment?

Everyone was excited; there was wild enthusiasm, and the war would certainly be over in a few months. It could all be a very pleasant interlude, and so he enlisted as a volunteer in the Fifteenth Pennsylvania Infantry Regiment some time in late April or early May, 1861, telling the recruiting officer that he was twenty-two years of age. His biography, published during his own lifetime in the Goodspeed *History of Tennessee*, indicates he could have been only eighteen years of age.

It is questionable if he really thought seriously about the issues at stake; the war was for him probably a relief after the weary toil of peddling—an adventure. He was determined to make of it an opportunity. Unlike the vast majority of his fellow soldiers he now sat down to study the language in earnest; in a relatively short time he became a noncommissioned officer, a corporal, and then began to aspire for the lieutenant's bars of a commissioned officer. Day and night, when the opportunity presented itself, he studied English and military tactics; he had no money for private instruction. Our information is not adequate to trace his career in every detail, but we do know that he was a good soldier, stood out in action, if only in a modest sense, acquired influential friends, and was finally presented to Simon Cameron, then Secretary of War. Cameron, a consummate politician, was the Pennsylvania political boss and was willing to look kindly upon this attractive, ambitious, and brave young German who wanted a commission. Upon the expiration of his period of enlistment he re-entered the service on October 7, 1861, as first lieutenant in Company B of the Ninth Pennsylvania Cavalry, the Lochiel Cavalry, which was sent West the following month to the Kentucky and Tennessee front. His regimental commander was Colonel E. C. Williams; his company commander, E. G. Savage. This was not a bad start for a young immigrant who was not yet a year in the country. Yet let it be remembered that it was not luck that had brought him this far; he had accomplished what he had through laborious and intensive study and under difficult circumstances. He was a young man of character.

As far as we know he had not written back home to the Kurtzigs since his arrival. No immigrant who set out for the American land of promise to pick up the gold lying in the streets ever cared to admit—certainly not to his relatives—that he had been a failure. Some immigrants, we know,

Army News.

The following co-religionists were either killed or wounded at the battle of Fredericksburg:

T. J. Heffernam, A, 163 N. Y., hip and arm.
Serg. F. Herrfukneckt, 7 " head.
M. Ellis, 23 N. J., hand.
Moses Steinburg, 142 Penn., legs bruised.
A. Newman, A, 72 " ankle.
Lt. H. T. Davis, 81 " arm.
J. Killenback, 4 N. J., head.
S. S. Vanuess, 15 " leg.
W. Truax, 23 " back.
J. Hirsh, 4 " "
Jacob Schmidt, 19 Penn., left arm.
Jos. Osback, 19 " wounded.
W. Jabob, 19 " left arm.
Lieut. Simpson, 19 " left leg.
Capt. Schuh, 19 " wounded.
C. M. Phillips, 16 Maine, cheek.
Lieut. S. Simpson, 99 Penn., leg.
R. Harris, 107 " thigh.
L. Brauer, wounded.
—— Wolf, 5 Penn., side.
R. Ellis, 2 " leg (slight).
S. Davidson, 186 " foot.
A. Valanstein, 105 N. Y, leg.
H Stottler, 136 Penn., leg.

The above are at the hospital of Second Division, First Army Corps, in charge of Chas. J. Nordquish.

Franklin's Left Grand Division.

Lieut. G. L. Snyder, B, 104 N. Y., killed.
W. Lewis, B, 104 N. Y., arm.
J. Meekles, 94 " dead.
— Shupfel, D, 94 " "
G. Stancliffe, 26 " "

All the above were buried on Dec. 14, near the hospital across the river, from the battlefield.

F. Strausser, 6 Penn., hand.
J. P. Marks, 16 Maine, thigh.
C. B. Marks, 16 " arm.
C. Nunemager, 121 Penn., finger.
W. Hermeken, 12 " leg and arm.
H. Morris, 8 Penn., ankles, knee, and shoulder.
J. Hartmann, arm amputated.
P. Hemninger, 2 Del., wounded.
G. Simpson, 4 " "
Joseph Heine, 20 Mass., "
Serg. A. Rice, 20 " "
J. Morrison, 19 " "
M. Lattman, 20 " "

The Civil War marked the first large-scale participation of Jews in the American military. Some eight thousand to ten thousand Jews, mostly recent immigrants, donned uniforms, and well over 500 gave their lives in battle. Following the Battle of Fredericksburg, December 11–15, 1862, which ended disastrously for the Union Army, the *Jewish Record of New York* published a long list of "co-religionists... killed or wounded at the battle." Courtesy of Jonathan D. Sarna and Scott-Martin Kosofsky deliberately lied about their disappointments and wrote home describing in detail the good fortune that existed only in their imagination. Gratz had preferred thus far to remain silent, but now that he had mounted the first rung of the ladder to success, he felt like crowing—just a little—to the folks at home. He had been promised a captaincy, and he set out to earn it; he was proud of what he had accomplished. Just a few months back he was a struggling peddler barely making both ends meet; when he had peddled around Carbondale no one wanted to know him; now he was on special duty as a recruiting officer with headquarters in Scranton, in the same neighborhood, and the best Jewish and Gentile homes were thrown open to him. Not many Jews could show a similar record of speedy achievement, he wrote. In this he was quite wrong. There were a number of German Jewish immigrants who had earned rapid promotion or made a brilliant career for themselves as speedily as this young man from Posen; a notable example was the gallant major of the Twelfth Alabama Infantry, Adolph Proskauer. "My dear ones, I beg you with all my heart not to be angry because I have gone to war," Gratz wrote home. "And should it be my destiny to lose my life, well I will have sacrificed it for a cause to which I am attached with all my heart, that is: the liberation of the United States." The Americanization of Louis A. Gratz was proceeding apace, yet it would be false to infer that, even though this young soldier had already risked his life on the field of battle, and even though he was ready at the moment to do it over and over again, he had forgotten his native land. His heart still lay in Germany with his father and his relatives and his dear friends. It is almost asking too much to expect a man—even a young man—who has been in a country less than a year completely to disavow and surrender his past. There is such a thing as indecent haste. Gratz wrote home that if he survived the war he intended to return to Germany!

On August 4, 1862, Lieutenant Gratz was discharged from the Ninth Pennsylvania Cavalry, now fighting in Kentucky, and on the 16th of the same month accepted a commission as major in the Sixth Regiment Kentucky Cavalry. The Sixth was short of officers, and this able young lieutenant was jumped to a majority, probably never holding a captain's commission. During the fall and early winter of 1862 he was busy with his regiment, scouting and fighting around Cumberland Gap and chasing General Morgan, the Confederate raider; by December he was already in command of the regiment, although only a major. The other regimental commanders in the brigade at this time had at least the rank of lieutenant-colonel. He was now twenty-two or twenty-three years old according to his service records, possibly only nineteen.

The spring of 1863 found the Sixth Kentucky Cavalry and Major Gratz in Tennessee protecting the right flank of Rosecrans, and on September the 19th and 20th he was in the bitter battle of Chickamauga. It was probably during the action at Crawfish Springs that he nearly lost his liberty—and his life. Through the inept leadership of the Union general, the Northern front was opened up and the Confederates under Bragg poured in. The Sixth was repeatedly flanked, and at times almost if not completely surrounded. Gratz had to make the difficult decision of surrendering or fighting his way through. He dreaded the prospect of rotting away in a Southern detention camp—every Union soldier knew of the horrors of Andersonville and Libby—and made up his mind that he would rather be shot in battle than be taken prisoner: he gave the order to his men to break through the encircling forces which heavily outnumbered his. It was a desperate dash for safety, and a costly one. One hundred and twenty of his men were captured, several—surprisingly few—were killed; the regimental chaplain was shot down at his side; his adjutant, ten paces behind him, was captured, and his orderly, three paces behind him, was shot dead off his horse.

The courageous conduct and presence of mind of Gratz at Chickamauga may have been one of the factors that induced General Samuel Powhatan Carter to place him on his personal staff on December 25, 1863. Carter was now stationed at Knoxville and in all probability it was at this time that Major Gratz learned to know the young lady whom he was ultimately to marry. In the summer of 1864 he made the march through Georgia with Sherman, and in the following spring, in March, he was in North Carolina serving as Acting Assistant Inspector General at the headquarters of the Second Division of the Twenty-Third Army Corps; in April, at Raleigh, he was appointed Acting Assistant Adjutant General for the Third Division. Three months later, on July 14, 1865, he was mustered out of the service at Edgefield, Tennessee, near Nashville.

In December, 1863, when Gratz was appointed to the staff of General Carter, he was already a seasoned cavalry officer who had seen a lot of service. Judging from a letter written to the folks back home a few months later, he was not only seasoned, but hardened. With all the bravura of the dashing cavalry officer who had earned his spurs on the field of battle, he talked toughly of exterminating the rebels. "Our army is standing on the soil of the South, our flag is waving in every rebel state." "We would have won this war before had it not been for the traitors in our own midst, right in the cabinet itself. If the patriotic feelings of the people would be appealed to, the war would be soon over. The call for 500,000 and the threat to draft the unwilling was a wise move. We shall yet wash away the stains of dishonor with our heart's blood." But even this magniloquent outburst of youthful patriotism could not help the young soldier hide from himself the distress and the suffering about him. He bitterly attacked the people of the South and exulted for a moment in their despair—was he trying to hide his own sense of guilt as one of the ravaging troops?—but in the next moment he wrote contritely: "I can assure you that I am often heartsick thinking of the distress of the people." In his thinking, in his feeling, he was completely at one with those with whom he had thrown in his lot. It is "our cabinet," "our army," "our battles." His Americanization had taken deeper root. There is no talk or postscript of returning permanently to Germany after the war. This land was to be his home.

This sentiment of "belonging" was reflected even more fully in General Order, No. 34, issued on June 17, 1865, at the Headquarters of the Third Division of the Twenty-Third Army Corps, at Greensboro, N.C. It was General Carter's valedictory to the men of this division as they were about to be mustered out of service, and was countersigned by the Acting Assistant Adjutant General, L. A. Gratz. It is safe to assume that this adjutant like most adjutants since time immemorial wrote General Order, No. 34, for his commanding officer, and that it expresses the sentiments and words of Major Gratz as much as those of the Major General. "Three or more years ago," the valedictory reads, "you left all that was dear to you to respond to the call made upon you by the country, to save it from disunion and to overthrow a wicked rebellion. . . . Nobly you rallied around our starry banner and vowed to save it, and by unfurling it over every inch of this great country, secure liberty to all and for all time to come. Gallantly have you kept your vow. Through your exertions and deeds of valor our country stands today more glorious than ever, the proudest among the proud, and the first among the free." In every sense of the word this immigrant was now an American.

Ever since Gratz had been detailed to the staff of General Carter—the famous sailor on horseback—he had had more time for himself. This mature and thoughtful young man realized the war would soon be over and knew that he would again have to go out and hustle for a living. When he was mustered out he was offered a colonelcy in the new army, but refused to accept it; he was interested only in active service and was beginning to tire of a soldier's life: he had been in for over four years. His English had improved, so much so that frequently he was taken for a native American. During his leisure moments at staff headquarters in 1864 and 1865 he had studied law religiously, on the promise of fellow officers, practicing lawyers back home, that they would prepare him for the bar examination in the shortest possible time.

The close of the war found him back in Knoxville, his old headquarters. There, in 1865, he soon hung out his shingle; and on October 18, he married Elizabeth Twigg Bearden, whom he described to his family as a beautiful and virtuous woman related to one of the oldest and best families in the state. Her father, Captain Marcus D. Bearden, was to be mayor of Knoxville from 1868 to 1870. Like many of the other lawyers of the early post-war period, Gratz had to do a lot of circuit traveling. Apparently he had plenty of work offered him, although the people were frequently too poor to pay; hard cash was scarce, and he had to be content with promissory notes which were as good as the harvest that was yet to come in. Judging from his letters of this period, the struggle was not too onerous, for he was a man of more than ordinary capacity and was soon making a modest but comfortable living. Years later he found lucrative clients, like the Knoxville Water Company, and the Grabfelder interests of Louisville. By the fall of 1867 he already owned his own home on the outskirts of town, had a large lot with a fine garden on it, and the beginnings of a fast-growing family. Ultimately Lizzie Bearden was to bear him five children.

Like other veterans of his day—and a later day!—he went into politics. He was twice elected city attorney of Knoxville, was the first mayor of North Knoxville after it was incorporated in 1889, served for four terms (1889–1892), and worked hard to establish adequate public schools in this new village. He saw that Knoxville was a growing town and anticipated its growth by laying out the Gratz addition to the city; Gratz Street still recalls this early enterprise.

He was also active since the Seventies in the national fraternal and benefit society, the Knights of Honor, an organization numbering hundreds of lodges and including many thousands of members, and in the 1880s became its Supreme Dictator. By 1893 he was living in Louisville, where he represented this order and served, at the same time, as private counsel for Mr. S. Grabfelder, the well-known whisky dealer who also had hotel interests in Knoxville. It was while on a business mission for Mr. Grabfelder that Gratz died of a heart attack on a train going from Louisville to Knoxville, on the night of September 19, 1907. At the time of his death his first wife had already died, and he was survived by his second wife, who also bore him several sons and daughters. All told he left twelve children. His widow, the former Miss Fiddler, had once been a Mrs. Kempshall.

The career of Louis A. Gratz, after he was mustered out of the service, was not atypical. It was the normal success story of the competent American lawyer who worked hard, acquired more or less wealth, attained a considerable degree of recognition from his colleagues, and left a family of sturdy church-going children. As students of American Jewry, however, we are not primarily interested in the typical career of this American citizen. Louis A. Gratz was not only an American, he was also a Jew by ethnos, and originally, at least, by religion. In Inowrazlaw, as a boy in his teens, the Jewish part of him was not inconsiderable. In the 1850s the Jews of this town had little to do with the Poles, and the German Gentiles still looked askance at Jews. Years before Gratz left town, during the post-Napoleonic period, Aunt Emma's father, a physician, had distinguished himself fighting an epidemic of typhus, and the Prussian authorities, as a reward, had offered to make him a district physician, but only on condition that he become a convert to Christianity. Conditions had improved somewhat since then, but complete civil and political rights—on paper— were not to be granted to Prussian Jewry until the 1860s. During this period the majority of the Jews in town still spoke a German Yiddish, kept kosher, went frequently, if not daily, to the synagogue, and, no doubt, many of them still sported the earlocks of the pious religionist. This was the outer form of the heritage that Major Gratz brought with him to these shores. What happened to it in America?

In September, 1867, the Major wrote home that since he had decided to remain in Tennessee, he was determined to become one with the people. This sounds almost like an apology to his orthodox Jewish relatives for marrying out of the faith. His "Jewishness"—that undefinable but not indefinite something—had been gradually slipping away from him. As far as we know, the noun and adjective "Jew" and "Jewish" do not occur in any of his letters after that of November, 1861. He had ample opportunity, had he so desired, to maintain close religious contacts with the Jewish community in the town of Knoxville in 1865. There were at least fifteen families there, and just about that time—it might have been a year earlier or a year later—they had established a confraternity, the Hebrew Benevolent Society, which also conducted religious services. The Knoxville Jewish records—woefully inadequate, it is true—offer no evidence that he joined the Jewish group. No doubt he had to make some sort of decision in his own mind as to whether he would affiliate himself actively with the Jewish religious group, and apparently the decision was in the negative. There is no indication in his obituary, in the *Knoxville Sentinel* for September 20, 1907, that he was even born a Jew. All this does not mean that he had no social relations with the little Jewish community; he could not have avoided meeting some of them every day, and, as a matter of fact, one of his friends was the cultured Bavarian Jewish immigrant, Squire Julius Ochs. Captain Ochs—he had served in the Fifty-Second Ohio Volunteers, a militia regiment—had come to town in 1864 and gone into business but had never achieved any degree of economic success. One of his boys, Adolph, had been compelled to go to work to help the family eke out an existence, and at eleven years of age he was already getting up every morning at five o'clock to deliver newspapers on his route. Louis Gratz, who knew the family well, must have seen the boy frequently, but certainly hardly dreamed that this little fellow was one day to become the owner and builder of *The New York Times*. Another son of the Squire, Milton B. Ochs, was acquainted with the Major, but never knew that he was a Jew.

Captain Ochs was a justice of the peace from 1868 to 1872, and Gratz must have brought some cases into his court during this period. The Squire was also the unpaid volunteer rabbi in town, but, as we suggested above, we have no way of knowing if the Major ever came to services even to hear his friend preach on the high holidays. We do know that Gratz reared his children as Christians. We may assume that the Squire and the Major met in the Grand Army of the Republic posts where they were both active, and when the former died in Chattanooga in 1888, the Major went there to serve as one of the pallbearers.

In the course of time Gratz forgot much of his native German, for his wife and children did not speak or understand the language, although for a few years he still nursed the hope of securing a diplomatic post in Prussia in order to be able to see his family once more. This hope was never realized; he never returned to the land of his birth.

SOURCES

The Gratz letters and the Kurtzig family material are in Heinrich Kurtzig, *Ostdeutsches Judentum* (Stolp, 1927). I wish to express my appreciation to Dr. Joshua Bloch of the New York Public Library for drawing my attention to this work. For a study of the orthodox Jewish background of Inowrazlaw in the middle nineteenth century, see A. Heppner and J. Herzberg, *Aus Vergangenheit und Gegenwart der Juden in Hohensalza* (Frankfurt a. M., 1907).

Further biographical data on the life of L. A. Gratz may be found in the following obituaries: *Knoxville Sentinel*, September 20, 1907; Louisville *Courier Journal*, September 20, 1907; *The Times* (Louisville), September 20, 1907; will of L. A. Gratz in Jefferson County Court, Kentucky, Will Book 28, 307; *History of Tennessee . . . with an historical and biographical sketch of the county of Knox and the city of Knoxville* (Nashville: Goodspeed Pub. Co., 1887), p. 968; communication from Milton B. Ochs of Chattanooga, dated January 13, 1948; W. Rule, *Standard History of Knoxville, Tennessee* (Chicago, 1900), pp. 125–142; M. U. Rothrock, *The French Broad-Holston Country* (Knoxville, 1946), p. 378; *Directory of the Knights of Honor in the United States for . . . 1877* (Greensburg, Pa., 1877).

For the military record of L. A. Gratz, consult also his service record in the War Department, The Adjutant General's Office, Washington, D.C.; F. B. Heitman, *Historical Register and Dictionary of the United States Army . . .* , 2 vols. (Washington, D.C., 1903); *War of the Rebellion,* consult the general index volume under "Louis A. Gratz" and "Samuel P. Carter," particularly the following references: Series I, vol. XX, part 1, 144–146; part II, 186; XXIII, part II, 580; XXX, part III, 275; XXXIX, part II, 75, 220; XLVII, part I, 995; part III, 189, 252, 398, 650, 651 (G.O., No. 34), 669; LII, part I, 361, 386–387. Consult also Thomas Speed, R. M. Kelly, and Alfred Pirtle, *The Union Regiments of Kentucky* (Louisville, 1897), for the history of the Sixth Kentucky Cavalry; *Report of the Adjutant General of the State of Kentucky . . .* , vol. I, 1861–1866 (Frankfort, Ky., 1866), pp. 136ff.; Samuel P. Bates, *History of Pennsylvania Volunteers, 1861–5 . . .* , vol. I (Harrisburg, 1869), pp. 142ff.; vol. III (Harrisburg, 1870), pp. 234ff.; *Annual Report of the Adjutant General of Pennsylvania . . . for the Year 1866* (Harrisburg, 1867), p. 499.

For the Ochs family and Knoxville Jewry, see: *Temple Beth El 80th Anniversary Celebration* (Knoxville, Tenn., 1947); *Inventory of the Church and Synagogue Archives of Tennessee, Jewish Congregations* (The Tennessee Historical Records Survey, Works Projects Administration, 1941); G. E. Govan and J. W. Livingood, "Adolph S. Ochs: The Boy Publisher," *The East Tennessee Historical Society's Publications*, no. 17 (1945); Gerald W. Johnson, *An Honorable Titan* (New York, 1946); *The American Israelite,* May 23, 1873; October 17, 1873; November 2, 1888, quoting the *Chattanooga Daily Times* for October 29, 1888.

Part V

|||||||||||||||||||||||||||||||||||||||||

The Home Front

Until recently the home front, the vast civilian terrain beyond the battlefield shaped and scarred by the Civil War, attracted only limited attention from historians. Over the past two decades, scholars have begun to fill this considerable lacuna, drawing on a trove of diaries, memoirs, and letters left by women and other noncombatants whose lives were nonetheless profoundly affected by the conflict. Whereas once attention was focused primarily on formal relief efforts—Bertram Korn devoted a chapter to the patriotic activities, medical care, charitable organization, and other institutional responses spurred by the war—interest has now shifted to the psychological and social effects of the war on those who remained behind when their sons, husbands, brothers, and fathers enlisted in the Union and Confederate armies.

This impact varied considerably. Jewish women living in the South were more likely to encounter devastation and deprivation directly. By contrast, the war probably provided an economic boon to Jewish women involved in the needle trades in Northern cities, offering employment for those able to sew uniforms and tents for military suppliers. The risks of enlistment were more evenly distributed. Battle and disease scythed through the ranks on both sides, returning veterans home crippled physically and psychologically or not returning them at all. We know relatively little of the toll of the war on Jewish families and even less about those left widowed, orphaned, or caring for the injured.

Our portrait of Jewish civilian life in the Confederacy is more richly hued than for that of their counterparts in the North because of the publication of several wartime diaries of Southern Jewish women. David Morgan, drawing on one such partially published account, offers a portrait of

Eugenia Levy Phillips, a fiery patriot and provocateur in the cause of the South. Born in Charleston in 1820, Phillips was a woman of wealth and status whose husband was a successful and well-connected lawyer. Morgan chronicles Phillips's repeated run-ins with Union officialdom after the outbreak of war, first in Washington, D.C., and later in New Orleans, where the family resettled. Shortly after the capture of the city, Phillips was confined for three months to Ship Island off the coast of Mississippi as punishment for displaying open contempt toward the Union army. Although others harbored strong feelings, Eugenia Phillips's act of defiance was atypical. The commitment of most Southern women, scholars have suggested, oscillated with the hardships and loneliness of wartime.

In contrast to the irrepressible Eugenia Phillips, Dianne Ashton offers a detailed study of the quiet defensive strategies that several Jewish women, North and South, pursued in order to maintain relationships with friends and family across political and religious divides. These bonds provided an essential source of succor and support during the war, particularly with the rise of anti-Jewish sentiments in both the Union and Confederacy. While Ashton underscores the significance of solidarity between Jewish women as a coping mechanism during the war, she also analyses the "delicate dance" enacted by these women in their public behavior and correspondence in order to maintain these fragile bonds. This performance required concealing divisive differences—clashing political loyalties or religious tensions—and instead emphasizing areas of concord and commonality: shared womanhood and friendship. In much the same way, Ashton demonstrates how women, depending on the circumstances, veiled or burnished their Judaism.

These essays substantially advance our understanding of the home front but also reveal the limitations of our knowledge of Jewish civilian life during the Civil War. More work must be done to broaden our picture beyond the South, revealing the toll of a wrenching war on all of American Jewry.

10

Eugenia Levy Phillips
The Civil War Experiences of a Southern Jewish Woman

David T. Morgan

War causes dislocation and misery in unpredictable ways—oftentimes to the unsuspecting civilian as well as to the soldier in the front lines. Women, far from the fields of battle, have been known to become involved indirectly and to suffer because of their involvement. And so it was during the Civil War with Eugenia Levy Phillips, who, probably more than any other Southern woman of prominent political connections and high social standing, paid a heavy price in humiliation and suffering for her abiding loyalty to the Confederacy. Here is a bizarre story, the story of a woman who seems to have courted trouble by refusing, in the words of her husband, to be discreet in expressing her convictions.

Eugenia Levy Phillips was the daughter of Jacob C. Levy and Fanny Yates Levy. She was born in Charleston, South Carolina, in 1820. Her father, also a native of Charleston, was a well-educated man and a successful merchant. He was director of the Union Insurance Company from 1830 to 1840, a delegate to the Knoxville Railroad Convention in 1836, and a member of the Charleston Chamber of Commerce from 1841 to 1847. Although a thoroughgoing Southerner, he was a Union Democrat who opposed nullification and secession. In 1848 he moved to Savannah, Georgia, where he lived until his death. Eugenia's mother was from Liverpool, England.[1]

On 7 September 1836, at age sixteen, Eugenia was married in Charleston to Philip Phillips, a lawyer who had served in the South Carolina

---

Reprinted with permission from *Jews of the South*, ed. Samuel Proctor and Louis Schmier (Macon, GA: Mercer University Press, 1984), 95–106, copyright © 1984 by Mercer University Press.

legislature and had stood forthrightly and firmly against the doctrine and ordinance of nullification in 1833. Following his term in the legislature, he had moved in 1835 to Mobile, Alabama, where he established a thriving legal practice. Not long after the wedding in 1836, Eugenia and her new husband left Charleston, heading for Mobile by railway, stagecoach, and riverboat.[2]

For nearly eighteen years Philip and Eugenia Phillips lived in Mobile. Their first house was in the western suburbs; their second was on the bay. Fire destroyed the house on the bay, along with nearly all the family's possessions. By this time Phillips, as attorney for the Bank of Mobile and an established lawyer handling 150 to 200 cases a year, enjoyed a handsome annual income of $8,000, and so the family recovered quickly from the disaster and continued to do well. In 1853, when Eugenia and Philip left Mobile, they had seven children and one on the way. Clavius, Fanny, Caroline (called Lina), Salvadora, Eugene, John Walker, and John Randolph were all born in Mobile between 1838 and 1850. William Hallett and Philip were born in Washington in 1853 and 1855, respectively.[3]

Philip Phillips had been a political activist in South Carolina, and so he was in Alabama. His involvement in politics led him to the chairmanship of the Alabama Democratic party, two terms in the state legislature in 1844 and 1851, and finally to a term in the United States House of Representatives in 1853. One term in Congress at an annual salary of less than one-third of what he was accustomed to making as a lawyer prompted him to refuse to stand for another term. He and his family did, however, remain in Washington, where Philip returned to his legal practice.[4]

From 1855 to 1861 Phillips's practice before the United States Supreme Court "slowly but steadily increased." Among those who obviously had every confidence in Phillips as an attorney was Edwin M. Stanton, former attorney general of the United States. Besides working together on legal matters, Phillips and Stanton were close personal friends who often discussed the bitter sectional conflict between the North and South. Other influential friends of Phillips and his family included Associate Supreme Court Justice James M. Wayne and Reverdy Johnson, a prominent Maryland congressman.[5] Not so friendly with the Phillipses, but well known to them, was Secretary of State William H. Seward. At one time during their prewar stay in Washington, when they lived near the Patent Office, Seward was their neighbor. He and Eugenia frequently quarreled over the issues that were dividing the North and South.[6]

MRS. PHILIP PHILLIPS
of Washington, D. C.

A portrait of Eugenia Phillips produced before the war. Used with Permission of Documenting the American South, The University of North Carolina at Chapel Hill Libraries.

The firing on Fort Sumter, which dramatically announced the beginning of the Civil War, had occurred just four months before Federal agents, on 24 August 1861, burst into the Phillips's home on I Street and declared all persons in the house under arrest. From top to bottom the house was searched, for the agents were convinced they would find evidence proving that the Phillipses were Confederate spies. Eugenia's family letters, which no doubt contained derogatory remarks about President Abraham Lincoln and the government, were in a box in the washstand. She managed to whisper to Phebe Dunlap, her "confidential maid," telling her to destroy the box. Eugenia trusted Phebe's "Irish shrewdness," and she was not disappointed; for on the pretext of being very thirsty and needing to leave for a drink of water, the maid, with the incriminating evidence tucked under her dress, got away from her guard long enough to burn the letters.[7]

The scene at the Phillips's home must have been the epitome of pandemonium. When Eugenia's daughter Fanny dropped a scrap of paper out of an upstairs window, it was picked up by a passing friend. Several of the distressed government agents went to great lengths to secure "this important document," as Eugenia sarcastically called it, only to find the words, "We are all arrested and treated with indignity." An unidentified woman visitor, who was a Roman Catholic, nervously crossed and recrossed herself and begged Eugenia to tell the agents that she had never sent any letters South and that she visited the Phillips's home only infrequently. The Phillipses were relieved when the distraught lady was released an hour or two later. Upon collecting all the family's correspondence that could be found, the agents departed, leaving soldiers to occupy the house and keep the Phillips family under house arrest.[8]

The occupation of the Phillipses' home lasted a week; but soon after the house was searched, Eugenia, two of her daughters, Fanny and Lina, and her sister, Martha Levy, were moved to the home of Rose Greenhow on 16th Street. Mrs. Greenhow was widely believed to be a Confederate spy and was also under arrest. Her house became the prison "where all the female Rebels could be better cared for," according to Eugenia Phillips. She described their situation at the Greenhow house: "So my two daughters, sister, and myself were thrust into two dirty, small attic rooms, evidently where negroes had lived, with no comforts of any kind. The stove (broken) served us for a table and washstand, while a punch bowl grew into a washbasin. Two filthy straw mattresses kept us warm, and Yankee soldiers were placed at our bedroom door to prevent our escape. Low men took charge of us, their conduct becoming so rude that one of the soldiers, filled with pity, wrote us a note while his watch came round, saying he would take a note to Mr. Phillips, who had not been arrested but was at home with the younger children that night."⁹

While the women were confined, Philip Phillips worked hard through Reverdy Johnson, Edwin Stanton, and Judge James Wayne to obtain their release. In one of the messages Eugenia received from her husband during her incarceration, she heard that their old neighbor, Secretary of State Seward, whom Eugenia bitterly labeled that "arch hypocrite," was behind the imprisonment. At one point during her confinement, Eugenia was incensed to learn the newspapers had reported her release and removal to the South under a flag of truce.¹⁰

Finally, on 18 September, after more than three weeks of being under arrest, the Phillips women were released, largely because of the intervention of Philip Phillips's powerful friends, especially Stanton. Meanwhile, Phillips had arranged through Seward for permission to take his family from Washington and head southward. He sold everything except his law library, entrusting it to a friend, and prepared to leave. The departure from Washington was facilitated by General Winfield Scott, who permitted Phillips to carry with him $5,000 in gold and furnished the steamboat that took the family to Virginia. A ten-day stay in Richmond afforded Phillips an opportunity to report his impressions of the Northern frame of mind with regard to the war. His report that the North was determined to restore the Union at the cost of "the last man and the last dollar" was not what Southern leaders wished to hear. According to Caroline (or Lina) Phillips Myers's account, written a half century later, Eugenia carried a coded message from Rose Greenhow in a ball of yarn and delivered it to President Jefferson Davis of the Confederacy.¹¹ What the message said remains unknown.

From Richmond the Phillips family went ultimately to New Orleans, where Philip opened a law office, only to find that "in time of war the laws are silent." Scarcity of legal business, as it turned out, was not his only problem. On 29 April 1862, Union forces commanded by General Benjamin F. Butler captured New Orleans. Given the compulsion of his wife and daughters to express their Southern sympathies so vocally, Phillips probably knew trouble was not far away now. Only two months passed before Eugenia's defiance brought the Phillipses to grief once more. On Saturday, 29 June 1862, a funeral procession for an officer in the Union army—one Lieutenant DeKay—passed beneath the balcony of the Phillipses' home. As it passed, Eugenia, standing on the balcony, burst into laughter and cheers. The next morning a soldier appeared at the Phillipses' home and informed Eugenia that he was under orders to take her to General Butler. A wave of apprehension swept over the family; but convinced that there must be some mistake, Eugenia, accompanied by her husband, went with the soldier to the customhouse where "the autocrat," as she caustically called Butler, presided. She noted that Butler "styled himself Christ's viceregent." When Philip Phillips was told that he could not go with his wife into Butler's chamber, Eugenia sat down and defiantly announced that only by dragging her would they get her in there alone. She won her point, as Butler relented and permitted Philip to accompany his wife.[12]

The confrontation with Butler was brief, for Eugenia's presence apparently made him seethe with anger. As she approached him, he screamed that she had been observed "laughing and mocking at a Federal officer," referring to her behavior on the balcony the day before. When the general continued his verbal abuse, Philip interrupted him and said he would tolerate only the language of a gentleman in the presence of his wife. At this Butler, "trembling with rage," ordered Phillips from the room, but he refused to go. Butler then slowly wrote out Special Order No. 150, which sentenced Eugenia Phillips to Ship Island, Mississippi, an island in the Gulf of Mexico, until further notice. Eugenia believed that Butler took his time so that she would throw herself on his mercy, but her "holy indignation" led her to stand, with arms folded, and look on with "silent contempt."[13]

Special Order No. 150 was highly explicit. It noted that Eugenia Phillips had already been imprisoned in Washington for "traitorous proclivities and acts." She was accused of training her children to spit on United States officers, and it was noted that one of them had done so. She and her husband had apologized, and had been forgiven, but now she had laughed and mocked during the funeral procession of Lieutenant DeKay, contemptuously giving as her explanation that she was in "good spirits" that day. Henceforth, she was to be regarded "as a uncommon, bad and dangerous woman stirring up strife and inciting to riot," and would be confined to Ship Island "till further orders." Only one female servant would be allowed to accompany her. She was to live in a house assigned to hospital purposes and have a soldier's ration, which she would have to cook herself. No written or verbal communications were to be allowed with her except through General Butler's office.[14]

When Butler was finished, Eugenia Phillips was taken to an adjoining room and locked up for the night, while Philip Phillip made his way home to a "heartbroken family." On the second day of her imprisonment, she was told that a steamboat would take her to Ship Island the next day. Her family packed her things, and her maid Phebe made preparations to accompany her. Eugenia's husband and sons went with them to the boat, as "old venerable men and others" removed their hats and stood in silence as Eugenia passed by.[15]

The boat ride lasted thirty-six hours, during which time Eugenia and Phebe were subjected to "whisky drinking, ribald talk unfit for a female ear." Upon arriving at the island, Eugenia was informed that her quarters were not ready and that she would have to spend another day on the boat. Already in a "nervous state," she announced that another day on the boat would drive her crazy or kill her. An officer, called Lieutenant Blodgett in Eugenia's diary and Captain Blodgett in her memoirs years later, had pity on her, and had her and Phebe rowed ashore in a boat. In her memoirs, written after the war, Eugenia described her island prison: "Ship Island is a sand bar, formed from the workings of the water all around. Not a tree or blade of grass shades the eye or person from the fearful heat. Neither man nor beast . . . found the island inhabitable. Having walked about one-fourth of a mile, Capt. B. suddenly stopped, saying he wished to prepare me for my home. In a path before me stood a box, or small room, fixed upright on a hill of sand."[16]

What Eugenia Phillips called a box or small room was actually a railroad boxcar. There can be little doubt that she and her maid spent a miserable summer on Ship Island, but in spite of the discomfort they suffered from the heat and the insects, they tried to make the best of a grim situation. Eugenia's diary and the letters she wrote to her family reveal that her spirit remained defiant and her tongue sarcastic. She spoke sneeringly of General Neal Dow, commander of the forces on Ship Island, calling him a "Black Republican." And when another female prisoner, named Mrs. LaRue, was released on 4 August Eugenia asked her to tell General Butler when she reached New Orleans that Mrs. Phillips was still in "good spirits." According to Eugenia's later memoirs, Butler dispatched someone once a week to inquire about her health, hoping she would beg and plead to be released, but she never did. She urged Philip to ask no favors, for she preferred rotting on Ship Island to asking Butler for anything.[17]

With regard to Eugenia's living conditions on Ship Island, General Butler's directions were not carried out. As noted, her first shelter was a railroad boxcar, not a hospital house, and when she was moved from the car, her new quarters turned out to be the former post office. Eugenia described it as looking much like a Southern barn that kept out neither wind nor rain. Mosquitoes and flies were so bad she reported that the mosquitoes established an early "curfew." She blessed the man who had invented the mosquito net.[18]

According to Butler's Special Order, Eugenia and Phebe were to cook their own food, a soldier's ration, but this did not work out in practice either. She recorded that at one point the cook took pity on them and attempted to make some bread they could eat; the bread they normally received was too hard to be eaten and could not be softened enough to make it edible. They thought, according to Eugenia, of trying to engage the services of a pile driver or of using steam to see if it could "penetrate the indomitable loaf." Besides hard bread, they had tongue one morning for breakfast and sardines the next; for dinner they had the same. The cook, whom Eugenia jokingly called "our chef de cuisine," would enter and announce, "Thar's you *brikfast* the best I could do." About the only comfort the women could take in their meals was that they were served in a pan that, from a distance, looked like silver. Therefore, they could imagine that the food was going to be of high quality.[19]

In addition to poor housing and almost inedible food, Eugenia found the inhabitants of Ship Island and their behavior quite distressing. She recorded in her diary that the island was the abode of "negroes, soldiers, contractors, sutlers, piddlars, black republicans, sailors, and Officers." Their manner of dress, especially officers walking about in their undershirts, offended her, and she complained that the air was "musical with curses and other elegancies of language." She was also bothered by the familiarity that existed between whites and blacks on the island, plus the constant arrival of runaway blacks whose coming brought a "jubilee of prayers, holy groans, and loud singing." Because she was a former slaveowner and a thoroughly Southern woman, this kind of behavior "aroused her indignation."[20]

To add to her misery, Eugenia at one point became ill during her confinement on Ship Island. Sometime between 9 and 20 August, she was so sick for a week that she could not lift her head without fainting. She experienced severe pain in her eyes and back, but the army doctor treated her "very skillfully," and Phebe never left her bedside. The illness no doubt broke her spirit a little, for she wrote Philip that she was no longer going to conceal from him all that she suffered. She became a little frightened in early September when a soldier died and the doctor reported that yellow fever might have been the cause. After Eugenia's illness and the yellow fever scare, Phebe's health broke down, and what Eugenia called her "chronic disease" began to worsen. Eugenia requested that Philip send someone else to her so that Phebe could go home.[21]

During those difficult, hot summer days Eugenia kept up her morale by reading such material as the *Deserted Village* and the *Vicar of Wakefield*, which she said she had read for the hundredth time. She also studied French to help pass the time. From her family she received loving letters and "creature comforts," which meant much to her. She was no doubt encouraged also by words of praise, such as those written to her by Amanda Levy, apparently a relative who lived in New Orleans. Amanda wrote, "Future historians will vie with each other for the honor of writing your biography." She also reported to Eugenia that pilgrimages two or three times a week to the Phillipses' home had become "quite the rage." Sympathy for her in New Orleans was "wide spread and real."[22]

While Eugenia was on Ship Island several false reports circulated, each claiming that she had been released, but it was not until three months had passed that she was finally permitted to leave her island prison. The exact date of her release and who was responsible for it are not known with certainty, although the evidence indicates that Reverdy Johnson had arranged it at the end of September. On 2 October she gave an account of her property to the provost marshal in New Orleans and admitted to being "an ENEMY of the United States." Sometime after making this declaration she appeared unexpectedly at the Phillipses' home. Immediately there ensued a great emotional scene during which family members laughed and wept. Eugenia had kept control of her nerves as long as she could, and then the family's emotional outburst caused her to break down. She later described what happened: "My brain appeared on fire. My nerves lost all control, and I fell fainting and paralyzed on the floor. My screams were heard over the neighborhood. I lost all consciousness, and physicians were summoned. I was pronounced in a very critical condition, and to be kept perfectly quiet, else the consequences would be fatal."[23]

Since Philip Phillips and his wife had refused to take an oath of allegiance to the United States, it was hardly possible for the family to remain in New Orleans. Consequently, Philip secured a passport through the Federal lines from General George F. Shepley, and at the end of October 1862, the Phillips family and other refugees left New Orleans by boat. After spending some time in Mobile, Alabama, and Marietta, Georgia,

Philip Phillips and his family settled down in LaGrange, Georgia, where they remained until after the war was over. There Eugenia Phillips took delight in "nursing the wounded and dying, alleviating in every way the desolation and misery which civil war surely brings."

By 1867 Philip Phillips was back in Washington, again practicing law. So successfully did he plead cases before the United States Supreme Court that he was eulogized in laudatory terms by important men upon his death in 1884. Eugenia, never forgetting what she went through in 1861 and 1862 because of her beliefs, lived to be eighty-one. She died in 1902.[24]

Surely many women suffered because of the Civil War. But Eugenia Phillips's experience is somewhat unique in that she was numbered among the very few women who were designated as "uncommon, bad, and dangerous." Actually she was, as her husband said, indiscreet but not dangerous. She refused to conceal her beliefs, and proudly proclaimed them in a belligerent manner. Looking back on her experience, one might not be able to endorse the cause that she so pugnaciously supported; but one can admire her courage and sympathize with her for suffering punishment that appears now to have been drastic and uncalled-for. She was twice a victim of overreaction by the Federal authorities. That she annoyed her enemies cannot be questioned; that she was dangerous to them is doubtful.

NOTES

1. Barnett Abraham Elzas, *The Jews of South Carolina* (Philadelphia, 1905), 194; Elizabeth H. Jervey, "Marriage and Death Notices from the *City Gazette* of Charleston," *South Carolina Historical and Genealogical Magazine* 44 (April 1943): 85.

2. Manuscript autobiography of Philip Phillips, 20–21, Phillips Family Papers, Manuscript Division, Library of Congress, Washington, DC; "Schirmer Diary," *South Carolina Historical and Genealogical Magazine* 69 (January 1968): 65.

3. Phillips Autobiography, 21, and the Legal Files, Phillips Family Papers.

4. William Garrett, *Reminiscences of Public Men in Alabama for Thirty Years* (Spartanburg, SC, 1975) 405–407; Manuscript journal of the Alabama House of Representatives, 1851, Alabama State Archives, Montgomery; Phillips Autobiography, 24–30.

5. Phillips Autobiography, 38; Edwin M. Stanton to Philip Phillips, 21 February 1861, Phillips Family Papers; Caroline Phillips Myers, "Memoirs of Events in 1861," Phillips-Myers Collection, Southern Historical Collection, University of North Carolina at Chapel Hill.

6. Myers, "Memoirs."
7. Jacob R. Marcus, ed., "Eugenia Phillips, Defiant Rebel," *Memoirs of American Jews* (New York, NY, 1974), 3:163–67; Phillips Autobiography, 42–43.
8. Marcus, "Eugenia Phillips, Defiant Rebel," 3:166–67.
9. Ibid., 167.
10. Ibid., 168–74; Myers, "Memoirs."
11. Jacob R. Marcus, ed., "Philip Phillips, Southern Unionist," *Memoirs of American Jews*, 3:152–53; Myers, "Memoirs."
12. Marcus, "Eugenia Phillips, Defiant Rebel," 3:180–85; Myers, "Memoirs."
13. Manuscript accounts of Eugenia Phillips's dealings with General Butler and her diary of the events of 1862 are in the Phillips-Myers Collection. The entry giving this particular information is dated 29 June 1862. Also see Marcus, "Eugenia Phillips, Defiant Rebel," 3:186–87.
14. Newspaper clipping of Special Order No. 150, Phillips-Myers Collection.
15. Marcus, "Eugenia Phillips, Defiant Rebel," 3:188–89; Diary of Eugenia Phillips, 1–3 July 1862, Phillips-Myers Collection.
16. Marcus, "Eugenia Phillips, Defiant Rebel," 3:190–91; Diary of Eugenia Phillips, 3 July 1862.
17. Marcus, "Eugenia Phillips, Defiant Rebel," 3:192–93; Diary of Eugenia Phillips, 3 July and 1, 6 August 1862.
18. Diary of Eugenia Phillips, 9 July 1862, and Eugenia Phillips to her friends and husband, 9 July 1862, Phillips-Myers Collection.
19. Diary of Eugenia Phillips, 9 July 1862, and Eugenia Phillips to her "Darling Household," 17 July 1862, Phillips-Myers Collection.
20. Diary of Eugenia Phillips, 9 July 1862.
21. Eugenia Phillips to Philip Phillips, 20 August and 4 September 1862, Phillips-Myers Collection.
22. Eugenia Phillips to her friends and husband, 9 July 1862; Eugenia Phillips to Fan and Flo [Phillips], 25 July 1862; Amanda Levy to Eugenia Phillips, 26 July 1862, Phillips-Myers Collection.
23. Marcus, "Eugenia Phillips, Defiant Rebel," 3:194–95; Jacob C. Levy to Martha and Emma [Eugenia's sisters], 24 July 1862; E. Warren Moise to Mrs. Frederick Myers, 16 October 1862; and Provost Marshal's Receipt to Eugenia Levy Phillips, Phillips-Myers Collection.
24. Marcus, "Eugenia Phillips, Defiant Rebel," 3:161, 195–96; Marcus, "Philip Phillips, Southern Unionist," 3:133, 154–60; "Biographical Information Contained in the Guide and Resolutions Made upon the Death of Philip Phillips"; and E. Warren Moise to Mrs. Frederick Myers, 16 October 1862, Phillips Family Papers.

11

Shifting Veils
Religion, Politics, and Womanhood in the Civil War Writings of American Jewish Women

Dianne Ashton

"If I do not keep the friends I have, I shall indeed be bereaved," wrote Emma Mordecai, a refugee from Richmond, Virginia, in May 1864. That belief guided Mordecai's adjustment to life in her sister-in-law's home in the Confederate countryside, where she had gone to escape the dangers and privations besieging Richmond as the armies of Lee and Grant fought fewer than ten miles away.[1] Although Mordecai faced greater danger than most American Jewish women, many of whom lived in the North, she was not alone in relying heavily on friendships for the duration of the war.

Jewish women of that era were thoroughly immersed in American culture. Prior to Eastern European immigration late in the nineteenth century, American Jews did not live in ethnic neighborhoods. Indeed, because so many Jews were small peddlers, they were sometimes forced by economic pressure to move to small towns where they could provide a town's sole general store. Even in large cities, Jewish neighborhoods of the kind that developed in industrial cities in the early twentieth century, neighborhoods that provided an all-encompassing Jewish subculture, did not exist. Prior to 1880, Jewish women in American towns and cities obtained schooling with Gentile peers, served a Gentile public in family stores, and socialized, at least occasionally, with non-Jewish friends, male and female. Many of these women joined charity organizations serving both Jews and

---

Reprinted with permission of Dianne Ashton from *Women and American Judaism: Historical Perspectives*, ed. Pamela S. Nadell and Jonathan D. Sarna (Hanover, NH: University Press of New England, 2001), 81–106, copyright © 2001 by Brandeis University Press.

non-Jews, and others wrote poetry and short stories for both Jewish and non-Jewish presses. Thus, when antisemitism increased sharply during the Civil War, on both sides of the Mason-Dixon line,[2] American Jewish women were personally challenged to navigate the cultural storm.

Civil War anti-Jewish sentiment can be traced to two trends. First, Americans both North and South used Christian religious rhetoric to justify their causes. Northern abolitionists argued that their Christian faith could not allow them to remain silent while slavery thrived, and Union soldiers marched to the "Battle Hymn of the Republic." The Union's military forces did not allow Jewish chaplains until 1862, after a protest by Jewish soldiers.[3] First in the North and later in the South, the belief that America played a pivotal role in bringing the second coming of Christ reached an apogee just before and during the Civil War.[4] Southern antisemitism was fueled in part by a more fundamentalist style reading of the New Testament than was common in most Northern churches.[5] The Confederacy went so far as to define itself as a Christian nation in its constitution. Southern clergy mounted frequent revivals among the troops, both to obtain God's favor and to enable soldiers to fight without fear of death. Historian Harry Stout explained that the Confederacy declared many fast days, a practice previously more common in the North, to bind the civilian populace to the war effort, to seek God's favor, and to enable civilians and troops alike to display their patriotism and piety—then defined as the same thing.[6]

In part because of the Confederacy's cultural traditions, and in part because it recognized that it lacked both the manpower and heavy artillery of the North, it relied heavily on winning God's favor for its chance of victory. A century later one writer described the Jesus of the South as a "constant presence ... perched on the shoulder of every believer."[7] That faith had penetrated the South by 1850, as Methodist and Baptist forms of Christianity, buttressed by cross-denominational revivals, replaced the earlier dominance of the more staid, patrician style of Episcopal Christianity.[8] Southern women especially depended on piety to effect victory because their cultural traditions expected women to be pious and because they, even more than their menfolk, lacked the military and political means of winning the war.[9] Those Confederates who did not help the South to win God's favor—by lack of reverence for Christ—were, by this logic, suspected of aiding the enemy.

At the same time, Victorian America as a whole moved away from traditional forms of piety and sought meaning in secular as well as religious pursuits. Historian Anne Rose has argued that this trend was evident among leading Americans in all regions of the country over the course of the century. Americans' experience of the Civil War, she insists, needs to be understood as an expression of the general cultural trends of the nineteenth century. The Victorian era's more individualized efforts to obtain a sense of personal meaning helped to shape America's experience of the war as well as to memorialize the war during the 1880s and 1890s.[10] Practical wartime factors contributed to this individualization of religion. The South lost much of its clergy and many houses of worship as men were drawn into the military and communal buildings were burned or converted into hospitals.[11] Thus, the resolution of religious conundrums was often left to individual effort and ingenuity.

The second reason for antisemitism linked prejudice and economics. One historian argues that Southern antisemitism was fueled by a widespread dislike of foreigners and the suspicion of merchants common in an agrarian society.[12] Yet the South as a whole cannot be said to have been anti-Jewish. As the economy of the South worsened and as the North sought to control espionage and contraband, the Shylock stereotype surfaced in both the North and the South. General U. S. Grant ordered all Jews removed from an area in western Tennessee in frustration over cotton trading across enemy lines. However, Grant's attitude was not universal. He took action despite his own father's appeal to him for special trading permission for a group of Jewish merchants. Democrats in Congress issued a resolution against the decree, and Lincoln rescinded it.[13] Public opinion in western Tennessee so favored the Jews there that "the order was completely ignored in certain communities."[14]

Both before the war and after it, Southern Jews held both elective and appointive political offices.[15] Prior to the war, Judah P. Benjamin was the first self-proclaimed Jew elected to the U.S. Senate (representing Louisiana), and he served as attorney general, secretary of state, and secretary of war to the Confederacy.[16] The Southern states varied in religious tolerance: although Louisiana elected Benjamin to national office and South Carolina elected and appointed Jews to various offices,[17] North Carolina maintained religious oaths that effectively banned Jews from public office until 1868. Denunciations of Jews became more commonplace during the Civil War and Reconstruction.[18] Southerners explained their defeat as God's chastisement for widespread sinfulness.[19] Across the South, both small merchants and public figures like Benjamin were blamed for the region's economic woes and its military defeat.[20] Newspapers and magazines in Richmond, Virginia, for example, sometimes referred to Jews as "Yankees among us" and depicted them as Shylocks.[21] Although Richmond's major industries were not in Jewish hands, Jews were among those blamed for the South's economic ills as the war dragged on.[22] Historian Anne Rose concludes that "public demonstrations of piety and the use of Christian concepts became more pronounced in the course of the war," in both North and South.[23]

For Jewish women of this period, antisemitism could not be said to have been universal and open but rather sporadic and threatening. To navigate that social and political turbulence, to maintain established ties, or to forge new alliances, Jewish women displayed either their patriotism, their religious piety, or their common understanding that good women are supposed to maintain family and social ties. Their personal perception of their own needs and of the degree of danger they faced determined their highly individualized shaping of their community during the Civil War. After determining whom they loved and needed and whom they could trust, they displayed those aspect of their own identities that would in turn enable them to present themselves as trustworthy. Through this delicate dance, they survived the war. For some Jewish women, the Civil War made additional critical demands on their religious practices, such as obtaining kosher meat and candles and finding suitable public worship. Consequently, they were forced to forge new alliances and to refashion their standards of meaningful association. In their diaries and letters these women reshaped religious identity, gender expressions, political loyalties, and personal relationships.

A decade ago, women's historians noted that by the early decades of the nineteenth century, women carried most of the responsibility for maintaining social relationships among kin. Moreover, this duty helped to define women's lives.[24] While this was less the case among Jewish extended families whose men were linked by business, synagogue, fraternal, or charitable activities, once those activities were broken, by war, women maintained family ties. To the extent that women accepted this role in both peacetime and wartime, they approached it with seriousness and sought ways to surmount challenges to its successful accomplishment. In many families, these ties linked both Jews and non-Jews, Yankees and Southerners.

Most of the women discussed in this essay also maintained family ties with Christians. These familial commitments provided a tradition of avoiding potential conflict while searching for commonalities to create social harmony. Emma Mordecai, Phoebe Yates Levy Pember, Rebecca Gratz, and Miriam Moses Cohen all sustained family and friendship relationships with Christians. During the Civil War these women learned to attend more carefully to the subtleties of these and similar problematic relationships.[25] By veiling differences, Jewish women were able to suppress potential dangers to social and familial relationships. At the same time, they could display their common identities as women, family members, or Jews. By adapting themselves to various measures of in-group memberships, women thus fashioned new meanings for the concepts of friendship, family, and community. During that war, when the determination of friend or foe was the degree to which an individual displayed shared values and commitments and when religion was made to serve political causes, Jewish identity could be a liability or an asset.

Jewish women used letters and diaries to express their own perceptions of their experiences to themselves and to others in ways that reshaped and strengthened communal ties during the crisis years of the Civil War. In that process, religion and politics were like shifting veils, lifted and lowered as the writers needed, reconstructing ideas and beliefs so as to find their place within their new communities. In so doing, these writers strengthened their communal bonds.

Emma Mordecai was born in 1812, in Warrenton, North Carolina, a younger child among twelve siblings. Her family maintained the Jewish Sabbath and dietary laws despite being the only Jewish family in town. Her father, Jacob Mordecai, was known both locally and nationally as one of the country's leading Hebraists, an acknowledged authority on Jewish law and lore. In Warrenton, a small town near the Virginia border, he directed, with the assistance of his wife and three older children, the highly successful Warrenton Female Academy, from 1809 until 1818.[26] His children continued the family's reputation for erudition, discipline, and scholarship. By the 1840s, Emma Mordecai, then living in Richmond, Virginia, held a responsible position in her congregation's Sunday school, published at least one article on Judaism, and attended synagogue regularly.[27]

As an unmarried woman, Emma Mordecai undoubtedly was more accustomed to depending on female extended family and friends than were women whose husbands had gone to war and for whom this behavior was new.[28] Nonetheless, when she left Richmond for the home of her sister-in-law, Rosina Young Mordecai, in rural Rosewood in 1864, Mordecai was anxious about adjusting to life on Rosina's farm. Although determined to subjugate her own preferences and desires to the household and communal responsibilities she took on in trade for food and shelter, Mordecai brought with her a blank diary. Diaries are often written to aid their authors in overcoming a crisis or in adjusting to change.[29] Mordecai's diary provides a secure place in which to review her new experiences and to shape her responses to them, thus providing her with an emblem of her identity. When she finally settled in at Rosewood, "in spite of some experience and all resolutions to the contrary [Mordecai] concluded to commence" keeping the diary. Subduing her fears of imminent catastrophe by focusing on the act of writing, Mordecai used her diary to help her enter the small local community at Rosewood and to reshape for herself the meanings of personal, familial, and communal experience.[30]

Mordecai's diary, written during 1864, vividly captures those pressures shaping her adjustment to life under new circumstances. In a diary, potentially the most private and freest expression of personal experience, we might hope to uncover resistance to communal ideals or perhaps opinions unusual for that time and place. Instead, Mordecai struggled to bind herself ever more tightly to her new community and to its standards of behavior and opinion. Her diary became a means both to express her fears and to overcome them, to command her behavior and through self-control and creativity, to shape it into acceptable and approved forms.

Especially in the nineteenth century, Jews throughout the United States borrowed and adopted the attitudes common to the regions in which they lived.[31] Mordecai shifted the priorities in her life in order to survive the difficulties of the Civil War. Friendship has been called a social trust and in this sense forms the basis for community.[32] One sociologist argues that community ought to be understood as symbols bounded by the shared ideas distinguishing "outsiders" and "insiders." Their members share common values, and because they do, they turn to each other in times of need. When changes occur either in the content of shared ideas or the social contexts determining who shares those ideas, communities are reshaped.[33] The letters and diaries written by Jewish women during the Civil War illustrate and explain the ways women strove either to remain within, to enter, or to transform communities torn by the war. Southern women relied on each other in new ways and made changes in their personal understanding of the meaning of womanhood that were born of necessity. Southern Jewish women's lives reflected these larger patterns. War underlined the differences in gender responsibilities; yet, as the war went on and as daily personal survival became more difficult, women relied more and more on themselves and on each other to cope with life without men. In that process, Southern traditions of male protection, aid, and supervision were altered.³⁴

As Mordecai begins her diary, she describes her emotions on leaving Richmond. She hopes she will be a "blessing and not a torment or inconvenience" to her host and sister-in-law Rosina, acutely aware that her safety and comfort depend upon her ability to keep Rosina happy.³⁵ This situation framed all her experience while at Rosewood and no doubt exacerbated Mordecai's need to control both her behavior and her fears. Rosina is, in Mordecai's phrase, "a good economist," a middle-aged woman who maintained hogs, horses, cows, chickens, three "servants," as Mordecai called them, and a vegetable garden, while caring for her teenage daughter.³⁶ All in all, Rosina's house was a fine place to be during the latter days of the Civil War, when food became scarce in the South.

Although Rosina and Emma might already be considered members of the same community—female Southerners and Virginians related by marriage—Rosina was a Christian, and Emma Mordecai was a Jew. Religious differences often mark an important boundary between communities. But these women constructed, under pressure of war, a new relationship in which womanhood outweighed all other determinants of community. Although some of Mordecai's siblings married non-Jews, as had her brother Augustus, Rosina's deceased husband, and although two of her sisters actually converted to Christianity, Emma Mordecai remained a Jew. She taught in her synagogue's Sunday school and wrote at least one book about Judaism for children.³⁷ Having previously worked to clarify and strengthen the distinction between Jews and Christians, she now believed she must find a way to accommodate her own religious life within her Christian sister-in-law's household.

In Richmond, Mordecai participated in Jewish communal celebrations. Indeed, she arrived at Rosina's home after spending Passover with a Jewish family. Once settled in at Rosewood, however, religion became for Mordecai an almost completely private matter. While at Rose's (as Mordecai called her sister-in-law), on Shabbat, Mordecai "read the service" in her room from her prayer book.³⁸ Occasionally, she visited Jewish family and friends in town for larger celebrations and rare synagogue attendance.³⁹ She made no secret of her religion, but neither did she display it before Rosina. Although in acknowledging one holiday, Mordecai wrote in her diary, "Blind and foolish are those children of Israel who persuade themselves that the laws given to them by the Unchanging One for them and their descendants to observe forever are not binding on them," nowhere does she mention maintaining Judaism's laws herself apart from the most rudimentary forms of worship.[40] Dietary laws, for example, would have marked a boundary between Mordecai and her Christian host, indicating that in some way they belonged to different communities. Yet Mordecai's account of her stay includes descriptions of dozens of shared meals and common preparations, with no reference to the Jewish dietary laws. In the 1840s, Mordecai had defended Judaism in the national periodical the *Occident and American Jewish Advocate*, and her father observed Jewish laws, but we do not know if Mordecai herself kept dietary laws in her own home.[41] However, despite her daily fears for her own safety that prompted her to prayer and despite copying into her diary the injunction against disobedience to God's laws, Mordecai apparently never increased her own level of observance while living in Rosina's home. It seems likely that she was unsure that she could afford to display marked religious difference while living in a Christian home. Rather, Mordecai accommodated herself to the responsibilities and rhythms of Rosina's household. She spent much of her time in mending and sewing clothes, doing domestic chores, and serving cold milk, biscuits, and fruit to the hungry Confederate soldiers who appeared on their porch or in their yard almost daily.

Most days, Mordecai took food from Rosewood to the wounded soldiers she tended in Seabrook Hospital, the General Winder Hospital, and St. Frances de Sales Hospital.[42] Her diary includes several sentences describing each hospital visit she made. In the rhetoric of Confederate patriotism she recorded her horror at the suffering of "pure, highminded" and "noble, uncomplaining, all enduring heroes."[43] She was also alarmed by the hospitals' shortages of staff and food. Yet when Rosina became ill, Mordecai barely mentioned any effort to care for her friend. Why the difference in the descriptions? It may be, as she admitted in one entry, that the hospital scenes appalled her, and her strong emotion prompted her to write. By writing about hospital conditions, she convinced herself of the importance of her labor there and persuaded herself to return. Tending Rosina at home, on the other hand, may have seemed so ordinary a part of woman's life it was unworthy of note. Mordecai wrote only curt sentences noting that Rosina was ill and spending much or most of several days lying on the couch or in bed.[44] Mordecai also may have resented Rosina's illness, which left more household responsibilities on her own shoulders. Patriotic fervor also seems to have influenced Mordecai. By 1864 the South had begun to romanticize its failed world, in part by idealizing the heroism of those who fought and suffered for their "lost cause." Mordecai's hospital scenes share that rhetoric.

Patriotic feelings, however, revealed another difference between the two women. By May 14, only six weeks after Mordecai arrived at Rosewood, the women had their first disagreement. When a mutual friend nearer the scene of the day's battle wrote assuring them that General Lee had won, Rosina doubted the report. Mordecai argued with her host over its credibility, angering Rosina by telling her that she "hugged worry with the closest affection." The two women did not speak until the next day, after Mordecai "used every means with [her]self to get into a right frame of mind," including confiding the incident to her diary. She apologized to Rosina the next morning, commenting, "If I do not keep the friends I have, I shall indeed be bereaved." The following day, a Sunday, Mordecai went to church with Rose and agreed that the preacher had made some "excellent remarks."[45] As Mordecai moved beyond veiling her Judaism to actively listening to and attending Christian worship, an important boundary between the two women, their religious difference, was temporarily erased in order to strengthen their household community and friendship. Until their political rift healed, Mordecai concluded that other areas of potential conflict, such as their religious differences, must be hidden.

On July 4, 1864, Mordecai avoided facing the imminent danger to her regional community, the South, by focusing on familial and local relationships. That day, as she expected to hear celebrations from the "Yankee gunboats" nearby, Mordecai encountered more Confederate "refugees," "exiles" from embattled Maryland and Petersburg, Virginia. She worried about how stragglers would be cared for, and while she fretted about civilians, she did not mention soldiers, despite the fact that she had spent most of the previous two months tending soldiers both in hospitals and at Rose's front door. She assured herself that "Yankee . . . guns can be destroyed if [Confederates] choose to do it," immediately dropping the subject of the Confederate suffering around her. Instead, she refocused on domestic scenes, and in the very next sentence, Mordecai described how her niece and nephew, enjoying a horseback ride, "looked very pretty and pleasant as they rode off under the trees."[46] In this passage, Mordecai deliberately avoided the issue of the impending destruction of the Confederacy by shifting her attention to her immediate familial community. Her diary describes countless visits to friends, relatives, and soldiers, visits by which she knitted her own life into the local community rent by the war. In this entry, the uncertainty and ambiguity of the war are replaced by the clarity and reassurance of happy familial events. In so doing she constructed an image of an intact community with which to suppress her fears of a broken Confederacy and subsequent threats to family members.

Thirty-one years after the war, Mordecai returned to the diary, filled in passages lost to paper-eating insects, and passed along this memorial of her life to younger relations.[47] By then a romantic image of the Old South had taken shape in popular American culture, a myth built in no small part by the published memoirs of Confederate generals and politicians.[48] Perhaps Mordecai embellished her accounts of hospital scenes at this later time when war memoirs were popular. Mordecai may have felt encouraged to return to her own Civil War diary by the memoir of Phoebe Yates Levy Pember, whose popular 1879 volume was based on the diary she kept while working as a head matron at Richmond's Chimborazo Hospital,[49] then the largest hospital in the world.[50] Pember, like Mordecai, veiled religious differences in order to construct her communal bonds and to bolster the friendships on which her own security depended.

Pheobe Yates Levy was born in Charleston, South Carolina, in 1823. Her father, Charlestonian Jacob Levy, met and married British-born Fanny Yates while visiting Liverpool, England, as a young man. After the young couple settled in Charleston, Fanny was reputed to have been the leader of "the best Jewish society." The Levys relocated to Savannah, Georgia, after the birth of their children. In the smaller town of Savannah, Jews and Christians mingled more freely than in Charleston, and this may have appealed to the couple.[51] Phoebe married a Gentile, Bostonian Thomas Pember, but was widowed in 1861 when he died of tuberculosis. She then returned to her family, which had moved on to Marietta, Georgia, but after only two months there began seeking a way to support herself elsewhere. According to her memoirs, she was uncomfortable living again in her parents' home. Like Mordecai, Pember was forced to seek some new way to survive during the Civil War. She arranged for a matron position at Chimborazo Hospital near Richmond through a friend, the wife of George W. Randolph, then the Confederacy's secretary of war. In December 1862, Pember began at Chimborazo by cleaning an unused kitchen and preparing a huge vat of chicken soup for the patients.[52]

Pember was the first woman to hold a matron's position at Chimborazo.[53] According to historians, the work of women—like Pember, Clara Barton, and the countless female nursing volunteers like Mordecai—consistently outshone that of male nurses during the Civil War. A Kentucky committee investigating hospital conditions discovered that patients

While nursing the wounded in the Confederate stronghold of Richmond during the Civil War, Phoebe Yates Levy Pember veiled her Judaism except when she could present it in a manner emphasizing her loyalty to the South and its cause. Courtesy of The Jacob Rader Marcus Center of the American Jewish Archives.

under the care of male nurses suffered a mortality rate double that of patients tended by female nurses.[54] Indeed, women's Civil War nursing, on both sides, assured that the nursing profession would remain a largely female field after the war. Some historians credit female nurses with helping advance women's suffrage by improving the image of women in the public mind.[55] The first modern nursing school opened in the United States only five years before Pember's diary appeared, and her book no doubt added to a growing effort among philanthropic women as well as nurses to advance professional education and public support for trained female nurses.[56] At the time that Pember began her work at Chimborazo in 1862, female nursing institutions in the United States were, in almost every case, linked to Christian religious orders or denominations. Florence Nightingale's well-known successes in transforming military nursing in Europe, only a few years before the American Civil War, came after her own training and labors in Catholic institutions.[57]

Although we do not know if Pember actually practiced Judaism, she made no secret of her heritage. In a letter to her sister, Louisianan Eugenia Levy Phillips, Pember remarked on the hypocrisy of Christian women who deemed forgiveness the hallmark of their religion yet relished revenge against Yankees, to the point, in the case of one woman, of hoping to use a Yankee's skull for a jewel box. At one moment, Pember so merged her Jewish identity to her Southern patriotism that she claimed relief that she, unlike her Christian friends, was "born of a nation that did not enjoin forgiveness on its enemies." She archly suggested that "until the war was over [every Southerner] should . . . join the Jewish church . . . and leave forgiveness alone."[58] Pember may well have been comforting her sister, who had been banished to Ship Island by Union general Benjamin Butler for three months to prevent her further inciting a riot against the Union occupiers. Eugenia was so outspoken in defending the South that some Union officials considered her a threat to the Northern war effort.[59] By sharing with her sister the common Christian view that Judaism did not enjoin forgiveness on its members, Pember turned an idea used by Christians to condemn Judaism into a measure of their own patriotism to the South.

Christmas 1864 found Pember at work. In a letter to a friend, the wife of Major General Gilmer, Pember described her efforts to provide a celebration for Christian patients in her hospital as well as to join in celebratory dinners at the homes of Christian friends and supervisors. In that letter, Pember began by emphasizing difficulties she faced as a woman, eliciting her friend's sympathy while avoiding the fact that, since she was not a Christian, she could not possibly celebrate this holiday as a Christian would. Yet that unstated fact grounds her day's experience. Others might ask why Pember hadn't gone to church. Because, she could reply, she was too busy working hard to make that day joyous for Christians.

Pember, like Mordecai, was reluctant to display her own Jewish identity before the Christians on whom she depended, unless she could present her Jewishness in a manner that underlined her loyalty to a shared Southern community. In her letter to Mrs. Gilmer, therefore, Pember needed some delicacy in describing her own working Christmas day. She began with a complaint that Christmas seemed like a week's worth of work. At a tedious dinner party at an officer's home on Christmas eve, a loud woman embarrassingly remarked on Pember's unmarried state and urged a match with another guest. The next morning at Chimborazo, Pember provided eggnog and cake for the whole division at 8:00 A.M., turkey and oysters for the inmates of the hospital at 2:00 P.M., and at 5:00 P.M. dressed for a "great dinner" at the home of a colonel. Telling her friend, "it seemed to me I lived a week during the twenty four hours which constituted Christmas," Pember assured her Christian friend that she respected her holiday sufficiently to participate in the celebrations that forged Christian communal identity, regardless of the effort involved.[60] At the same time, by describing distinctly *women's* labors and predicaments, she enhanced her link to Mrs. Gilmer on the grounds of shared womanhood. Thus, just as Mordecai did with Rosina, Pember veiled religious differences between herself and her friend in order to strengthen female commonality. Pember's actions no doubt also strengthened her position as matron by assuring military families and the directors of the hospital that she understood and would carry out the cultural and religious celebrations that they believed maintained Southern communal life.

For Mordecai, Pember, and other American women, navigating the turbulence of many Civil War relationships rested on an ability to command their language and subsequently to reshape and reconstruct communal ties. Although only sixteen years old at that time, Clara Solomon, of New Orleans, had already learned the important role language played in maintaining her own security. "There is no power like that of words," she wrote in 1862.[61] Indeed, Solomon so regarded her diary as an intimate friend that she named it Philemon and hoped it would serve her as a "comforting angel."[62] Solomon was one of six sisters; her parents were natives of South Carolina but had lived for some time in New Orleans by the outbreak of the war. Her father, a merchant, was forty-six when war broke out in 1861. Too old to serve as a soldier, he supplied the Confederate forces with clothing and other materials. At a local synagogue, Clara's older sister, Alice, a schoolteacher, rarely missed a Sabbath service. Clara herself enrolled at the local normal school. Although she never attended class on Saturdays, she seldom attended synagogue. Nonetheless, she relied on faith to help her cope with the casualties of war. On June 7, 1861, she concluded writing in her diary her complaints about war by insisting that "Divine Providence . . . doeth all things well."[63] The Solomon family, like nearly all Jewish families in the antebellum South, was largely integrated into the surrounding Gentile population.

Many marriages between Jews and Gentiles took place in Solomon's circle and in her own family.[64] New Orleans may have seen less antisemitism than any other important city in the country during the antebellum period.[65] Nonetheless, by age sixteen, when she wrote her diary, Clara Solomon had learned to withstand insults in silence, as her family seems to have done, at least during the war. When a Gentile friend lamented that a young man whom she liked was a Jew, Clara confided to her diary that she regretted having to listen to her.[66] Silent about antisemitism in public, teenaged Clara Solomon wrote extensively about her feelings only in her diary. Struck by the plight of a deaf-mute man who communicated via a slate and chalk, young Solomon considered his life a tragic one largely because he could not hear the laughter and condolences of friends.[67] "Necessity and war is the mother of invention," Solomon wisely wrote in 1862.[68]

Mordecai, Pember, and Solomon do not offer unique instances of Jewish women who balanced shifting commitments in order to survive the war. The letters of other Jewish women living during the Civil War reveal their conscious efforts to reshape and strengthen personal, familial, or communal relationships by either displaying or veiling religious or communal commitments. Antebellum Jews lived in all parts of the country by 1848 and did not take a united stand on the issue of slavery. Rather, their political views tended to reflect those of their region.[69] Yet, in contrast to those Jewish women who chose to veil religious differences when in the company of Christian women in order to secure social ties, for some Jews, religious ties became the means for maintaining relationships with Jews in other regions despite political differences. By deliberately avoiding explosive issues and concentrating on shared concerns, Jewish women maintained ties to families and friends in other regions. Mordecai and Pember had veiled religion in order to weaken or erase its potential to create a boundary between themselves and the women friends on whom they depended during the Civil War. Even young Clara Solomon learned by her teen years to control or modulate the display of her Jewish identity. By contrast, elderly Rebecca Gratz, a Philadelphia Unionist and devout Jew, relied on religious ties to secure her relationship with loved ones in the border state of Kentucky as well as in the Confederate South. In letters to her family, Gratz either veiled political disagreements that might divide her family, as they had divided other Americans, or displayed them in a way that supported and strengthened religious and familial ties.[70]

Born in 1781, Gratz was a middle child in a family of ten children. Her father, uncle, and brothers formed a family of merchants who had engaged in coastal shipping, land speculating, and dry goods trading for almost one hundred years, from the mid-eighteenth century through the Civil War. Gratz herself grew up in post-Revolutionary Philadelphia, and throughout her long life she remained convinced that the ideals of the American Revolution signaled a new era of freedom in human history. Gratz, like her older sister, and three brothers, remained single. During her life she helped to establish and lead five different benevolent organizations: the Female Association for the Relief of Women and Children in Reduced Circumstances (1801), the Philadelphia Orphan Asylum (1815), the Female Hebrew Benevolent Society (1819), the Hebrew Sunday School (1838), and the Jewish Foster Home (1855). When Gratz's younger sister, Rachel Gratz Moses, died in 1823, she brought Rachel's six children into her home until their father found a home nearby, and she continued to act as their mother. One of those children, Miriam Moses, married Southerner Solomon Cohen in 1836 and settled first in Charleston, South Carolina, and later in Savannah, Georgia.[71]

As early as the 1840s, when Solomon Cohen began speaking to audiences about the virtues of slavery, Gratz and her niece, Miriam Moses Cohen, began veiling their political differences and emphasizing their religious commonalities. Like Gratz, Miriam cared deeply about Judaism. In each letter the two women usually commented on some religious matter. For Miriam, discussions about religion provided a continuing bond with her aunt, and Miriam rarely disagreed with Gratz or raised issues that might cause friction. Miriam's husband, attorney Solomon Cohen, was an ardent and outspoken secessionist who owned several slaves and believed that Black slavery civilized both Whites and Blacks, an idea widespread in the South.[72] Rather than debate about slavery, the women talked of religion. When Jewish religious reformer Max Lilienthal wrote inspiring works about Jewish ideas, both women wrote admiringly about his work, despite Gratz's strident opposition to the movement for religious reform then popular among some American Jews. Miriam, like Gratz, worried about the thinness of Jewish resources in America—her own congregation lacked "a good hazan" (reader). And like her aunt, Miriam noted all work authored by Jewish women and thought a piece Emma Mordecai published in the Philadelphia-based *Occident and American Jewish Advocate* "quite well written."[73] Miriam's letters carefully maintained the bond between herself and her aunt across a distance that increasingly carried differences in cultural and political allegiances.

Like Mordecai, Pember, and Solomon, Gratz believed that harmonious relationships rested on well-controlled language. Reflecting her own high regard for self-discipline, Gratz disliked unbridled sentimentality in life and in literature. She believed that both domestic and world peace could be achieved only when individuals exercised rational self-control. In 1845 she complained to her new sister-in-law, Ann, the young wife of her brother Benjamin, then living in Lexington, Kentucky, that "female moralists sometimes laud candor as the . . . test of friendship—and care not how deeply they lacerate the feelings—and poison the peace of families."[74] It was a warning to Ann, a Christian raised in the South, to avoid conflict for the sake of family harmony. In keeping the Gratz family sentimentally united while dispersed geographically, the Gratz women wrote of domesticity, religion, or gossip. Southerners in the family commented on the beauties of gardens and nature; Northerners, on the inspiration of literature. These themes constituted part of what has been called a "female world of love and ritual."[75]

In May 1844, near the holiday of Shevuot (Feast of Weeks), Gratz's sister, Richea Gratz Hays, visited her daughter Rosa Marx in Richmond, Virginia. Rosa was working on a horticultural exhibit at Falls Plantation, when "Emma Mordecai . . . walked over, . . . starting the festival with us. I was invited to spend the holy days with Rebecca Myers and attend synagogue but I declined," Richea told her sister Rebecca. The women close to Gratz often discussed what she would think of the sermons and religious debates they heard. "Dear Rosa bought Mr. Salomon's and Mr. Leeser's sermons for the festival and read them to me. We thought of and talked of you and all our loved ones," Richea wrote to Gratz.

Richea Gratz Hays assured her sister that the younger generation of Jewish women in the South in their circle cared about Judaism. Rosa Hays Marx, Richea's daughter, wrote her own note to Gratz underneath her mother's text, assuring her aunt that she and her Jewish women friends had declined to attend a party because "it was the commencement of our holy days." Rosa also conveyed best wishes from Emma Mordecai, whose brother Alfred had married Richea's daughter Sara, and told Gratz that both young women hoped to see her in Richmond one day.[76] Assurances about Emma Mordecai's dedication to Judaism pleased and surprised Gratz. Gratz had been appalled when Emma's older sisters converted to Christianity. Gossiping about their conversion to her niece, Miriam Moses Cohen, Gratz insisted that their behavior would injure their characters as well as scandalize their father's memory. As those around her knew, Gratz believed that "we every day see the necessity of paying more attention to religious duties if we would not lose the dignity and honor of [Jewish] national character."[77] Her own life experience convinced Gratz that only when Jews honored their religion were they treated respectfully, and only by practicing their religion could they cultivate the self-discipline required for success in life.

Like her correspondence with Miriam, Gratz's mail from her Lexington, Kentucky, family limited itself to topics that would cause little friction. Although the Lexington Gratzes were staunch Unionists, Gratz's sister-in-law Ann was a Christian, and the two women confined their letters to uncontroversial topics. Both women discussed the details of domestic life and the beauties of nature. At Gratz's urging, Ann took up Shakespeare "with renewed spirit" and found it "elevating and refining, . . . thereby approximating us to our divine origin, perhaps as much as many of our clerical lecturers." This was the sister-in-law Gratz hoped for, one who could appreciate the spiritual benefits of reading Shakespeare. Through Shakespeare, popular in all classes of antebellum society, Gratz and Ann displayed their common identity as Americans. Moreover, by articulating his *moral* significance, Gratz and Ann echoed the central argument that, according to historian Lawrence A. Levine, "overcame general prejudice against theater."[78] More important for Gratz and Ann, Shakespeare provided them a secular source of shared spiritual and moral values and offered them common reference points for American culture. Encouraged, Gratz rewarded Ann by arranging to have four dresses, linen boots, thread, stockings, and a bonnet made for her sister-in-law.[79] Enmeshed in the details of each other's lives, Gratz's relationships with her Lexington family survived the political tensions otherwise dividing families across the nation.

The following winter, when Gratz's niece, Sarah Moses, visited her sister, Miriam Moses Cohen, in Savannah, Sarah could not help linking religion to the national unrest. From her sister's damp house she wrote of her concern for the nation's future. Like some other antebellum Americans, Sarah worried first about what God would think of the way the country had conducted its political life, in compromises between slave and free states, in untenable rulings about new territories, in allowing Indian treaties to be broken and innocents slaughtered, and in embarking on a war with Mexico to gain its land.[80] "Nations as a rule are punished for their sins and if we should now be involved in warfare—I should look upon it as the result of the unhallowed system of politics that has been indulged in for the last few years," Sarah wrote to Gratz.[81] Sarah's political sympathies echoed those of her aunt. Twelve years before Harriet Beecher Stowe's *Uncle Tom's Cabin* attacked slavery's devastation of Black domesticity, Gratz described her sympathy for Native Americans in language that revealed her concern for their domestic tragedies. She empathized with their "private sufferings" at the hands of Whites and admitted to "horror and shame" for attacks on Indian villages and families and to a "fear and dread" of "Indians" who "have so many wrongs to avenge."[82] Sentimental literature of the time condemned politics ruled solely by economics, and, in the North, political critiques increasingly voiced concern for violence to households and domestic life. Neither Gratz nor Stowe was alone in such views.[83]

Although Sarah Moses and Rebecca Gratz linked their anxieties for the political future of the nation to distress about domestic tranquility among families, a theme that grew increasingly powerful in the North in the years leading up to Civil War, Gratz's niece Miriam, Sarah's older sister, now a Southerner, seldom discussed politics with her Northern aunt. Instead, Miriam described religious and familial activities and the natural beauty of the South. "March is mellow sunshine, yellow jasmine in bloom. You scarcely meet anyone in the street without a sprig of it, even the horses are decorated with its bright flowers and the houses are perfumed with it." She repeated her love and concern for Gratz. Miriam talked about her father, Solomon Moses, whom she hoped would visit her for Passover, and about hosting a family celebration for Purim.[84] Miriam wrote only about family, religion, and nature, avoiding politics when corresponding with Gratz.

Few people could ever meet Gratz without learning about her religious beliefs, partly because she devoted so much time to religious activities. Even Congressman Frank Blair, Gratz's distant kin through her former Christian sister-in-law, Maria Gist Gratz, could not separate his impression of Rebecca from her dedication to her religion, honoring her, in 1842, as "Queen of the Jews."[85] Far from avoiding the topic of religion with those who did not share her beliefs, Gratz's faith was so much a part of her identity that it was impossible to be her friend without addressing religious issues.[86]

When Sarah Moses visited her sister, Miriam Cohen, in 1846, her letters to Gratz describing Jewish life in Savannah revealed that regional differences between North and South were beginning to affect the way American Jews understood their religious orientations. Sarah Moses saw regional and political loyalties threatening to split American Judaism, just as they did some Protestant denominations. Sarah told her aunt that, in the South, religious debates about tradition and Reform were recast in the language of the deepening national conflict. One Friday evening, Philadelphia Jewish leader Isaac Leeser visited the Cohen home, where "he had a long discussion . . . with the Levys—reform vs. anti-reform." Sarah wrote to her aunt: "The Southern Jews say that the Northern Jews will not believe that they can have any religion because they do not adhere to all the forms prescribed by the rabbis while the Southern Jews insist that the Northern and Conforming Jews lose all spirituality in blind adherence to what their fathers did before them."

Sarah, like Leeser and Gratz, opposed Reform but felt herself inadequate to the debate that evening. Knowing Gratz's eloquent defense of Jewish tradition, she remarked, "I wished for your aid." Sarah's frustrations were evident in her letter. "The discussion ended as it must do—by either party's remaining unconvinced," she concluded.[87] The discussion held little chance for resolution, embedded as it was in other, perhaps even more emotionally laden, political controversies.

But as if to erase the potential for family enmity her account described, Sarah immediately shifted her topic to depict domestic Judaism thriving despite controversy in the Cohen home. She assured Gratz that although interested in Reform, Miriam and her husband remained faithful Jews at home. "We kept Friday evening just as we do it at home, . . . [and] I read my prayers quietly the next evening and thought of you." To quell any fears she might have raised in her aunt, Sarah then praised Miriam's womanly virtues. She admired Miriam's self-discipline and composure. The more expressive and honest Sarah, soon to marry and move to Montreal, worried that she might never see her sister again. "How can I gain her well controlled nature?" she asked Gratz, "living in the present 'Heart within—God overhead'—with neither regrets for the past or fears for the future?" Sarah thought such self-control impossible for her to attain herself.[88]

Gratz herself used a similar device when writing younger brother Benjamin, living in Lexington, Kentucky, about her June 1860 visit to niece Miriam in Savannah. Benjamin Gratz, who, like his sister, opposed both slavery and secession, lost his son Cary, defending the Union at the Battle of Wilson's Creek. Gratz sought to minimize the potential for hostility between her brother and their niece, Miriam, by writing about Miriam's female world—domesticity and marriage. She wrote to Benjamin that "dear Miriam looks in full health and is the picture of contentment—no one can be happier in the domestic sense or more grateful to the Almighty giver of all good than she is—truly Mr. Cohen repays her tenderness and our great regard."[89] By displaying Miriam's womanliness and her own faith, Gratz veiled the political conflicts that separated her brother Benjamin from Miriam. Thus she hoped to erase potential family conflict.

There seems no question that Miriam's political views would have estranged her from her family. A grim 1861 letter employed Confederate political rhetoric and envisioned history's epitaph to the United States: "Here lies a people who in seeking the liberty of the negro, lost their own."[90] Echoing phrases common to Confederate speeches, Miriam wrote passionately to her aunt, outraged by the indictment of the Southern way of life frequently found in the pages of newspapers, magazines, and fiction published in the North. Quoting a phrase from Southern political speeches, Miriam believed the attack on Southern culture proved that "sickly sentimentality," as secessionists called the abolition movement, had enveloped "every class of [Northern] society." Moreover, she believed the cultural war against the South part of a concerted effort to "incite the poor [and] uproot the foundations of the Southern social system." She explained to her aunt that although Southerners found the North's "system of white labor, with all its oppression and wrongs . . . abhorrent," Southerners refrained from writing books and delivering sermons aimed at destroying the North's economic structure. For Miriam, that restraint on the part of Southerners proved their moral superiority to Northerners.[91] But after this outburst in 1861, Miriam wrote only of domesticity, religion, and nature when writing to Rebecca. Miriam's husband, Solomon Cohen, was a secessionist, but he, too, usually veiled politics and displayed religion when corresponding with Gratz. Solomon Cohen also sent Gratz clippings from newspapers about events in Savannah that swept the Cohens along in the country's turmoil. Miriam and Solomon Cohen fit so well into the White population of their own town that, after her death, one obituary called Miriam "a beautiful example of Christian character."[92]

Despite her own Unionist convictions and her outspoken temperament, the eighty-year-old Gratz kept silent on politics when writing to Miriam. Instead she separated the public war from the privacy of the family. Focusing on emotions, Gratz wrote that her "heart was sick with every days account of wrongs and outrages" but that with Miriam's letters before her, she could "look into [Miriam's] own loving heart." Indeed, Gratz insisted that her "one great consolation" was that between herself and Miriam "there was no war in [their] own hearts."[93]

But there was no hiding the fact that family members were preparing to battle on opposing sides. In July 1861, a few months after the war began, Gratz's nephew, Charles E. Etting, a cadet at West Point, wrote to her about his life there, filled with drills, rifle practice, and guard duty.[94] Gratz urged Benjamin, whose political views matched her own, to stay at home in Kentucky rather than visit her in Philadelphia, because travel was too dangerous and because "every man should be at the place where his influence for the good may be needed." Happy that Philadelphia was "decidedly Unionist," Gratz hoped that Kentucky was free "of secessionist principles or dangers and that our beloved Union may survive."[95]

War left Gratz in a state of "constant agitation," she explained to Benjamin's wife, Ann. She detested the way the war tore apart families and friends. "Every day," she complained, she heard an "account of wrongs and outrages perpetrated by kindred on each other—of familiar friends becoming bitter foes." The Non-Intercourse Law, passed in 1861, which limited communication between North and South, interfered with her correspondence with Miriam. Gratz asked individuals with special travel passes to convey letters for her. But travel across the Mason-Dixon Line was sharply curtailed, and six months sometimes passed between letters from her niece. Gratz told Ann that she didn't think it was fair for the law "to exist between" them: "I had a rare treat of a letter from Miriam Cohen through a private opportunity. . . . [It is] sad when the natural flow of familiar intercourse is to be either stolen or only accidentally enjoyed." She lamented not just for her own family but for "our late happy country." Gratz's own opinions echoed Lincoln's speeches.[96] It seemed to her that America's promise of a new era of peace and freedom might come to an end.

When Benjamin's son was killed in battle, Gratz wrote to Cary's stepmother, Ann, that the "outrages perpetrated by kindred on each other . . . [are] too appalling to be realized."[97] Gratz comforted Benjamin with the hope that he would be reunited with his son in another world. Benjamin's daughter Miriam also supported the Union. "My dear patriotic niece," Gratz wrote later, "my heart goes with you in all our triumphs."[98] But even Union victories failed to make Gratz happy. "I have so many dear [ones] scattered over the land," she explained. To Ann, she detailed her dilemma, as she watched those she loved and who loved one another arm themselves against each other. No doubt thinking of Miriam Moses Cohen, who as a child was supported by the Gratz brothers and who now stood with the Confederates in Georgia, Gratz detailed her emotional turmoil. "I have been reading some loving letters from some so near to me in blood and affections whose arms are perhaps now raised against those hearts at which they have fed." By the end of 1861, Gratz had "no faith in politicians" and thought only "Divine Providence" could convince national leaders that it was wrong to be "shedding Brothers blood in this unholy war."[99] The following year she quit discussing politics with Confederate sympathizers, after Benjamin had admitted to her that he behaved similarly.[100] Niece Miriam, fearing that Gratz would die while the Civil War still thwarted her communication with her aunt, in 1864 managed to have a birthday letter stamped "Flag of Truce."[101]

In 1865, when the Union had survived, Gratz began receiving reassuring letters from her family. Ann wrote that in Kentucky life was returning to normal and those who had fled were returning from Canada and elsewhere. With smooth delivery of the mails restored, Sarah Gratz Moses, now married to Henry Joseph, wrote weekly from Montreal, assuring Gratz that "your love, my darling aunt, is the treasure of my life—it warmed my orphan heart when God saw fit to remove my mother—and it has burnt steadily on without changes or diminution—and each year of my life I feel its influence."[102] Through the crucible of Civil War correspondence, Sarah had learned that by displaying piety and affection and veiling politics, she could remain within the Gratz family community despite geographic separation and new political loyalties. These Jewish women's personal writings, both diaries and letters, enabled them to survive the social traumas of the Civil War with communal lives intact.

For Emma Mordecai, a woman in her fifties, her diary helped to overcome potential family conflicts raised by differences in religious and political ideas. For young Clara Solomon, too, the act of writing in her diary provided a means to express ideas and emotions that might otherwise endanger her position in a community in which antisemitism was not uncommon. Both Solomon and Mordecai used their diaries to veil more public displays of their Jewish identities by providing a private arena in which they could express their ideas and feelings about their religion. Like Phoebe Yates Levy Pember and Miriam Moses Cohen, Solomon and Mordecai worked hard at making a place for themselves within their local communities in the South. Each of these women accomplished her goal in large part by veiling her religious difference from the Christians who played powerful roles in their worlds. Ultimately, the strategy of veiling helped Jewish women to remain within those communities that enabled them to survive during wartime despite an increase in anti-Jewish feeling.

For Philadelphian Rebecca Gratz, an elderly woman at the time of the Civil War but a dominating figure in her family, letters became the primary vehicle for keeping her scattered family united. By writing and asking about religious ideas, loyalties, disciplines, and activities, Gratz avoided mentioning the political conflicts that otherwise separated her from loved ones. When writing to her Christian sister-in-law in Kentucky, Gratz linked her expressions of piety to literary sources and modulated the expression of her own Unionist sympathies until they matched those common in Kentucky and so established a firm relationship with her new sister-in-law. Her strategy worked—the family relationships survived. Gratz certainly would have agreed with Clara Solomon's judgment on the power of words. Although Jews did not speak with a single voice,[103] the writings examined here suggest that individual Jewish women strove to reshape their local communities and their family ties through writing and language. The women had learned that through written texts they could both veil their differences from those whom they loved or needed while displaying their commonalities. Soon after the war, Jews, like many other Americans, either relocated to new regions or returned to communities and families that had been split by the war.[104] The sensitivity to social language that Mordecai, Pember, Solomon, Gratz, Moses, and Cohen evidenced in their writing helped them to survive the war and to provide entry to new communities and relationships that emerged at its end.[105]

NOTES

1. James McPherson, *Battle Cry of Freedom: The Civil War Era* (New York: Oxford University Press, 1988), 723–40.

2. Hasia R. Diner, *A Time for Gathering: The Second Migration: 1820–1880* (Baltimore: Johns Hopkins University Press, 1992), 158–60.

3. Jacob Rader Marcus, Foreword, *A Jewish Colonel in the Civil War: Marcus M. Spiegel of the Ohio Volunteers*, ed. Jean Powers Soman and Frank L. Byrne (Lincoln: University of Nebraska Press, 1981), viii.

4. Randall Miller, Harry Stout, and Charles Regan Wilson, eds., *Religion and the American Civil War* (New York: Oxford University Press, 1999), 22; Paul Boyer, *When Time Shall Be No More: Prophecy Belief in Modern America* (Cambridge, Mass.: Belknap, Harvard University Press, 1992), 47.

5. Bertram Wallace Korn, "American Judaeophobia: Confederate Version," in *Jews in the South*, ed. Leonard Dinnerstein and Mary Dale Palsson (Baton Rouge: Louisiana State University Press, 1973), 135–36.

6. Miller, Stout, and Wilson, *Religion and the American Civil War*, 11–14.

7. Eli Evans, *The Provincials*, rev. ed. (New York: Free Press, 1997), 121.

8. Christine Leigh Heyrman, *Southern Cross: The Beginnings of the Bible Belt* (New York: Knopf, 1997), 206–52.

9. Drew Gilpin Faust, *Mothers of Invention: Women of the Slaveholding South in the American Civil War* (New York: Vintage Books, 1996), 182–83.

10. Anne C. Rose, *Victorian America and the Civil War* (Cambridge: Cambridge University Press, 1992), 20–38.

11. Faust, *Mothers of Invention*, 185.

12. Korn, "American Judaeophobia," 135–36.

13. McPherson, *Battle Cry*, 622–23.

14. Seth Forman, "The Unbearable Whiteness of Being Jewish," *American Jewish History* 85:2 (1997): 129.

15. Ibid.

16. For a full account of Benjamin's political life, see Eli Evans, *Judah P. Benjamin: The Jewish Confederate* (New York: Free Press, 1988).

17. Mark I. Greenberg, "Becoming Southern: Jews of Savannah, Georgia, 1830–1870," *American Jewish History* 86:1 (1998): 63–68.

18. Leonard Rogoff, "Is the Jew White? The Racial Place of the Southern Jew," *American Jewish History* 85:3 (1997): 201.

19. Daniel Stowell, *Rebuilding Zion: The Religious Reconstruction of the South, 1863–1877* (New York: Oxford University Press, 1998), 33–49.

20. Evans, *Benjamin*, 193.

21. Myron Berman, *Richmond's Jewry, 1769–1976: Shabbat in Shockoe* (Richmond: University of Virginia Press, 1979), 176–78.

22. Ibid., 188; Miller, Stout, and Wilson, *Religion and the American Civil War*, 313.

23. Rose, *Victorian America*, 61.

24. Micaela Di Leonardo, "The Female World of Cards and Holidays: Women, Families, and the Work of Kinship," *Signs* 12:3 (1987): 440–53; Carroll Smith-Rosenberg, "The Female World of Love and Ritual," in *Disorderly Conduct: Visions of Gender in Victorian America* (New York: Knopf, 1985), 53–77.

25. Many thanks to Anne Rose for this insight, personal communication, December 14, 1997.

26. Sheldon Hanft, "Mordecai's Female Academy," *American Jewish History* 79:1 (1989): 72–93.

27. Richea Gratz Hays to Rebecca Gratz, May 27, 1844, Richmond to Philadelphia, Gratz Family Papers, collection 72, box 16, American Philosophical Society (thereafter APS).

28. Emma's brother, Major Alfred Mordecai, resigned his commission in the U.S. Army rather than fight against the South, but he sat out the war in Philadelphia rather than fight against the North. His decision was unpopular with both Northerners and Southerners. Berman, *Richmond's Jewry*, 173–74.

29. Steven E. Kagle and Lorenza Gramegna, "Rewriting Her Life: Fictionalization and the Use of Fictional Models in Early American Women's Diaries," in *Inscribing the Daily: Critical Essays on Women's Diaries*, ed. Suzanne L. Bunkers and Cynthia A. Huif (Amherst: University of Massachusetts Press, 1996), 44.

30. Emma Mordecai, *Diary*, TS, 1864, 1886, American Jewish Archives, Cincinnati, Ohio (hereafter AJA). This was Mordecai's second diary that we know of; her first was written almost twenty years earlier when she examined her family's disparate religious loyalties and resolved her own. Emma Mordecai Diary, 1838, Mordecai Family Papers, Southern History Collection, Chapel Hill, N.C.

31. Diner, *Time for Gathering*, 156–58; Bertram Korn, *American Jewry during the Civil War* (Cleveland: World Publishing Co., 1961), 2–16.

32. Janice G. Raymond, *A Passion for Friends: Toward a Philosophy of Female Attraction* (Boston: Beacon Press, 1986), 9.

33. Anthony P. Cohen, *The Symbolic Construction of Community* (London: Routledge, 1995), 10–30. Lynn Hankinson Nelson has argued that these relationships have epistemological import. "Epistemological Communities," in *Feminist Epistemologies*, ed. Linda Alcoff and Elizabeth Potter (New York: Routledge, 1993), 121–60.

34. Faust, *Mothers of Invention*, 248–54.

35. Mordecai, *Diary*, AJA, 1.

36. Ibid., 8.

37. Hanft, "Mordecai's Female Academy," 90; Hays to Gratz, May 27, 1844; Mordecai, *Diary*, AJA, 16.

38. Mordecai, *Diary*, AJA, 17, 30.

39. Ibid., 24.

40. Ibid., 42.

41. Miriam Moses Cohen to Rebecca Gratz, March 22, 1846, Gratz Family Papers, collection 72, box 16, APS.

42. Berman, *Richmond's Jewry*, 179.

43. Mordecai, *Diary*, AJA, 22.

44. Ibid., 56–60.

45. Ibid., 18–19
46. Ibid., 59.
47. Ibid., 56.
48. McPherson, *Battle Cry*, 197; C. Vann Woodward and Elizabeth Muhlenfeld, eds., *The Private Mary Chestnut: The Unpublished Diaries* (New York: Oxford University Press, 1984), xxv.
49. Bell Irvin Wiley, ed., *A Southern Woman's Story: Life in Confederate Richmond by Phoebe Yates Pember, Including Unpublished Letters Written from Chimborazo Hospital* (Jackson, Tenn.: McCowat-Mercer Press, 1959), 4.
50. McPherson, *Battle Cry*, 478; Richard Tedlow, "Judah P. Benjamin," in *Turn to the South: Essays on Southern Jewry*, ed. Nathan M. Kaganoff and Melvin I. Urofsky (Charlottesville, Va.: American Jewish Historical Society, 1979), 48.
51. James Hagy, *This Happy Land: The Jews of Colonial and Antebellum Charleston* (Tuscaloosa: University of Alabama Press, 1993), 53–54.
52. Wiley, *Southern Woman's Story*, 19.
53. Ibid., 6.
54. Faust, *Mothers of Invention*, 97.
55. McPherson, *Battle Cry*, 480; Wiley, *Southern Woman's Story*, 7.
56. Richard H. Shryock, *The History of Nursing* (Philadelphia: W. B. Saunders Co., 1959), 295; Susan Armeny, "Organized Nurses, Women Philanthropists, and the Intellectual Bases for Cooperation among Women, 1898–1920," in *Nursing History: New Perspectives, New Possibilities*, ed. Ellen Condliff Lagemann (New York: Teachers College Press, 1983), 16–17.
57. Shryock, *History of Nursing*, 269–77.
58. Quoted in Faust, *Mothers of Invention*, 206; see also Berman, *Richmond's Jewry*, 179.
59. Greenberg, "Becoming Southern," 66–67, 75.
60. Wiley, *Southern Woman's Story*, 158.
61. Clara Solomon, *The Civil War Diary of Clara Solomon: Growing Up in New Orleans, 1861–1862*, ed. Elliott Ashkenazi (Baton Rouge: Louisiana State University Press, 1995), 98.
62. Quoted in Faust, *Mothers of Invention*, 164.
63. Quoted in ibid., 192.
64. Solomon, *Civil War Diary*, 2–19.
65. Bertram Korn, quoted in Eli Evans, *The Provincials* (New York: Free Press, 1997), 205–6.
66. Solomon, *Civil War Diary*, 284.
67. Ibid., 98.
68. Quoted in Faust, *Mothers of Invention*, frontispiece.
69. Korn, "American Judaeophobia," 12–30; Tedlow, "Judah P. Benjamin," 49; Eli N. Evans, "Southern Jewish History: Alive and Unfolding," in Kaganoff and Urofsky, *Turn to the South*, 160.

70. Dianne Ashton, *Rebecca Gratz: Women and Judaism in Antebellum America* (Detroit: Wayne State University Press, 1998), 195–208.

71. Dianne Ashton, "Souls Have No Sex: Philadelphia Jewish Women and the American Challenge," in *When Philadelphia Was the Capital of Jewish America*, ed. Murray Friedman (Cranbury: N.J.: Associated University Presses, 1993), 34–45; Joseph Rosenbloom, "Some Conclusions about Rebecca Gratz," in *Essays in American Jewish History* (Cincinnati: American Jewish Archive, 1958), 171–86.

72. Greenberg, "Becoming Southern," 62–63.

73. Ashton, *Rebecca Gratz*, 203.

74. Rebecca Gratz to Ann Gratz, November 24, 1845, Rebecca Gratz Papers, P-9, American Jewish Historical Society (hereafter AJHS); quoted in Ashton, *Rebecca Gratz*, 198.

75. Smith-Rosenberg, "Female World," 73.

76. Ashton, *Rebecca Gratz*, 199; Richea Gratz Hays to Rebecca Gratz, May 27, 1844, Gratz Family Papers, Collection no. 72, box 16, APS.

77. Ashton, *Rebecca Gratz*, 200.

78. Lawrence W. Levine, *Highbrow/Lowbrow: The Emergence of Cultural Hierarchy in America* (Cambridge, Mass.: Harvard University Press, 1988), 39.

79. Ann Gratz to Rebecca Gratz, April 2, 1846, Gratz Family Papers, collection 72, box 16, APS.

80. Samuel Eliot Morison, *The Oxford History of the American People* (New York: Signet, 1972), 2:133–39, 261–64, 273–82; McPherson, *Battle Cry*, 48.

81. Sarah Gratz Moses to Rebecca Gratz, April 1846, Gratz Family Papers, collection 72, box 16, APS.

82. Rebecca Gratz to Miriam Moses Cohen, May 20, 1838, Miriam Moses Cohen Papers, Southern History Collection, University of North Carolina, Chapel Hill.

83. Ann Douglas, *The Feminization of American Culture* (New York: Avon Books, 1977), 73; McPherson, *Battle Cry*, 88–91; Jane Tompkins, "Sentimental Power: Uncle Tom's Cabin and the Politics of Literary History," *Glyph* 8 (1981): 4.

84. Miriam Moses Cohen to Rebecca Gratz, March 22, 1838, Miriam Moses Cohen Papers and Books, Collection no. 2639, Southern History Collection.

85. Frank Blair to Rebecca Gratz, November 13, 1842, Gratz Family Papers, collection 72, box 11; Hyman Gratz to Rebecca Gratz, August 2, 1847, Gratz Family Papers, collection 72, box 15, APS. Blair married Maria's sister Eliza Violet Gist in 1812 (Gist Genealogy, Genealogies file, AJA).

86. Mrs. Shroeder to Rebecca Gratz, July 20, 1847, Gratz Family Papers, collection 72, box 15, APS.

87. Ashton, *Rebecca Gratz*, 203.

88. Ibid., 203–4.

89. Rebecca Gratz to Benjamin Gratz, June 24, 1860, Rebecca Gratz Paper, manuscript collection 236, AJA.

90. McPherson, *Battle Cry*, 102, 230.

91. Ashton, *Rebecca Gratz*, 226.

92. Mrs. James T. Dent, clipping, Gratz Family Papers, box 11, APS.

93. Rebecca Gratz to Miriam Moses Cohen, n.d., Gratz Family Papers, collection 72, box 11, APS.

94. Charles Etting to Rebecca Gratz, July 14, 1861, Gratz Family Papers, collection 72, box 9, APS.

95. Rebecca Gratz to Ann Gratz, December 13, 1860, in *Letters of Rebecca Gratz*, ed. David Philipson (Philadelphia: Jewish Publication Society, 1929), 417–18.

96. McPherson, *Battle Cry*, 309.

97. Rebecca Gratz to Ann Gratz, June 8, 1861, Rebecca Gratz Papers, P-9, AJHS.

98. Rebecca Gratz to Miriam Gratz, August 24, 1861, Rebecca Gratz Papers, manuscript collection 236, AJA.

99. Rebecca Gratz to Ann Gratz, October 30, 1861, Rebecca Gratz Papers, P-9, AJHS.

100. Rebecca Gratz to Benjamin Gratz, Rebecca Gratz Papers, manuscript collection 236, AJA.

101. Miriam Moses Cohen to Rebecca Gratz, Savannah to Philadelphia, February 18, 1864, Gratz Family Papers, collection 72, box 9, APS.

102. Sarah Moses Joseph to Rebecca Gratz, December 27, 1865, Gratz Family Papers, collection 72, box 9, APS.

103. Diner, *Time for Gathering*, 156.

104. Ibid., 157.

105. Diane Lichtenstein's *Writing Their Nations: The Tradition of Nineteenth-Century American Jewish Writers* (Bloomington: Indiana University Press, 1992) analyzes the ways Jewish women modulated their American and Jewish identities in published writings later in the nineteenth century.

Part VI

|||||||||||||||||||||||||||||||||||||||||||

Jews as a Class

Historians used to trace the roots of American antisemitism to the post–Civil War era, usually to 1877, when the banker Joseph Seligman was excluded from the Grand Union Hotel in Saratoga Springs on account of his religion. Earlier slurs, scholars believed, were sporadic, insignificant, and without serious malicious intent.

Bertram W. Korn's *American Jewry and the Civil War* challenged this view, dealing extensively with what he characterized as "Judaeophobia" during the Civil War era. Northerners and Confederates alike, he showed, used Jews as a convenient scapegoat for the social and economic ills of the day, which the war exacerbated. Korn's revised edition argued that Civil War era antisemitism "was far greater in articulation, repetition, frequency, and in action too, than had ever before been directed against Jews in America."

Today, historians understand that antisemitism in the United States dates as far back as American Jewry itself; no era was completely free of its scourge. The spike in antisemitism during the Civil War reflected the tensions and frustrations of those perilous years. Prejudice, which found its primary outlet in persecutions of Catholics and African Americans during the dark years of the war, was likewise directed at Jews.

Gary L. Bunker and John J. Appel trace Civil War–era prejudice against Jews in popular culture, specifically the graphic images found in some of the leading magazines of the day. Cartoons, they show, regularly caricatured all traders and smugglers as "sharp-nosed" Jews, although, of course, most of them were not Jewish at all. Magazines likewise blamed Jews for the range of "shoddy" goods—substandard uniforms, weapons, foodstuffs, and the like—that corrupt wartime contractors supplied to the military. The implication, echoing a perennial antisemitic trope, was that Jews preferred to profit from the war rather than fight in it. Ethnocentrism, popular stereotypes, and Jewish visibility combined to shape the perception "that Jews as a class represented a threat to the outcome of war" (this volume, 328).

Two notorious episodes of wartime prejudice against Jews left a legacy of lasting significance. Notably, in both cases, Jews fought back and triumphed. The first, recounted here by Bertram W. Korn, was the battle to amend the military chaplaincy law, passed in 1861, that stipulated that a regimental chaplain be a "regular ordained minister of some Christian denomination." Protestant chaplains and, to the extent that they could, Catholic ones, made the most of their opportunity to influence the troops in the field. At their best, chaplains tended to soldiers' spiritual needs, helped them to overcome personal and family problems, and modeled virtuous and courageous behavior under fire. Jewish chaplains, by contrast, were officially barred from the ranks, putting Jewish soldiers at a great disadvantage and, in effect, rendering the Jewish faith illegitimate in the military. Two elected Jewish chaplains were rejected on account of the discriminatory law, setting off a national debate concerning the religious rights of non-Christians. Congress, encouraged by Abraham Lincoln, amended the law in 1862; Korn calls it "the first major victory of a specifically Jewish nature won by American Jewry in a matter touching the Federal government" (this volume, 342).

The second episode, now known as "the most sweeping" anti-Jewish official act in all of American history, was an order dated December 17, 1862, by General Ulysses S. Grant expelling "Jews as a class" from the entire territory under his command, including parts of Tennessee, Mississippi, Kentucky, and Illinois. The broader context for this order is provided here by John Simon, longtime editor of the Ulysses S. Grant Papers. He shows that Grant blamed Jews for the smuggling and cotton speculation that was rife throughout the area he oversaw. He concludes that Grant's rage was specifically ignited by the discovery that Jesse Grant, his own father, was engaged in cotton speculation, working with a Jewish firm. Since his relationship with his father was tension fraught and complicated, General Grant "displaced his anger," according to Simon (this volume, 358). Instead of lashing out at his father, he went after his father's Jewish partners and at "Jews as a class."

Steven Ash focuses on the impact of Grant's order on the Jews of Paducah, Kentucky. In Paducah, unlike many other places where Jews lived or worked, Grant's expulsion order was zealously enforced. "The Jews in Paducah," Ash shows, "became the focus for all the hatred and mistrust that the war had created and unleashed in the city." Expulsion was "the tragic culmination of longstanding attitudes" (this volume, 372).

Jews, for their part, lost no time in protesting Grant's order. Not only did they send letters and telegrams to the White House, but one of those expelled, Cesar Kaskel of Paducah, rushed to Washington and met personally with President Lincoln. Lincoln, it turned out, knew nothing of Grant's order, but instantly countermanded it. "I do not like to hear a class or nationality condemned on account of a few sinners," he told Jewish leaders a few days later.

Paradoxically, these antisemitic episodes ultimately affirmed and entrenched the Jewish claim to equality in the United States. Other manifestations of wartime antisemitism did not end so rapidly, or so positively; they continued throughout the war's duration, and in some cases beyond. As for Grant's order, after a few weeks of recriminations and a failed move by congressional opponents to censure Grant, the whole issue was forgotten. It was recalled, with a vengeance, when Grant ran for president in 1868.

12

"Shoddy" Antisemitism and the Civil War

Gary L. Bunker and John J. Appel

At the outset of the Civil War, the fruit of anti-Semitism was ripe for harvesting.[1] Ethnocentric beliefs expressed a preference for white, native-born Protestants. Because immigration between 1850 and 1860 had swelled the Jewish population,[2] and the tenets of Judaism did not match the popular standard of religious acceptability, Jews were automatically indicted on two of the three counts: the vast majority of Jews were not native-born; and, except for the anomaly of isolated conversions, few passed the litmus test of religious legitimacy.[3] Although historian John Higham identified General U. S. Grant's December 1862 expulsion of Jews from his jurisdiction "as the principal nativistic incident of the war years," the element of nativism in the cartoon medium had emerged as early as the summer of 1861.[4] Of course, nativism and religious difference continued to wield a vital force in the appraisal of Jews for the duration of the war and beyond.

Ethnocentrism was not the only national blemish. Pejorative economic and political stereotypes such as "avaricious," "exploitative," and "politically subversive"—the heritage of ages of prejudice—were commonplace in the American lexicon of anti-Semitism. Such beliefs added potency to an already virile ethnocentrism; the resultant effect markedly increased the probability of some form of intolerance. Because sensitivity to any assessment of perceived political subversion reaches its zenith in wartime, the circulation and availability of such beliefs was not a good omen for the image of Jews.

While ethnocentrism and stereotyping may be necessary elements in rationalizing ethnic beliefs, feelings, and behavior, neither alone nor

---

Reprinted, without some of the original illustrations, with permission from *American Jewish History* 82 (1994): 43–71, copyright © 1994 by the American Jewish Historical Society.

together do they constitute a sufficient condition for prejudice. For an ethnic group to become a significant target of derision or discrimination, that group must also be visible. The confluence of adverse living conditions in Europe, and the hope of expanded freedoms in the new world, spawned the demographic conditions essential for sharpened Jewish visibility. The sheer number and rapid influx of immigrants, the concentration of Jews in urban settings, and their cultural singularity—for example, the temporary language barrier for German Jews—accentuated real or imagined differences. Having attained a conspicuous standing, Jews became even more vulnerable to public censure.

Then, when it became apparent that some wartime contractors were providing substandard uniforms, food, weapons, and other military supplies at outrageous prices, the volatile mixture of ethnocentrism, stereotypical beliefs, visibility, and the unsettling climate of war promoted scapegoating against Jewish citizens.[5] Not long after the first shots were fired at Fort Sumter, illustrators for *Vanity Fair*, the *New York Illustrated News*, and *Phunny Phellow* began imputing to Jews subversive motives and conduct inimical to the Union military cause. Also in 1861, the exclusion of Jewish chaplains from the armed forces gave substance to the fear of concrete discrimination. Moreover, when "the army happened to arrest a trader or smuggler who was Jewish, his religion was noted in the record, though no other religion was."[6] This practice increased the chance for guilt by association. Eventually, the anti-Semitic behavior of influential military leaders such as Grant, Butler, Hurlbut, and Sherman further exposed the roots of institutional intolerance.[7] Arguably, the manifestation of anti-Semitism in the media and the military attested to the gradual infiltration of prejudice in some elements of the power structure. Thus ethnocentrism, stereotypes, visibility, expressions of perceived threat, and concrete support from some in key positions of authority constituted a formidable constellation of variables leading to various degrees of real or potential antipathy toward Jews.[8]

Unlike conventional historical investigations of anti-Semitism and the Civil War, this research does not use illustrations as mere visual aids but as primary source material.[9] The systematic deposition of graphic images left behind an unselfconscious record of anti-Semitism in periodicals such as *Vanity Fair*, *Phunny Phellow*, *Frank Leslie's Budget of Fun*, *Frank Leslie's Illustrated Newspaper*, *Harper's Weekly*, and the *New York Illustrated News*. A frequency tally of the visual record shows anti-Semitism peaking in

1861 and 1864. Among the magazines, the Frank Leslie publications and the *New York Illustrated News* were the major carriers of anti-Semitism. Dominating the themes were economic stereotypes, but in the context of war, these images also bore overtones of political subversion. During the Civil War period, a survey of illustrations tinged with anti-Semitism implicated Jews in several contexts: Ulysses S. Grant's General Order Number 11; smuggling goods between Confederate and Union lines; mediating foreign intervention; tampering with gold, cotton, and/or stock market prices; as camp followers seeking economic gain; and as the ubiquitous "shoddy." As we shall see later, the term "shoddy," as applied to anti-Semitism, gratuitously linked Jews with the production and distribution of inferior products to the military, allegedly jeopardizing the health and welfare of soldiers and the security of the nation. In terms of the number of illustrations from the above-mentioned categories, "shoddy" is the decisive anti-Semitic slur; therefore, "shoddy" came to represent the quintessential stereotype of the unpatriotic Jew.

The original meaning of "shoddy" was innocent enough. "'Shoddy,' properly speaking, is the short wool carded or worn from the inside of cloth, without fibre or tenacity, and with no capability of wear, and yet easily made into the semblance of more durable goods."[10] With the outbreak of the Civil War, the popular referent quickly changed. A spirit of profiteering accompanied the race to clothe, equip, and feed soldiers rushing into war.[11] Loose regulations and supervision fostered abuse by war contractors. The concomitance of exorbitant prices and inferior products led to investigations of graft and corruption. Soon, when "shoddy" referred to a product, it signified "any description of rotten or improper material."[12] But the word "shoddy" was also affixed to the alleged perpetrators who bilked the government and short-changed military personnel in dire need. "The 'boys' have nick-named the army contractors in general 'Shoddies,'" wrote a *Vanity Fair* correspondent from General Stone's column, "and when any of these personages make their appearance the cry of 'Shoddy! Shoddy!' goes up from all parts of the camp!"[13] Now the broadened referent included "swindling and humbug of every character"[14] or "a synonym for miserable pretence in patriotism."[15] The final step in the transformation of connotation was to libel an ethnic minority, Jews, with the label "shoddy."

Indeed, the cognitive process linking "the sons of Israel" from "Chatham Street" to the "shoddy" is preserved in these lines of doggerel from *Vanity Fair* in the "The Triumph of Israel":

> In times like these it is a real treat
> To ramble by the stalls of Chatham Street,
> Where, all day long, the sons of Israel
> With smiles obsequious their goods do sell;
>
> Viewed, as I have, the swindle-stitched disgrace
> Of uniforms daubed with sordid lace,
> With cheap tag-rags disguised, and paltry loops,
> Served out by mean contractors to our troops:
>
> The weak devices in moth-eaten felt
> That straight before the summer shower melt,
> The "petersham," enough to make a body
> Desponding, and that other sham, the "shoddy";
>
> Is it a wonder that one's mind replete
> Should turn to Sholomonsh of Chatham Street,
> Whose vilest "warranted to wash and wear"
> With those things favorably must compare?
>
> Go on, good Sholomonsh! by contrast crowned;
> Proceed: disseminate much virtue round:
> Continue; till for truth men look to you,
> "O! my prophetic soul, my Uncle!" do.[16]

At the time, an accusatory spirit, propagated by the excesses of unprincipled contractors, was rife in the land. Although the vast majority of allegations were generic rather than ethnic in origin, Jewish Americans felt the sting of malice. On July 22, 1861, the *New York Tribune* summarily tried Jews in the press by associating "speculators and Jew brokers" with the sale to the government of a bad batch of cattle.[17] As the connotation "shoddy" was repeatedly associated with Jews, symbolic conditioning offered a ready-made, seductive stereotype for those who sought gratification in condescension.

In November 1861, over the caption "Shoddy Patriotism," that stereotype was enthroned in cartoon form in the humor periodical *Phunny Phellow*. The dialogue in the subcaption lays bare the prejudice:

SHODDY PATRIOTISM.

Recruiting Sergeant—Come, Moses, rub up your patriotism, and join the Union forces.

Jew—Mine cot, no! I have as mooch as I can do to supply de army mit coot uniforms, upon vich I makes noting at all, s'elp me got!

"Shoddy Patriotism." Courtesy of the Providence Public Library, Special Collections.

> RECRUITING SERGEANT—Come, Moses, rub up your patriotism, and join the Union forces.
>
> JEW—Mine cot, no! I have as mooch as I can do to supply de army mit coot uniforms, upon vich I makes noting at all, s'elp me got![18]

The Jew in the cartoon declining service in the armed forces, bearing the title "shoddy," and betraying his foreign origin with broken English combine to underscore the image of the subversive Jew.

Words like "shoddy" and even "contractor" acquired not only negative but harsh meanings.[19] Moreover, severe measures were reserved for "shoddy" business practices. One illustrator for *Harper's Weekly* proposed hanging;[20] another suggested tar, feathers, and riding "shoddy" out of town on a rail.[21] A few lines of doggerel in *Vanity Fair* suggested that tears should not be shed if one Shoddy choked another.

> If a Shoddy
> Meet a Shoddy
> A-raking of his "rye,"
> And a Shoddy
> Chokes a Shoddy
> Need anybody Cry![22]

The *New York Tribune* described vultures as "human compared with monsters who furnish rotten blankets and rotten meat to the living in the camp."[23] These hostile images would not be easily forgotten. Furthermore, some cartoons were sufficiently ambiguous to allow the eye of the beholder to draw his or her own conclusions. For example, a cartoon in *Harper's Weekly* on the theme of "shoddy" featured some of the villains with elongated noses.[24] Although there may have been no artistic intent to denote ethnicity, the physiognomic stereotype was salient enough to allow for a projective response.[25] In any event, even generic allusions to the concept of "shoddy" were capable of eliciting anti-Semitic imagery. But "shoddy" was not the only manifestation of intolerance toward Jews.

Cartoonists found other pretexts for maligning Jews. Although these other images differed in emphasis from "shoddy," the elements were essentially the same. Economic and political stereotypes dominated the central motif. In December 1861, *Vanity Fair*'s H. L. Stephens caricatured the confederate "Exodus to Nashville" led by Judah Benjamin. A balloon caption

"Old Moses Davis to Prince Napoleon." Courtesy of the Providence Public Library, Special Collections.

further linked Judaism to the Confederate cause with the lamentation, "No more shall the children of Judah sing."[26]

Perhaps because of Judah Benjamin's southern political prominence, a cartoonist for the *New York Illustrated News* pictured Jefferson Davis as "Old Moses Davis," trying to persuade Prince Napoleon to favor the South.[27] The dialect emphasized the foreign element. "Now, my poy, come over to our side—don't go to the old man [Lincoln] on de utter side of de vay. Ve vill let you have de cotton at your own price—sheap. Come, my poy!"

One week later, the *New York Illustrated News* gratuitously shows Lincoln condoning anti-Semitism.[28] Lincoln confronts "Shylock" at the entrance of the *London Times*. "No Shylock—we did not come about the loan we have money enough, and to spare, at home. But we thought, since our English brethren had come to be ruled by such as you, and your

"John Bull and the American Loan." Courtesy of the Providence Public Library, Special Collections.

hirelings, yonder, that we had better keep an eye on you." In due time, Lincoln's decisive action, granting the full rights of chaplaincy to Jews and rescinding General Grant's ill-advised exclusionary policy, refuted any uncertainty as to where Lincoln stood on the matter of anti-Semitism. Marshaling the full weight of executive power to stave off discrimination was the most important Civil War act in behalf of Jews.

In comparison with other Jewish illustrations for 1861, the final image is serene. It touched on a universal theme. Where is there an army without soldiers complaining about the quality or quantity of the food?

Troopers from the Union ranks were no different. They bemoaned the steady diet of pork.[29] But the *New York Illustrated News* publicized the plight of the devout "Hebrew volunteer" complying with dietary laws.[30] The cartoon hardly qualified as anti-Semitic, although it did accent cultural distinctiveness.[31]

Ironically, two of the more blatantly offensive anti-Semitic actions, General Grant's Order Number 11 and the exclusion of Jews as chaplains in the armed forces, were not popular topics in the cartoon medium. In each instance, credit President Lincoln's bold, resolute act in reversing the tide, muting the potential effects of those discriminatory policies. Had Lincoln in any way countenanced the proposed exclusions, the results might have been devastating. *Vanity Fair*'s allusion to Lincoln's censure of Grant took the form of a "Hebrew Catechism." "Question—'What kind of evergreen might General Grant have represented by this time, had not the President come down upon him?' Answer—'A Jew Nipper.'"[32] Lincoln's action nullified Grant's ill-advised order, and the phrase "had not the President come down upon him" was of immeasurable worth to embattled Jews held hostage by prejudice.

But General Order Number 11 would come back to haunt Ulysses S. Grant.[33] In an 1882 meeting at Chickering Hall, Grant had apparently expressed "Sympathy for the Persecuted Jews in Russia." *Puck* magazine contrasted his 1862 order "excluding Jews from the Army" from his more recent remarks under the caption: "Then and Now 1862 and 1882."[34] "Army Order No. II" was symbolized by a crocodile skin draped around Grant. Although Grant was ostensibly weeping for the treatment of contemporary Jews, so were crocodile tears coming from the emblem of the 1862 policy. The cartoonist cleverly imputed to Grant disingenuous motives in the inscription "Jewish Vote 1884," floating in the giant pool of tears.

Nor was the 1862 exclusion easy for General Grant to explain when confronted with the facts while running as a candidate for the presidency in 1868. *Frank Leslie's Budget of Fun* juxtaposed Grant's unpleasant dream of a "Vision of Jerusalem" with an announcement in the *Tribune*: "The fact that the Jews have endorsed General Grant is a gratifying one."[35] The vision did not depict a happy reception for Grant in the Jewish community.[36] Grant's nightmare was full of unsettling hostility.

Although 1862 contained fewer negative visual images of Jews, the undercurrent of anti-Semitism continued its course. "The ambivalence toward Jews was captured in a poem from *Harper's Weekly* entitled "The Jew's Garden."[37] Although the poem praised "the little old Jew, so cheerful and fond of flowers," the poet made it clear that here was an exception to the rule. For another verse chanted the litany of scorn:

> And I thought, this old man here, to this day,
> May have lived by brokerage, cheat, and bribe—
> May have fawned, and lied, and clutched, and grown gray
> In the sordid curse of his tribe.[38]

In the early months of 1863, a gold panic on Wall Street sent the market into a tailspin and the media scurrying after a scapegoat. Although President Lincoln and Secretary of the Treasury Chase took the immediate brunt of the reproach, the Jews were not far behind the chain of denunciation. "Most of the heavy speculators were Jews," said a journalist for *Frank Leslie's Illustrated Newspaper*, "and they cut miserable figures as they rushed to and fro, foaming at the mouth, cursing with impotent rage Old Abe and Secretary Chase, who had brought this ruin on the house of their fathers."[39] Soon, illustrations followed in the wake of the economic turbulence, as the latent propensity for anti-Semitism became reality. Frank Bellew, artist for the Leslie publications, linked Jews and gold in his illustration labeled "A New Toy for the Rising Generation."[40] A cartoon in *Yankee Notions* announced in its caption a "Terrific Explosion of the Gold Bubble in the Camp of the Children of Israel."[41] In the *Budget of Fun*, a wary Secretary Chase plunders an unwary Jewish "Speculator in Gold" in a "Scene from the new pantomime of 'The Yellow Fever.'"[42] Meanwhile, the *New York Illustrated News*, in a sketch by H. J. Kurtz, used the atmosphere of antipathy to show "Jews Smuggling Goods Across the Potomac."[43] Yet a more discordant note of anti-Semitism was sounded with the appearance of a condescending cartoon in late 1863. Once again, the *Budget of Fun* was the sponsor in "The Golden Rule or The Wall Street Thermometer."[44] The gauge of a bull or bear market is shown in the countenance of Jewish faces expressing degrees of sadness or elation. At the left base of the illustration, the "fatted calf" is the focal point of worship, and, to the right, Jewish investors presumably determine the market's strength or weakness.

Although the images of "shoddy" tended to dominate 1864, there were exceptions. From the genre of political caricature, the *New York Illustrated News* ridiculed James Gordon Bennett, the editor of the rival *New York Herald*, calling him Shylock.[45] The economic stereotype of Jews is invoked in the caption. When a woman describes Bennett as wealthy, he replies:

"Service and Shoddy." Courtesy of L. Tom Perry Special Collection, Harold B. Lee Library, Brigham Young University, Provo, Utah.

"Wealthy, ah, dat ish von great mishtake, but I will advertise your book for seventy-five cents ze line, cash down, and no agents admitted."[46]

While the concept of "shoddy" was introduced in 1861 and made its presence felt in 1862 and 1863, it reached the apex of its influence in 1864. Moreover, the bonds of anti-Semitism to "shoddy" were strengthened with each repetition of association, and set in concrete roughly a year before the end of the war. When Henry Morford's book *The Days of Shoddy* was published in 1863, the author predicted that those days "will not end until the contest [Civil War] closes, and they may linger long after. While the nation remains in distress or society convulsed," continued Morford, "thieves (moral, social and pecuniary) will continue to embrace their opportunity."[47] Although Morford wrote about the generic "shoddy," and even went out of his way to disclaim that the type he was after was "the old clo' dealer of Chatham Street," he nevertheless pointed out that the old clothes dealer "advertised that he would pay the very highest price for cast-off clothing, as he had 'extensive orders from the government.'" Such allusions, together with his reference to "the slop-shops of Chatham Street," did not discourage readers from perceiving a relationship between Jews and "shoddy."[48]

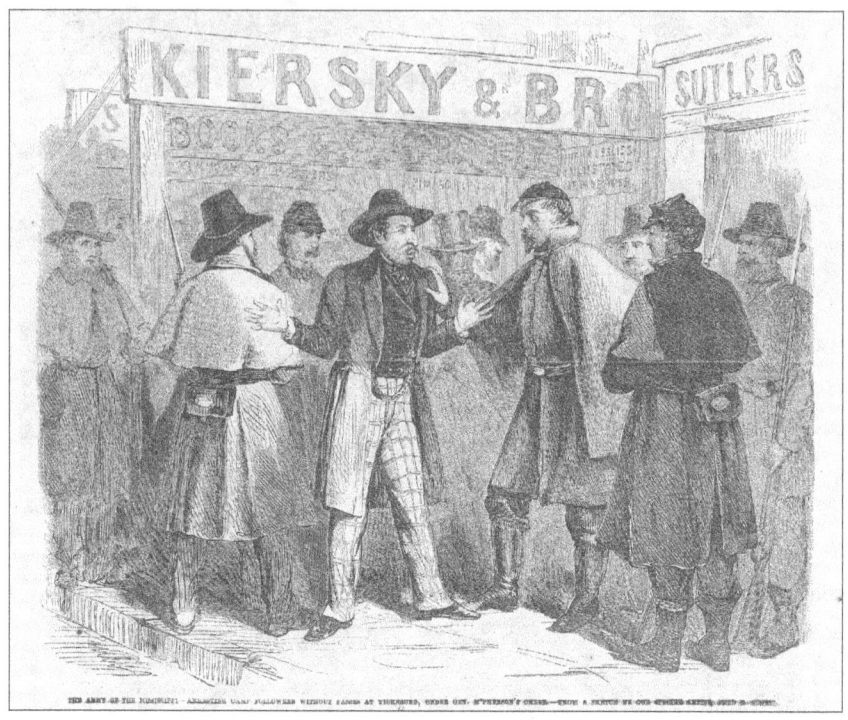

"The Army of the Mississippi." Courtesy of L. Tom Perry Special Collection, Harold B. Lee Library, Brigham Young University, Provo, Utah.

General references to "shoddy" in 1862 and 1863 lingered. Cartoon captions exclaimed: "The new camp blankets are so remarkably fine, that many of our soldiers use them for fishing-nets"; or elsewhere, "these 'shoddies' [our army blankets] are awful cold."[49] *Harper's Weekly* contrasted three sets of panels in a prominent illustration.[50] In the first, a soldier is exposed to the bitter elements of weather, while the shoddy contractor indulges his appetite at a bar. The second compares the grim circumstances of the soldier's wife with the lavish lifestyle of the contractor's spouse. The final panel contrasts soldiers in the life and death struggle of war as the purveyors of "shoddy" languish in leisure in a warehouse for distribution of "shoddy" goods. Finally, the *Cincinnati Daily Enquirer* implied that Rabbi Wise, who had declined the Democratic nomination for state senator, could have run on the other ticket with the help of "the Shoddy contractors."[51]

In 1864, *Frank Leslie's Illustrated Newspaper* described camp followers who, "in these days of conscription," shadowed the army to "avoid the draft."[52] Because camp followers were often associated with profiteering and "shoddy," this was an added dimension to the stereotype of disloyalty. The illustrator chose to select a Jewish figure as the representative camp follower.[53] The customary watch chain, the bejeweled tie, the gesturing hands, and the overall appearance fit the Jewish stereotype used by cartoonists to convey ethnic identification. What precipitated the illustration were the orders submitted by generals Sherman and McPherson to arrest any camp followers who did not have passes and to induct them into the army.[54]

In the spring, illustrators intensified the campaign of anti-Semitism. "Shoddy or the Vulture of the Camp" was now unmistakably Jewish.[55] The vulture imagery was as popular south of the Mason and Dixon line as it was north of it. The *Richmond Examiner* wrote that Jews "flocked as

"An Everyday Scene Everywhere." Courtesy of University of Chicago Library, Special Collections Research Center.

vultures to every point of gain."⁵⁶ But "shoddy" was the preeminent image.⁵⁷ A serialized epic poem, appearing in multiple numbers of *Budget of Fun*, reinforced the Jewish connection with "shoddy."⁵⁸ In May, the second segment of the poem, "The Adventures of the Shoddy Family," identified the home base as, of course, Chatham Street.

> Shoddy was "Snobby," and Chatham street air
> Never wafted to Madison Square⁵⁹

But the hub of the poem revolved around "Shoddy," the Jewish tailor and political subversive. An illustration on the same page as the poem entitled "Mr. Shoddy's way of Treating the Destitute" revealed just how Mr. Shoddy would fare in the poem. The cartoon pictures Mr. Shoddy as utterly calloused and insensitive to the needs of the poor. That same moral indifference is reflected in an early verse of the poem under the heading "The New Method of Bleeding—Shoddy's Patent":

> Upon the new system (Oh! let us adore it)
> Of bleeding the country, but not bleeding for it!
> "For surely," said Shoddy, wise-shaking his head,
> "Tis better by far thus to bleed than be bled;
> Let men be as brave and as bold as they can—
> A tailor is but the ninth part of a man,
> And therefore, of course, should make money for nine—
> Let others be men, be the tailor's part mine."

Later, a verse developed the idea of an aspiring Shoddy:

> No Shoddy, the tailor, began to aspire,
> A capital thief, an astonishing liar,
> He glowed with a rogue's and a patriot's fire.
> "Hurrah," thus he cried, "for the glorious flag!
> Hurrah for the money that's made out of rag!
> Hurrah for the stripes and hurrah for the stars!
> Hurrah for the fools who must go to the wars!
> I stay at my home, yet, as heaven well knows,
> I'm making more money than any who goes—
> For each one who goes to the war must be clad
> With a garment of mine, be it good, be it bad!"

Further, on the theme of "How the Death of a Customer May Sometimes be of Advantage to a Tailor," the poet wrote:

> If th' garment gives way, why, it matters me not
> A soldier can never complain when he's shot.
> Death shielded the doctor from sceptic and railer,
> And bullets will do much the same for a tailor!
> So Shoddy extended his trade and began.
> To be known by the world as a "rising, rich man."

In much the same way, the poet maligned Mrs. Shoddy as a crude, vulgar, upwardly mobile counterpart to her husband. As Mrs. Shoddy enters Tiffany's looking for diamonds, doggerel describes her central features:

> There enters a woman, she's ugly and course,
> As stout as an ox and as tall as a horse;
> She's red in the face and amazing in dress,
> More vulgar by far than all words can express.

In the same issue of *Budget of Fun*, an artist pits the unrefined Mrs. Shoddy against other women, who symbolize the respectable professions of "Commerce," "Science," and "Art," respectively.[60]

If another drop in gold prices and the stock market had triggered the most recent episode of anti-Semitism,[61] the grinding, frustrating stalemate in the Civil War also set nerves on edge. Whatever the complex causal forces, neither June nor July was a good month for Jews. It was no honor for Jews to be featured on the front page of *Budget of Fun*.[62] "Mr. Shoddy wants to kill the bird [the American eagle] that lays all the golden eggs," exclaimed the front page caption. One of the golden eggs was labeled "a fat contract." This "bogus speculation," declared the cartoon, was "The Height of Madness." Thus the powerful editorial cartoon had reduced Jews to the convenient status of scapegoat.

An equal dose of anti-Semitism was fed to the readers of *Frank Leslie's Illustrated Newspaper*. "Oh, horror! This year, whoso goeth down into the sea shore or elsewhere will be perpetually and irretrievably afflicted with Shoddy. Shoddy pere, Shoddy mere, and Mesdemoiselles Shoddy, the daughters, to say nothing of the worst of the lot, the youthful masculine scions of the House of Shoddy. . . . You will find them . . . trailing robes and glittering bracelets and Mr. Shoddy will jingle his massive chain . . .

And Mrs. Shoddy, in diamond ear-rings, will exclaim: 'This here coffee ain't fit for nothin'; And Miss Shoddy . . . will make a dead set at your young brother. . . . And young Shoddy will . . . drive you to the verge of desperation."[63] "You need not say you will not mix with such people," so avoidance was the only practical solution. "If you desire to escape Shoddy (and who would not?) you must make up your mind to farmhouses and rustic hotels, and abjure, for this season at least, Saratoga, Newport, Trenton Falls, Lake George etc.; and making a merit of necessity, enjoy the 'real country' for once in your life. You will not lose by it."

One week later, the *New York Illustrated News* picked up where the *Budget of Fun* and *Frank Leslie's Illustrated Newspaper* left off. The anti-Semitism was just as spirited and robust. Dressed in the trappings of the "Anti-Silk Movement," "Shoddy," noted the caption, was "left alone in its glory."[64] An accompanying textual description explained the meaning of the cartoon:

> Our picture with the above title exhibits Queen Fashion as she has lately appeared, clad as usual with all the taste of a lady, but not in the costly material of silk and satin she has been wont to wear. She will be seen seated in the aerial region, at the top of the engraving, surrounded by her attendants. These little Cupids are on the one side engaged in driving off the foreign merchants who come laden with luxuries, that in these times of fierce toil and strife are more than useless. With the means accruing from the savings thus made, good things are showered upon the sick and wounded in the hospitals, as is shown on the other side of the drawing. On the left a disciple of the praiseworthy queen is receiving homage from a new list of adorers—no brainless fops, possessed merely of wealth and the capacity to spend, bur men of heart and virtue, of science and art, the intellect of the land. The Queen of Fashion declares herself the queen of sense and sensibility. But one dissentient voice is heard. Shoddy spreads her ample skirts and comes rustling to the front. Her Jewish features are contorted with irate emotions as she surveys the good work about her. In her hand she holds a document, "What Mrs. Lincoln says." What did Mrs. Lincoln say when she was requested to join the movement?"[65]

During July, the *New York Illustrated News* turned the vise a notch tighter on Shoddy. A double-page illustration, celebrating Independence Day, displayed a series of patriotic images and lobbied for the presidential candidacy of McClellan over the incumbent Lincoln. On the one hand,

McClellan is shown riding on the back of the American eagle, ascending gracefully to the White House. On the other hand, Lincoln falls toward defeat in the symbolic waters of Salt River. Predictably, the sole exception to the patriotic imagery is the inclusion of "Shoddy consumed in extravagance."[66]

Two weeks later, one of the final wartime Shoddy cartoons portrays Shoddy wondering "if there isn't a chance for a little spec. here" in contracting for "onions for the soldiers."[67] As the pungent aroma from the onions draws tears from Shoddy, his insincerity is also exposed: "Onions for the soldiers, eh? Dear me! It's quite affecting."[68]

Just as suddenly as shoddy had emerged in the early months of the war, so it faded at the end. As Sherman occupied Atlanta and drove to the sea, generals Grant and Sheridan routed their foes, and Lincoln was reelected for a second term, the end of the conflagration was now in sight. Battlefield success had removed the venom of Copperheadism in the North and diffused a pall of gloom over the South. That same northern surge of optimism set a limit on the days of shoddy. Because shoddy was conceived and nurtured by the exigencies of war, the motives sustaining the anti-Semitic variant of shoddy rapidly diminished in strength as the surrender at Appomattox drew near. Happily, only a few remnants of the shoddy legacy survived the Civil War.[69]

At first glance, it is surprising that the fine scholarship on the Civil War and anti-Semitism has virtually ignored the concept of "shoddy."[70] Yet the omission is understandable because the idea was unobtrusively buried in the cartoon genre of the popular culture. Only by considering illustrations as primary sources were we able to uncover the significance of "shoddy" as a tool of anti-Semitism. Scattered references to "shoddy" did, indeed, appear in various written sources. However, it was the salience of "shoddy" in illustrations that spurred us on to look more carefully, widely, and assiduously for the pattern that eventually emerged. For us, this experience—from the often unpredictable odyssey of research—underscores the axiom that historians can ill afford to ignore or underestimate the significance of any obscure primary source as a clue in the investigative or interpretive process. In this case, the popular print category proved invaluable.

On the central issue of the relative importance of anti-Semitism during the period, we disagree with two fundamental arguments in David A. Gerber's recent analysis.[71] First, he asserts that "there is little evidence that the common types of prejudice . . . increased significantly during the Civil

War."[72] As an index of prejudice, Gerber uses "the appearance in literature, drama, art, and various facets of popular culture, such as cartoons, of negative imagery and stereotypes; or the informal verbalization of such negative views of Jews."[73] Our study explicitly addresses the degree of prejudice in the popular culture. Contrary to Gerber's thesis, we found significant changes in the frequency, prominence, and intensity of prejudice in the cartoons of the popular culture. Neither the antebellum or reconstruction era produced as malevolent, common, or conspicuous images of Jews. Typically, these cartoons were not buried in some remote corner of an illustrated periodical—rather, many were displayed prominently as front-, full-, half-, or even double-page spreads, and generally the tone was harsh and hostile.

Second, we differ with Gerber in his characterization of "ordinary anti-Semitism in the nineteenth century as a gradually broadening stream."[74] The substantial rise of anti-Semitism during the war and the rapid decline after the war do not fit a linear developmental model. Historically, war has not been kind to the treatment or image of Jews. The Civil War was no exception; it was not a minor eddy in the broadening stream. For some Americans, the dynamic climate of war transformed latent propensities for anti-Semitism into manifest realities of contempt and scapegoating. That anti-Semitism declined after the Civil War does not render its temporary status inconsequential.[75]

However, we also acknowledge the concurrent existence of causal factors which suppress as well as sponsor anti-Semitism. Our model of anti-Semitism takes these countervailing forces into consideration. For any significant degree of anti-Semitism to occur, two general conditions must be met. First, anti-Semitism must be rationalized; second, significant sectors of power must support its expression. We have already argued that the economic and political tensions and frustrations of war magnified the salience of ethnocentrism, popular stereotypes, and Jewish visibility. Hence the perception that Jews as a class represented a threat to the outcome of war was easier to rationalize. Then, when certain pockets of power in the military, the media, and elsewhere promoted anti-Semitism, the social problem increased.

On the other hand, to the extent that individuals with more enlightened values attacked the rationalization of anti-Semitism, or individuals in power restrained its overt manifestation, some forms of intolerance diminished. When a unified Jewish community appealed to a sensitive Abraham Lincoln to redress obvious grievances, as noted earlier, equalitarian, pluralistic, and democratic values neutralized the anti-Semitism associated with the policy on Jewish chaplains and U. S. Grant's order to exclude Jews from his district. As president, Lincoln was influential both as an opinion leader and power broker.

Yet if Lincoln's benign influence generalized to other forms of anti-Semitism, the effects are less discernible. Lincoln's rejection of anti-Semitic military policies did not extend to the civilian sphere and did not prevent anti-Semitic actions by some of his generals.[76] In the media, the theme of "shoddy," the purported manipulation of financial institutions, the alleged subversive complicity with the Confederacy, the supposed exploitation of military personnel by Jewish camp followers, and the claims of foreign intervention against the interests of the North continued unabated to plague the image of Jews. However effective the democratic restraints may have been, the rhetoric of anti-Semitism enjoyed the sanction of major illustrated periodicals throughout the duration of the war, including *Frank Leslie's Illustrated Newspaper*, *Frank Leslie's Budget of Fun*, the *New York Illustrated News*, and the comic press.

Although our study revolves around the relatively unexplored concept of "shoddy," the role of popular prints in the expression and documentation of prejudice, and the reaffirmation of the Civil War as a catalyst for anti-Semitism, our perception of the causes that support and suppress anti-Semitism agrees fundamentally with Jonathan Sarna's thesis of ambivalence.[77] Sarna portrayed the period as a contest between democratic and antidemocratic elements. Although we attack the problem differently than does Bertram Korn, our research also views the Civil War version of anti-Semitism as a potent strain.

Ironically, more than 30 years after the Civil War, the issue of Jewish loyalty was still hotly debated. At that time, Mark Twain attempted to bury the "common reproach" by recourse to "figures from the War Department."[78] "This slur upon the Jew," wrote Twain, "has done its work, and done it long and faithfully, and with high approval: it ought to be pensioned off now, and retired from active service." Lamentably, the retirement was only temporary.[79]

NOTES

1. The standard work on anti-Semitism and the Civil War remains Bertram Korn, *American Jewry and the Civil War* (Philadelphia, 1951).

2. "Exact statistics are unavailable, but we cannot be very far from the mark in estimating that at least two-thirds of the approximately one hundred and fifty thousand American Jews in 1860 were immigrants." Ibid., 1.

3. In time, a general susceptibility to racial explanations combined to argue in favor of biological determinism. In so doing, the notion of race was also invoked to characterize the behavior of Jews, Irish, Italians, and other hyphenated Americans. John Higham, *Send These to Me: Immigrants in Urban America* (Baltimore, 1984), 45–47.

4. John Higham, *Strangers in the Land: Patterns of American Nativism, 1860–1925* (New York, 1973), 12.

5. This study concentrates on anti-Semitism on the Union side of the conflict. For anti-Semitism in the Confederacy, see Korn, *American Jewry and the Civil War,* 175–188; and Eli N. Evans, *Judah P. Benjamin: The Jewish Confederate* (New York, 1988), 198–210.

6. Mark E. Neely, Jr., *The Fate of Liberty: Abraham Lincoln and Civil Liberties* (New York, 1991), 107–108. Bertram Korn also noted a comparable unfair practice of some northern newspapers. "An indication of the anti-Jewish tendency of the age was the common practice of Northern newspapers to identify as a 'Jew,' 'Israelite,' or worse yet, a 'German Jew,' any Jew who was apprehended in or suspected of carrying on disloyal activities. . . . This journalistic technique was at one and the same time the product of prejudice and an agency for its dissemination. It fixed ever more strongly in the mind of the reader the myth of the dishonest, law-breaking Jew. But it could never have been used unless there had been an acquaintance with the myth in the first place." Korn, *American Jewry and the Civil War,* 158.

7. General Sherman's fears that "the country will swarm with dishonest Jews who will smuggle powder, pistols . . . in spite of all the guards and precautions we can give" was typical of parallel decisions and behaviors of generals Grant, Hurlbut, and Butler. Korn, *American Jewry and the Civil War,* 148–149, 122, 153–154.

8. For a more complete exposition of this model, see the unpublished manuscript of Gary L. Bunker, "A Value-Added Model of Oppression," joint meeting of the Western and Rocky Mountain Psychological Associations, Reno, Nevada, April 27–30, 1989.

9. See John J. Appel, "Popular Graphics as Documents for Teaching and Studying Jewish History," in *A Bicentennial Festschrift for Jacob Rader Marcus,* ed. Bertram Wallace Korn (New York, 1976); and Rudolf Glanz, *The Jew in Early American Wit and Graphic Humor* (New York, 1973). For the application of this

historical approach to another maligned minority, see Gary L. Bunker and Davis Bitton, *The Mormon Graphic Image, 1834–1914* (Salt Lake City, 1983).

10. Henry Morford, *The Days of Shoddy: A Novel of the Great Rebellion in 1861* (Philadelphia, 1863), 774.

11. For a broad overview of this issue, see Fred Albert Shannon, *The Organization and Administration of the Union Army, 1861–1865*, 2 vols. (Cleveland, 1928).

12. Morford, *Days of Shoddy*, 174.

13. *Vanity Fair*, 23 November 1867, 230.

14. Morford, *Days of Shoddy*, 23.

15. Ibid., 174.

16. *Vanity Fair*, 10 August 1861, 71. In the text, two verses (the second and third) are omitted.

17. Shannon, *Union Army*, 1:73.

18. *Phunny Phellow*, November 1861, 5.

19. See "The Dream of the Army Contractor," *Vanity Fair*, 17 August 1861, 77; "The Song of Shoddy," *Vanity Fair*, 27 September 1861; and "The Contractor's Plaint," *Vanity Fair*, 8 February 1862, 73. The Secretary of War, Simon Cameron, was caricatured awash in a sea of questionable contracts. *Vanity Fair*, 21 September 1861, front page and 144.

20. *Harper's Weekly*, 24 August 1861, 531.

21. American Antiquarian Society, Samuel B. Woodward Collection, folder 3, no. 27.

22. *Vanity Fair*, 23 November 1861, 230.

23. *New York Tribune*, 25 May 1861, 4.

24 *Harper's Weekly*, 10 August 1861, 512.

25. "Levi—'It is the strangest thing, I have plenty of hair on my head but can't raise a mustache.' Friend of Levi—'Your nose makes too much shade, my boy; nothing can grow in the shade.'" *Comic Monthly*, August 1862, 3.

26. *Vanity Fair*, December 1861, 253.

27. *New York Illustrated News*, 19 August 1861, 256. Judah Benjamin was not always censured. *Harper's Weekly* applauded the selection of Judah P. Benjamin as Attorney-General of the Confederate States. *Harper's Weekly*, 1 June 1861, 341.

28. *New York Illustrated News*, 26 August 1861, 272.

29. Shannon, *Union Army*, 1:79.

30. *New York Illustrated News*, 9 September 1861, 304.

31. For some, one other cartoon may have conjured up anti-Semitic imagery. The artist portrays a "European Capitalist" in dialogue with Jefferson Davis. Davis asserts: "I can call millions across the vasty deep." To which the capitalist replies: "Ferry goot, but vill dey comes." *New York Illustrated News*, 11 November 1861, 32. The dialect and general appearance of the capitalist resemble Jewish images in other illustrations.

32. *Vanity Fair*, February 1863, 19.

33. For the particulars of the infamous order, see John Y. Simon, ed., *The Papers of Ulysses S. Grant* (Carbondale, Ill., 1979), 7:50–57.

34. *Puck*, 15 February 1882, 376.

35. *Frank Leslie's Budget of Fun*, October 1868, 16.

36. For the ramifications of the controversy engendered by the 1868 election, see Korn, *American Jewry and Civil War*, 132–133.

37. *Harper's Weekly*, 5 July 1862, 431.

38. Of course, these images only modestly sample the universe of contemptuous examples from 1862. For example, for the linkage of John Bull to Professor Rothschild, see *Comic Monthly*, September 1862, 8.

39. *Frank Leslie's Illustrated Newspaper*, 21 March 1863, 402. "There was as little truth in this accusation as in any other blanket generalization; the New York Jewish editors dared their secular colleagues to walk to the gold curb and count Jews, so certain were they that a very small proportion of Jews could be found there." Korn, *American Jewry and Civil War*, 161.

40. *Frank Leslie's Illustrated Newspaper*, 11 April 1863, 48. The same cartoon appears in *Frank Leslie's Budget of Fun*, June 1863, 5.

41. *Yankee Notions*, May 1863, 149.

42. *Frank Leslie's Budget of Fun*, June 1863, 4.

43. *New York Illustrated News*, 2 May 1863, 4. "The traffic carried on between the enterprising Jews on the Maryland shore and the needy rebels on the other side of the Potomac has become so extensive as to attract the special attention of the government." Ibid., 3. "It was not only the Jewish bankers of New York who were disloyal to the government, . . . so the rumors ran—but at every geographic point of contact between the Union and the Confederacy, Jews were supposed to be doing the actual work of supplying the South with goods and the necessities of war." Korn, *American Jewry and Civil War*, 162.

44. *Frank Leslie's Budget of Fun*, December 1863, 12.

45. *New York Illustrated News*, 30 April 1864, 432.

46. This was biting satire, because "James Gordon Bennett's widely read *New York Herald* displayed particular vehemence in its denunciation of Jews." Jonathan D. Sarna, "Anti-Semitism and American History," *Commentary*, March 1981, 43.

47. Morford, *Days of Shoddy*, 477.

48. Ibid., 182, 218. That individual Jews (or Christians) succumbed to the temptation of "shoddy" behavior is not contested; it was the generalization to a class of people that was offensive.

49. For the first reference, see *Vanity Fair*, 4 January 1862, 5. Both illustrations appear in *Pictorial History of the Southern Rebellion*, Providence Public Library, Vol. 3, p. 131.

50. *Harper's Weekly*, 24 October 1863, 677.

51. *Cincinnati Daily Enquirer*, 11 September 1863, in Korn, *American Jewry and Civil War*, 43.

52. *Frank Leslie's Illustrated Newspaper*, 23 January 1864, 283.

53. Ibid., 284.

54. For evidence of General Sherman's anti-Semitism, see Korn, *American Jewry and Civil War*, 148–149. About the same time, *Harper's Weekly* kept ethnicity salient by announcing the capture of "twenty-two rebels, . . . five Jews [and] ninety-nine Negroes." *Harper's Weekly*, 6 February 1864, 83.

55. *Budget of Fun*, April 1864, 5.

56. *Richmond Examiner*, 15 January 1863 and 20 December 1862, in Evans, *Judah P. Benjamin*, 200–201.

57. One magazine article conceded that Jews "have always been precursors of commercial greatness" and that "the Christian world has been especially hard upon the Hebrew," but the overall tone of the piece was ambivalent at best. *Frank Leslie's Illustrated Newspaper*, 30 April 1864, 82.

58. The serial poem "The Adventures of the Shoddy Family" first appeared in *Budget of Fun*, April 1864, 5.

59. *Budget of Fun*, May 1864, 5.

60. Ibid., 16.

61. "Gold in New York," *Frank Leslie's Illustrated Newspaper*, 7 May 1864, 103. See illustration, including Jews in the lower right-hand corner, on 104–105.

62. *Budget of Fun*, June 1864, front page.

63. "Out of Town," *Frank Leslie's Illustrated Newspaper*, 4 June 1864, 163.

64. *New York Illustrated News*, 11 June 1864, 520.

65. Ibid., 516.

66. *New York Illustrated News*, 9 July 1864, 584–585.

67. *New York Illustrated News*, 23 July 1864, 624.

68. Again the large watch chain and other subtle clues, such as the ostentatious dress of Mrs. Shoddy, are the nexus for anti-Semitism.

69. The title "Shody [sic] goods" does appear in a few early twentieth-century anti-Semitic valentine post cards. Yet "Shoddy" refers to the quality of the tailor's product, and does not have the same meaning as the Civil War connotation. For examples of these valentine post cards, see the private collection of John and Selma Appel.

70. Although the word "shoddy" is not indexed in Bertram Wallace Korn's *American Jewry and the Civil War*, the concept is included, for example, in an allusion to "shoddy contractors" on p. 43.

71. David A. Gerber, "Anti-Semitism and Jewish-Gentile Relations in American Historiography and the American Past," in *Anti-Semitism in American History*, ed. David A. Gerber (Urbana, Ill., 1986).

72. Ibid., 21. Gerber also argued "that there is little evidence that . . . discrimination and harassment increased significantly during the Civil War." Although our research does not focus on discrimination or harassment, an increase in prejudice generally paves the way for the more overt behavioral manifestations

of anti-Semitism. If the evidence is lacking with respect to acts of discrimination, significant attempts to discriminate were not. The controversies over the justification for Jewish chaplains and the general order of U. S. Grant are cases in point. That a presidential order was required to set these decisions aside argues at least for the genuine threat of increased discrimination. Furthermore, had Lincoln not then occupied the White House, favorable executive action may not have occurred.

73. Ibid., 20.

74. Ibid., 23. Although this is not a central issue for us, we do find some conceptual problem with defining any kind of anti-Semitism as "ordinary." While Gerber has carefully linked his definition of "ordinary" with specific conceptual referents, there is a temptation for the reader to think of the word "ordinary" euphemistically (i.e., as benign or inconsequential). We believe that Gerber does not intend that connotation. However, the common usage of the word may vitiate the intentional meaning.

75. Gerber appears to minimize Civil War anti-Semitism. "Because the brief Civil War experience of Jew-baiting by public officials failed to survive the war, analysis of the development of ideological anti-semitism and its political manifestations and of the breakdown of the usual moral, political, and cultural sanctions against the acceptance of anti-Semitic views among growing sectors of the population is best restricted to the period 1890 to 1950." Gerber, "Anti-Semitism and Jewish-Gentile Relations," 29.

76. Korn, *American Jewry and the Civil War*, 148–150, 154–155.

77. Sarna, "Anti-Semitism and American History," 44.

78. "Concerning the Jews," *Harper's Monthly*, September 1898. The background of this issue, along with the full reproduction of the above-cited article, appears in Mark Twain, *Concerning the Jews* (Philadelphia, 1985).

79. For a refurbished version of the negative image, see "The Modern War God," *Puck*, 25 January 1905, front page. Of course the full-blown fury of such beliefs manifested itself more recently and fully in the Holocaust.

Jewish Chaplains during the Civil War

Bertram W. Korn

The American tradition of the military chaplaincy is as old as the United States itself. Clergymen served with the armies of the individual colonies almost from the first battle of the Revolution, and provisions for the payment of chaplains were enacted by the Continental Congress as early as 1775. The first regular army chaplain was commissioned in 1781, immediately following due authorization by Congress in its legislation for a second regiment to supplement the small national military establishment. From then on, post and brigade chaplains were an accepted feature of the army table of organization.

These chaplains were all Protestants, though of varying denominations. The possible service of Roman Catholic chaplains received no official attention until the time of the Mexican War, when President Polk held several conferences on the subject with members of the American church hierarchy. Polk's suggestion that the bishops appoint two priests to serve with the army in a *civilian* capacity was adopted, but he apparently had no intention of recommending them for military appointments. During the 1850s Catholic priests served several military posts in the capacity of chaplain, but their official status is open to question. It was actually not until the Civil War that Catholic priests were explicitly granted the right to serve as army chaplains.[1]

There is no evidence that the legal status of Jewish chaplains was ever discussed prior to the Civil War, but once that fratricidal conflict had begun, with thousands of Jews enlisting in the armies of both the Union and Confederacy,[2] it was inevitable that these members of a minority faith

---

Reprinted with permission from *American Jewish Archives* 1 (1948): 6–22, copyright © 1948 by the American Jewish Archives.

would press for their right to be served by clergymen who could truly minister to their spiritual needs. The personal liberties and civil rights of members of all religious minorities had been safeguarded by a Constitution which carefully separated church from nation, although states like North Carolina lagged far behind in their application of this principle to their internal politics. The chaplaincy was, however, another realistic test of the equality which the Federal government theoretically accorded to all American citizens.

In the Confederacy, this equality was apparently recognized immediately upon the outbreak of hostilities. The acts providing for the appointment of chaplains in the Confederate military establishment merely stipulated that they should be "clergymen," with no denominational specifications.[3] There was probably not a sufficient number of Jews in any one Confederate regiment to warrant the election of a Jewish chaplain, but at least there was no *legal* barrier to such an appointment.

In this instance the Confederate Congress was more liberal and tolerant than its Washington counterpart, and it was in the North that the storm broke over the right of Jewish soldiers to chaplains of their own faith. The original Volunteer Bill, as reported to the floor of the House, required that regimental chaplains, who were to be "appointed by the regimental commander on the vote of the field officers and company commanders present," be "regularly ordained minister[s] of some Christian denomination."[4] On July 12, 1861, in a discussion of this proviso, an Ohio Congressman moved an amendment which would substitute the phrase "religious society" for the objectionable words "Christian denomination." The Congressman was Clement L. Vallandigham, who was later to become notorious for his leadership of the Copperhead movement and who was eventually arrested by military order and exiled across the Confederate border. Apparently on his own initiative and without any Jewish prompting, he spoke out clearly in defense of Jewish rights. "There is a large body of men in this country, and one growing continually, of the Hebrew faith," he said, "whose rabbis and priests are men of great learning and piety, and whose adherents are as good citizens and as true patriots as any in this country." Amplifying his remarks, he denounced the underlying implication of the bill that the United States is a Christian country, in the political sense, and branded the law as entirely unjust and completely "without constitutional warrant."[5] Vallandigham's appeal failed to move his fellow members of the House, or perhaps they paid no attention to his comments. At any rate, they rejected his amendment and passed the bill with its discriminatory clause intact.

This brief episode attracted very little notice. But perhaps because he also was an Ohioan and a member of the Democratic Party, Rabbi Isaac Mayer Wise did grasp its significance. He labeled the qualification clause an "unjust violation of our constitutional rights" and applauded Mr. Vallandigham for his staunch advocacy of the American conception of equality. But Wise was more furious than imaginative and had no constructive suggestion to offer to remedy the situation. His fear of dictatorship and of militarism ran away with his confidence in democratic action, and he could only urge his readers to remember this deliberate act of injustice and to hold their indignation in check until the end of the war, when surely they would be free to "square accounts."[6]

For all that Vallandigham, Wise, and the few others who were interested, knew, the question of the Jewish chaplaincy would remain a theoretical one. Wise himself had no inclination for personal military service since he was totally antagonistic to the purposes of the war. Fortunately for America and the Jew, however, the question did not remain a theoretical one and was not permitted to die for lack of excitement and interest.

In September, 1861, less than three months after the House had refused to sanction the service of Jewish chaplains, a YMCA worker happened to visit the military camp in Virginia where the 65th Regiment of the 5th Pennsylvania Cavalry, popularly known as "Cameron's Dragoons," was temporarily stationed. He was horrified to discover that a Jew, one Michael Allen of Philadelphia, was serving as the regimental chaplain, and promptly began such an agitation in the public press that ultimately the Assistant Adjutant General of the Army, George D. Ruggles, was forced to state in writing his official warning that "any person mustered into service as a chaplain, who is not a regularly ordained clergyman of a Christian denomination, will be at once discharged without pay or allowance."[7] Allen felt so humiliated that he resigned his commission on the excuse of ill health rather than suffer the dishonor of dismissal from the service, but the clamor raised by the zealous YMCA worker brought the issue before the public once again.[8]

Obviously, Allen had been elected without any deliberate intention on the part of his regiment's colonel and officers to disobey the law. They were probably ignorant of the Congressional bill which forbade them to designate a Jewish chaplain for their regiment even though the Commanding Officer, Colonel Max Friedman, and a large proportion of his officers and 1,200 men were Jewish.[9] And Allen had been a very fitting choice for the office. Born in Philadelphia, November 24, 1830, he was, from childhood, a pupil of the Rev. Isaac Leeser, the leading spokesman of American traditional Judaism, and for a time he undertook to follow, under his rabbi's guidance, a regular course of study for the Jewish ministry. Even after he abandoned this ambition, and unlike many other erstwhile rabbinical students, he remained close to Jewish affairs and preserved his relationship with Leeser. He taught classes for the Philadelphia Hebrew Education Society, and substituted for Leeser as *Hazan* (cantor) in the conduct of services, when that frequent traveler was out of town. The Rev. Samuel M. Isaacs, editor of the *Jewish Messenger*, wrote a few years later that Allen was "the only gentleman not actually a minister, accustomed and able to read the entire ritual according to the *Portuguese minhag* [rite]. He really deserves credit for the alacrity with which he has always responded to . . . calls [to act as *Hazan*], having frequently officiated at the Franklin street and Seventh street Synagogues of Philadelphia, and occasionally at the 19th street Synagogue of N.Y."[10] As a layman, Allen took a further leading role in Jewish communal affairs, and served as secretary to both the United Hebrew Beneficial Society and the Hebrew Education Society.[11]

Surely there was no one in the entire regiment better equipped by training as well as inclination to serve as its chaplain. During the two months of his service, Allen was not a Jewish chaplain, but the regimental chaplain for men of all faiths. On the New Year, the Day of Atonement, and the Feast of Tabernacles, as well as on the Jewish Sabbath, he went to Washington or Philadelphia to attend services. But on Sundays, he held his non-denominational services, consisting of brief Scriptural readings and a hymn or two, as well as a sermon. An entry in his diary for Sunday, September 8, 1861, reads: "Arose at 5 1/2 am. Very cool, pleasant and invigorating. 'Fast of Gedaliah.' Did not fast, not feeling able to do so. Had service at 8 o'clock. Lectured on 'Peace and Harmony.' All the officers and companies were present under command of Lieut. Col. Becker, and they all in their uniform looked very well."[12]

On that Jewish holiday, filled with remembrances of the pain of exile and the destruction of Jewish statehood, the chaplain preached a message about friendship and consideration to his men, without a single indication of the meaning of the day in his own religious thinking!

Indeed, one who reads over the manuscript copies of his sermons, preserved by his family, would never know they were written by a devout Jew. Of course, there is no reference to Christianity or its central figure, but neither is there any reference to the most pivotal of Jewish concepts.

Theologically, his sermons approached the various aspects of religion; immortality, ethics, faith, from a general and common Judaeo-Christian background. They were realistic, practical, down-to-earth talks, designed to touch the most basic problems of men stationed only a few miles from the battle-front: fear, restlessness, doubt, and homesickness. Chaplain Allen spoke of faith in God, "our shield and our buckler . . . in the hour of battle, of danger, and of tribulation." He urged them to prepare for the strife by learning the arts of the soldier as conscientiously as they could, because theirs was a "good and just cause . . . to save our country from the hands of the spoiler"; but he also pleaded for a spiritual preparation for the death that surely faced some of them. Never discussing political issues as such, he nevertheless took care that they came to have some understanding of his conviction that the Union was in danger, that the Confederacy was a rebellion against the Constitution, and that their erstwhile fellow-Americans were now their deadly foes. He never avoided the most difficult subjects: desertion, sex, obedience to superiors, the evils of camp life, but tried as best he could to impart a reasonable, loyal, and high ethical attitude to his men. Reverence for Deity and love of Scripture infused every sermon with a warmth and humanity which must truly have "endeared him to all." Those were words used by his friend, Alfred T. Jones, who gave an address when the regimental colors were presented to Colonel Friedman by a group of Philadelphia Jews in a formal ceremony on September 10. Jones said further, in the ornate fashion of his day, that Allen "taught the Word of God with pure unadulterated piety; he breathed into the ears of his hearers no sectarian hatred toward others, but labored zealously for their moral and spiritual welfare."[13]

In a passage of one sermon, Allen presented his own conception of some of the duties of the chaplain:

> I [must be] as one of you. . . . I must share with you, the pleasures and privations of a soldier's life, and I trust I shall be able to gain the esteem and confidence of each and every one of you. . . . [Since] there are many of you who are good and loyal *adopted* citizens of this our country, and as there are amongst you those not very well conversant with the English language, I wish you to consider me as your Teacher, and during your leisure hours in camp, should you wish to perfect yourself in the vernacular language of this country, I will be glad and willing to impart all the necessary information which my time and abilities will permit.

To teach, to inspire, in his own humble way—this was Allen's purpose in serving as substitute Rabbi, and as military chaplain. The "Cameron's Dragoons" were deprived of a sincere and superior religious mentor when Michael Mitchell Allen was forced to resign his office.

On the other hand, we must not overlook the fact that Allen was disqualified from serving as chaplain for two reasons: he was not a Christian, it is true, but neither was he a "regularly ordained clergyman." Even under the revised provisions of the following year which permitted rabbis to enter the military service, Allen would still have been ineligible. An unknown Philadelphian, writing a "letter to the editor" in an effort to clarify the issue which he felt had been unjustly confounded by accusations of intolerance, insisted that Allen's appointment had been called into question not because of his faith but because he was "a liquor dealer, . . . doubtless a very worthy man, but no clergyman."[14]

This editorial correspondent was not attempting to white-wash the War Department. Great as their excitement about Allen had been, the original letter from the YMCA had not complained about him but about "a number of Chaplains in our Pennsylvania regiments [who] are entirely disqualified . . . for the high and important position to which they have been raised";[15] and Ruggles's letter nowhere specified the Allen case, although it undoubtedly included it. Indeed, the election of non-clergymen to the office of chaplain plagued War Department officials and thoughtful Protestant leaders all during the war. It was a subject which obtained recognition and reference in many investigation reports and exposes. The Paymaster General of the Army, for instance, wrote to Senator Henry Wilson of Massachusetts on December 5, 1861, that: "I regret to say that very many holding this position [of chaplain] are utterly unworthy. . . . I think none should be appointed who did not come recommended by the highest ecclesiastical authority. . . . It is said one regiment employs a French cook, and musters him as chaplain to meet the expense."[16] Rabbi Isaac Mayer Wise took great delight in quoting the assertion of a Presbyterian journal that "two thirds of the chaplains in the army are unfit for their place,"[17] and offered his own personal testimony that at least two professed atheists of his acquaintance were serving as chaplains.[18] One of Lincoln's private secretaries, W. O. Stoddard, charged that military chaplains were, for the most part, "broken down 'reverends,' long since out of the ministry for incompetency or other causes, men who could not induce any respectable church to place itself under their charge," and quoted Lincoln's angry comment, that "I do believe that our army chaplains, take them as a class, are the worst men we have in the service."[19]

Colonel Friedman and his officers were undoubtedly distressed by this valid legal objection which complicated their determination to be served by a Jewish chaplain. They now realized that Allen would have had no right to serve as chaplain even if the law could be stretched to permit Jews to be elected to that position. So they resolved to try again. This time they would elect an ordained rabbi, but they would also take the precaution of electing a civilian who would not so easily be frightened into resigning, and who would have to apply directly to the Secretary of War for a commission. This would indeed be a test case which would determine whether discriminatory legislation against the Jews was to be enforced with the full knowledge and consent of the government and the people. Colonel Friedman lost no time in selecting the Rev. Arnold Fischel of New York City as the regiment's chaplain-designate. This was Mr. Fischel's introduction to the *cause célèbre* in which he participated for many months. His service in the Potomac area as a civilian chaplain, and his lobbying activities in the nation's capitol as the representative of the Board of Delegates of American Israelites, have been known for a long time, but the motivation behind his application for a commission has never been explained before.[20] The simple truth is that he sought the commission after his election by the officers of the regiment, in order to test the law and to secure a public statement about Jewish rights in the matter. His application was denied, of course, and ironically, the letter of rejection (warm and friendly as it was) was signed by the very same Simon Cameron, Secretary of War, in whose honor the "Cameron's Dragoons" was recruited and named.[21] To be fair to Cameron, we must understand that he had not dictated the law and that he had no choice about obeying it—but now there was no possible doubt of the interpretation of the law, and American Jewry had to recognize it.

These, then, are the circumstances: The illegal election of Allen; the exposé by the YMCA; Allen's chagrined resignation; then the election of Fischel as a test case; and, finally, the rejection of his application on the basis of the discriminatory clause. This was the chain of events which confronted American Jewry in late 1861 with the first instance of outright discrimination and legal inequity in the nation's history. It was a realistic situation, not a theoretical one, and it demanded a realistic solution. We shall not take the time here to chronicle and evaluate the lobbying campaign which lasted for almost a year and involved political pressures and techniques of every known variety (and which also revealed the alarming degree to which anarchy and indifference prevailed within American Jewry). Suffice it to say that, in July of 1862, Congress finally modified the chaplaincy requirements so that any "regularly ordained minister of some religious denomination" might, with the proper recommendations and qualifications, seek appointment as a chaplain.[22] This was, to the writer's knowledge, the first major victory of a specifically Jewish nature won by American Jewry in a matter touching the Federal government. But it was more than a Jewish victory and certainly more than the recognition of a blunder by Congress and the erasure of a mistake. Because there were Jews in the land who cherished the equality granted them in the Constitution, the practice of that equality was assured, not only for Jews, but for all minority religious groups. And Michael Allen, an innocent victim of national carelessness, was the direct cause of that democratic victory.

II

In July of 1862, then, it was permissible for rabbis to apply for commissions in either of two categories: as regimental chaplains, or as members of the newly organized hospital chaplaincy. And, as might be predicted, it was not long before President Lincoln received a communication in this regard—a month later, to be explicit. It was a petition from the Board of Ministers of the Hebrew Congregations of Philadelphia, requesting the appointment of a Jewish hospital chaplain for the Philadelphia area. This representative body had met on August 19, the letter said, and discussed the hospital problem. Two soldiers of the Jewish faith had already died without the consolation of prayers by a Jewish clergyman, and, since Philadelphia was increasingly becoming a "central depository for sick and wounded soldiers," more and more Jewish men would be sent to those hospitals. Although the Board had now contacted the hospital officials and were assured that their Secretary, the Rev. Isaac Leeser, would be notified of the admission of Jewish wounded, they nevertheless believed it advisable that a Jewish chaplain be officially appointed, and they suggested further that he be assigned not only to the Philadelphia hospitals but also to those located in "York, Harrisburg, Chester, and other towns at not too great a distance."[23]

John Hay, Secretary to Mr. Lincoln, wrote Leeser on September 6 that the President "recognizes the propriety of your suggestion, and will appoint a chaplain of your faith if the Board will designate a proper person for the purpose." The Board of Ministers was called to conference again, and after deliberating on the relative merits of their varied membership, selected the Rev. Jacob Frankel, minister of Rodeph Shalom Congregation of Philadelphia, then fifty-four years old, as their nominee for the commission. The President was informed of this action, and Frankel's commission arrived a few days later, duly signed by the President, together with all the requisite papers and directions.[24] Thus, on September 18, 1862, Jacob Frankel became the first American rabbi to be appointed a military chaplain.

The Rev. Frankel was a native of Grünstadt, Bavaria, where he was born on July 5, 1808. His family was one with a long musical tradition, and, at an early age, he set out on his first concert tour, through the Alsace-Lorraine district, with two brothers. His first position as cantor was in his native town. He next went to Mainz, where he remained for a number of years. In 1848, he applied for and was elected to, the position of Minister of Rodeph Shalom Congregation of Philadelphia. A pleasant and popular man, blessed with a stirring voice and a kindly disposition, the Rev. Frankel was greatly beloved by his congregation, and served it well until his retirement from the active ministry a year before his death on January 12, 1887. Contemporary descriptions of his gentle character and mild manner render it easy to understand why his fellow rabbis selected him from among their number to be honored with the chaplaincy assignment. Further evidence of his popularity can be discovered in the results of a good-humored election, in 1866, for the most popular rabbi in Philadelphia, incidental to a raffle to raise money for the new Jewish hospital. The Rev. Frankel's friends bought so many tickets that he had more votes than all the other ministers combined.[25]

Frankel's service as a chaplain extended for almost three years, until July 1, 1865, when the war had ended.[26] It was, of course, only a part-time activity, and his fellow rabbis assisted him in visiting the various military hospitals.[27] A small fund was placed at his disposal for purchasing inexpensive gifts and necessities for the men he visited, but the men were most grateful for the gift of his voice. Frequent were the occasions when they asked him to sing during his rounds in the hospitals; and many were the men, wounded and well, who came to his synagogue whenever they could to hear his inspired chanting of the service. As best he could, Chaplain Frankel arranged for religious furloughs for ambulatory cases during the High Holy Days and at the Passover. In his typical summarizing style, Leeser wrote, after Frankel was mustered out, that the latter had "faithfully

The military chaplaincy law having been amended, Abraham Lincoln appointed Jacob Frankel as the first Jewish hospital chaplain in the United States military. Here is his commission signed by Lincoln with "the advice and consent of the Senate." Courtesy of The Jacob Rader Marcus Center of the American Jewish Archives.

discharged the duties incident to the office, and the Jewish soldiers in the hospitals in this vicinity were properly cared for under his supervision."[28] Frankel so cherished this war-time experience that he framed his commission, signed by Lincoln and Stanton, and had it hung on the wall of his home, where it remained until his death. It has been a treasured possession of his family ever since.

Frankel and the other Jewish hospital chaplain who served during the Civil War have all but been ignored by writers who have somehow assumed that because it was different, the hospital chaplaincy was inferior to the regimental chaplaincy. This is a historical error completely unwarranted by the facts. Both hospital and field chaplains were enrolled in the volunteer army and were appointed to office on temporary commissions. Indeed, all hospital chaplains were commissioned by the President and the War Department, whereas many regimental chaplains were appointed by governors and other state officials. Equal remuneration was provided for both types of service by Congressional law—the pay of a cavalry captain—but neither was responsible for the military duties of that rank. The same uniform regulations were applied to the chaplain in the field and the chaplain in the hospital: neither wore a military uniform; they were both instructed to wear their customary civilian garb.[29] Hospital chaplains were subject to the same type of military discipline as regimental chaplains, and were equally responsible to their military superiors. For purposes of centralized efficiency, all hospital chaplains were subordinate to the Surgeon General of the Army, and assigned by him to hospitals in the cities of their residence, where, in turn, they were supervised by the Surgeons in charge.[30] Regimental chaplains, on the other hand, were subject to the orders of their colonels. It was a fortunate decision to place all hospital chaplains under a single authority, for they could never have successfully fulfilled their essential role within the complicated and often contradictory structure of state and national military authority.

Much of the confusion regarding the two types of appointments has resulted from the very history of the hospital chaplaincy itself: it was new for the entire country as well as for the American-Jewish community. No such office had existed prior to the Civil War, and Congress alone might never have created it even then. The urging of various Protestant ministers and of Archbishop John Hughes of New York[31] was necessary to convince President Lincoln of the desirability of such a new departure and then he did not wait for Congressional action; instead he requested certain clergymen to act as hospital chaplains, and pledged that at the first opportunity he would press Congress to legalize their appointments. He fulfilled his promise in his Annual Message to Congress on December 3, 1861, and such a bill was finally enacted in May 1862 (without any denominational provisions), a short time before the bill was passed which revised the regimental chaplaincy qualifications.[32]

III

In his report to the readers of *The Occident* informing them of the steps taken to secure a commission for the Rev. Frankel, Isaac Leeser had urged his colleagues in New York, Baltimore, St. Louis, and Cincinnati, to organize themselves as the Philadelphia rabbis had, and to apply in a similar fashion for Jewish chaplaincy appointments for the benefit of the Jewish soldiers in their areas.[33] This suggestion was never adopted by those rabbis, but another representative Jewish body did make application for a hospital chaplaincy. The Board of Delegates of American Israelites, through its President, Henry I. Hart, petitioned the President on October 6, 1862, for an appointment as hospital chaplain for the Rev. Arnold Fischel, who had, from December of 1861 to the following April, carried on such duties in the Potomac area as the civilian representative of the Board, in much the same capacity as Jewish Welfare Board workers during World Wars I and II. Fischel richly deserved such official recognition for his noteworthy and unique activities. His work had come to a halt only because the member congregations of the Board failed to contribute adequate funds to pay his expenses. But now that chaplaincy appointments were obtainable it was more than fitting that the Board should recommend him to Mr. Lincoln and ask that he be assigned to the hospitals in Washington and vicinity with which he was already so familiar. This letter of application[34] was endorsed by John Hay, Lincoln's secretary, in these words: "The President directs me to refer the enclosed to the notice of the Surgeon General and to inquire whether a Jewish chaplain is needed here." No other notation was made on the letter and there is no answer to it in the files of the Board of Delegates' correspondence, which have been carefully preserved.

At any rate, Fischel never received a commission and never served as a military chaplain. The noteworthy service he performed was as a civilian. Our knowledge of his later career is extremely hazy, but it is reported that he returned to Holland shortly after this episode, although the date is uncertain.[35] This was a disappointing conclusion to the war career of a rabbi who should, by virtue of his interest in, and efforts in behalf of, the Jewish soldiers of the Union Army, have been privileged ultimately to serve as an officer of that Army.

There were not enough rabbis in Louisville, Kentucky, to form a Board of Ministers, but the entire Jewish community of Louisville was conscious enough of the Jewish war wounded in Kentucky hospitals to initiate a public movement to secure the appointment of a Jewish chaplain for that area. Prominent non-Jewish citizens joined together with Jews, and urged Robert Mallory, a Kentucky member of the House of Representatives from 1859 to 1865, to seek a commission for the Rev. Bernhard Henry Gotthelf, the rabbi of Adath Israel Congregation of Louisville. This public movement coincided with the furor over General Grant's anti-Jewish General Order No. 11, which had so many repercussions in the state of Kentucky—indirect evidence that the majority of non-Jews in this area where Jews were accused of disloyalty did not share the suspicions of Grant's staff officers. The petition met with success, and the Rev. Gotthelf received his appointment on May 6, 1863, although his commission dated his rank from February 16.[36]

The Rev. Gotthelf, born in Bavaria on February 5, 1819, had come to the United States at the age of twenty-one, and served congregations in the East, including Keneseth Israel of Philadelphia, of which he was the first cantor and preacher, prior to his call to Louisville in 1851. After the Civil War he moved to Vicksburg, Mississippi, where he ministered to Anshe Chesed Congregation until his death in 1878, a victim of the yellow fever epidemic which swept the whole Southland that year. The inscription on his tombstone records his life and character in these laudatory terms: "a wise teacher, a faithful minister, a tender husband, a devoted father, a good man."[37]

So successful had been the campaign to convince the American public of the right of rabbis to serve as military chaplains, that the news of Mr. Gotthelf's appointment was noted in the public press, although chaplaincy appointments (for Christians, at least) were by that date quite commonplace. The editor of the Louisville *Journal* celebrated the occasion in these words:

> An Excellent Appointment.—We are gratified to announce that President Lincoln has appointed the Rev. B. Gotthelf, the minister of the German Jewish Congregation of this city as Hospital Chaplain, to be stationed here. The fact that a very respectable number of Jewish soldiers have been and

still are receiving medical treatment at our hospitals having been brought to the notice of the Hon. Robert Mallory, he made an application for the appointment of Mr. Gotthelf, which we took pleasure, with other citizens, in endorsing. These invalids can now enjoy the instruction and consolation of a minister of their own faith, and we are, therefore, convinced that the appointment was as timely as it is well merited.[38]

A careful search for family papers and examination of contemporary periodicals has disclosed only one interesting detail of the Rev. Gotthelf's twenty-eight months of chaplaincy service (he was mustered out of the Army on August 26, 1865). Since the responsibility of the Civil War chaplain towards his men included the provision of various items of comfort and entertainment, the Rev. Gotthelf was eager to obtain reading matter for his men, most of whom were German-Jewish immigrants. During January and February of the final year of the war, he made a tour of the larger Jewish communities of the midwest to secure donations in cash, and in books, to establish German language libraries in the various military hospitals under his jurisdiction. An editorial in *The Israelite* endorsing the purposes of this trip conveyed the information that "there are almost always from 2,000 to 3,000 sick and wounded German soldiers in [the Louisville] hospitals, among them from 200 to 300 Israelites."[39] Undoubtedly the libraries were to be assembled for the use of all German-speaking patients, non-Jews as well as Jews. Perhaps this was the first example of that type of non-denominational service which Jewish chaplains and war service agencies rendered so frequently during the subsequent wars of the United States.

In Cincinnati, at least, Rabbi Wise's assurance that "Mr. G., well known to our readers, will find the encouragement this matter deserves," was not disappointed. Beth El Lodge of B'nai B'rith appointed a special committee to assist Mr. Gotthelf in the project, as did other Jewish lodges in the community. There is no record of the other cities which Gotthelf visited, or of the general success of his tour,[40] but the whispered word of criticism, which seems to make the lives of so many rabbis miserable, pursued even this meritorious mission of beneficence. One William Kriegshaber of Louisville was compelled later to send a public letter of retraction to *The Israelite*, apologizing for some bitter reflections on the character of the Rev. Gotthelf and of his mission which he had written to friends in Cincinnati.[41] This episode marks the sum total of the information available concerning Gotthelf's military career. It was unfortunately typical of Jewish interests during the Civil War that once Jewish chaplains were appointed, their work was all but ignored by the Jewish press, and the more glamorous military exploits of individual Jews received the greater amount of publicity.

NOTES

1. See *The United States Army Chaplaincy* (War Department Pamphlet 16-1), Washington, DC, 1946, for a detailed study of the historical development of the Army Chaplaincy.

2. See statistics and lists of Jews in the Union and Confederate armies and navies in Simon Wolf, *The American Jew as Patriot, Soldier and Citizen*, Philadelphia 1895.

3. *Journal of the Congress of the Confederate States of America 1861–1865*, Washington, DC, 1904, II, pp. 160, 196. Ella Lonn (*Foreigners in the Confederacy*, Chapel Hill 1940, p. 265) erroneously refers to the Rev. Jacob Frankel, who will be discussed later in this essay, as a Confederate chaplain. Miss Lonn obviously misread a vague phrase in the authority which she cites, Mrs. Townes R. Leigh, "The Jews in the Confederacy," *Southern Historical Society Papers* XXXIX, p. 178, where it is not clearly stated that Frankel was a Union chaplain. No rabbi is known to have served as a chaplain in the Confederate Army.

4. *War of the Rebellion: . . . Official Records of the Union and Confederate Armies*, Washington, DC, 1880–1901, III, I, p. 154. (Hereafter abbreviated *WROR*).

5. *Congressional Globe*, Washington, DC, 1861, 37th Congress, First Session, p. 100. Vallandigham later took pleasure in reminding his fellow Congressmen that he had called the injustice of this measure to their attention months before they were deluged with protests from their constituents; ibid., Second Session, Part I, pp. 156–57.

6. *The Israelite* VIII, No. 3, p. 23, July 19, 1861. Perhaps this was yet another reason for Wise's unabating opposition to the Republican administration and his mounting loyalty to the Democratic Party. Wise was willing to stand as Democratic nominee for State Senator in Ohio in the same election of 1863 in which Vallandigham was narrowly defeated for the gubernatorial office. See this writer's essay on "Isaac Mayer Wise on the Civil War" in *Hebrew Union College Annual* XX, Cincinnati 1947. An editorial in the *Jewish Messenger* (X, No. 9, p. 68) on Nov. 1, 1861, indicates that its editors were not oblivious to the problem, but had failed to comment upon it because they were convinced that it was an oversight and that "no discrimination against our co-religionists, was in any way intended, and . . . that Congress, at its next session, will modify the act." Obviously the father and son editorial team, Samuel M. and Myer S. Isaacs, were either ignorant of the facts or blind to their meaning: Vallandigham's motion was defeated—the House had acted deliberately.

7. Philadelphia *Sunday Dispatch*, Oct. 20, 1861. There were undoubtedly many other cases in which the appointment of chaplains of minority faiths was attacked publicly. Carl Sandburg, in *Abraham Lincoln: The War Years*, New York 1939, II, p. 230, records the visit to Washington of a delegation of Philadelphia clergymen to urge Lincoln not to appoint a certain Universalist minister as chaplain, because "he believes that even rebels themselves will be finally saved."

8. His resignation was accepted on Sept. 26. Special orders No. 79, Headquarters, Army of the Potomac, in *Records of the War Dept., Office of the Adjutant General, Volume 403, Orders and Special Orders*, in the National Archives.

9. Wolf, *American Jew as Patriot, Soldier and Citizen*, pp. 484–85. The law was passed only a few days before Allen enlisted (July 18, 1861, according to *Records of the Veterans Administration*, WO 1204831, in the National Archives). The officers could hardly have known of the prohibitory clause. New York *Tribune*, Oct. 31, 1861.

10. *Jewish Messenger* XIX, No. 23, p. 4, June 15, 1866.

11. Ibid. X, No. 7, p. 52, Oct. 4, 1851; Henry S. Morais, *The Jews of Philadelphia*, Philadelphia 1894, p. 245.

12. P. 5 of an eleven-page diary kept by Allen during the weeks his regiment was encamped near Washington, in the possession of Mrs. Clarence Michael Allen of New York, daughter-in-law of M. M. Allen.

13. In a letter to the Philadelphia *Sunday Dispatch*, Oct. 20, 1861.

14. Philadelphia *Sunday Dispatch*, Oct. 27, 1861.

15. Philadelphia *Enquirer*, Oct. 12, 1861, p. 8.

16. *WROR* III, I, p. 728.

17. *Presbyterian Banner*, cited in *The Israelite* IX, No. 2, p. 14, July 11, 1862.

18. *The Israelite* VIII, No. 6, p. 45, Aug. 9, 1861; No. 9, p. 70, Aug. 30, 1861.

19. W. O. Stoddard, "White House Sketches," New York *Citizen*, Oct. 6, 1866, quoted in David R. Barbee, "President Lincoln and Doctor Gurley," *Abraham Lincoln Quarterly*, March 1948, p. 7.

20. *Jewish Messenger* X, No. 12, p. 93, Dec. 13, 1861, and various items in the Board of Delegates of American Israelites correspondence files in the library of the American Jewish Historical Society (notably Letter No. 37 from Myer S. Isaacs, Secretary of the Board, to the Rev. Fischel, Nov. 27, 1861) established the authenticity of his appointment by the officers of the regiment. Some of Fischel's activities are chronicled in the mis-named article by Myer S. Isaacs, "A Jewish Army Chaplain," in *Publications of the American Jewish Historical Society*, No. 12 (1904), pp. 127–37. The Rev. Fischel's contract as lecturer at the Shearith Israel Synagogue in New York was about to expire on Oct. 31, 1861, and was not expected to be renewed. He was, therefore, seeking a new position. *Shearith Israel Trustees' Minutes* VI, p. 477, passim.

21. *Jewish Messenger* X, No. 12, p. 93, Dec. 13, 1861.

22. *WROR* III, I, p. 154; III, III, pp. 175–76.

23. *The Occident* XX, No. 7, pp. 325–28, Oct. 1862.

24. Ibid. The appointment was signed by the President on Sept. 10, and forwarded by the Surgeon General on Sept. 15. *Records of the War Dept., Office of the Adjutant General,* in the National Archives. The commission printed on p. 13 was sent to Frankel two years later when his appointment was renewed.

25. Morais, *Jews of Philadelphia,* pp. 73–74; Edward Davis, *The History of Rodeph Shalom Congregation, Philadelphia, 1802–1926,* Philadelphia 1926, pp. 61, 98–100.

26. Records of the War Dept., Office of the Adjutant General, in the National Archives.

27. See the Rev. Leeser's pass, addressed to "Surgeons in Charge of USA General Hospitals, Department of the Susquehanna," requesting that he be permitted to visit sick Jewish soldiers, signed March 30, 1864. In Dropsie College Library, Leeser Collection.

28. *The Occident* XXII, No. 5, pp. 234–35, Aug. 1865. Other details from miscellaneous clippings in the possession of Mr. Joseph Frankel, New York, grandson of Jacob.

29. *General Orders of the War Department, 1861–1863,* New York 1864, I, p. 177. Allen wore a uniform (see p. 8), as did certain other chaplains, because he had enlisted as an officer of the line before his election as chaplain.

30. For the military orders concerning the appointment and assignment of hospital chaplains, see *WROR* III, II, pp. 67, 222, 276; IV, III, p. 496.

31. See Carl Sandburg, *Abraham Lincoln: The War Years,* II, p. 44, for pertinent quotations from Lincoln's correspondence on this subject.

32. *WROR* III, I, pp. 712, 721.

33. XX, No. 7, pp. 325–28, Oct. 1852.

34. No. 18878-9 of the Robert Todd Lincoln Collection, Manuscript Division, Library of Congress.

35. Isaacs, "A Jewish Army Chaplain," pp. 130–31. *The Jewish Record* reported several times that Fischel intended to return to America, but these expectations were never fulfilled. See, for example, V, No. 22. p. 2, Feb. 24, 1865. [See Jonathan Waxman, "Arnold Fischel: 'Unsung Hero' in American Israel," *American Jewish Historical Quarterly* 60 (June 1971): 325–43.]

36. *The Israelite* IX, No. 45, p. 357, May 15, 1863; *Records of the War Department, Office of the Adjutant General, Vol. XI, Officers of Signal Corps and Hospital Chaplains,* in the National Archives.

37. Letters from Rabbi Stanley Brav, Vicksburg, Oct. 23, 1947, and Mr. Harold Gotthelf (grandson of the rabbi), Vicksburg, Nov. 18, 1947; *Keneseth Israel 90th Anniversary Booklet,* Philadelphia 1937.

38. Cited in *The Israelite* IX, No. 45, p. 357, May 15, 1863.

39. XI, No. 30, p. 237, Jan. 30, 1865.

40. Ibid., No. 34, p. 269, Feb. 17, 1865.

41. Ibid., No. 39, p. 309, March 24, 1865.

14

That Obnoxious Order

John Simon

"That obnoxious order," Julia Dent Grant called it. She disliked *General Order Number Eleven,* issued by her husband, Major General Ulysses S. Grant, on December 17, 1862. The order read:

> I. The Jews, as a class, violating every regulation of trade established by the Treasury Department, and also Department orders, are hereby expelled from the Department. II. Within twenty-four hours from the receipt of this order by Post Commanders, they will see that all of this class of people are furnished with passes and required to leave, and any one returning after such notification, will be arrested and held in confinement until an opportunity occurs of sending them out as prisoners unless furnished with permits from these Head Quarters. III. No permits will be given these people to visit Head Quarters for the purpose of making personal application for trade permits.

Why did Grant issue such an order? This remains a puzzle with only a partial solution. On the day of the order's issue, Grant advanced into Mississippi along the line of the Mississippi Central Railroad, and reached Oxford. From there he instructed Major General William T. Sherman to lead an expedition down the Mississippi River to Vicksburg, the ultimate objective of Grant's campaign.

Though he planned a pincer's movement on the Confederate citadel, Grant knew relatively little about the strength of the army before him or of the Vicksburg defenses. Already two Confederate cavalry commanders,

---

Reprinted with permission from *Civil War Times Illustrated* 23:6 (1984): 12–17, copyright © 1984 by Civil War Times.

Major General Earl Van Dorn and Brigadier Nathan B. Forrest, were preparing to cut Grant's supply line. They struck three days later, Van Dorn at Holly Springs, Mississippi, Forrest further north in Tennessee.

On December 17, Grant knew that his army had advanced deep into Mississippi with a tenuous supply line, that enemy forces remained intact and mobile, and that his army ran the risk of fighting the same Confederate forces on separate fields. Given his military anxieties, he could hardly be expected to devote enough thought to matters of trade. But such concerns constantly intruded.

Grant's victory at Fort Donelson, Tennessee, in February 1862 had cracked the Confederate defense line in Tennessee, opening part of the cotton kingdom to Federal occupation, and through the year, as U.S. armies advanced, more of the plantation South came within Federal lines. The outbreak of war had so increased the value of cotton in the North and in Europe that planters continued to grow it, despite the Confederate embargo. By the end of the year, Grant's advance carried him toward the richest plantations, some storing both 1861 and 1862 crops.

A confused and ambivalent U.S. Government policy on trade provided generous loopholes for the enterprising and unscrupulous. When war began, Secretary of the Treasury Salmon P. Chase moved immediately to halt the shipping of "munitions of war" to the Confederacy, but not until August 1861 did President Abraham Lincoln give the Treasury authority to regulate trade with insurrectionary regions. Chase believed that trade should follow the flag, and as armies moved southward, Treasury agents gave permits to loyal citizens to resume normal commerce. Such a policy, Chase believed, would reconcile citizens to the Federal government and benefit the Northern economy through the flow of needed Southern products.

What looked sound and sensible from Washington looked disgraceful from army headquarters in Mississippi, where everyone knew how often goods traded by "loyal" persons behind the lines seeped southward to the Confederacy in exchange for cotton. The war had cut off the supply of cotton to New England mills and the world market, multiplying traditional prices. The government expected the army to seize captured and abandoned cotton for sale to benefit the Treasury, thus defraying the staggering cost of war and ending the cotton famine. But as the army advanced, patriotic Confederates burned their cotton, rather than lose their hoards without payment and help the North win the war. Rebels aware of the imminent arrival of the enemy and reluctant to torch their only capital asset did have an alternative. Traders or their agents who slipped through the lines offered gold, weapons, or medicine in return for these doomed bales. Such illegal and unpatriotic practices were lucrative enough to warrant the risk, and speculators who bought the cotton stood to make sufficient profit to enable them to bribe officers and officials to look away or even to assist as they smuggled cotton through the lines. Once through the lines, cotton might pass through different hands on the way to market, and smuggled bales, looking the same as those from occupied regions, defied efforts to trace their origin.

Wartime cotton trade in the Mississippi Valley outraged patriotic Northerners, soldiers and civilians alike. Unscrupulous traders enabled Confederates to fight more effectively by supplying gold and scarce goods, deprived the U.S. Treasury of revenue, and corrupted the military. Officers and journalists frequently blamed this trade on Jews. When the war began, some 150,000 Jews lived in the United States, about two-thirds of whom, born abroad, had crossed the Atlantic for much the same reasons motivating other recent immigrants from Europe. Like other immigrants, they more often settled in the North than the South, and disproportionately in cities. Whether or not they were disproportionate participants in the wartime cotton trade cannot be determined, but contemporaries wrote as if they were. An 1863 investigation of cotton-buying in the Mississippi Valley involved hundreds of soldiers and civilians, only four of them Jewish. Some ugly remarks about "Jew traders" may have been intended as insults to non-Jewish traders, but nonetheless had the effect of strengthening the impression that Jews dominated the cotton business.

Seeking the roots of this prejudice requires turning to the mass immigration of earlier years. In one decade, 1845–1854, 2,939,000 newcomers, largely from Germany and Ireland, added some 14.5 percent to the population of the United States. Such enormous numbers created social, economic, and political strains on Americans who called themselves natives, a group that always excluded the Indians. The sins of the Irish included voting Democratic and practicing Catholicism, the latter a source of outrage to many Protestants who found difficulty enough in tolerating each other. Between 1834 and the late 1850s, religious rioting erupted in many cities, and some twenty Catholic churches were burned in places ranging from Maine to Texas. Resentment of foreigners and their religions gave rise to political groups of nativists. This reached high tide in the Know-Nothing surge of 1854 and the American Party of 1856. Before thinking better of it, Grant attended one meeting of a Know-Nothing lodge after his rejection for the post of county engineer in St. Louis in favor of a German immigrant.

Immigration ebbed and the slavery controversy grew as the Civil War approached, but nativism never disappeared. Tensions and animosities from the preceding decade provided tinder awaiting a spark. Ethnic and religious stereotypes remained a staple for newspaper articles. Cotton speculation, a risky and immoral enterprise, would naturally attract Jews and Yankees, some assumed, so the stereotypes and accusations circulated unencumbered.

Before the Civil War, American Jews lacked national organization, and generally those North or South followed regional politics and practices. Rabbis who took stands on slavery usually reflected their location, but one in New York City had defended slavery as sanctioned by the Bible, while another in slaveholding Baltimore acquired a reputation as an Abolitionist.

When war began, Jews enlisted in local regiments much like their fellow citizens. Ultimately, an estimated 10,000 Jewish soldiers served North and South. But, especially in the North, many Jews enlisted in regiments in groups. When Grant issued *General Order Number Eleven*, the highest ranking Jewish officer in his command, Lieutenant Colonel Marcus M. Spiegel, 120th Ohio, son of a German rabbi, was with his regiment on Sherman's expedition to Vicksburg.

Although Jews were more numerous in the North, they were more prominent in the South, if only because Judah P. Benjamin, former U.S. Senator from Louisiana, held (at various times) three different Cabinet posts in the Confederate Government. Confederates were not, however, immune to the anti-Semitism embodied in Grant's orders. Critics of Benjamin in the South as well as the North constantly harped on his ancestry. Confederates in Thomasville, Georgia, asserting that German Jews passed counterfeit money and raised prices through speculation, demanded their expulsion from Thomasville. Prejudice pervaded both North and South; Grant hardly invented it.

Grant's imperial Department of the Tennessee stretched from northern Mississippi to Cairo, Illinois; and from the Mississippi River to the Tennessee River. Within this domain, he delegated administrative duties to subordinates while concentrating his attention on the armies moving southward. But he could not ignore the civil problems of his department. Both Grant and Sherman vehemently but fruitlessly protested current trade regulations as fostering fraud and corruption. Constantly vexed by the cotton trade, Grant fell prey to the pervasive anti-Semitism of the day.

On July 26, 1862, Grant telegraphed from Corinth, Mississippi, to his subordinate at Columbus, Kentucky. "Examine the baggage of all speculators coming South, and, when they have specie, turn them back. If medicine and other contraband articles, arrest them and confiscate the contraband articles. Jews should receive special attention." On November 9, he telegraphed to Major General Stephen A. Hurlbut at Memphis: "Refuse all permits to come south of Jackson for the present. The Israelites especially should be kept out." The following day, Grant instructed his superintendent of military railroads: "Give orders to all the conductors . . . on the road that no Jews are to be permitted to travel on the Rail Road southward from any point[.] They may go north and be encouraged in it but they are such an intolerable nuisance. That the Department must be purged for them[.]" Even so, when Colonel John Van Deusen Du Bois issued orders on December 8 expelling "Cotton-Speculators, Jews and other Vagrants" from Holly Springs, Grant immediately ordered them revoked as violating instructions from Washington encouraging cotton shipping from the South.

Grant's prompt revocation of Du Bois's order makes more puzzling his issuance of similar orders within a few days. The timing suggests that Grant's rage was ignited by the arrival of his father in Mississippi to buy cotton for a Jewish firm in Cincinnati in return for one-quarter of the profits. Jesse R. Grant was no simpleton ensnared by crafty speculators. A shrewd and aggressive businessman, he rose from poverty to affluence through attention to business. A neighbor remembered him as one willing "to follow a dollar to hell."

Jesse's relationship with his son was complex. It was the father who had arranged the son's appointment to West Point, but Ulysses said, "I won't go." Later, young Grant responded, that "he thought I would, *and I thought so too if he did.*" When Ulysses resigned from the army fifteen years later, his father-in-law rather than his father tried to help him establish a farm, and when necessity eventually drove him to his family's leather store in Galena, Illinois, he worked for a younger brother for a less-than-generous salary.

Jesse's efforts to defend his son in newspapers and to gain military appointments for friends embarrassed the general. But Ulysses never broke with his father, and through his rise to fame during the Civil War frequently wrote to him, apparently seeking his approval. However, Jesse's attempt to use his paternity as a source of cotton profits was the last straw. On the eve of his father's arrival, Ulysses complained of "speculators whose patriotism is measured by dollars & cents. Country has no value with them compared to money." Suddenly he realized that his father fit this condemnation. Ulysses displaced his anger, lashing out at his father's Jewish partners.

Grant's anger appeared even more clearly in a letter written the day the orders were issued, addressed to Assistant Secretary of War Christopher P. Wolcott.

> I have long since believed that in spite of all the vigilance that can be infused into Post Commanders that the Specie regulations of the Treasury Dept. have been violated, and that mostly by Jews and other unprincipled traders. So well satisfied of this have I been that I instructed the Commandg Officer at Columbus to refuse all permits to Jews to come south, and frequently have had them expelled from the Dept. But they come in with their Carpet sacks in spite of all that can be done to prevent it. The Jews seem to be a privileged class that can travel any where. They will land at any wood yard or landing on the river and make their way through the country. If not permitted to buy Cotton themselves they will act as Agents for some one else who will be at a Military post, with a Treasury permit to receive Cotton and pay for it in Treasury notes which the Jew will buy up at an agreed rate, paying gold. There is but one way that I know of to reach this case. That is for Government to buy all the Cotton at a fixed rate and send it to Cairo, St Louis or some other point to be sold. Then all traders, they are a curse to the Army, might be expelled.

Grant's reference in his orders to Jews as a "class" made no sense and created considerable confusion in enforcement. Several officers asked whether the orders applied to Jewish sutlers, the licensed traders who accompanied regiments. At least one Jewish officer resigned. Captain Philip Trounstine, 5th Ohio Cavalry, writing from Moscow, Tennessee, explained that he was "either fortunately or unfortunately born of Jewish parents," that he owed "filial affection to my parents, Devotion to my Religion, and a deep regard for the opinion of my friends" and could "no longer, bear the taunts and malice, of those to whom my religious opinions are known."

Information about enforcement within the Department of the Tennessee remains hazy, but the orders were zealously enforced at Paducah, Kentucky, where Jews were expelled on twenty-four-hour notice. Entire

Henry Mack, who had made his fortune as a clothing merchant and manufacturer, was one of the largest suppliers of uniforms to the Union Army during the war, and a prominent member of Cincinnati's Jewish community. In December 1862 he entered into fateful partnership with Jesse Grant to speculate in cotton. Jesse's son Ulysses S. Grant had recently been appointed as commander of the Department of the Tennessee, controlling a vast territory that served as a major conduit for trade in illicit Southern cotton. Jesse Grant and Henry Mack hoped to profit from this familial connection. Instead Ulysses S. Grant was enraged by his father's efforts at influence peddling, perhaps contributing to the vehemence of his General Order Number 11. Courtesy of The Jacob Rader Marcus Center of the American Jewish Archives.

families were driven from their homes. Two women lying ill were exempt; two army veterans were not. In his inaugural address in 1869, President Grant stated: "I know no method to secure the repeal of bad or obnoxious laws so effective as their stringent execution." Nowhere had this been more effectively demonstrated than in Paducah, where Jewish leaders began a protest eventually heard in Washington.

Cesar F. Kaskel of Paducah, barred from telegraphing Grant under terms of the orders, telegraphed to Lincoln instead. Then he proceeded toward Washington, along the way visiting or writing to Jewish leaders to create pressure against the orders. Kaskel headed toward the right man. During the 1850s, Lincoln had flatly rejected any political advantage through harnessing nativism and in 1855 wrote:

> I am not a Know-Nothing. That is certain. How could I be? How can anyone who abhors the oppression of negroes, be in favor of degrading classes of white people? Our progress in degeneracy appears to me to be pretty rapid. As a nation, we began by declaring that "all men are created equal." We now practically read it "all men are created equal, except negroes." When the Know-Nothings get control, it will read "all men are created equal, except negroes, and foreigners, and catholics." When it comes to this I should prefer emigrating to some country where they make no pretence of loving liberty—to Russia, for instance, where despotism can be taken pure, and without the base alloy of hypocracy.

Lincoln apparently knew nothing about Grant's orders until Kaskel arrived. After hearing Kaskel, Lincoln wrote a note—unfortunately lost—to Major General Henry W. Halleck.

In response, on January 4, 1863, Halleck sent Grant a characteristically cautious telegram. "A paper purporting to be a Genl Order No. 11 issued by you Dec 17th had been presented here. By its term it expels all Jews from your Dept. If such an order has been issued, it will be immediately revoked." On the following day, Colonel John C. Kelton in Halleck's office wrote to Grant, "Permit me to inform you unofficially the objection taken to your Genl Order No 11. It excluded a whole class, instead of certain obnoxious individuals. Had the word 'pedler' been inserted after Jew I do not suppose any exception would have been taken to the order. Several officers and a number of enlisted men in your Dept are Jews. A Govr of one of the Western states is a Jew." Kelton presumably meant Governor Edward Salomon of Wisconsin, who was a Lutheran.

People of the period knew far more about stereotypes than they knew about Jews. Just how successfully Grant and his subordinates could identify Jews remains problematical; had Grant known more about Jews, he would have remembered those who fought in his army.

Halleck himself wrote to Grant on January 21: "It may be proper to give you some explanation of the revocation of your order expelling all Jews from your Dept. The President has no objection to your expelling traders & Jew pedlars, which I suppose was the object of your order, but as it in terms prescribed an entire religious class, some of whom are fighting in our ranks, the President deemed it necessary to revoke it."

After receiving Halleck's telegram, Grant revoked the orders. Consequently, Congress tabled censure resolutions introduced in the House and Senate. *General Orders Number Eleven* might then have been forgotten. But its author entered politics.

Presidential campaign pressures forced Grant to write something for publication on a topic he did not want to discuss, and through the remainder of his life he chose to maintain public silence about his expulsion of the Jews. The incident received no mention in the two volumes of his *Memoirs* and even today is better known in American Jewish history than in Civil War history. Grant's wife, however, remembered his speaking of "that obnoxious order" and of the Congressional resolutions which he said were deserved, "as he had no right to make an order against any special sect."

15

Civil War Exodus
The Jews and Grant's General Order No. 11

Stephen V. Ash

The popular mind commonly envisages the Civil War in images of battlefield heroics and exalted statesmanship to the exclusion of the more petty manifestations of the human spirit—greed, hatred, prejudice. But the latter were epidemic in America in the 1860s, spawned and nurtured by the virulent nature of the world's first modern war. An event in late 1862—the forced removal of innocent Jewish families from Paducah, Kentucky—exemplifies this ugly phenomenon clearly and brings to light some less familiar aspects of America's experience during those years. Though historians have not ignored this episode altogether, they have not yet fully accounted for it. This essay, examining sources never before used in this connection, explores the background of events in Paducah to show that the incident, far from being fortuitous, was in fact the climax to a story of evolving social turmoil in wartime America.

In mid-December 1862, the world seemed a cheerless place to Ulysses S. Grant. The more the general reflected upon the exasperating circumstances in which he found himself, the more disconsolate he became. In a letter to his sister Mary he allowed himself an uncharacteristic moment of self-pity. "For a consciencious [sic] person, and I profess to be one," he said, "this is a most slavish life."[1]

Grant was writing from his headquarters in Oxford, Mississippi, the farthest point of advance in his first campaign down the Mississippi Valley against the Confederate stronghold at Vicksburg. While General William T. Sherman massed a second force upriver in preparation for a

---

Reprinted, with minor abridgement, with permission of Stephen V. Ash from *The Historian* 44 (August 1982): 505–523, copyright © 1982 by Phi Alpha Theta.

surprise amphibious assault on the city, Grant and his men found themselves alone, advancing more and more deeply into Rebel territory along a fragile railroad line in the hope of decoying the main body of the enemy away from the Vicksburg defenses. Confederate cavalry under Nathan Bedford Forrest and Earl Van Dorn flitted annoyingly around the flanks of the army, popping up at inopportune moments. Swarms of "contraband" slaves trailed behind the blue-clad troops, creating extra problems of administration and supply. To add to Grant's woes, he was the object of swelling criticism from the victory-starved Northern public for the alleged shortcomings of his strategy; publicly he sloughed off these attacks, but privately he admitted the "mortification" they caused him.[2] And as though these vexations were not enough to keep him overworked and miserable, Grant was forced to deal daily with another problem so thorny and maddening that it often made all the rest seem facile by contrast. This was the question of cotton.

There were those who claimed that cotton was what the war was really all about. Whether this is true or not, it is certain that cotton became a crucial issue after the conflict began. At the heart of the matter was the fact that the South had cotton and much of the rest of the world wanted it. Abraham Lincoln tried at first to deny the Rebels the benefits of foreign trade by keeping all of the cotton in the South, but he soon had to reconsider the matter. Certain industries and businesses in Europe and America depended heavily on the cotton trade, and they worked vigorously to persuade the president to lift his strict embargo. Border states, particularly Kentucky, wanted trade with the South kept open, and Lincoln, at least early in the war, was afraid to risk offending them. Furthermore, his own armies needed limited amounts of cotton for such articles as tents. The necessity for compromise between the opposing demands of war and politics soon became obvious to Lincoln. Within a few weeks after Fort Sumter, the president and Treasury Secretary Salmon P. Chase resolved to relax the land blockade enough to allow limited trade in those parts of the Confederacy in Union hands; that is, as Chase phrased it, they decided "to let commerce follow the flag." This policy was welcomed at first by sympathetic army officers who recognized that destitute Southerners in occupied areas often had nothing of value left in the world but a few bales of cotton. Restrictions were gradually lifted so that by the summer of 1862 military authorities were under orders to provide "all possible facilities" for moving cotton out, and in September alone 14,000 bales worth three million dollars were shipped up the Mississippi.[3]

This measure remedied certain problems but unfortunately begat a multitude of others. The whole policy was probably as mismanaged as any government operation of the war. The worst mistake was that, in the great tradition of American free enterprise, no one ever considered granting the government a monopoly of the cotton trade. Instead, private individuals were licensed to follow the armies and deal in cotton. In 1862, as Northern troops marched into the heart of the Cotton Belt and the commodity's price skyrocketed to three or four times its prewar value, hopeful buyers flocked to the occupied towns, hot on the scent of cotton deals. Official regulations governing the trade were vague and often contradictory, and no one was even sure whether the army or the Treasury Department had ultimate authority. Chase himself conceded that the whole problem was "exceedingly arduous and perplexing," and nearly impossible to resolve satisfactorily.[4]

Worst of all, the burgeoning trade attracted a good number of men of dubious character; and the enormous profits to be made seduced others who had begun honestly, so that the whole affair rapidly degenerated into something close to an orgy of corruption. The scene in the Mississippi Valley in 1862 tends to affirm the assertion of one Southerner that cotton made "more damn rascals on both sides than everything else" during the war. A scandalized correspondent of the *Chicago Tribune* described the spectacle at Grant's supply base in Mississippi in December: "If ever a community were insane, or afflicted with a disgusting moral malady, it is the crowds of speculators and vagrants which have congregated at Holly Springs to deal in cotton—they have 'cotton' on the brain—every one of them."[5]

Grant and his generals fumed bitterly about the necessity of tolerating and even abetting this carnival of greed while trying to carry on the war. Army headquarters was constantly besieged by speculators importuning the commanding general for permits and transportation. Even worse, traders traveling back and forth through the lines carried vital military intelligence to the enemy, or so Grant believed, as well as passing gold to the Confederates with which they could purchase war supplies abroad. Grant was also convinced that it demoralized his troops to be used to protect this trade for the benefit of rapacious and unscrupulous civilians whose "patriotism is measured by dollars & cents." "I will venture that no honest man has made money in West Tennessee in the last year," he declared in 1863, "whilst many fortunes have been made there." Sherman was equally incensed. "We cannot carry on war and trade with a people at the same time," he grumbled. "Of course our lives are nothing in the scales of profit with our commercial people."⁶

Inevitably some military men were themselves lured into the trade by the dazzling vision of a quick fortune. A War Department agent reported from Memphis, with some hyperbole, that "every colonel, captain, or quartermaster is in secret partnership with some operator in cotton; every soldier dreams of adding a bale of cotton to his monthly pay." A *New York Times* correspondent on the Mississippi wrote that he had met officers "who, six months ago, could scarcely raise sufficient money to buy a clean shirt, but who to-day have a 'clean' half million."⁷

The resentment felt within the army toward the cotton trade and its avaricious agents was natural and understandable. But what grew out of this general animosity was a malevolent strain of bigotry. A good many of the cotton speculators hounding the army were Jewish, and (whatever their actual proportion among the traders) the Jews came to epitomize in the eyes of Grant and his men the worst characteristics of all the speculators. The terms *Jew* and *trader* were in fact often used synonymously. Virtually every diatribe delivered against the speculators by army officers or others in the Mississippi Valley in 1862 betrayed a core of anti-Semitism. Sherman habitually denounced "Jews and speculators" in the same breath, and Grant ordered officers dealing with traders to take special precautions with the "Isrealites [sic]." A Treasury Department agent informed Secretary Chase in May that the booming cotton business was drawing "swarms of Jews and a good many white men." Newspaper correspondents with the army were also infected by this pervasive prejudice; they sent regular reports to their readers back home about the nefarious activities of the "pork-hating descendants of Abraham" and the "oleaginous children of Israel."⁸

The fact is that the Jews were neither the most numerous nor the most iniquitous of the legion of sharpers following the army; their peccadilloes were certainly no greater than the misdeeds of any number of crooked Yankees, Treasury agents, and army officers. But the Jews were active, and in a largely rural, old-stock population they were easily identifiable by their manners, accents, and surnames. And, too, they bore the burden of ancient stereotypes. The Jews thus became for Grant and his harassed officers a convenient symbol of all the frustrations and annoyances with which they were contending. By late 1862 Grant's army was operating in an atmosphere of growing intolerance which would lead ultimately to tragic consequences.

As Grant began his Mississippi campaign in November, he was reconciled to the necessity of permitting trade but determined to exercise strictly what little discretion he retained in the matter. He was authorized to regulate the traders in his military department (which included northern Mississippi, the western parts of Kentucky and Tennessee, and Cairo, Illinois), and soon there issued from his headquarters a series of orders requiring licenses for trading, forbidding the use of government transportation to haul cotton, and designating the areas where the license holders could travel and do business. During the next weeks, Grant energetically enforced these edicts and others from the Treasury Department, frequently availing himself of his prerogative to expel violators from his department.[9] He thus went as far as he could to check the worst abuses, but he still felt constrained by the letter of government instructions. When the provoked post commander at Holly Springs promulgated a sweeping order in early December designed to banish all traders from the town, Grant was forced, though reluctant, to overrule it.[10]

But complaints about the speculators and reports of violations continued to pour into headquarters. As usual these reports emphasized the miscreancy of the Jews, and Grant, predisposed to believe such allegations, was soon entirely convinced that the Jews were the main, indeed the only, perpetrators. He drew a distinction between the Jews and other traders, called them an "intolerable nuisance," and repeatedly instructed his subordinates to endeavor to keep them out of the department altogether.[11] His disposition was not improved when he learned that his own father had formed a cotton speculating partnership in Cincinnati with a group of Jewish merchants and had come down the river to wheedle a trading license from his son.[12]

By mid-December, as Grant sat writing his sister and bemoaning his "slavish life," his spirits had reached low ebb. The military campaign had been proceeding at an irritating crawl; the Northern press and public had become increasingly querulous and the speculators more bothersome. The climax came on December 17. As Grant recalled later, the mail that evening brought a batch of complaints about the Jews in his department, forwarded to him from army headquarters in Washington. There may also have been some implicit or explicit reprimand for allowing their mischief to continue.[13] At any rate, Grant had had enough. Hastily he wrote out or dictated General Orders No. 11.[14] As the order was being copied and sent out, Grant's chief of staff, John A. Rawlins, raised objections to its discriminatory intent. But Grant was adamant. "Well, they can countermand this from Washington if they like," he declared, "but we will issue it anyhow."[15]

Undoubtedly, as Grant later claimed, the order was in great part the product of haste, petulance, and thoughtlessness. The strain of weeks of campaigning and public attacks on him may have warped Grant's judgment. Yet, at the same time, General Orders No. 11 was a logical culmination of the history of anti-Semitism in Grant's army and his own intensifying bigotry, a culmination shaped by the penchant of the soldier for quick and decisive remedies based on military considerations alone. "During war times these nice distinctions were disregarded," Grant explained some years afterwards. "We had no time to handle things with kid gloves."[16]

Grant's men did not need to be reminded that kid gloves were unnecessary, and in the vicinity of the army they began to carry out the order with alacrity. Jews were singled out and given notice to leave without delay. One group in Holly Springs was even refused rail transportation and had to trudge forty miles to Memphis on foot. When one of the group, Lazarus Silberman of Chicago, tried to telegraph Grant's headquarters for confirmation of the order, he was arrested, clapped into jail, and forced to cool his heels overnight. Military officers, no doubt relishing the long-awaited chance to rid the army of this scourge, did not waste time considering mitigating circumstances in individual cases; the fact of a man's Jewishness was enough. Four hapless Northern Jews who had been detained in the Confederacy since the start of the war and had at last been permitted to leave were making their way towards Grant's lines; unluckily, they arrived in Oxford on December 18; they were arrested, dispossessed of their baggage, horse, and buggy, and sent on their way north with a gratuitous warning not to return. Reportedly, some Jews who were legitimate residents of the area were sent packing along with the rest.[17] Gentile speculators were not molested, and their lucrative activities continued unabated.[18] (Ironically, many would see their fortunes literally go up in smoke a few days later when Van Dorn's cavalry made a surprise attack on the base at Holly Springs and destroyed it, cotton and all.)

The remarkable thing is that the whole affair very nearly ended here. The terms of the order included Grant's entire department, but outside the immediate environs of the main body of the army there was almost no attempt at enforcement. Though Jewish speculators were trading at many towns along the river, local commanders apparently were not annoyed by their presence, or they interpreted the order to apply only to the area around army headquarters. Perhaps, as was reported of General Jeremiah Sullivan at Jackson, Tennessee, some thought the directive was unjust and simply refused to comply with it. Others may never have received the order in the confusion following the Holly Springs raid. Whatever the reasons, outside of northern Mississippi the order was practically a dead letter.[19] But there was one conspicuous exception, and what happened there brought the whole matter to the attention of the nation and vividly illustrated the intolerance and hatred emerging in the Mississippi Valley under the stress of war.

The dissemination of orders from Grant's remote headquarters was slow, and it was not until late December that General Orders No. 11 reached the desk of Provost Marshal L. J. Wardell at Paducah, in western Kentucky fifty miles up the Ohio River from its confluence with the Mississippi. But whereas others had ignored the order, Wardell determined to enforce it with a vengeance, and here Grant's careless haste bore its bitterest fruit. Bad as the order was, Grant had meant it to apply only to Jewish cotton speculators following the army. But his ill-considered wording was not explicit. Seizing on this technicality, Captain Wardell set about to remove from Paducah every Jewish man, woman, and child living there. Terse official notices were dispatched to the thirty or so Jewish heads of families, commanding them "to leave the city of Paducah, Kentucky, within twenty-four hours after receiving this order." That most of these Jews were well-established and longtime residents, that none was involved with cotton speculation in Grant's far-off army, and that at least two had served in the Union army, was of no consideration. Hurriedly these people locked up their homes and shops and embarked on a river steamer going up the Ohio River toward Cincinnati, almost abandoning a baby in the pandemonium. Only two sick women were allowed to stay behind.[20]

Why Paducah? What can account for the extraordinary turn of events in this town, alone among all in Grant's command? That the original intent of the order could have become so perverted there was probably due less to the individual prejudice or unthinking obedience of Provost Marshal Wardell than to the volatile situation that had been unfolding in Paducah during the war. Paducah was a microcosm of the wartime Mississippi Valley. In it can be discerned, in a peculiarly intensified form, all the instability, tension, and conflict which convulsed the whole region during the turbulent war years. As so often happens, growing social, political, and economic pressures in Paducah would find an outlet in actions against a helpless minority.

Any reasonably perceptive observer in 1861 might have anticipated the turmoil that Paducah would experience in the coming years. While the slave state of Kentucky was saved for the Union, political sentiment in Paducah was deeply divided, as it was in many river towns with commercial ties to the lower South. The city was first occupied in September 1861 by a small force under Grant, who noted the prevalence of Rebel flags and flagrant acts of disloyalty. A bitter contest ensued between the unionist and secessionist factions for political control of Paducah; some believed that only the federal military presence prevented outright violence. The troops did in fact ensure that the unionists would prevail in Paducah; but pro-Southern sympathy remained widespread (probably even preponderant), and the conflict simmered throughout 1862. Friction was aggravated by the influx into the city of hundreds of pro-union refugees from Tennessee, resentful at finding themselves in less than hospitable surroundings. Furthermore, even within the dominant political coalition, harmony was ephemeral; the army, local unionists, and federal civilian authorities all competed for power and frequently clashed.

The political strife spilled over into the economic sphere. Paducah in the antebellum period was a prosperous and important entrepôt in the Mississippi–Ohio River trade, but with the war Southern sources and markets were cut off, trade declined, and competition among Paducah's merchants for the remaining commerce intensified. In the autumn of 1861 the federal government declared western Kentucky to be under "insurrectionary influence," and the Treasury Department took control of all trade in the region to prevent commercial intercourse with the Confederacy. In Paducah a board of loyal merchants was empowered to rule on the fitness of others who applied for the required trade permits; needless to say, political allegiance was the prime consideration, and policy was explicitly directed toward favoring loyal citizens at the expense of secessionists. The unionists' political and economic hegemony was thus established, but their hold was tenuous and their uneasiness did not diminish.

A third complicating and unsettling factor in Paducah was the presence there of a growing number of runaway slaves; confrontations cropped up frequently between citizens and the army over the return of these contrabands. Though the forthcoming Emancipation Proclamation would not legally apply to Kentucky, all Paducahans could sense the specter of social upheaval that the war had inevitably raised.[21]

In this environment, cupidity, suspicion, and fear found fertile soil and flourished. Accusations of treachery, corruption, and malfeasance, often linked to personal animosities or economic rivalries, rent the town. The Treasury Department worried that the Paducah board of trade members, who were all merchants themselves, would be unable to resist the temptation to use their power to enhance their own fortunes. The government thus endeavored to keep a close watch over the board's activities. "Too many checks cannot be established," warned W. P. Mellen, the Treasury Department's special agent for the Ohio Valley. The board of trade in its turn accused the Treasury Department's deputy collector in Paducah of ignoring its recommendations in order to give special privileges to a select group of merchants, "who are always Union men so long as it affords exclusive benefits"; one of the favored establishments was the same dry-goods store where the deputy collector was employed as a clerk.

In April 1862, a New York firm complained to the Secretary of the Treasury that it was anxious to engage in some tobacco deals in Paducah but knew for a fact that the Treasury official in charge there was himself illicitly trading in tobacco. That summer the military entered the fray by charging the same official with willfully permitting large quantities of salt to go into Rebel territory through the agency of some notoriously disloyal characters, in return for valuable Southern staples. Some months earlier the military had itself been the target of vilification. A cabal of ambitious junior officers and Paducah civilians undertook to discredit and unseat the town's military commander, arraigning him in anonymous letters to the newspapers for incompetence, disloyalty, and overly lenient treatment of slaveholders. Washington was apprised of these "underground workings," however, and an informal army investigation confirmed the commander's contention that it was all a "base conspiracy." But another officer who took command at Paducah later in the year was not so lucky. He fell victim to attacks from another camp when local conservatives denounced him as an abolitionist for his reluctance to return runaway slaves and succeeded in securing his removal. That officer in reply damned his accusers as "secesh and negro Union men." Sometime afterward Paducahans divided acrimoniously over the issue of a board of trade member, accused by one faction of outright secessionism, bribery, and favoritism.[22]

To some extent this epidemic of suspicion and recrimination in Paducah remained general and diffuse, turning everyone against everyone else. But, as the accusations were increasingly aimed in a single direction, one common theme did emerge. The Jews in Paducah soon became the focus for all the hatred and mistrust that the war had created and unleashed in the city.

The relations between Paducah's gentiles and its small but growing Jewish community had been amicable before the war. But in the troubled months following the occupation, the Jews became increasingly suspect. Agent Mellen of the Treasury Department advised in October 1861 that continued government regulation of trade was absolutely necessary in Paducah to control the "rascally conduct" of secessionists and Jews. A naval lieutenant patrolling the Ohio River the following December declared that the sizable smuggling operations still carried on between Paducah and the North were being perpetrated "as usual chiefly by Jews." The town's Jews as a whole were almost universally assumed to be disloyal (though one was in fact vice-president of the local Union League), and several were openly challenged and forced to swear an oath of allegiance. The board of trade decided in advance that Jewish merchants, as known traitors and smugglers, would not be granted permits. One board member informed them when they objected to this policy that if they were not willing to enlist in the army they should not be allowed to trade, and Mellen gloated that he would allow the Jews to "stew a while" under this treatment. Given this pre-existing popular and official state of mind in Paducah with regard to the Jews, the events of December 1862 are comprehensible if nonetheless inexcusable. Manifestly, the unconscionable enforcement there of General Orders No. 11 was not a mere coincidence, but rather the tragic culmination of longstanding attitudes.[23]

The removal of the Jews was an accomplished fact by December 29, but it was not to go unchallenged. To their everlasting credit, the Jews of Paducah rose to the occasion and refused to submit humbly to their fate. While hurriedly making preparations to leave the city, a group of Paducah's Jewish merchants, including Cesar and J. W. Kaskel and the Wolff brothers, dispatched an indignant telegram to President Lincoln, condemning the order as an "enormous outrage on all law and humanity" and begging for the president's "immediate interposition." Beyond this they took steps to communicate with the larger Jewish congregations up the Ohio River, to publicize the affair, and to send emissaries directly to Washington seeking revocation of the order. On December 30, while aboard a steamboat on the Ohio, Cesar Kaskel wrote out a report of the events in Paducah and saw that it was published in the newspapers. Pausing in Cincinnati long enough to collect letters of recommendation from influential Jews, he then headed for Washington, followed by one of the Wolff brothers. Another Paducah merchant, Abraham Goldsmith, stopped at Louisville, where he aroused the Jewish community, and then traveled

Cesar J. Kaskel, a merchant in Paducah, Kentucky, rallied opposition against General Order Number 11 following his expulsion from his home. After telegraphing Abraham Lincoln to protest the edict that "place[d] us as . . . outlaws before the world," he rushed down to Washington to personally plead that it be revoked. Courtesy of The Jacob Rader Marcus Center of the American Jewish Archives.

on to Cincinnati to help organize a protest delegation there. Within a few days of the expulsion of their Paducah coreligionists, Jews all along the Ohio River had been stirred to action.[24]

Meanwhile Cesar Kaskel was hurrying to Washington, where he arrived on Saturday, January 3. He wasted no time in presenting his letters of introduction and explaining his mission to Congressman John A. Gurley of Cincinnati. Together the two men then went to the White House, where Kaskel related his story to the president and observed that Lincoln's initial disbelief turned to amazement when he was shown a copy of General Orders No. 11 along with the written order for Kaskel's dismissal from Paducah. The president's response was unhesitating. Instantly he forwarded a countermand to General-in-Chief of the Army Henry W. Halleck, who also expressed doubts about Kaskel's report until the same proof was offered. Halleck's telegraphed order went out to Grant the next day, January 4. Perhaps by this time Grant's temper had cooled, and he had begun to appreciate what he had wrought. Without a murmur, he revoked his "infamous order" on January 6.[25]

Given the patent injustice of Grant's order, Lincoln could hardly have done otherwise than to annul it, once it was brought to his attention. But he went to some pains to explain his feelings later in the week when the Jewish delegations from Louisville and Cincinnati finally arrived and obtained an audience. To these gentlemen the president reiterated how astonished he had been to learn of the order and stated his belief that "to condemn a class is, to say the least, to wrong the good with the bad. I do not like to hear a class or nationality condemned on account of a few sinners." He added that he felt no prejudice against Jews himself and would not tolerate it in others. The assemblage, which included Isaac Wise, editor of the *Cincinnati Israelite* and later revered as the "founder of American Judaism," left the half-hour conference deeply impressed by the president's obvious frankness and sincerity.[26]

Cooler heads had thus prevailed, wrongs had been righted, and the Jews returned to their homes and businesses. But as word of the episode spread, thoughtful people, Jew and gentile alike, spoke out in condemnation. Most vociferous, understandably enough, was the small but articulate Northern Jewish community. Jewish protests took several forms— meetings and resolutions, letters to the government and to newspapers, and editorials in Jewish journals. Their most common theme was the iniquity of any decree which proscribed an entire religious group because of the misbehavior of a few. Frequent remark was made also of the machinations of the Yankee cotton speculators by comparison with whom the Jews were practically innocent, and of the outstanding patriotism of the Jews as a whole, some of whom had "offered up their blood on the altar of their country." Many American Jews were recent refugees from Old World persecution, and this irony did not escape them. "Is this country the much-boasted home of the free?" one Jew demanded. "Can it now be truthfully stated that America is the 'asylum of the oppressed'?" Contrasting Lincoln's liberalism with the actions of Grant and his officers, another expressed confidence that "he who sets the slaves free will not permit [others] to bring the Jews back into bondage." Personal attacks on Grant were plentiful and often vitriolic, ranging from demands for an apology or his removal to denunciations of him as a "liar," an accomplice in cotton dealings, and one of a company of "indolent, whisky-drinking, barroom Generals." "A day of reckoning will surely come," one editorial darkly prophesied; "Ulysses S. Grant is a *marked man*." The fervent outburst of an Indianapolis Jew revealed how he and many others must have felt as they apprehensively sensed the growing intolerance in the Mississippi Valley: "In the name of justice, in the name of common sense, and in the name of all that is true and righteous, when will these contemptible outrages cease?"[27]

Much of the non-Jewish press took up the cause of the Jews, adducing similar arguments, although somewhat more dispassionately and without the tirades against Grant. The *Philadelphia Public Ledger* condemned the order and reminded its readers of the many contributions of Jews from ancient times to the present. The *New York Times* attacked the order first for its "atrocious disregard" for the rules of English grammar and then went on to assert that the war had brought out in many a gentile "degrees of rascality . . . that might put the most accomplished Shylocks to the blush." The *Times* also expressed regret that the "freest nation on earth" had experienced "a momentary revival of the spirit of the medieval ages," and on a practical note warned that the order might have the effect of affronting certain powerful European Jews.[28]

Through all of this Lincoln maintained a policy of silence, obviously hoping that the disagreeable affair would blow over as quickly as possible. Though he had willingly expressed his humanitarian sentiments in private, his political instinct would not let him do so publicly, for that might be construed as a rebuke to Grant. He did not censure Grant's action (beyond the reproach implicit in his overruling of it), and he did not oblige the general to make a public apology as some had demanded. But others were not quite ready to let the matter die, for Lincoln's political foes saw here a splendid opportunity to embarrass the administration by castigating a general so closely identified with it. Before long the issue began to take on a distinctly political flavor. Within the Jewish community a split was evident between the friends of the administration, who applauded Lincoln's decisive action and were gratified at the matter's speedy resolution, and an anti-administration element which took a more militant stand and threatened political retaliation against the Republicans. Gentile sentiment seemed also to divide along party lines. Democratic newspapers were loudest in their excoriation of the order, while Republican journals sought to ignore or minimize it, or even in some instances to vindicate its author outright. The *Washington Republican* scoffed at warnings of Jewish political reprisals by declaring that Grant was "worth more to the cause than the votes of the whole Jewish nation resident in our midst." *The Daily Morning Chronicle* in the same city furnished its readers with a detailed history of the malefactions of the Jews in Grant's department and concluded that "if there was no good reason, there was, at least, some excuse" for the order.[29]

As it happened, Congress was in session; thus, during the second week of January, Capitol Hill became the focal point of the national debate over Grant's culpability. In the House George H. Pendleton of Ohio, a leader of the Peace Democrats, proposed a resolution condemning both the order and President Lincoln as commander-in-chief. This was quickly tabled by a 56–53 vote after Elihu Washburne of Illinois, Grant's old friend and sponsor, objected that it "censures one of our best generals without a hearing." (Washburne, who kept himself well informed on affairs in Grant's army, had the previous day written privately to Lincoln to dissuade him from countermanding General Order No. 11, lauding it as the "wisest order yet made by a military command.") In the Senate a similar resolution (minus the censure of Lincoln) was offered by Lazarus W. Powell of Kentucky, who accompanied it with a dramatic account of the events in Paducah and a windy harangue against military interference in civilian affairs. Since Lincoln had taken office, Powell had cultivated the image of a sort of Democratic watchdog of civil rights; and here he reached new heights of indignation, professing to have seen citizens' rights everywhere "stricken down and trodden under foot" and calling for a rebuke of Grant to serve as a warning to others. But his oratory fell on deaf senatorial ears. Republicans raised the same objection Washburne had made in the House, and the resolution was easily tabled by a lopsided 30–7 vote.[30]

In both houses party politics mainly determined the electoral results. Democrats voted overwhelmingly to pass the resolutions, Republicans to shelve them. With secure Republican majorities in both House and Senate, Grant was safe from a potentially damaging censure and Lincoln from political discomfiture. If the Democrats had indeed hoped to deliver from all of this a lively political issue, they were disappointed at the stillbirth. Republicans were more than glad to let the matter drop.

In fact, as Grant, Lincoln, and the Republican party were no doubt gratified to observe, the whole affair of General Order No. 11 burned itself out rather quickly and without serious political consequences. Outside of Jewish circles it was not long discussed; Washington and the popular press soon moved on to more exciting issues.[31] Most Jews seemed mollified, if not completely satisfied, by the outcome of the affair and did not desert the Republicans on account of it. The incident did not perceptibly impede Grant's rising star; his military campaign went on, despite setbacks, to eventual victory at Vicksburg (though cotton speculators, Jew and gentile both, continued to plague him to the end of the war).

But the significance of the event transcends its limited contemporary impact. If one explores the history of the General Order No. 11 episode, and similar events occurring elsewhere, one gains insights into the interaction of the social, economic, political, military, and psychological aspects of America's Civil War and sees that the lofty deeds of statesmanship and arms deemed to be the decisive acts of the war occurred within a context of inglorious societal turbulence. General Orders No. 11 was not an isolated instance, for the traumatic nature of the Civil War generated an undercurrent of anxiety and conflict which could and did surface frequently in a somewhat familiar pattern of animosity and bigotry. Repeatedly the targets were Jews, although the grisly experience of innocent blacks in the New York City draft riots of 1863 and the bloody Memphis and New Orleans race riots of 1866 proved that other scapegoats could easily be found. To a great extent, however, all of these occurrences represented but a brief spasm of mindless hostility which subsided once the strains of war had eased. Ironically, Paducah, Kentucky, where wartime tensions were so dramatically translated into anti-Semitism, would in 1871 elect a Jewish mayor.[32]

NOTES

1. Grant to Mary Grant, 15 December 1862, in John Y. Simon, ed., *The Papers of Ulysses S. Grant*, 8 vols. to date (Carbondale and Edwardsville, Illinois, 1967–), 7: 44.
2. Ibid.
3. Samuel R. Curtis to Henry W. Halleck, 10 August 1862, *The War of the Rebellion: A Compilation of the Official Records of the Union and Confederate Armies* (Washington, D.C., 1880–1901), ser. 1, vol. 13, 552–53 (hereafter cited as *OR*); Halleck to Grant, 2 August 1862, ibid., vol. 17, pt. 2, 150; Robert F. Futrell, "Federal Trade with the Confederate States, 1861–1865: A Study of Governmental Policy" (Ph.D. diss., Vanderbilt University, 1950), 98. The complicated history of federal cotton policy, which can only be briefly sketched here, is more fully examined in the following sources: Allan Nevins, *The War for the Union*, 4 vols. (New York, 1959–71), 3: 346–64; E. Merton Coulter, "Effects of Succession upon the Commerce of the Mississippi Valley," *Mississippi Valley Historical Review* 3 (1916–17): 275–300; E. Merton Coulter, "Commercial Intercourse with the Confederacy in the Mississippi Valley, 1861–1865," *Mississippi Valley Historical Review* 5 (1918–19): 377–95; A. Sellew Roberts, "The Federal Government and Confederate Cotton," *American Historical Review* 32 (1926–27): 262–75; Thomas H. O'Connor, "Lincoln and the Cotton Trade," *Civil War History* 7 (1961): 20–35; Ludwell H. Johnson, *Red River Campaign: Politics and Cotton in the Civil War* (Baltimore, 1958), passim; and Futrell, "Federal Trade," passim.
4. Nevins, *War for the Union*, 3: 350.
5. Futrell, "Federal Trade," 460; *Chicago Tribune*, 18 December 1862.
6. Ulysses S. Grant, *Personal Memoirs of U. S. Grant*, 2 vols. (New York, 1885), 1: 399–400; Grant to Mary Grant, 15 December 1862, in Simon, ed., *Papers of Grant*, 7: 44; Grant to Salmon P. Chase, 31 July 1862, ibid., 5: 255; Benjamin P. Thomas, ed., *Three Years with Grant, as Recalled by War Correspondent Sylvanus Cadwallader* (New York, 1955), 22; Grant to Chase, 21 July 1863, *OR*, ser. 1, vol. 24, pt. 3, 538; Sherman to John A. Rawlins, 30 July 1862, ibid., vol. 17, pt. 2, 140–41; Sherman to his wife, 31 July 1862, in M. A. DeWolfe Howe, ed., *Home Letters of General Sherman* (New York, 1909), 229–30. See also Bruce Catton, *Grant Moves South* (Boston, 1960), 347–50.
7. Charles A. Dana to Edwin M. Stanton, 21 January 1863, *OR*, ser. 1, vol. 52, pt. 4, 331; *New York Times*, 25 December 1862.
8. Sherman to his wife, 31 July 1862, in Howe, ed., *Home Letters of General Sherman*, 229–30; Grant to Stephen A. Hurlbut, 9 November 1862, in Simon, ed., *Papers of Grant*, 6: 283; W. P. Mellen to Chase, 27 May 1862, Press Copies of Letters Sent, vol. 30, Records of the General Agent, Miscellaneous Records of Civil War Special Agencies, U.S. Treasury Department, Record Group 366, National Archives (hereafter cited as RG 366, NA); *New York Times*, 25, 26 December 1862. See also Simon, ed., *Papers of Grant*, 7: 51–52; and ibid., 52n.

9. General Orders No. 8, 19 November 1862, in Simon, ed., *Papers of Grant*, 6: 333–34n.; Grant to Charles A. Reynolds, 10 December 1862, ibid., 7: 9n.; Grant to Theodore S. Bowers, 11 December 1862, Letters Sent, Department of the Tennessee, U.S. War Department, Record Group 393, National Archives (hereafter cited as RG 393, NA); Grant to Christopher P. Wolcott, 17 December 1862, in Simon, ed., *Papers of Grant*, 7: 56–57; and ibid., 52n.

10. Joseph Lebowich, "General Ulysses S. Grant and the Jews," *Publications of the American Jewish Historical Society*, no. 17 (1909), 77 (hereafter cited as *PAJHS*); Grant to John V. D. DuBois, 9 December 1862, in Simon, ed., *Papers of Grant*, 7: 8; General Orders No. 2, Post of Holly Springs, 8 December 1862, ibid., 9n.

11. Grant to Hurlbut, 9 November 1862, in Simon, ed., *Papers of Grant*, 6: 283; Grant to Joseph D. Webster, 10 November 1862, ibid., 283n.; Grant to Wolcott, 17 December 1862, ibid., 7: 56–57; Grant to Sherman, 5 December 1862, ibid., 6: 393–95.

12. Catton, *Grant Moves South*, 352–53. Catton's assertion that Grant's father was unsuccessful in his mission is contradicted by an article in the *New York Daily Tribune*, 19 September 1872, describing a lawsuit later brought by the elder Grant against his erstwhile partners. That on at least one previous occasion Grant had used his position to secure a permit for a friend is shown in Mellen to Chase, 7 October 1861, Press Copies of Letters Sent, vol. 30, Records of the General Agent, RG 366, NA. See also Simon, ed., *Papers of Grant*, 7: 53n.

13. Grant's comments on the incident are found in four postwar public statements. See text of his interview with Rabbi E. B. M. Browne, 27 August 1875, in Bertram Korn, *American Jewry and the Civil War* (1951; New York, 1970), 279n.; Grant to I. N. Morris, 14 September 1868, *New York Times*, 30 November 1868; Rawlins to Lewis N. Dembits, 6 May 1868, *New York Herald*, 23 June 1868; Adam Badeau to Simon Wolf, 22 April 1868, in Simon Wolf, *The Presidents I Have Known from 1860–1918* (Washington, D.C., 1918), 65–66. Grant does not refer to the incident in his memoirs. No written reprimand such as Grant mentioned has been located among his papers or in army headquarters records.

14. Simon, ed., *Papers of Grant*, 7: 50. The proper numerical designation of this order has been a matter of some confusion, which is now clarified in the most recently published volume of the *Papers of Grant*. Originally issued as No. 11, the order was soon after altered to 12 in all the official records because a No. 11 had been promulgated some weeks previously in regard to a court martial proceeding. By the time the error was detected, however, the misnomer No. 11 had gained currency and has since stuck; it was perpetuated in *OR* and the standard account of the order in Korn, *American Jewry and the Civil War*. The editor of *The Papers of Grant* establishes that No. 12 is the technically correct appellation but chooses nevertheless to call the order No. 11, apparently to avoid confusion; and it will be so designated in this essay. Readers should be cautioned, however,

that the order appears as No. 12 in virtually all contemporary official documents. See Simon, ed., *Papers of Grant*, 7: 50-51n.

15. James H. Wilson, *The Life of John A. Rawlins . . .* (New York, 1916), 96.

16. Interview with Rabbi E. B. M. Browne, 27 August 1875, in Korn, *American Jewry and the Civil War*, 279n.

At the time and in the years since, a number of alternate explanations of Grant's action has been offered by his sympathizers and detractors both, and the ensuing debate could be the subject of a whole essay. Grant's enemies claimed that he had been prevailed upon by gentile speculators who were attempting to corner the cotton market by removing Jewish competition. Some went so far as to accuse Grant himself of complicity in speculation. These were baseless accusations for which no real evidence has ever been offered. Some of Grant's admirers tried to show that the order was written by a subordinate in Grant's absence and without his knowledge, or that Grant did write the order but was using the term "Jew" loosely to refer to all traders. The most persistent story of all was that Grant had received from Washington on December 17 a direct order to expel the Jews. All these explanations are contradicted by the weight of the evidence. Grant's contemporary correspondence and later remarks, which are all very consistent, indicate that the order was aimed at Jews alone and was issued by him and on his own initiative. No order from Washington has ever been found (nor did Grant say or imply that there was one). What the facts do show plainly is that Grant was convinced that the Jews among the traders were a nuisance and a danger to the army, and that his best course of action was to remove them.

The various pieces of evidence bearing on this whole question are summarized and assessed in Korn, *American Jewry and the Civil War*, 138-42, 154-55; Lebowich, "General Ulysses S. Grant and the Jews," 71-79; Catton, *Grant Moves South*, 354-55; Kenneth P. Williams, *Lincoln Finds a General*, 5 vols. (New York, 1956), 4: 178-79, 512-14n.; Lloyd Lewis, *Letters from Lloyd Lewis Showing Steps in the Research for His Biography of U. S. Grant* (Boston, 1950), 20-21, 24-25; Simon, ed., *Papers of Grant*, 7: 51-53n.; and William S. McFeely, *Grant: A Biography* (New York, 1981), 123-24. These authors do not arrive at identical conclusions. Catton finds Grant guilty only of loose wording. Korn and Lewis accept the contemporary reports which claimed that the order originated in Washington, though these reports seem to have more the character of army rumor and partisan polemic than of hard evidence. Korn does imply, however, that what Grant received may have needed no prodding. Lebowich, Williams, Simon, and McFeely give Grant full responsibility for General Orders No. 11. Williams, however, fails to appreciate the general prejudice against the Jews and the very real distinction he drew between the Jews and other traders. Simon suggests and McFeely agrees, that Grant's perturbation over his father's involvement with the Jewish traders "provides a psychological explanation for the orders, though hardly a justification."

17. *Israelite* (Cincinnati), 2 January 1863; *Jewish Messenger* (New York), 9 January 1863; Korn, *American Jewry and the Civil War*, 123–24.

18. This is indicated in a December 22 letter from an army correspondent to the *Daily Missouri Democrat* (St. Louis), 5 January 1863, which mentions the continued presence of speculators. See also J. Russell Jones to Elihu Washburne, 21 December 1862, Elihu Washburne Papers, Manuscript Division, Library of Congress (hereafter cited as Washburne Papers, LC). Jones was an old friend of Grant who was following the army and speculating in cotton.

19. This is based on my examination in the National Archives of headquarters' and provost marshals' records of the various subdistricts and posts in Grant's department, none of which indicates any cognizance of the order. Also, contemporary Jewish newspapers report the expulsion of specific individuals only in northern Mississippi and Paducah, Kentucky (to be discussed below), though they received information from many sources. It is possible that Jews were removed quietly in other places, however; and in fact the *Israelite* of 23 January 1863 says that despite General Sullivan's refusal to carry out the order "he was forced after 4 days to enforce it." A historian of the Jews of Memphis states flatly that none was removed there, but offers no explanation of why not; Korn is in error in saying that it was because Memphis was not part of Grant's command. See Rabbi James A. Wax, "The Jews of Memphis: 1860–1865," *West Tennessee Historical Society Papers*, no. 3 (1949): 74; Korn, *American Jewry and the Civil War*, 281n. The editor of Grant's papers concludes that the order was generally enforced in Grant's department but cites no specific removals outside of Mississippi and Paducah. See Simon, ed., *Papers of Grant*, 7: 53n.

20. The Paducah post records for this period in the National Archives are fragmentary and the story of events there must be reconstructed from other sources. See letter of C. J. Kaskel, *Cincinnati Daily Enquirer*, 2 January 1863; speech of Senator Lazarus Powell, 9 January 1863, *Congressional Globe*, 37th Cong., 3rd sess., 245–46 (Powell was in possession of written testimony from Paducah residents); and Korn, *American Jewry and the Civil War*, 123. The post commander at Paducah was Colonel Silas Noble, who was removed shortly after this incident but for reasons not connected with it.

21. Evidence of the political, economic, and social turmoil in Paducah is found in the following sources: Grant to John C. Fremont, 6 September 1861, in Simon, ed., *Papers of Grant*, 2: 196; S. Ledyard Phelps to Andrew H. Foote, 30 December 1861, ibid., 3: 425–26; Fred G. Neuman, *Story of Paducah* (Paducah, Ky., 1920), 37–39; O. P. Weigart to Andrew Johnson, 3 June 1862, in LeRoy P. Graf and Ralph W. Haskins, eds., *The Papers of Andrew Johnson*, 5 vols. to date (Knoxville, Tenn., 1967–), 5: 435–37; Alvin Hawkins to Johnson, 14 December 1863, Andrew Johnson Papers, Manuscript Division, Library of Congress; Mellen to Chase, 5 November 1861, Press Copies of Letters Sent, vol. 30, Records of the General Agent, RG 366, NA; John E. L. Robertson, "Paducah: Origins to Second

Class," *Kentucky Historical Society Register* 66 (1968): 123–26; Silas Noble to Elihu Washburne, 25, 31 December 1862, Washburne Papers, LC; Isaac W. Bernheim, *History of the Settlement of Jews in Paducah and the Lower Ohio Valley* (Paducah, Ky., 1912), 31–33; Chase to Mellen, 10 September 1861, Letters Received: Secretary of the Treasury, Records of the General Agent, RG 366, NA; Chase to Mellen, 12 November 1861, ibid.; Chase to Warren Thornberry, 11 October 1861, ibid.; Mellen to R. K. Williams, 25 December 1861, Letters Received: General, ibid.

22. Mellen to Chase, 25 September 1861, Press Copies of Letters Sent, ibid.; Chase to Mellen, 20 November 1861, enclosing J. H. Gardner to Chase, 13 November 1861, Letters Received: Secretary of the Treasury, ibid.; George Harrington to Mellen, 12 April 1862, ibid.; George Harrington to Mellen, 20 August 1862, enclosing E. A. Paine to Chase, 10 August 1862, ibid.; John Lellyet to Johnson, 14 January 1862, in Graf and Haskins, eds., *Papers of Andrew Johnson*, 5: 97–98, 98n.; Halleck to Lorenzo Thomas, 15 January 1862, *OR*, ser. 1, vol. 7, 929; Catton, *Grant Moves South*, 87–89; Noble to Washburne, 25, 31 December 1862, Washburne Papers, LC; Paducah Papers: Case of William Grief, 1863, Records of the General Agent, RG 366, NA.

23. Robertson, "Paducah," 124; Bernheim, *History of the Settlement of Jews*, 23–25; Mellen to Chase, 6 October 1861, Press Copies of Letters Sent, Records of the General Agent, RG 366, NA; Phelps to Foote, 30 December 1861, in Simon, ed., *Papers of Grant*, 3: 425–26; Post of Paducah, Kentucky: Names of Secessionists and Suspected Persons Who Have Not Taken the Oath, Etc. (September 1862), RG 393, NA; Morris U. Schappes, ed., *A Documentary History of the Jews in the United States, 1654–1875* (New York, 1971), 703n.; Mellen to Chase, 19 October, 5 November 1861, Press Copies of Letters Sent, Records of the General Agent, RG 366, NA. It is significant that although a few Paducah gentiles protested the expulsion of their Jewish fellow-townspeople, no word of comment was ever recorded by the city council. See speech of Senator Powell, 9 January 1863, *Congressional Globe*, 37th Cong, 3rd sess., 245–46; Robertson, "Paducah," 124.

24. Cesar F. Kaskel, et al., to Lincoln, 29 December 1862, *OR*, ser. 1, vol. 17, pt. 2, 506 (also in Simon, ed., *Papers of Grant*, 7: 54–55n.); Schappes, ed., *Documentary History of the Jews*, 703n.; *Cincinnati Daily Enquirer*, 2 January 1863; *Israelite*, 16, 23 January 1863.

25. Halleck's telegram is in *OR*, ser. 1, vol. 17, pt. 2, 530, and in Simon, ed., *Papers of Grant*, 7: 53n. Grant's revocation is in ibid., 54n. Additional interesting details on Kaskel's activities are found in Isaac Markens, "Lincoln and the Jews," *PAJHS*, no. 17 (1909): 118–19, which unfortunately cites no sources.

While Lincoln was no doubt unaware of Grant's action until the meeting with Kaskel, Halleck was almost certainly feigning ignorance in order to avoid embarrassment. Army headquarters records show that on December 31 Halleck had received the original telegram of protest from Kaskel and the others in Paducah but that he had merely endorsed it and sent it on to Grant by mail for a report. There is no record in Lincoln's papers of his having seen this telegram, though it was addressed to him; it was probably routed routinely to army headquarters. See Simon, ed., *Papers of Grant,* 7: 51–55n. There is also no record of a written countermand from Lincoln to Halleck—it may have been relayed through Kaskel.

26. *Israelite,* 16, 23 January 1863. For information on Wise, see James G. Heller, *Isaac M. Wise: His Life, Work and Thought* (New York, 1965), and Jacob R. Marcus, *Studies in American Jewish History: Studies and Addresses by Jacob R. Marcus* (Cincinnati, 1969), 180–94.

27. Protest meetings in St. Louis and New York are noted in the *Chicago Tribune,* 7 January 1863, and the *Jewish Messenger,* 9 January 1863. Others were held in Chicago and Philadelphia, besides the Cincinnati and Louisville meetings already mentioned. Letters of protest to the government are reprinted in Simon, ed., *Papers of Grant,* 7: 55n. The quotations are from the *Cincinnati Daily Enquirer,* 2, 9 January 1863; *Daily Missouri Democrat,* 5 January 1863; *Jewish Messenger,* 16 January 1863; *Israelite,* 16 January 1863. Other examples are in the *Israelite,* 2, 23, 30 January 1863; *Jewish Messenger,* 9 January 1863; *Washington Daily Morning Chronicle,* 8 January 1863.

28. *Philadelphia Public Ledger,* 13 January 1863, quoted in *Israelite,* 30 January 1863; *New York Times,* 18 January 1863.

29. Schappes, ed., *Documentary History of the Jews,* 472–73, 702–3n.; *Washington Republican* quoted in Korn, *American Jewry and the Civil War,* 128; *Washington Daily Morning Chronicle,* 6 January 1863.

30. *Congressional Globe,* 37th Cong., 3rd sess., 184, 222, 245–46; Washburne to Lincoln, 6 January 1863, quoted in John Y. Simon, "From Galena to Appomattox: Grant and Washburne," *Journal of the Illinois State Historical Society* 58 (1965): 177.

31. For a discussion of Grant's order as an issue in 1868 see Korn, *American Jewry and the Civil War,* 132–38, and Joakim Isaacs, "Candidates Grant and the Jews," *American Jewish Archives* 17 (1965): 3–16.

32. Robertson, "Paducah," 124, 129–31. Korn, *American Jewry and the Civil War,* 154–88, offers numerous other examples of Northern and Southern anti-Semitism. He was the first historian to explore these outbreaks in depth and to explain them as a reflection of underlying wartime tension; his work endures as the standard account of the Jewish experience in the Civil War. Other historians who have examined the whole history of anti-Semitism in America generally conclude that it was not prevalent until the social upheaval of the late nineteenth century gave birth to it, though they usually note the Civil War years as a significant exception.

It is interesting to note that Grant himself, after the war, never again showed any anti-Semitic prejudice. He was in fact friendly with many Jews and helpful to them as president. See Lebowich, "General Ulysses S. Grant and the Jews," 79; Korn, *American Jewry and the Civil War*, 144–46; and Evelyn L. Greenberg, "An 1869 Petition on Behalf of Russian Jews," *American Jewish Historical Quarterly* 54 (1964–65): 278–95. Historians of American Judaism have emphasized the significance of the General Orders No. 11 episode in the development of the Jewish community. See Philip S. Foner, *The Jews in American History, 1654–1865* (New York, 1945), 74n., and Korn, *American Jewry and the Civil War*, 217–19. Many have also noted in the same connection the importance of the other major controversy involving Jews during the Civil War, i.e., the creation of a Jewish chaplaincy. See Korn, *American Jewry and the Civil War*, 56–97, for a full discussion.

Part VII

Aftermath

Jews emerged from the Civil War with greater self-assurance and a renewed determination to make a place for themselves in American society. Toward these ends, some Jews moved South, seeking to take advantage of economic opportunities during Reconstruction as the South struggled to rebuild.

Thomas D. Clark examines an economic niche that attracted many Jews to the devastated region: country storekeeping. The sudden demise of the plantation system radically reshaped the Southern economy and opened new vistas for enterprising middlemen. Farmers were eager to purchase merchandise and supplies and needed intermediaries to distribute their crops to distant markets. The itinerant trade, which initially drew Jews into the agrarian South, exposed many peddlers to the promises of this underexploited rural economy. The introduction of the crop lien system, allowing farmers to borrow against their future harvest, seeded this new and fertile commercial field. Peddling scattered these seeds broadly. Once packpeddlers had raised sufficient capital and found a promising location, they settled and opened rural stores. Although Clark's picture is largely accurate, Elliot Ashkenazi has demonstrated in *The Business of Jews in Louisiana, 1840–1875*, that these broad trends preceded the Civil War.

Clark argues that the often roseate depiction of the Jewish country storekeeper as a mercantile jack-of-all-trades—performing an eclectic mix of social and commercial functions that ranged from undertaker to postmaster and mongering as much in gossip as merchandise—neglects their role in establishing sophisticated "systems of capitalization and distribution . . . in a bankrupt region" (this volume, 388). By extending credit to farmers, collecting agricultural and commerce intelligence, and underpinning the operations of wholesale merchants and speculators, "furnishing merchants" linked rural markets to the national economy. This system, Clark demonstrates, was not wholly benign, sometimes trapping farmers in a cycle of debt, even as it enabled storekeepers to accumulate land and transferable skills in brokerage and contracting.

Clark's analysis of the Jewish economic experience in the South underplays the fraught racial and political dynamics of Reconstruction and understates the simmering antisemitism that lingered after the war. Beyond the unflattering stereotypes that depicted Jews as opportunistic carpetbaggers, we still know surprisingly little about the texture of Jewish life in the small towns and country byways of the region over the decades after the Civil War ended. Likewise, we know little about the experience of veterans or about the impact of returning Jewish veterans on communal life in both North and South. Jacob Rader Marcus's essay on Louis Gratz (included in chapter 9) demonstrates that the war expanded the horizons of some, exposing them to a broader swathe of America, widening their social circles, teaching them managerial and other skills, and imbuing them with confidence. This single example should be tested against others.

Even as the Civil War receded into history, memories of the devastating conflict remained fresh. This was especially true in the South, where Jews in the war's wake developed their own non-Christian version of the "Religion of the Lost Cause" that linked them to their white neighbors. They associated their tragedy with Jewish tragedies back to the destruction of the ancient temple in Jerusalem, memorialized their war dead, and joined in the cult of Confederate martyrdom through monuments and memorials to Southern war heroes.

Across the country, the 1868 Republican presidential campaign of General Ulysses S. Grant cast a national spotlight on Jews, as Democrats sought to strengthen the political fortunes of their candidate, Horatio Seymour, by recalling Grant's 1862 order barring "Jews as a class" from his war zone. Never before had a Jewish issue carried such weight in national politics.

Joakim Isaacs's treatment of this episode is significant for what it reveals about the political behavior of Jews in the immediate postwar years. While Grant's opponents bid for Jewish votes, some Jews, he shows, felt torn between conflicting loyalties—to the Republican Party and to the Jewish people. Grant's apology—"I do not pretend to sustain the order"—did much to mollify his Republican supporters, and Grant won the election handily. But memories of General Order No. 11 shaped Grant's subsequent relationship with the Jewish community. As if seeking to make amends, he went out of his way as president to appoint Jews to public office, to respond to Jewish concerns, and to reassure Jews of his support.

16

The Post–Civil War Economy in the South

Thomas D. Clark

The Confederate soldier straggling home after Lee's surrender at Appomattox came home to ruin. Many Southern towns and all of the railroads were laid waste by the invading Union Army. Four years of conflict had taken a terrific toll of property and human life. More important even than this was the fact that Southern energy was depleted not only during the war but for many years to come in the future. No historian can ever estimate the price of total destruction in many parts of the South because much of this was in the form of loss of highly potential human leadership. Many a bright young Southerner went to a soldier's grave who in the years ahead might have given the South the necessary impetus to bring about changes.

Even though Southern economy was greatly disrupted and displaced it was not pushed out of the grooves of its old procedures. Unhappily the idea that cotton was king was so deeply impressed upon the Southern mind before 1860 that it became within itself a cause to be defended. Cotton was a prime commodity during the war in both domestic and foreign trade. Smugglers had slipped thousands of bales out of the region, farmers had hidden their crops from the invaders, and the United States Government held other hundreds of thousands of bales in warehouses. No one knew at the war's end how many bales of raw cotton were available. One thing, however, was clear—cotton was bringing a good price, and it seemed that Southern farmers could begin all over again devoting their attention to the production of this staple crop.

Reprinted, with minor abridgement, with permission from *American Jewish Historical Quarterly* 55 (June 1966): 424–432, copyright © by the American Jewish Historical Society.

There was little actual choice for hosts of Southerners after 1865 but to become yeoman farmers. It is true, of course, that the plantation survived, but not in its old forms with its large labor force of slaves. A bigger difference was the fact that cotton farmers now had to find some way to finance production. They were faced actually with the primary challenge of making a subsistence living from the soil, but even this required some kind of a system of capitalization. Farmers had no capital, no seed, fertilizer, or equipment with which to farm. They had no organized market on which to sell their produce if they grew it.

In much of the region merchants suffered the same disaster as did their customers. They were without credit, and their store shelves stood barren of merchandise. Transportation facilities were so badly disrupted that shipment of goods was next to impossible. Goods themselves were difficult to obtain from Southern sources; thus it was necessary to turn to other sections for supplies. The booming Civil War economy had brought about the creation of great storehouses of goods in the North. There merchants and manufacturers were in search of new customers to take up the slack created by the coming of peace.

One of the most serious mercantile losses to come out of the war for the South was the disappearance of the factorage system. No longer could factors find customers who could promise to meet their obligations within a year, or ever as for that matter. No longer was this unique system of agricultural supply and credit able to survive, yet its passing created an enormous vacuum which stifled Southern agricultural economy. This old system had depended upon the plantation, slavery, and cotton. Two of these were gone.

In the factor's place there appeared the wholesale merchants in Louisville, St. Louis, Baltimore, Charleston, Cincinnati, New Orleans, and Mobile. Many of these houses were operated by Jewish merchants who had either survived the war or were quick to see the opportunity for trade on a new basis of merchandising in the post-war South. This was especially true of merchants in the Ohio and Mississippi valleys, and in Charleston. The challenge to these merchants lay not so much in the field of merchandising as in helping to devise systems of capitalization and distribution which would work in a bankrupt region. The South was a rich potential market, but it had no fluid security and no money.

No longer could wholesalers wait for customers to come to their doors. They now had to develop the trade themselves. It was necessary to send agents or "drummers" into the region to organize crossroads or furnishing stores geared to the floundering agricultural economy. These agents selected likely storekeepers, stocked their shelves with merchandise, and gave them some elementary instructions in the business of storekeeping. No one, in fact, knew much about operating the new credit system. For the most part drummers were Confederate veterans who spoke a common language from a common experience with their customers. They were highly successful both in the organization of new stores and in the sale of their employers' goods.

It is doubtful that there was ever organized anywhere on the globe a system of merchandising so thoroughly integrated with the economy of the daily lives of common everyday people as was the Southern general store. The country store was not confined solely to the South, nor to the post-war period. New Englanders were masterful storekeepers, and about their counters they developed much of the rich folklore associated with this rural trade. The general store existed everywhere. It went in lock-step across the continent with the great westward movement. It existed in mining towns, at cattle railheads, at county seats, and even in the fur trade centers. There were general stores to supply the trade wherever there were customers with money to buy merchandise. The Southern country store, however, differed from these in several aspects. First it was closely integrated with a staple crop agricultural system; its customers were dirt poor, seldom handling as much as ten dollars in cash in a year's time; the stores were centers of supply for vast lists of merchandise which ranged from Hoyt's Cologne to the coarsest sort of farm implements; they sold fertilizers, livestock, feed, fencing, and burial supplies. The merchants were postmasters, bankers, special agents for all sorts of businesses, undertakers, social correspondents, professional referees for the general local character, cotton buyers, news media, members of school boards, of church boards, and officials of the local lodges.

As cotton buyers the merchants served the much broader function enabling the staple crop agricultural system to function. On the other hand they were necessary agents of the highly speculative cotton trade. Without the furnishing merchant neither farmer nor cotton speculator could have survived. The merchant was the eyes and ears for both speculator and wholesale merchants. It was he who kept account of the conditions of crops, the growing seasons, the reliability of farmers, the validity of local integrity, and the capacity of his community to purchase a given amount of merchandise. These were truly little businessmen, but in the aggregate they were highly important.

In 1867 the General Assembly of Georgia enacted one of the first agricultural lien laws. This act was patterned after an earlier steamboat law which created a legal facility for securing and collecting debts contracted for productive purposes. Specifically the agricultural lien law permitted a moneyless and propertyless yeoman farmer to mortgage an unplanted crop for the purpose of securing supplies to sustain him in the growing season. Otherwise the little white farmer and the newly freed Negroes would have found themselves without means of supplying the meagerest subsistence while they produced a crop. In turn the lien contract permitted furnishing merchants to discount their paper to wholesale houses, and wholesale houses to banks, sometimes as far away as New York City.

By 1880 there was a furnishing or general store at almost every crossroad in the South. No village or town was without its large general stores. Back of these were many rich human stories in entrepreneurial activity. Suppliers tried to select bright young men who under other circumstances might have gone into one of the professions, but lacking funds and education the bright youths turned to storekeeping. At Dewey Rose, Georgia, officials of the Louisville and Nashville Railroad Company persuaded J. T. Hewell to open a store, and when he demurred that he might go broke, he was asked if he had money. When he said, "No," the promotion agent asked, "How in hell can you go broke when you ain't got nothing?" This young Hewell had never pondered. At any rate such a philosophy evidently put the proposition in a new light, for soon a long-barreled house was serving a thriving trade as a store-cotton market and freight station.

Elsewhere plantation owners, army sutlers, adventurous ex-soldiers, Alsatian Jews, and enterprising native yeoman sons opened stores. Sidney Andrews, a Northern newspaper reporter, saw Northern men coming south with their stocks of goods and letters of credit. They saw in the reconstruction South an opportunity to make their fortunes.

Many a Southern store had its beginnings in a humble peddler's pack. There was a close affinity between the peddler with all his worldly goods wrapped in a canvas bag, and the poor cotton farmers whose hopes for the future were wrapped up in a cotton lien note. The Alsatian Jew was a hero, and he has remained largely unnoted and unsung by the historians. He walked thousands of miles over dusty or muddy roads bearing on his back heavy packs of merchandise, or he bumped over impassable roads in one-horse wagons. One can only wonder what dreams or what frustrations these people had. One thing was clear: they got a full concept of what the struggling South was like. Like the old Methodist circuit riders

In the decades after the end of the war, peddling drew many Jews to an agrarian South that had been devastated by the conflict. Once peddlers had raised sufficient capital and found a promising location, they often settled and opened rural stores. These enterprising country storekeepers became linchpins in the rural economy. Courtesy of the Library of Congress.

they had time in their travels to think through their problems, and no doubt to plan for future operations of stores.

The Jewish pack peddler replaced the old Yankee who had come south prior to the war selling nutmegs, clocks, tinware, and anything else that a backwoods customer could be tempted to buy. Like the Yankees, the Jews were of a humorous turn of mind. They understood the whimsical Southern rural nature and could joke with their customers. They might even have carried "budgets" of local news about with them. Unhappily many of them became the butts of rural country practical joking.

Few things brought the isolated rural family more excitement than the visitation of a pack peddler. A circle was cleared out before the fireplace, chairs and beds were pushed back, and the peddler was given a place of honor in the middle of the floor. With a flourish he undid his stout leather fastenings, and then rolled back the awning-striped cover of his pack to expose his wares. With subtlety of salesmanship he placed his bright colored cloths in the first bag to be opened. When his canvas roll was opened there came a rush of smells. Odors of sachets, cheap perfumes, soap, leather goods, and spices filled the room. It was like bringing a country store right up to the most isolated country hearth.

Jostling around the countryside, these peddlers dreamed of the day when at last they could back their wagons under the shed and turn their tired old horses out to graze. They searched for just the right spots to open stands, and when they located them, they emptied their packs onto store shelves and went into business in permanent locations.

Already the peddlers knew their trade. They had learned whom to trust and whom to watch. Old friends who had traded generously with them in their horse-and-wagon days were given advantages of lower prices and, frequently, little presents or lagniappes for old time's sake.

There is a long history of merchandising and personal relationships which remains unexplored in the location of Jewish merchants in Southern towns. Almost every town had one or more of these merchants who made modest beginnings and advanced his mercantile career as the South moved further away from the reconstruction years. Possibly a major portion of the dry goods and clothing sold in the Southern small towns were sold by these merchants. A good example of such a business was that developed by David Ades in Lexington, Kentucky. He came to that town as a small merchant and developed the Lexington Dry Goods Company, which sold yard goods to all of Eastern Kentucky. The smaller retailers really clothed the South either by the sale of cloth or ready-made clothing.

There was another side to this story: the local Jewish merchants in a great majority of cases became well-known citizens of the towns. They were members of the lodges, served on all sorts of boards and committees, were sources of advice, and oftentimes gave a sound leadership in the organization of banks. To a great extent they set the styles of their communities because they had the outside purchasing contacts from which they imported new goods and styles into their trade. Where stores evolved through the stages of general store to department store these merchants were to have a marked influence on the taste of their customers.

The Jewish population of the South after 1870 represented a facet in another phase of Southern history. Clearly the South needed an ingenious population if its resources were to be profitably exploited. There was deep animosity against the freed slave in some quarters, and serious doubts that he would be able to make a major contribution for a long time to come in improving regional economy. There were two sources which could supply the South with new blood: the foreign immigrant and the Yankee migrant. The Southern states joined in their efforts to attract immigrants to their region. Between 1870 and 1900 state-maintained immigration agencies produced hundreds of thousands of pamphlets, leaflets, handbooks, special reports, resource surveys, and land prospectuses. These were translated into several foreign languages and were widely distributed in countries which fed the large numbers of immigrants into the great stream flowing into North America.

The South was equally as solicitous in its attempts to attract Northerners to the region. It was felt that they would bring industry and ingenuity which would help to correct many economic failures. All sorts of seductive inducements were offered. The region offered up its rich lands, timber, and mineral resources as bait. Booklets proclaimed the virtues of Southern society, described the educational dreams of the region, boosted towns which they hoped would soon grow into cities, proclaimed cotton as king, and described the new railroads which in a short time would be in operation. Almost any sort of a promise was made to attract the flow of Northern population and capital into the South.

Generally speaking the campaigns to attract the Yankee and European immigrants to the South were failures. Few European immigrants came into the region. They either failed to understand the promises of success there, or they wished to escape having to compete with the Negro. They no doubt were afraid they could not grow cotton and tobacco. In the case of the German immigrants they were rather well-informed about conditions in North America before they left home. German agents plodded through the South gathering detailed statistics, bits of economic information, notes on capital supply and industries, railroads, the nature of the towns, the position of the Negro, and Southern politics. They produced ponderous reports which often compared the South unfavorably with the expanding agricultural belt in the Northwest.

Remarkably few European immigrants came to the South. A fair number of Jewish newcomers came below the Potomac. They were uninfluenced by the reports which favored agriculture. Their interests lay elsewhere, and the South offered opportunities which could not have appealed to other immigrants. Jewish farmers were fairly rare, and few engaged in businesses which brought them into competition with the Negro.

It is a remarkable fact that large masses of Southerners were free of feelings of anti-Semitism. This was true for several reasons: they were so deeply prejudiced against Negroes and Catholics that they had little room to hate the Jews. Too, they were schooled in the Old Testament, and much of their religious imagery was the same as the Jew's religious imagery. Jews were quiet and unobtrusive in the practice of their religion, and never offered competition to the rock-ribbed Protestant South. Economically the Jew seldom if ever competed directly with the Southerner in his main economic activities.

The Southern agricultural system underwent many crises before the great revolution began in 1920. Passionately Southern farmers attempted to reinstate cotton as the king of their staple crops. This, however, became less possible with the passage of years. The ruinous system of agricultural credits which had been established by the enactment of the lien laws made farmers poorer after each crop year. No agricultural system anywhere could have survived the handicaps which the Southern agrarian economy faced. Between 1870 and 1900 foreign cotton growers began to compete with those of the South. Prices dropped continuously until the late 1880s, when they fell below the cost of production. Lands were exhausted by the eternal drive to meet the last year's expenses, and families were forced into a state of abject poverty or had to leave the South to make new beginnings of their lives. There were cotton farmers who, of course, succeeded in producing the staple, but they were few and far between. Cotton came to symbolize poverty for the man who grew it. Tobacco offered little more promise. In places farmers were thrown into open warfare by the drop in prices paid the producer.

Southern agriculture for almost a half century was the subject of bitter editorializing. All sorts of reformers begged for a change in agricultural procedures in the South. They assailed the cotton system, the merchants, the trusts, and the fertilizer and cotton distributors and buyers. So eloquent a critic as Henry W. Grady of the *Atlanta Constitution* published a bitter denunciation of the cotton system in 1881 in *Harper's Magazine*. M. B. Hammond of Columbia, South Carolina, and Charles Otken of Mississippi upbraided the cotton system in highly intelligent books. Almost every country editor in the South scolded their subscribers for their failures to change their system of farming. Yet the South remained wedded to cotton, tobacco, sugar, and rice as staples until after 1920.

No one received more severe scoldings than did the furnishing merchants. They were charged with overpricing their goods, of selling cheap and shoddy merchandise, of charging exorbitant rates of interest, of discriminating among their customers, and generally of driving the Southern farmer into complete failure. Some of these charges in specific instances no doubt were true. The merchant, however, was caught up in the same unhappy bind as his customers. In the examination of literally hundreds of accounts this author is not convinced the discriminations were in quite the precise areas as charged by earlier critics. Staple agriculture and the lien laws were chief offenders.

An analysis of accounts made after extensive examination of general store records indicate the common failings of the lien laws and the furnishing stores. Both of these seem to involve land in their final settlement; and for most merchants, land, valued at low prices, was often the only safe security available. There was involved in land dealing, however, the exceedingly delicate question of foreclosure, and not even the hardest-hearted furnishing merchant relished the opprobrium which was likely to result from the public sale of chattel goods and land for debt. It was much simpler to secure the transfer of ownership of property in quiet private negotiations than to stand exposure to criticism by public sale. It was in this way that many furnishing merchants accumulated large tracts of land, and sometimes men who started out as merchants became larger farmers who gradually came to run their stores as adjuncts to their farming activities. Doubtless many merchants insured the future success of their stores by building up a controlled trade upon their private domains. So prevalent did the custom of giving land as security become that it was common practice in much of the South to speculate on the amount of mortgage every man had on his farm and as to the probable date on which he would have either to secure an abundance of providential assistance or be foreclosed.

Some merchants made money from their stores. Some of them were able to accumulate a considerable amount of cash savings. Others accumulated little money, but came to own large holdings of land. Most of them were able to build comparatively good homes, but it is doubtful that many of them grew rich in the business. When the boll weevil reduced the cotton crop, and when competition of cash stores developed an expansion of industry, the old-line furnishing business went into eclipse in the South. Its end came only after merchants had committed countless sins against real Southern agricultural progress, and had been properly criticized for it in the newspaper and periodical press, and even in books. But the question remains, what part did the furnishing merchant play? Actually he was never an originator of anything. He was the most direct means by which the lien laws were made to work as a source of credit and banking for his community. His safe bulged with thousands of liens and mortgages. His store was both a source of supply and a market facility.

He facilitated the one-crop system of agriculture, and as a special agent for the fertilizer companies he sold guano in April to be paid for at high November prices plus an exorbitant profit and interest charge. Also, he helped to channelize an enormous amount of extra-regional capital into the South.

There were Jewish country merchants who succeeded in the general merchandising business. At Lorman, Mississippi, the Cohn brothers developed an enormous rural trade, and their store became a rather highly specialized departmental business ranging from the sale of dry goods to the sale of farm implements, wagons, and carriages. Scattered over the South were other stores operated by merchants who had immigrated to the South. The major merchandising role of the Jewish businessman, however, was in the establishment of small-town specialty stores, and in the organization of the large wholesale houses in the central towns which recovered from the losses of the Civil War. There is not a Southern city whose main business streets are not lined with department stores and wholesale houses which grew out of this era. Contrary to popular notion the Jewish merchant found the South almost as good a base of operation as the East.

The reputation of Bernard Baruch of Charleston, South Carolina, is too well known to be repeated here, but it was in the New South that this famous American first found his bearings. Two Jewish lads of Southern origin personify to a high degree the success of men who were cast in the hard years of Southern reconstruction. Samuel S. Fels was born in the isolated backwoods community of Yanceyville, North Carolina. There in a great rambling general merchandising house he got his first taste of business. Perhaps the old store still stands unless progress or the ravages of time have not destroyed it. This imaginative young merchant moved away to Philadelphia to develop the Fels-Naphtha business, which was of national importance. He was founder and benefactor of the Samuel S. Fels Fund, a non-profit philanthropic foundation established in 1935.

One of the most exciting personal histories of any Southerner was that of Adolph S. Ochs. Ochs was the son of German immigrants who came to America in the great rush of 1848. In 1877 this young man moved from Knoxville to Chattanooga to begin his newspaper career. He had worked in the *Knoxville Chronicle* office, and now at nineteen he was setting forth on an independent career. Out of his partnership with Franc M. Paul in ownership of the Chattanooga *Daily Dispatch* grew the Chattanooga *Times*, and subsequently the ownership of the New York *Times*. In 1880

Adolph Ochs brought his parents to Chattanooga, where Julius Ochs became the first real lay Rabbi in that city. In time the influence of Och's Southern *Times* was to play a major role in helping to develop the South in the post–Civil War years. The immigrant Jewish newcomer and the New South largely grew up together.

The history of the people and of the region are inseparably linked. It would be impossible to consider Southern economic and social history with any degree of thoroughness without also considering the history of the Southern Jewish people.

17

Candidate Grant and the Jews

Joakim Isaacs

General Grant and "The Hebrew Race"

In 1868, when the Republican Party nominated General Grant for President, for the first time since the founding of the United States, the idea of a Jewish vote and the question of a Presidential candidate's alleged anti-Semitism became a central political issue. The Jewish community at the time was not organized as it is today. The age of the Anti-Defamation League was in the future, and the B'nai B'rith, the only large Jewish organization, busied itself with internecine quarrels over whether meetings should be opened with a prayer and whether Gentiles should be admitted to membership. The B'nai B'rith kept completely aloof from the political question.

In fact, the stimulus for arousing Jewish protest did not come primarily from Jewish groups, but rather from the Democratic press. The Democrats, badly shaken by the loss of the Southern wing of the party during the war and stung by Republican accusations that they had opposed the war effort and were traitors to their country, now faced an uphill struggle which pitted the most popular Union general against New York Governor Horatio Seymour. In seeking all the support they could get and searching for issues to employ in the campaign, the Democrats naturally looked to Grant's Order No. 11 and the 300,000 Jewish votes.[1] The *New York Herald*, a leading Democratic journal, pointed out that attracting Jewish support might help the campaign in two ways. "This thing is at least certain, that

---

Reprinted, in abridged form, with permission from the *American Jewish Archives* 17:1 (1965): 3–16, copyright © by the American Jewish Archives.

against General Grant every influence of money and votes that can be controlled by the Hebrew race in the United States will be put forth with acrimonious activity; and their power is by no means to be despised."[2] The *Herald* felt that the "Hebrews" would not forgive General Grant, especially since he had singled them out and had used the word "Jew," which the paper felt had offensive connotations, instead of the more genteel appellation of "Hebrew" or "Israelite."[3]

The *Herald* was only one of many Democratic papers that sought to arouse the "Jewish vote." The *Atlanta Constitution* pointed to the great pertinacity with which the Jews clung to their "nationality," and the paper was sure that Grant would get few Jewish votes.[4] At the same time as the Democratic papers sought to inflame the Jewish vote by appeals to their religious loyalty, they attempted to explain just why Grant was an anti-Semite. The *New York World* spoke of Grant's order "as the brutal order which expelled hundreds of inoffensive Jewish citizens who were peacefully attending to their own affairs miles away from the scene of conflict," and called upon Jews and all Americans to countermand Grant, just as Lincoln had countermanded Order No. 11.[5]

The *La Crosse* (Wisconsin) *Daily Democrat*, in a front-page article, alleged that a cotton speculator, seeking from General Grant a permit to trade behind the Union lines, had offered Grant one-quarter of the profits. Grant had refused, insisting that he wanted a greater share of the profits. The Jew then offered Grant a one-eighth share, which Grant accepted. When Grant got his share, an adjutant expressed surprise that the amount was so small, and, when told about the deal which Grant had made, he explained to Grant that one-eighth was less than one-quarter. As the story continues, it was then that Grant became a confirmed anti-Semite.[6] This story in varying detail was given wide circulation in the Democratic press.

Who Drove the Hebrews from His Camp?

Not content with this jocular explanation alone, the Democrats revived the case of *Grant v. Mack Brothers* in attempting to give Grant's anti-Semitism a more substantial base and to link the general with the illegal cotton trade. The story of this law suit began in December, 1862. Jesse Grant, the general's father, like his Jewish fellow citizens, saw opportunity knocking on his door in the form of cotton trading. While Jesse Grant lacked what many Jews had in the way of capital, he did have a son in a position to be of great help to him;

so he began a two-pronged attack. First, he wrote his son soliciting his aid, and at the same time he negotiated a deal with the Mack Brothers, a firm of Cincinnati Jews. According to the terms, Jesse Grant was to receive a quarter of the profits for using his influence with his son to secure cotton permits.

Jesse Grant's plan was foiled because of total lack of cooperation from his son. Letters to Jesse's son, as well as a personal trip to the front, all failed to budge General Grant from his uncooperative position.[7] Jesse Grant then turned around and attempted to place the blame for the failure of the enterprise on the Mack Brothers, who had since withdrawn from the agreement. Jesse sued the Mack Brothers in the Cincinnati Superior Court for breach of contract. The case was argued before Judges George Hoadly and Bellamy Storer, who dismissed the case on the grounds that, if Jesse Grant had used his privileged position with his son to get a permit, then such an agreement was illegal and could not be enforced in the court; on the other hand, if Jesse Grant had asked for a permit legally, then the contract was void, for Jesse's role would not have sufficed to warrant payments. Either way the court refused to enforce the contract.[8]

While the case attracted little press attention when it was decided, it was revived and "played up" in the Democratic press in 1868. The Democratic press sought to prove that, since Order No. 11 had followed closely on the heels of the Grant–Mack Brothers disagreement, the Order's real aim had been to bar Jewish traders like the Mack Brothers from trading directly, without barring their capital from being employed in the trade by Gentiles like Jesse Grant.[9] Despite protests from the Macks, who were all leading Republicans and argued that the facts were entirely different, the press continued its attack. The following poem is typical:

> Who drove the Hebrews from his Camp,
> Into the Alligator swamp
> Where everything was dark and damp?
> Ulysses
> Who wrothy at those faithless Jews
> Who kept "pa's" share of Cotton dues,
> All further permits did refuse?
> Ulysses
> Who licensed chaps that would divide
> With father Jesse, Argus-eyed,
> Who claimed the hair and eke the hide?
> Ulysses![10]

The attempt by the Democratic press to arouse Jewish voters deeply concerned at least one Republican journalist, Joseph Medill, who said in a letter to Elihu Benjamin Washburne, one of Grant's campaign managers in Washington:

> I want to write to you on several subjects, and will put them all in one letter. First, what can be done in regard to that general order of General Grant issued in 1862 expelling "all Jews as a class" from his department? We have in this city [Chicago] at least six hundred Republican Jews headed by General Edward S. Solomon [Salomon]. . . . The General has written to Grant but has received no answer.
>
> It would only be necessary for General Grant to write a letter to Solomon or some other influential Jew saying that he has no prejudice against Jews, that he is in favor of full toleration of all religious opinions; that his subsequent experience in the army convinced him that other classes of men were just as likely to violate army regulations in relation to trading with the enemy, as Jews.
>
> Something to this effect would molify the Jews and give us a good many thousand votes. The Jews of Cincinnati and St. Louis are numerous enough to defeat our ticket in both cities, and they are strong enough to hurt us in Chicago also, as they include many of our most active Republicans. That they are deeply grieved by [the] General's order is undoubted. The Copperheads [the Northern Democrats] are making a handle of the matter in all parts of the country and we shall lose large numbers of Jew votes among them besides converting them into very active bitter opponents."[11]

The majority of the Republican press, however, remained silent, secure in the knowledge that Grant's popularity would bring him victory despite Democratic attacks. An Indiana newspaper, however, angry at all the appeals to the Jewish vote in the Democratic press, editorialized as follows:

> The Jews are all Democrats anyhow. We never heard of a Jewish soldier, during the War, on either side. They did not care an itinerant tinker's cuss how the War terminated. Their object was to make money out of it. They formed mainly the myriad of army vultures that preyed constantly and mercilessly on the poor, half-naked, hungry soldiers. For every Republican Jew that, by the sort of reasoning of the *Courier* [Democratic] and other similar journals, are to be induced to vote against Grant, a dozen decent, honest Christian White men will vote for him.[12]

Jews or Citizens

Editorials in the Democratic press and attacks like the above in Republican papers all combined to place the Jews in a dilemma. How were they to treat Grant's candidacy? Should they declare that a person's religion and his Americanism were separate and vote for Grant, if they were Republicans, or should they react, and vote, as Jews? The Jewish community was divided as to the best method to approach the situation.

Isaac M. Wise, a Reform Jewish leader and the editor of *The Israelite*, felt that a Jew always had to react as a Jew. Wise began his attacks on Grant months before Grant received the nomination. As early as February, 1868, he declared:

> Worse than General Grant none in this nineteenth century in civilized countries has abused and outraged the Jew. . . . If there are any among us who lick the feet that kick them about and like dogs run after him who has whipped them, if there are persons small enough to receive indecencies and outrages without resentment . . . we hope their number is small![13]

When Grant was nominated, Wise accelerated his attacks. He could not understand the argument that one could be an American in politics and a Jew in religion and never mix the two.

> We have been trying quite seriously to make of our humble self two Isaac M. Wises. The one who is a citizen of the State of Ohio and the other who is a Jew, but we failed and we failed decidedly. . . . The duties and wishes of the Jew as such being in no wise in conflict with those of the citizen, we being both the Jew and the citizen to the public forum and to the synagogue, before our God and our Country.[14]

Other Jews disagreed with Wise. A letter, signed "Julius" and published in *The Cincinnati Commercial*, declared:

> What does Dr. Wise care what becomes of the country? Whether we are making a living or not? He has a salary fixed during his life. . . . But how can we as Israelites seek to place in power a set of men who have been trying with all their might to destroy the Government our only refuge? . . . I think when we go to the polls next November our religious feeling ought to be entirely banished from our mind.[15]

Samuel M. Isaacs, in his paper *The Jewish Messenger*, also attacked the Wise position and argued that Jews should refrain from forming Jewish protest groups. He favored action through existing political organizations. In an indirect reference to Wise, Isaacs declared that "Israelites are too intelligent and too self-asserting to be driven, or led by their ministers, especially in matters that have no connection with religion."[16] Isaacs feared the consequences of political parties using the Jewish religion for their own purposes and questioned strongly the sincerity of the sudden solicitude for Jewish rights exhibited by the Democratic press.[17]

The Jewish voters were thus faced with conflicting advice, and the letters which filled the columns of the Jewish press and the regular press reflected this anxiety. One group agreed with Wise and insisted that Jews could not vote for Grant. They felt that Grant's Order had given an insight into his mind and showed that the nineteenth-century spirit of liberalism had totally escaped him. Therefore, as a man of the past he was unfit to rule a great and liberal nation. Others favored excusing Grant because of the difficult circumstances facing him at the time the Order was given; they called for the "Yom Kippur" spirit of forgiveness to permeate the air. Still another group took the position that, regardless of what Grant had done against the Jews, the Republicans should be supported as the party of Lincoln and human freedom. Perhaps the most extreme statement of this position was a letter written by a Jew to the *Illinois Staatszeitung* and reprinted on the front page of the *Missouri Democrat*:

> I am a Jew, when Saturday, the seventh day, comes; I am one on my holidays; in the selection and treatment of my food; it was always written on my doorposts; it is always to be spoken in my prayers; and it always is to be seen in my reverence for my Bible, that I am a Jew. . . . But it is different when I . . . take a ballot in order to exercise my rights as a citizen. Then I am not a Jew, but I feel and vote as a citizen of the republic, I do not ask what pleases the Israelites. I consult the welfare of the country. If that party in whose hands I believe the welfare of the country, so far as the advancement of human rights was concerned, was the safest, were to place a Haman at the helm of state, and if the opposite party, whose nonexistence I believe would be better for humanity and my country, were to place Messiah at their head, make Moses the Chief Justice, and call the Patriarchs to the Cabinet, I should say, "Prosper under Haman, my fatherland, and here you have my vote, even if all the Jew in me mourns."[18]

I Do Not Sustain That Order

Some Jews felt that the situation called for action, not words. Mass meetings were held by Jewish groups in many states. The one given the most publicity in the press was held in Memphis, Tennessee. Speeches were given urging that the only position Grant deserved to be elevated to was the one occupied by Haman in the last moments of his career.[19] Naturally, these mass meetings were denounced by the Republican press as well as by those Jewish newspapers which felt that direct political action was not in the best interest of the Jewish people. Commenting on the Memphis meeting, one Republican paper declared:

> We have had a big meeting of Jews here, to denounce General Grant for the order issued in his absence by his Adjutant excluding Jew traders from the army lines. Nearly every Jew that figured in this meeting was, it is notorious here, a contraband dealer, who grew much during the war by trading to both sides. The order was wrong because it was aimed at a whole sect, but a more unmitigated set of scoundrels than the Jew traders who were engaged in running goods through the army lines, it would be hard to find anywhere. The idea of such men, whose lives were disgraceful to their religion and race, meeting to denounce General Grant because his subordinate issued an order [so the paper claimed] which reflected on all Jews, and which General Grant almost immediately annulled, is absurd.[20]

Throughout the campaign a group of leading Republican Jews hoped that the whole issue could be avoided by a strong statement on the part of General Grant. One of the most active Jews in the campaign, Simon Wolf, interceded through one of Grant's advisors, Adam Badeau, to get a statement from the general. Grant answered through Badeau that he felt no animosity toward Jews, but had merely been trying to eliminate the evils of speculation.[21] This statement satisfied Simon Wolf, but did not quiet the agitation in the press. Finally, Grant, probably stung by the invectives in the press, answered with a forthright statement a letter of Adolph Moses forwarded by Grant's friend, I. N. Morris. Grant declared that he had received hundreds of letters about Order No. 11 and, although he had followed his usual practice of not answering them, in deference to Mr. Morris, he was replying to Mr. Moses:

I do not pretend to sustain the order.

At the time of its publication, I was incensed by a reprimand received from Washington for permitting acts which Jews within my lines were engaged in. There were many other persons within my lines equally bad with the worst of them, but the difference was that the Jews could pass with impunity from one army to the other, and gold, in violation of orders, was being smuggled through the lines, at least so it was reported. The order was issued and sent without any reflection and without thinking of the Jews as a sect or race to themselves, but simply as persons who had successfully (I say successfully instead of persistently, because there were plenty of others within my lines who envied their success) violated an order, which greatly inured to the help of the rebels.

Give Mr. Moses assurance that I have no prejudice against sect or race, but want each individual to be judged by his own merit. Order No. 11 does not sustain this statement, I admit, but then I do not sustain that order. It never would have been issued if it had not been telegraphed the moment it were penned, and without reflection.[22]

Grant's statement as to his motives in issuing Order No. 11 accords with the explanation which he gave the War Department the day after the order was issued.[23] This explanation, however, was not known, and the letter to Moses, written in mid-September, came too late to influence the campaign in any way. While it is impossible to know how many Jews voted against Grant because of Order No. 11, the evidence from letters to the press is that most Jews supported the candidate of the party of their choice and rationalized their choice accordingly, although undoubtedly Grant did lose some Jewish votes as the result of Order No. 11.

Without Further Comment

Isaac M. Wise and those that followed his lead found themselves in an awkward position when Grant was elected. They feared that they had created animosity toward the Jews in the heart of the man who was now the Chief Executive. Wise, through an editorial in *The Israelite*, beat an ignominious retreat and, seizing on the Grant-Moses correspondence, declared it now clear that Grant was not an anti-Semite and had merely been misled by the sinister cotton speculators' lobby.[24]

THEN AND NOW.—1862 AND 1882.

"OH, NOW YOU WEEP, AND I PERCEIVE YOU FEEL
THE DINT OF PITY. THESE ARE GRACIOUS DROPS."

Democrats continued to remind Jews of General Order Number 11 even after Grant was out of the White House. In this cartoon printed in the satirical journal *Puck* in February 1882, Grant's public expression of sympathy for persecuted Jews in Russia is questioned ("crocodile tears") in light of his order of twenty years before. Courtesy of the Library of Congress.

Grant himself, once he became President, proved a friend of the Jews and appointed many to posts at home and abroad. He sided with the Jews in the controversy raised by Harry Bergh of the A.S.P.C.A. over the alleged cruelty practiced by Jews in the slaughtering of animals.[25] Grant refused in his later career to discuss Order No. 11 and failed to mention it in his memoirs. An inquiry made to Grant's son, Frederick D. Grant, about the omission elicited the reply that his father had wanted to let the controversy die without further comment.[26]

Thus, despite the circumstantial evidence against Grant, it would seem that he was a product of his time—filled with the common images of the Jew as a Christ-killer, usurer, and shrewd businessman. This stereotyped picture probably made Grant easily susceptible to the belief that the chief offenders in the cotton trade were the Jews and that, through the deviousness of their character, they were able to succeed to a greater degree than the more "righteous" Gentiles. As is common with many who have a fixed prejudice against a group, Grant nevertheless had close friendships with individual Jews. His appointment of Jews like Edward S. Salomon and David Eckstein to diplomatic posts abroad and his offer of the post of Secretary of the Treasury to Joseph Seligman, as well as his close friendship with Simon Wolf, all bear out this fact.[27] Thus, considering the many individual Jews whose services, ability, and friendship he valued, it is not surprising that Grant denied that he was an anti-Semite, even though he had written Order No. 11.

With the end of Grant's Presidency, the question of just how the American Jewish community should react to political anti-Semitism ceased to be a problem until, under the impetus of pogroms abroad, America's Jews were finally forced to find a common ground of unity with which to develop effective organs of protest. Because these groups were organized to combat foreign anti-Semitism, they assumed a bipartisan political structure. It was not until 1892 that the political parties again became cognizant of the Jewish vote, but this time both party platforms agreed in censuring the Russian Czar for his treatment of the Jews.

The controversy over partisan political activity by American Jews in defense of their interests was thus resolved, and American Jewry avoided the attendant dangers of allowing itself to become a monolithic political group readily available for use as a political football by opposing parties.

NOTES

1. *Jewish Chronicle* (London), June 19, 1868.
2. *New York Herald*, as quoted in *Jewish Chronicle* (London), January 28, 1868.
3. Ibid.
4. *Atlanta Constitution*, June 14, 1868.
5. *New York World*, July 18, 1868.
6. *La Crosse Daily Democrat*, June 12, 1868; Brick Pomeroy, the editor of this newspaper, was a severe critic of President Lincoln, and his newspaper specialized in vilification and slander of the President, the war, and the Republican Party.
7. William Best Hesseltine, *Ulysses S. Grant, Politician* (New York: Dodd, Mead and Co., 1935), pp. 30–31.
8. *La Crosse Daily Democrat*, July 18, 1868.
9. *New York World*, August 10, 1868.
10. *La Crosse Daily Democrat*, August 19, 1868.
11. Medill to Washburne, June 16, 1868 (Washburne Mss., Library of Congress).
12. Quoted, with no further identification, in the *La Crosse Daily Democrat*, June 26, 1868.
13. *The Israelite*, February 28, 1868.
14. Ibid., June 26, 1868.
15. *Cincinnati Commercial*, August 26, 1868.
16. *Jewish Messenger*, June 1, 1868.
17. Ibid., July 3, 1868.
18. *Missouri Democrat*, July 30, 1868, as reprinted from the *Illinois Staatszeitung*, July 18, 1868.
19. *Washington National Intelligencer*, July 25, 1868.
20. *Cincinnati Commercial*, July 28, 1868.
21. Joseph Lebowich, "General Ulysses S. Grant and the Jews," in *PAJHS*, XVII (1909), 71.
22. *The Israelite*, November 27, 1868.
23. Robert Scott, *War of the Rebellion: A Compilation of the Official Records of the Union and Confederate Armies*, Series 1, Vol. XVII Part II (Washington, D.C.: Government Printing Office, 1887), p. 421.
24. *The Israelite*, November 27, 1868.
25. According to a legend in my family, Grant was moved by my grandfather's book (Aaron Z. Friedman's *Tub Taam, or Vindication of the Israelitish Way of Killing Animals*, translated from the Hebrew by Laemmlein Buttenwieser [New York, 1876]) to eat only ritually slaughtered meat in the latter part of his life.
26. Isaac Markens, "Lincoln and the Jews," in *PAJHS*, XVII (1909), 122.
27. Bertram W. Korn, *American Jewry and the Civil War* (Philadelphia: Jewish Publication Society, 1951), p. 146.

For Further Reading

Bertram W. Korn's *American Jewry and the Civil War* (2nd ed., Jewish Publication Society, 1961; 3rd ed., 1970; reissued in 2001) remains the definitive work on its subject. First published in 1951, it set a new standard for objectivity and research and posed most of the central questions that historians have grappled with ever since. Robert N. Rosen's *The Jewish Confederates* (University of South Carolina Press, 2000), a well-illustrated and more passionate treatment, synthesizes the literature on Jews in the Confederacy. For selected primary sources, see Morris U. Schappes, *A Documentary History of the Jews in the United States, 1654–1875* (3rd ed., Schocken, 1971); the excellent collection of documents posted online at http://www.jewish-history.com/civilwar/Default.htm; and the two "Civil War Centennial" issues of *American Jewish Archives*: volume 13:1 (April 1961), dealing with the South, and volume 13:2 (November 1961), dealing with the North. See also Isidore S. Meyer's invaluable catalogue of the 1961 Civil War Centennial exhibit in New York and Washington, DC, published as *The American Jew in the Civil War* (American Jewish Historical Society, 1962), and also as a special issue of *Publications of the American Jewish Historical Society* 50 (June 1961).

Memoirs and diaries illuminate many aspects of the Civil War experience of Jews. The three volumes of Jacob Rader Marcus, *Memoirs of American Jews, 1775–1865* (Jewish Publication Society, 1955) contain abundant material bearing on the Civil War, especially in volume 3. Other published memoirs include A. E. Frankland, "Kronikals of the Times—Memphis 1862," *American Jewish Archives* 9 (October 1957): 83–125; Septima M. Collis, *A Woman's War Record* (G. P. Putnam's Sons, 1889); Phoebe Yates Pember, *A Southern Woman's Story: Life in Confederate Richmond*, originally published in serial form in *The Cosmopolite* in 1866 (available online at http://www.mdgorman.com/Hospitals/pember_memoir_cosmopolite.htm), and in book form in 1879 and (edited by Bell Irvin Wiley) in 1959; Isaac Hermann, *Memoirs of a Veteran Who Served as a Private in the 60's in the War between the States* (Byrd, 1911); Louis Leon, *Diary of a Tar Heel Confederate Soldier* (Stone, 1913) and online at http://docsouth.unc.edu/fpn/leon/leon.html; "Diary of Private Louis Merz, C.S.A. of West Point Guards," *Bulletin* (Chattahoochee Valley Historical Society) 4 (November 1959): 17–47; *The Civil War Diary of Clara Solomon: Growing Up in New Orleans 1861–1862*, edited with an introduction by Elliott A. Ashkenazi (Louisiana State University Press, 1995); *A Jewish Colonel in the Civil War: Marcus M. Spiegel of the Ohio Volunteers*, ed. Jean Powers Soman and Frank K. Byrne (University of Nebraska Press, 1994), originally published as *Your True Marcus: The Civil War Letters of a Jewish Colonel* (Kent State University Press 1985); Stanley B. Weld, "A Connecticut Surgeon in the Civil War: The Reminiscences of Dr. Nathan Mayer," *Journal of the History of Medicine and Allied Sciences* 19:3 (July 1964): 272–286; Saul Viener, "Rosena Hutzler Levy Recalls the Civil War," *American Jewish Historical Quarterly* 62 (March 1973): 306–313; Raphael J. Moses, *Last Order of the Lost Cause: The Civil War Memoirs of a Jewish Family from the "Old South*," ed. Mel Young (University Press of America, 1995); and Edward Rosewater, "The War between the States: Reminiscences of Edward Rosewater, Army Telegrapher," *American Jewish Archives* 9 (October 1957): 128–138; a typescript of Rosewater's full diary is available online at http://www.americanjewisharchives.org/aja/FindingAids/Rosewater.htm.

The question of Jewish involvement in American slavery exploded into the public arena in 1991 with the publication, by the Nation of Islam, of *The Secret Relationship between Blacks and Jews*. Early, somewhat polemical refutations of its charge that Jews dominated the slave trade came from Harold Brackman, *Ministry of Lies: The Truth behind the Nation of Islam's "The Secret Relationship between Blacks and Jews"* (Simon Wiesenthal Center, 1994); Nat Trager, *Empire of Hate: A Refutation of the Nation of Islam's "The Secret Relationship between Blacks and Jews"* (Coral Reef Books, 1995); and Saul S. Friedman, *Jews and the American Slave Trade* (Transaction, 1998). More important scholarly studies of the subject include Seymour Drescher, "The Role of Jews in the Transatlantic Slave Trade," *Immigrants and Minorities* 12 (July 1993): 113–125; David Brion Davis, "Jews in the Slave Trade," *Culturefront* (Fall 1992): 42–45; idem, "Jews and the Children of Strangers," *Slavery and Human Progress* (Oxford University

Press, 1984); idem, "The Slave Trade and the Jews," originally published in the *New York Review of Books* (December 22, 1994) and reprinted in idem, *In the Image of God: Religion, Moral Values and Our Heritage of Slavery* (Yale University Press, 2001); as well as Virginia Bever Platt, "'And Don't Forget the Guinea Voyage': The Slave Trade of Aaron Lopez of Newport," *William and Mary Quarterly*, 3d. ser., 32:4 (1975): 601–618; and Eli Faber, *Jews, Slaves, and the Slave Trade: Setting the Record Straight* (New York University Press, 1998).

Far too little has been written about nineteenth-century Jewish supporters of slavery. Jonathan D. Sarna, *Jacksonian Jew: The Two Worlds of Mordecai Noah* (Holmes & Meier, 1981) tracks the increasingly proslavery statements of one of America's foremost antebellum Jewish lay leaders; John A. Forman, "Lewis Charles Levin, Portrait of an American Demagogue," *American Jewish Archives* 12 (October 1960): 150–194, provides an unusual account of a Jewish anti-Catholic "Know Nothing" nativist, who also opposed the forces of antislavery; and Eli Evans provides the best account of the slaveholder, Louisiana senator, and Confederate leader, *Judah P. Benjamin: Jewish Confederate* (Free Press, 1988).

The antislavery positions of pre–Civil War Jews have, unsurprisingly, elicited far more attention. Chris Monaco discovered and published the 1828 pamphlet by Moses Elias Levy, *A Plan for the Abolition of Slavery Consistently with the Interests of All Parties Concerned* (Wacahoota Press, 1999), also reprinted in *American Jewish Archives Journal* 51 (1999): 109–154. Kate E. R. Pickard, in *The Kidnapped and the Ransomed: The Narrative of Peter & Vina Still after Forty Years of Slavery* (W. T. Hamilton, 1856), discusses the role of Joseph and Isaac Friedman of Tuscumbia, Alabama, who helped purchase Still's freedom. The 1995 Bison Books edition of this work (University of Nebraska Press, 1995) includes a valuable introduction published in 1970 by Maxwell Whiteman on Jews in the antislavery movement as well as an important new introduction by Nancy L. Grant. Older studies include Max J. Kohler, "Jews and the American Anti-Slavery Movement," *Publications of the American Jewish Historical Society* 5 (1897): 137–155, and 9 (1901): 45–56; James A. Wax, "Isidor Bush: American Patriot and Abolitionist," *Historia Judaica* 5 (1943): 183–203; Louis Ruchames, "The Abolitionists and the Jews," *Publications of the American Jewish Historical Society* 42 (1952): 131–155; Leon Hühner, "Some Jewish Associates of John Brown," *Publications of the American Jewish Historical Society* 23 (1915): 55–78; Martin Litvin, *The Journey* (Galesburg Historical Society, 1981), a biography of August Bondi that discusses his involvement with John Brown; and Yuri Suhl, *Ernestine Rose and the Battle for Human Rights* (Reynal & Company, 1959). Rose's antislavery writings may be found in Paula Doress-Worters, *Mistress of Herself: Speeches and Letters of Ernestine L. Rose, Early Women's Rights Leader* (Feminist Press, 2008).

Bertram W. Korn opened up the subject of "The Rabbis and the Slavery Question," devoting a full chapter of his *American Jewry and the Civil War* to this subject. Valuable primary sources, including Moses Mielziner's much discussed "Slavery amongst the Ancient Hebrews," which factored in Rabbinic debates of the era, and "Documents Relative to the American Jewish Pulpit and the American Slavery Agitation," may be found in Ella McKenna Friend Mielziner, *Moses Mielziner* (s.n., 1931). For the views of Isaac Leeser, see Lance J. Sussman, *Isaac Leeser and the Making of American Judaism* (Wayne State University Press, 1995), and for more on Isaac M. Wise's views, see Bertram W. Korn, "Isaac Mayer Wise on the Civil War," *Hebrew Union College Annual* 20 (1947): 635–658, reprinted in Korn's *Eventful Years and Experiences* (American Jewish Archives, 1954), 125–150, and James G. Heller, *Isaac M. Wise: His Life, Work and Thought* (Union of American Hebrew Congregations, 1965). William Warren Rogers, "In Defense of our Sacred Cause: Rabbi James K. Gutheim in Confederate Montgomery," *Journal of Confederate History* 7 (1991): 112–122, looks at a Southern rabbi during the war.

Some eight to ten thousand Jews fought in the Civil War. Simon Wolf, *The American Jew as Patriot, Soldier and Citizen* (Levytype, 1895), first told their story at length. As Adam Mendelsohn explains in his introduction to this volume, Wolf's book "was intended to serve explicit political ends." For other broad accounts of Jewish Civil War soldiers, see Harry Simonhoff, *Jewish Participants in the Civil War* (Arco, 1963); Mel Young, *Where They Lie: The Story of the Jewish Soldiers of the North and South whose deaths . . . occurred during the Civil War, 1861–1865* (University Press of America, 1991); and Irving I. Katz, *The Jewish Soldier from Michigan in the Civil War* (Wayne State University Press, 1962). Robert Shosteck offers a detailed portrait of a Union soldier in "Leopold Karpeles: Civil War Hero," *American Jewish Historical Quarterly* 52 (March 1963): 220–233; and Samuel Rezneck portrays "The Strange Role of a Jewish Sea Captain in the Confederate South," *American Jewish History* 68 (September 1978): 64–73. Patricia Spain Ward, *Simon Baruch: Rebel in the Ranks of Medicine, 1840–1921* (University of Alabama Press, 1994), contains excellent chapters on the practice of wartime medicine by a Jewish doctor in the Confederacy.

Many Jewish communities were deeply affected by the Civil War, particularly those divided in their loyalties or in the path of the battling armies. Isaac Fein, "Baltimore Jews during the Civil War," *American Jewish Historical Quarterly* 51 (1961): 67–86 (parts of which appear in this volume); Robert Shosteck, "The Jewish Community of Washington, D.C. during the Civil War," *American Jewish Historical Quarterly* 56 (March 1967): 319–347; and Stanley F. Chyet, "Ohio Valley Jewry during the Civil War," *Historical and Philosophical Society of Ohio Bulletin* 21 (July 1963): 179–187 depict border communities. Myron Berman, *Richmond's Jewry, 1769–1976: Shabbat in Shockoe* (University Press of Virginia, 1979), contains an excellent chapter entitled "Bloody Battles—Richmond Jewry and the Civil War." Fedora Small Frank, "Nashville Jewry during the Civil War, *Tennessee Historical Quarterly* 39 (Fall 1980), 310–322; and James A. Wax, "The Jews of Memphis, 1860–1863," *West Tennessee Historical Society Papers* 3 (1949): 39–89, portray the war as experienced in Tennessee's largest Jewish communities. Belinda Gergel and Richard Gergel, *In Pursuit of the Tree of Life: A History of the Early Jews of Columbia, South Carolina, and the Tree of Life Congregation* (Tree of Life Congregation, 1996), contains a memorable depiction of "The Civil War and Its Aftermath" in a city torched by General William T. Sherman's troops.

Jewish women in particular "shouldered a range of responsibilities brought on by wartime exigencies." Hasia Diner explores this topic in the article on the "Civil War" in *Jewish Women in America: An Historical Encyclopedia,* ed. Paula E. Hyman and Deborah Dash Moore (Routledge, 1997), 1:230–232, also available online at http://jwa.org/encyclopedia/article/civil-war-in-united-states. For more on Jewish women during the Civil War, see Stanley R. Brav, "The Jewish Woman, 1861–1865," *American Jewish Archives* 17 (April 1965): 34–75.

Antisemitism, a product of many of the same tensions and frustrations that elsewhere found their outlet in persecutions of Catholics and African Americans, flared both in the North and in the South during the war years. For more on the battle to overturn the clause that limited chaplains in the North to ministers "of some Christian denomination," see Jonathan Waxman's biographical appreciation of Arnold Fischel, who led the battle to change the law: "Arnold Fischel: 'Unsung Hero' in American Israel," *American Jewish Historical Quarterly* 60 (June 1971): 325–343. "The Diary of Chaplain Michael M. Allen, September, 1861," the Jewish chaplain forced to resign prior to the law's being changed, was published by David de Sola Pool in *Publications of the American Jewish Historical Society* 39

(December 1949): 177–182. Bertram W. Korn chronicles the life of Ferdinand Leopold Sarner, the first properly elected Jewish regimental chaplain in the Civil War, in *American Jewish Archives* 1 (1948): 18–22.

A large literature explores Ulysses S. Grant's General Orders No. 11, barring "Jews as a class" from his war zone. The most important contribution, besides those appearing in this volume, is volume 7 of *The Papers of Ulysses S. Grant*, ed. John Simon (Southern Illinois University Press, 1979), esp. 50–56, where the major documents are gathered. See also Joseph Lebowich, "General Ulysses S. Grant and the Jews," *Publications of the American Jewish Historical Society* 17 (1909): 71–79; and Isaac Markens, *Abraham Lincoln and the Jews* (1909), available online from Google Books and in *Publications of the American Jewish Historical Society* 17 (1909), which also deals more broadly with Lincoln's relationship with the Jewish community. For more on Lincoln and the Jews, see David G. Dalin and Alfred J. Kolatch, *The Presidents of the United States and the Jews* (Jonathan David, 2000), 70–81; Emanuel Hertz, *Abraham Lincoln: The Tribute of the Synagogue* (Bloch, 1927); and a forthcoming volume by Gary Phillip Zola. On the Jewish businessman who teamed with Grant's father to obtain Southern cotton, see Michael W. Rich, "Henry Mack: An Important Figure in Nineteenth-Century American Jewish History," *American Jewish Archives* 47 (1995): 261–279. For the antisemitism of General Benjamin F. Butler, see *Publications of the American Jewish Historical Society* 29 (1925): 117–128.

The Confederacy likewise experienced antisemitism. Lauren F. Winner, in "Taking Up the Cross: Conversion among Black and White Jews in the Civil War South," *Southern Families at War: Loyalty and Conflict in the Civil War South*, ed. Catherine Clinton (Oxford University Press, 2000), 192–209, chronicles the way "Protestant Confederates blamed Southern Jews when any aspect of the war effort went wrong, accusing them of espionage, racketeering and conspiracy." She concludes that, in response to prejudice, numbers of Jews—Blacks as well as Whites—abandoned their faith for that of the majority; indeed, she argues that "the Civil War era saw more Jewish conversions to Christianity than any period prior to the war." More research into this provocative question is required.

The best known antisemitic incident of the Confederacy took place in 1862 when a committee of citizens in Thomasville, Georgia, accused local Jewish merchants of extortion, counterfeiting, and unpatriotic behavior and ordered them out of town. Harmony between Jews and their neighbors soon resumed, and no Jews ever were actually required to depart.

Still, the "Thomasville incident" has spawned a scholarly literature; see Richard M. McMurray, "Rebels, Extortioners and Counterfeiters: A Note on Confederate Judaeophobia," *Atlanta Historical Journal* 22 (Fall–Winter 1978): 45–52; Louis Schmier, "Notes and Documents on the 1862 Expulsion of Jews from Thomasville, Georgia," *American Jewish Archives* 32 (April 1980): 9–22; and Mark I. Greenberg, "Ambivalent Relations: Acceptance and Antisemitism in Confederate Thomasville," *American Jewish Archives* 45 (1993): 13–30.

With the war's end, the South entered a long, painful era of Reconstruction. Contemporaries believed, in the words of Mark Twain, that "after the war . . . the Jew came down in force, set up shop on the plantation, supplied all the negro's wants on credit, and at the end of the season was the proprietor of the negro's share of the present crop and of part of his share of the next one." See Mark Twain [Samuel Clemens], "Concerning the Jews" (1899), reprinted in Arnold A. Rogow, *The Jew in the Gentile World* (Macmillan, 1961), 269. In the absence of any serious history of Reconstruction-era Southern Jewish life, it is impossible to know how much of this was true. For some initial scholarship, besides Clark's essay in this volume, see Canter Brown, Jr., "Philip and Morris Dzialynski: Jewish Contributions to the Rebuilding of the South," *American Jewish Archives* 44 (Fall–Winter 1992): 516–539; and Elliott Ashkenazi, *The Business of Jews in Louisiana, 1840–1875* (University of Alabama Press, 1988), esp. 27–30, as well as his "Jewish Commercial Interests Between North and South: The Case of the Lehmans and the Seligmans," *American Jewish Archives* 43 (Spring–Summer 1991): 24–39.

Index

1868 presidential election, 399–409; Democratic press, role of, 399–402, 404, *407*; General Order No. 11 as issue, 44, 386, 399–402, 405; *Grant v. Mack Brothers* as issue, 400–401; Grant's alleged antisemitism as issue, 399–401, 405–406; Jews in America, role of, 403–404; Wise and, 403–404, 406

Abodath Israel (Szold), 185
abolitionism, 123–156; before 1850s, 125–126; among Jews of the South, 114; antebellum Jewish abolitionists, 124, 125–144; as anti-immigrant, 158; antisemitism/Judeophobia among abolitionists, 123–124, 126, 145–151, 231; Biblical sanction for slavery, debate over, 133–136, 157, 167, 184, 186; British abolitionists, 69–70; Christian clergy in North, 168; in Civil War historiography, 8, 12, 16; displaced social elites in, 130; dissenting religious attitudes, 131–134; Einhorn and, 8, 124, 135, 137, 158, 167, 185–186; environmentalist arguments in, 136–137; equal/human rights arguments in, 137, 145, 154, 186; European abolitionists, 69–70; evangelism and, 123, 124; fear of antisemitic backlash, 126; French abolitionists, 69–70; Haskalah and, 131–132; in Jewish Civil War historiography, 4, 8; *Jewish Encyclopedia* entry on, 47; Jewish oppression and slavery, parallels between, 137–139; Jewish radicals (48'ers) and, 127–130, 158, 182; Jewish support for, 124; Jewish unwillingness to participate in, 125; Jewish women in, 16, 137, *138*, 147–149; Judeophilia among abolitionists, 124, 150–155; Know Nothings, 164; liberal European beliefs, 133; in Massachusetts, 168; Missouri conventions (1861 to 1863), 129; northern opponents of, 132; obstacles to, 133; Orthodox Judaism, 130–131, 136, 142n24; parental guidance, role of, 130; Protestant abolitionists, 132; racialist arguments in, 136–137, 139; Raphall-Heilprin debate, 134–136; as reckless agitation, warmongering, 123, 145, 178n26; Reform Judaism, 131–134; as sickly sentimentality, 298; Wise and, 123–124, 135, 158, 165, 168

Abraham Lincoln: The Tribute of the Synagogue (Hertz), 12
Adams, Charles Francis, 39
Adams, John Quincy, 230, 231
Addison, Joseph, 69
Ades, David, 392
Adler, Adolphus, 128
Adler, Cyrus, 4–5, 7
Adler, Hannah, 104
Adler, Henry, 240
Adler, Jacob, 99
Adler, Samuel, 90
"Adventures of the Shoddy Family" (poem), 324
Allen, Michael, 337–341, 342

Alsatian Jews, 390–391
American and Foreign Anti-Slavery Society, 125
American Census of Social Statistics, 127
American Jew as Patriot, Soldier and Citizen (Wolf), 5–7, 28–29, 197, 237
American Jewish Archives, 91, 92
American Jewish Historical Society, 7, 145
American Jewry and the Civil War (Korn): on General Order No. 11, 43; influence, 1, 17, 18–19, 123; Judeophobia during Civil War, worsening of, 307, 383n32; Ruchames on, 145–146; on Zacharie, 41–42
American Party, 355
American Society for Promotion of National Unity, 134
Americans All (Leonard), 13–14
"An Everyday Scene Everywhere" (illustration), 323
Andrews, Mary, 95
Andrews, Sidney, 390
Angel, Myer, 96
antisemitism, 307–334; among abolitionists, 123–124, 126, 145–151, 231; Benjamin as focus of, Judah P., 15, 38–39, 169, 231, 235, 356; in cartoons, 307, 316–322, 326–327, 328; chaplain controversy, Union Army (*see* chaplains, Jewish); cotton speculation and, 366; Du Bois's order expelling Jews, 357; expulsion of Jews from Tennessee command (*see* General Order No. 11); factors inflaming, 307, 312–313, 320, 325; factors suppressing, 328–329, 393–394; fear of, 126; Gerber on, 327–328, 333n72, 334n74, 334n75; Grant's, 357, 368, 383n32, 399–401, 405–406; in graphic images, 312; importance during Civil War, 327–328; in Jewish Civil War historiography, 4–5, 11; Jewish women and, 282; in newspaper articles, 325–326; in the North, 28, 42, 230–231; in Northern newspapers, 330n6; peak years, 312–313; periodicals featuring, 312–313, 329; in poems, 313–314, 324–325; proslavery arguments, resemblance to, 133; during Reconstruction, 386; "shoddy" as a figure of speech, 307–308; "shoddy" theme, 311–334; in the South, 28, 42, 280, 281, 292, 356; in the South during Reconstruction, 393–394; stereotypes, camp follower, 323; stereotypes, economic, 311, 313, 316–317, 320–321; stereotypes, moral, 233–234, 323; stereotypes, physical, 307, 316; stereotypes, political, 311, 313, 316–317; Twain on, 329; underlying trends, 280–282
"The Army of the Mississippi" (illustration), 322
Ashkenazi, Elliot, 385
Ashkenazic Jews, 85n41, 127
Atlanta Constitution (newspaper), 400

Badeau, Adam, 405
Baer, Marx, 239
Baker, Max, 13
Baltimore: 48'ers in, 182; 1856 election campaign, 190; Einhorn on, 192–193; Einhorn's flight from, 8, 137, 191–192; German Jews in, 158, 181, 182; Jewish population, 181; Know Nothings in, 190; as "mobtown," 189–191; rabbis in, 157–158, 183 (*see also* Einhorn, David; Illowy, Bernard; Rice, Abraham; Szold, Benjamin); synagogues in, 182–183; Wise on, 192
Bancroft, Frederic, 101
Banks, Nathaniel P., 40
Barrett, Jacob, 99
Barton, Clara, 288
Baruch, Bernard, 30, 233, 396
Baruch, Herman, 233
Baruch, Simon, 30–31, 231, 233
Bearden, Elizabeth Twigg, 261
Bearden, Marcus D., 261
Becker, Daniel, 97
Beecher, Henry Ward, 134
Bell, John, 205
Belles, Beaux and Brains of the Sixties (De Leon), 31, 111
Bellow, Frank, 320
Belmonte, Diogo Nunes, 64, 80n21
Bendavid, Isaac, 5
Benet, Stephen Vincent, 37, 217
Benjamin, I. J., 10, 116–117, 229–230
Benjamin, Jacob, 128, 139
Benjamin, Judah P., 37–39, 234–237; antisemitism against, 15, 38–39, 169, 231, 235, 356; in cartoons, 316–317; Confederacy, contributions to, 23n53; Confederacy, flight from, 5, 244; as Confederate attorney general, 234–235, 281; as Confederate secretary of state, 235, 281; as Confederate secretary

of war, 235, 281; as Confederate spymaster, 38, 235–237; daughter, 88; Davis and, Jefferson, 37, 235, 237; distinctions bestowed on, 117; Fillmore and, 234; government positions held by, 36–37; intelligence, his, 10, 14, 18; intermarriage, 9; in Jewish Civil War historiography, 9–10, 12, 14, 15, 16; Judaism, lack of interest in, 9, 17; Kohler and, 9–10; Korn on, 17; monument to, 17; photo, 236; plantation of (Bellechasse), 88–89; reputation of, defense of, 9–10; as Senator from Louisiana, 227, 281; sister, 40; sisters, 88; slavery, defense of, 109; slaves, arming of, advocacy of, 109; slaves, ownership of, 8; Supreme Court, nomination to, 234; wife, 88; Zacharie and, 39

Bennett, James Gordon, 320–321
Bergh, Harry, 408
Birney, James G., 130
Black Jack, Battle of, 128
Black Reconstruction in America (Du Bois), 4
Blair, Frank, 296
Bledsoe, A. T., 241
Bloom, Herbert, 80n21, 80n23
B'nai B'rith, Alabama branch, 17–18
Board of Delegates of American Israelites, 341, 346
Board of Ministers of the Hebrew Congregations of Philadelphia, 342
Bondi, August, 128, 130, 137, 139
Booker, Armistead, 99
Booth, John Wilkes, 235
Boston Evening Transcript (newspaper), 230
Boston Journal (newspaper), 231–232
Boyajian, James, 59, 85n40
Boyd, Belle, 237
Brandenburg African Company, 64
Brandon, David Perayra, 93
Brazil Company, 64, 82n29
Breckinridge, John C., 205
Brock, Eric, 237, 239
Brown, John, 128, 139, 204–205
Buchanan, James, 134, 157, 162, 166
Burnard, Trevor, 63
Busch, Isidor, 130, 137
Business of Jews in Louisiana (Ashkenazi), 385
Butler, Benjamin F. "Beast": New Orleans, capture of, 271; Phillips and, Eugenia, 31–32, 266, 272–274; Special Order No. 150, 272, 274; "The Woman Order," 32

Cameron, Simon: Fischel and, 341; Gratz and, 256; Maryland legislators, arrest of, 191; Mordecai and, Alfred, 213, 216
Cameron's Dragoons, 337, 341
Cantor, Reuben, 97
Cardozo, Isaac, 106
Cardozo, Jacob N., 106, 110
Cardozo, Moses N., 96
Carter, Samuel Powhatan, 259, 260
Century of Jewish Life (Elbogen), 13
Chamlee, Roy Z., Jr., 235
Chancellorsville, Battle of, 36, 242–243
Channing, William Ellery, 231
chaplains: Catholic, 335; in civilian capacity, 335; in Confederate States Army, 336; field chaplains, 345; hospital chaplains, 342, 345–346; non-clergymen as, 340–341; non-denominational services, 338, 348; Protestant, 335; regimental chaplains, 338, 342, 345; requirements for, modification of, 342; responsibilities, 348; uniform regulations, 345
chaplains, Jewish, 335–351; cartoons and, 319; controversy over, 337, 340, 341–342; equality before the law, 336; exclusion of, 308, 312, 318, 319, 333n72, 336–337, 342; first appointed, 343; full rights for, 318, 319, 328–329, 342–346; in Jewish Civil War historiography, 11; Lincoln and, 318, 319, 328–329, 342–346, 347; Vallandigham and, 336–337; Volunteer Bill qualification clause, 336–337; Wise and, 171, 337, 340; year allowed in Union Army, 280. *See also* Allen, Michael; Fischel, Arnold; Frankel, Jacob; Gotthelf, Bernhard Henry
Chapman, Maria, 105
Charleston Daily Courier (newspaper), 232
Chase, Salmon P.: in cartoons, 320; Free Soil movement, 164; gold panic (1863), 320; Know Nothings, 164; trade with the South, 354, 364–365; Wise and, 162, 164
Chesapeake (Union frigate), 239
Chestnut, Mary, 32, 233, 241
Chicago Tribune (newspaper), 36, 365
Chickamauga, Battle of, 36, 259
Child, Lydia Maria, 231
Cincinnati, 158, 162, 164, 169–170. *See also* Wise, Isaac Mayer

Cincinnati Commercial (newspaper), 403
Cincinnati Enquirer (newspaper), 45, 322
Cincinnati Israelite (newspaper), 374
Citron, Jack, 239
Civil War historiography: abolitionism, 8; consensus view in, 3; early debates, 2; Jewish contributions (*see* Civil War historiography, Jewish); reconciliationist interpretations, 3, 4–5, 6, 7–8, 18; Reconstruction as subject, 9
Civil War historiography, Jewish, 1–26; amateur historians, role of, 2, 3–4, 197; American historiographic mainstream and, 3; antisemitism as subject, 4–5, 11; Benjamin's place in, Judah P., 9–10, 12, 14, 15, 16; chaplaincy controversy as subject, 11; in children's literature, 12–14; consensus view, influence of, 3; eras of, 1; first book in, 43; homefront as a subject, 265; Jewish bravery as subject, 3, 5–7, 197; Jewish-Christian comity as subject, 4; Jewish contributions to war efforts as subject, 3, 12; Jewish loyalty as subject, 5–7, 8, 18, 23n53; Jewish soldiering as subject, 19; Jewish support for abolitionism as subject, 8, 12, 16; Jewish women as subject, 16; Lincoln's place in, 10–13, 14, 16, 18; military history, role of, 197–198; mythologizing and romanticism in, 1–2, 18–19; political imperatives, responses to, 18; reconciliationist interpretations, influence of, 4–5, 7–8, 18; Reconstruction, avoidance of, 3, 19; slavery as subject, 3, 7–9, 12, 16; in textbooks, 12–14; women's diaries, 265–266; World War II on, effect of, 14–16
Clayton, Daniel, 96
Cletherall, James, 94
Cobb, Thomas R. R., 38
Cohen, Abraham, 34
Cohen, Barnet A., 89, 106
Cohen, Barnet Owens, 106, 108
Cohen, Benjamin Phillip Owens, 106–108
Cohen, David, 89
Cohen, Eleanor H., 111
Cohen, Emily, 108
Cohen, Gustavus A., 239
Cohen, J. S., 96
Cohen, Jacob, 92, 93
Cohen, Jacob I., 94–95

Cohen, Joseph, 95
Cohen, Marx, 89, 239
Cohen, Miriam Moses, 233, 283, 293–294, 296–300
Cohen, Mordecai, 89
Cohen, Moses A., 106–107
Cohen, Naomi, 28
Cohen, Perry, 104
Cohen, Philip Melvin, 111
Cohen, Samuel, 107–108
Cohen, Sheldon, 104
Cohen, Solomon: Biblical sanction for slavery, 228; distinctions bestowed on, 117; on Lincoln's election, 231; secessionist, 293; slave owner, 293; slavery, defense of, 111–112, 298; support for the South, 232; veiling of political differences, 298–299
Cohn brothers (of Lorman, Mississippi), 396
Communications on the Subject of Slave Immigration (Heydenfeld), 109
Cone, Herman, 99
Confederacy. *See* South
Confederate martyrdom, cult of, 386
Confederate States Army, 227–251; chaplains, 336; Cross of Honor winners, 30; enlisted men, 237–240; "Fronthals" in, 30; hometown companies, 238; Jews in, 6–7, 18, 29–31, 219, 232–234, 237–240 (*see also* Gratz, Louis A.); officers, 240–243; quartermasters, 240–242; reasons for joining, 232–234; revivals among the troops, 280; Richmond Light Infantry Blues, 239–240
Connell, Maria Bryan, 230
Conway, Moncure D., 114, 170
Copperheads (Peace Democrats), 158, 171, 175, 327, 376
Craig, Henry K., 209, 210–211, 212–216
crop lien system, 385

Daily Commercial (newspaper), 174–175
Daily Enquirer (newspaper), 172, 174–175
Daily Morning Chronicle (newspaper), 376
Daily Times (newspaper), 174–175
Dana, Charles A., 43
Daniel, John M., 235
Darmstadt, George, 104
Darmstadt, Joseph, 96
David (Confederate torpedo boat), 29
Davis, Benjamin, 93, 102
Davis, David Brion, 48

Davis, Jefferson: Benet on, 37; Benjamin and, Judah P., 37, 235, 237; in cartoons, 317; Greenhow and, 271; Mordecai and, Alfred, 207, 218; Myers and, Abraham Charles, 241; Zacharie and, 41
Davis, Mrs. Jefferson, 241
Davis, Natalie Zemon, 85n41
Davis, Varina Howell, 235
Davis family (of Petersburg, Virginia), 102
Days of Shoddy (Morford), 321
D'Azevedo, Rachel, 92–93
De Cordova, Jacob, 110
De La Motta, Jacob, 92–93, 98
De Leon, Camden, 230–231
De Leon, Edwin, 110–111, 230–231
De Leon, Thomas Cooper: *Belles, Beaux and Brains of the Sixties*, 31, 111; on Benjamin, Judah P., 235; on Myers, Abraham Charles, 240; on Pember, Phoebe Yates, 33; on Phillips, Eugenia, 32
Deborah (weekly publication), 161
DeKay, Lieutenant, funeral procession for, 271–272
Democratic Party: chairman, 230; Copperheads (Peace Democrats), 158, 171, 175, 327, 376; General Order No. 11, 281, 376–377; German Jews, 181; pro-Southern New York Democrats, 134; Wise and, 337, 349n6
Democratic press in 1868 election, 399–402, 404, 407
Der Deutsche Correspondent (newspaper), 181–182
Der Wecker (newspaper), 182, 188, 191
Dial (journal), 114–115
Dinnerstein, Leonard, 229
Donald, David, 130
Douglas, Stephen A., 105, 158, 168
Dow, Neal, 273
draft riots, 377
Drescher, Seymour, 48
Du Bois, John Van Deusen, 357
Du Bois, W. E. B., 4, 12
Dunlap, Phebe, 270, 273, 274
Dunning, William, 3, 18
Dutch West India Company, 60–61, 62, 64, 80n23, 81n24

Eastern European Jews, 126–127
Eckstein, David, 408

Eichberg, Frederick, 173
Einhorn, David, 185–190; 48'ers and, 185; abolitionism, 8, 124, 135, 137, 158, 167, 185–186; on Baltimore, 192–193; Baltimore, flight from, 8, 137, 191–192; emancipation, support for, 124; Hungary, flight from, 137; Lincoln and, 186, 193; photo, *187*; Raphall and, 134–135, 186–188; on Reform Judaism, 132; on religion, 188; religion and church, distinction between, 186; religious reform, advocate of, 158; secession, 193; *Sinai* (magazine) (see *Sinai*); slavery, 188; "social justice" view of Jews' responsibility towards society, 115, 189–190; Tuska and, 188–189; *War with Amalek*, 190
Elbogen, Ismar, 13
Eliot, Charles, 13
Elizer, Elisha, 96
Ellis, John W., 206
Elvas, António Fernandes de, 59
Elzas, Barnett, 237
Emancipation Proclamation, 12
Emerson, George B., 152
Encounters with Emancipation (Cohen), 28
Etting, Charles E., 299
Evans, Eli, 235
Evening Post (newspaper), 208
Ezekiel, Catherine, 233
Ezekiel, Herbert, 234, 237
Ezekiel, Moses, 232

Faber, Eli, 48, 63, 65
Falk, Louis, 14
Farber, Isaac, 104
Farmer's Register (journal), 111
Fels, Samuel S., 396
Felsenthal, Bernhard, 16, 137–139, 228
Female Association for the Relief of Women and Children in Reduced Circumstances, 293
Female Hebrew Benevolent Society, 293
Fillmore, Millard, 234
Fischel, Arnold, 341
Floyd, John B., 208
Foner, Philip, 16–17, 18
Foote, Henry S., 38, 235
Forrest, Nathan B., 30, 354, 364
Fort Blakely, Battle of, 31
Fortune, Stephen Alexander, 84n37

Frank Leslie's Budget of Fun (magazine): antisemitism in, 312, 320, 324–325, 329; on Grant, Ulysses S., 319
Frank Leslie's Illustrated Newspaper (newspaper): antisemitism in, 312, 320, 325–326, 329; on camp followers, 323
Frankel, Jacob, 343–345, 346
Franklin and Armfield, 102
Frauenthal, Max, 30
Fredericksburg, Battle of, 257
Fredman, J. George, 14
Friedenwald, Joseph, 191
Friedman, Isaac, 113–114
Friedman, Joseph, 113–114
Friedman, Max, 337, 339, 341
"Fronthals," 30
Fundamental Constitution of Carolina, 229

Gall, Jacob, 239
Gallagher, Gary, 233
Gallinger, J. S., 17
Garrison, Helen, 147
Garrison, William Lloyd: anti-Catholic sentiments, 146–147; Gottheil and, 149–150; Heilprin and, 129; Judeophilia, 150–151; Judeophobia, 123, 146–150, 155, 231; mother, 130; Noah and, 149, 231; Rose and, Ernestine L., 147–149
General Order No. 11, 43–45, 353–384; 1868 presidential election, 44, 386, 399–402; abolitionists and, 126; *American Jewry and the Civil War* on, 43; cancellation of, 44, 45; Congressional debate over Grant's culpability, 376–377; cotton speculators in Mississippi Valley, 43–45, 308, 354–358, 364–367; Democratic Party, 281, 376–377; enforcement in general, 368–369; enforcement in Paducah, Kentucky, 308–309, 358–360, 363, 369–372; Grant on, Julia Dent, 353; Grant on, Ulysses S., 44, 358, 361, 367–368, 405; Grant's father, cotton speculation by, 357–358, 367; Grant's responsibility for, 380n16; Halleck and, 360–361, 374, 382n25; Higham on, 311; Jewish protests, 374–375, 376, 377; Kaskel and, Cesar F., 43–44, 309, 360, 372–374; Lincoln, cancellation by, 44, 45, 308–309, 318, 319, 329, 333n72, 361, 374, 375–376; nativism, 355–356; non-Jewish press on, 375; numerical designation, proper, 379n14; provisions, 43, 308, 353; Republican Party, 376–377; Wise and, 44, 45, 171
General Order, No. 34, 260
Genovese, Eugene, 18
Gerber, David A., 327–328, 333n72, 334n74, 334n75
German Jews: in Baltimore, 158, 181, 182; Democratic Party, 181; in Georgia, 356; mass migration of, 126–127; Reform Judaism, 131; Republican Party, 28; slavery, 181–182, 228; in the South, 112–113
Gettysburg, Battle of, 31, 34, 36, 243
Glazer, Simon, 13
Gleitzman, Isaac, 30
Glikl bas Juda Leib, 85n41
Goff, Richard, 241
Goldback, Abraham, 238
Goldsmith, Abraham, 372–374
Gomez, Lewis, 96
Gorgas, Josiah, 207
Gottheil, Gustav, 149–150
Gotthelf, Bernhard Henry, 347–349
Grabfelder, S., 261
Gradis family (of Bordeaux, France), 65, 82n29
Grady, Henry W., 394
Graetz, Heinrich, 12
Grand Union Hotel (Saratoga Springs), 307
Grant, Frederick D., 408
Grant, Jesse R., 308, 357–358, *359*, 367, 400–401
Grant, Julia Dent, 353, 361
Grant, Mary, 363
Grant, Ulysses S., 355–361, 399–409; 1868 presidential election, 44, 386; antisemitism of, 357, 368, 383n32, 399–401, 405–406; cartoon of, *407*; cotton speculators, attitude toward, 43, 45, 281, 308, 356–357, 365–367, 408; Du Bois's order expelling Jews, revocation of, 357; father and, 357–358, 367 (*see also* Grant, Jesse R.); *Frank Leslie's Budget of Fun* on, 319; General Order No. 11, responsibility for, 380n16; on General Order No. 11, 44, 358, 367–368, 405; Halleck and, 360–361, 374; Jewish attacks on, 375; Jewish office holders, appointment of, 386, 408; Knefler and, 36; Know Nothings, 355–356; Lincoln and, 375–377; mathematical skills, disparagement of his, 400; on repealing bad laws, 360; Solomon and, Edward, 402;

Vicksburg campaign, 353–354, 363–364, 367; Wolf and, 405, 408
Grant v. Mack Brothers, 400–401
Gratz, Ann, 294–295, 299–301
Gratz, Benjamin, 298
Grätz, Heinrich, 253
Gratz, Louis A., 253–264; Americanization of, 258, 260, 262–263; Cameron and, 256; children, 262, 263; death, 261–262; early life, 253–254; emigration, 254; General Orders, No. 34, 260; in Inowrazlaw, 253–254, 262; law practice, 261; military service, 198, 256–260; as peddler, 255–256; political career, 261; postwar life, 198–199; wife, 261, 262
Gratz, Maria Gist, 296
Gratz, Rebecca, 293–300; Cohen and, Miriam Moses, 293–294, 297–300; Cohen and, Solomon, 232; family ties with Christians, maintenance of, 283, 294–295; Gratz and, Ann, 294–295, 299–301; Native Americans, sympathy for, 296; Shakespeare, interest in, 295; veiling of political differences, 293–294, 298–300, 301
Grayzel, Solomon, 13
Greeley, Horace, 135
Greenbaum, Michael, 139
Greenhow, Rose, 32, 270–271
Greenhut, Joseph B., 34–36
Guinea Company, 62
Gumpertz, Sydney, 14
Gurley, John A., 374
Gutheim, Emily (nee Jones), 100
Gutheim, James K., 100, 243–244

Halleck, Henry W., 44, 360–361, 374, 382n25
Hammond, M. B., 394
Hampton's Legion, 239
Harby, Isaac, 110, 231
Hardee, William J., 207
Harper's Weekly (magazine): antisemitism in, 312, 316, 319–320, 322; on cotton system during Reconstruction, 394
Hart, Henry I., 346
Hart, James F., 239
Hart, Nathan, 96
Hart, Philip, 92, 93
Hartman, Isaac, 127
Haskalah, 131–132
Hay, John, 342–343, 346

Hays, Moses Michael, 152–153
Hays, Richea Gratz, 294–295
Hebrew Benevolent Society, 262
Hebrew Education Society, 338
Hebrew Ladies Memorial Association for the Confederate Dead, 244
Hebrew Sunday School, 293
Hebrew Union Veterans Organization, 7
Hebrews in America (Markens), 4
Heilprin, Michael, 4, 124, 128–129, 134–136
Heller, Maximilian, 35
Henry the Navigator, 55
Herald of Freedom (newspaper), 153–155
Herbert, Hillary, 29
Herschell, Constance, 104
Hertz, Emanuel, 12
Hewell, J. T., 390
Heydenfeld, Solomon, 109
Higham, John, 311
Hirsch, Aaron, 112–113
Hirsch, Isaac, 232–233
Hirsh, Herman, 238
Hirsh, Sam, 238
History of Israel (Glazer), 13
History of the Jewish People (Margolis and Marx), 13
History of the Jews (Graetz), 12
History of the Jews (Grayzel), 13
History of the Jews in Modern Times (Raisin), 12
History of the Jews in the United States (Levinger), 13
History of the Jews of Richmond (Ezekiel and Lichtenstein), 234
History of the Rise and Fall of the Slave Power in America (Wilson), 150
Hoadly, George, 401
Hochheimer, Henry, 158, 184
Holmes, Emma, 230
Huger, Benjamin, 206, 212
Hughes, John, 345
Hunt, Samuel, 150
Huntsville Times (newspaper), 17
Hurlbut, Stephen A., 357
Hutzler, Moses, 238
Hyams, Henry, 37, 227–228, 244
Hyams, Samuel, 96

Illinois Staatszeitung (newspaper), 404
Illowy, Bernard, 158, 183–184

Immigrants and Minorities (journal), 48
Isaacs, David, 105
Isaacs, Isaiah, 93–94
Isaacs, Myer, 10–11, 18
Isaacs, Myer S., 349n6
Isaacs, Samuel F., 97
Isaacs, Samuel M., 338, 349n6, 404
Isabel (Confederate steamer), 29
Israel, Jonathan, 80n21, 82n29, 84n37
Israel, Marx, 239
Israel, Menasseh ben, 85n41
Israelite (weekly newspaper): on 1868 presidential election, 406; on abolitionists, 165, 178n26; on Buchanan's call for National Fast Day, 166; on Christianization of the country, 178n27; on dissolution of the Union, 165–166, 177n13; first issue, 161; on Gotthelf, 348; payment for, 165; on refusing to preach politics, 166–167, 169–171; on secession, 165; on slavery, 167; subscribers to, 170–171; Wise in, 165–168

Jacobi, Abraham, 129–130
Jacobs, George, 229
Jacobs, Levy, 104
Jacobs, Solomon, 94, 98
James, Duke of Courland, 64
Jefferson, Thomas, 229
Jewish chaplains. *See* chaplains, Jewish
Jewish Confederates (Rosen), 30–31, 199
Jewish Encyclopedia, 7, 10, 47
Jewish Foster Home, 293
Jewish Legion of Valor (Gumpertz), 14
Jewish Messenger (weekly): editor, 338; Isaacs and, Samuel M., 404; Jewish support for the Union, call for, 231; on Jewish volunteers, 169–170; Raphall-Heilprin debate, 135
Jewish Record of New York (newspaper), 257
"Jewish Soldiers in the Union Army" (*North American Review*), 5
Jewish War Veterans of the United States, 7
Jewish women. *See* women, Jewish
Jews (American): 1845–1854 immigration, 355; 1850 population, 126–127; 1860 population, 27, 181; 1868 presidential election, 403–404; Alsatian, 390–391; Americanization of, 45; Ashkenazic, 85n41, 127; Civil War historiography by (*see* Civil War historiography, Jewish); congregations'

unwillingness to accept Negroes, 104; correspondence between political views and those of their region, 292, 356; cotton trade, participation in, 355, 366; Eastern European, 126–127; ethnic neighborhoods, 279; German (*see* German Jews); Lincoln on, 44; New World colonies, value to, 48; political neutrality, preference for, 28; political status achieved by, 116–117; Republican Party, 377, 386, 402; Sephardim (*see* Sephardim Jews); as Shoddy Contractors, 174–175; "social justice" view of Jews' responsibility towards society, 115, 139
Jews, Slaves and the Slave Trade (Faber), 48
Jews and Blacks in the Early Modern World (Schorsch), 49
Jews Come to America (Masserman and Baker), 13
"The Jew's Garden" (poem), 319–320
Jews in American History (Foner), 16–17
Jews in American Wars (Fredman and Falk), 14
John Brown's Body (Benet), 37
"John Bull and the American Loan" (cartoon), *318*
Johnson, Andrew, 39
Johnson, Reverdy, 268, 271, 275
Jones, Alfred T., 339
Jones, Emily (later Emily Gutheim), 100
Jones, Israel I., 100
Jones, John Beauchamp, 242
Jones, Samuel, 92, 93
Joseph, Henry, 300
Journal (Louisville newspaper), 347–348
Journal of Negro History, 4
Judaism: obedience to established governments, 234; Orthodox Judaism, 130–131, 136, 142n24; Reform Judaism, 131–134, 139, 297; "social justice" view of Jews' responsibility towards society, 115, 139

Kalender und Jahrbuch fur Israeliten (periodical), 129
Kapeles, Leopold, 34
Kaskel, Cesar F.: General Order No. 11, 43–44, 309, 360, 372–374; Lincoln and, 43–44, 309, 360, 372–374; photo, *373*; Wise and, 44
Kaskel, J. W., 372
Kauffman, George and Samuel, 104
Kaufman, David S., 109

Kaufman, Sigismund, 127
Kelton, John C., 360
Key to Uncle Tom's Cabin (Stowe), 102
Kidnapped and the Ransomed (Packard), 113–114
Klein, Martin, 83n31
Knefler, Frederick, 36
Knights of Honor, 261
Know Nothings, 164, 190, 355–356, 360
Knoxville Sentinel (newspaper), 263
Kohler, Max, 7–10, 18, 75n7, 167, 177n20
Korn, Bertram: on abolitionist leaders, 126; *American Jewry and the Civil War* (see *American Jewry and the Civil War*); antisemitism in Northern newspapers, 330n6; antisemitism issue, approach to, 329; on Benjamin (Judah P.), 17; formal relief efforts, emphasis on, 265; on Jewish participation in slave trade, 49; Jewish soldiers, inattention to, 197; on rabbis, 157; on Southern Jews, 228, 234; on Wise, 177n20
Kossuth, Louis, 128
Krackowitzer, Ernest, 129–130
Kriegshaber, William, 348
Kursheedt, Edwin, 238–239
Kurtz, H. J., 320
Kurtzig, Aron, 254, 256
Kurtzig, Emma Kühlbrand, 254, 256, 262

La Crosse Daily Democrat (newspaper), 400
Laidley, Theodore T. S., 206
Lake, Richard, 66
Lamar, Gazaway B., 208, 210
Lambert, W. C., 93
Lawton, Alexander R., 241
Lazarus, Benjamin D., 98
Lazarus, Marx E., 114–115
Lebeson, Anita, 13
Lee, Robert E., 235, 241, 287
Leeser, Isaac: on Allen, 338; Biblical sanction for slavery, 167; Board of Ministers of the Hebrew Congregations of Philadelphia, 342; on Frankel, 343–345, 346; Jews and Americans, places for, 189; on Rice, 182
Lehman, Emanuel, 29
Lehman, Herbert, 29
Lehman, Mayer, 29
Leon, Lewis, 233
Leonard, Oscar, 13–14
Leopard (British man-of-war), 239
Leovy, Henry J., 237

Leslie, Frank, 313
Levi, Marcus, 97
Levin, Jacob, 100
Levine, Lawrence A., 295
Levinger, Lee, 13
Levy, Affey, 104
Levy, Alexander, 93
Levy, Amanda, 275
Levy, Benjamin, 93, 104
Levy, Chapman, 89, 92
Levy, Charlotte, 97
Levy, Eugene Henry, 111, 238–239
Levy, Eugenia. *See* Phillips, Eugenia
Levy, Ezekiel J., 239–240
Levy, Fanny Yates, 267
Levy, J., 89
Levy, J. C., 227
Levy, Jacob C., 267, 288
Levy, Joseph, 240
Levy, Leopold, 238
Levy, Lewis B., 97
Levy, Martha, 270
Levy, Moses, 89, 96, 124
Levy, Peter, 104
Levy, Phoebe. *See* Pember, Phoebe Yates
Levy, Richard, 104
Levy, Sampson, 238
Levy, Samuel Yates, 227
Levy, Sarah, 92
Lexington Dry Goods Company, 392
Liberator (newspaper), 147–149, 151
Lichtenstein, Gaston, 234, 237
Lilienthal, Max, 293–294
Lincoln, Abraham: 1860 presidential election, 191; chaplains, hospital, 345–346; chaplains, Jewish, 318, 319, 328–329, 342–345, 347; cotton speculators, attitude toward, 43; Einhorn and, 186, 193; General Order No. 11, cancellation of, 11, 44, 45, 308–309, 318, 319, 329, 333n72, 361, 374, 375–377; gold panic (1863), 320; Gotthelf and, 347; Grant and, Ulysses S., 375–377; Halleck and, 44; in Jewish Civil War historiography, 10–13, 14, 16, 18; on Jews, 44; Kaskel and, Cesar F., 43–44, 309, 360, 372–374; on Know Nothings, 360; Mordecai and, Alfred, 205, 216; Phillips and, Eugenia, 270; trade with the South, 354, 364–365; Wolf and, 28; Zacharie and, 12, 39, 41–42
"Lincoln and the Jews" (Markens), 11–12

428 Index

Lindo, Alexandre, 66
Locke, John, 229
Lopez, Aaron, 48
Lopez, David, 29
Lopez family (of Newport, Rhode Island), 65
Lovejoy, Elijah P., 130
Lucassen, Jan, 85n41
Lyons, Isaac, 89

Mack, Henry, 359
Mack Brothers, 401
Magnus, Katie, 4–5
Mallory, Robert, 347, 348
Marchand, Albert G., 230
Marcus, Jacob Rader, 17, 124
Margolis, Max, 13
Markens, Isaac, 4, 11–12
Marks, Mark, 96
Marx, Alexander, 13
Marx, Charley, 238
Marx, Rosa Hays, 294–295
Marzagalli, Silvia, 82n29
Masserman, Paul, 13
Maximilian, Emperor of Mexico, 41
May, Samuel, 146, 152–153
Mayer, Maurice, 104
Maynadier, William, 215, 217
McCall, Samuel Walker, 13
McClellan, George, 326
McCragg, William O., Jr., 131
McMaster, John Bach, 3, 18
McPherson, James, 232
McPherson, James Birdseye, 323
Medill, Joseph, 402
Meinnart, Amelia, 239
Meinnart, Isaac, 239
Mellen, W. P., 371, 372
Memoir of Samuel J. May (May), 152–153
Mendez family (of Bordeaux, France), 82n29
Michelbacher, Max, 229, 243
Mielziner, Moses, 135
Miller, Joseph, 58–59
Minhag America (Wise), 161
Minis, Abigail, 89
Missouri Democrat (newspaper), 404
"Mr. Shoddy's way of Treating the Destitute" (poem), 324
Mittledorfer, David, 238
Mobile Daily Advertiser and Chronicle (newspaper), 96

Moïse, Abraham, 92
Moise, Edwin, 37
Moise, Edwin Warren, 228
Moise, Justine, 104
Monaco, Chris, 124
Monk, Henry Wentworth, 41–42
Morais, Sabato, 130, 131, 142n24, 167
Morais, Samuel, 130, 142n24
Mordecai, Alfred, 201–225; 1860 election, attitude toward, 205; abolitionism, attitude toward, 202; Benet on, 217; birthplace, 201; brother Augustus, 219, 285; brother George, 204, 205, 206, 207, 212, 213–214, 218, 219; brother Samuel, 205, 211, 218, 219; brother Solomon, 219; Brown's Harpers Ferry raid, attitude toward, 204–205; Cameron and, 213, 216; Craig and, 209, 210–211, 212–216; daughter Laura, 212; Davis and, Jefferson, 207, 218; dissolution of the Union, attitude toward, 202, 212; divided loyalties problem, 201, 205–206, 211–213; emancipation of slave by, 113, 204; father's family, 202; job search, 219–220; Lincoln and, 205, 216; Maynadier and, 215, 217; in Philadelphia, 218, 220; photo, *203*; Porter and, 214–216; Republican Party, attitude toward, 205; request for transfer to California, 213–215; resignation of his commission, 113, 216–219; secession, attitude toward, 212; self-determination, attitude toward, 204; sister Caroline, 206; sister Ellen, 218; sister Emma (*see* Mordecai, Emma); slavery, attitude toward, 202–204, 212; son Alfred, 218–219; South, investments in, 205, 219; Southern extremists, attitude toward, 202; Southern offers, entreaties, 206–207, 213–214, 218; Southern relatives, 204; suspicions of, 207–211, 213, 218; United States Military Academy, 201; Watervliet Arsenal, command of, 201, 204–205, 208–209, 211, 213, 214–217, 218; wife Sara, 202, 206, 211, 212, 216, 219, 295; Wool and, 208–211
Mordecai, Augustus, 219, 285
Mordecai, Benjamin, 231–232, 294
Mordecai, Emma, 283–288; brother Alfred, 214 (*see also* Mordecai, Alfred); brother Augustus, 283; Christian worship, attendance at, 287; Cohen and, Solomon,

111–112; family ties with Christians, maintenance of, 283–287; father Jacob, 283, 286; friendships, reliance on, 279; hospitals, volunteer work in, 286–287; Mordecai and, Rosina Young, 283–287; Norris and, 91–92; in *Occident and American Jewish Advocate*, 286, 294; patriotism of, 286–287; on Richmond during Reconstruction, 244; sisters' marriages, 285; veiling of political differences, 287–288; veiling of religious differences, 285–286, 292–293
Mordecai, George W., 111
Mordecai, Harry, 104
Mordecai, Jacob, 283
Mordecai, M. C., 29
Mordecai, Rosina Young, 283–287, 285–287
Mordecai, Samuel, 111
Morford, Henry, 321
Morgan, John Hunt, 258
Morris, I. N., 405
Mortara case (abduction of Edgardo Mortara), 126
Moses, Adolph, 405–406
Moses, Isaiah, 89
Moses, J. F., *103*
Moses, Joshua Lazarus, 31
Moses, Major, 91
Moses, Miriam (later Miriam Moses Cohen), 293
Moses, Octavia Harby, 239
Moses, Perry, 239
Moses, Rachel Gratz, 293
Moses, Raphael J., 89, 117, 238
Moses, Sarah, 295–296
Moses, Sarah Gratz, 300
Moses, Solomon, 96, 296
Moses, Solomon, Jr., 96
Moses versus Slavery (Gottheil), 150
Motta, Sarah A., 92
Mumford, Thomas J., 152
Murat, Achille, 89
Myers, Abraham Charles, 240–242, 244
Myers, Caroline (or Lina) Phillips, 271
Myers, Marian, 241
Myers, Rebecca, 294
Myers, Samuel, 94

Napoleon III, 41
Nathans, Isaac, 104
Nathans, Nathan, 89
Nation (magazine), 129
Nation of Islam, 47–48
nativism, 355–356
Nevins, Allan, 44
New Ironsides (Union warship), 29
"New Method of Bleeding–Shoddy Patent" (poem), 324–325
New York Daily Tribune (newspaper), 134–135
New York Herald (newspaper), 40, 41, 320, 399–400
New York Illustrated News (newspaper): antisemitism in, 312–313, 317–318, 320–321, 326–327, 329; on cultural distinctiveness of Jewish troops, 319
New York Sunday Messenger (newspaper), 149
New York Times (newspaper): on Democratic Party, 230; on General Order No. 11, 44, 375; influence of, 397; Ochs and, Adolph, 263, 396–397
New York Tribune (newspaper), 129, 314, 316, 319
New York World (newspaper), 40, 400
Nightingale, Florence, 290
Noah, Mordecai: Garrison on, William Lloyd, 149, 231; Quincy on, 151; Rogers on, 153–155; stereotypes of, 123
Non-Intercourse Law (1861), 299
Norris, Sarah P., 91–92
the North: antisemitism in, 28, 42, 230–231; Jewish loyalty to, 6–7, 8, 18, 23n53, 34–37, 157; Jewish women in, 265; political sentiment in river towns with ties to the South, 370; political status achieved by Jews in, 116–117; trade with the South, 364–365. *See also* Union Army
North American Review (journal), 5
Nunes, James, 105
Nunes, Moses, 105
Nunes de Costa, Jeronimo, 82n28, 82n29
Nunes de Costa family (of Amsterdam and Hamburg), 64

Occident and American Jewish Advocate (journal), 100, 286, 294, 346
Ochs, Adolph, 30, 263, 396–397
Ochs, Bertha, 30
Ochs, Julius, 30, 263, 397

Ochs, Milton B., 263
"Old Moses Davis to Prince Napoleon" (cartoon), *317*
Olmsted, Frederick Law, 97
Oppenheimer, Reuben, 192
Orthodox Judaism, 130–131, 136, 142n24. *See also* Isaacs, Samuel M.; Leeser, Isaac; Raphall, Morris Jacob; Rice, Abraham
Os Magnatas do Tráfico Negreiro XVI e XVII (Salvador), 76n12
Osawatomie, Kansas, raid on, 128
Otken, Charles, 394
Ottolengui, Jacob, 99
Outlines of Jewish History (Magnus), 4–5, 7
Owens, Catherine, 106

Packard, Kate E. R., 113–114
Packwood, Theodore, 88
Paducah, Kentucky, 308–309, 358–360, 363, 369–372, 377
Park, Robert Emory, 242, 243
Parker, Theodore, 231
Patriotism of American Jewry (McCall), 13
Paul, Franc M., 396
Peace Democrats (Copperheads), 158, 171, 175, 327, 376
peace plan, Monks's, 41–42
peace plan, Zacharie's, 41
Pember, Phoebe Yates (nee Levy), 288–291; Chimborazo Hospital, 31, 33, 288–290; family ties with Christians, maintenance of, 283; photo, *289*; sister, 290 (*see also* Phillips, Eugenia); *Southern Woman's Diary*, 31; veiling of religious differences, 288, 291, 292–293; whiskey barrel, standing guard over, 33; on women of the South, 233
Pember, Thomas, 288
Pendleton, George H., 376
Philadelphia Hebrew Education Society, 338
Philadelphia Orphan Asylum, 293
Philadelphia Public Ledger (newspaper), 375
Phillips, Caroline (called Lina), 268, 270, 271
Phillips, Clavius, 268
Phillips, Eugene, 268
Phillips, Eugenia (nee Levy), 267–277; Butler, run-in with, 31–32, 266, 272–274; children, 268, 272; Greenhow and, 270–271; house arrest, 270–271; husband (*see* Phillips, Philip); imprisonment on Ship Island, 32–33, 272, 273–276, 290; Lincoln, derogation of, 270; maid (*see* Dunlap, Phebe); oath of allegiance, refusal to take, 275; parents, 267; photo, *269*; sister, 290 (*see also* Pember, Phoebe Yates); Special Order No. 150, 272, 274; spying by, 31–32; sympathy for, 275; Union soldiers/dead, contempt for, 266, 271–272, 273
Phillips, Fanny, 268, 270
Phillips, John Randolph, 268
Phillips, John Walker, 268
Phillips, Philip: Butler and, 272–273; emancipation, attitude toward, 109–110; house arrest, 270; law practice, 268, 276; nullification, opposition to, 267–268; oath of allegiance, refusal to take, 275; political activism, 268; Scott and, 271; slavery, opposition to, 31; Stanton and, 268, 271; wife (*see* Phillips, Eugenia)
Phillips, Philip, Jr., 268
Phillips, Salvadora, 268
Phillips, Ulrich Bonnell, 7–8
Phillips, Wendell, 130
Phillips, William Hallett, 268
Phunny Phellow (magazine), 312, 314–316
Pilgrim People (Lebeson), 13
Pinner, Moritz, 139
Polk, James K., 335
Polock, Solomon, 89
Porter, Horace, 214–216
Postma, Johannnes, 61
Powell, Lazarus W., 376
Poznanski, Gustavus, Jr., 232
"Principles of Emancipation" (Lazarus), 114–115
Proskauer, Adolph, 36, 242–243, 258
Prosser, Gabriel, 239
Puck (magazine), 319, *407*
Putman, Sallie, 242

Quincy, Edmund, 123, 151–152, 155, 231

"Rabbi Raphall" (poem), 135
rabbis, 157–196; abolitionism, defenders of, 158 (*see also* Einhorn, David; Felsenthal, Bernhard; Morais, Sabato); in Baltimore, 157–158, 183 (*see also* Einhorn, David; Illowy, Bernard; Rice, Abraham; Szold, Benjamin); Confederacy, support for (*see* Gutheim, James K.; Michelbacher, Max);

correspondence between religious positions and positions on slavery, 158, 183, 356; divided loyalties among, 157–159; Korn on, 157; reconciliation/self-determination, defenders of, 158 (*see also* Hochheimer, Henry; Szold, Benjamin; Wise, Isaac Mayer); slavery, defenders of, 158 (*see also* Illowy, Bernard; Leeser, Isaac; Raphall, Morris Jacob)

race riots, 377

Raisin, Max, 12

Randolph, George W., 288

Raphael, Solomon, 94

Raphall, Morris Jacob: Einhorn and, 134–135, 186–188; proslavery sermon, 134–136, 157, 167, 189, 228; slavery, defense of, 8; Wise and, 177n20

Rapp, Wilhelm, 139

Raule, Benjamin, 64

Rawlins, John A., 367–368

Rebel War Clerk's Diary (Jones), 242

Reconstruction: antisemitism during, 386; in Civil War historiography, 9; Confederate martyrdom, cult of, 386; crop lien system, 385; in Jewish Civil War historiography, 3, 19; "Religion of the Lost Cause," 386; the South during (*see* South during Reconstruction); Southern Jewish experience of, 244, 385–386

Reform Judaism, 131–134, 139, 297. *See also* Einhorn, David; Wise, Isaac Mayer

religion: abolitionism and dissenting religious attitudes, 131–134; church distinguished from, 186; correspondence between religious positions and positions on slavery, 158, 183, 356; Einhorn on, 188; individualization of, 281; religious cleansing of Europe's Atlantic littoral, 54, 55–56

"Religion of the Lost Cause," 386

Reminiscences of Charleston (Cardozo), 110

Reminiscences (Wise), 123

Republican Party: 1860 presidential campaign, 136; Free Soil movement, 164; General Order No. 11, 376–377; Jews and, 377, 386, 402; Jews and, German, 28; Mordecai and, Alfred, 205; Wise and, 158, 164, 175, 349n6

Rhodes, John Ford, 3, 6, 18

Rice, Abraham, 182–183

Richards, Leonard L., 130, 132

Richmond Enquirer (newspaper), 38, 241

Richmond Examiner (newspaper), 235, 323–324

Richmond in By-Gone Days (Mordecai), 111

Richmond Light Infantry Blues, 239–240

Ripley, James W., 213, 215–216

Rivera family (of Newport, Rhode Island), 65

Roanoke Island, Battle of, 239–240

Rogers, Nathaniel Peabody, 153–155

Roosevelt, Franklin, 13–14

Rose, Anne, 281, 282

Rose, Ernestine L., 137, *138*, 147–149

Rosen, Robert, 30–31, 33

Rosenberg, Betty, 104

Rosenheim, Philip, 232, 238, 239

Rosewater, Edward, 11–12

Rothschild, Salomon de, 37, 116, 228

Rothschild, Sam, 99

Royal Adventurers Trading, 63

Royal African Company (RAC), 63, 65

Royal Guinea Company, 55

Ruchames, Louis, 123–124, 126

Ruffin, Edmund, 111

Ruggles, George D., 337, 340

Salomon, Edward, 360, 408

Salvador, José Goncalves, 76n12

Saratoga Springs, New York, 307

Sarna, Jonathan, 329

Sartorius, Philip, 99

Sasportes, Catherine, 104

Savage, E. G., 256

Savannah Daily News (newspaper), 241

Schappes, Morris, 17, 18

Schlessinger, Louis, 127–128

Schorsch, Jonathan, 49

Schurz, Carl, 36

Scott, Winfield, 210, 271, 211n1

secession: Cohen and, Solomon, 293; Einhorn and, 193; Illowy and, 183–184; Jewish support for, 228, 230–231; Jews blamed for, 230; Mordecai and, Alfred, 212; Wise on, 165, 167, 169

Secret Relationship between Blacks and Jews (Nation of Islam), 47–48

Seddon, James A., 29

Seixas, Abraham Mendes, 100–101

Seixas, Gershom Mendes, 100

Seligman, Joseph, 307, 408

Sephardim Jews: Atlantic slave trade, 60, 62, 70, 76n12, 85n41; mercantile connections, 127
"Service and Shoddy" (illustration), *321*
Seward, William H., 129, 268
Seymour, Horatio, 386, 399
Shakespeare, William, 295
Sharpsburg, Battle of, 242
Sheftall, Mordecai, 96
Shepley, George F., 275
Sherman, William Tecumseh: camp followers, arrest of, 323; cotton speculators, attitude toward, 43, 45, 356–357, 365–366; Gratz and, 259; Knefler and, 36; Vicksburg campaign, 353, 363–364
"Shoddy Patriotism" (cartoon), 314–316
Silberman, Lazarus, 368
Simmons, Anna Maria, 92
Simons, Samuel, 105
Sinai (magazine): abolitionism, support for, 186; demolition of its shop, 191; Einhorn and, 182, 183; in Philadelphia, 192; on Tuska, 188–189
slave trade, 47–86; African slave trade, 70–71, 76n10, 83n31; Ashkenazic Jews, 85n41; Atlantic and Baltic states' participation in, 59–60; in Barbados, 63; Brandenburg African Company, 64; in Brazil, 59, 61, 66, 67; Brazil Company, 64; British slave trading, 63, 65, 69, 84n37; in Caribbean colonies, 61–62, 63, 67; categories of traders, 98–103; cost-benefit calculation, responsiveness to, 53; creation myth of, 53–54, 70; in Curaçao, 62, 72; Dutch slave trading, 60–62, 69, 80n21; Dutch West India Company, 60–61, 62, 64, 80n23, 81n24; early medieval slave trade, 76n10; French slave trading, 63–64, 65; full-time traders, 101–103; Guinea Company, 62; in Jamaica, 65–66, 84n37; Jewish investors in, 63, 80n23; Jewish merchants in, 48, 62, 71; Jewish middlemen/agents in, 61–63, 64, 80n21; Jewish participation in, 47–48, 49, 53–54, 60, 67, 68–69, 75n7, 76n10, 98–103; Korn on, 49; "Middle Passage," 52, 54, 60, 81n25; by national carrier, 53; New Christians' participation in, 56–59, 60, 61, 66, 67–68, 70, 71–72, 85n41; Old Christians' participation in, 56–57, 58, 68, 69; part-time traders, 99–101; personal traders, 98–99; phase, first (1500-1640), 52, 53, 55–59; phase, second (1640-1700), 52, 53, 59–64, 68–69; phase, third (1700-1807), 52, 53, 64–66, 69; Portuguese slave trading, 59, 66, 67–68, 70, 76n12; reexport trade, 65–66, 81n25; religious cleansing of Europe's Atlantic littoral, 54, 55–56; Royal Adventurers Trading, 63; Royal African Company (RAC), 63; Royal Guinea Company, 55; Sephardim Jews, 60, 62, 70, 76n12, 85n41; Sombart on, 53–54, 70; South Sea Company, 84n37; state sponsorship of, 55, 60; in Suriname, 72, 85n41; transit slave trade, 61–62, 63; triangular trade, 52, 54; working Europeans implicated in, 83n32
slavery, 87–121; Biblical sanction for, 133–136, 157, 167, 184, 186, 228; court cases brought against slaves by Jews, 95–96, 97; defenders of, 8; in development of Jewish life in Old South, 117; Einhorn on, 188; emancipation, possibility of, 95, 98, 107; emancipation of slaves by Jews, 93–95, 113–114; environmentalist arguments for, 136–137; establishment Protestantism, 132; German Jews, 181–182, 228; Jewish acceptance of, 115–117, 127–128, 228–230; in Jewish Civil War historiography, 3, 7–9, 12, 16; Jewish oppression and, parallels between, 137–139; Jews as harsh taskmasters, 95–96; Jews as owners of slaves, 88–90, 150, 228–229, 293; Jews involved in apprehending/punishing slaves, 96; Jews involved in business dealings with blacks, 96–98; miscegenation involving Jews, 104–108; opinions of Jews about slavery, 108–115; racialist arguments for, 136, 139; Raphall and, 8; religious positions and positions on, correspondence between, 158, 183; runaway slaves, 370, 371; in the South, 87–121; treatment of slaves by Jews, 91–93; wills of slave owners, 91; Wise on, 167, 177n20
Smith, Abraham, 229
Smith, Goldwin, 5–6
Solomon, Alice, 292
Solomon, Benjamin, 95–96
Solomon, Clara, 291–293, 300–301
Solomon, Edward, 36, 402
Sombart, Werner, 53–54, 70

Sorin, Gerald, 130, 132
the South: acceptance of Jews, 229; antisemitism in, 28, 42, 280, 281, 292, 356; German Jews in, 112–113; God's favor, reliance on, 280; Jewish acclimation in, 90, 115–117; Jewish aristocrats, 36–37; Jewish auctioneers, commission merchants, brokers, 99–101, 229; Jewish communities in, 227; Jewish loyalty to, 6–7, 8, 18, 23n53, 31–33, 157 (see also Benjamin, Judah P.; Mordecai, Alfred); Jewish merchants or professionals, 88–89, 385–386; Jewish peddlers/store-keepers, 89–90, 99, 228–229, 385–386; Jewish plantation overseers, 89; Jewish population, 228; Jewish women in, 265; Northern blockade, effect of, 42, 240; Northern trade with, 354, 364–365; plantation system, demise of, 385; political status achieved by Jews in, 116–117, 227–228, 230, 281, 356; rabbinical support for, 243–244; Reconstruction period (see South during Reconstruction). See also Confederate States Army; slavery
the South during Reconstruction, 387–397; Alsatian Jews, 390–391; antisemitism, 393–394; campaigns to attract immigrants, 393; cotton farming, 387–388, 394; factorage system, disappearance of, 388; furnishing merchants/general stores, 388–390, 394–396; land dealing, 395; lien laws, 390, 394, 395; merchants, 388, 392; peddlers, 390–392; specialty stores, 396; staple agriculture, 395; successful Jews, 396–397; tobacco farming, 394; wholesale houses, 396
South Mountain, Battle of, 242
South Sea Company, 65, 84n37
Southern Woman's Diary (Pember), 31
Soutro, Max, 189–190
Special Order No. 150, 272, 274
Spiegel, Marcus M., 356
Spitz, Hyman, 190–191
Spotsylvania Court House, Battle of, 30, 243
spying: by Benjamin, Judah P., 38, 235–237; by Boyd, 237; by Greenhow, 270; by Phillips, Eugenia, 31–32; by Zacharie, 40–41
Stampp, Kenneth, 18
Stanton, Edwin: Frankel and, 345; Phillips and, Philip, 268, 271; Solomon and, Edward, 36; Zacharie and, 41

Stanton, Elizabeth Cady, 130
Stephens, H. L., 316–317
Stern, Abraham, 104
Stern, Emanuel, 91
Stewart, James Brewer, 130, 132
Stikes, Augustus, 242
Still, Peter, 113–114, *148*
Stix, Louis, 112
Stoddard, W. O., 340
Storer, Bellamy, 401
Stout, Harry, 280
Stowe, Harriet Beecher, 102, 111, 136
Straus, Julius, 238
Straus, Lazarus, 113
Straus, Oscar, 113, 117, 228, 229
Strode, Hudson, 17
Stuart, J. E. B., 238
Sullivan, Jeremiah, 369
Sumner, Charles, 129
Swierenge, Robert, 85n41
Sycles, Simon, 238
Szold, Benjamin, 158, 183, 184–185
Szold, Henrietta, 4–5

Tappan brothers (Arthur, Benjamin, Lewis), 130
Thalheimer, Gus, 238
Thalheimer, Walter, 97
Thompson, Jacob, 237
Thornton, John, 57–58
Times (Chattanooga newspaper), 396
Tobias, Joseph, 94
Touro, Judah, 113
"The Triumph of Israel" (poem), 313–314
Trounstine, Philip, 358
Tuska, Simon, 188
Twain, Mark, 329
Twiggs, David Emanuel, 240

the Union, dissolution of: *Israelite* on, 165–166, 177n13; Mordecai and, Alfred, 202, 212; Wise on, 165
Union Army: all-Jewish companies, 36, 198; Congressional Medal of Honor winners, 29, 34; conscription, resistance to, 172; Department of the Tennessee, 356–357; desertions from, 172; Jewish chaplains (see chaplains, Jewish); Jews in, 18, 29, 169–170, 198, 218–219, 356 (see also Gratz, Louis A.; Mordecai, Alfred)

Union Party, 171
United Daughters of the Confederacy, 30
United Hebrew Beneficial Society, 338

Valentine, Isaac, 232
Vallandigham, Clement L., 171–172, 175, 336–337, 349n6
Van Dorn, Earl, 354, 364, 368
Vanity Fair (magazine), 312, 313–314, 316–317, 319
Verlinden, Charles, 76n10
Vlessing, Odette, 80n23

Wade, Benjamin, 231
Walker, William, 128
War with Amalek (Einhorn), 190
Wardell, L. J., 369
Warrenton Female Academy, 283
Washburne, Elihu, 376, 402
Washington Chronicle (newspaper), 44
Washington Republican (newspaper), 376
Wasserman, Levi, 240
Wayne, James M., 268, 271
Weiner, Theodore, 128, 139
Weis, Julius, 112
Wensley, a Story with a Moral (Quincy), 151–152
Wessolowsky, Charles, 234
West, Nancy, 105
Western hemisphere, Jewish population centers (1500-1800), 72–73, 85n41
White, Richard, 93
Whitlock, Philip, 234
Wilderness, Battle of the, 34
Williams, E. C., 256
Wilson, Henry, 150, 169, 231, 340
Wilson, Woodrow, 3, 18
Wilson's Creek, Battle of, 298
Winslow, Warren, 206
Wise, Isaac Mayer, 161–180; 1868 presidential election, 403–404, 406; abolitionism, antagonism toward, 123–124, 135, 158, 165, 168; on Baltimore politics, 192; Bene Israel Congregation, 175; Buchanan and, 162; chaplain controversy, 171, 337, 340; Chase and, 164; *Cincinnati Israelite* (newspaper), 374; Congregation B'nai Yeshurun, 161, 173, 175; *Deborah* (weekly newspaper), 161; Democratic nomination for Ohio State Senate, 158, 172–175, 180n42, 322, 349n6; Democratic Party, 337, 349n6; Douglas and, 168; General Orders No. 11, 44, 45, 171; on Gotthelf, 348; *Israelite* (weekly newspaper) (see *Israelite*); Kaskel and, Cesar F., 44; on Lincoln, 12; as middle-of-the-roader, 168; *Minhag America*, 161; Peace Democrats (Copperheads), 158, 175; personality, 176; photo, 163; post-1860 election attitudes, 164–165; Raphall and, 177n20; Republican Party, 158, 164, 175, 349n6; Ruchames on, 145–146; secession, 165, 167, 169; sectional self-determination, 158; slavery, 167, 177n20; Talmud Yelodim Institute, 161, 173
Wolcott, Christopher P., 358
Wolf, Simon: *American Jew as Patriot, Soldier and Citizen*, 5–7, 28–29, 197, 237; Congressional Medal of Honor winners, 34; Grant and, Ulysses S., 405, 408; influence, 18; Lincoln and, 28
Wolfe, Benjamin, 96
women, Jewish, 279–306; abolitionism and, 16, 137, 138, 147–149; antisemitism and, 282; Christian worship, attendance at, 287; family ties with Christians, maintenance of, 282–283, 294–295; friendships, reliance on, 279; hospitals work, 31, 33, 286–287, 288–290; non-Jewish neighborhoods, 279–280; in the North, 265; patriotism, 286–287; social relationships, maintenance of, 282; solidarity between, 266; in the South, 265; veiling of political differences, 287–288, 297, 298–300, 301; veiling of religious differences, 285–286, 288, 291, 292–293; veiling strategies, usefulness of, 301; wartime diaries, 265–266, 284, 300–301. *See also* Cohen, Miriam Moses; Gratz, Rebecca; Mordecai, Emma; Pember, Phoebe Yates
Woodward, C. Vann, 12, 18
Wool, John E., 208–211

Yankee Notions (magazine), 320
Yates, Fanny, 288
YMCA, 337, 340, 341
Yulee, David Levy, 39, 109, 124, 230

Zacharie, Isachar, 12, 39–42
Zionism: Rogers on, 153–155; Szold and, Benjamin, 184–185

About the Editors

JONATHAN D. SARNA is the Joseph H. and Belle R. Braun Professor of American Jewish History at Brandeis University and Chief Historian of the National Museum of American Jewish History. An elected member of both the American Academy of Arts and Sciences and the American Academy of Jewish Research, he has written, edited, or coedited more than twenty-five books, including *American Judaism: A History,* winner of the Jewish Book of the Year award from the Jewish Book Council.

ADAM MENDELSOHN is Assistant Professor of Jewish Studies and Director of the Center for Southern Jewish Culture at the College of Charleston.

www.ingramcontent.com/pod-product-compliance
Lightning Source LLC
Chambersburg PA
CBHW051932290426
44110CB00015B/1952